The Evolution of Management Thought

Seventh Edition

Daniel A. Wren
David Ross Boyd Professor *Emeritus*
The University of Oklahoma

and

Arthur G. Bedeian
Boyd Professor *Emeritus*
Louisiana State University and A&M College

WILEY

VP AND EDITORIAL DIRECTOR	George Hoffman
EDITORIAL DIRECTOR	Veronica Visentin
EXECUTIVE EDITOR	Lisé Johnson
SPONSORING EDITOR	Jennifer Manias
EDITORIAL MANAGER	Gladys Soto
CONTENT MANAGEMENT DIRECTOR	Lisa Wojcik
CONTENT MANAGER	Nichole Urban
SENIOR CONTENT SPECIALIST	Nicole Repasky
PRODUCTION EDITOR	Ameer Basha
PHOTO RESEARCHER	Alicia South-Hurt

This book was set in 10/12 TimesLTStd by SPi Global and printed and bound by Strategic Content Imaging.

Founded in 1807, John Wiley & Sons, Inc. has been a valued source of knowledge and understanding for more than 200 years, helping people around the world meet their needs and fulfill their aspirations. Our company is built on a foundation of principles that include responsibility to the communities we serve and where we live and work. In 2008, we launched a Corporate Citizenship Initiative, a global effort to address the environmental, social, economic, and ethical challenges we face in our business. Among the issues we are addressing are carbon impact, paper specifications and procurement, ethical conduct within our business and among our vendors, and community and charitable support. For more information, please visit our website: www.wiley.com/go/citizenship.

ISBN: 978-1-119-40027-1 (PBK)
ISBN: 978-1-119-40013-4 (EVAL)

Library of Congress Cataloging-in-Publication Data:

Names: Wren, Daniel A., author. | Bedeian, Arthur G., author.
Title: The evolution of management thought / by Daniel A. Wren, David Ross
   Boyd Professor Emeritus, The University of Oklahoma, and Arthur G.
   Bedeian, Boyd Professor Emeritus, Louisiana State University and A&M
   College.
Description: Seventh edition. | Hoboken, NJ : John Wiley & Sons, Inc., [2018]
   | Includes index. |
Identifiers: LCCN 2017015035 (print) | LCCN 2017025244 (ebook) | ISBN
   9781119400172 (pdf) | ISBN 9781119400080 (epub) | ISBN 9781119400271 (pbk.)
Subjects: LCSH: Management—History. | Management—Philosophy.
Classification: LCC HD30.5 (ebook) | LCC HD30.5 .W73 2018 (print) | DDC
   658.009—dc23
LC record available at https://lccn.loc.gov/2017015035

The inside back cover will contain printing identification and country of origin if omitted from this page.
In addition, if the ISBN on the back cover differs from the ISBN on this page, the one on the back cover is correct.

To Leon, Maude, and Karen
my links with the past;
To Jonathan, Laura, and Lynda;
and to another generation,
Karen Nicole, Tanner Main, Ethan Daniel, Sarah Lynn, and Caitlyn Claire
my links with the future.

To Varsenick and Arthur Bedeian
for reasons lost to history;
To Lynda, Katherine, and TAB;
for every reason;
To Anna-Kennon, Kate McGee, Laura Gabrielle, and Elizabeth Jane
for making me so very happy.

Brief Contents

Contents

12   Scientific Management in Retrospect   214

Part 3   The Social Person Era   227

13   The Hawthorne Studies   229

20   Organizational Behavior and Organization Theory   339

21   Science and Systems in an Information Age   362

About the Authors

Daniel A. Wren, PhD, the University of Illinois, is David Ross Boyd Professor of Management *Emeritus* and Curator *Emeritus* of the Harry W. Bass Business History Collection at The University of Oklahoma. He has served as president of the Southern Management Association, as chairman of the Management History Division of the Academy of Management, is a Founding Fellow of the Southern Management Association and a Fellow of the Academy of Management. He has been honored as a member of the Oklahoma Higher Education Hall of Fame and has received the Distinguished Educator Award from the Academy of Management for his contributions "as the foremost management historian of his generation." His research has appeared in numerous scholarly journals, and he is the author of *Collegiate Education for Business Administration at The University of Oklahoma: A History*; *White Collar Hobo: The Travels of Whiting Williams*; and coauthor with Ronald G. Greenwood of *Management Innovators: The People and Ideas That Have Shaped Modern Business.*

Arthur G. Bedeian, DBA, Mississippi State University, is a Boyd Professor *Emeritus* and former Ralph and Kacoo Olinde Distinguished Professor of Management at Louisiana State University and A&M College. A past-president of the Academy of Management and former dean of the Academy's Fellows Group, he has also served as president of the Foundation for Administrative Research, the Allied Southern Business Association, the Southern Management Association, and the Southeastern Institute for Decision Sciences. He is a Founding Fellow of the Southern Management Association, and a Fellow of the International Academy of Management, the American Psychological Association, the Society for Industrial and Organizational Psychology, and the Association for Psychological Science. Among his honors, he has received the Academy of Management's Distinguished Educator and Service Awards, Ronald G. Greenwood Lifetime Achievement Award, and Richard M. Hodgetts Distinguished Career Award. A former editor of the *Journal of Management*, he has been on 18 editorial boards,

including the *Academy of Management Review*, *Journal of Applied Psychology*, *Leadership Quarterly*, *Organizational Research Methods*, *Journal of Management History*, *Management & Organizational History*, and *Academy of Management Learning & Education*. He has served on various government committees, twice chaired the J. William Fulbright Foreign Scholar Board, and been an external or panel reviewer for the National Science Foundation, the National Academy of Science, and the National Research Council of Canada.

Preface

Over the past half-century, the authors have come to more fully appreciate that everything about management as an academic discipline—its language, its theories, its models, and its methodologies, not to mention its implicit values, its professional institutions, and its scholarly ways—comes from its inherited traditions. The formal study of management, however, is relatively new. To adapt a line from Ebbinghaus, whereas the practice of management has a long past, the study of management as a discipline has but a short history.[1]

Our challenge as we have explored this history and prepared each edition of *The Evolution of Management Thought* has been to recognize that, like all historians, we are a product of our own personal interests and biases. Subjectivity is inherent at every stage of historical knowledge. As historical meaning can only be established in retrospect, even "historical 'facts' are strongly embedded in interpretation."[2] Despite their best efforts, "[h]istorians may strive for objectivity, but . . . they cannot completely escape from their own historical moment, their culture, or their own past."[3] Thus, before moving ahead to Chapter 1, we forewarn our readers that because history is not an objective science, how things "really were" can never be fully known.

In further complication, given that it is impossible to rewind time, the historical record is inevitably spotty and fragmentary. There are many missing links. It is hence seldom (if ever) possible to establish an unquestioned chain of antecedents and consequences leading to a specific event. Moreover, although there are those who argue that to "see the world truly" one must "survey the whole stream of time in one comprehensive vision,"[4] we find that efforts to do so all too frequently make history medicinal, reducing historical knowledge to a drab meshing of abstract and impersonal forces. The study of history need not be a slog through time. To avoid pointless excess associated with a mere chronicling of past events and to give texture to the people and ideas discussed, we have attempted to offer flecks of color when appropriate.

We strongly believe that contemporary scholarship within the management discipline suffers to the extent that it lacks an appreciation of the past's impact on modern thinking. To learn that others in the past have traveled the same intellectual byways offers reassurance that progress in scholarship is a multigenerational endeavor. Joining us in an appreciation of the "past as prologue," March has argued, and we concur, the pursuit of knowledge involves the improvement of ideas "as they evolve through generations of individual scholars and scholarly communities, each building on those who went before and providing a base for those who follow." Further echoing our own sentiments, March has exulted "the benefits and beauties of being connected to a boundless past of cumulative scholarship that can anticipate a boundless future in which the ideas of today mature and develop into complex wonders of future knowledge."[5]

---

[1] Hermann Ebbinghaus, *Abriss der Psychologie* [*Outline of Psychology*] (Leipzig: Verlag von Veit & Comp., 1908), p. 1. The original Ebbinghaus quote reads: "Die Psychologie hat eine lange Vergangenheit, doch nur eine kurze Geschichte."

[2] Geoffrey Jones and Tarun Khanna, "Bringing History (Back) into International Business," *Journal of International Business Studies* 37(4) (July 2006), p. 465.

[3] Alert L. Hurtado, *Herbert Eugene Bolton: Historian of the American Borderlands* (Berkeley, CA: University of California Press, 2012), p. 165.

[4] Bertrand A. M. Russell, "Mysticism and Logic," *Hibbert Journal* 12(4) (July 1914), p. 795.

[5] James G. March, "Research on Organizations: Hopes for the Past and Lessons from the Future," *Nordiske Organisasjonsstudier* 1(1) (1999), pp. 80, 81.

Like its predecessors, *The Evolution of Management Thought* (7/e) seeks to capture the "benefits and beauties" of this past as a basis for expanding our intellectual horizons. As Sarason has warned, however, "we can be unfortunate prisoners of time and place unless our education builds into us schemata that aid us in taking distance from our time and place."[6] Toward this end, every chapter in this edition has been rigorously reviewed and systematically updated to convey an appreciation of the narrative past underlying the evolution of management thought. Our intent has been to place various theories of management in their historical context, showing how they developed as thinking about the nature of work, the nature of human beings, and the nature of organizations has changed across time. With this in mind, we caution readers to avoid the folly of judging the past by latter-day standards.

History may be portrayed using any number of complementary approaches. The following account presents a chronological history of management thought. In doing so, it makes no claim at being encyclopedic in its coverage nor is it meant to suggest that progress is always linear. With respect to the former, our aim was not to write a history of everything that has happened within the management discipline since the beginning of time. Indeed, as Elliott writes: "No narrative is ever fully comprehensive, no explanation total, and the balance between description and analysis is painfully elusive."[7] Concerning the latter point, within a four-part chronological structure (Early Management Thought; The Scientific-Management Era; The Social-Person Era; and Moving Onward: The Near Present), we move back and forth through time highlighting unsuspected connections and, as suggested above, exhort readers to eschew what might be called "straight-line thinking" in associating individual factors with specific events.

We have chosen a chronological structure not only because a "consideration of time sequences is crucial to any kind of history writing,"[8] but because we believe it best creates a feeling for the *zeitgeist* of the people and ideas that compose the management discipline's intellectual heritage. Moreover, we realize that in distinguishing between various eras or periods in time, different boundaries could have been employed. This said, as Logan has observed: "History has few 'natural' lines of fracture." We thus remind readers that the boundaries we have selected "are not the boundaries of what really happened at a given place or time; rather, they are boundaries [we have chosen] about that place and time – a story that has a workable beginning and end."[9]

In addition, we should perhaps also comment on the title *The Evolution of Management Thought*. It has been said that "A teacher must either treat history as a catalogue, a record, a romance, or as an evolution."[10] We have selected the latter. Our use of the term "evolution" in both title and text is meant to refer to the historical development of management thought over time. We have no intention of calling to mind Darwin's theory of evolution by natural selection "in which randomly generated traits survive and spread because they provide some edge in the competition for survival and reproduction."[11] We have no Darwinian theory of evolution to promulgate and would find it impossible to manhandle the facts to fit one.

The continuing interest of scholars who care about the evolution of management thought and the students who find value in the lessons history provides made this edition possible.

---

[6] Seymour B. Sarason, *The Making of an American Psychologist* (San Francisco: Jossey-Bass Publishers, 1988), p. 277.

[7] John H. Elliot, *History in the Making* (New Haven, CN: Yale University Press, 2013), p. 94.

[8] Ernst Mayr, *The Growth of Biological Thought: Diversity, Evolution, and Inheritance* (Cambridge, MA: Harvard University Press, 1982), p. 2.

[9] Cheryl A. Logan, "Shaping and Owning the Boundaries of a Book," *History of Psychology* 16(3) (August 2013), pp. 217, 218.

[10] Henry Adams, *The Education of Henry Adams* (Boston, MA: Houghton Mifflin Company, 1918), p. 300.

[11] John R. McNeill, [Review of the book *A Foot in the River*]. *Wall Street Journal* (February 29, 2016), p. A11.

Over the years, the authors have had the privilege of training several generations of gifted graduate students who have gone on, as eminent historians, to shape the study of management thought. We are proud of their contributions to our knowledge of the past and, in particular, the leadership they have provided chairing the Management History Division of the Academy of Management. This latter group is comprised of Paula Phillips Carson, the late Kerry David Carson, Shawn M. Carraher, Franz T. Lohrke, Milorad M. Novicevic, Roland E. Kidwell, and Stephanie Case Henagan. Several esteemed colleagues who propelled management history into the limelight as a scholarly endeavor and from whom we learned so much are now deceased. In particular, we wish to remember Claude S. George, Jr.; John F. Mee; Richard J. Whiting; W. Jerome Arnold; Ronald G. Greenwood; James C. Worthy; Richard M. Hodgetts; Alfred A. Bolton; William B. Wolf; William F. Muhs; and Charles D. Wrege. Their unique insights and contagious enthusiasm continue to inspire us. We remain indebted to John D. Breeze, W. Jack Duncan, Peter B. Petersen, and David D. Van Fleet for their decades of friendship and contributions to expanding our knowledge about the management discipline's past.

Among the many individuals who aided in locating original source materials, we are indebted to Leah S. Loscutoff, Head of Archives and Special Collections, Samuel C. Williams Library, Stevens Institute of Technology for aid in navigating the Frederick Winslow Taylor Collection; Patrizia Stone, Research Archivist, Kheel Center for Labor Management Documentation and Archives, Cornell University for locating items in the Charles D. Wrege Research Papers; Regina Scannell Greenwood for access to the Ronald G. Greenwood Collection, University Archives, Alvin Sherman Library, Nova Southeastern University (Fort Lauderdale, FL); Kenneth F. Thomas, Senior Manuscript Specialist, State Historical Society of Missouri–St. Louis for combing the records of the International Association of Machinists and Aerospace Workers (District 9); Keith W. Rabiola and Lee C. Grady, Public Services Librarian and Senior Reference Archivist, respectively, Archives Division, Wisconsin Historical Society Library–Madison for searching the Wisconsin State Federation of Labor Papers, the John R. Commons Papers and the Richard T. Ely Papers; Nicole Potter and Nicole C. Westerdahl, Reference Assistant and Reading Room Supervisor, respectively, Special Collection Research Center, Syracuse University Libraries for material from the Collis Porter Huntington Papers; Sarah Roberts, Acquisitions Archivist, University Archives and Historical Collections, Michigan State University Libraries for consulting the Nels Peter Alifas Papers; Traci JoLeigh Drummond, Archivist, Southern Labor Archives, University Library, Georgia State University (Atlanta) for scouring the Archives of the International Association of Machinists and Aerospace Workers; Jennifer G. Eidson, Assistant Labor Collections Archivist, Special Collections and University Archives, University of Maryland Libraries for an introduction to the AFL-CIO Archives, and Alison Barnard, Norfolk Record Office, The Archive Centre (Norwich, United Kingdom) for assistance in locating records pertaining to Rev. Morgan Powell.

It has been a pleasure working with Regina Scannell Greenwood and Julia Kurtz Teahen in developing PowerPoint slides to accompany this new edition. The slides feature photographs, charts, and other visual materials that enliven and augment the companion text. Eric C. Taylor deserves particular mention for reviewing page proofs and providing invaluable comments and suggestions. At John Wiley & Sons we wish to express our appreciation to Lisé Johnson, Executive Editor; Jennifer Manias, Development Editor; Alicia South-Hurt, Photo Researcher; Janet Wehner, Project Manager; and Gladys Soto, Editorial Manager, Content Enablement & Operations, who cheerfully saw the present edition through its various stages from manuscript to print. Ameer Basha, Production Editor, provided valuable support throughout. We thank staff at SPi Global for copyediting. Finally, we want to acknowledge Melba K. Staub and Jacob J. Fontenot, Middleton Library, Louisiana State University, for obtaining material through the Interlibrary Loan Service, as well as their colleague Rebecca N. Kelley, Research & Instruction Services Librarian, for fulfilling—at record speed—countless acquisition requests.

No book fully achieves the intentions of its creators. We would thus welcome being told of any discrepancies in the following pages, as well as receiving additional information or materials that might be incorporated into a future edition. In closing, we remain grateful for the suggestions and encouragement of the many people who have used previous editions of *The Evolution of Management Thought* in the classroom and in their own research.

Daniel A. Wren
Norman, Oklahoma

Arthur G. Bedeian
Baton Rouge, Louisiana

July 4, 2017

Early Management Thought

part

1

Part 1 traces developments in management thought up to the scientific-management era in the United States. After a brief introduction to the role of managers in organizations, it examines examples of early management thought and then demonstrates how economic, social, political, and technological changes set the stage for the Industrial Revolution. This revolution created unprecedented managerial challenges in the emerging factory system and led to the need for the formal study of organizations and management. The genesis of modern management thought is found in the work of early pioneers who sought to solve the challenges created by the embryonic factory system. Part 1 concludes by tracing this genesis of management thought in the United States and examining early experiences with the developing factory system, the work of early management writers, and the cultural framework in the United States before the scientific-management era.

A Prologue to the Past

chapter

1

A Cultural Framework
  The Economic Facet
  The Social Facet
  The Political Facet
  The Technological Facet
People, Management, and Organizations
  The Human Being
  Organizations and Management
Summary

The practice of management is ancient, but the formal study of management, based on an evolving body of knowledge, is relatively new. Rarely, if ever, in human history has an activity emerged as fast as management and proven so indispensable so quickly. For a broad working definition, management may be viewed as the activity whose purpose is to achieve desired results through the efficient allocation and utilization of human and material resources. Management thought, the evolution of which is our primary focus, is the existing body of knowledge about the functions, purpose, and scope of management.

The goal of this book is to trace the evolution of management thought from its earliest informal days to the present. The study of management, like the study of people and their cultures, is an unfolding story of changing ideas about the nature of work, the nature of human beings, and the nature of organizations. The methodology used in the study of management is analytic, synthetic, and interdisciplinary. It is analytic in examining people who made significant contributions, their backgrounds, their ideas, and their influence. It is synthetic in combining trends, movements, and environmental forces to form a conceptual framework for understanding the changing nature of management thought. It is interdisciplinary in the sense that it includes—but moves beyond—traditional management thinking to draw upon economic history, sociology, psychology, social history, political science, and cultural anthropology to examine management thought from a cultural and historical perspective. The objective is not only to understand what management thought was but also to explain why it developed as it did.

We thus study the past to illuminate the present. Management history as a separate area of study is, however, generally neglected in most schools of business administration. A smattering of history is taught at various levels, but the instruction generally lacks depth, direction, and unity. In his 1838 poem "A Psalm of Life," Henry Wadsworth Longfellow said, "Let the dead Past bury its dead!"[1] but there is much to be said for resurrection. We live and study in an age characterized by myriad approaches to management. Students encounter quantitative, behavioral,

---

[1] Henry Wadsworth Longfellow, "A Psalm of Life," *The Knickerbocker* 12(4) (October, 1838), p. 189.

functional, and other approaches in their various management courses. Although such a variety may be intellectually stimulating, it presents students with a fragmented picture of management and assumes that they have the ability to integrate these various approaches for themselves.

In many cases, this burden is far too great. Management history as a separate area of study provides a conceptual framework for integrating the various approaches to management. A study of the past contributes to a more logical, coherent picture of the present. Without a knowledge of the past, individuals have only their own limited experiences as a basis for thought and action. As one scholar commented, History is a "universal experience – infinitely longer, wider, and more varied than any individual's experience."[2] The study of history thus equips students with an appreciation of past answers and present alternatives to the dilemmas of contemporary life. Lawrence distinguished between *historical research* (inquiry into past persons and events) and *historical perspective* (using history as raw material for understanding the present). The object of historical perspective is to "sharpen one's vision of the present, not the past . . . . It pushes thinking about alternative explanations for phenomena, helps identify more or less stable concepts, and expands research horizons by suggesting new ways of studying old questions."[3] Smith noted: "Reading, exploring, and discussing history can provide students with opportunities to acquire knowledge of their field and its practices, gain wisdom, and develop and use judgment."[4] Present pedagogy can, thereby, be improved, knowledge expanded, and insights gained by examining the lives and labors of the management discipline's intellectual ancestors. By tracing the sources of our ideas about management, we can better understand the nature of work, the nature of human beings, and the nature of organizations. Moreover, in understanding the growth and development of large-scale enterprises, the dynamics of technology, the ebb and flow of cultural values, and the changing assumptions about the nature and nurture of people, we can better equip students with the skills required for future positions of responsibility.

Today is not like yesterday, nor will tomorrow be like today; yet today is a synergism of all our yesterdays, and tomorrow will be the same. Mark Twain reputedly said that "History never repeats itself, but sometimes it rhymes."[5] History teaches many lessons and, as Shakespeare observed, perhaps the most important is: "What's past is prologue."[6]

A Cultural Framework

How have our concepts of managing organizations evolved throughout history? To understand the dynamics of this evolution requires a cultural framework for analyzing the development of management thought. Management is not a closed-end activity as managers make decisions within a given set of cultural values and institutions. Rather, management is an open system in which managers affect, and are affected by, their environments.

Culture is the sum total of a society's "knowledge, belief, art, morals, law, custom, and any other capabilities and habits" that are transmitted from generation to generation.[7] As culture is a very broad subject, the chapters that follow are limited to a consideration of those specific

---

[2] Basil H. Liddell Hart, *Why Don't We Learn From History?* (London: George Allen and Unwin, 1972), p.15.

[3] Barbara S. Lawrence, "Historical Perspective: Using the Past to Study the Present," *Academy of Management Review* 9(2) (April 1984), pp. 307, 311.

[4] George E. Smith, "Management History and Historical Context: Potential Benefits of Its Inclusion in the Management Curriculum," *Academy of Management Learning & Education,* 6(4) (December 2007), p. 524.

[5] The prefatory phrase "History never repeats itself" does appear in Mark Twain and Charles Dudley Warner, *The Gilded Age: A Tale of To-Day* (Hartford, CT: American Publishing Company, 1874), p. 430. An earlier reference to history's "mystic rhyme" may be found in [Review of *A History of the Church in Russia* by Andrew N. Mouravieff] *The Christian Remembrancer: A Quarterly Review* 10(50) (October 1845), p. 264.

[6] William Shakespeare, *The Tempest*, Act 2, Scene I.

[7] Edward B. Tylor, *Primitive Culture: Researches into the Development of Mythology, Philosophy, Religion, Art, and Custom,* vol. 1 (London: John Murray, 1871), p. 1.

economic, social, political, and technological ideas that influence managing an organization. Human behavior is a product of past and present cultural forces. The discipline of management is likewise a product of the economic, social, political, and technological forces of the past and present. As Bedeian has observed, "past arrangements – institutions, roles, cultural forms – are not simply superseded, but transformed and recombined to produce the present. In this sense, the past repeatedly informs and reinforms the present such that the search for understanding is never finished."[8] Modern students of management may examine present organizations and read contemporary authors, yet all too often have little appreciation for the background of our technologies, political institutions, and economic policies. Management thought did not develop in a cultural vacuum; managers have always found their jobs affected by the existing culture.

In the study of modern management, the past must be examined to see how our communal heritage was established. In practice, the economic, social, political, and technological facets of our culture are closely interrelated and interact to form a cultural framework; they are delineated here and throughout the following pages only for ease of presentation. Further, our attention shall be confined to the portions of our culture that apply most directly to managing an organization, omitting other cultural phenomena, such as art, literature, and music.

The Economic Facet

The economic facet of culture is the relationship between people and resources. Humans or nature may create resources; the term denotes both tangible objects and intangible efforts that may be utilized to achieve some stated end. Physical resources include land, buildings, raw materials, semifinished products, tools, and equipment or other tangible objects. Technology—our understanding of the art and applied science of making and using tools and equipment—has advanced at varying rates in different eras and, consequently, influences how resources are used at any given time in history.

Human thought and effort are also resources because they enable the design, assembly, shaping, and performing of other activities that result in the production of goods or services. The allocation of scarce resources to produce and distribute goods and services has, therefore, been accomplished in various ways throughout history. Heilbroner characterized different methods of allocating resources by tradition, by command, and by market forces.[9] The traditional method of allocating resources operates on past societal precepts under which technology is basically static, occupations are passed down from one generation to the next, agriculture predominates over industry, and social and economic systems remain essentially closed to change. The command method is a central agency (or person) imposing its dictates on an economic system to determine how resources are both allocated and utilized. This economic commander-in-chief may be a monarch, a fascist dictator, or a collectivist central-planning agency that decides what is to be produced, levels of prices and wages, and how economic goods and services are to be distributed. The market method, which Heilbroner noted is a relatively recent phenomenon, relies on an impersonal network of forces and personal decisions to allocate resources. Prices, wages, and interest rates are set by a bargaining process between those who furnish a product or service and those who want it. This provides for best meeting the needs and wants of consumers and no central agency or prior cultural precepts intervene. In actual practice, modern societies employ all three methods of allocating resources. Although our history has been predominantly influenced by tradition and command methods, we will see later that the market

---

[8] Arthur G. Bedeian, "Exploring the Past," *Journal of Management History* 4(1) (1998), p. 4. See also Arthur G. Bedeian, "The Gift of Professional Maturity," *Academy of Management Learning & Education* 3(1) (March 2004), pp. 92–98.
[9] Robert L. Heilbroner, *The Making of Economic Society* (Englewood Cliffs, NJ: Prentice-Hall, 1962), pp. 10–16.

method, as an economic philosophy, created the need for a formal body of management thought. In brief, technological advancements and the prevailing balance of methods for allocating resources have a significant bearing on how managers go about their jobs. A tradition-directed economy circumscribes the managerial role with prior precepts and a command orientation makes managers executors of decisions made by a centralized authority, but the market system opens the way to the competitive use of resources, which stimulates growth in the supply of goods and services.

The Social Facet

The social facet of culture refers to relations among people in a given culture. Humans do not live alone, but find advantages in forming groups for mutual benefit or for furthering personal goals. In forming groups, people of differing needs, abilities, and values come together. Out of this heterogeneity, some homogeneity must evolve or a group will not survive. Thus, participants form a "contract," which encompasses shared beliefs, attitudes, and behaviors to ensure a group's survival. This unwritten, but nevertheless binding contract includes an implicit agreement regarding how to best combine and coordinate efforts for accomplishing various tasks.

Values, or cultural standards of conduct defining the propriety of a given type of behavior, are another part of social interaction. Thus, ethics in interpersonal relations is an age-old problem. Economic transactions, deeply embedded in social trust, are an integral part of a societal network. Values vary across cultures and eras, and managerial efforts are affected by the relations among individuals and groups and by a culture's prevailing social values.

The Political Facet

The political facet of culture is the relationship between individuals and sovereign states, and includes the legal and political arrangements for establishing social order, as well as the protection of life and property. The absence of social order is anarchy; unless there is some provision for the protection of rational from irrational actors, economic, social, and political chaos will prevail. Where order begins, however, anarchy ends. Political institutions that bring stability take various forms, ranging from a representative government to a monarchy or dictatorship. Political assumptions about the nature of humanity range from a belief in democratic self-government to a need for a ruling elite (or one person) to impose its will on others based on the assumption that people cannot, or will not, govern themselves. Provisions for property, contracts, and justice likewise vary according to the nature of political institutions. In a democracy, people have private property rights, the freedom to enter or not to enter into contracts, and an appeal system for justice. Under a ruling elite, however, the right to hold and use private property is severely restricted, freedom to contract is limited, and justice depends on the whims of those in power. The management of organizations is affected by a culture's political institutions and form of government, by the power to hold or not hold property, by the ability to engage in contracts for the provision of goods and services, and by the appeal mechanisms available to redress grievances.

The Technological Facet

The technological facet of culture is the art and applied science of making tools and equipment. Historians refer to past eons such as the Stone Age, the Iron Age, and the Bronze Age when humans first made tools. Over the intervening centuries, technology has advanced, sometimes rapidly, other times more slowly, giving rise to the world's contrasting cultures.

Technology is a means to an end that can produce beneficial as well as detrimental results. Landes has warned us

> that the wresting and exploitation of knowledge are perilous acts, but man must and will know, and once knowing, will not forget . . . the marriage of science and technology are the climax of millennia of intellectual advance. They have also been an enormous force of good and evil, and there have been moments when the evil has far outweighed the good. Still, the march of knowledge and technique continues, and with it the social and moral travail.[10]

Perilous as it may be, "the wresting and exploitation of knowledge" has transformed global industry and trade from labor intensive to capital intensive and, ultimately, to knowledge intensive.

Technology often advances slowly in tradition-bound or closed societies because it threatens the status quo. Kieser has written of medieval guilds, which kept

> production and selling conditions for all members as equal as possible. No [guild] master should be able to gain an advantage at the expense of his co-masters . . . . The master was only allowed to employ a restricted number of journeymen . . . and he was not allowed to choose these men himself . . . Wages and working hours were uniformly regulated. The pursuit of customers was strictly forbidden . . . Innovations were suppressed.[11]

Tradition-bound or closed societies that cling to past precepts stifle innovation and offer little incentive to seek new knowledge, to explore, or to experiment. Technologies, their basic science, are limited by the status quo that discourages innovations in education, free inquiry, and taking the risk necessary for the discovery of new things.

The technology facet of culture makes a difference in how organizations are managed, and we will see examples of how it affects the economic, social, and political facets of a nation's culture. By applying science in an artful manner, we have the potential of influencing all facets of our culture. In his First Annual Message to Congress on January 8, 1790, George Washington encouraged the promotion of science, saying, "Knowledge is in every country the surest basis of public happiness."[12] This quest for knowledge, and improvements in technology through advances in science, must be never ending, impelling us to learn, to do better, to live better.

Interacting to form a whole, the economic, social, political, and technological facets of any culture are useful tools for examining the evolution of management thought, as a nation's cultural framework affects its managers and the available means for providing goods and services.

People, Management, and Organizations

We now turn to a consideration of basic elements underlying the study of management as an activity and as a discipline. Even before people began to record their activities, they encountered the necessity of managing their efforts in cooperative endeavors. As an overview, Figure 1.1

---

[10] David S. Landes, *The Unbound Prometheus: Technological Change and Industrial Development in Western Europe from 1750 to the Present* (Cambridge, England: Cambridge University Press, 1969), pp. 555, 524. For a global perspective on the impact of technology on a nation's wealth, see idem, *The Wealth and Poverty of Nations: Why Some Are So Rich and Some So Poor* (New York: W. W. Norton, 1998).

[11] Alfred Kieser, "Organizational, Institutional, and Societal Evolution: Medieval Craft Guilds and the Genesis of Formal Organizations," *Administrative Science Quarterly* 34(4) (December 1989), p. 553.

[12] George Washington, "Speech of the President of the United States to both Houses of Congress," January 8, 1790, p. 5. Available online at http://memory.loc.gov/mss/mgw/mgw2/025/1251007.jpg

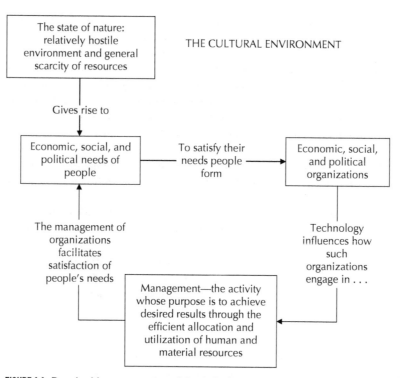

THE CULTURAL ENVIRONMENT

FIGURE 1.1 **People, Management, and Organizations.**

begins with "the state of nature" and traces the quest for need satisfaction through organizations. Management, an activity essential to organized endeavors, facilitates the efficient allocation and utilization of human and material resources to satisfy human needs.

The Human Being

The human being is the fundamental unit of analysis in the study of history, the study of organizations, and the study of management. Humans have always faced a relatively hostile environment characterized by scarce food supplies, inadequate shelter, and, in general, a paucity of other resources with which to satisfy their manifold needs. Humans are biologically weaker than many other species. To explain their survival, we must look beyond physical prowess for other characteristics that have enabled humans to control and manipulate the natural environment.

The answer to the question of why humans have survived is found in their ability to reason. In the long evolutionary process, it was not always the most physically fit who survived. Rather, it was the most cognitively capable who fashioned tools and weapons, mastered the use of fire, developed the ability to think conceptually, advanced their power of communication, and engaged in group activities that required a marked degree of planning and coordination. These were the people who fashioned clubs and spears for defense, who created implements for tilling the soil, and who cooperated with one another to give humans a differential advantage over their natural enemies.

Paleoanthropologists have constantly pushed our knowledge of humankind further and further into the past.[13] They have studied the origins of *Homo habilis*, "handy man," who fashioned tools;

---

[13] For example, see Donald Johanson and Maitland A. Edey, *Lucy: The Beginnings of Humankind* (New York: Simon and Schuster, 1981).

Homo erectus, who possessed bipedal ability; and *Homo sapiens,* the thinker. Humans are thinkers, doers, and makers; they are active, creative, and ever changing in their quest to better themselves and their species. Their most basic needs are physiological: food, water, shelter, sleep, and oxygen necessary for physical survival. Beyond these basic needs, social needs most probably arose out of the drive to reproduce and, thus, to select a mate. In turn, families became the most elementary unit forming human groups. With time, survival of families being a shared goal, humans found that they could better protect and enhance their welfare by forming groups or tribes for mutual advantage in gathering food, defense, and child care. As Bronowski concluded: "We are joined in families, the families are joined in kinship groups, the kinship groups in clans, the clans in tribes, and the tribes in nations. This is the most primitive revelation of a hierarchy of organization, layer upon layer that links the present to the past of man's existence."[14]

Early humans found that the knowledge and skills of one generation must be transmitted to the next if they were to survive. Such were the elementary beginnings of knowledge transfer through education. In forming groups and living with one another to satisfy their mutual goals, humans needed a way to ensure the viability of their families, kinship groups, clans, tribes, and, ultimately, nations. They formed elementary political units with agreed-upon codes governing economic, social, political, and often religious behavior. Out of their common economic, social, and political needs, organized human activity began.

Organizations and Management

As humans have evolved, so have organizations. Early humans found that they could magnify their own abilities by working with others and could thereby better satisfy their respective needs. Varying individual natural skills and abilities led to the recognition that some people were better at certain tasks than others. Group tasks were, thus, logically differentiated; that is, there was a division of labor to take advantage of natural skills and abilities. Once labor was divided, some agreement had to be reached about how to structure and interrelate various activities to accomplish desired ends. As the number of activities necessary to accomplish an end grew in number, it became necessary to group tasks and develop a hierarchy of authority to assure adequate coordination across activities. Perhaps the wisest, the strongest, the eldest, or the most articulate of a group became its leader, assigning tasks based on skill and ability. In any case, groups had to achieve some unity of agreement about what was to be done, how, and who would be responsible for expending the required effort.

The elements leading to the initial emergence of organizations are essentially the same throughout history. *First,* there had to be a goal, a purpose, an objective, or something to be accomplished. Perhaps it was the annual berry picking, the hunt, the sowing of a crop, or the defense from marauding nomads. *Second,* people had to be sufficiently attracted to a goal so as to participate. They had to perceive that it was in their best interest to share in accomplishing a goal. The genesis of organized group activities can be found in people's attraction to others as a means of satisfying their own individual needs. *Third,* those joining together to form a group required resources necessary for goal accomplishment. Both human and physical resources were required: people with requisite skills and abilities, weaponry, tools, and other implements that supported goal attainment. *Fourth,* the activities of group members had to be structured in such a way as to further goal accomplishment. If each member proceeded without coordinating their efforts, the result would be chaos. *Finally,* as undertakings became complex, groups soon discovered that goal accomplishment was more likely if someone was assigned the task of keeping the whole group on course. Someone had to resolve differences of opinion, decide on strategy and

---

[14] Jacob Bronowski, *The Ascent of Man* (Boston, MA: Little, Brown and Company, 1973), pp. 95–96.

timing, and, in a word, manage the people and activities necessary to succeed. This emergence of managing as a distinct role was to become an essential aspect of all cooperative endeavors.

Throughout the course of their entire history, humans have participated in organizations (whether families, kinship groups, clans, tribes, nations, pop-and-pop groceries, or *Fortune* 500 companies) and organizations have existed to serve the needs of people. These needs are reflected in manifold arrangements for the transmission of knowledge from one generation to the next, for the protection of life and property, and, in general, for the provision of a seemingly unlimited variety of goods and services. As the human species' conceptual ability has been refined through evolution, people have refined their understanding of the art of arranging physical and human resources toward purposeful ends. We call this art "management."

SUMMARY

Our ideas about people, management, and organizations have evolved throughout history. Likewise, our knowledge of how to manage has also evolved within a cultural framework comprised economic, social, political, and technological facets. Accordingly, as management thought is a product of the prevailing cultural environment, it must be examined within this framework. People seek to satisfy their natural economic, social, and political needs through organized efforts. Toward this end, organizations naturally form as individuals seek to satisfy their needs through group action. In doing so, people enlarge on their own specialized talents to protect themselves, to enrich their lives, and to otherwise satisfy their manifold needs. The coming chapters will focus on how our ideas about management as a body of knowledge and management as activity have developed over time.

Management Before Industrialization

Historically, industrialization is a relatively recent phenomenon. Humans existed for eons before the great advances in power, transportation, communications, and technology that came to be known as the Industrial Revolution. Before industrialization, organizations were primarily family-, church-, military-, or government-related. Some individuals engaged in economic undertakings (e.g., barbers, bakers, blacksmiths, cabinetmakers, cobblers, millers, tailors, wheelwrights), but not on a scale comparable to what emerged following the Industrial Revolution. Nevertheless, there was still a need for management in conducting military campaigns and in administering household, civic, and religious affairs. This chapter examines management in early civilizations prior to the Industrial Revolution. It also discusses the changing cultural values in these civilizations that led to the Industrial Revolution.

Management in Early Civilizations

The Near East

As group affiliations evolved from families to nations, the establishment and management of authority became a challenge. In families, authority rested in a patriarch or a matriarch, but in nations, there was often a conflict between chiefs and priests, the former claiming secular power and the latter heavenly dominion. From this struggle and divided authority came the idea of a priest-ruler or divine king. A king was not a King until ordained by priests, a tradition that long endured.

One such divine king was Hammurabi (ca. 2123–2071 BCE), who ruled over Babylon, between the Tigris and Euphrates rivers and near modern Baghdad—an area that is often referred to as the Cradle of Civilization. Hammurabi believed his right to rule emanated from the sun god Shamash, and in 2250 BCE Hammurabi issued 282 laws he claimed to have received from Shamash. These laws governed business dealings, personal behavior, interpersonal relations, punishments, and a host of other societal matters. Law 104, for example, is the first historical reference to a form of accounting. It required an agent acting on behalf of a merchant to provide the merchant with a receipt for the money value of any goods with which the agent was being entrusted and, in turn, to be given a receipt for any money the agent returned the merchant for the sale of the goods. Hammurabi's Code, as the laws became to be known, also regulated wages and fees, such as fixing surgeons' fees and wages paid to "builders, brickmakers, tailors, stonemasons, boatmen, herdsmen, and laborers."[1] In 604 BCE, when Nebuchadnezzar was King of Babylonia, weavers of cloth were paid in food, with the quantity received dependent upon each spinner or weaver's output. This was before, and possibly influenced, the later biblical notion, "If anyone will not work, let him not eat" (2 Thess. 3:10), or, in the words of the Prophet Muhammad (d. 632 CE), "He who neither worketh for himself, nor for others, will not receive the reward of God."[2] In the case of weavers, the reason for working was clear. In Hammurabi's Code, however, there was no incentive to do more than required because wages were regulated. Thus, here were early examples of bureaucratic authority and differing ideas about incentives, motivation, and workplace performance.

The Far East

The ancient Chinese civilization occasionally opened its doors to let Westerners peek in. The oldest known military treatise was written by the Chinese general Sun Tzu (544–496 BCE). He wrote of marshaling an army into subdivisions, establishing gradations of military rank, and using gongs, flags, and signal fires for communications. Sun Tzu advocated lengthy deliberations and sound plans before going into battle: "Thus do many calculations [i.e., plans] lead to victory, and few calculations to defeat." He commented on the distinct roles of line and staff managers and boldly advised: "The general that hearkens to my counsel and acts upon it, will conquer . . . . The general that hearkens not to my counsel nor acts upon it, will suffer defeat."[3] It appears that the challenges of managing line and staff relations are over 2,500 years old. Sun Tzu also provided strategic decision-rules for generals:

> This is the art of offensive strategy . . . . When ten to the enemy's one, surround him . . . . When five times his strength, attack him . . . . If double his strength, divide him . . . . If equally matched you may engage him . . . . If weaker numerically, be capable of withdrawing . . . . And if in all respects unequal, be capable of eluding him.[4]

If the rivalry among business competitors to achieve goals such as increased market share and higher profits is considered a surrogate for war, "competitive strengths" can be compared to "forces," and "competitor" to "enemy," and we can see an early pillar of modern management strategy.

---

[1] Will Durant, *The Story of Civilization*, vol. 1: *Our Oriental Heritage* (New York: Simon & Schuster, 1935). p. 231. See also Robert F. Harper, *The Code of Hammurabi, King of Babylon, About 2250 B. C.* (Chicago, IL: University of Chicago Press, Callaghan & Co., 1904). Originally written circa 154 BCE.

[2] Prophet Muhammad, *The Sayings of Muhammad*. Abdullah al-Māmūn al-Suhrawardy, ed. (London: A. Constable, 1905), p. 2.

[3] Sun Tzu, *Transcription of the Text of Sun Tzu on the Art of War: The Oldest Military Treatise in the World*, trans. Lionel Giles (London: Luzac, 1910), pp. 27, 26.

[4] Sun Tzu, *The Art of War,* trans. Samuel B. Griffith (Oxford: Oxford University Press, 1963), pp. 79–80. Originally written in circa 513 BCE.

Confucius (ca. 551–479 BCE) and his followers have also had a lasting influence on Eastern thinking about virtuous behavior, including benevolence toward others, achieving practical wisdom in making sound decisions, avoiding extremes, and living an exemplary life. Virtue was highly desirable in those holding positions of responsibility. In Confucius's time, the highest respectable goal was service in the Chinese government: merchants ranked only slightly above convicts in social esteem. The competition for governmental posts was severe, and Confucius believed that only individuals of proven merit and ability should hold public offices. Merit exams, based on Confucian advice, began during the Han dynasty (206 BCE–220 CE). Merit as a basis for selection would in time lead to merit ratings (performance appraisals) for promotions. Although the record is spotty, the Sung dynasty started a merit-rating system around 962 CE. Research also indicates that the ancient Chinese had difficulties with bureaucracy, much as we do today. Selecting officials based on their ability as a classical scholar, for instance, did not always bring the best administrators to office. Corruption and manipulation by officials and lesser functionaries was common, leading to numerous attempts to reform the Chinese civil-service bureaucracy.[5]

The Chinese civil-service was organized in a fully developed hierarchy of differing ranks perhaps as early as 1000 BCE, long before Confucius. Indeed, the Confucian philosophy was in contradiction to the legalist philosophy of that time. So-called "legalists" sought to use imperial rewards and punishments based on a system of laws to ensure performance, whereas Confucius advocated cultivating and improving people's moral nature to secure cooperation. How ancient this struggle between the formalists and the humanists, the system and the individual! There is also evidence that the Chinese were familiar with the division of labor and departmentalization as early as 1 CE. For example, an inscription on a rice bowl from this period indicates that it was made in a government workshop where there was specialization among individual artisans divided into various departments. The workshop was divided into three departments: accounting, security, and production.[6] Such artifacts enable us to understand the earliest roots of management.

In other parts of the ancient Far East, Kauṭilya (also known Chanakya; ca. 332–298 BCE) was a noted and feared minister to Chandragupta Maurya, the greatest statesman of Hindu India. Kauṭilya's *Arthaśāstra*, a treatise on statecraft, contained advice on establishing and maintaining economic, social, and political order. Kauṭilya cautioned that it was difficult to find competent public officials because humans "are naturally fickle-minded, and like horses at work exhibit constant change in their temper." Further, "it is impossible for a government servant not to eat up, at least, a bit of the king's revenue."[7] To maintain order, he advised close controls, severe punishment, the use of workplace spies, and various ploys to test employee loyalty. Kauṭilya's assumptions about human nature are as modern as they are ancient, as are the prescriptions he provided on maintaining order. Although he was largely unknown in the Western world, we find his advice reflected in the words of others. Kauṭilya also wrote on the desired traits for administrators ("of high family . . . wise . . . eloquent . . . intelligent, possessed of enthusiasm . . . affable") and how to select employees using interviews and checking references. He commented further on consulting staff advisers ("consult three or four"), establishing departments with directors, and preparing detailed job descriptions for various offices.[8] Kauṭilya's writings highlight the antiquity of many management concepts and assumptions.

---

[5] Richard L. A. Sterba, "Clandestine Management in the Imperial Chinese Bureaucracy," *Academy of Management Review* 3(1) (January 1978), pp. 69–78.

[6] Rodger D. Collons, "Factory Production – 1 A.D.," *Academy of Management Journal* 14(2) (June 1971), pp. 270–273.

[7] Kauṭilya, *Arthaśāstra* [*The Science of Political and Economic Relations*], trans. Rudrapatna Shamasastry (Bangalore: Government Press, 1915), pp. 77, 79. Originally written between second-century BCE and third-century CE.

[8] *Ibid.*, pp. 16, 32.

Egypt

The ancient Egyptians developed extensive irrigation projects as an adjunct to the annual overflowing of the Nile River. Their engineering feats in building the Great Pyramids of Giza and the Canal of the Pharaohs (forerunner of the modern Suez Canal) were marvels superior to anything the Greeks and Romans later constructed. Mining and most engineering projects were government monopolies and required developing an extensive civil service to administer. The labor force for such projects consisted of both freemen and slaves. Strong cultural traditions bound individuals to occupations, and chains and whips took care of other labor problems.

There is evidence that the early Egyptians were aware of limits to the number of laborers one overseer could supervise. Excavated engravings suggest a ratio of about ten laborers to one overseer. Excavations have also revealed distinctive dress for overseers and laborers. Overseers wore kilts or robes, whereas laborers were dressed to represent their trade or occupation.[9] The "rule of ten" as a limit on an overseer's "span of control" was an Egyptian practice that can be found in numerous civilizations, as we shall see shortly.

The most important official in ancient Egypt was the *vizier*, who served the pharaoh as chief political advisor, as well as supervised the administration of the country. It is from the word *vizier* that; we derive the word *supervisor*. The existence of a vizier was recorded as early as 1750 BCE. One of the best-known viziers was the Hebrew-Israelite named Joseph, who had been sold into bondage by his brothers. Because of Joseph's ability to forecast the future, the pharaoh Apophis made him vizier. This was a clear delegation of authority, leaving spiritual matters in the hands of Apophis and secular matters in Joseph's care. As vizier, Joseph was the second most powerful person in ancient Egypt. He was a director, organizer, coordinator, and decision maker. Under Joseph's direction, an elaborate bureaucracy was developed to measure the level of the Nile River—on which every part of the economy depended—to forecast grain production and revenues, allocate these revenues to various governmental units, and supervise all industry and trade. This involved some rather sophisticated (for the times) management techniques, including forecasting, planning, division of labor and departmentalization, and a well-trained "professional" bureaucracy to function.

The Hebrews

The Old Testament is a story of a people in the quest of a land. In addition to Joseph, other great leaders of the Hebrew people combined spiritual and secular powers, including Abraham (ca. 1900 BCE), Moses (ca. 1300 BCE), and David (ca. 1000 BCE). After these great leaders had passed away, tribal leadership became the task of judges, who led by virtue of possessing spiritual power, or what has come down to us as "charisma." The book of Judges in the Bible tells how twelve judges, in successive reigns amounting to 410 years, held sway over Israel.

It is very likely, however, the Egyptians provided the seeds for the management concepts found in the Bible. Joseph was sold into slavery, rose to be Apophis's vizier, and gained valuable administrative experience. Moses, while in captivity in Egypt, observed the Egyptian "rule of ten." The Bible tells us that on the advice of his father-in-law, Jethro (thus making Jethro the first known management consultant), Moses "chose able men from all over Israel and made them judges over the people—thousands, hundreds, fifties, and tens. They were constantly available to administer justice. They brought the hard cases to Moses but judged the smaller matters themselves" (Exod. 18:25–26). Thus, Moses employed the most fundamental control technique, management by exception, as well as established a more orderly structure for tribal management.

---

[9] W. M. Flinders Petrie, *Social Life in Ancient Egypt* (Boston, MA: Houghton Mifflin, 1923), pp. 21–22.

Other managerial advice can be found in the Bible: "Without deliberation, plans come to nothing; where counselors are many, plans succeed" (Prov. 15:22). This bears a marked resemblance to the advice of Sun Tzu, who was a continent and many years away. For controlling, we are told: "Where there are many hands, lock things up" (Eccles. 42:6).[10] Leadership, delegation, span of control, planning, organizing, and controlling were managerial practices found among ancient peoples.

Greece

Will Durant captured the essence of the rise and fall of many civilizations in writing, "a nation is born stoic, and dies epicurean."[11] In the stoic phase of this cycle, adversity breeds cohesion and deprivation fosters initiative. Self-control, thrift, hard work, and an orderly life bring prosperity. As affluence reigns, self-control becomes self-indulgence, thrift becomes a vice, industry and perseverance yield opportunism, and social order breaks down. Epicureans take no thought for the morrow, and decline begins. As historian Basil H. Liddell Hart noted, the downfall of a civilization "tends to come not from the direct assaults of foes but from internal decay."[12] This cycle was true for Greece and for Rome.

The institutions, art, language, drama, and literature of ancient Greece form a significant part of Western culture. Greek economic philosophy, however, was antibusiness. Trade and most commerce were considered beneath the dignity of Greek patricians. Prestige was directly proportional to the amount of time a person spent engaged in leisurely pursuits. The liberation of the mind was considered the highest ideal of human development. Physical labor was for slaves. Business and agriculture were for freedmen or resident foreigners. Affairs of state were controlled by an oligarchy of privileged citizens and their descendants. All others were denied the privilege of citizenship.

Socrates (469–399 BCE) observed that managerial skills were transferable: "[the] management of private concerns differs from that of public concerns only in magnitude . . . neither can be carried on without men . . . and those who understand how to employ [others] are successful directors of private and public concerns, and those who do not understand, will err in the management of both."[13] Plato (ca. 428–348 BCE), a pupil of Socrates, remarked on human diversity and how this led to the division of labor:

> I am myself reminded that we are not all alike; there are diversities of natures among us which are adapted to different occupations. . . . And, if so, we must infer that all things are produced more plentifully and easily and of a better quality when one man does one thing which is natural to him and does it at the right time, and leaves other things.[14]

This notion that a division of labor optimized productivity would persist for nearly 2,000 years, forming the basis for organizing work and determining how to best utilize individual differences in knowledge, skills, and abilities.

---

[10] For other examples, see Sterling R. McLean, *The Evolution of Principles of Organization Structure* (Unpublished dissertation, University of Texas, Austin, TX, 1961); Robert L. Hagerman, "Accounting in the Bible," *Accounting Historians Journal* 7(2) (Fall 1980), pp. 71–76.

[11] Durant, *The Story of Civilization*, vol. 1: *Our Oriental Heritage*, p. 259.

[12] Basil Henry Liddell Hart, *Why Don't We Learn from History?* (London: G. Allen & Unwin, 1946), p. 49.

[13] Xenophon, [*Socrates's*] *Memorabilia and Oeconomicus,* trans. Edgar C. Marchant (Cambridge, MA: Harvard University Press, 1968), p. 189. Originally written circa 421 BCE.

[14] Plato, *The Republic of Plato,* 3rd ed. trans. Benjamin Jowett (Oxford: Clarendon Press, 1888), p. 50. Originally written circa 380 BCE.

Aristotle (384–322 BCE), a student of Plato, provided numerous insights into management and organization. Examples from his classic *Politics* include:

On the specialization of labor: "[E]very work is better done which receives the sole, and not the divided attention of the worker."

On departmentalization: "[E]very office should have a special function [and one question is] should offices be divided according to the subjects with which they deal, or according to the persons with which they deal?"

On centralization, decentralization, and delegation of authority: "We should also know when local tribunals are to have jurisdiction over many different matters, and when authority should be centralized; for example, should one person keep order in the market and another in some other place, or should the same person be responsible everywhere?"

On synergy: "The whole is naturally superior to the part."

On leadership: "[H]e who has never learned to obey cannot be a good commander."[15]

Aristotle's *Nicomachean Ethics* (ca. 350 BCE) guided Western thought for millennia on how we should conduct ourselves in our relations with others. Borrowing from Plato, Aristotle described the cardinal virtues of prudence (practical wisdom in making rational choices), temperance (moderation and self-control), courage (fortitude and endurance), and justice (the equitable exchange of goods and the fulfillment of contractual obligations). He observed that achieving virtuous behavior required teaching, experience, and time for developing one's disposition to act appropriately by doing the right thing at the right time for the right reasons.

In his *Metaphysics,* Aristotle advanced the thesis that reality is knowable only through the senses and through reason. By rejecting mysticism, Aristotle became the father of the scientific method and established the intellectual foundation for the Italian Renaissance, which we will discuss shortly. Eventually, this spirit of scientific inquiry would form a basis for scientific management (Chapter 7).

Another Greek, Xenophon (ca. 430–354 BCE), described the advantages of the division of labor (ca. 370 BCE):

[T]here are places [workshops] even where one man earns a living by only stitching shoes, another cutting them out, another by sewing the uppers together, while there is another who performs none of these operations but only assembles the parts. It follows, therefore, as a matter of course, that he who devotes himself to a very highly specialized line of work is bound to do it in the best possible manner.[16]

In 146 BCE, Greece fell to the Romans, a hardy stock of people from the banks of the Tiber River. Greece destroyed itself by depleting its forests and natural resources, by internal moral decay, by political disorder, and by decimating its leadership through revolts and counterrevolts. Despite its antibusiness sentiment, ancient Greece sowed the first seeds of democracy and saw the advent of decentralized participatory government, the first attempts to establish individual liberty, and the beginnings of the scientific method, as well as provided early insights into the division of labor, departmentalization, delegation of authority, and leadership.

Rome

According to legend, Rome was founded by the twin brothers Romulus and Remus on April 27, 753 BCE. Rome was born "stoic" and conquered the decaying Hellenic civilization. The Romans

---

[15] Aristotle, *The Politics of Aristotle,* vol. 1, trans. Benjamin Jowett (Oxford: Clarendon Press, 1885), pp. 137–138, 105, 74. Originally written 4th-century BCE.

[16] Xenophon, *Cyropaedia*, vol. 2, trans. Walter Miller (London: W. Heinemann, 1914), p. 333. Originally written circa 370 BCE.

developed a quasi-factory system to manufacture armaments for their Imperial Legion, to produce earthenware for a world market, and, later, for making textiles to be sold for export. The famous Roman road system was built to speed the distribution of goods, as well as to rapidly move legionnaires to dissident colonies. Patrician Romans inherited the Greek disdain for trade and left business activities in the hands of plebeians and freedmen.[17] As a growing external trade in foodstuffs, animal products, and materials for manufacturing and construction required commercial standardization, the Romans established a guaranteed system of measures, weights, and coins. The first resemblance to a corporate organization appeared in the form of joint-stock companies, which were involved in fulfilling government contracts for necessary war supplies and equipment.[18] There was a highly specialized labor force that, with few exceptions, worked in small shops owned by independent artisans. Men who shared a common occupation (e.g., sack-carriers, grain measurers, barge-men, and ship pilots) joined together to form guilds (*collegia*). These, however, did not function as unions to control wages, hours, or conditions of employment, but to screen members and punish any who stole or were otherwise corrupt, so as to protect a guild's reputation.[19] The Roman Republic (and later Empire) governed all aspects of economic life: it levied tariffs on goods, fined monopolists, and regulated trade guilds. Large-scale organizations could not exist because joint-stock companies were prohibited for any purpose other than the execution of government contracts.

The Roman Army followed the "rule of ten," although its application varied from time to time. The Roman cavalry had *decuriones,* units of 10 horse soldiers, with 3 decuriones constituting a *turma* and 10 *turmae* (300 cavalry) supporting a legion. Centurions commanded *centuries* of some 100 men, and these centuries were organized into cohorts, with 10 cohorts making up a legion. Thus, the Roman genius for order and discipline established units to perform certain tasks, as well as a hierarchy of command or authority to ensure performance. Other Roman contributions to our shared heritage came chiefly from law and government, which were manifestations of a concern for order. Roman law became a guide for later civilizations, and the Roman separation of legislative and executive powers provided a model system of checks and balances for later constitutional governments.

The Roman Catholic Church

From its seedbed in the Middle East, Christianity faced theological as well as organizational challenges. As the Christian faith spread, novel sects (each interpreting the Bible differently) multiplied, and the first blush of a youthful theology threatened to become an adolescence of diversity. Early congregations operated independently, each defining its own doctrine and conditions for membership. Bishops became heads of various local churches, and presbyters and deacons began to appear as their assistants. By the third-century CE, an ascending hierarchy based on rank was more apparent, with the addition of subdeacons and acolytes, who assisted with personal and secretarial duties, and exorcists and readers, who performed liturgical duties. Bishop Cornelius enumerated these ranks in a message to Fabius of Antioch (251 CE). At the Council of Arles (314 CE), some bishops were made superior to others, giving rise to a chief bishop, the Bishop of Rome. At the Council of Nicaea (325 CE), the Bishop of Rome was given primal authority and proclaimed "rector of the whole church," and given the title Pope. The outcome was centralized doctrine and temporal authority in Rome and the Papacy. Conflict between centralized and decentralized authority has, however, reappeared throughout history, not only in early Christianity but also in other organizations. In modern terms, church leaders of all faiths have perceived a need to institutionalize, that is, to specify policies, procedures, ecclesiastical doctrine, and differences in authority. This is a recurring challenge even today, given the need for unanimity of purpose, yet discretion for local challenges and conditions.

---

[17] James W. Gilbart, *Lectures on the History and Principles of Ancient Commerce* (London: Smith, Elder and Co., 1847), p. 223.

[18] Peter Temin, *The Roman Market Economy* (Princeton, NJ: Princeton University Press, 2013), p. 188.

[19] *Ibid*., pp. 109–110.

Feudalism and the Middle Ages

Scholars coined the phrase "Middle Ages" to identify the period in Western European history from the fall of Rome to the beginning of the Italian Renaissance. Slavery became uneconomical in the late-Roman era, between the second- and eighth-centuries CE: the upkeep of slaves was costly, and they showed no particular enthusiasm for their work. The abolition of slavery came not with moral progress but with economic change. Developing freedmen as tenant farmers simply proved to be more economical. The growth of large estates and the political disorder following the fall of Rome in 476 CE led to economic, social, and political chaos, ripe for the emergence of feudalism, as local powers took over the functions of a central authority. Feudalism, as a cultural system, prevailed in Europe from about the ninth- to tenth-centuries CE. At the base of feudalism were serfs, who tilled plots of land owned by manorial lords, much like modern sharecroppers, and were given military protection in exchange for a portion of their crops. Feudalism bound serfs to a lord, set rigid class distinctions, established a landed aristocracy that endured to the Industrial Revolution, and stifled improvements in education, thereby making poverty and ignorance the hallmark of the masses. It is no wonder that some historians prefer to call this period the Dark Ages.

Although some writers romanticize the Middle Ages for chivalry, the Crusades, a healthy agrarian life, and dignity of the artisan, it was a rather bleak time in history. Many of the problems typically associated with the Industrial Revolution actually began during this period. People razed the forests for fire wood, ignoring any reforestation needs, and overgrazed or carelessly tilled open lands. As the forests diminished, coal became a more important source of fuel, thus creating air pollution. Eleanor of Provence, Queen consort of England, was forced from her castle at Nottingham in 1257 by the coal smoke and fumes from a nearby village. Water pollution resulted from human and animal waste flowing from open sewers into surrounding streams. Conditions grew worse until the British parliament passed the first known antipollution legislation in 1388, almost four centuries before the Industrial Revolution.[20] These were nasty, brutish times, but developing events would lead to better days.

The Revival of Commerce

Feudalism saw the spread of Christianity (specifically Roman Catholicism) as the nobility funded religious activities in return for divine favor. The spread of Christianity, in turn, gave birth to the Crusades, as those who fought to defend the Church were promised indulgences absolving their past sins. Two centuries of religious fervor had left the Holy Land in the hands of Muslims, and Christian Europe was seething. The Crusades also stimulated commerce by opening new trade routes and exposing parochial, feudal Europe to the wealth of the Middle East. This new worldliness weakened the Roman Catholic Church's influence and also disrupted feudalism as thousands of aristocrats died young and many others went bankrupt because they could not repay money borrowed to crusade. Further, embarking on their journeys with invincible religious conviction, the Crusaders returned with the realization that Middle Eastern culture was in many ways superior in manners, morals, trade, industry, and warfare.

Another eye-opener was the return of a Venetian trader, Marco Polo (1254–1324), from China, Tibet, Burma, and India in 1295. In addition to his fantastic tales of a previously unseen part of the world, he told how the Tartar (actually, Tatar) tribes of Mongolia and Manchuria organized their armies: "[The Chief] puts himself at the head of an army of a hundred thousand horses . . . and appoints an officer to the command of ten men, and others to command a hundred,

---

[20] Jean Gimpel, *The Medieval Machine: The Industrial Revolution of the Middle Ages* (New York: Holt, Rinehart and Winston, 1976), pp. 75–85.

a thousand, and ten thousand men respectively . . . by this arrangement each officer has only to attend to the management of ten men or ten bodies of men."[21] How did the Tartars, having never before visited or been visited by the West, arrive at this "rule of ten"? For that matter, how did the Incas, a civilization that flourished from about 1200 to 1532 in what is roughly modern Peru and Chile, have "a decimal system of control, with overseers of ten, a hundred, a thousand, and up to ten thousand people"?[22] History often reveals more than it resolves.

The cultural eye-opening of the Crusades led to a more secular life in Europe through a weakening of religious bonds. Interest arose in exploration, and a new spirit of trade and commerce undercut feudalism. New markets, new ideas, the rise of towns, the first seeds of a middle class, freer circulation of money and credit instruments, and the resurgence of political order created the base for both the Italian Renaissance (which began in the late fourteenth century) and the ensuing Protestant Reformation (1517–1648) in Western Europe.

Before the Industrial Revolution, how were goods produced? Many products were made or grown in the home for a family's use. Other products, however, came from two basic methods of industrial organization: guilds and the domestic system of production. Guilds, as far as we know, existed primarily between 1100 and 1500 and consisted of two types: merchant guilds, which were the buyers and sellers of goods, and craft guilds, which were the makers of goods. Within craft guilds, there was a hierarchy of descending authority, from masters to journeymen to apprentices. Masters owned workshop tools and raw materials; journeymen were paid workers who had finished their apprenticeship, but had not yet opened their own shop; and apprentices were those who were learning a craft. Each town or village typically regulated the number of masters in each craft, the number of apprentices in a workshop, and the *maximum* wages an apprentice could earn. If an apprentice ran away, wanted posters were circulated and law enforcement authorities were sent to retrieve the culprit. Local officials, who forbade the entry of products from outside a village and, in turn, taxed or licensed guilds to pay for such protection, shielded each guild from competition. As we noted in Chapter 1, craft guilds also suppressed innovations.

Guilds regulated quality and acted to control certain types of work: for example, craft-guild rules prohibited shoemakers from tanning hides, which was the job of tanners, and weavers from dyeing cloth, which was the job of dyers. Conversely, tanners and dyers also had to stick to their own work. Thus, craft guilds used division of labor to gain greater job control. The modern union practices of controlling job access, defining guild jurisdiction, and restricting encroachment by members of other guilds is a legacy of early craft guilds.

Members of merchant guilds were intermediaries in trade, buying raw materials to sell to individual producers who made items that the merchants would then pay for and sell. Merchants were thus the cornerstone of what was called the domestic, or "putting-out," system of production. A merchant procured raw material and contracted with individuals or families who, using their own equipment, to produce items in their homes and then return them to the merchant for a wage. The faults of the domestic system lay in simple tools and technology, with little incentive for improvement, and in the inefficiencies of small-scale production with a limited division of labor. As the volume of trade grew, the domestic system of production proved inefficient, and the need for more capital, the benefits of specialized labor, and the economies of scale of a centralized workplace led to the factory system.

In the domestic system, however, we find an early example of what is now termed "transaction cost economics," the idea that, in some instances, a managerial hierarchy may allocate resources more effectively than a marketplace (to be discussed further in Chapter 16). The domestic system

---

[21] Marco Polo, *The Travels of Marco Polo* (New York: The Modern Library, 1954), p. 92. Originally written in 1298.
[22] John Hemming, "The Lost Cities of the Incas," in Joseph J. Thorndike, Jr., ed., *Discovery of Lost Worlds* (New York: American Heritage Publishing, 1979), p. 263.

of production relied on negotiating contracts with individuals who would work in their homes and the price that would be paid for their output set a basis for determining the prevailing market price. Working from their homes, individuals could labor at their own pace, making supply unpredictable for merchants. With no monitoring of performance, quality often suffered. Payment for performance provided an incentive, however, for timely output. At any point, a merchant could have contracts with numerous individuals or families, making the monitoring of performance even more difficult. With the emergence of steam power and the factory system, we will see how a central workplace and a managerial hierarchy facilitated dependable production, reduced risk and uncertainty, and yielded advantages over the domestic system.

Growing trade also required improved accounting methods. Although traders and bankers such as Francesco Datini of Prato and Genoa and the Medicis of Florence were using the essentials of double-entry bookkeeping as early as 1340,[23] a Franciscan monk, Luca Pacioli, first described this advance in his *Summa de Arithmetica, geometrica, proportioni, et proportionalita* in 1494.[24] Pacioli's system was the first information system for management: it provided merchants with information on cash and inventory and enabled a check on cash flow, but did not keep track of costs. It would be some 400 years before any advancements were made in double-entry bookkeeping.

As trade expanded, more souls were placed in jeopardy with respect to the prevailing Roman Catholic Church doctrine against charging interest to earn personal profit as opposed to helping others. Saint Thomas Aquinas, a thirteenth-century theologian, had addressed the issue of justice in trade matters with the idea of a "just price," which was the market, or prevailing, price. In 1468, Dominican Friar Johannes Nider extended this notion by developing certain trade rules (we might call them a code of ethical conduct), which, if followed, would assure merchants that their transactions were just. For example, the rules declared that goods should be "lawful, honorable, and useful"; that prices should be just; that sellers should beware (*caveat venditor*) and not engage in "trickery" or "intimidation" or sell to "simpletons," who would not be informed buyers; and that those who buy "looking for nothing but a rise in prices [i.e., financial speculators], sin most gravely."[25] Nider's trade rules were published at Cologne in about 1468 and reprinted ten times by 1490. This was the first publication to focus on business ethics, and its early publication and appeal suggest that a concern for ethical trade practices has a long history. As one author summarized Nider's message for today:

> Nider's thoughts are surprisingly modern . . . . Through his eyes we see the moral dilemmas of the past and of the present; the moral choices that must be made in everyday life in business and our personal conduct; and the need for guidelines that provide the ropes to keep us from falling. Nider addressed evergreen issues that ethicists faced in the past and encounter in the present – that laws alone cannot deflect human frailties nor chicanery; that ultimate responsibility for one's actions cannot be avoided; and that virtuous conduct is necessary in exchange relationships.[26]

Feudalism was dead, interred by expanding trade, growing urbanization, the creation of a merchant class, and the development of strong central governments. The age of industrialization had, however, not yet arrived. New wine was fermenting, straining old societal containers. What was needed now was a new spirit, a new sanction for human effort.

---

[23] Morgen Witzel, *Builders and Dreamers: The Making and Meaning of Management* (London: Prentice Hall, 2002).

[24] Luca Pacioli, *Summa de Arithmetica, geometrica, proportioni, et proportionalita* [*Summary of Arithmetic, Geometry, Proportions and Proportionality*] (Venice: Paganino Paganini, 1494).

[25] Johannes Nider, *On the Contracts of Merchants*, trans. Charles H. Reeves, ed. Ronald B. Shuman (Norman, OK: University of Oklahoma Press, 1966), pp. 38–45. Originally written circa 1430 and originally published circa 1468.

[26] Daniel A. Wren, "Medieval or Modern? A Scholastic's View of Business Ethics, *circa* 1430," *Journal of Business Ethics* 28(2) (November 2000), p. 117.

Cultural Rebirth

The new wine that was straining the old societal containers was a trinity of forces that would eventually lead to the Industrial Revolution and a cultural rebirth. These forces established the cultural foundations of an industrial age that brought people from subservience to a newfound freedom in allocating resources, in social relations, and in political institutions. The rediscovery of classical music and art and renewed interest in reason and science epitomized the Renaissance ("Rebirth") that sprang up in Italy beginning in the late fourteenth century and, subsequently, spread throughout Western Europe. The Renaissance gave Europe a new culture and is seen as marking the transition from medieval to modern times. Three ethics, or standards for cultural conduct, interacted in practice to change prevailing values toward people, work, and profits. The *Protestant ethic*, which flowed from the Protestant Reformation, ended the near millennium-old religious hegemony of the Roman Catholic Church in Western Europe. The *liberty ethic* imposed legal limits on political power by promoting representative government. The *market ethic* brought forth the notion of a market-directed economy. The outcome of the resulting cultural rebirth was the creation of a new environmental ethos that would lead to the formal study of management.

The Protestant Ethic

During the Middle Ages, the Roman Catholic Church dominated life in Western Europe and provided the hope of an afterlife as the only consolation for one's worldly plight. With the Church as superstate, the admonitions of doctrine against lending for personal profit, against desiring anything from this world other than subsistence, and against materialistic trade perpetuated the notion of business as a necessary evil. The complete domination of life by the Church led people to think not of this world, but of the other; not of gain, but of salvation. According to the Church, the self-interest of trade diverted people's thoughts from God to personal gain, from obedience to initiative, and from humility to activity.

The loosening of religious bonds following the end of the Crusades in 1487 and the spread of general prosperity through the revival of commerce was bound, sooner or later, to lead to a revolt aimed at reforming the beliefs and practices of the Church. Although other individuals had previously protested papal authority and Catholic doctrine, monk Martin Luther is generally considered the architect of what became known as the Protestant Reformation. Legend holds that on October 3, 1517, he nailed to the door of All Saints' Church in Wittenberg (Saxony) a one-page printed list of 95 theses (a list of questions and propositions) challenging the teachings of the Church. The theses are generally believed to have been the catalyst for the Protestant Reformation, which divided the Church and launched over a century of religious conflict in Europe. Although Luther protested many of what he considered the Church's abuses, especially the sale of indulgences guaranteeing remission of sins and entry into Heaven, he agreed with the Church on other matters. In particular, like the Church, he condemned charging interest for personal gain, considered trade a "nasty business," and spoke out vehemently against the Fuggers, the leading commercial family in Germany.

John Calvin was inspired by Luther and, like Luther, believed in predestination, the notion that all events are willed by God. Calvin believed that God had determined that some ("the elect") were predestined for eternal salvation, whereas others, who God knew would not follow his teachings, were doomed to ever-lasting damnation. Calvin's doctrine of predestination gave a new spirit to his followers. Because everything was predetermined, everyone should believe that they are among the elect and have the courage to overcome the tribulations of their earthly existence.

Did Luther's and Calvin's belief in predestination provide a religious basis for capitalism? Max Weber would answer in the affirmative, by arguing that the *spirit of capitalism* evolved from

Protestant Reformation. Weber made a clear distinction between an irrational, unlimited greed for gain and the "rational capitalism" of what he termed the Protestant ethic:

> The impulse to acquisition, pursuit of gain, of money, of the greatest possible amount of money, has in itself nothing to do with capitalism. This impulse [to acquisition] has been common to all sorts and conditions of men at all times and in all countries of the earth, wherever the objective possibility of it is or has been given. It should be taught in the kindergarten of cultural history that this naïve idea of capitalism must be given up once and for all. Unlimited greed for gain is not in the least identical with capitalism, and is still less its spirit. Capitalism *may* even be identical with the restraint, or at least a rational tempering, of this irrational impulse. But capitalism is identical with the pursuit of profit, and forever *renewed* profit, by means of continuous, rational, capitalistic enterprise. For it must be so: in a wholly capitalistic order of society, an individual capitalistic enterprise which did not take advantage of its opportunities for profit-making would be doomed to extinction.[27]

Weber began his search for an explanation of the capitalistic spirit by noting the overwhelming number of Protestants among business leaders, entrepreneurs, highly skilled laborers, and more highly technically and commercially trained professionals. In Weber's view, Luther developed the idea of a calling in the sense of a task set by God, a life task. This was a new idea originating in the Protestant Reformation and became a central dogma of Protestant denominations. It discarded the Roman Catholic Church's notion of "monastic asceticism," which demanded poverty, and replaced it with ascetic Protestantism, which only condemned the enjoyment of wealth. Protestantism urged individuals to fulfill the obligations imposed on them in this world, that is, their calling (German *Beruf*), and to do so with a clear conscience. It regarded involvement in worldly affairs as the highest form of moral activity and gave the performance of earthly duties a religious significance and approval. Everyone's occupation was a calling, and all were legitimate in the eyes of God. Weber did not say that Luther intended capitalism to follow from his idea of occupations as a calling; on the contrary, this idea was later refined to become the success-oriented spirit of capitalism. The idea of a calling did place a new interpretation on the purpose of life: instead of waiting for Judgment Day, a person should choose and pursue an occupation, not for the purpose of material gain beyond one's needs, but because it was Divine will. Stated differently, everyone was to labor in this world for the glorification of God. All people had to consider themselves among the elect, and if they did not, this was seen as an absence of faith. People were, thus, to engage in worldly activity to guarantee God's grace. In practice, this came to mean that "God helps those who help themselves".[28]

According to Weber, whereas Protestantism held that people should fulfill their required religious duties conscientiously their good works did not need to form a "rationalized system of life" focusing on the promise of a future in heaven to offset the pain and deprivation of the present. They could use their good works to atone for particular sins, to better their chances for salvation, or as a sort of insurance premium for later years. To make a sharper distinction, Weber described the demands of Calvinism:

> The God of Calvinism demanded of his believers not single good works, but a life of good works combined into a unified system. There was no place for the very human Catholic cycle of sin, repentance, atonement, release, followed by a renewed sin. Nor was there any balance of merit for a life as a whole which could be adjusted by temporal punishments or the [non-ascetic] Churches [of the Protestant Reformation] means of grace.[29]

---

[27] Max Weber, *The Protestant Ethic and the Spirit of Capitalism,* trans. Talcott Parsons (New York: Charles Scribner's Sons, 1958), p. 17. Originally published in 1904.

[28] Algernon Sidney, *Discourses Concerning Government* (London: I. Littlebury, 1698), p. 166.

[29] Weber, *The Protestant Ethic*, p. 117. For an elaboration of various rendition of Weber's thesis, see Milan Zafirovski, "The Weber Thesis of Calvinism and Capitalism – Its Various Versions and Their 'Fate' in Social Science," *Journal of the History of the Behavioral Sciences* 52(1) (Winter) 2016, pp. 41–58.

Calvinists were therefore required to live a life of good works, not an inconsistent series of wrongs balanced by repentance, atonement, and forgiveness. Weber saw this as a keystone in developing a spirit of effort and gain; people were no longer able to give free rein to irrational impulses, but were required by dogma to exercise self-control over their every action. People proved their faith by worldly activity, acting with zeal and self-discipline.

This new Protestantism, which Weber also characterized as Puritanism, did not condone the pursuit of wealth for its own sake, for wealth would lead to pleasure and to all the temptations of the flesh. Instead, activity became the goal of a good life. Numerous corollaries developed in practice: (1) wasting time was the deadliest of sins, because every hour wasted was negating an opportunity to labor for God's glory; (2) a willingness to work was essential: "He who will not work shall not eat" (2 Thess. 3:10 as quoted above); (3) the division of labor (and resulting specialization) was a result of Divine will because it led to a higher degree of skill and improvement in the quality and quantity of production and, hence, served the good of all; and (4) consumption beyond basic needs was wasteful and therefore sinful: "Waste not, want not."[30] According to Weber, each of these ideas had a significant impact on the motivations of people, leading to a spirit of enterprise.

Intense activity moved people from a contemplative life to one of continuous physical and mental labor. Willingness to work placed the motivational burden on individuals, and their self-directed, self-controlled lives gave them an internal gyroscope. The division of labor placed each person in a calling and required a person's best, and the nonspecialized worker demonstrated a lack of grace. The Protestant ethic postulated that God desired profitability, that this was a sign of grace, and that to waste anything and reduce profits or to forgo what might be a profitable venture worked against God's will. By not seeking luxury, people created a surplus or profit from their labors. The created wealth was not to be consumed beyond a person's basic needs, and, thus, the surplus was to be reinvested in new enterprises or in the improvement of present ventures.

Protestantism (Puritanism) provided specific guidelines for the creation of a capitalistic spirit. Weber believed that people had a duty to work, a duty to use their wealth wisely, and a duty to lead self-denying lives. An unequal distribution of worldly goods was divine providence at work because everyone has different talents and, therefore, reaps unequal rewards. Wealth was no assurance of heaven, and the poor did not need to worry as long as they performed their calling properly. For Weber, the spirit of capitalism evolved from the Protestant ethic, which equated spiritual worth and temporal success. With no room for self-indulgence and with the tenets of self-control and self-direction, a new age of individualism had been born.

A Criticism of the Weberian Thesis

Every thesis generates an antithesis, and Weber's Protestant ethic was no exception. English economist Richard H. Tawney reversed Weber's thesis and argued that capitalism was the cause and justification of Protestantism, not the effect. Tawney noted that Roman Catholic cities were chief commercial centers, that Roman Catholics were leading bankers, and that the capitalistic spirit was present in Italy, southern Germany, and Flanders in the fifteenth century, far in advance of the sixteenth- and seventeenth-century influences that Weber discussed. According to Tawney, "Is it not a little artificial to suggest that capitalist enterprise had to wait, as Weber appears to imply, till religious changes had produced a capitalist spirit? Would it not be equally plausible, and equally one-sided, to argue that the religious changes were themselves merely the result of economic movements?"[31]

---

[30] *Ibid.*, pp. 157–173. The proverb "Waste not, want not," has origins dating back to Richard Edwards, *The Paradise of Dainty Devices* (London: Printed for Robert Triphook and William Sancho, 1810). Originally written in 1576.

[31] Richard H. Tawney, Foreword to Weber's *Protestant Ethic*, p. 8. Whereas Weber and earlier writers addressed traditional Roman Catholicism, Michael Novak noted changes in Catholicism that challenged the exclusivity of a "Protestant Ethic." See Novak's *The Catholic Ethic and the Spirit of Capitalism* (New York: Free Press, 1993) and *Business as a Calling* (New York: Free Press, 1996).

In Tawney's view, the rise of capitalism was action and reaction, molding and, in turn, being molded by other significant cultural forces. The Renaissance brought a new focus on reason, discovery, exploration, and science; all were challenges to the monolithic authority of the Roman Catholic Church. In doing so, it promised a new social order in which there would be mobility for all; it signaled the mastery of people over their environment, counter to the opposite view common throughout the Middle Ages.[32] A growing economic life posed new challenges for religious doctrine, and merchants and artisans engaged in profit-making activities regardless of dogma. Though the Protestant Reformation had begun as a religious reform movement, it was seized by an emerging merchant class and bent to its own economic needs, as it sought a religion that would sanctify and a sovereign state that would legalize its capitalistic impulses. As one authority has commented, the Protestant religion and capitalism went "hand in hand like bride and groom."[33]

With two sets of assumptions, two different conclusions could be reached: (1) Weber's notion that religious institutions changed and then the spirit of capitalism abounded; or (2) Tawney's view that economic motivation was steam pushing on the lid of religious authority until the safety valve of a change in dogma (i.e., the Protestant Reformation and its later proliferation into various sects) could sanction economic efforts.

Modern Support for Weber

Despite the criticisms of Weber's thesis that religion can influence economic growth, there is modern evidence that Protestants hold different values toward work. In *The Achieving Society,* David C. McClelland began a search for the psychological factors that were generally important for economic development. The principal factor he isolated was the "need for achievement," or in the shorthand version, *n ach*. McClelland's search was both historical and cross-cultural, and his findings support Weber's thesis. First, McClelland found that high *n ach* was essential to engaging in entrepreneurial activities; second, high *n ach* in a society was significantly correlated to rapid economic development; and third, certain ethnic, religious, and minority groups showed marked differences in *n ach*. He found that children of Protestants had higher *n ach* than children of Roman Catholics, and children of Jews had still higher *n ach*. McClelland concluded that individualistic religions, personified by various Protestant denominations, tended to be associated with a high *n ach*, whereas authoritarian religions, such as traditional Roman Catholicism, tended to have a lower need for achievement. He did concede, however, that there are wide variations among various modern Roman Catholic communities.

What was involved in the need for achievement was not so much the need to reach certain goals (such as wealth, status, respect), but the need to enjoy success. Wealth was a way of keeping score, not a goal. In this regard, McClelland argued that the entrepreneurial personality was characterized by special attitudes toward risk taking, a willingness to expend energy, an eagerness to innovate, and a readiness to make decisions and accept responsibility. Historically, the concern for achievement appeared in a culture some 50 or so years before a rapid rate of economic growth and prosperity. McClelland found this to be true in ancient Greece (before its Golden Age), in Spain during the Middle Ages (before the Age of Exploration), and in England during two different periods. The first period was from 1500 to 1625 when Protestantism was growing in strength concurrently with a need for achievement. The second period came in the eighteenth century just prior to the Industrial Revolution. The reasoning that McClelland used to support Weber was basically thus: (1) the Protestant Reformation emphasized self-reliance rather than reliance on others in all facets of life, and (2) Protestant parents changed child-rearing practices to teach

---

[32] Richard H. Tawney, *Religion and the Rise of Capitalism* (London: John Murray, 1926), pp. 61–63.
[33] Max I. Dimont, *Jews, God, and History* (New York: Simon and Schuster, 1962), p. 233.

self-reliance and independence. McClelland and his associates empirically demonstrated that these practices led to a higher need for achievement in sons and a higher need for achievement led to spurts of economic activity such as those characterized by Weber as the spirit of capitalism.[34] McClelland was, therefore, able to draw an empirical relationship between the influence of Protestantism and Weber's spirit of modern capitalism.

Lenski summarized, evaluated, and presented evidence both for and against Weber's belief in a Protestant ethic. On balance, he found the evidence more in favor of Weber than against. In an attempt to define the relationship between religious affiliation and the ability of people to move upward in their careers, Lenski explored the relationship between vertical mobility and individual characteristics, such as aspirations, ambition, and attitudes toward work. He found that Jews were the most mobile, followed by Protestants, and then Roman Catholics. Lenski believed this variation could be explained by differences in achievement motivation and attitudes toward work. In contrast, Roman Catholics held neutral attitudes toward work and labored for reasons other than the satisfaction that came from work itself. In Lenski's view, "Catholics continued to regard work primarily as a necessary evil; a consequence of Adam's fall and a penalty for sin. By contrast, Protestants came to view it as an opportunity for serving God, or, in the Deist version, for building character."[35]

The implications of McClelland's and Lenski's findings can be far reaching for contemporary society. Not only did McClelland and Lenski provide empirical support for Weber's contentions, but their findings also suggest that need for achievement can be developed in individuals and, in turn, instilled in entire nations. In underdeveloped countries, the challenge may be underachievement; if so, an inculcation of a need for achievement may be one means for furthering economic growth and prosperity.

The Liberty Ethic

Given the implications of a need for achievement and the sanctioning of individual rewards for performance, to grow economically, a nation's political system must be conducive to personal liberty. The divine right of kings, the aristocracy of the manor lord, the exercise of secular authority by the Roman Catholic Church, and serfdom as an ascribed status were not favorable conditions for developing an industrialized society. During the eighteenth century and the so-called Age of Enlightenment, political philosophers championed equality, justice, the rights of citizens, and governance by the consent of those governed. These ideas threatened the existing order by challenging the prevailing view of the relationship between citizens and their states.

As a standard for cultural conduct, the liberty ethic challenged political theory that called for the domination of the many by the few. It found its best proponents in Nicollò di Bernado dei Machiavelli and Thomas Hobbes. Machiavelli, an out-of-office administrator and diplomat in the city-state of Florence, wrote *The Prince* in 1513.[36] He was an experienced observer of the intrigues and machinations of Florence and the Roman Catholic Church and set forth a how-to book for a ruler or an aspiring ruler. *The Prince*, dedicated to Lorenzo di Piero de Medici, was an exposition on how to rule—not how to be good or wise—but how to rule successfully. Machiavelli identified three routes to the top: "fortune," "ability," and "villainy." Those who rose through their good fortune had little trouble in reaching the top, but had difficulty maintaining their position because they depended on the goodwill of others and were indebted entirely

---

[34] David C. McClelland, *The Achieving Society* (Princeton, NJ: Van Nostrand, 1961), pp. 47–53. See also John W. Atkinson and Norman T. Feather, eds., *A Theory of Achievement Motivation* (New York: John Wiley & Sons, 1966).

[35] Gerhard Lenski, *The Religious Factor: A Sociological Study of Religious Impact on Politics, Economics, and Family Life* (Garden City, NY: Doubleday, 1961), p. 83.

[36] Nicollò di Bernado dei Machiavelli, *The Prince*, trans. Luigi Ricci (New York: New American Library, 1952). Written in 1513, but not published until 1532 because of its controversial nature.

to those who elevated them. Those who succeeded by ability endured a thousand difficulties en route, but would be able to maintain their position more easily. Those who employed villainy, an oft-chosen path in Machiavelli's Florence, used methods that would gain power, but not glory; afterward, their crown would always rest uneasily as they awaited the next usurper or palace revolt.[37]

Machiavelli's basic assumption about human nature was indicative of his rationale for the type of leadership he advocated: "whoever desires to found a state and give it laws, must start with assuming that all men are bad and ever ready to display their vicious nature, whenever they may find occasion for it."[38] To cope with these brutes, rulers were justified in pursuing any leadership style that suited their purpose. Rulers should be concerned with having a good reputation, but not with being virtuous; should they have to choose between being feared and being loved, it was better to be feared; and above all, rulers must be both like a lion and like a fox, employing force and deceit. Machiavelli wrote of rulers, but not of the ruled; of power, but not of rights; and of ends, but not of means. He influenced the later ideas of British historian Lord Acton about power corrupting, and absolute power corrupting absolutely.[39] "Machiavellian" has come to connote those who are unscrupulous, crafty, and cunning in policy. For his time, and perhaps for ours, Machiavelli personified the command philosophy of governance.

Thomas Hobbes's *Leviathan* (1651) was a later argument for strong central authority. In Hobbes's view, humans originated in a state of nature, without civil government, and he proceeded to the conclusion that some greater power, the Leviathan, must exist to bring order from chaos.[40] This greater power (a commonwealth or an independent state) became sovereign in either of two ways: by natural force or when people voluntarily submit to someone in the confidence that in return they will be protected against all others.[41] It made no difference to Hobbes whether the Leviathan was secular or ecclesiastical, as long as it regulated all overt conduct and expression, whether civil or religious. The sovereign ruled all, and individuals were subordinate to those who ruled.

In the history of human liberty, John Locke's essay, *Concerning Civil Government* (1690), stands as a defining contribution to political theory and as an instigator of political action. It articulated the principles of the "Glorious Revolution of 1688," which brought about fundamental changes in the English constitution. It also set the stage for the Revolutionary War in the United States (1775–1783) by inspiring the authors of the Declaration of Independence, adopted by the Second Continental Congress meeting in Philadelphia on July 4, 1776, as well as Jean Jacques Rousseau to write *Of Social Contract, or Principles of Political Right*, which helped launch the French Revolution. Perhaps no other person has had such a profound effect on political theory and action. Locke attacked the divine right of kings, whose proponents traced the belief that monarchs were divinely empowered to the *Book of Genesis* and Adam's God-given right to rule his children. Further, he set forth some new concepts of authority: "who shall be Judge whether the Prince, or Legislative, act contrary to their Trust? . . . To this I reply; The People shall be Judge."[42]

[37] Daniel A. Wren and Ronald G. Greenwood, *Management Innovators: The People and Ideas That Have Shaped Modern Business* (New York: Oxford University Press, 1998), pp. 191–194.
[38] Nicollò di Bernado dei Machiavelli, "Discourses on the First Ten Books of Titus Livius" in *The Historical, Political, and Diplomatic Writings of Niccolo Machiavelli,* vol. 2, trans. Christian E. Detmold (Boston, MA: J. R. Osgood, 1882), p. 104. Originally written circa 1517.
[39] John Emerich Edward Dalberg-Acton, "Letter to Mandell Creighton (April 5, 1887)," in *Historical Essays & Studies*, eds. John Neville Figgis and Reginald Vere Laurence (London: Macmillan and Co., 1907), p. 504.
[40] Thomas Hobbes, *Leviathan, or, the Matter, Form, and Power of a Common-Wealth Ecclesiastical and Civil* (London: Printed for Andrew Crooke, at the Green Dragon in St. Paul's Churchyard, 1651), p. 1.
[41] *Ibid.*, p. 88.
[42] John Locke, *Two Treatises of Government: In the Former the False Principles & Foundation of Sir Robert Filmer & His Fllowers, Are Detected & Overthrown; the Latter Is an Essay Concerning the True Original, Extent & End of Civil Government* (London: Printed for Awnsham Churchill, at the Black Swan in Ave-Mary-Lane, by Amen-Corner, 1690), p. 269. Printed in 1689, but dated 1690.

This new concept found more explicit support in the Declaration of Independence:

> We hold these truths to be self-evident, that all men are created equal; that they are endowed by their creator with certain inalienable rights; that among these are life, liberty, and the pursuit of happiness. That to secure these rights, governments are instituted among men deriving their just powers from the consent of the governed.[43]

Locke's work is so broad that it is possible here only to sample its main contributions: first, people are governed by a natural rule of reason and not by the arbitrary rules of tradition or the whims of a central authority; and second, civil society is built on private property. The law of nature ("natural law") and reason commands one not to harm another's possessions, and individuals enter into a civil society to preserve more perfectly their liberty and property, which are then protected by both natural law and civil law. Because people have a natural right to property, a political entity cannot take their property, but rather must protect their right to ownership.

Locke was a Puritan in the England of Oliver Cromwell, who was considered by some to be a dictator, but by others a hero of liberty. Locke's writings influenced Adam Smith (discussed below) and were the basis for Rousseau's views on human nature. In the emergence of the philosophical Age of Enlightenment, Locke put forth a new civil order: (1) a law based on reason, not arbitrary dictates; (2) a government deriving its powers from the governed; (3) liberty to pursue individual goals as a natural right; and (4) private property and its use in the pursuit of happiness as a natural and legally protected right. These four ideas interwove in practice to form a solid political foundation for industrial growth. They gave sanction to laissez-faire economics and the pursuit of individual rewards, protected against the confiscation of private property, guaranteed contract rights, and created a justice system that treated all people equally.

The Market Ethic

Economic thinking was basically sterile during the Middle Ages because localized, subsistence-level economies required no commercial framework. People only recognized two factors of production: land and labor. Simply stated, in most of the world, people primarily produced food on small farms for their own consumption. Capital as an input factor was scorned and usury was damned. Any idea that management was a primary input that afforded a comparative advantage was completely lacking.

In the sixteenth and seventeenth centuries, however, the reemergence of strong national identities began to reshape economic thought. As new lands previously unknown were discovered through exploration, new trade routes and new products created international markets. The ensuing growth in world trade resulted in an economic philosophy known as "mercantilism" that placed governments in a central role, financing and encouraging international commerce to build strong national economies. In consequence, nations soon intervened in all economic affairs, engaged in federal economic planning, and, to the extent possible, regulated private economic activity.[44] Mercantilism eventually fell of its own weight. It went awry as it tried to keep alive failing enterprises, curbed private initiative, imposed elaborate bureaucratic controls, and fostered wars and trade rivalries that destroyed the very markets it was trying to gain. Mercantilism was a philosophical contradiction in Age of Enlightenment. Mercantilists thought only of a nation's power, whereas the philosophy of the enlightenment championed individual rights and viewed all human institutions in terms of the contribution they made to individual happiness.

---

[43] Thomas Jefferson, *Declaration of Independence* (Philadelphia, PA, 1776), p. 1. Miscellaneous Papers of the Continental Congress, 1774–1789; Records of the Continental and Confederation Congresses and the Constitutional Convention, 1774–1789, Record Group 360; National Archives. Available at http://www.archives.gov/global-pages/larger-image.html?i=/historical-docs/doc-content/images/declaration-of-independence-1.jpg&c=/historical-docs/doc-content/images/declaration-of-independence.caption.html

[44] John Fred Bell, *A History of Economic Thought,* 2nd ed. (New York: Ronald Press, 1967), p. 53.

In the eighteenth century, the Physiocratic school of economic thought emerged to challenge mercantilism. François Quesnay, its founder, maintained that wealth did not lie in gold and silver, but sprang from agricultural production. He advocated laissez-faire capitalism, meaning that governments should leave marketplace mechanisms alone; for Quesnay, a nation's economy had a natural order, and government intervention interfered with both. Adam Smith (1723–1790), a Scottish political economist, was not a Physiocrat per se, but was influenced by the idea that a nation's economy had a natural order. In *The Wealth of Nations,* Smith founded what is known as the classical school of economics. Smith thought that mercantilist tariff polices were destructive and that, rather than protecting industry, actually penalized efficiency and, consequently, misallocated a nation's resources. He felt that economic activity should be regulated solely by marketplace forces and competition. The "invisible hand" of the marketplace would ensure that resources flowed to their most efficient use and yielded the greatest return. In this way, the self-interests of each person and nation, acting in a completely competitive market, would bring about the fullest prosperity for all. As Smith stated it:

> As every individual, therefore, endeavors as much as he can both to employ his capital in the support of domestik industry, and so to direct that industry that its produce may be of the greatest value; every individual necessarily labours to render the annual revenue of the society as great as he can. He generally, indeed, neither intends to promote the publick interest, nor knows how much he is promoting it. By preferring the support of domestik to that of foreign industry, he intends only his own security; and by directing that industry in such a manner as its produce may be of the greatest value, he intends only his own gain, and he is in this, as in many other cases, led by an invisible hand to promote an end which was no part of his intention. Nor is it always the worse for the society that it was no part of it. By pursuing his own interest he frequently promotes that of the society more effectually than when he really intends to promote it. I have never known much good done by those who affected to trade for the publick good.[45]

Adam Smith. Library of Congress.

For Smith, the division of labor was a pillar of marketplace competition. He cited the example of pin makers: when each performed a single or limited number of tasks rather than a broad range of duties, they could produce 48,000 pins a day, whereas one worker alone could produce no more than twenty pins per day. He admitted that this was a trifling example, but he found the same principle operating successfully in many industries:

This great increase of the quantity of work which, in consequence of the division of labour, the same number of people are capable of performing, is owing to three different circumstances: first, to the increase of dexterity in every particular workman; secondly, to the saving of the time which is commonly lost in passing from one species of work to another; and lastly, to the invention of a great number of machines which facilitate and abridge labour, and enable one man to do the work of many.[46]

---

[45] Adam Smith, *An Inquiry Into the Nature and Causes of the Wealth of Nations* (London: W. Strahan and T. Cadell in the Strand, 1776), vol. 2, bk. IV, ch. 2, p. 350. This solitary mention of the "invisible hand" was also used in an economic context in Smith's *The Theory of Moral Sentiments* (London: W. Strahan and T. Cadell, 1759), pt. IV, ch. 1, p. 466.

[46] Smith, *Wealth of Nations,* vol. 1, bk. I, ch. 1, pp. 9–11. An appreciation of the consequences of the division of labor may be traced to early Greek and Chinese philosophers. See Guang-Zhen, *The Division of Labor in Economics: A History* (New York: Routledge, 2012).

Although Smith saw the benefits of the division of labor, he also foresaw its dysfunctional consequences:

> The man whose whole life is spent in performing a few simple operations . . . naturally loses, therefore, the habit of [mental] exertion, and generally becomes stupid and ignorant as it is possible for a human creature to become. . . . His dexterity at his own particular trade seems . . . to be acquired at the expense of his intellectual, social, and martial virtues.[47]

Smith argued that it was the province of governments, through public education, to overcome the division of labor's debilitating effects. In his view, manufacturers, to gain productivity, must rely on the division of labor. Smith believed that the division of labor benefited all society and provided an economic rationale for the factory system. As he reasoned, when markets were limited, the domestic system of production could meet market needs. As a nation's population grew, however, and new markets opened, the benefits of division of labor and economies of scale associated with the factory system would gain momentum.

The first edition of *The Wealth of Nations* was published in March 1776 and was sold out in 6 months. The second edition (1778) incorporated minor changes, but the third edition (1784) introduced substantial revisions, including Smith's concern for joint-stock or limited liability firms. During Smith's time joint-stock companies in England such as the East India Company and the Hudson Bay Company were established by either royal charter or by an act of Parliament. Apparently, investors in general preferred to form joint-stock companies rather than "private copartnery," or partnerships, and Smith had doubts about this arrangement:

> The directors of such [joint-stock] companies, however, being the managers rather of other people's money than of their own, it cannot well be expected, that they should watch over it with the same anxious vigilance with which the partners in a private copartnery frequently watch over their own. Like the stewards of a rich man, they are apt to consider attention to small matters as not for their master's honour, and very easily give themselves a dispensation from having it. Negligence and profusion, therefore, must always prevail, more or less, in the management of the affairs of such a company.[48]

At the time, the largest employers were textile firms, and these were not capital intensive. Yet, Smith anticipated that the separation of ownership from day-to-day control and the resulting rise of salaried managers had a potential downside. Those who managed "other people's money" incurred less personal risk (except for, perhaps, the loss of their jobs) and, thus, Smith felt, would be less vigilant and prudent in their duties.

When Smith first began writing during the early stages of the Industrial Revolution, he attracted a large number of vocal supporters and found fertile ground for his ideas. His views were in tune with the philosophy of the Enlightenment and the interest of newly emerging entrepreneurs who wished to sweep away the restrictions of mercantilism and the controlling power of the landed aristocracy. The market ethic provided a rationale for private initiative rather than mercantilism, competition rather than protectionism, innovation rather than economic stagnancy, and self-interest rather than a nation's power as a motivating force. In brief, the market ethic was another standard for cultural conduct that changed prevailing values toward people, work, and profits, and led to a cultural rebirth that created a new environment that would give rise to the formal study of management.

---

[47] *Ibid.*, vol. 2, bk. V, ch. 1, pp. 366–367.
[48] *Ibid.*, 3rd ed. (1784), vol. 2, bk. 5, ch. 1, pp. 123–124. Compare this with the New Testament allegory of the hired shepherd who abandons the flock he is tending when he sees a wolf. John 10: 11–13.

SUMMARY

Early management thought was dominated by cultural values that were antibusiness, antiachievement, and largely antihuman. Industrialization could not emerge when people were bound to their stations in life, when monarchs ruled by central dictates, and when people were urged to take no thought of individual fulfillment in this world, but rather wait for the hereafter. Before the Industrial Revolution, economies and societies were essentially static, and political values involved unilateral decision-making by a central authority. Although some early advancements in management practice appeared, they were largely localized. Organizations could be run on the divine right of a king, an appeal to dogma among the faithful, and on rigorous military discipline. There was little or no need to develop a formal body of management thought under these circumstances.

Three forces were interacting and combining to provide for a new age of industrialization. Characterized as ethics, or standards governing human conduct, they illustrate how economic, social, and political attitudes were changing and led to a cultural rebirth. The ethics discussed were in reality a struggle between a traditional and a newly emerging society. The Protestant ethic was a challenge to the central authority of the Roman Catholic Church and a response to human needs in the here and now; the liberty ethic reflected the ancient struggle between monolithic and representative forms of government; and the market ethic was a gauntlet flung before the landed gentry, who preferred mercantilism. These are age-old struggles: government control versus individual liberty, human rights and due process versus whimsical autocracy, and centralization versus decentralization. The struggle goes on.

This cultural rebirth would establish the preconditions for industrialization and, subsequently, the need for a rational, formalized, systematic body of knowledge about how to manage. The emergence and refinement of marketplace economies required managers to be more creative and better informed about how to effectively manage an organization. Faced with a competitive, changing environment, managers had to develop a body of knowledge about how best to utilize resources. People began thinking of individual gain and had to be accommodated in some logical managerial framework. The emergence of modern management had to be based on rational methods of decision making; no longer could organizations be operated on the whims of a few. This change did not come suddenly, but evolved over a long period of time as prevailing culture changed. How these changes came about and how they affected the evolution of management thought is an intriguing story.

The Industrial Revolution: Challenges and Perspective

3

The Industrial Revolution in Great Britain
  The Steam Engine
  Management: The Fourth Factor of Production
Management Challenges in Early Factories
  The Labor Challenge
    Recruitment
    Training
    Discipline and Motivation
  The Search for Managerial Talent
  Management Functions in the Early Factory
Cultural Consequences of the Industrial Revolution
  Working Conditions
  Child and Female Labor
Summary

The Industrial Revolution heralded a new age for civilization. The accompanying cultural rebirth had created new social, economic, and political conditions ripe for advances in science and technology. Subsequent improvements in technology made possible large combinations of physical and human resources and ushered in the "factory system," wherein standardized goods were mass produced in large quantities and replaced the "domestic system," in which individual workers fabricated goods in small workshops or in their own homes (see Chapter 2). This chapter examines the salient characteristics of the Industrial Revolution and the managerial challenges it created, and attempts to achieve some perspective on the resulting cultural consequences.

The Industrial Revolution in Great Britain

Industrial progress is always closely tied to advancements in science and technology. In the fifteenth-century, German Johannes Gutenberg (1400–1468) perfected the first movable-type printing press in Europe and began an information revolution that continues today. Although medieval scientists had attempted to deduce physical laws from the writings of Plato, Aristotle, Saint Augustine, and the Bible, a new age of scientific inquiry first emerged in the sixteenth and seventeenth centuries as religious bonds loosened. This revolution in scientific thought was the product of individuals such as Francis Bacon, Nicolaus Copernicus, Galileo Galilei,

William Gilbert, William Harvey, and Isaac Newton and established the foundation for the technological advancements that were to follow.

Ever since humans began to develop methods for tilling the soil, making weapons, and weaving cloth, there have been advancements in technology, the art and applied science of making and using tools and equipment. Technology has been evolving and advancing for thousands of years, but a series of technological advances in late-eighteenth-century England marked the beginning of what was to become known as the Industrial Revolution, an era in which technology developed more rapidly than ever before. The essence of the Industrial Revolution was the substitution of machine power for human, animal, wind, water, and other natural sources of energy. Deane, in pinpointing the emergence of the Industrial Revolution, illustrated the difference between preindustrialized and industrialized societies. Preindustrial societies are characterized by low per capita income, economic stagnation, dependence on agriculture, little specialization of labor, and limited geographic market integration. Industrial societies are characterized by rising or high per capita income, economic growth, low dependence on agriculture, extensive specialization of labor, and widespread geographic market integration.[1] Based on these characteristics, Deane concluded that the shift in England from a preindustrial to an industrial society became most evident in 1750 and accelerated thereafter.

The Steam Engine

In Chapter 2 we considered the two primary methods of pre-industrialized production: the domestic system and medieval craft guilds. In both methods, the scale of production was small, the product markets limited, and work was labor intensive rather than capital intensive. In the domestic system, merchants provided raw materials to families who, working from their homes, spun, bleached, dyed, or performed whatever tasks were necessary. Thus, we find the ancient source of family names for weavers, dyers, tailors, fullers, and so on. In some instances, skilled artisans worked in craft shops, where work was passed from one stage to another. For example, tanners did their work, passed it along to curriers and, in turn, came shoemakers and saddlers, who converted cured leather into finished products. Labor was specialized, capital investment low, and humans, animals, wind, water, and other natural sources (rather than machine power) were sources of energy.

England's largest industry during the Industrial Revolution was textiles.[2] From its overseas colonies came cotton, wool, and other fibers to be cleaned, combed, and spun on into cloth. Mechanical improvements in the textile industry preceded the Industrial Revolution. John Kay began the mechanization of weaving with his "flying shuttle" in 1733. In 1765, James Hargreaves changed the standard position of a spinning wheel from horizontal to vertical, stacked multiple spindles on top of one another, and wove eight threads at once by turning them all with a single pulley and belt. He called his gadget the "spinning jenny" (after his wife) and added more spindles and power until he could weave 128 threads at a time. In 1769, Richard Arkwright invented a "water frame" that stretched cotton fibers into a tighter, harder yarn. By 1776 he employed 5,000 workers in his factories. In 1779, Samuel Crompton introduced the "spinning mule," which integrated aspects of Hargreaves's spinning jenny and Arkwright's water frame.[3]

Despite these mechanical improvements, the steam engine was at the heart of the Industrial Revolution. The steam engine was not new: Hero of Alexandria (10 CE–70 CE) invented the first steam-powered engine for the sake of amusement. Others had built models, but encountered design problems. Thomas Newcomen developed a steam-propelled engine to pump water from

---

[1] Phyllis M. Deane, *The First Industrial Revolution* (Cambridge, England: Cambridge University Press, 1965), pp. 5–19.

[2] For a discussion of the origins of the Industrial Revolution in textiles, see John Styles, "Fashion, Textiles and the Origins of Industrial Revolution," *East Asian Journal of British History* 5 (March 2016), pp. 161–190.

[3] Richard L. Hills, "Hargreaves, Arkwright and Crompton: Why Three Inventors?" *Textile History* 10(1) (October 1, 1979), pp. 114–126.

coal mines that were flooding as shafts went deeper and deeper. Trained as a maker of scientific instruments, James Watt developed his first workable steam engine in 1765. Needing financial support, he formed a partnership with an ironmaster, Matthew Boulton, who would be called a "venture capitalist" in modern terminology. In 1776, Watt's first engine was sold to John Wilkinson for use in driving machinery in his Bersham Ironworks. To set a price, an agreement was reached that the steam engine would be rated by the number of horses required to do an equivalent amount of work; hence the derivation of the word *horsepower* for a unit of power. The standard unit of measurement for power, the watt, is named in James Watt's honor.

Until 1782, however, Watt's engines were used only to pump water and to power blowing engines for blast furnaces. In 1781, Watt made his greatest technological breakthrough when he transformed the up-and-down motion of a drive beam into a circular motion. This led to a host of new uses for steam power such as lifting coal and ore from mines, supplying power for breweries and oil mills, and, eventually, powering railway locomotives and steamships. In 1788, Watt patented a fly-ball governor, allowing steam to flow at a controlled rate. This first cybernetic system operated on a centrifugal principle: as an engine sped up, arms on a rotating shaft rose and steam intake vents closed, reducing power intake; as an engine slowed, the arms dropped, allowing more power.

James Watt. Universal History Archive/Getty Images.

George Williamson, *Memorials of the Lineage, Early Life, Education, and Development of the Genius of James Watt* (Edinburgh: Printed for the Watt Club by Thomas Constable, 1856), p. 120.

The historian Arnold Toynbee noted that two men, Adam Smith (see Chapter 2) and James Watt, were the most responsible for destroying the old England, building a new one, and launching the world toward industrialization. Smith brought about a revolution in economic thought, and Watt a revolution in the use of steam power.[4] Harnessed to the wheels of a hundred industries, the steam engine provided more efficient and cheaper power for ships, trains, and factories, revolutionizing English commerce and industry. Steam power reduced production costs, lowered prices, and expanded product markets. A spirit of innovation led to inventions, inventions led to factories, and factories led to a need for direction and organization. Cost-reducing inventions similarly lowered the price of goods, thereby expanding product markets that required more workers, more machines, and mass production on a recurring and regular basis. Mass production brought quality goods within the financial grasp of the many rather than only the few who had been able to afford them previously. As economist Joseph A. Schumpeter noted, mass production meant that a factory girl could have silk stockings as well as a queen.[5]

Capital was needed to finance larger industrial undertakings, and the individuals who could amass the required capital began to bring together workers and machines under one central authority. Instead of laboring in their homes, weavers, for example, were assembled in a common workplace with a steam engine to power their looms; similarly, combers, bleachers, dyers, and so on found their efforts shifting from their homes to large factories. As these workers came into a shared workplace, there was a greater need for monitoring and coordinating their efforts. The factory system proceeded irregularly in various industries, but the new age of industrialization was evident. A new power source had been perfected, large amounts of capital were required, and the need for efficient and effective performance became increasingly evident. The fledgling factory system soon toddled forth to create an abundance such as the world had never seen.

---

[4] Arnold Toynbee, *Lectures on the Industrial Revolution of the 18th Century in England* (New York: Humboldt Publishing, 1884), p. 90.
[5] Joseph A. Schumpeter, *Capitalism, Socialism, and Democracy* (New York: Harper & Brothers, 1942), p. 67.

Management: The Fourth Factor of Production

Before the Industrial Revolution, economic theory focused on two factors of production: land and labor. With the emergence of the factory system, however, the Roman Catholic Church's admonitions against materialistic trade and profits loosened, and capital was soon recognized as an indispensable and legitimate third factor of production. At the same time, with the unprecedented growth in the factory system, the importance of a fourth factor of production became increasingly evident: the entrepreneur. Richard Cantillon (1680–1734), an Irishman who moved to Paris and made a fortune in currency speculation, appears to have been the first to use the word "entrepreneur" in an economic sense. His pre–Industrial Revolution *Essay on the Nature of Commerce*, published some years after his death, used the word entrepreneur very loosely.[6] He considered anyone who bought or made a product at a certain cost to sell at an uncertain price to be an entrepreneur, including farmers, water-carriers, brewers, milliners, chimney sweeps, landowners, and capitalists employing labor. "[I]n all cases, however, the entrepreneurial role remains distinctly that of someone making decisions under uncertainty."[7]

Cantillon's *Essay* influenced the thinking of French economist François Quesnay (1694–1774), leader of the so-called Physiocrats, who believed that agriculture was the source of all wealth. In contrast to Cantillon's loose use of the word entrepreneur, however, Quesnay held that the operators of large farms were the only true entrepreneurs, as agriculture alone was capable of producing an economic surplus. Writing after Cantillon, Jean-Baptiste Say (1767–1832) advised that, to be successful, an entrepreneur needed many qualities that are rarely possessed by one person. As he explained, the entrepreneurial role

> . . . requires a combination of moral qualities, that are not often found together. Judgment, perseverance, and a knowledge of the world as well as of business. [The entrepreneur] is called upon to estimate, with tolerable accuracy, the importance of the specific product, the probable amount of the demand, and the means of its production: at one time he must employ a great number of hands; at another, buy or order the raw material, collect labourers, find consumers, and give at all times a rigid attention to order and economy; in a word, he must possess the art of superintendence and administration.[8]

Say noted that, whereas some entrepreneurs were the sole owners of a business, more frequently they owned only a share, having borrowed funds from others or having entered into partnerships. Thus, in starting a business, entrepreneurs assumed an additional risk as they sought to manage the factors of production to earn a profit by satisfying consumer demand. For their "industry," Say considered entrepreneurs to be a fourth factor of production, deserving additional compensation beyond a return on their own capital or that borrowed from someone else. Naturally, as a business grows, an entrepreneur acting alone cannot direct and control all of its activities. It, thus, becomes necessary to hire and delegate tasks to subordinates, a business's first nonowner employees. Delegation has been referred to as the "primordial act" in the creation of a corporate structure.[9] As the number of subordinates rises, an intermediary or agent (perhaps a foreman or supervisor) becomes necessary, and subordinates no longer receive instructions directly from the entrepreneur. At this point, "a pattern of coordination, a systematic ordering of positions and duties which defines a chain of command and makes possible the administrative integration of specialized functions" must be established.[10] With further growth, this process repeats itself and,

---

[6] Richard Cantillon, *Essai sur la Nature du Commerce en Général* [*Essay on the Nature of Trade in General*] (Londres, France: Chez Fletcher Gyles, 1756). Written between 1730 and 1734.

[7] Mark Blaug, *Great Economists Before Keynes* (Cambridge, England: Cambridge University Press, 1986), p. 38.

[8] Jean-Baptiste Say, *A Treatise on Political Economy*, vol. 2, trans. Clement R. Princep (London: Longman, Hurst, Rees, Orme, and Brown, 1821), p. 72. Originally published in 1803.

[9] Philip Selznick, "Foundations of the Theory of Organization," *American Sociological Review* 13(1) (February 1948), p. 25.

[10] *Ibid.*

as the number of foremen increases, it becomes necessary to hire department managers and, as the number of department managers increases, it becomes necessary to hire division managers and so on, until a full corporate structure emerges. Managers and operative employees at each level are responsible for making decisions within a broader framework of policies established by the entrepreneur. As subordinates are grouped into departments and divisions, and the number of links in an organization's scalar chain of command increase, first-time challenges invariably arise in ensuring that all its interrelated parts move in unison toward the same goal.

Management Challenges in Early Factories

In a similar manner, as organizations grew with the emerging factory system, entrepreneurs and managers in general faced challenges unlike those ever encountered before. The Roman Catholic Church could organize and manage its properties because of accepted dogma and the devotion of its faithful; armies and other military organizations could control a large number of personnel through a rigid hierarchy of discipline and authority; and governmental bureaucracies could survive without having to face competition or show a profit. Managers in the new factory system could not resort to any of these devices to ensure effective and efficient performance.

The Industrial Revolution spawned a number of industries, and the early 1800s were characterized by the growth of large firms operating in increasingly competitive environments. For these firms, pressure to grow came from the need to achieve economies of scale to compete more efficiently. Some advocated resisting the pressure to grow; for example, the Committee on Woollen Manufacturers of 1806 argued against large factories, claiming that merchants could save on capital investment and would not need to "submit to the constant trouble and solicitude of watching over a numerous body of Workmen."[11] Notwithstanding such claims, competition demanded growth. A major factor restraining sustained growth was an absence of individuals experienced in meeting the challenges inherent in managing a large factory. Many entrepreneurs, thus, found themselves on the horns of a dilemma: technology and capital made a large-scale production possible, and competitive forces made the economies of scale imperative, but at the same time, as factories increased in size, managerial challenges unlike any faced before emerged.

The Labor Challenge

Once an entrepreneur decides to embark on a venture, capital has to be raised to secure a power source, machinery, buildings, tools, and so forth. As suggested in the previous section, once an organization grows, it becomes necessary to hire managers and other employees. Workforce development, however, is not an easy task. Broadly conceived, it has three aspects: recruitment, training, and motivation.

Recruitment

The existing labor force at the time of the Industrial Revolution consisted largely of unskilled agrarian workers, and the shift from a small workshop, a farm, or a family-operated operation to a large factory could be tumultuous. In addition, workers often had to be enticed to pull up roots from a long-familiar milieu and go to a brawling, bustling city for employment. Andrew Ure (see Chapter 4) and others complained that large factories were uncongenial to the era's typical laborer, who was accustomed to a domestic or agrarian life, and did not easily adapt to the monotony of machine-paced work, regular year-round hours, and impersonal discipline.[12]

---

[11] "Report from the Committee on the State of the Woollen Manufacture of England," *Journals of the House of Commons* 61 (1806), p. 69.
[12] Andrew Ure, *The Philosophy of Manufactures: Or an Exposition of the Scientific, Moral and Commercial Economy of the Factory System of Great Britain* (London: Charles Knight, 1835), p. 15.

As a consequence, they were thought to be restless, shiftless, and deviant. Chemical manufacturer Roebuck and Garbett, for instance, moved its factory from Birmingham, England, to Prestonpans, Scotland, "to escape the independence of the local workers for the 'obedient turn of the Scots'."[13] One observer described early textile weavers as fiercely independent and generally insubordinate. For the most part, they were Puritans and were as opposed to the factory regimen as they were to the Church of England.[14]

The transition from farm to factory was eased for some workers, however, by the prospects of a steadier job and higher wages. Agrarian workers were accustomed to a subsistence living derived from the vagaries of soil and seasons. Studies of labor mobility in England during the early Industrial Revolution showed that workers were moving toward the north and west, where factories were primarily located. This demonstrated a "sensitivity of labor to wage incentives," as workers now had an opportunity to improve their standard of living.[15] Of course, not all workers responded to the prospect of higher wages, preferring agrarian or craft pursuits.

Particularly vexing to employers, however, was the shortage of skilled labor. Some high-skilled workers did exist in small scattered guilds and workshops, but they were generally more resistant to factory life. The Woolcombers Guild, for example, resisted mechanization and factory work, preferring their guild tradition. In the midlands of England—the center of the British textile industry—wool combers were in such short supply that this advertisement appeared: "To WOOL-COMBERS. Wm. TOPLIS and Co. have opened a Free Shop, at Mansfield, the County Nottingham, for Combers from any Part of the Kingdom. - The Prices given are equal to any society [guild] and good steady workmen may make very handsome wages."[16] Employers also had to offer inducements to skilled workers and to make major concessions to retain them. The loss of essential workers could shut down an entire factory. James Watt had pressing problems with finding workers who could cut and fit valves and cylinders to the proper tolerances; indeed, many of his early failures were of execution, not design. Richard Arkwright was forced to schedule his skilled workers for extra hours due to a shortage of qualified labor. Many iron mills kept their furnaces going even in slack times to keep from losing trained employees. Employers used every possible medium to advertise for workers, and one authority reported that children and paupers were employed after other sources of labor were absorbed.[17] In brief, it was difficult to recruit a workforce that had the qualifications necessary to perform skilled factory jobs. Labor mobility was enhanced by wage incentives, but traditions bound some to their trades and others to their agrarian life.

Training

Training was a second major management challenge faced by the emerging factory system. Once workers were recruited, they often had to be taught the skills necessary for factory life. Literacy was uncommon, and basic education was lacking; drawings, instruction sheets, and machine operations demanded an ability to read, to figure, and to respond with a predictable manner. Training was conducted largely by oral instruction, demonstration, and trial and error. New employees were taught how to operate a machine or process a piece of material by their coworkers. Standardized methods were unheard of, and workers blithely followed the example of others who knew little more than they. Traditional prejudices against anything new added to the challenge. Moreover, workers were largely unaccustomed to abiding by the accuracy and tolerances demanded for the manufacture of interchangeable parts that were the basis for mass production.

---

[13] Sidney Pollard, "Factory Discipline in the Industrial Revolution," *Economic History Review* 16(2) (December 1963), p. 255.

[14] Richard Guest, *A Compendious History of the Cotton-Manufacture: With a Disproval of the Claim of Sir Richard Arkwright to the Invention of Is Ingenious Machinery* (Manchester, England: Joseph Pratt, 1823), pp. 40–43.

[15] Robert M. Hartwell, "Business Management in England during the Period of Early Industrialization: Inducements and Obstacles," *Nebraska Journal of Economics & Business* 8(3) (Summer 1969), p. 66.

[16] *Northampton Mercury* (Northamptonshire, England), November 17, 1792, p. 2.

[17] Stanley D. Chapman, *The Early Factory Masters: The Transition to the Factory System in the Midlands Textile Industry* (Newton Abbot, England: David & Charles, 1967), p. 168.

The haphazard acquisition of knowledge from coworkers or inept supervisors, a lack of standardized methods, and worker resistance to new methods posed serious challenges for efficient and predictable performance. Employers resorted to developing their own schools to teach elementary arithmetic, geometry, and other necessary skills. Jobs were specialized to ease instruction. The goal was not only efficiency, but also meeting the practical challenge of finding workers to train. In short, industrialization required an educated workforce, something sorely lacking in the early days of the Industrial Revolution.

Discipline and Motivation

A third challenge encountered in the emerging factory system was that of discipline and motivation. Accustomed to the independence and self-sufficiency of agrarian and domestic life, workers had to develop habits of industry, such as punctuality and regular attendance, as well as to accept supervision and the mechanical pacing of their work. Moreover, the factory system demanded a different type of discipline: it required regularity instead of bursts of effort, and standardization in place of individual craftsmanship. This new discipline, however, did not come easily. Worker attendance was irregular. Ecclesiastical feasts honoring martyrs and saints, some lasting days, drove high levels of absenteeism as workers stayed at home to celebrate. Further, some tended to work in spurts—laboring long hours, collecting their wages, and then disappearing for countless days of dissipation. As one contemporary, Rev. Morgan Powell, commented, "[I]f a person can get sufficient [money] in four days to support himself for seven days, he will keep holiday the other three; that is, he will live in riot and debauchery."[18] Some workers took a weekly holiday they called Saint Monday, which meant either not working or working very slowly at the beginning of a week. To combat the problem of feast days, some early employers resorted to using traditional holidays for company-sponsored outings to build loyalty, break the monotony of everyday life, and cement relationships with workers. For example, Arkwright held a feast for 500 employees at his Cromford mill in 1776, and Matthew Boulton hosted 700 at his Soho plant.

Machine smashing, although sporadic, was another disciplinary problem. Most machine destruction, a common tactic of early weavers, however, antedated the perfection of the steam engine and the growth of large factories. In 1753, John Kay's flying shuttle and other inventions were smashed and his home destroyed by workers protesting his laborsaving machinery. James Hargreaves suffered a similar fate at his Blackburn mill in 1768. Operators of traditional handspinners were convinced that his spinning jenny would put them out of work, so they raided Hargreaves's house and smashed his machines. Machine smashers became known as Luddites, a term that supposedly originated with Ned Ludd, who smashed two spinning frames in a fit of anger.

The Luddite movement never had a unified purpose or a single leader. Scattered groups did the smashing, each proclaiming they were following orders from the fictitious "General Ludd." The name "Luddite" was first used in 1811, when a rash of machine breaking occurred, primarily in the hosiery-knitting trade around Nottingham. These protests, however, appeared to be based on grounds other than fear of unemployment resulting from technological advancement. In Nottingham, wages were falling, unemployment was rampant, and food prices were rising as a result of a government policy restricting imports. Machine smashing was a convenient way to demonstrate dissatisfaction, although other latent forces—not technology per se—are what caused increased unemployment.[19] Measures taken against the Luddites were rather draconian. Three Luddites who had assassinated a mill owner were hanged at York in 1813. Public fears of further violence

---

[18] [Morgan Powell], *A View of Real Grievances, with Remedies Proposed for Redressing Them; Humbly Submitted to the Consideration of the Legislature* (London: The Author, 1772), p. 143. For a collection of similar statements on the "deleterious effects of high wages," dating back to 1690, see: Edgar S. Furniss, *The Position of the Laborer in a System of Nationalism: A Study in the Labor Theories of later English Mercantilists* (Boston: Houghton Mifflin, 1920), p. 125n. Originally prepared as a dissertation, Yale University, New Haven, CT, 1918.

[19] Malcolm I. Thomis, *The Luddites: Machine Breaking in Regency England* (Hamden, CT: Archon Books, 1970), pp. 41–73.

led to more Luddites being hanged (Nottinghamshire, Lancaster, and Chester), and the movement soon died for lack of leadership.

Attempts to maximize worker effort in this era's factories fell into three categories: Positive inducements (often referred to as "carrots"), negative sanctions (commonly known as "sticks,"), and efforts to build a new factory ethos. Broadly speaking, business operators during this time period embraced poet and philosopher Ralph Waldo Emerson's conclusion that "Mankind is as lazy as it dares to be."[20] "Carrots" were opportunities to earn more money through wage incentives; thus, worker pay was based on performance. Wage incentives represented a major break with tradition. As noted, economists of the seventeenth- and eighteenth-century mercantilist school believed that income and the supply of labor were negatively related; that is, as wages rose, workers would choose to go spend their money, returning only after it had been spent and more was needed. This viewpoint is evident in the conclusion of two wool merchants who worked under the domestic system. The first noted, "It is a fact well known to those who are conversant in the matter, that scarcity, to a certain degree, promotes industry,"[21] to which the second added, "a reduction of wages in the woolen manufactures would be a national blessing and advantage, and no real injury to the poor. By this means we might keep our trade, uphold our rents, and reform the people in the bargain."[22]

The view that the hungriest worker was the best worker justified keeping wages low to ensure an abundant, motivated workforce. Adam Smith expressed a contrasting view, however:

> The wages of labour are the encouragement of industry, which, like every other human quality, improves in proportion to the encouragement it receives. . . . When wages are high, accordingly, we shall always find the workmen more active, diligent, and expeditious than where they are low. . . . Some workmen, indeed when they can earn in four days what will maintain them through the week, will be idle the other three. This, however, is by no means the case with the greater part. Workmen, on the contrary, when they are liberally paid by the piece, are very apt to over-work themselves, and to ruin their health and constitution in a few years. . . . If masters [employers] would always listen to the dictates of reason and humanity, they have frequent occasion rather to moderate, than to animate the [work] of many of their workmen.[23]

With an appeal to moderation, Smith disagreed with the tradition that wages must be kept at a subsistence level and that the best workers were the hungriest. Rather, he held that high wages brought out the best in people and that they would work harder to earn more. Often called the "economic man" assumption, this break with mercantilist theory offered the opportunity for individual rewards based on initiative.

The emerging factory system largely continued the domestic system practice of payment based on output. Wage incentives were used more widely in operations that were labor intensive, that is, where the cost of labor was a large part of total cost and where payment could be tied to individual performance. For example, in the late 1700s, almost one-half of the British cotton-mill workers were on piece rates, as were workers in Boulton and Watt's engine shops. In coal mining, which emphasized teamwork, group piecework plans were tried, but were generally

---

[20] Ralph Waldo Emerson quoted in Edward Atkinson, *The Industrial Progress of the Nation: Consumption Limited, Production Unlimited* (New York: G. P. Putnam's Sons, 1890), p. 11.

[21] John Arbuthnot (of Mitcham.), *An Inquiry Into the Connection Between the Present Price of Provisions, and the Size of Farms: With Remarks on Population as Affected Thereby. To Which Are Added, Proposals for Preventing Future Scarcity* (London: T. Cadell, 1773), p. 93.

[22] John. Smith, *Chronicon Rusticum-commerciale: Or Memoirs of Wool & Being a Collection of History and Argument Concerning the Woolen Manufacture and the Woolen Trade in General*, vol. 2, (London: T. Osborne, 1747), p. 308. See also William Hutton, *The History of Birmingham*, 3rd ed. (Birmingham, England: Thomas Pearson, 1795), p. 97.

[23] Adam Smith, *The Wealth of Nations* (1776), vol. 1, bk. I, ch. 8, p. 100.

ineffective.[24] Performance standards, meanwhile, were based on the average time necessary for completing a job rather than on a careful study of the job itself and the time it should take to complete.

"Sticks," negative sanctions, were practices for which the early factory system is frequently criticized. Corporal punishment, especially of children, was used, though historians disagree on its frequency and severity. The prevailing attitude toward children, even in respectable homes, was (as the medieval saying suggested), they should be seen and not heard and, in the spirit of Proverbs 13:24, that to spare the rod was to spoil the child. In the context of the period, employers treated children as they were accustomed to being treated at home.[25]

Graduated fines were a more common method of discipline: the penalty at one mine for being absent on a Monday morning was 2 shillings and 6 pennies; workers at one mill were fined 5 shillings for "singing, swearing, or being drunk."[26] This was a fairly large portion of a worker's pay. On December 1, 1797, Samuel Oldknow, considered one of the most progressive employers of the early factory period, posted the fines shown in Figure 3.1 at his Mellor Mill at Derbyshire, England.[27]

A third method of motivation was oriented toward creating a new factory ethos. The goal was to use religious morals and values to create "proper" attitudes toward work. To this end, workers were encouraged (often on company time) to read the Bible, regularly attend church, and exhorted to avoid the deadly sins of laziness, sloth, and avarice were the methods used to encourage positive attitudes toward work. A coalition of employers and ministers admonished the populace to guard against these moral depravities, which were not only sinful but also led to a lackadaisical, dissipated workforce. The London Lead Company, for instance, dismissed workers for "tippling [drinking intoxicating liquor], fighting, night rambling, mischief and other disreputable conduct."[28] Doubtless, this moral suasion emanated from more than a concern for workers' souls. Pollard presented a succinct statement of these attempts at creating a new ethos: "[T]he drive to raise the level of respectability and morality among the working classes was not undertaken for their own sakes, but primarily, or even exclusively, as an aspect of building up a new factory discipline."[29]

Figure 3.1 Fines at the Mellor Mill at Derbyshire, England, 1797. George Unwin, *Samuel Oldknow and the Arkwrights: The Industrial Revolution at Stockport and Marple* (Manchester: The University Press, 1924), p. 198.

The Search for Managerial Talent

In addition to the challenges of finding, training, and motivating operative employees, there was also the task of finding qualified managers. As outlined earlier, as organizations grew, the ability

---

[24] E. Brian Peach and Daniel A. Wren, "Pay for Performance from Antiquity to the 1950s," *Journal of Organizational Behavior Management* 12(1) (Spring 1992), p. 12.

[25] Chapman, *Early Factory Masters*, p. 203.

[26] Sidney Pollard, *The Genesis of Modern Management: A Study of the Industrial Revolution in Great Britain* (Cambridge, MA: Harvard University Press, 1965), p. 187.

[27] George Unwin, *Samuel Oldknow and the Arkwrights: The Industrial Revolution at Stockport and Marple* (Manchester: The University Press, 1924), p. 198.

[28] George H. Mennell, "Discussion," on Arthur Raistrick, "The London Lead Company, 1692–1905," *Transactions of the Newcomen Society* 14(1) (1933), p. 156.

[29] Pollard, *Genesis of Modern Management*, p. 197.

of owner-entrepreneurs to supervise their employees diminished, and an intermediate level of supervision became necessary. Judging from early literature, salaried managers (i.e., those in the layer of management below an owner-entrepreneur), were usually illiterate workers promoted from the ranks because they evidenced a greater degree of technical skills or had the ability to keep discipline. Typically, they were paid only a little more than their subordinates and were at times attracted to a managerial position because it gave them the power to hire their spouses and children. Untrained in the intricacies of supervising others, these managers were left on their own to develop a supervisory style. Problems were met and solved on an ad hoc basis. The general view was that success or failure to produce results depended on the character of a manager, on personal traits and idiosyncrasies, and not on any generalized concepts of leadership. Other potential sources of managerial talent included relatives, presumably hired on the assumption that they were more trustworthy or would act to preserve their potential inheritance. This practice also provided family members with training that would help secure ownership for future generations. Another source of possible talent was the countinghouse; entrepreneurs recruited talented bank clerks and tellers, thinking they probably had both business and financial acumen. On-the-job training (OJT) was used to develop necessary managerial knowledge.

The transformation of Great Britain from an agrarian to an industrial society occurred at a time when there was no ready supply of either trained or experienced managers. At the time, there was no common body of knowledge about how to manage. The formal training of managers supplemented OJT with instruction in production techniques, sources and characteristics of materials, machine operations, trade practices, and the legal obligations of firms. This training was oriented toward a specific industry (cotton, woolen, mining, or whatever) and did not readily lend itself to broader generalization. Managers, trained in one industry, were bound to that industry; to move to another they would need to learn new skills. Furthermore, there was no universal set of expectations about how a manager should act. Codes of conduct were developed for specific industries and gave advice about a manager's responsibility for safety, the security of plant and equipment, design standards for engineering, and procedures to follow in safeguarding an owner's interests.

Scotsman James Montgomery (1771–1854) prepared what were most probably the first management texts.[30] Montgomery's managerial advice was largely technical in nature; he advised how to discern quality and quantity of work, how to adjust and repair machinery, how to keep costs down, and how to "avoid all *unnecessary* severity"[31] in disciplining subordinates. He noted that a manager must be "just and impartial – firm and decisive – always on the alert to prevent rather than check faults, after they have taken place"[32] This latter comment was perceptive and indicates an early understanding that the control function is both forward and backward looking. Montgomery's advice, however, was written for those in the cotton industry and, like most other early writers, he did not seek to develop any generalized principles of management.

Montgomery was so highly regarded as a manager that he was brought to the United States in 1836 to become superintendent of the York Mills in Saco, Maine. This gave Montgomery the opportunity to conduct what was probably the first comparative study of management through the analysis of different economies. He found that the United States had higher production costs, paid higher wages (including wages for women), but had lower material costs. British firms had lower costs, paid lower wages, but paid more for raw materials. The relative competitive efficiency resided in Great Britain, in Montgomery's opinion, because the British firms were better

[30] James Montgomery, *The Carding and Spinning Master's Assistant; or the Theory and Practice of Cotton Spinning* (Glasgow: J. Niven, Jr., 1832); *idem, The Cotton Spinner's Manual or a Compendium of the Principles of Cotton Spinning* (Glasgow: J. Niven, Jr., 1835). Also see James P. Baughman, ed., "James Montgomery on Factory Management, 1832," *Business History Review* 42(2) (Summer 1968), pp. 219–226.

[31] James Montgomery, *The Theory and Practice of Cotton Spinning: or, The Carding and Spinning Master's Assistant: Showing the Use of Each Machine Employed* (Glasgow: J. Niven, Jr. 1832), p. 219.

[32] *Ibid.*, p. 256.

managed.[33] Montgomery's study was of cotton mills only, but it gives some idea of the differing states of managerial knowledge in the United States and Great Britain in 1840.

Early managerial salaries left much to be desired. First-line supervisors, or overlookers, were paid little more than their subordinates. Often, salaried managers were paid on the basis of their social class rather than on the extent of their responsibility. By 1800, however, Pollard noted that the shortage of managerial talent had forced payment based on the job and not the person.[34] By 1830, the pay of salaried managers had risen rapidly and compressed the differential between their pay and that of owner-managers. By the mid-nineteenth century, John Stuart Mill observed that those who managed others had to possess a higher "intelligence factor," that is, "something acquired through education, both formal and informal and on the job learning."[35] Those who were superintendents of others faced many nonroutine obligations dealing with complex problems, justifying their higher salaries. Mill disagreed with Adam Smith's concern about the separation of ownership and management (see Chapter 2). The "zeal" of hired managers could be stimulated by connecting "their pecuniary interest with the interest of their employers, by giving them part of their remuneration in the form of a percentage on the profits."[36]

In Great Britain, but not in France or Italy, the status of entrepreneurs was rising by the mid-nineteenth century, inducing many young people to seek their fortunes in commerce, or at least to become a junior partner in a large firm. Second- and third-generation offspring of founder-entrepreneurs afforded more status to salaried managers. They tended to delegate more to and depend more on these professional managers. Perhaps their affluence, built by the success of preceding generations, made them less desirous of becoming personally involved in daily workplace activities; or perhaps their firms had grown to such a size and the fund of managerial talent had reached such a point that finding reliable subordinates was easier than it had been for their predecessors. This stands in contrast to early factories, where the challenges of finding and developing managerial talent were acute. There were no business schools for recruiting and no systematic programs for developing managers, and managerial skill was judged in a localized, idiosyncratic matter.

Management Functions in the Early Factory

In addition to the demands of staffing a factory, the task of acquiring and retaining trained workers, early managers faced planning, organizing, and controlling challenges similar to those faced by managers today. In planning operations, early factories required more farsightedness than during the domestic system of production. As the factory system developed, managers became more rational, more pragmatically interested in laying a foundation for long-term growth rather than short-term speculative gains. Mines required long-range planning to develop untapped ore veins, and factories required costly equipment. As capital was sunk, managers had to be more aware of the long-term implications of their decisions. Examples of planning in the early factory are few, and those that do exist are largely technically oriented rather than comprehensive in scope and application. Robert Owen and Richard Arkwright led the way in preplanning factory layout. Their requirements, or principles, emphasized workflow orderliness and factory cleanliness.

[33] James Montgomery, *The Cotton Manufacture of the United States of America Contrasted and Compared with That of Great Britain* (London: John N. Van, 1840), p. 138.

[34] Pollard, *Genesis of Modern Management*, p. 139.

[35] P. Bruce Buchan, "John Stuart Mill – Contributions to the Principles of Management: The Intelligence Factor," *British Journal of Management* 4(2) (June 1993), p. 71.

[36] John Stuart Mill, *Principles of Political Economy with Some of Their Applications to Social Philosophy*, vol. 1 (Boston, MA: C. C. Little & J. Brown, 1848), p. 187.

Factory technology demanded planning power sources and connections, arranging machinery and space for smooth workflow, and reducing confusion through well-placed materials. The Boulton and Watt's engine shops also stressed factory layout and developed detailed systems for controlling materials and parts. They engaged in rudimentary production planning, work flow, and assembly.[37] The use of standardized, interchangeable parts made planning necessary, both in product design and execution. Watt's son (James Watt, Jr.), saw at an early stage that standard parts would make controlling production easier, and that detailed planning and proper execution would ensure final products meet specifications. Standard parts also eased product repairs and reduced both company and customer spare part inventories, thus simplifying inventory stock control.

In organizing, managers at each level are limited to a large extent by the caliber of the managers below them. Early departmentalization, or the grouping of activities, was often based on the number of partners or relatives. With a gesture toward egalitarianism, each partner or relative became a department head with one or two salaried managers to assist in supervising subordinates. It has been estimated that by 1820, there was an average of one first-line supervisor for every 28 millhands in the cotton industry.[38] Similar ratios were apparent in mining, dockyards, and construction, suggesting that firms in these industries were also relatively flat, with few levels of management. These small firms were typically family-owned and managed, staff personnel were little more than clerks, and they were rarely fully integrated. For example, although cotton mills might spin wool into fiber, they generally relied on other firms or agents to fabricate and merchandise a final product, such as garments and home textiles.

There is evidence that within the textile industry technology played an important role in how activities and relationships were structured in the emerging factory system.[39] In the beginning, most textile workshops followed a batch processing technology; that is, there were relatively short runs of manufacturing a quantity of like products, followed by another batch of slightly different products, and so on. This description seems to characterize the textile industry until the early 1800s.

As new steam-power applications were developed, another technological advancement further increased efficiency: power-driven machines were arranged in the sequence necessary to make a finished product. This "flow technology" resembled a mass-production assembly line, with an output of large quantities of standardized products made at a lower per unit cost, intended for a mass market. With this increase in production, it became more economical to specialize labor even further. Unlike a moving assembly line as we know it today, products were moved from one stage of production to another by carts, workers, chutes, and so on. Departments were established for individual operations. As hinted at above, with more departments came the need for another level of management to coordinate work as it flowed from one stage to another. The consequence was a growth in the scalar chain-of-command, creating a taller hierarchical structure and the need for more elaborate procedures and systems to integrate a firm's activities. It appears that early textile firms long ago discovered that technology affects an organization's structure. Early batch-production methods allowed more informality; however, the application of steam-driven power led to a new factory technology, which required more formality in organization design.

In controlling performance, entrepreneurs faced numerous challenges. Needing to delegate authority to cope with larger undertakings because they could no longer personally oversee all

---

[37] Eric Roll, *An Early Experiment in Industrial Organisation: Being a History of the Firm of Boulton and Watt, 1775–1805* (London: Longmans Green and Co., 1930). The development of relatively advanced managerial techniques at Boulton and Watt is credited to the founders' sons, Matthew Robinson Boulton and James Watt, Jr. (p. xv).

[38] Pollard, *Genesis of Modern Management*, p. 135.

[39] Stanley D. Chapman, "The Textile Factory before Arkwright: A Typology of Factory Development," *Business History Review* 48(4) (Winter 1974), pp. 468–473.

operations, they found that the shortage of trained and trusted salaried managers had raised concerns about accountability. As Adam Smith observed, salaried managers who would exercise the same vigilance over other people's money as over their own were rare. Accounting had not advanced since Luca Pacioli's time (see Chapter 2), and the use of financial information for making operating decisions was uncommon. Managers kept account books to record earnings, wages, purchases, and sales, but few managers used these accounts as an aid to decision making. Josiah Wedgwood, manufacturer of various pottery products, was one of those few, and he refined his accounts until he was able to use them in setting prices, fixing potters' piece rates, determining the percentage of selling expenses to sales, and tracing the embezzlement of certain funds by his head clerk.[40] It would be more than a century before better costing techniques were developed.

Through trial-and-error experience, early entrepreneurs attempted to cope with the challenges of managing a factory. The emphasis on technical rather than managerial challenges was probably due to the available technology and the pressure to keep abreast of competitors. Management was deemed a localized matter, not subject to generalization, and success was thought to depend on the personal qualities of individual managers, not on their grasp of broader principles. Management was a personal art, not a discipline; pragmatic, not theoretical; and parochial, not universal.

Some individuals, however, were attempting to fill the void in management knowledge. Their efforts are the subject of Chapter 4. Before moving ahead, though let us attempt to gain a perspective on the cultural impact of the Industrial Revolution.

Cultural Consequences of the Industrial Revolution

The consequences of the Industrial Revolution were not only technological but also cultural. New machines, new factories, and new cities shook people's tradition-based roots and demanded participation in a changing era. In the hearts of many, the agrarian life before industrialization has been idealized. Critics have charged that capitalism, together with its offspring—the market and factory systems—ended a golden age of equality and freedom. More specifically, the criticisms have been that people were enslaved to the owners of capital; that they became little more than a marketplace commodity, that capitalists exploited child and female labor, and that industrialization created poverty, urbanization, and pollution among other societal ills. Let us examine some of these criticisms and attempt to gain a perspective on the cultural consequences of the Industrial Revolution.

Working Conditions

Economics earned its sobriquet, "the dismal science," during the mid-nineteenth century.[41] The Rev. Thomas R. Malthus set out to disprove the optimism of Adam Smith and other classical economists with his contention that as the world's population increased geometrically, its food supply would at best increase only arithmetically.[42] Thus, Malthus believed that because the world's population is limited by the means of subsistence, and because the masses tend to reproduce beyond this limit, there could be no improvement in their condition. He felt that government relief of the poor

---

[40] Neil McKendrick, "Josiah Wedgwood and Cost Accounting in the Industrial Revolution," *Economic History Review* (2nd series) 23(1) (April 1970), pp. 45–67.

[41] The name "the dismal science" was coined by Scottish historian Thomas Carlyle in *Fraser's Magazine for Town and Country* 40(240) (December 1849), p. 672.

[42] Thomas R. Malthus, *An Essay on the Principle of Population, As It Affects the Future Improvement of Society* (London: J. Johnson, 1798).

only encourages a population increase, drives food prices up, and leaves the poor no better off. The only answer for Malthus was to restrict the supply of labor and to encourage self-restraint in the growth of the masses. His was a hopeless view of people as no more than marketplace commodities, basically powerless to overcome the world's natural limitations.

David Ricardo did not appear much more optimistic. His "iron law of wages" stated that in the long run real wages would tend to stabilize at some minimum level, which would provide workers with just enough means to subsist.[43] Utopian socialists, such as Robert Owen (see Chapter 4), saw people as powerless in their environment and wanted to replace marketplace individualism with a communal life. The Utopians did not write of the necessity of revolt, but felt they could achieve change through their writings and example. An opposite view was developed by Karl Marx and Friedrich Engels, who advocated the need for force as the midwife of history. In their view, because workers were powerless and kept at a subsistence level by their capitalist factory masters, they had to unite to break their chains. Although the writings of Marx and Engels were more political essays than economic analyses, they did reflect a dismal view of the world shared by some economists.[44]

Were people powerless and exploited by capitalism? The masses had spent the previous thousand or more years surviving at a subsistence level as agrarian peasants tied to a feudal landlord. Under mercantilism, the British government regulated wages to keep them low so as to maintain a favorable balance of trade, and, as we saw earlier, it was a common belief that low wages provided an incentive to work. The Industrial Revolution did not create poverty; it inherited it. With Adam Smith came a new market-based philosophy that high wages made people more diligent. The rise of capitalism released people from drudgery through laborsaving machines, making them more productive. It also offered jobs that were better paid for less effort.[45] It is difficult to agree with Marx and Engels that workers were exploited by their factory masters: as described, the shortage of labor (especially skilled) diminished the power of factory owners to exploit labor; and second, workers' real wages steadily rose from 1790 to 1830, improving "well above the level of mere subsistence."[46] For those who were willing to learn the necessary skills, new machines and methods made them more productive and raised their wages, which, in turn, added industrial efficiency, reduced the prices of goods, and increased their real income. Incentive-payment plans held out a promise of economic betterment for the common masses; no longer tied to remitting a tithe to a feudal lord, individuals could, through their own effort, enhance their well-being.

Working conditions and the "time-discipline" needed for scheduling tasks in a factory compared to an agrarian setting have also been cited by critics as examples of how the golden age of equality and freedom was lost. Hopkins, however, studied a heavily industrialized region of England and concluded "that there was no marked deterioration of working conditions during the classic period of the Industrial Revolution . . . [and] to suggest that . . . the majority of workers . . . were forced to . . . become the slaves of a new time discipline is really a very doubtful proposition, and its unthinking repetition can serve only to perpetuate a historical myth."[47] Claims of worker exploitation should be considered against this; through performance incentives, increased wages, rising real income, steady employment, and regular hours, workers were improving their lot beyond a subsistence level.

---

[43] David Ricardo, *The Principles of Political Economy and Taxation* (London: Dent, 1911), pp. 57, 61–63.

[44] For example, see Karl Marx, *Das Kapital: Kritik der politischen Oekonomie* [Capital: Critique of Political Economy], vol. 1: *Der Produktionsprocess des Kapitals* [*The Process of Capitalist Production as a Whole*] (Hamburg: Verlag von Otto Meissner, 1867); Friedrich Engels, *The Condition of the Working-Class in England in 1844*, trans. Florence Kelley Wischnewtzky (London: Swan Sonnenschein & Co., 1892).

[45] Friedrich A. Hayek, "History and Politics," in *idem*, ed., *Capitalism and the Historians* (Chicago, IL: University of Chicago Press, 1954), pp. 15–16.

[46] Thomas S. Ashton, "The Standard of Life of the Workers in England: 1790–1830," in Hayek, *Capitalism*, p. 158.

[47] Eric Hopkins, "Working Hours and Conditions during the Industrial Revolution: A Re-Appraisal," *Economic History Review* 35(1) (February 1982), pp. 63, 66.

Child and Female Labor

Child and female labor were not inventions of the Industrial Revolution. The domestic system of production and agricultural life required the participation of all and were built on families as the basic economic unit. One authority noted that child labor "was at its worst and greatest height before anybody thought of a factory."[48] Child and female workers were found primarily in textile manufacturing, where the technology was simple, and rarely in other sectors. Employers would have preferred a mature, stable, adult workforce, but such workers were scarce and hard to attract. Concern in Great Britain over child-labor practices led to two parliamentary investigations: the first in 1819, at the behest of Robert Owen, and chaired by Sir Robert Peel, himself an employer of children, and the second, in 1832, by the Committee on the "Bill to Regulate the Labour of Children in the Mills and Factories of the United Kingdom."[49] Extensive and detailed evidence was collected in both inquiries. Children often began working a twelve-hour day at age five. This practice was widespread in cotton, wool, flax, and silk mills. In both inquiries, informants described prevailing hours (long), wages (low), working conditions (often extremely poor), and the methods of discipline (often harsh). Overall, however, there is evidence that "the Industrial Revolution [did] not increase exploitation [but] gradually improved the situation of children. . . . Industrialization, far from being the source of the enslavement of children, was the source of their liberation."[50] Industrialization created more jobs and better jobs; as workers' nominal and real wages rose, child labor declined.

Female workers were attracted to factory work to pay off farm debts or to build dowries, for the opportunity of finding a husband, or to supplement their family income. One observer, Paul Mantoux, felt that entrepreneurs were "tyrannical, hard, sometimes cruel: their passions and greeds were those of upstarts. They had the reputation of being heavy drinkers and of having little regard for the honour of their female employees."[51] Mantoux was guilty of overgeneralization; ample examples can be given, such as Josiah Wedgwood, Jr., Matthew Robinson Boulton, James Watt, Jr., John Wilkinson, Robert Owen, and a host of others, for whom there is no evidence of loose and fancy-free behavior toward female employees.[52] Furthermore, in contrast, with the traditional norm of paying what was "suitable" for women's work, Burnette found that, during the Industrial Revolution, "Women seem to have been paid market wages, and the assertion that women were paid customary [i.e., traditional] wages needs to be revised."[53] There was also great concern that unemployed females would be forced by circumstances into prostitution, but Bisset Hawkins, a physician, presented evidence from Manchester, England, that of the 50 prostitutes who had been apprehended in the previous 4 years (1829–1833), only 8 had been employed in factories, whereas 29 came from the ranks of former household servants.[54]

Evidence concerning child and female labor is contradictory; most testimony hints at the moral degradation of factory life, but hard statistics are lacking. It appears that emotional

---

[48] Cyrus Redding, *An Illustrated Itinerary of the County of Lancaster* (London: How and Parsons, 1842), p. 39.

[49] *Reasons in Favour of Sir Robert Peel's Bill, for Ameliorating the Condition of Children Employed in Cotton Factories; Comprehending a Summary View of the Evidence in Support of the Bill, Taken before the Lords' Committees in the Present Session of Parliament* (London: W. Clowes, 1819); *Report from the Committee on the "Bill to Regulate the Labour of Children in the Mills and Factories of the United Kingdom": with the Minutes of Evidence, Appendix and Index* (London: House of Commons, 1832).

[50] Clark Nardinelli, "Were Children Exploited during the Industrial Revolution?" in Paul J. Uselding, ed., *Research in Economic History* 11 (1988), p. 268.

[51] Paul J. Mantoux, *The Industrial Revolution in the Eighteenth Century,* trans. Marjorie Vernon (New York: Macmillan Co., 1928), p. 397.

[52] For comments on these and other examples, see William O. Henderson, *J. C. Fischer and His Diary of Industrial England 1814–51* (London: Frank Cass & Co., 1966). Individuals such as Mantoux undoubtedly existed, as they do in all ages, but Fischer maintained that they were not representative of the era.

[53] Joyce Burnette, "An Investigation of the Female-Male Wage Gap during the Industrial Revolution in Britain," *Economic History Review* 50(2) (May 1997), p. 278.

[54] "Medical Reports by Dr. Hawkins," in Factories Inquiry Commission, "Second Report of the Central Board of His Majesty's Commissioners Appointed to Collect Information in the Manufacturing Districts, as to the Employment of Children in Factories, and as to the Propriety and Means of Curtailing the Hours of Their Labour," *Preliminary Papers* 21(519) (1833), D3, p. 4.

and religious overtones were given more credence, isolated instances were ballooned, and no thorough studies compared the past with the conditions at that time. As textile technology advanced and as income rose, child labor decreased dramatically before the passage of legislation regarding the employment of children.[55] What critics have overlooked is the fact that capitalism was slowly but surely releasing children from the workforce. As better machines were developed to perform simple jobs, it became uneconomical to employ children. It was an economic force—broadening capitalism—not legislative fiat nor a moral rebirth that freed children from loom rooms.[56] As for legislation and governmental bodies, it was the Poor Law Authorities, a government office that sent paupers into factories. Paupers were often poor or deserted children legally in the care of government authorities who sent them to whomever would provide for their care and feeding.

To understand the critics of the factory system, it is necessary to consider the era's Victorian values. The Victorian period began before Queen Victoria ascended the throne in 1837.[57] Victorian values concerning employing women and children and adherence to strict standards of personal and social morality began forming around 1800. Economic and social conditions had been worse before the Industrial Revolution, but the values of Victorian-era writers such as Charles Dickens, evidenced in his novels such as *Oliver Twist* (1838) and *Hard Times* (1854), advanced a basis for criticizing the emerging factory system.

Evidence suggests that the factory system led to a general rise in the standard of living in industrialized nations (something lacking in the previous thousand years), to falling urban death rates, and decreasing infant mortality. These factors led to a population explosion in Great Britain: the number of inhabitants increased from 6 million in 1750 to 9 million in 1800 and to 12 million in 1820. Further, infant mortality before the age of five fell from 74.5 percent in 1730–1749 to 31.8 percent in 1810–1829. Some 30 percent of the decline in infant deaths may be attributed to Edward Jenner's discovery of a vaccine to prevent smallpox. At the same time, improvements in agriculture, progress in sanitation, and advances in midwifery and hospital care between 1760 and 1815 also contributed to a decline in mortality.[58] Robert L. Heilbroner pointed out that factory life, even with urban poverty, represented an improvement over agrarian life in a domestic-production system. Poverty was not new; it had just been collected in one place—cities—and made more easily visible to the legislators, intellectuals, and others. Isolated and scattered, agrarian poverty did not shock the sensibilities, but next door and down the street, it became a bane. Heilbroner further answered Industrial Revolution critics saying that their judgments were political and not economic. Great Britain of that period was characterized by a surging interest in individual rights, social justice, and political reform; the populace had "a critical temper of mind before which any economic system would have suffered censure."[59] Criticism was directed at managers-entrepreneurs, not because they were to blame, but because they were a convenient symbol of change.

One cannot blame capitalism for the unsavory conditions and practices of the Industrial Revolution. The factory system inherited child and female labor, poverty, and long working hours from the past; it did not create them. The new age that capitalism created, through the factory system, offered people the means for a better life.

---

[55] Clark Nardinelli, "Child Labor and the Factory Acts," *Journal of Economic History* 40(4) (December 1980), pp. 739–755.

[56] William H. Hutt, "The Factory System of the Early Nineteenth Century," in Hayek, *Capitalism*, p. 184.

[57] John W. Osbourne, *The Silent Revolution: The Industrial Revolution in England as a Source of Cultural Change* (New York: Charles Scribner's Sons, 1970), pp. ix–xi.

[58] Mabel C. Buer, *Health, Wealth and Population in the Early Days of the Industrial Revolution* (London: G. Routledge & Sons, 1926), p. 29. Estimates of English birth and death rates for the period in question vary. For a discussion on this point see Edward A. Wrigley and Roger S. Schofield, *The Population of England 1541–1871: A Reconstruction* (London: Edward Arnold, 1981).

[59] Robert L. Heilbroner, *The Making of Economic Society* (Englewood Cliffs, NJ: Prentice-Hall, 1962), pp. 85–86.

SUMMARY

The Industrial Revolution created a new age and a revised set of managerial challenges. People's needs were becoming more complex as they sought to adjust to city and factory life. Industries were being reshaped by the demands for heavy infusions of capital, by the division of labor, and by the need for efficient and predictable performance. Organizations needed to innovate and compete in a market economy; this created pressures for growth and the economies of scale obtained from large-scale production and distribution. Economic theory recognized that entrepreneur-managers performed a distinct role in successfully combining the traditional three factors of production in the ever-growing factory system. With size came the need for salaried managers; the need for a capable, disciplined, trained, motivated workforce; and the need for rationalizing the planning, organizing, and controlling of operations in early enterprises. The next chapter examines some early management pioneers who proposed solutions for coping with the challenges presented by the growing factory system.

chapter 4

Management Pioneers in the Early Factory

A prevailing theme in the preceding chapters has been the relationship between the evolution of management thought and prevailing cultural values. The factory system of production posed new challenges for owner-entrepreneurs, salaried managers, and society-at-large. This chapter focuses on four individuals who pioneered solutions to these challenges. History leaves a notoriously scanty scent. Records have been lost, materials intended for one-time or temporary use have been destroyed, and notable ideas may never have been committed to writing. Judgments about the past, thus, must often be made with incomplete and uncertain information. Of the early management pioneers, history has provided the best records for four unique individuals: Robert Owen, Charles Babbage, Andrew Ure, and Charles F. Dupin.

Robert Owen: The Search for a New Harmony

Robert Owen (1771–1858), introduced in Chapter 3, was a paradox in the turbulent early years of the Industrial Revolution. Although a successful entrepreneur, he attempted to halt the era's growing industrialism and what he saw as its accompanying evils. A Utopian socialist, Owen called for a "new moral order" based on a drastic "social reorganization." He envisioned a new industrial society that was to be a combination of agricultural and industrial commune. Owen's vision harkened back to an earlier and more primitive time. Philosophically, he viewed people as powerless in a new age of machinery, held in the grips of revolutionary forces that destroyed moral purpose and social solidarity.

Early Managerial Experiences

A self-made man imbued with the self-confidence that typified the earliest entrepreneurs, Owen, at age 18, founded his first factory, a cotton mill, in Manchester, England. It was an era of conflict, when many manufacturers were becoming wealthy supplying military matériel. As discussed in Chapter 3, Arkwright's new water frame, Hargreaves's jenny, Crompton's mule, and Watt's steam engine made large factories more common. Owen described his introduction to managing as a co-owner of a machine shop: "I looked very wisely at the men in their different departments, although I really knew nothing. But by intensely observing everything, I maintained order and regularity throughout the establishment, which proceeded under the circumstances far better than I had anticipated."[1] Owen was subsequently hired as a manager by Peter Drinkwater, owner of Piccadilly Mills, with the understanding that he would ultimately become Drinkwater's partner. Still with only a modicum of experience, Owen applied himself to his new position:

> I looked grave, – inspected everything very minutely, – . . . I was with the first [workers] in the morning, and I locked up the premises at night, taking the keys with me. I continued this silent inspection and superintendence day by day for six weeks, saying merely yes or no to the questions of what was to be done or otherwise, and during that period I did not give one direct order about anything. But at the end of that time I felt myself so much master of my position, as to be ready to give directions in every department.[2]

Owen, left on his own by Drinkwater, made a success of the mill. He rearranged the equipment, improved the working conditions, and achieved a great deal of influence over his subordinates. He later attributed his success to his "habits of exactness" and knowledge of human nature. Following a disagreement with Drinkwater concerning his pending partnership, Owen left Piccadilly Mills in 1795 to become a partner in the New Lanark Mills, located in New Lanark, Scotland. At New Lanark, he encountered a labor shortage and noted, "[I]t was then most difficult to induce any sober, well-doing family to leave their home to go into cotton mills as then conducted."[3] This difficulty influenced Owen's labor policies, and he began forming a vision for a new society. Between 400 and 500 parish apprentices—paupers or deserted children, furnished by the Poor Law Authorities to whomever would take them (see Chapter 3)—were employed at New Lanark. The children worked 13 hours per day, 6 days a week. Owen continued to employ children, but tried to improve their living and working conditions by cutting their work day to 10.75 hours, setting 10 years as the minimum age for employment, providing meals and rest breaks, and stressing mill safety. In addition, he sought to reshape the whole village of New Lanark, including its streets, houses, sanitation, and school.

While at New Lanark, Owen began to also form new ideas about the welfare of society as a whole. Industrial progress, he felt, was inadequate to support the growing population. In 1821, he prepared a report for the citizens of Lanark Parish stating his belief that "manual labor, properly directed, is the source of all wealth and of national prosperity."[4] In Owen's view, the dominant economic and social challenge was to develop agriculture, using intensive methods of cultivation, to feed more people. He therefore prepared a plan to do the following:

1*st*, To cultivate the soil with the spade instead of the plough.

2*d*, To make such changes as the spade cultivation requires, to render it easy and profitable to individuals, and beneficial to the country.

---

[1] Robert Owen, *The Life of Robert Owen, Written by Himself*, vol. 1 (London: Effingham Wilson, 1857), p. 23.

[2] *Ibid.*, p. 29.

[3] *Ibid.*, p. 58.

[4] *Idem, Report to the County of Lanark of a Plan for Relieving Public Distress and Removing Discontent by Giving Permanent, Productive Employment to the Poor and Working Classes* (Glasgow: Wardlaw & Cunninghame, 1821), p. 1.

3*d*, To adopt a standard of value, by means of which the exchange of the products of labor may proceed without check or limit, until wealth shall become abundant that any further increase to it will be useless and will not be desired.[5]

Owen asserted that this would create jobs, enabling more people to be employed, thereby increasing their ability to consume England's industrial output. The notion of creating more arduous, menial jobs flew in the face of the technological progress that was being made at that time. It was a preface, however, to his vision of a communal society.

In managing New Lanark for over a quarter century, Owen sought to avoid disciplinary problems with employees. Like other manufacturers who had attempted to create a new factory ethos, he tried to use moral suasion rather than corporal punishment in such situations.[6] He developed one particularly unique device, the "silent monitor," to aid discipline. Using silent monitors, Owen awarded four types of marks to his superintendents, and they in turn rated their subordinates. These marks were translated into color codes: black, blue, yellow, and white, in ascending order of merit. A silent monitor (a small wooden block) was mounted on each weaver's loom and the four sides painted to match the code. At the end of each day, the marks were recorded, translated, and the matching side of the block turned outward. Owen reported that he "passed daily through all the rooms, and the workers observed me always to look at these telegraphs, – when black I merely looked at the person and then at the colour, – but never said a word to one of them by way of blame."[7] The silent monitor motivated laggards to improve and, supposedly, induced white block (good) workers to sustain their performance. It was a precursor of modern management's posting of sales and production data to encourage hard work and good behavior.

The Call for Reform

Predating Mayo, Roethlisberger, Likert, and others who have urged concern for a firm's human resources (see Chapters 13 and 15), Owen explained his rationale for a new moral order:

> [Y]ou will find that from the commencement of my management I viewed the population [the labor force] . . . as a system composed of many parts, and which it was my duty and interest so to combine, as that every hand, as well as every spring, lever, and wheel, should effectually co-operate to produce the greatest pecuniary gain to the proprietors. . . . Experience has also shown you the difference of the results between [a] mechanism which is neat, clean, well-arranged, and always in a high state of repair; and that which is allowed to be dirty, in disorder, without the means of preventing unnecessary friction, and which therefore becomes, and works, much out of repair. . . . If, then, due care as to the state of your inanimate machines can produce such beneficial results, what may not be expected if you devote equal attention to your vital machines [employees], which are far more wonderfully constructed?[8]

Owen chided his fellow manufacturers for not appreciating the profound effect of human factors on workers' productivity. He charged that they would spend thousands on the best machines, yet

---

[5] *Ibid.*, p. 10.

[6] For a commentary on early British manufactures influenced by Owen's reform efforts, see Lee D. Parker, "Corporate Social Accountability through Action: Contemporary Insights from British Industrial Pioneers," *Accounting, Organizations and Society* 39(8) (November 2014), pp. 632–659.

[7] *Idem, Life of Robert Owen*, pp. 136–137. The electric telegraph had not been invented; Owen used "telegraph" to mean viewing a record of performance from a distance.

[8] *Idem, A New View of Society, or, Essays on the Formation of the Human Character: Preparatory to the Development of a Plan for Gradually Ameliorating the Condition of Mankind*, 2nd ed. (London: Longman, Hurst, Rees, Orme, and Brown, 1816), pp. 72–73.

buy the cheapest labor. They would expend time improving machines and cutting costs, yet make no investment in their human resources. Owen appealed to their pecuniary instincts, claiming that money spent on improving labor "would return you, not five, ten, or fifteen per cent for your capital so expended, but often fifty, and in many cases a hundred per cent."[9] He claimed a 50 percent return at New Lanark and said it would shortly reach 100 percent. Owen asserted that it was more profitable to show equal concern for people, and that doing so also served to "prevent an accumulation of human misery."[10]

Robert Owen, 1845. Portrait of Robert Owen by John Cranch, 1845, Indiana Historical Society.

Accounting records from the New Lanark Mill indicate that Owen's estimates of return on investment and profits were only slightly exaggerated. The mill's partners took 5 percent of their investment as a return to capital and then prorated the remaining profits according to each partner's interest in the partnership. During Owen's time at New Lanark (1799–1828), his approximate share of gross profits was £128,500 (British pounds), plus 5 percent of his £130,000 capital (£6,500 per year). His annual return on investment typically exceeded 15 percent and, from 1811 to 1814, some 46 percent.[11]

Owen's partnership in New Lanark was profitable, but there were doubts whether this was due to his labor policies. One biographer noted that profits in the cotton-spinning industry at that time were so great, averaging 20 percent or more on capital invested, that any labor policy could have been profitable. He concluded: "In fact the margin of profit was so wide that we need scarcely look for any other explanation of Owen's success as a manufacturer."[12] Whatever the reason for Owen's own success, he deplored the commercialism of the time. He declared an intellectual war on capitalism and also attacked the Church of England because, in his view, it condoned the new industrial age and its accompanying evils. Owen's views were considered radical and made it more difficult for him to persuade others of the need for reform. He felt that the crucial error of all established religions was a belief in the doctrine of human responsibility. Owen held that humans were creatures of their material and moral environments, relatively incapable of escaping their surroundings without a moral rearmament through education. Contrary to the Church of England's view that good character was promoted by the promise of rewards and punishment, especially in the hereafter, Owen felt that a person's character developed only if one's material and moral environments were conducive. To this end, in about 1813, he became more politically active and, as described in Chapter 3, in 1819, proposed legislation to prohibit employing any child under the age of 10 and to limit the workday to 10 hours, with no night work for children.

A second biographer suggested that, frustrated in his attempts to reform society, some felt Owen was slightly mad in 1817.[13] Failing to achieve his goals in Great Britain, Owen read an ad in the *London Times* that offered some 30,000 acres for sale in Posey County, Indiana, in the United States. The sellers were a religious society, the Harmonians, followers of George Rapp; the asking price was £30,000, and the acreage was situated along the Wabash River.

[9] *Ibid.*, p. 74.

[10] *Ibid.*, p. 77.

[11] John Butt, "Robert Owen as a Businessman," in *Robert Owen, Prince of Cotton Spinners,* ed. *idem,* (Bristol: David & Charles, 1971), pp. 199–201, 211–13.

[12] Frank Podmore, *Robert Owen, a Biography* (New York: Appleton, 1924), p. 642.

[13] George D. H. Cole, *Robert Owen* (Boston: Little, Brown, and Company, 1925), p. 149.

In the decade or so that the Harmonians had farmed the land, some 2000 acres had been cleared for vineyards, orchards, and gardens; machine shops and a saw mill, as well as cotton and woolen mills, had been erected; and numerous brick and log dwellings had been completed.

Owen acquired the property, known as New Harmony, and set out to create a utopian community. Owen's primary goal was to provide for the happiness of the community's members. A new currency would be created based on labor credits, there would be no division of labor, everyone would receive a general education, and although community members would be trained for jobs, they would be able to work in other jobs as they wished. Freedom of speech was guaranteed, and women were granted the same rights and privileges as were men. Owen promised to give New Harmony to the community's members.

News about New Harmony spread quickly. By the time it opened, 800 people were ready to move the community formerly occupied by 700 Harmonians. Although the sheer number of people that moved to New Harmony was a burden, a more serious challenge arose from the nature of the new arrivals. There were some dedicated people who were aware of Owen's beliefs and took them as their own, but there were also those who had heard that New Harmony was a place where you could work a little, or not at all, and you would still be fed, clothed, and housed. For a few months, the excitement of the new venture kept everyone's morale high, but steadily the exhilaration and novelty began to wear thin. Due to lack of brewers, the brewery was idle. Because there were no millers, the grain mill was idle. With only a few dozen farmers, the task of feeding a population soon swollen to nearly 1000 became increasingly difficult. Although New Harmony was by no means ready to collapse, these and other difficulties left many dispirited. Owen assumed the position of governor, but many felt that in reassuming his previous position of complete authority, he was abandoning his promise to turn New Harmony over to the community's members. Owen tried to reorganize the community, but gave up, leaving in 1827.[14]

After New Harmony, Owen found himself both financially and emotionally broken. He had thought that what he had learned and applied in his New Lanark cotton mills could be applied to all society. Owen, however, was unable to persuade others that his new moral order was realistic rather than utopian. As a reformer, Owen devised laws for helping the poor and proposed solutions to decrease unemployment. He proposed Villages of Cooperation, like New Harmony, which would be agriculture-based, with the sharing of any surplus. Owen fought against Thomas R. Malthus's belief that, because the world's population is limited by means of subsistence and the masses tend to reproduce beyond this limit, there can be no improvement in their condition (see Chapter 3). He argued that no one would hunger if all shared. Owen deplored the division of labor's mind-numbing and debilitating effects (see Chapter 2); in his ideal world, each person would do a number of different jobs, switching easily from one to another. For Owen, the evils of the wage system and capitalism maintained life at a subsistence level. In 1833, Owen returned to England and helped create the Grand National Consolidated Trades Union. Renamed the British and Foreign Consolidated Association of Industry, Humanity and Knowledge, Owen was appointed the association's Grand Master. By 1834, however, the association ceased to function. Nevertheless, Robert Owen sowed the first seed of concern for the human side of management.

[14] John H. Hoagland, "Management before Frederick Taylor," in Billy Goetz, ed., *Proceedings of the Annual Meeting of the Academy of Management* (1955), pp. 15–24. See also *idem, Charles Babbage - His Life and Works in the Historical Evolution of Management Concepts* (Unpublished dissertation, Ohio State University, Columbus, OH., 1954); *idem,* "Historical Antecedents of Organization Research," in William W. Cooper, Harold J. Levitt, Maynard W. Shelly II , eds., *New Perspectives in Organization Research* (New York: John Wiley & Sons, 1964), pp. 27–38.

Charles Babbage: The Irascible Genius

To call Charles Babbage (1791–1871) an "irascible genius" is to pay him the highest compliment, for he fitted both qualities.[15] Babbage was distinctly ahead of his time. He held Isaac Newton's (Lucasian) chair of mathematics at Cambridge University, although it seems that he never delivered a lecture there. Babbage sought to apply technology to replace human effort and, in doing so, earned a place in history as the patron saint of Operations Research and Management Science (see Chapter 21). He theorized and applied a scientific approach to management long before the scientific-management era began in the United States (see Chapter 7). Born in Devonshire, England, the son of a wealthy banker, Babbage used his inheritance in a lifelong quest "into the causes of all those little things and events which astonish the childish mind."[16] He remarked that his first question after receiving a new toy was always, "Mamma, what is inside of it?" and he also invariably broke open the toy if her answer was unsatisfactory. The value of Babbage's work was recognized by

Charles Babbage, circa 1860.
"Obituary," *The Illustrated London News* (59) (November 4, 1871), p. 424.

few of his contemporaries, and his neighbors generally considered him a crackpot. His personal traits were not endearing to those who disturbed his meditations. To retaliate against the ubiquitous English organ-grinders that gathered outside his house, he repeatedly summoned the police who seemed powerless to stop the "music," even when he was lying on his deathbed. In response to his pleas for quiet so he could continue his work, organ-grinders, fiddlers, brass bands, and other assorted street musicians, accompanied by what Babbage referred to as "ladies of elastic virtue and cosmopolitan tendencies,"[17] responded by playing louder and longer in front of his home. One friend wrote, "He spoke as if he hated mankind in general, Englishmen in particular, and the English Government and Organ Grinders most of all."[18]

The First Computer

Babbage's scientific output was phenomenal. He demonstrated a small working model of the world's first automatic calculator, his Difference Engine, in 1822. It returned results to six decimals and provided solutions for second-order difference equations. Ninety-one years later, its basic principles were being employed in Burroughs's accounting machines. Babbage had received grants totaling £17,000 from the Chancellor of the Exchequer, Sir Robert Peele, to develop his Difference Engine. His irascibility, however, cost him similar backing for his Analytical Engine, a versatile general-purpose computer capable of any mathematical operation, which was a successor to his Difference Engine. As early as 1833, Babbage had conceived a calculating machine that could, in effect, scan a stream of instructions and automatically put them into operation. Touring a textile mill in Lyon, France, he saw looms weaving complex patterns, such as brocades, by means of holes punched in cards. A silk weaver, Joseph Marie Jacquard, drawing on earlier inventions by Basile Bouchon (1725), Jean-Baptiste Falcon (1728), and Jacques de Vaucanson (1740), had developed a mechanical loom. In Jacquard's loom, "horizontal steel rods with springs

---

[15] Maboth Moseley, *Irascible Genius: A Life of Charles Babbage, Inventor* (London: Hutchinson & Co., 1964).

[16] Charles Babbage, *Passages from the Life of a Philosopher* (London: Longman, Green, Longman, Roberts, & Green, 1864), p. 7.

[17] *Ibid.*, p. 314.

[18] Bertram V. Bowden, "A Brief History of Computation, in *idem*, ed., *Faster than Thought: A Symposium on Digital Computing Machines* (London: Sir Isaac Pitman & Sons, 1953), p. 18.

at the end 'sense' the holes punched in a rectangular piece of cardboard. When a rod 'feels' a hole it passes through and activates a mechanism for lifting the appropriate warp thread, which is then skipped in the weaving, while the other threads are regularly woven. The way the holes are punched programs the pattern."[19] In extending Jacquard's innovation, Babbage used punch cards for storing information, as well as for guiding machine operations. Building on Babbage's work, a half-a-century later, Herman Hollerith created a punched-card tabulating machine to input data for the 1890 U.S. Census.[20] Perhaps even more significantly, Babbage's innovativeness anticipated by some twenty years the binary system (zero/one, off/on, yes/no, true/false) developed by English mathematician George Boole (1815–1864) for comparing mathematical functions. Boole's work later formed the basis for the electrical switches used by modern digital computers to process logical expressions.

Babbage's Analytical Engine, the first digital computer able to perform any calculation, had all the basic elements of today's computers. It had a "store" (or memory device), a "mill" (or arithmetic unit), a punch-card input system, external memory storage, and conditional transfer.[21] In retrospect, Babbage's genius was not in the calculating power of his engine but in the mechanization of the organizing and logical control of mathematical functions.[22] The Analytical Engine was capable of raising numbers to the second and third powers and extracting the root of a quadratic equation. Babbage also conceived an "apparatus for printing on paper, one, or if required, two copies of the results" of a computer program's output—a Victorian version of a modern printer.[23] Babbage encountered so many problems in constructing his Analytical Engine that he was never able to build a full-scale model. He not only had to invent tools and tool shapers and design lathes to machine the hand-fitted steel and die-cast pewter gear wheels of his Analytical Engine, he also had to develop his own abstract notation when standard mechanical drawing symbols proved inadequate.[24] Shortly before Babbage's death in 1871, he wrote: "If I survive some few years longer, the Analytical Engine will exist, and its works will afterwards be spread over the world."[25] For more than a century his work would lie dormant, waiting other times and other people to advance his seminal ideas.

One of the few bright spots in Babbage's life was his friendship with Augusta Ada King (1816–1852), the Countess Lovelace, wife of William King, 1st Earl of Lovelace, and the estranged daughter of the poet Lord Byron. The countess had a gift for mathematics and engineering, and was one of the few who really understood Babbage's work. She wrote treatises that expressed his ideas better than he could, and wrote programs for his Analytical Engine. She warned people against becoming dependent on the engine, which "has no pretentions whatever to *originate* anything . . . [and would] do whatever we *know how to order it* to perform."[26] Together with Babbage, Countess Lovelace developed a system for applying the Analytical Engine to mathematically handicap horse races. The system was unsuccessfully, and twice the countess had

---

[19] Molly Gleiser, "The Looms of Lyons," *Datamation* 25(9) (September 1979), p. 220.

[20] George E. Biles, Alfred A. Bolton, and Bernadette M. DiRe, "Herman Hollerith: Inventor, Manager, Entrepreneur – A Centennial Remembrance," *Journal of Management* 15(4) (December 1989), pp. 603–615.

[21] In computer terminology, conditional transfer refers to the "if" statement: that is, instructing the computer "if such and such occurs, follow this path; if not, proceed in the normal sequence of control."

[22] Daniel A. Wren, "A Calculating Genius," *Knowledge Management* 2(5) (May 1999), p. 104.

[23] Details of Babbage's printing apparatus are provided in Harry W. Buxton, *Memoir of the Life and Labours of the Late Charles Babbage, Esq. F.R.S.*, ed. Anthony Hyman (Cambridge, MA: MIT Press, 1988), p. 182. Written between 1872 and 1880.

[24] Leopold Froehlich, "Babbage Observed," *Datamation* 31(5) (March 1985), p. 122.

[25] Babbage, *Passages from the Life of a Philosopher*, p. 449. In 1991, a team at London's Science Museum succeeded in constructing a full-scale model of the Analytical Machine using Babbage's original drawings. It weighs 3 tons, is 11 feet long, 7 feet high, and 18 inches deep, with 4,000 parts and is capable of calculating numbers up to 31 digits. Doing so, however, requires turning a crank nearly 27,000 times. "Calculator Designed in 1894 Works," *Morning Advocate* (Baton Rouge, LA) December 13, 1991, p. 4A.

[26] A. A. L. [Augusta Ada Lovelace], "Translator's Notes to M. Menabrea's Memoir," *Scientific Memoirs, Selected from the Transactions of Foreign Academies of Science and Learned Societies and from Foreign Journals* 3(12) (1843), p. 722.

to pawn the Lovelace family jewels to pay her gambling debts.[27] Undaunted by her losses (though Lord Lovelace was upset), Babbage continued his work and developed programs for his Analytical Engine that were a forerunner of modern business-gaming techniques. Babbage also developed a program to play tick-tack-toe and chess that computed the best possible combinations of positions as far as three moves in advance. In addition, he was the era's outstanding cryptologist.

Analyzing Industrial Operations

Inevitably, Babbage's inquisitive mind and wide interests led him to write about management. His most successful book, *On the Economy of Machinery and Manufactures*, was published in 1832. Babbage became interested in management as a result of difficulties he encountered constructing his Analytical Engine. Searching for solutions, Babbage visited a wide variety of British and French factories. In the aforesaid book, he not only described tools and machines and discussed the "economical principles of manufacturing" but also, in the true spirit of inquiry, analyzed operations and their expense, the kinds of skills involved, and suggested improvements.[28]

Babbage was interested in machinery, tools, the efficient use of power, developing counting machines to check totals, and the economic use of raw materials. He developed a "method of observing manufactories," which was closely akin to a scientific, systematic approach to the study of industrial operations.[29] As part of this method, he prepared a list of questions about capital investment (large or small), raw materials, required tools and machinery, necessary labor, waste, wholesale prices, and so on. In essence, it was the same procedure that an operations analyst or a consultant would use today in approaching a method-based analysis. Babbage emphasized the difference between "making" products in small workshops and "manufacturing" or operating on a larger scale, which necessitated carefully arranging the "whole system of [the] factory" to reduce production costs.[30] He recognized that success in a capitalist market economy calls for industry, integrity, and talent.

On the human side, Babbage recalled the Luddite movement (see Chapter 3) and pleaded with workers to recognize that a properly designed factory system was to their benefit: "It is of great importance that the more intelligent amongst the class of workmen should examine the correctness of these views; because . . . the whole class may . . . be led by designing persons to pursue a course, which . . . is in reality at variance with their own best interests."[31] Babbage's attempts to show the mutuality of interests between workers and factory owners were somewhat similar to what Frederick W. Taylor said 75 years later (see Chapter 7). According to Babbage,

> the prosperity and success of the master manufacturer is essential to the welfare of the workman . . . whilst it is perfectly true that workmen, as a class, derive advantage from the prosperity of their employers, I do not think that each individual partakes of that advantage exactly in proportion to the extent to which he contributes to it. . . . It would be of great importance, if in every large establishment the mode of payment could be so arranged, that every person employed should derive advantage from the success of the whole; and that the profits of each individual should advance, as the factory itself produced profit, without the necessity of making any change in the wages.[32]

---

[27] Margot Strickland, *The Byron Women* (New York: St. Martin's Press, 1974), pp. 209–210.

[28] Charles Babbage, *On the Economy of Machinery and Manufactures* (London: Charles Knight, 1832), pp. 94–96. It should be noted that although Babbage's discussion of expenses is somewhat similar to an early form of cost accounting, it differed from modern cost accounting, in that, it described costs rather than analyzing what costs ought to be, as under a standard cost system.

[29] *Ibid.*, pp. 93–97.

[30] *Ibid.*, p. 99.

[31] *Ibid.*, p. 192.

[32] *Idem*, *On the Economy of Machinery and Manufactures*, 3rd ed. (London: C. Knight, Pall Mall East, 1833), pp. 250–251.

Babbage's profit-sharing plan had two facets: a portion of workers' wages would depend on factory profits, and a worker *"should derive more advantage from applying any improvement he might discover . . . than he could by any other course of action."*[33] In other words, workers would receive a fixed salary based on the nature of their tasks, plus a share of a firm's profits and a bonus for any suggestions that improve a factory's performance. Babbage saw a number of advantages in his proposal: (1) each worker would have a direct interest in a firm's prosperity, (2) each worker would be stimulated to prevent waste and mismanagement, (3) every department would be improved, and (4) "it would be the common interest of all to admit [hire] only the most respectable and skillful [workers]." In effect, work groups, operating under a profit-sharing plan, would act to screen out those who would reduce their share of profits. Finally, Babbage saw his plan as removing the necessity for "combinations of workers" because their interests would be the same as those of their employers. With a mutuality of interests, neither would oppress the other and all would prosper.

Beyond his scientific contributions, Charles Babbage made significant advancements in understanding the challenges of the emerging factory system. His analytic approach to the study of manufacturing, his recognition of the need for new incentives to enlist labor cooperation, and his emphasis on a mutuality of interests between workers and employers made him a visionary pioneer in the evolution of management thought.

Andrew Ure: Pioneering in Management Education

Andrew Ure. Wellcome Library, London.

Dr. Andrew Ure . . . : A Slight Sketch. (London: Baines, 1876), frontispiece.

Andrew Ure (1778–1857) provided academic training for fledgling managers in the early days of the factory system. He studied at Edinburgh and Glasgow universities, receiving his MD from the latter in 1801. In 1804, Ure was elected to the Chair of Natural Philosophy at Anderson's Institute in Glasgow, where he remained until 1839. Dr. John Anderson had lectured on science at the University of Glasgow and in his will had proposed that the eponymous institute be founded to teach "the whole range of human knowledge to both sexes." The institute was the first technical college to focus on educating members of the "artisan class."[34] Educational pressures for technically trained workers and managers soon shifted the composition of Ure's classes from factory workers to clerks, warehousemen, artisans, and shopkeepers; from these classes, salaried managers for the ever-growing factory system were to be recruited. Ure knew the French engineer and management writer Charles Dupin, and when Dupin visited Great Britain in 1818, Ure escorted him around Glasgow's factories. Dupin commented that many of the factories' managers were Ure's former students. Ure acknowledged this, writing that his onetime students were "spread over the [United] Kingdom as proprietors and managers of factories."[35] Dupin's work was influenced by Ure and, in turn, may have influenced Henri Fayol, another pioneer whose ideas underlie modern-management theory (see Chapter 10).

---

[33] *Ibid.*, p. 254.

[34] For more about Anderson and Anderson's Institute, see James Muir, *John Anderson: Pioneer of Technical Education and the College He Founded* (Glasgow: J. Smith, 1950).

[35] Andrew Ure, *The Philosophy of Manufactures: Or an Exposition of the Scientific, Moral and Commercial Economy of the Factory System of Great Britain* (London: Charles Knight, 1835), p. viii.

Principles of Manufacturing

Ure was deeply concerned with industrial education. Writing in his 1835 book, *The Philosophy of Manufactures: Or an Exposition of the Scientific, Moral and Commercial Economy of the Factory System of Great Britain*, he provided a systematic account of manufacturing principles and processes. In Ure's judgment, the essential principle in manufacturing was "to substitute mechanical science for hand skill . . . [and to provide] for division or the graduation of labour among artisans."[36] Although Ure devoted a large portion of his 1835 book to the technical challenges of manufacturing cloth from silk, cotton, wool, and flax, he eventually dealt with the challenges of factory management. Ure sought a plan for automatically preventing individual mill-hands from stopping work as they pleased and, thereby throwing an entire factory into disorder. He believed that workers had to recognize and not resist the benefits of mechanization. According to Ure's plan to prevent work stoppages, the tasks necessary to manufacture a final product had to be "arranged and connected" in such a way as to achieve a harmony of the whole. To this end, Ure felt that in every establishment there were "three principles of action, or three organic systems; the mechanical, the moral and the commercial."[37]

Although Ure's explanation of these principles did not entail a clear-cut plan for organizing a factory system, he did seek to place them in the framework of a "self-governing agency." "Mechanical" referred to production techniques and processes, "moral" to the condition of personnel, and "commercial" to sustaining a manufactory through selling and financing goods and services. Ure treated the mechanical principle of action at length; the moral aspect reflected a pro-management stance. As the factory system of Ure's day was under attack from a number of quarters, he set out to defend his industrial practices. He argued that, as a group, factory workers were treated better with regard to "personal comforts" than artisans or others in nonindustrial establishments. They ate better, held jobs that were less physically demanding (due to the nature of the machines they operated), and were better paid. In Ure's view, rather than appreciate these advantages, workers who engaged in strikes, sabotaged equipment, and caused other capital losses for their employers were agitating against their own best interests. Rebutting investigations into child labor, Ure noted that most of the investigators and their supporters had never visited the factories they found so offensive; he also engaged in character assassination, charging that one investigation witness was an atheist, one a tavern keeper, and one "an assaulter of women." To further counter the investigators' accusations, Ure claimed that children employed in factories lived in well-kept cottages, received both practical and religious education, and were better fed and enjoyed better health than children in general. He also noted that children employed in agriculture were paid half their factory counterparts' wages and received no education or training. Citing Factory Inquiry Commission reports,[38] Ure concluded that the incidence of disease, the dietary habits, and the general state of health of factory workers were better than the general population.

To illustrate workers' nonappreciation of employers' concerns for their health, Ure cited an instance in which large ventilating fans had been installed in one factory to reduce the foul air. Instead of thanking the factory owner, however, the workers complained that the freshened air had increased their appetites, and, therefore, they were entitled to a corresponding wage increase! The factory owner reached a compromise with his workers by running the ventilating fans only half the day,

---

[36] *Ibid.*, p. 20.

[37] *Ibid.*, p. 55.

[38] Factories Inquiry Commission, "First Report of the Central Board of His Majesty's Commissioners Appointed to Collect Information in the Manufacturing Districts, as to the Employment of Children in Factories, and as to the Propriety and Means of Curtailing the Hours of Their Labour," *Parliamentary Papers* 20(450) (1833); *idem*, "Second Report of the Central Board of His Majesty's Commissioners Appointed to Collect Information in the Manufacturing Districts, as to the Employment of Children in Factories, and as to the Propriety and Means of Curtailing the Hours of Their Labour," *Parliamentary Papers* 21(519) (1833); *idem*, "Supplementary Report of the Central Board of His Majesty's Commissioners Appointed to Collect Information in the Manufacturing Districts, as to the Employment of Children in Factories, and as to the Propriety and Means of Curtailing the Hours of Their Labour," 2 vols. (London: House of Commons, 1834).

thereafter hearing no more complaints about foul air or appetites. Ure defended the factory system, seeing more benefits than disadvantages accruing to society. Some of his statements in defense of factory working conditions, however, would seem contestable.[39] He contended, for instance, that mill-workers suffered no harm from working at temperatures ranging up to 150° F or that their ill-health was due to eating too much bacon that was often putrid.[40]

Ure based many of his conclusions on data extracted from an 1833 survey report on the employment of children in factories.[41] The survey was conducted for the Factories Inquiry Commission by Samuel Stanway, a Manchester public accountant. Focusing on responses collected from 151 cotton mills, Stanway reported that the average mill worker labored for 69 hours per week. Of 48,645 "hands," approximately half were female and about 41.29 percent were under the age of 18, with 47.5 percent of this latter group between ages 14 and 18.[42] Based on records provided by Manchester mill-owner Thomas Houldsworth, Ure also drew a comparison between the wages paid to cotton-spinners in 1804 and 1833. Over this period, the work week for adult male cotton-spinners declined from 74 to 68 hours, while their average weekly wage increased from 60 to 65 shillings and 3 pence. Ure further noted that the purchasing power (real wages) of the 65 shillings was greater in 1833 than the 60 shillings in 1804. For example, in 1804, 60 shillings would buy 117 pounds of flour and 62.5 pounds of meat; in 1833, 65 shillings and 3 pence would buy 267 pounds of flour and 85 pounds of meat.[43] Ure concluded that progress in the cotton industry outpaced that in agriculture where workers who were still earning subsistence incomes. He did acknowledge that, although child and female labor were widely used in cotton mills, this was no different than had been the case in the domestic system in which individual workers fabricated goods in small workshops or in their own homes (see Chapter 2) or in either agriculture or coal mines. For Ure, rising real wages, a trend toward shorter and more regular hours, and advancing mechanization were the hallmarks of English cotton mills. Although Ure's focus on cotton mills precludes a general statement about English management in the mid-nineteenth century, the evidence he marshaled does suggest an increase in mechanization and a growing realization of long hours and harsh working conditions endured by men, women, and children.

Charles Dupin: Industrial Education in France

A second individual who pioneered in industrial education was a French mathematician, economist, politician, and engineer. Baron Pierre Charles François Dupin (1784–1873) was particularly known for his interest in mathematics and mechanics. As noted earlier, Dupin had visited Great Britain on various occasions (1816–1819) and observed the results Andrew Ure was obtaining in educating those working-class men and women.[44] In 1819, Dupin was named professor of mathematics and economics at the Conservatoire des Arts et Métiers in Paris.[45] He must have

[39] Wilfred V. Farrar, "Andrew Ure, F.R.S., and the Philosophy of Manufactures," *Notes and Records of the Royal Society of London*, 27(2) (February 1973), pp. 318, 395.

[40] Ure, *The Philosophy of Manufactures,* pp. 385 and 395.

[41] Factories Inquiry Commission, *Supplementary Report of the Central Board of H. Maj. Commissioners Appointed to Collect Information in the Manufacturing Districts, as to the Employment of Children in Factories, and as to the Propriety and Means of Curtailing the Hours of Their Labour,* pt. 1 (London: House of Commons, 1834), pp. 134–140.

[42] Andrew Ure, *The Cotton Manufactures of Great Britain Systematically Investigated*, vol. 1 (London: Charles Knight, 1836), pp. 334–342.

[43] *Ibid.*, vol. 2, p. 447. See also *Report from the Select Committee on Manufactures, Commerce, and Shipping; With the Minutes of Evidence, and Appendix and Index* (London: House of Commons, 1833), p. 319.

[44] Charles Dupin, *Voyages dans la Grande-Bretagne, entrepris relativement aux services publics de la guerre, de la marine, et des ponts et chaussés, en 1816, 1817, 1818 et 1819* [*Travel in Great Britain Undertaken in connection with the public services of war, navy, and bridges and highways, in 1816, 1817, 1818 and 1819*], vol. 3: *Commerciable de LaGrande-Bretagne* [*Commerce of Great Britain*] (Paris: Bachelier, 1824).

[45] Paul Tannery, "Dupin" in Brethelot Drefus, ed., *La Grande Encyclopedie: Inventaire Raisonné des Sciences, des Lettres et des Arts* [*The Great Encyclopedia: Inventory of Science, Letters and the Arts*], vol. 15, (Paris: Lamirault, 1886), p. 81. See also Académié des Sciences, *M. Le Baron Dupin: Discours Prononcés a ses Funéraillis le 21 Janvier 1873 et Éloge Historique lu a l'Académie des Sciences le 2 Avril 1883* [*Baron Dupin: Speeches at His Funeral on January 21, 1873 and Eulogies Read at the Academy of Sciences on April 2, 1883*] (Nevers, France: G. Valliére, 1902).

immediately initiated his own curriculum, for in 1831 he wrote: "For twelve years I have had the honor of teaching geometry and mechanics applied to the arts, in favor of the industrial class, I have dedicated the first and last sessions of each year to the general consideration of the most important questions affecting the well-being, education, and morality of the workers, to the progress of national industry, and to the development of all means of prosperity that work can produce for the splendor and happiness of our country."[46] One of Dupin's colleagues at the conservatory was Jean-Baptiste Say, a professor of political economy. As noted in Chapter 3, Say considered entrepreneurs to be a fourth factor of production. Because Say and Dupin taught their classes "at half-past eight o'clock in the evening, when the . . . artisans and working mechanics have completed the labours of the day," it is reasonable to assume that both Say and Ure influenced Dupin's view of management.[47] Dupin's contribution to the practice of management lie in the influence he had on the course of French industrial education and, though there is no direct historical support, perhaps on the later work of Henri Fayol. As will be discussed in Chapter 10, Fayol is widely credited with being the first writer to distinguish between technical and managerial skills and to argue for the necessity of teaching management. Examine this passage from Dupin, however, written over 8 decades before Fayol's major published work:

Charles Dupin, 1820. Julien Léopold Boilly, *Recueil de Portraits de Personnages Célèbres Faisant Partie des Quatre Différentes Classes Académiques de l'Institut Lithographies par Boilly Fils,* ed. Institut Royal de France (Paris: Blaisot, circa 1823), plate 9.

> It is to the director of workshops and factories that it is suitable to make, by means of geometry and applied mechanics, a special study [*étude spéciale*] of all the ways to economize the efforts of workers. . . . [F]or a man to be a director of others, manual work has only a secondary importance; it is his intellectual ability [*force intellectuelle*] that must put him in the top position, and it is in instruction such as that of the Conservatory of Arts and Crafts, that he must develop it.[48]

The aforementioned special study [*étude spéciale*] of all the ways to economize the efforts of workers would focus on technical instruction rather than manual work and feature instructions taught by Say, Dupin, and Ure. Fayol, who was educated as an engineer in France, could possibly have read Dupin as a student and been influenced in his own thinking about the importance of teaching management.

Hoagland reported that by 1826 Dupin's views on management had been presented in 98 French cities to more than 5,000 workers and supervisors.[49] Because his lectures were published and translated into 8 languages, the number of people he influenced was no doubt much larger.[50] Dupin also demonstrated a rudimentary grasp of time study and the need to balance workloads after labor was divided: "When [the] division of work is put into operation the most scrupulous attention must be exercised to calculate the duration of each type of operation,

[46] Charles Dupin, *Discours sur le Sort des Ouvriers, Considéré dans ses Rapports avec l'Industrie, la Liberté et l'Ordre Public: Prononcé dans la Séance de Clôture de son Cours, le 19 Juin, au Conservatoire des Arts et Métiers* [*Lecture on the Fate of the Workers, Considered in its Relations with Industry, Freedom and Public Order: Pronounced in the Closing Session of its Course, June 19, at the Conservatory of Arts and Crafts*], (Paris: Bachelier Librairie, 1831), p. 1.
[47] "Conservatoire des Arts et Métiers [de Paris]," *Revue Encyclopédique, ou Analyse Raisonnée* 24(10) (October 1824) p. 846.
[48] *Dupin, Discours,* pp. 12–13.
[49] John H. Hoagland, "Management before Frederick Taylor," p. 21.
[50] Roberto Romani, *National Character and Public Spirit in Britain and France, 1750–1914* (Cambridge, England: Cambridge University Press, 2002), p. 101.

in order to proportion the work to the particular number of workers that are assigned to it."[51] He wrote of the need to provide workers with clear, concise instructions for most efficiently producing desired work and for studying each industry to find and publish the most effective means of accomplishing different tasks.

Dupin's published lectures were not so much an examination of management as they were an exhortation to remove industrial strife. He also recognized worker uneasiness stemming from the increasing mechanization of French industry, discussed the work of James Watt (see Chapter 3), and stressed mechanization's benefits to workers, managers, and society. Regarding the dangers of technological displacement, Dupin noted that before Watt's first steam engine was introduced in 1776, British industry employed fewer than one million people; by 1830, this number had grown to over three million and combined with advances in machinery to equate to the power of seven million workers. For Dupin, this was ample proof that mechanization created, rather than destroyed, jobs. Evidently the French had their Luddites, and Dupin indicated that such resistance to mechanization was futile. As a solution, he called for widespread industrial training to permit agrarian and unskilled workers to share in the growing industrial prosperity: "He who perfects the machines tends to give them the advantage over the worker; he who perfects the worker, gives him the same fighting chance, and makes the machine serve his well-being, instead of having to suffer from their competition. Let us concern ourselves with man involved with the difficulties of the work and of the industry."[52] These were insights applicable not only to early nineteenth-century France, but also to industrial life in the twentieth and twenty-first centuries.

The Pioneers: A Final Note

The four pioneers discussed in this chapter were instrumental in sowing the seeds of a management discipline. At its best, however, the outgrowth of these seeds was sparse and rudimentary. What prevented the emergence of a formal body of management thought during this early period rather than some three-quarters of a century later? Why would Frederick W. Taylor, and not Charles Babbage, receive credit for founding scientific management? In retrospect, the reasons are manifold. First, early writings emphasized specific techniques and not managing per se. In an age of expanding technology, it was difficult to separate the role of management from the technical and commercial aspects of running a firm. Managers in this era were more concerned with finance, production processes, selling, and acquiring labor—all of which were indeed critical at the time—rather than with developing principles or generalizations about management. An analogy might be that of young children learning to walk: the motor urge is so great and consumes so much of their energy and attention that the development of speech is slowed. As walking is perfected, speech blooms. At the dawn of the Industrial Revolution, managers were just learning to walk in the new factory system; the technical and human challenges consumed so much of their time that they had little left over for formulating general principles of management.

Second, the era was dominated by the technical genius, the inventor-pioneer, and the owner-entrepreneur. Success or failure was more likely to be attributed to their individual intelligence or skill rather than to any generalized ideas about what talents managers needed to be successful. Each industry and its challenges were considered unique and, hence, the lessons learned in one setting were considered inapplicable in another. Finally, the limits of disseminating knowledge

---

[51] Charles Dupin, *Géométrie et Méchanique des Arts et Métiers et des Beaux-Arts* [*Geometry and Mechanics of Arts and Crafts and Fine Arts*], vol. 3 (Paris: Bachelier, 1826), p. 128.
[52] Dupin, *Discours,* p. 9.

must be considered. Few were literate, books were expensive, and schools were oriented toward either studying the classics or training artisans. Although scholars read the books of other scholars, it is unlikely that Babbage, Dupin, and Ure were widely read by practicing managers of the day. The lessons taught by Say, Ure, and Dupin reached managers in only a relatively small number of factories.

SUMMARY

The genesis of modern management thought occurred in Great Britain and, to a lesser extent, France. Robert Owen appealed to the heart, as well as to the pocketbook, in his search for a New Harmony between humans and machines. Charles Babbage appealed to the mind, became the grandfather of scientific management, and applied science to management before Taylor. Andrew Ure shared his experiences and observations, developing working-class managers for the new factories that heralded the Industrial revolution. Following Ure's lead, Dupin and Say launched industrial education in France. With the emergence of management thought in Great Britain, our story now moves to the development of "systematic" management in the United States.

chapter

5

The Industrial Revolution in the United States

The nineteenth century in the United States was an era of rapid expansion and growth. An English colony just 24 years earlier, and torn by half a decade of internecine strife in mid-century, the fledging nation was to become the world's leading political and industrial force by 1900. Indeed, by the early twentieth century, the manufactruing output of the United States surpassed that of Britian, Germany, and France combined.[*] This chapter focuses on the Industrial Revolution in the United States, the industries it spawned, and the work of various management pioneers from this era.

Antebellum Industry and Management

The territory that became the United States was part of the British Empire from 1607 to 1776. For the settlers that came to the 13 colonies that eventually formed the original states of the United States of America, the lure was manifold: social betterment, economic opportunity, religious freedom, and political separation. No element explains the whole, for the nation that emerged was a conglomerate, defying a single identification or explanation. The early colonists included aristocrats, felons, tramps, and petty criminals, as well as budding tycoons. Efforts to develop colonial manufacturing were discouraged by Great Britain, as it did not want competition from goods made in its own colonies. The Wool Act (1699), prohibiting colonists from exporting wool, and the Hat Act (1732), limiting the export of colonial-made hats, are but two prominent examples of laws restricting the manufacture, sale, and exportation of colonial goods. Two 1776 documents, however, tolled the end of mercantilist policies intended to favor British traders: the Declaration of Independence in the United States and Adam Smith's *The Wealth of Nations* in Great Britain (see Chapter 2). The former was a declaration of national independence and the latter was a declaration of economic freedom.

---

[*]Noam Maggor, Brahmin Capitalsim: Frontiers of Wealth and Populism in America's Gilded Age (Cambridge, MA: Harvard Univerity Press, 2017), p. ix.

Between 1776 and 1787, the ideas of Adam Smith (see Chapter 2) were widely read and discussed in the United States. Political leaders such as Benjamin Franklin, who commented on draft chapters of *The Wealth of Nations* for Smith,[1] objected to a strong government role in economic matters. Smith's laissez-faire philosophy was consistent with the views of America's Founding Fathers, including James Madison, Alexander Hamilton, Thomas Jefferson, and, of course, Franklin. Ratified in 1787, the United States Constitution, Article I, Section 8, gave the U.S. Congress the power to impose and collect taxes, borrow money, coin money, fix standards of weights and measures, punish counterfeiters, issue patents, and "regulate commerce with foreign nations and among the several states." With these exceptions, the U.S. government was to maintain a hands-off approach to private economic affairs and act primarily to ensure uniformity and order among the several states. Political and social conditions in the United States during the nineteenth century were favorable to capitalism and economic expansion. The United States was rich in natural resources, with a growing labor supply. Many colonial merchants made their fortunes in trade. These fortunes, aided by the sobriety and thrift of colonial Puritanism, made increasing amounts of capital available for entrepreneurial ventures. Three colonial merchants, William Almy, Smith Brown, and Moses Brown, of Providence, Rhode Island, provided the capital that brought the Industrial Revolution to the United States.

Early Industrial Development

British textile manufacturers were particularly concerned about colonial competition. To protect its mills, Great Britain prohibited both the export of textile machinery and the emigration of skilled mechanics who knew how to build and repair it.[2] To be allowed to emigrate to the United States, Samuel Slater (1768–1835), an experienced builder and mechanic who had worked with Richard Arkwright, the British textile pioneer (see Chapter 3), claimed to be a farmer. At the time, cloth was made in hundreds of homes by farm wives and their daughters, "put out" by various merchants who provided raw materials under the domestic system, and occasionally made in a few small textile factories with hand looms. In 1789, William Almy (1761–1836) and Moses Brown (1738–1836) established the first water-powered textile factory in the United States. Brown foresaw tremendous possibilities in Arkwright's more advanced water frame. Learning of Brown's interest in running his looms with hydropower instead of human power, Slater offered his services to replicate Arkwright's water frame. The result was the nation's first water-powered textile mill, built at Pawtucket, Rhode Island, in 1790. Striking out on his own in 1798, Slater developed what became known as the "Rhode Island System." Following the practice in Great Britain, the Rhode Island System consisted of a sole proprietorship or mill partnership that produced fine yarn and employed entire families (including children) to do weaving in their homes. Slater supervised mill operations, assisted by his sons, his brother, and other relatives.

By 1808, the United States boasted 15 textile mills, over half of them connected with Slater and his various associates. The War of 1812 with Great Britain led to a further surge in U.S. textile manufacturing. Francis Cabot Lowell, a prominent New England merchant, had visited Great Britain and seen textile looms driven by waterwheels. He returned to the United States and founded the Boston Manufacturing Company of Waltham, Massachusetts, to apply this new technology. Rather than emulating Slater's Rhode Island System, what was known as the Waltham

---

[1] John F. Watson, *Annals of Philadelphia, Being a Collection of Memoirs, Anecdotes, & Incidents of the City and Its Inhabitants from the Days of the Pilgrim Founders* (Philadelphia, PA: E. I. Carey & A. Hart, 1830), pp. 514–515. See also Thomas D. Eliot, "The Relations between Adam Smith and Benjamin Franklin before 1776," *Political Science Quarterly* 39(1) (March 1924), pp. 67–96.

[2] Theodore F. Marburg, "Aspects of Labor Administration in the Early Nineteenth Century," *Bulletin of the Business Historical Society* 15(1) (February 1941), pp. 1–10.

System used joint-stock companies and a corporate form of ownership; did not put out work to people working from their homes, but integrated spinning and weaving so as to manufacture textiles in large quantities; hired nonfamily supervisors and managers; and relied on adult female labor.

The Waltham System had become the dominant method of textile manufacturing by 1816. Slow to change, Slater and his associates waited almost a decade before giving up the Rhode Island System.[3] In 1827, Slater became one of the few mill owners to use steam-driven power looms at his Steam Cotton Manufacturing Company in Providence, Rhode Island. Whereas other manufacturers depended on hydropower, Slater was able to regularize production and employment by relying on steam power. He also began to integrate spinning and weaving, ending the putting-out system. As Slater's mills became more successful, operating in some 15 separate locations by 1835, he began to hire professional managers. Slater pioneered the use of factory ledgers to determine the cost of producing a yard of cloth and vertically integrated his business holdings, moving forward to establish a sales office in New York City and backward by employing buyers to locate and purchase raw materials. Slater offers an excellent example of an early U.S. entrepreneur who strategically responded to technological, as well as foreign and domestic competitive pressures.

The first U.S. textile mills provide insights into early ideas about organization structure and management. As outlined in Chapter 3, as organizations grew in size and number of locations, the ability of owner-entrepreneurs to directly supervise all their employees diminished, and intermediate levels of supervision became necessary. There is also evidence of emerging staff positions. A mill manager was often "assisted by a superintendent, a technically trained man, and there were overseers with technical responsibilities that cut across the operations of the mill: overseers of repairs . . . or of belting."[4] Thus mechanics, woodworkers, and other skilled workmen were employed and still others were made supervisors and technical overseers. Reflecting Dupin's distinction between technical and managerial skills (see Chapter 4), supervisors did not need both technical and managerial ability, but could rely on specialists in these areas.

Slater's Rhode Island System and Lowell's Waltham System also differed in their labor policies. To attract enough workers for its mills, Slater's Rhode Island System was patterned after the British practice of employing entire families and, consequently, resulted in more child labor. In contrast, the Waltham System was designed to recruit female workers to its mill towns by furnishing boarding houses. These "mill girls" were mainly young women between the ages of 15 and 30. They were hired from neighboring farms by agents who toured the countryside, emphasizing the moral and educational advantages of factory work.[5] The mill girls had to be in at 10:00 pm, and their conduct was carefully monitored by a housemother.

Even English novelist Charles Dickens (see Chapter 3), a vocal critic of the British factory system, praised the Waltham System. He reported that the Waltham mill girls were clean, healthy, and well mannered. Dickens felt British mill-owners could learn much from the Waltham example.[6] Nonetheless, the Waltham System was less successful in retaining a labor force; Ware estimated that the typical New England cotton-mill girl stayed at her job for only a year.[7] The introduction of steam-powered looms, however, had a dramatic effect on the employment of child labor in Rhode Island: "with the mechanization of picking and weaving in the early 1820s, Pawtucket's factory system had reached maturity and as a consequence had come to rely increasingly on adult factory

---

[3] Barbara M. Tucker, *Samuel Slater and the Origins of the American Textile Industry, 1790–1860* (Ithaca, NY: Cornell University Press, 1984), pp. 99–124.

[4] Steven Lubar, "Managerial Structure and Technological Style: The Lowell Mills, 1821–1880," in Jeremy Atack, ed., *Business and Economic History* 13 (March 1984), p. 21.

[5] Thomas C. Cochran and William Miller, *The Age of Enterprise* (New York: Harper & Row, 1961), p. 19.

[6] Charles Dickens, *American Notes for General Circulation*, vol. 1 (London: Chapman and Hall, 1842), pp. 156, 163–164. Corroborating evidence for Dickens's observations may be found in William Scoresby, *American Factories and Their Female Operatives* (Boston, MA: W. D. Ticknor Co., 1845).

[7] Norman Ware, *The Industrial Worker: 1840–1860* (Gloucester, MA: Peter Smith Co., 1959), p. 149.

labor."[8] Consequently, the evils commonly found in Britain were increasingly absent in U.S. textile mills. Employers were paying high wages to attract and retain their workers, child labor was not as prevalent, and abuses were less frequent and less severe.[9]

Overall, U.S. workers were less resistant to the introduction of machinery than their British counterparts. They also took a different stance with respect to organized labor. As a legacy of legislation regulating British guilds, combinations of workers were viewed as conspiracies in restraint of trade and, therefore, illegal. Although local craft unions made some headway in the United States, they often ran into court-ordered injunctions when they sought to strike. In a landmark 1842 case (*Commonwealth v. Hunt*), the Massachusetts Supreme Court held that labor combinations were not illegal per se, though if they were organized for an unlawful purpose, or used criminal means to accomplish their goals, they were subject to prosecution.[10] The Court's ruling thus established that workers had the right to strike or use peaceful coercion to raise wages. In addition, the Court ruled that unions could require "closed shops" in which all workers were required to be union members. Although these rulings only applied in Massachusetts, it discouraged attempts in other states to prosecute unions on conspiracy grounds. In brief, early U.S. industrial development was fostered by economic, social, political, and technological forces that encouraged work, thrift, innovation, and competition. The Industrial Revolution in the United States began in textiles, but would soon spread throughout other industries.

The American System of Manufacturing

In 1851, the Great Exhibition of the Industry of All Nations was staged in London at the Crystal Palace. What amazed visitors the most was the U.S. exhibit featuring Alfred C. Hobbs's unpickable locks, Isaac M. Singer's sewing machine, Samuel Colt's repeating pistol, and Cyrus H. McCormick's mechanical reaper. Not only were these products superior to those made in other nations, they also were all made in a unique fashion—the parts were built to such exacting standards that they were interchangeable, so a person could pick up the necessary parts at random and assemble a complete product. This unique feature became known as the American System of Manufacturing.

To conclude that the development of interchangeable parts was solely an U.S. innovation, however, would be inaccurate. As early as 1436, the Arsenal of Venice (Italy) was manufacturing warships using standard parts. For example, all bows were built to fit any arrow, a single type of rudder fit all stern posts, and deck furnishings and riggings were largely uniform.[11] Armorers in Switzerland, France, and other countries had also followed this principle in their work; however, no one had previously used interchangeable parts in industry until Hobbs, Colt, Singer, McCormick, and other U.S. manufacturers. What could have happened in the United States to lead to this new application?

In the United States, as elsewhere, the use of interchangeable parts began in arms manufacturing. Early private contractors, such as Eli Whitney and Simeon North, had made small batches of arms using interchangeable parts, but with limited success.[12] The Springfield (Massachusetts) Armory was established in 1795 as a central workshop to bring weapons makers together to produce armaments, although it did not really begin to apply improved management techniques

[8] Gary B. Kulik, *The Beginnings of the Industrial Revolution in America: Pawtucket, Rhode Island, 1672–1829* (Unpublished dissertation, Brown University, Providence, RI, 1980), p. 341.
[9] Ross M. Robertson, *History of the American Economy* (New York: Harcourt Brace Jovanovich, 1955), p. 184.
[10] *Commonwealth v. Hunt*, 45 Mass. 111 (1842).
[11] Frederic Chapin Lane, *Venetian Ships and Shipbuilders of the Renaissance* (Baltimore, MD: Johns Hopkins Press, 1934), pp. 211–212.
[12] More information about Eli Whitney and the American system of manufacturing can be found in Robert S. Woodbury, "The Legend of Eli Whitney and Interchangeable Parts," *Technology and Culture*, vol. 1 (1960), pp. 235–253. See also Robert C. Ford, "The Springfield Armory's Role in Developing Interchangeable Parts," *Management Decision* 43(2) (2005), pp. 265–278.

until Lt. Colonel Roswell Lee became civilian superintendent in 1815. Lee reorganized the armory, centralizing authority and establishing defined areas of responsibility. An early piece-rate accounting system in which workers were paid based on units of output rather than a day-rate was developed and later used to monitor labor and material costs. With a division of labor, specialization also increased: in 1815, there were 34 different occupational specialties; in 1820, 86; and by 1825, 100.[13] Weapons were made by specialists rather than by general metal- and wood-workers. Innovative metalworking machines for barrel channeling, stock making, and milling small parts were introduced. With more accurate measurement devices, parts could be manufactured to closer tolerances, which increased their interchangeability. Colonel Lee also tightened discipline, with a policy that prohibited "scuffling or playing of Ball or other proceedings that have a tendency to impede . . . the progress of work." He further declared: "From and after the 15th day of April 1816 no Rum, Gin, Brandy, Whiskey, or ardent Spirits of any kind will be suffered to be carried or drunk in or about the public work shops at this place."[14] Although the Springfield Armory was government-owned, it nonetheless provides insight into the early development of modern private-sector factories. The armory's division of labor, authority structure, cost controls, plant-wide accounting system, inspection and quality techniques, and advanced metalworking were all crucial to the American System of Manufacturing.

The improvements introduced by Lee at the Springfield Armory were unique in both governmental and private sectors. A survey commissioned by the U.S. Secretary of the Treasury, Louis McLane, in 1832 provided a partial census of the nation's manufacturers. In the 10 states surveyed, there were 106 manufacturers with $100,000 or more in assets; 88 of these were in textiles, 12 in iron making, and the remaining 6 produced nails and hoops, axes, glass, paper, flour, and hydraulic equipment (viz., fire pumps and fire engines). Only 36 of these manufacturers employed 250 or more workers; of these, 31 were textile factories, 3 iron works, a nail and hoops works, and an axe factory.[15] In 1832, the Springfield Armory employed 246 people, so it was among the period's largest manufacturers. Other than textile mills and a few iron works though, most nongovernmental organizations were relatively small, employing an average of 10 to 12 workers. The McLane report also indicated that most manufacturers were family-owned and managed as sole proprietorships or partnerships, and there were few corporations. Finally, steam power was rarely used, as the manufacturers primarily relied on water power. Recalling Andrew Ure's study of Lancashire cotton mills during this same period (see Chapter 4), there are remarkable similarities in the size and how the manufacturers were managed, with the British ahead in using steam power.

In short, U.S. private-sector manufacturers before 1835 were small, family-run, and water-powered. In the 1840s and 1850s, however, U.S. entrepreneurs unleashed a host of products that would revolutionize industry in both the United States and Great Britain. The management techniques pioneered at the Springfield Armory and elsewhere provided the basis for the later manufacture of shovels, sewing machines, clocks, locks, watches, steam engines, reapers, and other products. What visitors admired at the Crystal Palace was the result of a long chain of developments—beginning at the Springfield Armory and spreading to private industry. Mass production had not yet been perfected, but its antecedents were present.

---

[13] Merritt Roe, *Harpers Ferry Armory and the New Technology: The Challenge of Change* (Ithaca, NY: Cornell University Press, 1977), p. 83.

[14] Roswell Lee quoted in Alex MacKenzie, *Springfield Armory* (Charleston, SC: Arcadia Publishing, 2015), p. 19. See also Russell I. Fries, "British Response to the American System: The Case of the Small-Arms Industry after 1850," *Technology and Culture* 16(3) (July), 1975, pp. 377–403.

[15] U. S. Congress, *Documents Relative to the Manufactures in the United States, Collected and Transmitted to the House of Representatives, in Compliance with a Resolution of Jan. 19, 1832* by the Secretary of the Treasury [McLane Report], 22nd Congress, 1st Session, H. R. Document 308, 2 vols. (Washington, DC: Printed by Duff Green, 1833). The data in this paragraph were compiled by Alfred D. Chandler III, and reported in Alfred D. Chandler, Jr., "Anthracite Coal and the Beginnings of the Industrial Revolution in the United States," *Business History Review* 46(2) (Summer 1972), p. 143.

The Railroads: Pioneering in U.S. Management

Whereas in the early 1800s textile mills represented the largest private enterprises in the United States, a transportation and communication revolution was on the horizon. Development of the iron rail, flanged wheel, and steam locomotive began around 1830. U.S. canals and waterways, both natural and artificial, primarily carried commercial freight. Opposed initially by canal operators, who were feared its competition, by 1850, the rail industry had introduced a new dimension to life in the United States. The rail industry in the United States began in 1815 when Colonel John Stevens III obtained the nation's first railroad charter from the New Jersey state legislature.[16] Deemed eccentric, Stevens could not obtain financial backing until 1830, when he and others built the 23-mile-long Camden and Amboy Railroad. For constructing the first U.S. steam-powered locomotive, Stevens is known as the Father of American Engineering. After the Camden and Amboy, other lines, such as the Chesapeake & Ohio and the Baltimore & Ohio, were built and expanded, until by 1850, 9,000 miles of track extended all the way into Ohio. These railroads would create a revolution in transportation and, as we shall see, emphasized managing in a systematic fashion. First, however, let us examine a concurrent revolution in communication, the telegraph.

The Communication Revolution

Tom Standage reminds us that, as humans, we are chronocentric; that is, we have

> . . . the egotism that one's own generation is poised on the cusp of history. . . . [W]e are repeatedly told that we are in the midst of a communications revolution. But the electric telegraph was, in many ways, far more disconcerting for the inhabitants of the time than today's advances are for us. . . . Heavier-than-air flying machines were, after all, thought by the Victorians to be totally impossible. But as for the Internet – well, they had one of their own.[17]

The "Victorian Internet" that Standage refers to was the telegraph, the invention of Samuel F. B. Morse, who built on a long line of scientific discoveries about electricity and magnetism. The possibilities of "distance signaling" through metal wires were developed by Morse in 1832, but not patented until 1837, the same year William F. Cooke and Charles Wheatstone obtained a British patent and installed 13 miles of telegraph wires on poles along Britain's Great Western Railroad. Morse gained a competitive advantage by developing a code, consisting of dots and dashes, which became the standard format for transmitting telegraphic messages.

The telegraph provided the beginnings of a nationwide communication system. An experimental telegraph line was completed between New York and Washington, DC, in 1844, and by 1860 about 50,000 miles of wires and poles crisscrossed the eastern United States. Usually built by railroads along their rights-of-way, the telegraph was used to coordinate train departures, as well as handling commercial and personal messages. The impact on business communication was dramatic—where it might take days, weeks, or months for messages to be sent and received by mail, the telegraph shrank the world of words. News items could be sent by the telegraph, enabling daily newspapers to keep their readers informed of the world's events; stock prices were

---

[16] For an account of John Stevens's various activities, including his anticipation by 3 years of Fulton's steamboat, see Dorothy Gregg, "John Stevens: General Entrepreneur," in William Miller, ed., *Men in Business* (New York: Harper & Row, 1957), pp. 120–152. Across the Atlantic, Britain's George Stephenson demonstrated a locomotive able to pull 36 wagons of coal and flour 9 miles in 2 hours on a level track in 1825. Britain's first intercity line between Manchester and Liverpool opened in 1830.

[17] Tom Standage, *The Victorian Internet: The Remarkable Story of the Telegraph and the Nineteenth Century's On-Line Pioneers* (New York: Walker and Company, 1998), p. 213.

sent across the nation to investors from trade exchanges via ticker tape; money could be transferred by wire; a cable under the Atlantic Ocean connected the United States to Great Britain and the European continent. Credit for the first electronic commerce belongs to Richard W. Sears, who in 1886 was working as a telegrapher and railroad-station agent. He used his position to sell a shipment of gold-filled watches through other station agents along the Minneapolis & Saint Louis Railroad. Sears would soon partner with Alvah C. Roebuck to found Sears, Roebuck & Co.

These technological revolutions in transportation and communication would sweep away local trade barriers, open new lands for settlement, extend product markets and reshape distribution strategies, and provide an inexpensive, rapid, year-round means for travel and commerce.

The Age of Rails

Railroads were truly the United States' first big business. The textile industry, though growing and dominating the Northeastern states, never developed into the size and scope of the railroads. Textile mills remained relatively small—the Springfield Armory rarely employed more than 250 people, and capital investment in industry was relatively limited. The railroads, however, grew to such a size and complexity that means had to be developed to cope with massive financial requirements, integrate thousands of miles of rail line, spread huge fixed costs, and handle a labor force dispersed over a wide geographical area. These new demands required innovations in managing the first U.S. industry national in scope. Unlike manufacturers, railroad operations were spread across hundreds of miles, thus making communications a significant challenge. Investments in track and rolling stock were immense, and extensive long-range planning was required to prevent large fixed capital outlays from being invested in the wrong markets. Passenger safety and preventing damage to or loss of cargo were critical. Road-way maintenance and scheduling eastbound and westbound traffic required coordination, and standing rules and policies had to be developed to guide decentralized operations.[18]

The original 23-mile track of the Camden and Amboy line required little in the way of management. Other lines, however, grew in scope and distance. In 1841, after a series of rail accidents, including a head-on collision between two passenger trains, the Western Railroad (Massachusetts) established defined areas of responsibility and a clear hierarchy of authority to prevent future mishaps. Another large line, the Baltimore & Ohio (B&O), was reorganized in 1847 by Benjamin Latrobe II to separate rail operations from finance and to establish machine shop and road-way maintenance departments. Although the Western and the B&O lines responded to growth with new organization structures, it was the New York and Erie Railroad that pioneered systematic management in the United States.

Daniel C. McCallum: System and Organization

Daniel C. McCallum was born in Scotland, but came to the United States in 1822.[19] He received some elementary schooling in Rochester, New York. Rather than learning to be a tailor like his father, McCallum left home (and school) to become an accomplished carpenter and architect. He joined the New York and Erie Railroad Company ("the Erie") in 1848. McCallum showed a talent for management, as well as engineering, and became superintendent of the Susquehanna

---

[18] Alfred D. Chandler, Jr., ed., *The Railroads: The Nation's First Big Business, Sources and Readings* (New York: Harcourt, Brace & World, 1965), pp. 9–10.

[19] Personal data on McCallum are from [W. Jerome Arnold], "Big Business Takes the Management Track," *Business Week*, April 30, 1966, pp. 104–106; Charles D. Wrege and Guidon Sorbo Jr., "A Bridge Builder Changes a Railroad: The Story of Daniel Craig McCallum," *Canal History and Technology Proceedings* 24 (March 19, 2005), pp. 183–218.

Division, where he developed an early set of procedures to govern rail operations. Faced with difficulties in rail integration and high accident rates, the Erie's owners appointed McCallum general superintendent in May 1854. In June 1854, defying McCallum's operating rules, the Erie's rail workers went on a 10-day strike, demanding shorter hours or more pay.

To McCallum, sound management was based on good discipline, specific and detailed job descriptions, frequent and accurate performance reports, pay and promotion based on merit, a clearly defined hierarchy of authority, and personal responsibility and accountability. He laid down the following general principles for assuring the Erie's efficient management:

1. A proper division of responsibilities.

2. Sufficient power conferred to enable the same to be fully carried out, that such responsibilities may be real in their character.

Daniel C. McCallum, circa 1865.
Brady National Photographic
Art Gallery/Library of Congress.

3. The means of knowing whether such responsibilities are faithfully executed.

4. Great promptness in the report of all derelictions of duty, that evils may be at once corrected.

5. Such information to be obtained through a system of daily reports and checks, that will not embarrass principal officers, nor lessen their influence with their subordinates.

6. The adoption of a system, as a whole, which will not only enable the General Superintendent to detect errors immediately, but will also point out the delinquent.[20]

To enact these principles, McCallum first required all Erie workers to wear a prescribed uniform with insignia indicating their primary duties and rank. Second, he developed comprehensive rules to limit workers' ability to do their tasks as they pleased. For instance, Rule 6, "Run Safe First, Fast Afterwards," enjoined engineers to "take all the time necessary to run safe . . . acting under the assumption that every switch was out of place, and a train standing on the main line."[21] Enginemen were told they would be accountable for "running off a switch," even if a switchman were at fault.

Finally, in 1855, McCallum developed an organization plan that depicted the Erie's lines of authority, its division of labor among operating units, and its communication lines for reporting and control. When depicted as a vine, the Erie's board of directors and president were positioned at the plan's base; its five operating divisions, plus the staff service departments of engine repairs, car, bridge, telegraph, painting, treasurer's, and secretary's offices were shown as branches; local freight and ticket forwarding offices were displayed as leaves; subordinate supervisors, crews, and so on to the lowest element were rendered as smaller leaves. Adherence to formal lines of authority was to be absolute:

> The enforcement of a rigid system of discipline . . . is indispensable to success. All subordinates should be accountable to, and *be directed by their immediate superiors only*; as obedience cannot be enforced where the foreman in immediate charge is interfered with by a superior officer giving orders directly to his subordinates.[22]

---

[20] Daniel C. McCallum, "Superintendent's Report," in *Reports of the President and Superintendent of the New York and Erie Railroad to the Stockholders for the Year Ending September 30, 1855* (New York: Press of the New York and Erie Railroad, 1856), p. 35.
[21] "Engineers' Strike on the New York and Erie Railroad," *The Engineer* 2 (October 31, 1856), p. 589. See also Walter Licht, *Working for the Railroad: The Organization of Work in the Nineteenth Century* (Princeton, NJ: Princeton University Press, 1983), pp. 246–247; Edward Harold Mott, *Between the Ocean and the Lakes: The Story of Erie* (New York: J. S. Collins, 1900), p. 433.
[22] McCallum, "Superintendent's Report," p. 40.

McCallum saw no exceptions to this "unity of command principle"; to do otherwise would disrupt his control system, which was based on personal accountability.

McCallum also developed an information system that was likely the most advanced of its day. He used the telegraph to make operations safer, coordinate rail traffic by requiring hourly reports showing the position of every train in the Erie system, collect daily passenger and cargo reports, and disseminate monthly planning, ratemaking, and market analysis reports. He designed a clever cross-check control system by requiring both freight and passenger conductors to report on train movements, loadings, damaged freight, and so on; by comparing the reports, he could readily spot discrepancies and dishonesty.

McCallum's general principles were successful from management's point of view, but trouble was brewing. The Erie's enginemen had never forgiven McCallum for "infamous Rule 6"; 29 engineers had been dismissed for breaking the rule and for violating various other safety standards. A 6-month strike ensued. McCallum was unable to replace the striking engineers and resigned, along with Erie's president, in 1857. He had, however, earned the highest praise of Henry V. Poor, the eminent editor of the *American Railroad Journal* and spokesperson for the industry. Poor later had some doubts about McCallum's approach, but agreed that his general principles contributed to efficient management.

All the same, McCallum's managerial days were not over. While on the Erie, he had invented and patented (in 1851) an inflexible arched truss bridge. He established McCallum Bridge Company in 1857 and built bridges throughout the country. In 1862, he was asked by Secretary of War Stanton to manage the nation's railways, with the power to seize and operate any rail line necessary to the Union States' success during the War Between the States. By the end of the war, he was a major general. His main feat was supplying General William Tecumseh Sherman's 200-day Atlanta campaign. Using principles developed on the Erie, McCallum "was able to transport supplies for 100,000 men and 60,000 animals for 360 miles from the supply base on a single-track railroad with turnouts" in Sherman's "March to the Sea."[23] After the war, McCallum served as a consultant for the Atlantic and Great Western and the Union Pacific railroads. Failing health led to his early retirement to Brooklyn, New York, where he wrote poetry. His best-known poem was "The Water-Mill," which advised:

> Possessions, power, and blooming health, must all be lost at
> last,
> "The mill will never grind with water that is past."[24]

McCallum's approach to management lived on, despite his setbacks at the Erie. Poor widely publicized McCallum's work, and others applied and extended, his general principles. For instance, Albert Fink, vice president and general superintendent, Louisville, Nashville, and Great Southern Railroad Company, developed a cost-accounting system that used information flows, classification of costs, and statistical-control devices. It became a model for modern corporate control.[25] As early as 1847, the B&O Railroad used an internal auditor to check on receipts and disbursements. External auditing by independent public-accounting firms also began as early as 1854, as stockholders sought to verify reports submitted from professional managers. [26]

Dynamic growth, geographical separation of previously connected activities, and separation of ownership and management were the driving forces for systematizing railroad management.

---

[23] Wrege and Sorbo, p. 207. For a further account of McCallum's wartime efforts, see Thomas Weber, *The Northern Railroads in the Civil War* (New York: Columbia University Press, 1952).

[24] Daniel C. McCallum, *The Water-Mill; and Other Poems* (Brooklyn, NY: Privately printed, 1870), p. 10.

[25] Albert Fink, "Cost of Railroad Transportation, Railroad Accounts, and Governmental Regulation of Railroad Tariffs," Extract from the *Annual Report of the Louisville & Nashville Railroad Company for the Year Ending June 30, 1874* (Louisville, KY: Printed by John. P. Morton, 1875).

[26] James L. Boockholdt, "A Historical Perspective on the Auditor's Role: The Early Experiences of the American Railroads," *Accounting Historians Journal* 10(1) (Spring 1983), pp. 69–86.

The most faithful adoption of McCallum's general principles came on the Pennsylvania Railroad. J. Edgar Thomson and Thomas A. Scott applied McCallum's ideas on handling a labor force dispersed over a wide geographical area, formal lines of authority, communications, line and staff duties, measuring performance, and cost accounting. As it were, the Pennsy (as it was known), enjoyed the benefits of McCallum's principles, not the Erie, where they had been originally developed. Working on the Pennsy, a young Scottish immigrant learned McCallum's principles from Thomson and Scott; his name was Andrew Carnegie, and he will enter our story again shortly.

Henry V. Poor: A Broader View of Management

Henry V. Poor, through his position as editor of the *American Railroad Journal*, endeavored to become the rail industry's conscience. Whereas McCallum spoke of rail operations, Poor took a broader perspective in appraising the industry's power and vital role in the nation's daily life. Poor was well educated and came from a more select background than McCallum; Poor was thoroughly imbued with the uniquely American romance and optimism of the nineteenth century.[27] As editor of the *Journal* in the years prior to the War Between the States, Poor made it the leading business periodical of the day and a reliable source of information for rail investors and managers. His editorials not only discussed equipment, facilities, expansion, and legislation but also the financial status of different rail lines. After the war, Poor's *Manual of Railroads in the United States* continued his efforts to document the finances of rail lines across the nation.[28] Poor's life paralleled the growth of railroads from their infancy to maturity; from their role in opening new lands for the United States' westward expansion to ultimately binding the plains, mountains, and valleys of the United States with a web of steel.

In its early years, the ill-managed and financed Erie was one of Poor's favorite essay topics. The advent of McCallum's management reforms soon made Poor its biggest booster. Poor saw a need for professional managers, rather than speculators and promoters, to build the nation's railway system. Poor looked for a science, or system, of management. Drawing on McCallum's general principles, Poor proposed three fundamental principles for a "science of management": organization, communication, and information.[29] *Organization* was basic to all management: There had to be a clear chain command from top to bottom with a clear designation of duties and responsibilities. *Communication* meant devising a method of reporting throughout an organization to give top managers a continuous and accurate accounting of operations. Finally, *information* was "recorded communication"; Poor saw the need for systematically compiled and analyzed operating reports on costs, revenues, and rail rates so as to understand and improve performance. This third principle was an early appearance of a database concept in which information is collected and analyzed to identify patterns in key factors essential to a business's success. McCallum's influence on Poor's thinking is readily apparent, and his third principle can be traced to Albert Fink's cost-accounting system that used information flows, classification of costs, and statistical-control devices for corporate control.

Just as McCallum's general principles were becoming widely known, in large part due to *American Railroad Journal* editorials, Poor began having doubts about whether organization, communication, and information were adequate principles to encompass the entirety of a manager's job. Poor visited Great Britain in 1858 to survey its more mature railway system. On his return, he wrote about "the grave difficulties of adapting human capabilities and current business practices and institutions to the severe requirements demanded by the efficient operation of large-scale

---

[27] Alfred D. Chandler, Jr., *Henry Varnum Poor: Business Editor, Analyst, and Reformer* (Cambridge, MA: Harvard University Press, 1956), p. 8. In a side note, Chandler was Poor's great-grandson.

[28] Poor established *Poor's Publishing* in 1860 to provide financial information about other industries; in 1941, a merger with *Standard Statistics* created the *Standard and Poor's Industry Surveys* of today.

[29] Chandler, *Poor*, pp. 146–147.

administrative units."[30] Both in Great Britain and on the Erie, Poor saw worker resistance developing in response to "systematic management." The tighter control required to bring order from chaos, the limiting of individual discretion in performing tasks, and the rigid hierarchical specifications of a formal organization were all leading to worker protests. Such protests have seemingly been a common feature of other periods in which workplace changes were underway. Poor, however, thought the protests were extreme and defended the need for systematization: "We do not see how a great road like the Erie can be successfully conducted in any other manner,"[31] that is, except through order, system, and discipline.

Accordingly, Poor began to look for some broader principles to overcome the risk of "regarding man as a mere machine, out of which all the qualities necessary to a good servant can be enforced by the mere payment of wages." He recognized, however, that "[d]uties cannot be always prescribed, and the most valuable ones are often voluntary ones."[32] In Poor's view, rigid guidelines prescribing performance criteria and increased bureaucracy reduced individual initiative and would inevitably lead the railroads to the difficulties found in the military and government. His solution was to call for a style of leadership that would overcome dullness and routine by infusing the railroads with an esprit de corps. Top managers should become "the soul of the enterprise, reaching and infusing life, intelligence and obedience into every portion of it. This soul must not be a fragmentary or disjointed one giving one direction to the head, another to the hands, and another to the feet. Wherever there is lack of unity there will be a lack of energy – of intelligence – of life – of accountability and subordination."[33]

In anticipating Fayol's unity of direction principle by 60 years (see Chapter 10), Poor felt the primary challenge faced by top managers was assuming and convincing subordinates to assume a total-systems perspective. He believed that to be leaders, top managers should not only know all aspects of a railroad's operation and administration, but also able to handle people and prevent interdepartmental conflicts that could destroy unity of purpose. Poor contended that breakdowns in leadership came from two sources: selection on some basis other than ability or training, and lack of an information system to pinpoint weak managers. His plea for hiring professional managers ran counter to the downside premonitions Adam Smith voiced nearly a century earlier regarding those who managed "other people's money" (see Chapter 2).

Emerging Governance Issues

Early textile mills were largely owned and managed by individual entrepreneurs or two or more partners. The money was "all in the family," so to speak. Requirements for accounting and financial reporting were consequently reduced. As recounted in Chapter 3, Adam Smith felt there was a danger in joint-stock, limited-liability firms, where ownership and management were typically separated as he believed that rarely did anyone watch over "other people's money" as they would over their own. Smith was deceased by the time this concern was confronted by British railways, as they acquired capital and debt on a scale unknown to any previous human endeavor.

George Hudson, a friend of the British railway pioneer and innovator George Stephenson, envisioned a network of rails covering the whole of England, Scotland, and Wales. In 1844, Hudson began promoting assorted ventures to raise capital for new lines and for acquiring existing right-of-ways. Under British law, each joint-stock company was authorized by a separate Act of Parliament, leading to varying charter requirements. At the time, there were no general rules for accounting and financial reporting, and corporate law was in its infancy. The railways held a romantic fascination for investors, leading to waves of rampant stock speculation, or, in more

---

[30] *Ibid.*, p. 151.

[31] Henry V. Poor, "Lease of the Erie Railroad," *American Railroad Journal* 32 (July 2, 1859), p. 424.

[32] *Idem*, "New York and Erie Railroad" *American Railroad Journal* 32 (January 15, 1859), p. 41.

[33] Henry V. Poor, "English Railways and Their Management," *American Railroad Journal* 31 (September 4, 1858), pp. 561–562.

modern terms, "irrational exuberance." It has been estimated that by 1845, £71 million (British pounds) had been invested in railways, and another 620 new rail schemes amounted to £563 million, equivalent to more than two-thirds of the British national debt.[34]

Hudson took advantage of these speculative impulses and, by 1849, nearly one-third of Britain's 5,000 miles of rail lines were under his management or control. In addition, he had raised money to buy land, build docks, and form canal companies. He was, as all Britain knew, the "Railway King."[35] His operations extended from Brighton and Southampton in the southeast to Edinburgh in the northeast. Unfortunately, his machinations offer perhaps the earliest example of top-management malfeasance. He paid dividends out of capital, both existing and borrowed; inflated railway-traffic counts and revenue; published false financial statements; and, in one instance, bought iron rails from one of his lines for £9 each and sold them to another he owned for £11, pocketing a £6,000 profit.

The British Parliament passed a Companies Clauses Consolidation Act in 1845 to bring some uniformity to corporate charters, to require "full and true" accounts, and to mandate that three directors and a firm's chief executive sign and verify its annual balance sheet.[36] This legislation, however, did not stop Hudson's chicanery; his dishonesty led to shareholder investigations and lawsuits. His estimated ill-gotten gains amounted to £598,785.[37] Hudson went into exile, and his creditors were never fully satisfied.

How does this brief account of George Hudson fit into the history of United States' economic development and Poor's plea for professional managers who were also leaders? Poor kept abreast of railroad developments abroad and addressed governance issues in his editorials. For example, he complained that railroads did not separate operating costs from construction expenses, thus hiding such costs from investors. It was common practice to book operating costs as a construction expense, hence leading to higher profits and extra dividends.

What was the path to reform? According to Poor, who believed "the germ of all improvement is *knowledge*,"[38]

> . . . the only way to introduce honesty into the management of railroads, is to expose every thing in or about it, to the public gaze. Concealment in either case is certain to breed disease. Instances are very rare in which integrity is preserved unless strict accountability is exacted. Such accountability to the public should be exacted from directors of railroads. . . . For the dishonesty and incapacity in the management of railroads the holders of their securities have in a great measure to thank themselves. They put them in charge of a body of men, responsible to no authority, who soon come to practice concealment, either to escape the consequences of mistake or dishonesty. The perpetuation of their power is an easy matter, so long as they can sustain themselves by the various modes resorted to for *borrowing*.[39]

Poor lashed out against railroad promoters and speculators and endorsed a laissez-faire economic philosophy by calling for unrestricted competition. He argued that governments should not regulate rates, and the only legislation necessary was that to protect "honest rational men" from dishonest promoters. Poor insisted that the rapid development of the U.S. railroads was "proof that reliance on the self-interest of individuals operating under conditions of unrestricted competition resulted in the greatest good for the greatest number."[40] He argued that by giving stockholders and the public full information, by employing professional managers, and by

---

[34] John J. Glynn, "The Development of British Railway Accounting, 1800–1911," *Accounting Historians Journal* 11(1) (Spring 1984), pp. 103–118.

[35] Richard S. Lambert, *The Railway King, 1800–1871* (London: George Allen and Unwin, 1934).

[36] Companies Clauses Consolidation Act, (8 Vict c. 16) (1845). Available at http://origin-www.legislation.gov.uk/ukpga/Vict/8-9/16/contents.

[37] *Ibid.*, p. 273.

[38] Henry V. Poor, "Railroad Dishonesty and Remedy," *American Railroad Journal* 29 (April 26, 1856), p. 364.

[39] *Idem*, "How to Improve the Management of Railroads," *American Railroad Journal* 30 (June 20, 1857), p. 392.

[40] Chandler, *Poor*, p. 260.

protecting rational from irrational investors, the railroads could fulfill their proper role in the nation's economy.

Henry V. Poor addressed issues that managers still face today and will continue to confront in the future. His belief that the role of government is to protect, not control, illustrates a recurring theme of management rights vis-à-vis government responsibilities. Poor's search for order out of chaos without diminishing individual incentive and dignity also remains a recurring challenge.

SUMMARY

In 1790, New York City was the largest metropolis in the United States, with a population of 33,131; next came Philadelphia, with 28,522 residents; and then Boston, with 8,300. Even the largest city was smaller than the student body at some of today's state universities. In 1790, some 90 percent of the nation's estimated total population of 3,231,533 was engaged in agriculture. From declaring independence in 1776 to 1860, the United States made unmatched progress. Textile mills provided inexpensive clothing to a growing national market; railroads spread further westward from their beginning along the East Coast until they reached the Pacific Ocean, opening new lands and opportunities; the telegraph delivered messages across vast distances; and mechanical devices such as the sewing machine and the reaper caused others to envy the American System of Manufacturing.

The nineteenth century was a defining era in the development of today's modern corporation. The domestic system of putting-out work in homes was disappearing. It was initially replaced by family- and partner-owned and managed small-scale firms powered by steam engines. Capital requirements increased with the first railroads, the telegraph enabled firms to grow and achieve economies of scale. This growth created the need for professional managers. If one views a firm as an input-throughput-output system, inputs come from external markets in the form of people, capital, technology, and other resources. Through an emerging hierarchy of managers, firms grow so as to transform an ever larger number of inputs into market outputs to meet mounting consumer demand. Considering this dynamic, it is easy to see how the nineteenth century helped shape the nature of today's corporations.

A male born in Massachusetts in 1789 could expect to live 34.5 years; a female 36.5 years. By 1855, these lifespans had risen to 38.7 and 40.9 years, respectively. Not only were people living longer in the United States, but they were living better: real wages (purchasing power) surged 16 percent between 1820 and 1860 (1913 = 100).[41] By 1860, the U.S. census estimated that 1,311,246 people were employed in manufacturing; 21 percent of these were females.[42] The percentage of child workers employed in manufacturing had begun declining as early as 1840.[43] Times were changing, life was better, and this was only the dawning of the Industrial Revolution in the United States.

---

[41] Edgar W. Martin, *The Standard of Living in 1860: American Consumption Levels on the Eve of the Civil War* (Chicago, IL: University of Chicago Press, 1942), pp. 220, 415.

[42] Bureau of the Census Library, *Manufacturers of the United States in 1860; Complied from the Original Returns of the Eighth Census, Under the Direction of the Secretary of the Interior* (Washington, DC: Government Printing Office, 1865,) p. 742.

[43] Claudia Goldin and Keith Sokoloff, "Women, Children, and Industrialization in the Early Republic: Evidence from the Manufacturing Censuses," *Journal of Economic History*, 42(4) (December 1982), p. 748.

Industrial Growth and Systematic Management

When the Industrial Revolution reached the United States in the early nineteenth century, its impact was soon felt in textile and machine manufacturing, and along the nation's canals and railroads. The War Between the States from 1861 to 1865 was a tragic pause in the United States' march toward global industrial leadership. Accordingly, this chapter describes the continued growth of U.S. enterprises following the conclusion of the War, discusses the accompanying emergence of systematic management, and examines the nation's economic, social, political, and technological environment on the eve of the scientific-management era.

The Growth of U.S. Enterprises

No student of business history had a keener eye for the growth of large-scale enterprises than Alfred D. Chandler, Jr.[1] In his early work, Chandler delineated four phases in the development of what would become known in the United States as "Big Business": (1) "initial expansion and accumulation of resources"; (2) "rationalization or full use of resources"; (3) "expansion into new markets and lines to help assure the continuing full use of resources"; and (4) "development of a new structure" to enable continued growth. For different firms, these phases started and ended at different times, depending on the current state of technology and their ability to react to

---

[1] The subsequent discussion draws on Alfred D. Chandler, Jr., *Strategy and Structure: Chapters in the History of the Industrial Enterprise* (Cambridge, MA: MIT Press, 1962); *idem, The Visible Hand: The Managerial Revolution in American Business* (Cambridge, MA: Belknap Press of Harvard University Press, 1977); *idem* and Takashi Hikino, *Scale and Scope: The Dynamics of Industrial Capitalism* (Cambridge, MA: Belknap Press of Harvard University Press, 1990).

and capitalize on market opportunities. In the latter part of the nineteenth century, companies such as Standard Oil of New Jersey and the American Sugar Refining Company were forming and would fit into Chandler's initial expansion and resource-accumulation phase.

Chandler further noted two periods of industrial growth: (1) horizontal growth from 1879 to 1893 and (2) vertical growth from 1898 to 1904. *Horizontal growth* occurred when producers in similar fields combined through mergers, pools, or trusts to achieve economies of scale in production. During the years 1879 to 1893, firms in the oil, beef, sugar, tobacco, rubber, and liquor, and other industries merged and grew to better control their markets, gain financial leverage, and lower production costs. *Vertical growth* occurred when firms entered one or more additional stages in a production-marketing chain. *Backward vertical-integration* occurred when a firm acquired raw material sources or suppliers; *forward vertical-integration* occurred when a firm established marketing outlets for its own products. For example, a petroleum refiner might move backward to explore, acquire oil leases, drill, and build pipelines to its refinery; it would move forward by acquiring wholesale agents and, perhaps, its own retail gas stations.

In addition, Chandler found a close connection between advances in transportation and communication, like the railroad and the telegraph, and the initial expansion and accumulation of resources necessary for enterprise growth. When modes of transport were crude and slow, product markets were largely local, so there was little or no need to increase production volume. Thus, the domestic system of manufacturing was entirely appropriate to its time, as it served small markets requiring limited capital investment. With the advent of steam engines in the Industrial Revolution, and their use to power locomotives and steamboats, markets were extended and mechanized as large-scale production was needed to meet unprecedented demand. Advances in communication, such as the telegraph, encouraged producers, suppliers, and distributors to pursue regional and international markets. Improved transportation and communication made it possible to produce and market in volume; thus, production could be done in large batches or in a continuous process, and firms could seek mass-market distribution. With these increases in output and distribution came a need for greater capital intensity, and as capital investments in facilities and equipment rose, per-unit production costs were minimized until output could be maintained at an optimal level. In Chandler's terms, capital-intensive industries had to operate at a "minimum efficient scale" (that is, at a level that resulted in the lowest per-unit costs) to attain a competitive advantage. With a cost advantage, prices could be lowered and markets extended, and eventually the whole cycle of mechanization, greater output, lowered prices, increased distribution volume, and so on would be repeated.

There are limits, of course, to the cost advantages of large-scale production and mass marketing. A firm can only profitably gain market share if it can lower its production costs. In Chandler's explanation, the key to profit is not in capacity (the potential to produce or sell in volume), but in how well a firm is managed. There must be a smooth flow of inputs (employees, materials, supplies, and so on) through a production process (throughput) such that the value of the resulting output is greater than the cost of additional inputs and production. This residual balance is the necessary profit for replenishing inputs and beginning the cycle once again. Chandler's analysis showed that a firm's success (i.e., ability to earn a sufficient profit) over the long term largely depended on how well its inputs-throughputs-and-outputs are managed. As we view the latter half of the nineteenth century in the United States, we can see how advanced production processes for making steel, refining sugar and corn products, milling grains, canning, packaging, and other advancements led to larger enterprises, but as Chandler's analysis showed, sound management differentiated those that were successful from those that were not. Andrew Carnegie and the growth of the Carnegie Steel Company (founded in the mid-1870s) offers a prototype example of the cycle Chandler identified as underlying successful enterprises.

Carnegie and the Rise of Big Business

The name Andrew Carnegie conjures a portrait of a manager who built an empire in steel and left a fortune in the millions. But where did Carnegie learn his management skills? Carnegie, an immigrant like so many other entrepreneurs of his era, first found work as a telegrapher. Thomas A. Scott, superintendent of the Pennsylvania Railroad's Western Division, hired young Carnegie as his personal telegrapher to assist in dispatching trains over the Division's mountainous main line. Carnegie learned fast and made his mark one day when he untangled a traffic tie-up following a derailment. Scott was absent at the time, and Carnegie sent out orders using Scott's initials. He was rewarded for this usurpation of authority, and his initiative led to a change in a protocol that had only permitted Scott, as superintendent, to issue dispatch orders. Carnegie learned railroad management from Scott and J. Edgar Thomson, who, as mentioned in Chapter 5, had applied Daniel C. McCallum's general principles to the Pennsylvania Railroad. At age 24, Carnegie became superintendent of the Western Division, which at the time was the largest sector of the nation's largest railroad. Under his supervision, rail traffic quadrupled, track mileage doubled, and the Division had the lowest ton-per-mile costs of any railroad in the nation. Carnegie was asked to be the Pennsy's General Superintendent in 1865, but he declined because he wanted to strike out on his own.

Andrew Carnegie, circa 1878. Andrew Carnegie, *Autobiography of Andrew Carnegie*, ed. By John C. Van Dyke (London: Constable & Co., Ltd., 1920), following p. 214.

To understand Carnegie and his impact on management thinking, it is necessary to examine the development of the steel industry. Steel is the sinew of any industrial economy. Iron, because of its impurities, caused many problems for early machine designers and factory owners. The race to remove the impurities followed different paths in Great Britain and the United States. In 1847, Kentuckian William Kelly perfected a process for removing impurities from iron ore during smelting by injecting it with a blast of hot air. Unfortunately, Kelly did not apply for a patent until 1857, a year after Henry Bessemer had obtained a patent for the same basic process in Great Britain. In 1865, the steel industry in the United States was neither vertically nor horizontally integrated. Some firms owned furnaces that smelted iron ore into pig iron (i.e., iron produced from iron ore and coke); others operated rolling mills and forges that converted pig iron into decarbonized bars or slabs; and still others infused these bars or slabs with extra carbon and rolled them into steel for rails, nails, wire, or whatever. Between each of these independent operations, marketing intermediaries linked producers, each taking a profit for the services they provided. After Carnegie saw the Bessemer process in operation, he realized it could be used for mass-producing steel. He decided to forego railroading to concentrate on steel because, as he explained, "Every dollar of capital or credit, every business thought, should be concentrated upon the one business upon which a man has embarked. He should never scatter his shot. . . . The rule, 'Do not put all your eggs in one basket,' does not apply to a man's life work. Put all your eggs in one basket and then watch that basket, is the true doctrine – the most valuable rule of all."[2]

Using the Bessemer process, Carnegie began to vertically integrate the stages required for the production of steel and, thus, eliminate the intermediaries' profits. He succeeded in reducing the amount of time it took to produce a ton of steel so that he could lower prices and gain market share. He used cost accounting to assist in setting prices to undersell his competitors, many of whom did not know their true costs. Carnegie integrated backward into iron and coal mines and other steel-related operations to ensure an uninterrupted flow of raw materials to run his furnaces

---

[2] Andrew Carnegie, *The Empire of Business* (Garden City, NJ: Doubleday, Page & Company, 1913), p. 74.

at full capacity and to move from iron ore to finished steel more quickly. By combining the new Bessemer process with Daniel McCallum's general principles, Carnegie had developed a recipe for success that was soon emulated by firms in other industries.

On the Pennsylvania Railroad, Carnegie had learned how to measure performance, control costs, and delegate authority. These lessons fueled his success in the steel industry.[3] Until 1908, and the invention of the open-hearth furnace, the Bessemer process was the basis for the world's steel industry. In the mid-1870s, iron rails cost $100 per ton; by 1900, one ton of steel rails cost $12. Perhaps that was Carnegie's greatest philanthropy, or, as Jonathan Swift expressed it in Lemuel Gulliver's travels: "[W]hoever could make two ears of corn, or two blades of grass to grow upon a spot of ground where only one grew before would deserve better of mankind, and do more essential service to his country than the whole race of politicians put together."[4] To unscramble the metaphor, Carnegie combined technology and sound management to create more jobs, reduce prices, expand product markets, and advance industrial development. In 1868, the United States produced 8,500 tons of steel compared with 110,000 in Great Britain; in 1879, the countries' outputs were nearly equal; but by 1902, the United States produced 9,138,000 tons and Great Britain 1,826,000. U.S. industry was showing its mettle.

The Emergence of Systematic Management

The steel industry illustrates the scale and pace of industrial growth following the War Between the States. Steel was not the only industry, however, to thrust the American System of Manufacturing into world prominence. As further technological advances were made in transportation, communication, machine making, and power sources, old industries were revitalized and new ones emerged. As noted, Chandler saw initial expansion and accumulation of resources as part of the first phase in the development of Big Business in the United States.

Daniel C. McCallum introduced systematic management to the railroads. Andrew Carnegie learned his lessons well and created a steel colossus. As other firms and other industries began to grow, they too faced the challenge of managing a large-scale enterprise. They needed to plan ahead to acquire labor, materials, equipment, and capital; to organize by dividing labor, delegating authority, and grouping activities into departments; to lead and motivate by providing performance incentives and building strong interpersonal relationships; and to control by comparing actual to realized plans and taking corrective actions when necessary. With growth there also came the need to formalize communications, especially in written memos and reports. Yates has shown how, between 1850 and 1920, business communication changed as oral and informal modes of communication gave way to written documents.[5] During this era, however, there was no real appreciation of the skills required by a successful manager. A great deal of emphasis was placed on technical or financial knowledge, but very little on how to plan, organize, lead and motivate, and control. Faced with ever larger enterprises, how could managers learn to manage better?

Engineers and Economists

Engineers played a large role in building canals and railroads and in designing and installing industrial machinery. Thus, they frequently became factory managers; examples we have

---

[3] Parallels between McCallum and Carnegie are discussed in Harold C. Livesay, *Andrew Carnegie and the Rise of Big Business* (Boston, MA: Little, Brown, 1975).

[4] Jonathan Swift, *Travels into Several Remote Nations of the World*, vol. 1 (London: Benjamin Motte, 1726), p. 129.

[5] Jo Anne Yates, *Control through Communication: The Rise of System in American Management* (Baltimore, MD: Johns Hopkins University Press, 1989).

discussed include Samuel Slater, Daniel McCallum, and others. The professionalization of engineering began with the formation of the American Society of Civil Engineers in 1852, followed by the American Institute of Mining Engineers in 1871. Neither of these groups, however, was interested in the challenges confronting the era's factory managers. The first forum for those interested in factory management appears to have been the *American Machinist,* an "illustrated journal of practical mechanics and engineering" that began in 1877. In 1878, James Waring See, writing under the pen name Chordal, began submitting a series of letters to the *American Machinist's* editor.[6] See was a veteran of working in and supervising machine shops. He established a successful practice as a consulting engineer and used his letters to describe machine-shop practices and management. He advocated a work system based on two principles: "a place for everything and everything in its place" and "specific lines of duty for every man."[7] See noted that good workers rarely made good supervisors and that good supervisors should not "bully" their workers, but should be tactful and understanding. *Soldiering*, or deliberately working as slowly as one dared, at the same time trying to make one's supervisor believe one was working fast, existed and could be handled best if a supervisor had an "understanding with [the worker] that he is to work for you five days a week for pay, and soldier one day at his own expense . . . One week day idle in a busy man's life will make him feel glad to get into the shop for five days of occupation."[8] See also advocated paying above-market wages to attract better qualified workers, standardizing tools, and other techniques for better factory management. Other than to readers of the *American Machinist,* See's writings remained relatively obscure for a century. It would appear, however, that his experiences and advice may have influenced later writers even though his work was not explicitly cited.

The *American Machinist* also had a hand in another signal event of the period, the formation of the American Society of Mechanical Engineers (ASME) in 1880. The ASME first met at the Stevens Institute of Technology, Hoboken, New Jersey. Its purpose was to address issues of factory management neglected by the other engineering groups. In what is considered a landmark meeting, the ASME convened at Chicago on May 25–28, 1886. On May 26, Henry R. Towne (1844–1924), an engineer, cofounder of the Yale Lock Company, and president of the Yale & Towne Manufacturing Company, presented a paper "The Engineer as an Economist." Towne observed that

> There are many good mechanical engineers; there are also many good "businessmen"; – but the two are rarely combined in one person. But this combination of qualities . . . is essential to the management of industrial works, and has its highest effectiveness if united in one person . . . the matter of shop management is of equal importance with that of engineering . . . and the *management of works* has become a matter of such great and far-reaching importance as perhaps to justify its classification also as one of the modern arts.[9]

Because no group seemed to be concerned with "the management of works," Towne proposed that the ASME create an Economic Section to act as a clearinghouse and forum for shop management and shop accounting. Shop management would deal with the subjects of organization, responsibility, reports, and all that pertained to the executive management of works, mills, and factories. Shop accounting would treat the questions of time and wage systems, determination and allocation of costs, methods of bookkeeping, and all that pertained to manufacturing accounts.

[6] William F. Muhs, Charles Wrege, and Arthur Murtuza, "Extracts from Chordal's Letters: Pre-Taylor Shop Management," in Kae H. Chung, ed., *Proceedings of the Annual Meeting of the Academy of Management* (1981), pp. 96–100.
[7] James W. See, "Extracts from Chordal's Letters," *American Machinist* 2(15) (August 16, 1879), p. 6.
[8] Idem, "Extracts from Chordal's Letters," *American Machinist* 3(13) (March 27, 1880), p. 4.
[9] Henry R. Towne, "The Engineer as an Economist," *Transactions of the American Society of Mechanical Engineers* 7 (1886), pp. 428–429. See also Ion Georgiou, "Engineers as Economists: A Study in Gilded Age Sensibilities," *Management & Organizational History* 9(1) (January 2014), pp. 69–91.

Immediately following Towne's presentation, in the same afternoon session, a second significant paper was delivered at the 1886 ASME meeting by Captain Henry Metcalfe, an intellectual heir of the Springfield Armory's Roswell Lee (see Chapter 5). In 1881, at the Frankford Arsenal (near Philadelphia) and the Watervliet Arsenal (Troy, New York), Metcalfe had installed a shop-order system of accounts that used cards to coordinate and control work as it flowed through a shop.[10] These cards accompanied the work and were used to record the labor and materials required at each step in a production process. When an order was finished, direct costs (such as labor and materials) and indirect costs (administrative overhead) could then be easily identified. In the discussion that followed Metcalfe's presentation, Frederick W. Taylor commented that Midvale had been using a similar system for the past 10 years, except that it used a central office and clerks, rather than supervisors, to handle all the paperwork. Taylor had joined the ASME in 1886. We shall learn more about Taylor in Chapter 7.

Almost all the discussion following the session in which Towne and Metcalfe presented their papers dealt with the shop-order system of accounts. Towne's proposal to create an Economic Section within the ASME received scant notice. Despite evidence that managers were coming from technical schools, such as the Stevens Institute of Technology, and that their duties were managerial rather than technical,[11] only four other papers on management subjects were presented at ASME meetings from 1887 to 1895.[12] This minimal attention may have been due to a lack of clarity about the skills a successful manager required. A manager at the time was part engineer, part businessman, and part accountant. The emphasis was on shop or manufacturing management and not on general management. Shop management, in particular, focused on machine shops, where the trend had been to move from small-batch production to larger scale output based on the American System of Manufacturing. The principal challenges shop managers faced were technical. They were seldom called on to display other management skills.

One early writer noted that large-scale manufacture required the "utmost system . . . necessary in every detail [for] the economy and uniformity of production."[13] Thus, "system" in this context referred to developing rules, standards, and procedures to handle increased output. It would include topics such as die-setting standards, machine tolerances, job scheduling, quality and quantity of work, coordination of work flow through routing, wage incentives, accounting for costs, assigning responsibility, and handling labor problems such as soldiering.[14]

In contrast to the ASME membership, picking up on Jean-Baptiste Say's earlier work (see Chapter 3), there was a resurging appreciation among economists of the importance of entrepreneurs and professional managers as a factor of production. An economist of this period, Edward Atkinson, noted that a "difference in management will alter results, in the same place, at

---

[10] Henry Metcalfe, "The Shop-Order System of Accounts," *Transactions of the American Society of Mechanical Engineers* 7 (1886), pp. 440–468. This paper was a summary of Metcalfe's pioneering book in cost accounting, *The Cost of Manufactures and the Administration of Workshops, Public and Private* (New York: John Wiley and Sons, 1885). See also William H. Reid, "The Development of Henry Metcalf's Card System of Shop Returns at Frankford Arsenal," *Journal of Management* 12(3) (Fall 1986), pp. 415–423.

[11] The Stevens Institute of Technology had 600 graduates between 1872 and 1896; of these, 230 (38 percent) were in executive positions by 1900. William D. Ennis, "The Engineering Management of Industrial Works," *Engineering Magazine* 22 (November 1901), pp. 241–246.

[12] Hirose noted, however, that some mechanical engineers favored scientific management; only in 1920 did the majority of ASME members agree to a separate division of management. See Mikiyoshi Hirose, "The Attitude of the American Society of Mechanical Engineers toward Management: Suggestions for a Revised Interpretation," *Review of Economics and Business* (Kansai University) 25 (September 1996), pp. 125–148. See also *idem, The Management Thought of the Engineers: The Emergence of Industrial Management in America, 1880–1920* (Tokyo: Bunshindō, 2005).

[13] Oberlin Smith, "System in Machine Shops," *American Machinist* 8 (October 31, 1885), p. 1.

[14] Joseph A. Litterer, *The Emergence of Systematic Management as Shown by the Literature of Management from 1870 to 1900* (Unpublished dissertation, University of Illinois, Urbana, IL, 1959), released in book form by Garland Press, New York, 1986. See also *idem,* "Systematic Management: The Search for Order and Integration," *Business History Review* 35 (Winter 1961), pp. 461–476; *idem,* "Systematic Management: Design for Organizational Recoupling in American Manufacturing Firms," *Business History Review* 37(4) (Winter 1963), pp. 369–391.

the same time, in the use of similar machinery."[15] Economist Alfred Marshall and his wife Mary Paley Marshall (also an economist) noted that, to be successful, the manager of a large enterprise almost always requires rarer abilities and expensive training, as he "must look far ahead, and wide around him; and he must be continually on the look out for improved methods of carrying on his business, . . . [and devote] all his energies to planning and organizing, to forecasting the future and preparing for it.[16]

In noting that managers must devote energy to forecasting, planning, and organizing, the Marshalls hinted at the "functions of management" long before they were identified by Henri Fayol (see Chapter 10). The Marshalls also commented on division of labor, but advised that it need not lead to monotonous jobs "when the work is light, and the hours of work not excessive."[17] Further, they discussed economies of scale, as well as the internal economies that could be attained by more efficient management. In this latter sense, the Marshalls' view that allowing firms to operate in a free-market was the best means for allocating resources anticipated by more than a half-century the work of Nobel Laureate Ronald Coase (Chapter 16).

These musings were a prelude to Alfred Marshall's fame as the founder of the Cambridge (England) or Neoclassical School of Economic Thought. Like Say, Marshall considered "organization" to be as an "agent" of production and recognized the differential advantage that a high-energy manager with exceptional ability could provide. As he explained:

> A manufacturer of exceptional ability and energy will apply better methods, and perhaps better machinery than his rivals: he will organize better the manufacturing and the marketing sides of his business; and he will bring them into better relation to one another. By these means he will extend his business; and therefore he will be able to take greater advantage from the specialization both of labour and of plant. Thus he will obtain increasing return and also increasing profit.[18]

Economists, such as the Marshalls, had less impact than mechanical engineers in the early development of management thought. To mechanical engineers such as Towne, Metcalf, and Taylor, a manager's primary challenges related to shop management, not managing an overall enterprise. Yet, a much broader issue concerned the relationship between labor and capital, or what was termed "the labor question."

The Labor Question

In Chapter 4, we reviewed criticisms of the factory system of production in Great Britain and the Victorian sense of conscience with respect to subjecting women and children to long hours and harsh working conditions. Speaking from their hearts, U.S. reformers also attacked the American System of Manufacturing. One of the most outspoken critics was Washington Gladden, a Columbus (Ohio) Congregational minister, local politician, and social reformer who listed the major problems of the day as labor unrest, intemperance, poverty, slums, and child and female labor.[19] Gladden believed that solutions to labor unrest resided largely in organizing workers into strong unions to resist employer demands, sharing company profits with labor, and requiring arbitration to settle labor–management disputes. Temperance was essential: the greatest evil was alcohol, because it contributed to an ever-widening circle of ills, including slums, family disintegration,

---

[15] Edward Atkinson, *The Distribution of Products; or, The Mechanism and the Metaphysics of Exchange* (New York: G. P. Putnam's Sons, 1885), p. 62.

[16] Alfred Marshall and Mary Paley Marshall, *The Economics of Industry* (London: Macmillan, 1879), p. 139.

[17] *Ibid.*, p. 56.

[18] Alfred Marshall, *Principles of Economics*, 8th ed. (New York: Macmillan, 1920), p. 614.

[19] Washington Gladden, *Working People and Their Employers* (Boston, MA: Lockwood, Brooks, and Company), 1876. See also Jacob H. Dorn, *Washington Gladden: Prophet of the Social Gospel* (Columbus, OH: Ohio State University Press, 1966).

and poverty. As Richard T. Ely, one of the early proponents of the Social Gospel Movement (see Chapters 9 and 12), put it: ". . . drink [is] the poor man's curse so often, and so often the rich man's shame."[20] Social Gospel advocates held that, above all, society must be Christianized and the Golden Rule applied by both labor and management. They felt a duty to reform social and economic conditions, especially in the workplace. Rather than wait for a gradual improvement in the quality of life found in poorer neighborhoods, they argued for immediate action in improving personnel-administration and industrial-relations policies. They appealed for profit sharing, the right to organize unions, impartial workplace arbitration, and the freedom to establish worker cooperatives, as well as for legislation governing the hiring and firing practices, the employment of women and children, and workplace sanitation.[21]

Whereas Social Gospel reformers defined the labor question broadly, engineers and economists saw workplace issues in a more limited manner. Methods and systems would improve factory efficiency, but there had to be an incentive to assure worker cooperation and performance. Some managers, such as James W. See, argued that low employee productivity was due to the deliberate restriction of output. He contended that many employees worked in spurts, took it easy when their supervisor was absent, and achieved less than they were capable. The one thing that engineers and economists felt they could do to address this situation was to only pay for work performed.

Another English economist, David Schloss, reported that workers disliked piecework-pay systems that compensated a set amount for each unit of work completed because "the difficulty of satisfactorily fixing a piece-wage is very great" and often depended upon an employer's idea of how quickly work should be done.[22] Employers were also prone to "nibble their piece-wages down," or gradually increase the amount of work expected for the same pay. Schloss also reported on the mistaken belief that there was a fixed amount of work to be done in the world and, by working more slowly, the available work could be spread more evenly over a work force so that all would be employed. He attributed this belief, known as the "lump of labor fallacy," to how expected output was determined.[23] In all too many cases, an individual employee's output reflected a trade-off between what employers could cajole and pressure from coworkers to produce less. If employees did too little, they incurred their employers' wrath and risked being dismissed. If an employee did too much, coworker pressure to hold back production would increase. Thus, a day's work was a compromise between contending forces.

Although there were doubts about the wisdom of paying for work performed rather than time worked, there appeared to be a connection between higher pay, lower per-unit costs, and greater productivity. Atkinson observed that "the cheapest labor is the best-paid labor; it is the best-paid labor applied to machinery that assures the largest product in ratio to the capital invested."[24] He reasoned that if an employer paid low wages, output would also be low; but if workers were paid well and provided with the proper tools, output would be high. Another economist, Jacob Schoenhof, compared wages across various countries and found those that paid the highest wages had the lowest labor costs. Thus, nail makers in Pittsburgh were paid 10 times as much as those in Great Britain, yet the nails they produced were priced at one-half as much.[25] This paradox of high wages and low costs resurfaces in the scientific-management movement as discussed in Chapters 11 and 12.

If high wages lead to increased productivity and lowered costs per unit, and the possibility of higher profits, then the obvious solution resided in linking a firm's profits and worker performance.

---

[20] Richard T. Ely, *The Labor Movement in America* (New York: Thomas Y. Crowell, 1886), p. ix.

[21] For the views of Social Gospel proponents, see the chapters in William E. Barns, ed., *The Labor Problem: Plain Questions and Practical Answers* (New York: Harper & Brothers, 1886); for an alternative view of the labor question, see Simon Newcomb, *A Plain Man's Talk on the Labor Question* (New York: Harper & Brothers, 1886).

[22] David F. Schloss, "Why Working-men Dislike Piece Work," *Economic Review* 1 (1891), p. 313.

[23] *Idem, Methods of Industrial Remuneration* (London: Williams and Norgate, 1892), p. 38.

[24] Atkinson, *Distribution of Products*, p. 63.

[25] Jacob Schoenhof, *The Economy of High Wages: An Inquiry into the Cause of High Wages and Their Effect on Methods and Cost of Production* (New York: G. P. Putman's Sons, 1892), p. 226.

The benefits of a firm sharing its profits based on worker performance were recognized as early as 1775 by the French economist Anne Robert Jacques Turgot and practiced by Maison Leclaire, a Parisian house-painting contractor. Proponents believed that profit sharing would encourage workers to produce more at less cost because they would share in the benefits. By 1887, over 30 U.S. firms had adopted some form of profit sharing, including John Wanamaker Dry Goods, Pillsbury Flour, Procter & Gamble, and Yale & Towne Lock Company.[26] Yale & Towne, however, dropped profit sharing when its president, Henry R. Towne, realized that "the interest of each participator in the profit fund is largely affected by the actions of others whom he cannot control or influence, and that what he may earn or save for the common good may be lost by the misman-agement or extravagance of others."[27] Consequently, Towne argued for determining the present cost of a product and sharing any reduction in cost due to each individual worker's increased efficiency or increased economy in the use of materials (or both). Each worker would be guaran-teed an annual wage, but, in addition, would receive a pro-rated portion of the resulting cost savings on the basis of his yearly earnings. As Towne explained:

> Supposing, then, that at the end of the year it was found that the cost per unit of product had been reduced from $1 to 95 cents, that the total gain thus resulting was $800; and that the aggregate wages paid during the year had been $10,000. One-half of the gain would be $400, which would equal 4 per cent on earnings during the year. This is equivalent to two weeks' extra wages, no mean addition to any income, and accounting, even in the case of a laborer earning $1.50 per day, to cash a dividend of $18 at the end of the year.[28]

Frederick A. Halsey criticized profit-sharing and pay-for-work performed systems.[29] He felt that any profit-sharing system that based its distributions on collective rather than individual efforts was unfair and expressed concern about rate-setting abuses in piece-rate incentive plans. Under the Halsey "premium plan," each day workers are expected to produce a specified minimum output and receive a premium for any excess, with the "amount of this premium being based on the excess, and being *less per unit of product than the old wages cost*." Halsey offered the following example:

> Taking round numbers for convenience, suppose a workman to be paid three dollars per day of ten hours and to produce one piece of a certain kind per day. The wages cost of the produce per piece is obviously three dollars. Now, under the premium plan the proprietor says to the workman: "If you will reduce the time on that piece I will pay you a premium of ten cents for each hour by which you reduce the time." If a reduction of one hour is made the first result to the employer is to save the wages of thirty cents for the hour which has been saved, but against this is to be placed the ten cents earned as a premium, leaving a net gain of twenty cents to the employer and net increase of ten cents to the employee.[30]

In 1895, Frederick W. Taylor proposed a rate-setting and piece-rate system as a "step toward partial solution of the labor problem."[31] His solution will be compared to the Towne and Halsey plans in Chapter 7. Moving forward, the systematic-management movement was now in firmer hands, with more coherent direction. Its foundations had been prepared: a forum for sharing

[26] Nicholas P. Gilman, *Profit Sharing between Employer and Employee* (Boston, MA: Houghton Mifflin, 1889); Mary W. Calkins, *Sharing the Profits* (Boston, MA: Ginn, 1888).

[27] Henry R. Towne, "Gain Sharing," *Transactions of the American Society of Mechanical Engineers* 10 (1889), p. 600.

[28] *Ibid.*, pp. 504–605.

[29] Frederick A. Halsey, "Premium Plan of Paying for Labor," *Transactions of the American Society of Mechanical Engineers* 12 (1891), pp. 755–764.

[30] *Idem*, "Experience with the Premium Plan of Paying Labor," *American Machinist* 22(9) (March 9, 1899), pp. 180–118.

[31] Frederick W. Taylor, "A Piece Rate System, Being a Step Toward Partial Solution of the Labor Problem," *Transactions of the American Society of Mechanical Engineers* 16 (1895), pp. 856–903.

management practices had been established, a nascent literature was developing, the so-called labor question was being debated, and the need for rationalization or full use of resources had become apparent. Systematic management was a prelude to what came to be known as "scientific management," the topic of the following two chapters.

Big Business and Its Changing Environment

No nation can undergo a transformation as the United States did during the last half of the nineteenth century without substantial repercussions. An examination of the U.S. response to its changing environment is necessary to understand the forces that would shape the twentieth century. We have considered what Chandler believed to be the first phase in development of large-scale enterprises (i.e., initial expansion and accumulation of resources) and the accompanying emergence of "systematic management." Let us look beyond these developments to examine evolving notions of business and society, the beginnings of a national labor movement, the new technologies that transformed how people lived, and the changing relationship between government and business.

Business and Society: Barons or Benefactors?

Virtuous conduct seldom makes news. Historians and journalists are awed by the extraordinary, and more frequently than not overemphasize those individuals who are ruthless and unscrupulous to the detriment of those quiet, sturdy, responsible people who, unheralded, are true productive builders. As a case in point, criticism of business operators and their practices began to appear primarily in the latter third of the nineteenth century. Although the origins are obscure, one early reference described Cornelius Vanderbilt as a "medieval baron," drawing an analogy to the feudal lords who built castles along the Rhine River to exact tolls from those who passed by. The epithet *robber barons* appeared later. In time, it became so popularized that the public often equated any rich and famous business operator with someone who was ruthless and unscrupulous. It would be impossible to examine all those deemed to be robber barons, but a few thumbnail sketches will reveal why Matthew Josephson, who coined the phrase "robber barons,"[32] felt that some business operatorss were behaving in socially irresponsible ways.

Vanderbilt gained control of the New York and Harlem railroad by manipulating its stock and bribing the New York state legislature. Daniel Drew had the dubious honor of being the first to engage in what came to be called "watering stock." He had purchased a herd of cattle with an enlistment bonus from his army days. In transporting the cattle to market, he fed them salt to make them thirsty, and then after providing them all the water they could drink, sold at a very large profit some temporarily overhydrated cattle. Together with Jay Gould and Jim Fisk, Drew turned to railroading and soon gave the Erie line its reputation for mismanagement in the days following Daniel C. McCallum departure. The builders of the Central Pacific Railroad—the Big Four—Collis P. Huntington, A. Leland Stanford, Sr., Mark Hopkins, and Charles Crocker bribed lawmakers to obtain free government land, rail franchises, and favorable legislation. One year Huntington paid $200,000 to get a bill through the U.S. Congress; he later complained to David D. Colton, Central Pacific's Financial Director, that Congress was costing up to a half-million dollars a session and moaned: "I am fearful this Democratic Congress will kill me."[33]

---

[32] Matthew Josephson, *The Robber Barons: The Great American Capitalists, 1861–1901* (New York: Harcourt, Brace Jovanovich, 1934), p. vii.

[33] Letter from Collis P. Huntington to David D. Colton, August 1, 1876, p. 1. Collis Porter Huntington Papers, Box 140, Special Collections Research Center, Syracuse University Libraries, Syracuse, NY.

Not all of the robber barons were railroad men. John D. Rockefeller combined audacity and cunning in building the South Improvement Company and the Standard Oil Trust. By conspiring with railroads, he was able to extract rebates on the cost of transporting his oil, as well as that of his competitors. Andrew Carnegie at one point owned or controlled two-thirds of the nation's steel industry. A strike at the Homestead (Pennsylvania) plant of Carnegie Steel in 1892 earned Carnegie poor press when with a force of Pinkerton detectives (hired to protect the plant), who were brutally stoned and beaten by striking workers. State militia troops moved in on the order of Governor Robert E. Pattison and secured the plant for nonunionized replacements; in the process, four Pinkerton agents were killed and 300 wounded.[34] Men such as Rockefeller and Carnegie represented, at least for Josephson, the most unsavory lot in U.S. business.

What motivated the robber barons? For some social historians, it was the publication of Charles Darwin's 1859 book *On the Origin of Species by Means of Natural Selection, or the Preservation of Favoured Races in the Struggle for Life*.[35] Darwin's book introduced his theory that species evolve across generations through a process of natural selection. He claimed that there was a continual "struggle for existence" in nature, in which only the fittest would survive. Some scholars applied Darwin's theory to society. The result was "Social Darwinism."[36] The phrases "struggle for existence" and "survival of the fittest" suggested a competition or battle for the resources needed to survive, and that only the most fit would win. Social Darwinists argued that society's progress depended on a selection process based on unrestricted competition, and used Darwin's theory to justify class distinctions and inequities in wealth. They believed that legislation and charity intended to thwart this process would redound to society's detriment by weakening the human species. For some, the robber barons' success proved that, in a competition for resources, only the most fit would "advance up the social ladder of success," whereas the "unfit" would remain on the lower rungs and, eventually, be eliminated through natural selection. For these Social Darwinists, the unrestrained business practices of the robber barons were morally justified, as Darwin's theory asserts that society's progress depends on the survival of the fittest. This view, however, was then, as now, open to debate.

As one observer noted, in general, business operators of the late nineteenth and early twentieth centuries were pragmatic doers who did not read Darwin (or Adam Smith's musings on market-place forces and competition) and cared little for abstract social and economic theories.[37] Another agreed: "[I]t is not true that this commitment [to notions of competition, merited success, and deserved failure] was grounded on Darwinian premises . . . very few businessmen of the 1870's or 1880's knew enough of Darwin . . . to turn biology to the uses of self-justification."[38] What can be concluded about the effect of Social Darwinism on the thinking and practices of those in business? The economics of the "robber-baron era" led to mergers rather than to cutthroat competition, as Social Darwinism would predict. For example, Chandler saw Rockefeller's efforts to build Standard Oil as an attempt to benefit from economies of scale rather than as an effort to monopolize the oil industry. Under Rockefeller, the cost of a gallon of kerosene (lamp oil) went from 1.5 cents before the Standard Oil Trust was formed to less than one-half of 1 cent by 1885.[39] Hardly an indication of exclusive control and, in turn, monopoly profits. Before the discovery and refining of oil, animal fat was used for lubricating wheels and gears, and before

---

[34] Joseph F. Wall, *Andrew Carnegie* (New York: Oxford University Press, 1970), p. 559.

[35] Charles Darwin, *On the Origin of Species by Means of Natural Selection, or the Preservation of Favoured Races in the Struggle for Life* (London: John Murray, 1859).

[36] Richard Hofstadter, *Social Darwinism in American Thought* (Philadelphia, PA: University of Pennsylvania Press, 1944), p. 4.

[37] Edward C. Kirkland, *Dream and Thought in the Business Community, 1860–1900* (Ithaca, NY: Cornell University Press, 1956), pp. 14, 18. Another who shared this pragmatic view is Peter d'A. Jones, "Introduction," in *The Robber Barons* Revisited, *idem*, ed. (Boston, MA: D. C. Heath, 1968), pp. v–xi.

[38] Raymond J. Wilson, "Darwinism and Social Ethics" in *Darwinism and the American Intellectual: A Book of Readings*, *idem*, ed. (Homewood, IL: Dorsey Press, 1967), pp. 93–94.

[39] Alfred D. Chandler, Jr., "The Emergence of Managerial Capitalism," *Business History Review* 5(4) (Winter 1984), pp. 473–503.

kerosene, whale oil was used for lighting. Saving the world's whales was not Rockefeller's intention, but the distillation of crude oil into kerosene saved them from extinction. Earlier, we saw that Carnegie drove down the price of steel, which may have been his greatest philanthropic achievement. The Big Four paid bribes when corrupt politicians, willing to sell their votes to the highest bidder, considered payoffs a normal "cost of doing business." Similarly, when Ezra Cornell sought a charter from the New York state legislature to found a college at Ithaca, he had to strike a "bargain" with the "friends of Geneseo College" who, in return for a $25,000 "gift" to the college, assured him the votes necessary for obtaining the charter. As Cornell noted in his "cipher" book, "Such is the influence of corrupt legislation."[40]

It is highly doubtful that those in business found much guidance in Social Darwinism. Rather, it appears that in an era of change the so-called robber barons were highly visible targets for progressive critics:

> Thus the creation of the Robber Baron stereotype seems to have been the product of an impulsive popular attempt to explain the shift in the structure of American society. . . . [M]ost critics appeared to slip into the easy vulgarizations of the "devil-view" of history which ingenuously assumes that all misfortunes can be traced to the machinations of an easily located set of villains – in this case, the big businessmen of America.[41]

Rising in counterpoint to Social Darwinism was another set of ideas that came closer to grasping the policies and practices of the nineteenth-century business world. These ideas flowed from the Social Gospel movement. People such as Washington Gladden saw the Social Gospel movement as Christianity in action. We will return to the Social Gospel movement in Chapters 9 and 12, and discuss how it led to improved personnel practices.

Another set of developments also suggests that those in business at the turn of the nineteenth century were far more generous than typically portrayed. Business philanthropy is as ancient as business itself. "Captains of Industry,"[42] a phrase coined by Thomas Carlyle, have been patrons of arts and letters, underwriters of community projects, donors to religious groups, and endowers of educational institutions. No one questioned the right of the era's business philanthropists to give away some or all of their fortunes; after all, it was their money to do with as they pleased. But what of this new phenomenon, the corporation? Could its managers and directors give a portion of its profits to underwrite nonbusiness endeavors?

The notion of limited charter powers and the belief that corporate officers hold property for the benefit of stockholders combined to form the nineteenth-century legal basis for corporate philanthropy. A case precedent in 1881 involved the Old Colony Railroad, whose corporate officers had agreed to underwrite the 1872 World's Peace Jubilee and International Music Festival held in Boston. Despite the fact that the railroad benefitted from increased passenger traffic because of the jubilee, the Massachusetts Supreme Court ruled in favor of its shareholders that the officers' action was *ultra vires* (i.e., outside the railroad's chartered powers).[43] In 1883 in Great Britain, the West Cork Railroad Company attempted to compensate its employees for the loss of their jobs occasioned by its dissolution. In ruling against the railroad, Lord Justice Bowden stated: "Charity has no business to sit at boards of directors *qua* charity . . . [the directors] can only spend money which is not theirs, but the company's, if they are spending it for purposes which are reasonably incidental to the company."[44] What might or might not be "reasonably

[40] Carl L. Becker, *Cornell University: Founders and Founding* (Ithaca, NY: Cornell University Press, 1943), pp. 103–107, 154.

[41] John Tipple, "The Anatomy of Prejudice: Origins of the Robber Baron Legend," *Business History Review* 33(4) (Winter 1959), p. 521.

[42] Thomas Carlyle, *Past and Present* (New York: William H. Colyer, 1843), p. 149.

[43] *Davis v. Old Colony Railway Company*, 131 Mass. 258 (1881).

[44] *Hutton v. West Cork Railroad Company*, 23 Chancery Division Reports 654 (1883), pp. 426, 425.

incidental" would receive some clarification in what is known as the Steinway case. The New York State Supreme Court allowed piano manufacturer Steinway and Sons to buy an adjoining tract of land to be used by its employees for a church, library, and school. The Court reasoned that the employees would benefit, so there was a definite *quid pro quo* accruing to the corporation's well-being through better workplace relations.[45] In short, the law is fairly clear that corporations are chartered to do specific things, that managers and directors are trustees of shareholder-owned property, and that directors can give away assets only if it is to a corporation's measurable benefit to do so. Each of the preceding cases limited the power of directors to engage in corporate philanthropy. This power was extended in 1953 with the *A. P. Smith Manufacturing v. Barlow et al* case.[46] The Smith directors donated $1,500 to Princeton University for general educational purposes. A group of shareholders sued, claiming that the donation was outside the powers granted to the directors under the company's charter. The New Jersey Chancery Court held that the directors had acted within their rights to further corporate (and not personal) ends. It should be mentioned that, on the Federal level, the Revenue Act of 1935 included a clause that permitted corporations to deduct up to 5 percent of their net income for charitable contributions.[47] It is now accepted that directors, acting on behalf of corporations, may engage in general philanthropy for the public interest.

Although corporate philanthropy might be questioned, it seems unlikely that the hand of individual charity would be nipped. Individual philanthropy would be the vehicle for expressing the social conscience of nineteenth-century business operators. Only a few of the great business philanthropists of this era can be mentioned here.[48] Ezra Cornell's pioneering advancements in telegraphy earned him a fortune as founder of the Western Union Company and, in turn, provided the money to endow Cornell University; William Colgate aided people in following John Wesley's admonition that "Cleanliness is next to godliness"[49] by manufacturing soap, and he and his heirs gave so much to a college that it changed its name in his honor; Moses Brown, Samuel Slater's partner, founded Rhode Island College in Providence (1770), which became Brown University in 1804; Johns Hopkins, founder of the Baltimore & Ohio Railroad, founded the Baltimore university that bears his name; and Cornelius Vanderbilt made a large bequest in 1873 that converted a small Methodist seminary in Nashville into a major university.

There were more: Joseph Wharton, whose $100,000 grant to the University of Pennsylvania in 1881 underwrote the nation's first school; Edward Tuck, who honored his father with a gift of $300,000 to Dartmouth College to start the Amos Tuck School of Administration and Finance (1899); A. Leland Stanford, Sr., who honored his son's memory with a university (1891); John Stevens, whose will established an institute of technology in Philadelphia (1870); and James B. "Buck" Duke, who created a $40-million-dollar trust fund for Trinity College (later renamed for the Duke family). Good fortune did not smile on all colleges who hoped for a philanthropist. In 1867, Daniel Drew signed a $250,000 promissory note to endow a Methodist theological seminary in Madison, New Jersey. The seminary started its work, but Daniel Drew went bankrupt and was unable to deliver the promised money. Nonetheless, the seminary was named Drew University.

Other philanthropists are better known. Rockefeller endowed the University of Chicago (1896), gave millions to a general education fund for educating African-Americans throughout the South, financed historically black colleges and universities such as Spelman in Atlanta, Georgia, and made key gifts to what is now Rockefeller University. By the time of his death in 1937, he had given half-a-billion dollars to ensure the future of the foundation that bears his

---

[45] *Steinway v. Steinway and Sons*, 40 N.Y.S. 718 (1896).
[46] *AP Smith Manufacturing Co v Barlow*, 98 A.2d 581 (NJ 1953).
[47] *Revenue Act of 1935*, Pub. L. No. 74-407, 49 Stat. 1014, 1016, Section 102(c), (1935).
[48] For an extensive list, see Daniel A. Wren, "American Business Philanthropy and Higher Education in the Nineteenth Century," *Business History Review* 57(3) (Autumn 1983), pp. 321–346. See also Mark Sharfman, "Changing Institutional Rules: The Evolution of Corporate Philanthropy, 1883–1953," *Business and Society* 33(3) (December 1994), pp. 236–269.
[49] Richard Watson, *The Life of the Rev. John Wesley, A. M.* (New York: S. Hoyt & Co., 1831), p. 180.

family name. During his lifetime, Carnegie gave away $350 million of his fortune. Libraries, a university, and a foundation are enduring monuments to his expressed "stewardship of wealth philosophy."[50] Despite such generosity, in 1915, Frank P. Walsh, chairman of the United States Commission on Industrial Relations and whom we will read more about in Chapter 11, questioned whether the Rockefeller, Carnegie, and other foundations were potential "menaces to society." In hearings sparked by the 1914 Colorado coal-mine strike that culminated in the Ludlow Massacre, in which some dozen miners and their families were killed by the Colorado National Guard at a Rockefeller-family-owned mine, Commission members expressed concern that "improperly administered" foundations might actually increase rather than lessen the "evil" they sought to remedy, and that this would especially be the case in the future should they fall into "evil hands." Philanthropy by company-sponsored foundations was seen as intruding on the province of government, and reflected a fear that bequests given at the direction of men such as Rockefeller and Carnegie might exercise "a great influence on the public mind," allowing foundations to increase their control over public institutions, colleges and universities, government, and the masses.[51]

Times have changed: income and inheritance taxes make it difficult to accumulate the wealth of a Rockefeller or Carnegie, the legal question of corporate philanthropy has been clarified (as we shall see in Chapter 22), and public expectations about the role of business in society have changed. Individually and collectively, however, we remain the beneficiaries of the so-called robber barons uncommon largess. More recent philanthropists include Nike co-founder Phil Knight who has given more than a half-billion dollars to the Oregon Health Sciences Center and donated more than $100 million dollars to the Stanford University Graduate School of Business; former Citigroup CEO Sandy Weil, who has given more than $600 million dollars to Cornell Medical Center; and hedge-fund manager John Paulson, who has donated $100 million dollars to the Central Park Conversancy in New York City. This list could be extended *ad infinitum*.

Business and Labor: Uneasy Relations

As noted in Chapter 5, in 1842 the Massachusetts Supreme Court ruled in *Commonwealth v. Hunt* that workers had the right to strike or use peaceful coercion to raise wages. At the time, in the United States, labor organizations were found among craft workers, such as those in the building trades, and among so-called brotherhoods of railway employees. Efforts to form general unions across trades or industries were generally less successful. One of the nation's first union federations, the National Labor Union, headed by William H. Sylvis (1828–1869), sought to supplant the employer–employee wage system with cooperative production, in which workers would pool their resources, supply their own labor, and manage their own factories. The Noble Order of the Knights of Labor (organized in 1867) sought an 8-hour workday, establishment of a bureau of labor statistics, protection against child labor, government ownership of railroads and telegraph lines, abolition of national banks, and a graduated federal income tax to raise money for government services and programs.

Labor violence in the 1880s and 1890s fueled public fear of unions. The Molly Maguires terrorized the Pennsylvania coalfields with murders and other atrocities. The Haymarket Affair (1886), in which the Knights of Labor tried to enforce a general strike in Chicago, led to several deaths. The Homestead Steel strike (1892) and the Pullman strike (1894) were other examples of violence brought about by confrontations between labor and management. Public fear of radicals and anarchists, who were often equated with legitimate union organizers, kept the union

---

[50] Andrew Carnegie, "Wealth," *North American Review* 148 (391) (June 1889), pp. 653–665.
[51] *Industrial Relations, Final Report and Testimony Submitted to Congress by the Commission on Industrial Relations*, vol. 9 (Washington, DC: U.S. Government Printing Office, 1916), pp. 8110–8111, 8171, 8179, 8316.

movement at a relative standstill as a percentage of the U.S. labor force. Total union membership grew from 300,000 members in 1870 to 868,000 in 1900; however, in 1870, only five percent of the total U.S. labor force was organized; this percentage declined in the 1880s and 1890s, but recovered and rose to 4.8 percent by 1900.

In contrast to the National Labor Union and the Knights of Labor, the American Federation of Labor (AFL), organized in 1886 as a federation of trade unions, was successful in achieving its goals.[52] The AFL concentrated on immediate economic gains for its members rather than on distant political reforms. Under Samuel Gompers's presidency, AFL membership increased from over 600,000 in 1887 to some 2,865,000 at the time of Gompers's death in 1924.[53] In general, however, workers had to wait for other times and a changing public opinion to legitimize their attempts to unionize.

Immigration provided a steadily growing work force to meet the labor needs of a rapidly expanding industrial economy: Chinese were brought in to build railroads, and Irish, Germans, and Swedes populated the nation's coalfields and steel mills. After 1880, another flow of Slavs, Poles, and Italians added to a growing work force. The increased supply of labor, however, did not result in lower wages. Daily wages and annual earnings in manufacturing increased 59 percent between 1860 and 1890, and real wages (the purchasing power of the workers' incomes) increased 60 percent from 1860 to 1890 (1.6 percent compounded annually).[54] Wage earners benefited from the growth of U.S. industry in terms of both employment and real income.

Inventive and Innovative Impulses

We earlier noted the influence of railroads in creating a national market for a growing array of manufactured goods. When the Union Pacific and the Central Pacific railroads met at Promontory, Utah, in 1869, a golden spike driven by A. Leland Stanford commemorated the last link in a transcontinental railroad connecting east and west. The miles of track in the United States would increase from 35,000 in 1865 to 193,000 by 1900. Technological advancements made rail travel more pleasurable: steel rails replaced iron rails; George Pullman introduced the sleeping car in 1865; and George Westinghouse developed the air brake in 1868, making rail travel safer. The westward expanding railroads fostered a retailing revolution, as we shall see, by creating greater time and place utility through mass distribution. Although the railroads facilitated interstate commerce, they also made it more complicated because there were no established time zones. It could be noon in Chicago, 12:30 pm in Pittsburgh, and 11:45 am in St. Louis, creating confusion for shippers and travelers. The solution was four time zones, based on sun time at the 75th, 90th, 105th, and 120th meridians west of Greenwich, England. Standard times were adopted by the nation's railroads in 1883 and U.S. Congress in 1918.

The remarkable spirit of inventive and innovative impulses that shaped the era's technological advances were due to a number of prime movers, individuals whose ideas created new wealth. As Locke expressed it, "for wealth to be created, individuals must create it . . . *prime movers . . .* moved society forward by the force of their own creative imagination, their own energy, and their own productive capacity."[55] These individuals pushed to advance the nation's capacity to produce more, to create jobs, and to devise means of making, moving, and packaging a cornucopia of consumer products that had no precedent.

---

[52] Trade or craft unions organize workers in a particular industry along trade or craft lines; examples include the carpenters' union, electricians' union, and painters' union. In contrast, industrial unions organize all the workers in a particular industry regardless of craft or trade; examples include automobile workers, steel workers, mine workers, and shipbuilders.

[53] Philip A. Taft, *The A. F. of L. in the Time of Gompers* (New York: Harper & Brothers, 1957), pp. 52, 362.

[54] Ross M. Robertson, *History of the American Economy*, 3rd ed. (New York: Harcourt Brace Jovanovich, 1973), pp. 379–380.

[55] Edwin A. Locke, *Prime Movers: Traits of the Great Wealth Creators* (New York: American Management Association, 2000), p. 7.

Telegraph was the companion of railroads in this unprecedented period of economic growth. Chandler described this growth in terms of *scale* and *scope*: (1) economies of scale occur when the increased size of a single operating unit producing or distributing a single product reduces the per-unit cost of production or distribution; (2) economies of scope result when processes within a single operating unit are used to produce or distribute more than one product.[56] Carnegie's vertical integration in the steel industry achieved economies of scale by reducing unit costs; economies of scope were realized by manufacturing a variety of different steel products. As scale and scope expanded, an increasing number of managers were needed to plan, coordinate, and monitor a firm's activities. With the rail system, telegraph, and Alexander Graham Bell's telephone, it became possible to produce, transport, and sell to national and global markets leading to further economies of both scale and scope.

Large-scale enterprises in the last half of the nineteenth century were entirely different than the localized, family-owned and managed, and labor-intensive firms of the first half of the century. To mention all of the "prime movers" of this latter period would require several books. Some, such as Thomas Edison and George Westinghouse, transformed how electricity is transmitted and controlled. Rockefeller's lamp oil market would be superseded by electricity. The Bell Telephone Company, created in 1875, eventually became the American Telephone & Telegraph Company in 1885. Elisha Gray invented the first facsimile machine for transmitting handwriting via telegraph in 1877. With improvements in communication and transportation, came the first mass-marketers, chain-retailers, mail-order houses, and grocery chains such as the Great Atlantic & Pacific Tea Company, which by 1878 operated 70 stores. Refrigerated rail cars transformed the meat-packing industry, bringing perishable products to distant markets. The American System of Manufacturing enabled mass production of Isaac Singer's sewing machines and Cyrus McCormick's mechanical reaper. Christopher L. Sholes sold his typewriter patent to E. Remington & Sons in 1873. Andrew Carnegie's stronger, lighter, structural steel enabled high-rise buildings, whereas Elisha Otis's elevator made the trip to the top easier and safer. These were a few of the prime movers whose inventive and innovative impulses were the basis for large-scale enterprises in manufacturing, communications, marketing, distilling, refining, transporting, and food processing that created a material abundance unparalleled in the history of the world.

Business and Government: Seeds of Reform

The U.S. government during the nineteenth century was not noted for its progressiveness. The patronage system (also known as the spoils system), in which the political party in power awarded government positions to friends and relatives, had prevailed since the nation's founding. Calls for government reform went unanswered. In 1883, shortly after the assassination of President James Garfield by a disappointed office seeker, the U.S. Congress passed the Civil Service Act, establishing the permanent Civil Service Commission. Better known as the Pendleton Act, after its senatorial sponsor, its intent was to bring qualified employees, rather than political favorites, to government and to provide some stability in public affairs. In this new environment, the seeds of government reform found fertile ground in the systematic-management movement emerging in the private sector.

Credit for introducing systematic management to government belongs to Woodrow Wilson, then a young professor at Bryn Mawr College. In 1887, Wilson recognized that civil-service reform must extend beyond the need for qualified public employees to perform the functions

---

[56] Chandler and Hikino, *Scale and Scope*, pp. 17–28.

of government. To this end, Wilson recommended "administrative study to discover, first, what government can properly and successfully do, and, secondly, how it can do these proper things with the utmost possible efficiency and the least possible cost either of money or of energy."[57] The study of government, according to Wilson, had focused more on politics and not enough on how to manage the public's business. After all, "the field of administration is a field of business . . . removed from the hurry and strife of politics. . . . The object of administrative study is to rescue executive methods from the confusion and costliness of empirical experiment and set them upon foundations laid deep in stable principle."[58] Later, as the 28th President of the United States (1913–1921), Wilson brought improved systems and methods to government.

As the federal government during this era narrowly construed the U.S. Constitution's commerce clause, there were but few efforts made to regulate business practices. The first attempts to do so were aimed at abuses by the railroads. In 1869, Massachusetts passed legislation establishing a railroad commission with authority to set and enforce shipping rates; the Granger laws, passed in the late 1860s and early 1870s by several Midwestern states, regulated the prices charged to farmers by railroads and grain elevator operators; and the Interstate Commerce Act of 1887 became the first Federal act to regulate the railroads' monopolistic practices. Beyond the railroads, the Sherman Antitrust Act of 1890 was the first Federal act to outlaw monopolistic practices "in restraint of trade." Poorly written and narrowly interpreted, it was generally ineffective. The Wilson-Gorman Tariff Act of 1894 imposed the first peacetime national income tax. It levied a 2 percent personal tax on all incomes above $4,000 and a 2 percent tax on all corporate net income. In 1895, the Supreme Court declared the Wilson-Gorman Tariff Act's income tax provision unconstitutional. Passed in 1913, the Constitution's Sixteenth Amendment allowed Congress to levy an income tax. In brief, the nineteenth-century economic and political environments remained relatively laissez-faire, true to the precepts of Adam Smith; the twentieth century would stand in stark contrast.

SUMMARY OF PART 1

Part 1 traced developments in management thought up to the scientific-management era in the United States. After a brief introduction to the role of managers in organizations, it reviewed the first attempts at management in early civilizations and discussed how changing cultural values set the stage for the Industrial Revolution. The Industrial Revolution posed new challenges for owner-entrepreneurs, salaried managers, and society-at-large. The efforts of four individuals—Robert Owen, Charles Babbage, Andrew Ure, and Charles Dupin—who pioneered solutions to these challenges were discussed. Part 1 concluded by examining the continued growth of U.S. enterprises following the War Between the States, the emergence of systematic management, and the nation's economic, social, political, and technological environment on the eve of the scientific-management era.

Figure 6.1 presents a synopsis of early management thought. It opens by noting that people have manifold needs and wants, which they seek to satisfy through organized endeavors. Whereas early civilizations generally placed a low value on economic exchange and held a parochial view of management as an independent activity, a cultural rebirth established preconditions for industrialization. The Industrial Revolution in England beget the factory system, which posed unprecedented managerial challenges. The efforts of Robert Owen, Charles Babbage, Andrew Ure, Charles Dupin, and others (such as Daniel McCallum and Henry Poor) in meeting these challenges are noted. Finally, the expansion of U.S. industry following the War Between the States led to systematic management, a prelude to the scientific management-era, our next topic.

---

[57] Woodrow Wilson, "The Study of Administration," *Political Science Quarterly* 2 (2) (June 1887), p. 197.
[58] *Ibid.*, pp. 209–210.

**FIGURE 6.1 Synopsis of
Early Management
Thought.**

The Scientific-Management Era

Part 2 begins by reviewing the life of Frederick W. Taylor and the scientific-management movement. Taylor left an indelible mark on the management disciple. His work was, and still remains, revolutionary. Taylor, however, was not alone in spreading the gospel of efficiency. He was joined by others who would apply, adapt, and refine scientific management. Carl G. Barth, Henry L. Gantt, Frank and Lillian Gilbreth, Harrington Emerson, and Morris L. Cooke were among the most prominent individuals flying the scientific-management banner. Though the work of Taylor and his followers dominated scientific management's early years, Part 2 continues by examining social forces in play during the same period and how they affected industrial psychology, industrial sociology, and industrial relations. Together, these forces set the stage for later developments in labor–management relations, the human-relations school of management, and, eventually, the field of organizational behavior. Part 2 next considers the ideas of Henri Fayol, a French manager-engineer, who was the first writer to advance a formal statement of management elements and principles, and Max Weber, a German economist-sociologist, who addressed the more fundamental issue of how organizations should be structured. As the scientific-management movement grew in the United States, it sparked attention in other parts of the world, including Western and Eastern Europe, Japan, China, and Australia. Part 2 concludes with a retrospective view of the economic, social, technological, and political conditions that composed scientific management's cultural environment.

The Advent of Scientific Management

Earlier chapters reviewed the transformation of U.S. industry in the years following the War Between the States. The Industrial Revolution in Great Britain initially spread across the Atlantic Ocean with the mechanization of textile manufacturing. Given the westward migration of settlers, the Industrial Revolution was most evident in the railroad industry. The nation's railroads also provided a cost–effective means for transporting manufactured goods, raw materials, and food. The seeds of the modern industrial corporation—the forerunner of today's *Fortune* 500 company—were sown during this era. As noted in Chapter 5, early railroad pioneers were among the first to feel the need for improved management. Daniel McCallum introduced systematic management on the Erie Railroad, and his ideas influenced other railway operators and Andrew Carnegie in steel. Railroads opened new product markets, and the telegraph connected the nation for financial, production, marketing, and other transactions.

Another stage of the Industrial Revolution began in the latter half of the nineteenth century. It grew out of a complex, uneven, and interacting outcome of technological advances, changing power sources, evolving labor–management relations, and a desperate need to reconcile these factors through improved managerial practices. As engineers were vital in developing and installing advances in technology and power, it was natural that they became a prime source of ideas for meeting new management challenges. Henry R. Towne, for example, called for engineers to look beyond the technical side of manufacturing and become involved in increasing the managerial efficiency of industrial operations. One of the engineers who responded to Towne's call was Frederick W. Taylor, and he is the focal point of this chapter.

Frederick W. Taylor: The Early Years

Frederick Winslow Taylor (1856–1915) was born in Germantown, Pennsylvania. His father was a fairly prosperous lawyer of Quaker stock and his mother traced her Puritan roots to a Plymouth, Massachusetts, ancestor who arrived in Colonial America in 1629.[1] Taylor's early education was liberally sprinkled with the classics, the study of French and German, and three-and-a-half years' schooling and travel in Europe. His parents originally intended that he should follow his father's footsteps and consider a career in law. Accordingly, in 1872, Taylor entered Phillips Exeter Academy in Exeter, New Hampshire, to prepare for Harvard University. Indicative of the stiff competition among students at Phillips Exeter, one of Taylor's instructor's, George A. Wentworth, used a stop watch to see which of his students could most quickly solve math problems.[2] Taylor's zeal and restless energy led to late nights and long hours, eventually impairing his eyesight and causing headaches. Although he graduated in 1872 at the head of his class and passed the Harvard entrance exams with honors, and eyeglasses would ultimately solve the vision and headache problems, Taylor decided to turn away from further study. His parents suggested that he become an engineer. So, at the age of 18, he began an apprenticeship as a machinist and patternmaker for the Enterprise Hydraulic Works (Philadelphia), a pump-manufacturing company owned by family acquaintances.[3] Taylor's decision to enter an apprenticeship was not unusual. Upper class Philadelphians had long been educated in this manner. It was an accepted means of developing elite mechanical engineers. As was customary with apprentices from better-off families, Taylor started his four-year apprenticeship at no wage. During his second year, he earned $1.50 a week. By his fourth year he was pocketing the princely sum of $3.00 a week. At Enterprise, Taylor developed empathy for the workers' point of view; he could swear with the best of them and admired the pride they took in their craftsmanship. He noted, however, what he called "bad industrial conditions," worker restriction of output, poor management, and lack of harmony between labor and management.

Taylor at Midvale

Having completed his apprenticeship, Taylor joined, again through family connections, the Midvale Steel Company (Philadelphia, Pennsylvania), in 1878.[4] Midvale specialized in the manufacture of locomotive wheels and railway axles. The economic consequences of the financial panic of 1873 lingered, and positions were scarce. Taylor consequently took a job as a laborer. Midvale, under the presidency of William Sellers, one of the nineteenth century's most prominent machine-tool inventors, was among the leading steel firms of the era. There Taylor rose from common laborer to clerk, to machinist, to gang boss of machinists, to machine-shop supervisor, to master mechanic in charge of all repairs and maintenance, and to chief engineer—all in 6 years.

---

[1] The life of Taylor is a popular subject for biographies. A much-cited source is Frank Barkley Copley's authorized biography, *Frederick W. Taylor: Father of Scientific Management*, 2 vols. (New York: Harper & Brothers, 1923). Other useful sources are Charles D. Wrege and Ronald G. Greenwood, *Frederick W. Taylor, the Father of Scientific Management: Myth and Reality* (Homewood, IL: Business One Irwin, 1991); Daniel Nelson, *Frederick W. Taylor and the Rise of Scientific Management* (Madison, WI: University of Wisconsin Press, 1980); and Robert Kanigel, *The One Best Way: Frederick Winslow Taylor and The Enigma of Efficiency* (New York: Viking, 1997).

[2] Aleksey Tikhomirov, "'The First Case of Scientific Time-Study That I Ever Saw . . .'," *Journal of Management History* 17(4) (2011), pp. 356–378. Wentworth was one of the era's foremost mathematicians and the author of textbooks that sold well over a million copies. He taught at Phillips Exeter for more than 40 years. See "Wentworth, George Albert," in *The National Cyclopædia of American Biography*, vol. 10 (New York: James T. White & Company, 1900), p. 106.

[3] Robert Kanigel, "Frederick Taylor's Apprenticeship," *Wilson Quarterly* 20(3) (Summer 1996), pp. 44–51. See also Andrew Dawson, *Lives of the Philadelphia Engineers: Capital, Class and Revolution, 1830–1890* (Burlington, VT: Ashgate, 2004), pp. 226–246.

[4] Charles D. Wrege and Ronald G. Greenwood, "The Early History of Midvale Steel and the Work of Frederick W. Taylor: 1865–1890," *Canal History and Technology Proceedings* 11 (1992), pp. 145–176.

Taylor's 12 years at Midvale (1878–1890) were a time of experimentation, during which he gained invaluable insights that would be the basis for his later ideas about proper management. Realizing that he lacked a "scientific education," he took a home-study course in mathematics and physics at Harvard University. He then enrolled in a home-study course from Stevens Institute of Technology (Hoboken, New Jersey). Without ever having been on campus, except to take his entrance examination and each of his required course examinations, Taylor graduated with a degree in mechanical engineering in 1883. Given that Taylor was able to immediately pass many of his exams in French, German, history, and so on, due to his experience abroad and to general reading, he was able to graduate in about two-and-a-half years, all the while fulfilling his duties at Midvale.

As Taylor received no formal management training at Midvale, he relied solely on his own experiences in fulfilling his supervisory duties. The company had established a piece-rate pay plan that he knew to be ineffective from his days as a laborer. Midvale's owners believed that laborers would produce more if they were paid a fixed "piece rate" for each unit produced than if they received a flat day rate. When Taylor became gang boss, he learned otherwise. He quickly realized that output was unnecessarily low due to a practice called "soldiering," whereby (as described in Chapter 6) laborers deliberately worked as slowly as they dared, at the same time trying to make their bosses believe they were working fast. Indeed, he estimated that gang output was only one-third of what was possible.

Taylor distinguished between two types of soldiering. "Natural soldiering" proceeded from "the natural instinct and tendency of men to take it easy"; "systematic soldiering" came from the workers' "more intricate second thought and reasoning caused by their relations with other men."[5] Inspiring or forcing workers to come up to the mark could overcome natural soldiering. Systematic soldiering posed a different challenge, and managers for years had been attempting to cope with the tendency of workers to deliberately "underwork." Taylor understood that workers soldiered for several reasons. First, they feared that if they worked faster, they would complete their jobs and be laid off; second, based on their experience of being paid by the piece, if they produced more, management would likely cut the piece rate governing their wages and they would end up doing more work for the same take-home pay; and third, they adhered to rule-of-thumb work methods handed down from generation to generation.[6] Taylor placed the blame on management, not on the workers, for he thought that it was management's responsibility to design jobs properly and offer appropriate performance incentives to overcome worker soldiering.

In no small part, soldiering arose out of a "lump of labor" theory, which as discussed in Chapter 6, held that there was a fixed amount of work to be done in the world, so any increase in the amount each worker produced reduced the number of available jobs.[7] A flat daily or hourly wage rate encouraged soldiering, because workers had no incentive to produce more today than yesterday. Pay was based on attendance and position, not on effort. Working harder brought no reward and, thus, workers were actually encouraged to be lazy. Piece-rate systems, in use long before Taylor's time, sought to encourage individual productivity by paying workers on the basis of their output, but such systems had generally been failures; standards were often poorly set, employers cut pay rates as increased output became the norm, and workers hid their shortcut methods to keep management ignorant of how fast work could be performed. Not surprisingly,

---

[5] Frederick W. Taylor, *Shop Management* (New York: Harper & Brothers, 1903), p. 30. Originally published in the *Transactions of the American Society of Mechanical Engineers*, 24 (1903), pp. 1383–1456.

[6] Frederick W. Taylor, *The Principles of Scientific Management* (New York: Harper & Brothers, 1911), pp. 15–16. Originally written in 1909 for publication in the *Transactions of the American Society of Mechanical Engineers*, but was withheld because, in part, the Meetings Committee felt it overstated the "universal applicability" of its claims. Taylor subsequently circulated the book privately in 1911 and arranged for it to be serialized as three installments in *The American Magazine*, March, 1911, through May, 1911. For further details, see Carol Carlson Dean, "The Principles of Scientific Management by Frederick W. Taylor: The Private Printing," *Journal of Management History* 3(1), 1997, pp.18–30.

[7] John Wilson, "Economic Fallacies and Labour Utopias." *Quarterly Review* 131(261) (1871), pp. 229–263.

workers developed a consensus about how much each should produce and earn, not only to protect themselves, but to also avoid sanctions being placed on the less capable. Management was seemingly unaware of the resulting inefficiencies.

Taylor's initial experiences as a machine-shop supervisor resulted in a bitter encounter with Midvale's machinists. He told the machinists he knew they could work faster and he was going to see that they did. Taylor started by showing them how to use metalworking lathes to achieve more output with little additional effort. The machinists refused to follow his instructions. Taylor then turned to training apprentice machinists. Facing established output norms, however, they promptly disavowed Taylor's methods. Taylor admitted, "I was up against a stone wall. I did not blame . . . these laborers in my heart; my sympathy was with them all of the time."[8] In an effort to force the machinists to work faster to earn the same daily pay, Taylor cut the prevailing piece rate. The machinists retaliated by breaking and jamming their machines and "warned that he had better abandon his practice of going home along a railway track where he could be easily attacked, or else carry arms." Taylor countered by imposing a system of fines (the proceeds going to a worker benefit fund) for damaged equipment and giving notice that "he was going to continue to go on his accustomed way and would go unarmed."[9] After three years, the machinists finally gave in and adopted Taylor's methods. This bitter experience taught Taylor a valuable lesson. He realized a business is a system of human cooperation that will be successful only if all concerned work toward a common goal. Never again would he impose fines, and he would later establish strict rules against rate cutting. More important, Taylor realized a new industrial system was essential for preventing such bitter labor–management encounters. Taylor set out to develop such a system.

Portrait of Frederick W. Taylor, circa 1900. Frederick W. Taylor Collection. Special Collections and Archive, Stevens Institute of Technology, Hoboken, NJ.

The Search for Science in Management

Taylor thought he could overcome soldiering by determining how each job could be done most efficiently and then establishing performance standards. He believed once workers saw that performance standards had been set "scientifically," rather than on guesswork and tradition, there could be no appeal and their motivation to soldier would be eliminated. The problem was in defining "a fair day's work" for each job. Taylor set out to determine what the workers *ought* to be able to produce with their equipment and materials. This was the beginning of what was to be called "scientific management," that is, the application of the scientific method to empirically establish the most efficient way to perform a job. He was not asking workers to produce more with the same effort, but more with improved methods and conditions. Taylor had concluded that labor–management conflict was due to ignorance on both sides. Management expected and workers were ready to provide "a fair day's work" for "a fair day's pay." Neither side, however, knew what constituted a day's work. Both relied on vague impressions that led to continuing disputes.

---

[8] *Hearings before Special Committee of the House of Representatives to Investigate the Taylor and Other Systems of Shop Management under Authority of House Resolution 90* (Washington, DC: U.S. Government Printing Office, 1912), vol. 3, p. 1413.
[9] "The Father of Scientific Management," *The Outlook* 109 (March 31, 1915), p. 755.

Recalling the lessons he had learned at Phillips-Exeter from his teacher George A. Wentworth, time study became the foundation of Taylor's work. With a stopwatch, weight scale, and tape, he literally measured the distances workers and materials traveled. Gradually, he determined that a large share of both effort and materials was needlessly wasted because of improper management. Some critics would question the originality of Taylor's work. Charles Babbage had previously used a watch to record the labor operations and times necessary for manufacturing pins.[10] In 1912, a subcommittee of the American Society of Mechanical Engineers (ASME) issued a report on time study that made no mention of Taylor's work, but referenced Babbage and Adam Smith (see Chapter 2). Taylor contributed to a discussion of this report in an effort to clarify his concept of time study and answer those who doubted the originality of his work.

> Time study was begun in the machine shop of the Midvale Steel Company in 1881. . . . It is true that the form of Tables 1 and 2 [from Babbage's 1835 book *Economy of Machinery and Manufacture*] is similar to that of the blanks recording time study, but here the resemblance ceases. Each line in Table 2, for instance, gives statistics regarding the average of the entire work of an operative who works day in and day out, in running a machine engaged in the manufacture of pins. This table involves no study whatever of the movements of the man, nor of the time in which the movements *should* have been made. Mere statistics as to the time which a man takes to do a given piece of work do not constitute "time study." "Time study," as its name implies, involves a careful study of the time in which work *ought* to be done . . . [rather than] the time in which the work actually was done.[11]

Unlike Babbage, Taylor used time study for inferential rather than descriptive purposes. Rather than simply describe "what is," Taylor used time study to discover "what was possible" in improving job performance. Taylor's time study had two phases: *analysis* and *synthesis*. In analysis, each job was broken into its elementary movements. Nonessential movements were discarded and the remainder carefully examined to determine the quickest and least wasteful means of performing a job. These elementary motions were then described, recorded, and indexed, along with the amount of time required to cover unavoidable delays, minor accidents, and rest. In the second stage, synthesis, the elementary movements were combined in the correct sequence to determine the time and the exact method for performing a job. This phase also led to improvements in tools, machines, materials, methods, and the ultimate standardization of all elements surrounding and accompanying a job.[12]

The Quest for Improved Performance Incentives

The search for effective performance incentives for increasing output is probably as old as humanity.[13] Piece work, or paying a fixed rate for each unit produced, was the basis of the "putting-out" or domestic system of production, and was used before and during the Industrial Revolution (see Chapter 3). As U.S. industry developed after the War Between the States, numerous schemes were proposed for paying labor. These included Henry Towne's gain sharing and Frederick Halsey's premium plan (see Chapter 6). In a paper presented to the ASME in 1895, Taylor criticized both Towne and Halsey plans and proposed a new alternative.[14] In Taylor's opinion, a weakness in the Towne and Halsey plans was that they took present worker output as their

---

[10] Charles Babbage, *On the Economy of Machinery and Manufacturers* (London: Charles Knight, 1832), pp. 138–152.

[11] *Ibid.*, p. 226.

[12] Taylor, *Shop Management*, pp. 149–176.

[13] E. Brian Peach and Daniel A. Wren, "Pay for Performance from Antiquity to the 1950s," *Journal of Organizational Behavior Management* 12(1) (Spring 1991), pp. 5–26.

[14] Frederick W. Taylor, "A Piece-Rate System, Being a Step Toward Partial Solution of the Labor Problem," *Transactions of the American Society of Mechanical Engineers* 16 (1895), pp. 856–883. See also Wrege and Greenwood, *Frederick W. Taylor, the Father of Scientific Management*, p. 20.

performance standard. In contrast, Taylor proposed a new three-part plan that extended an earlier piecework-system developed by Charles A. Brinley at Midvale Steel: (1) observation and analysis through time study to set output standards and pay rates; (2) a differential piecework-system in which a higher rate per piece is paid if work is done in less time than specified, and a lower rate is paid if it is done in more time than allowed; and (3) "paying men and not positions."

In Taylor's opinion, profit sharing failed because it discouraged personal ambition by allowing all to share in profits regardless of their contribution, and because of the "remoteness of the reward." In recognizing this shortcoming, Taylor showed an appreciation of Aristotle's (383–322 BCE) *principle of temporal contiguity*; that is, the importance of the timing between a stimulus and a response in conditioning behavior, and reflected Taylor's view that sharing profits at the end of a year gave little incentive for improved daily performance.

In his 1895 paper, Taylor had clearly put the onus on management to establish daily output standards rather than following the established practice of allowing workers to determine how jobs should be performed. In commenting on the audience remarks that followed his paper presentation, Taylor said he was "much surprised and disappointed that elementary rate-fixing has not received more attention during the discussion."[15] In Taylor's view, those present evidently did not realize that proper performance standards had to be determined before establishing a fair-piece rate. Under Taylor's plan, a special department analyzed each job and then set a performance standard and pay scale instead of relying on guesswork and tradition. Taylor's notion of "paying men rather than positions" was designed to partially address soldiering, but primarily intended to reward individual initiative. Taylor also understood he was dealing with humans as well as material and machines. He readily acknowledged that "There is another type of scientific investigation . . . which should receive special attention, namely, the accurate study of the motives which influence men."[16]

Taylor's 1895 ASME paper also outlined his initial view of unions, especially with respect to regulating wages and conditions of employment:

> The [author] is far from taking the view held by many manufacturers that labor unions are an almost unmitigated detriment to those who join them, as well as to employers and the general public.
>
> The labor unions . . . have rendered a great service not only to their members, but to the world, in shortening the hours of labor and in modifying the hardships and improving the conditions of wage-workers. . . .
>
> When employers herd their men together in classes, pay all of each class the same wages, and offer them any inducements to work harder or do better than the average, the only remedy for the men lies in combination; and frequently the only possible answer to encroachments on the part of their employers is a strike.
>
> This state of affairs is far from satisfactory and the writer believes the system of regulating wages and conditions of employment of whole classes of men by conference and agreement between the leaders, unions and manufacturers to be vastly inferior . . . to the plan of stimulating each workman's ambition by paying him according to his individual worth, and without limiting him to the rate of work or pay of the average of his class.[17]

Taylor, thus, in his early writing, saw no need for unions under his piece-rate pay plan. Unions, to foster class solidarity, insisted that their members all be treated the same. For Taylor, this prevented union members from fulfilling their personal ambitions. Rather than being encouraged to better themselves, in Taylor's mind, unions stifled individual initiative. Taylor's view of unions, however, would evolve over time.

---

[15] Taylor, "Piece-Rate System," pp. 902–903.
[16] *Idem, Principles of Scientific Management*, p. 119.
[17] *Idem*, "Piece-Rate System," p. 882; also in *idem, Shop Management*, pp. 185–186.

Taylor's comments on properly setting performance standards, establishing a fair-piece rate, and relations between labor and management anticipated his belief that the concerns of employee and employer should be based on a "mutuality of interests." Countering the assumption that if workers earned more, they did so at their employer's expense, Taylor advocated a system that would benefit both employer and employee. In doing so, he addressed the contradiction inherent in the "paradox of high wages and low costs," which on the surface appear to be diametrically opposed concepts (see Chapter 6). Rather than employers' attempting to buy the cheapest labor and paying the lowest wages possible, in the belief that high wage rates were accompanied by high per-unit costs, Taylor showed that high wages could be associated with low costs. Taylor advocated paying first-class workers a high wage, thereby encouraging them to produce more under standard, efficient conditions with no greater expenditure of effort. The result would be greater productivity and, hence, lower per-unit costs, making higher wages possible. Taylor reasoned that high wages and low costs were possible by using scientific principles to empirically establish the most efficient way to perform each worker's job. Throughout history, it had been taken as self-evident that workers could produce more only by working harder or longer. Taylor showed that the real potential for increased output was not "working harder" but "working smarter." Toward this end, Taylor said that management should strive to ensure that each workman . . .

(*a*) . . . be given as far as possible the highest grade of work for which his ability and physique fit him.

(*b*) . . . be called upon to turn out the maximum amount of work which a first-rate man of his class can do and thrive.

(*c*) . . . when he works at the best pace of a first-class man, . . . be paid from 30 per cent to 100 per cent according to the nature of the work which he does, beyond the average of his class.[18]

The notion that workmen should be given the highest grade of work to perform based on their ability and physique indicated that Taylor was aware of the need to match abilities to job requirements and the continuing need to do so. As he explained:

> It becomes the duty of those on the management's side to deliberately study the character, the nature, and the performance of each workman, with a view to finding out his limitations on the one hand, but even more important, his possibilities for development on the other hand; and then, as deliberately and as systematically to train and help and teach this workman, giving him, wherever it is possible, those opportunities for advancement which will finally enable him to do the highest and most interesting and most profitable class of work for which his natural abilities fit him, and which are open to him in the particular company in which he is employed. This scientific selection of the workman and his development is not a single act; it goes on from year to year and is the subject of continual study on the part of the management.[19]

To this Taylor later added: "Scientific management does not come into existence until the owners of the establishment, all of the managers of the establishment, have the building up of their men, the development of their men, as absolutely the first thought in their minds."[20]

Taylor's use of the term "first-class man," however, caused him much grief, especially when explaining it to others. In testimony before a special committee of the U.S. House of Representative

---

[18] *Idem, Shop Management*, pp. 28–29.
[19] *Hearings before Special Committee of the House of Representatives to Investigate the Taylor and Other Systems of Shop Management*, vol. 3, p. 1394.
[20] Frederick W. Taylor, "Competitive Profit Sharing," *Greater Efficiency: Journal of the Efficiency Society* 3(6) (March 1914), pp. 25–26.

charged with investigating "the Taylor and other systems of shop management," Taylor defined what it meant to be a "first-class man" by describing a workman who did not meet his definition:

> I believe the only man who does not come under "first-class" as I have defined it, is the man who can work and will not work. I have tried to make it clear that for each type of workman some job can be found at which he is first class, with the exception of those men who are perfectly well able to do the job but won't do it.[21]

Under these terms, non-first-class workmen would be those who were physically or mentally unsuited for the work to which they had been assigned (in which case they should be retrained or transferred to another job for which they were suited) or who were unwilling to give their best. In setting pay rates for each job, Taylor wrote that performance standards should be set at the pace a first-class worker "can keep up for a long term of years without injury to his health. It is a pace under which men become happier and thrive."[22] Taylor anticipated what today is considered sound human-resource management, that is, matching workers' abilities to assigned jobs.

It was management's task to identify the work for which employees were best suited and provide them with incentives to give their best. Taylor's views on first-class workers were intertwined with his personal philosophy of "the will to get there," the success drive that was the basis of his own life. It was his observation that individuals differ not so much in brains, but in their will to achieve.[23] First-class workers were people with ambition and who were suited to their work. They were not super humans, as the term later came to connote.

Task Management

Taylor's task management extended the systematic-management movement that emerged in the nineteenth century as the scale and scope of enterprises grew. It focused on establishing an orderly workflow, determining the quickest and least wasteful means of performing different tasks, training workers in how tasks could be performed more efficiently, and monitoring time, cost, and quality of performance. Time study did not ask workers to do more in the same way, but to use the most appropriate movements and best materials and equipment to meet scientifically determined performance standards.

Taylor defined management as "knowing exactly what you want men to do, and then seeing that they do it in the best and cheapest way." He added that no concise definition could fully describe the art of management, but that "the relations between employers and men form without question the most important part of this art."[24] Taylor saw unevenness in traditional shop management and foremen who lacked the special knowledge necessary to plan, teach, and supervise workers. As a remedy, he purposed that workers be instructed by teachers known as "functional foremen," who would bring specialized knowledge to the workplace.[25] As a foreman at Midvale, Taylor employed assistants to prepare instruction cards and perform other associated clerical duties. Over time, he gave these assistants more and more responsibility and additional duties.

---

[21] *Hearings to Investigate the Taylor System*, vol. 3, p. 1451.

[22] Taylor, *Shop Management*, p. 25.

[23] Copley, *Taylor*, vol. 1, p. 183.

[24] Taylor, *Shop Management*, p. 21.

[25] *Ibid.*, p. 138. The term "foreman" dates to the fourteenth century, originating in the trade guilds of Europe. "In those days when the men wanted to talk to management, there was always someone of mature judgment, probably a little older, a well-skilled man, who could talk a little on his feet. When the men got together, they referred to 'John Anderson, fore'; and he became the foreman; he was the man who came to the fore; therefore, he was a foreman." Testimony of Clarence C. Carlton, Hearings Before the Committee on Military Affairs, U.S. House of Representatives, 78th Congress, 1st sess. on H. R. 2239, H. R. 1742, H. R. 1728, and H. R. 922, *Full Utilization of Manpower*, March 31, 1943 (Washington, DC: Government Printing Office, 1943), p. 104.

The typical manager of this period was not considered much of a planner, and Taylor sought to overcome this shortcoming by creating a planning department.

In the planning department, an "order of work route clerk" determined work flow and the most efficient assignment of workers and machines; and an "instruction card clerk" furnished written information on necessary tools and materials, the prevailing piece rate, performance premium, and other operating directions. A "time and cost clerk" maintained time tickets and recorded the costs associated with each work order; and a "shop disciplinarian" kept a record of each worker's "virtues and defects," served as a "peacemaker," and selected and discharged employees, as necessary.

Taylor realized that this division of responsibilities required that workers were properly trained. He, thus, saw "the necessity of systematically teaching workmen how to work to the best advantage."[26] Taylor sought "expert teachers," chosen for their knowledge, skill, and experience, to become functional foremen. The emphasis was on "teacher" and parenthetically adding a title for their duty: "One of these teachers (called the inspector)" was responsible for output quality; "the second teacher (called the gang boss)" was in charge of all work up to the time it was machined; "the third teacher (called the speed boss)" took over while work was being machined, determined the tools, the required cutting operations, and appropriate machines; and "the fourth teacher (called the repair boss)" was in charge of machinery care and maintenance.[27]

Functional foremen (Figure 7.1) replaced the traditional single foreman with four clerks responsible for planning and four teachers for instructing and monitoring shop performance. Instruction would be individualized: "All workmen engaged in the same kind of work do not require the same amount of individual teaching and attention," depending on aptitude and experience. Taylor added there were opportunities for worker suggestions: "Whenever a workman proposes an improvement, it should be the policy of management to make a careful analysis of the new [proposed] method [and] . . . whenever the new method is markedly superior to the old, it should be adopted [and] . . . the workman should be paid a cash premium for his ingenuity.[28]

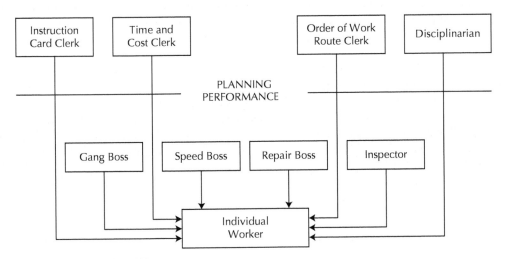

FIGURE 7.1 Taylor's Functional Foremen.
(Adapted from Frank B. and Lillian M. Gilbreth, *Applied Motion Study,* New York: Sturgis & Walton Co., 1917, preceding p. 23.)

---

[26] Taylor, *Principles of Scientific Management*, p. 122.
[27] *Ibid.*, pp. 123–124.
[28] *Ibid.*, pp. 125 and 128.

Functional foremanship was appropriate for exercising specialized knowledge and instructing workers in new methods and motions. It made coordinating different workshop activities more difficult, however, as no one person had responsibility for overall workshop performance. This appears to be a violation of the unity of command principle—that is, no person should report to more than one superior so as to eliminate the possibility of receiving conflicting orders. Taylor believed that this would not generally occur as workers were responsible to only one boss/clerk for each activity. In situations where conflicts did arise, Taylor stipulated that an over-foreman was to be consulted and, if a conflict could not then be settled, an assistant superintendent was to arbitrate any outstanding differences. Where initially this would take time, Taylor held that over time an "unwritten code of laws by which the shop is governed" would be established.[29]

Functional foremanship never became widespread in practice. It offered a limited view of planning, and the unwritten code Taylor believed would develop for shop governance all too often failed to materialize. As functional foremanship has evolved to the present, specialized knowledge is exercised through *functional authority* over specialized tasks rather than over individual workers. The value of staff specialists would be recognized in time, but primarily in assisting general managers to juggle the many demands of a large organization. This would especially be the case when it came to dealing with either specialized areas (such a legal matters) or significant exceptions from planned performance. In this way, those activities requiring specialized knowledge or immediate attention (the "exceptions") can be promptly and knowledgably addressed. The "exception principle" was one of Taylor's more important contributions:

> Under it the manager should receive only condensed, summarized, and *invariably* comparative reports, covering . . . all of the exceptions to past averages or to the standards . . . both the especially good and especially bad exceptions . . . leaving him free to consider broader lines of policy and to study the character and fitness of the important men under him.[30]

Taylor believed that all authority should be based on knowledge, not position or title, and that the exception principle would improve efficiency by allowing managers time to focus on their most pressing and significant concerns over both the long and short term.

Taylor: The Manager and the Consultant

Taylor's years at Midvale Steel had been full: increasing responsibilities and numerous promotions; teaming with his brother-in-law, Clarence M. Clark, to win the inaugural U.S. Natioanl Lawn Tennis Association's amateur doubles championship in 1881 at Newport (RI); a mechanical engineering degree from Stevens Institute in 1883; marriage to Louise M. Spooner in 1884; experiments on cutting metals and machine belting; and developing the essentials of task management all made for a busy 12 years. In 1890, he left Midvale to join the Manufacturing Investment Company (MIC), a paper fiber manufacturer owned by financier J. Pierpont Morgan and other investors.[31] Taylor's experiences as superintendent at MIC's newest mill, in Madison, Maine, were far from satisfactory. Taylor felt that the mill's operational difficulties were due to a new papermaking process it had installed, whereas its owners believed that Taylor lacked the broad executive experience necessary to bring the process online. In May 1893, Taylor resigned

---

[29] *Idem, Shop Management*, pp. 108–109.
[30] *Ibid.*, p. 126.
[31] Daniel Nelson, "Scientific Management in Transition: Frederick W. Taylor at Johnstown, 1896," *Pennsylvania Magazine of History and Biography* 99(4) (October, 1975), pp. 460–475. See also *idem*, "The Making of a Progressive Engineer: Frederick W. Taylor," *Pennsylvania Magazine of History and Biography* 103(4) (October, 1979), pp. 446–466.

from MIC. The Madison mill closed the following month. Taylor expressed contempt for financiers who were interested only in "making money quickly" and had "absolutely no pride of manufacture."[32] Taylor's experience at MIC would not be his last encounter with owners who, in Taylor's opinion, were resistant to change and only interested in an immediate return on their investments. MIC filed for bankruptcy in 1899.

Taylor's contempt for financiers aside, he did come away from MIC with a more complete understanding of managerial accounting and, in particular, managing and reducing business expenses. During Taylor's tenure at MIC, R. Somers Hayes, a former railroad manager, had revamped the company's accounting system and hired William D. Basley, an experienced railroad accountant, to oversee the system. Basley had worked for the Newark and Hudson Railroad, which was controlled by the Erie Railway, where Daniel C. McCallum had developed accounting and reporting systems in the 1850s (see Chapter 5). Taylor was impressed by Hayes's and Basley's methods, which would later form the basis of his own accounting system.[33] With his newly acquired knowledge of accounting and his engineering background, Taylor decided to become a consulting engineer for management.

One of Taylor's clients was the Johnson Company (Johnstown, Pennsylvania). Asked, in 1896, to increase the efficiency of the Steel Motor Works and the Lorain Steel Railway Company, both subsidiaries of the Johnson Company, Taylor developed a system to track the cost of raw materials. He also devised a routing chart showing how all the parts composing the Steel Motor Works' principal product, electrical streetcar motors, were assembled.[34] Taylor worked closely with Tom L. Johnson, the Johnson Company's founder; Arthur J. Moxham, who worked in the company's comptroller's office; and T. Coleman du Pont, company general manager. Moxham, together with Pierre du Pont who was associated with Lorain Steel, later adopted Taylor's cost-accounting system at the E. I. du Pont de Nemours and Company.[35] Alfred D. Chandler has suggested that it is likely that General Electric Company was also influenced by Taylor's cost and routing procedures.[36]

Another of Taylor's clients was Simonds Rolling Machine Company (Fitchburg, Massachusetts), where (in 1897) he conducted experiments in the manufacture of bicycle ball-bearings. In the final stage of the manufacturing process, 120 women inspected ball-bearings for flaws. Over a period of time, Taylor gradually shortened the work day from ten-and-a-half to eight-and-a-half, introduced morning and afternoon rest periods, identified the best inspectors, and put the women on a piecework-pay schedule. The interaction of these changes was complex, and it would be difficult to fix causes and results. The outcome, however, was that 35 women were able to do the work previously done by 120, as output increased from 5 million to 17 million bearings per month, inspection accuracy improved by two-thirds, wages were averaging 80 percent to 100 percent higher for fewer hours, and "each girl was made to feel that she was the object of especial care and interest on the part of management."[37] While at Simonds, Taylor also

---

[32] Copley, *Taylor,* vol. 1, p. 388.

[33] Charles D. Wrege, "Nineteenth Century Origins of 'Bookkeeping under the Taylor System,'" in Kae H. Chung, ed., *Proceedings of the Annual Meeting of the Academy of Management* (1983), pp. 106–110. See also Nelson, *Taylor,* pp. 54–55.

[34] Michael Massouh, "Technological and Managerial Innovation: The Johnson Company, 1883–1889," *Business History Review* 50(1) (Spring 1976), pp. 66–67.

[35] H. Thomas Johnson, "Management Accounting in an Early Integrated Industrial: E. I. Du Pont de Nemours Powder Company, 1903–1912," *Business History Review* 49(2) (Summer 1975), p. 194. See also Rosita S. Chen and Sheng-Der Pan, "Frederick Winslow Taylor's Contributions to Cost Accounting," *Accounting Historian's Journal* 7(2) (Fall 1980), pp. 1–22; Murray C. Wells, "Taylor's Contributions to Cost Accounting: A Comment," *Accounting Historian's Journal* 9(2) (Fall 1980), pp. 69–77.

[36] Alfred D. Chandler, Jr. *The Visible Hand: The Managerial Revolution in American Business* (Cambridge, MA: Belknap Press of Harvard University Press, 1977), p. 430.

[37] Taylor, *Principles of Scientific Management*, pp. 95–96. See also Chris Nyland, "Taylorism and Hours of Work," *Journal of Management History* 1(2) (1995), pp. 8–25.

introduced the Hayes and Basley accounting system to classify expenses, distribute overhead costs, and improve materials handling and control.

Taylor's most challenging and controversial consulting assignment was for the Bethlehem Iron Company in South Bethlehem, Pennsylvania.[38] Taylor came to Bethlehem Iron (later Bethlehem Steel Company) in 1898, at the request of its largest stockholder, Joseph Wharton, who sought Taylor's assistance in decreasing the company's overhead costs and improving its overall efficiency. At the time, Bethlehem's management was under federal investigation for overcharging and price colluding on defense contracts. From Taylor's initial hiring, the company's top managers resented his assertiveness. Taylor felt that many of the top managers were unqualified, having gained their positions due to family connections rather than their ability. After much opposition, Taylor was finally able to convince Bethlehem's owners to reorganize the company, but not without further alienating the company's top managers. These managers, in turn, sought every opportunity to subvert Taylor's efforts.

Taylor established a central planning department, organized a tool crib and parts storeroom, and implemented the cost-accounting system he had developed for Steel Motor Works. To assist in his work, Taylor brought in Sanford E. Thompson, who had probably conducted more time studies than Taylor ever dreamed possible; Henry L. Gantt, who had worked with Taylor at Midvale; Carl G. Barth, a mathematics whiz; Dwight V. Merrick, who became a leading authority on time study; James Gillespie, who had been involved with time studies at Simonds Rolling Machines Company; and J. Maunsell White III, who had earlier helped Taylor with a series of metal-cutting experiments (discussed below).

In 1899, the price of pig iron rose sharply, and Bethlehem promptly sold 10,000 tons from its inventory. Shipping the iron by rail required that it be manually loaded onto gondola cars. The iron had been cast as 92-pound ingots or "pigs." At the time, Taylor and Thompson were preparing a handbook on the elements of work. The required loading provided an opportunity for them to gather information for the handbook on the time required to perform this type of work. Taylor asked James Gillespie and Hartley C. Wolle to collect the desired information. The workers who loaded the pig iron were known as "pig-iron handlers." They were paid a fixed "piece rate" for each ton loaded. Gillespie and Wolle selected 10 of the "very best men" and ordered them to work at "maximum speed." During the first 10-hour day, the workers loaded 75 long-tons each (2,240 pounds = a long ton), filling one gondola car. The tons loaded per day had previously averaged about 12.5 long-tons per worker. Based on these figures, Gillespie and Wolle, factoring in time for unavoidable delays and rest, set a new output standard at 45 long-tons per worker per day. Taylor then set the piece rate at $.0375 per ton, which meant that the first-class worker who met the new 45 long-ton standard would earn $1.85 per day. Because the average flat day rate for a common laborer at Bethlehem was $1.15 per 10-hour day, the new piece rate represented a more than 60 percent increase in pay.

Taylor used the pig-iron-handling story to illustrate the savings that could come from carefully examining even menial jobs. On June 4, 1907, a stenographer was hired to record a talk Taylor gave at his home, Boxly, in Chestnut Hill (Pennsylvania). Taylor described how he selected one of the pig handlers for Gillespie and Wolle to study: "I picked out a Pennsylvania Dutchman . . . and said 'Noll are you a high priced man?'"[39] Henry Knolle (later changed to Noll) became the focal point of Taylor's comments on how to secure higher performance by paying workers on a "piece rate." Noll was then 27 years old, 5 feet 7 in. tall, weighed 135 pounds. He was singled out

[38] Daniel Nelson, "Taylorism and the Workers at Bethlehem Steel, 1898–1901," *Pennsylvania Magazine of History and Biography* 101(4) (October, 1977), pp. 487–505.

[39] Charles D. Wrege, "F. W. Taylor's Lecture on Management, 4 June 1907, an Introduction," *Journal of Management History* 1(1) (1995), pp. 4–7; the stenographer's transcript follows on pp. 8–32.

because he had been observed trotting "back home for a mile or so after his work in the evening . . . [and was known as someone who placed] a very high value on a dollar."[40]

When *The Principles of Scientific Management* was published, Noll became "Schmidt" in Taylor's account of how the Pennsylvania Dutchman was convinced to load 47.5 tons of pig iron per day. Although the story of Schmidt has entered the management literature as an example of Taylor's scientific study of work, its veracity has been challenged. Wrege and Perroni examined various versions of Taylor's story, as well as a report prepared by Gillespie and Wolle, and noted numerous discrepancies. Among these discrepancies were the reasons for Bethlehem selling pig iron from its inventory, the amount to be loaded, the method of loading, the number of pig-iron handlers, how the workers were selected, and so on. Wrege and Perroni reached the conclusion that the Schmidt story was, to borrow their phrase, a "pig-tale," an embellishment by Taylor of the truth.[41] Over the years, evidence has mounted to suggest that, as judged by Barth, Taylor "greatly exaggerated what had been accomplished at Bethlehem."[42]

Taylor's intent may have been to use pig-iron handling to illustrate the application of scientific management to even menial jobs requiring only physical labor, but he omitted facts that more fully conveyed what actually occurred. As reported by Gillespie and Wolle, there were three "first-class" workers, not one. Joseph Auer and Simon Conrad joined Noll in this elite group. At times, Conrad loaded more tons than Noll: on June 1, 1899, 70.7 long-tons for Conrad, 48 long-tons for Noll; on June 2, 1899, 55.7 long-tons for Conrad, 68.3 for Noll; and on June 3, 1899, 70.9 long-tons for Conrad, 39.7 for Noll, and 30.1 long-tons for Auer. The story of Schmidt, as told by Cooke and retold by Taylor, oversimplified what actually occurred at Bethlehem, but made the power of Taylor's methods more memorable. Some may think that Auer, Conrad, and Noll were exploited, working day in and day out to achieve the new piece rate. They, however, never worked more than three days without going back to a flat day-rate. Indeed, for the duration of the pig-iron study, March 10 to May 31, 1899, records indicate that Conrad and Noll worked a total of 36 days on the new piece rate and 41 on the flat day-rate.[43]

Although Taylor referred frequently to the pig-iron study as a success, its design was less than ideal, making it difficult to draw firm conclusions regarding the effects of the new piece rate. Gillespie and Wolle arbitrarily set a 40 percent time allowance for rests and delays; Taylor likewise did so for the per-ton piece rate; and Noll and the other pig-iron handlers studied were not randomly selected. Even so, the results were impressive: labor costs fell from $.072 per ton under a flat day-rate to $.033 per ton under a piecework schedule; and the pig-iron handlers averaged a 60 percent increase in wages.

Despite Taylor's success in reducing Bethlehem's labor expenses, its top managers continued to oppose his other efforts, especially his cost-accounting system. Writing in September, 1898, Taylor described the system he was introducing at Bethlehem as "in general the modern railroad

---

[40] Taylor, *Principles of Scientific Management*, pp. 43–44. See also James Gillespie and H. C. Wolle, "Report on the Establishment of Piecework in Connection with the Loading of Pig Iron, at the Works of the Bethlehem Iron Co., South Bethlehem, PA," June 17, 1899, Frederick Winslow Taylor Collection, Samuel C. Williams Library, Stevens Institute of Technology, Hoboken, NJ, Files 32A and 32J.

[41] Charles D. Wrege and Amadeo G. Perroni, "Taylor's Pig-Tale: A Historical Analysis of Frederick W. Taylor's Pig-Iron Experiment," *Academy of Management Journal* 17 (March 1974), pp. 6–26. Later, Wrege and Greenwood, in *Taylor*, p. 102, wrote that the "pig-tale" was "prepared by Taylor's assistant, Morris L. Cooke." The mystery remains: the penmanship was Cooke's, but were the words Cooke's or Taylor's? See also Charles D. Wrege and Regina Ebert Greenwood, "Frederick W. Taylor's "Pig Iron Loading Observations" at Bethlehem, March 10. 1899–May 31, 1899: The Real Story," *Canal History and Technology Proceedings* 17 (1998), pp. 159–201; Charles D. Wrege and Beulah M. Wrege, "Searching For the Insignificant: Thirty-Eight Years of Successful Historical Research in Bethlehem, Pennsylvania, and Elsewhere: 1957–1995," *Canal History and Technology Proceedings* 23 (2004), pp. 155–212.

[42] Letter from Carl G. Barth to L. Arthur Sylvester, December 21, 1925, Charles D. Wrege Research Papers, 1925–2013, Box 6, Folder 65, Kheel Center for Labor-Management Documentation and Archives, Cornell University Library. See also Kanigel, *The One Best Way*, p. 397.

[43] Charles D. Wrege and Richard M. Hodgetts, "Frederick W. Taylor's 1899 Pig Iron Observations: Examining Fact, Fiction, and Lessons for the New Millennium," *Academy of Management Journal* 43(6) (December 2000), p. 1287.

system of accounting adapted and modified to suit the manufacturing business."[44] This was the Hayes–Basley accounting system that Taylor had learned at MIC and adapted and applied in various companies. Taylor abhorred the futility of postmortem accounting that provided annual, semiannual, or monthly reports that were received too late for managerial action. At Bethlehem, he moved the cost-accounting function to the new planning department he had established. The planning department generated cost figures coincident with daily operations reports. Costs then became an integral part of daily planning and control, not a subject for analysis long after they had been incurred. The system was effective, in fact, so much so that Bethlehem's top managers tried to stop its implementation. Apparently they did not care for an accurate and timely appraisal of their performance. Taylor eventually lost in his struggle to introduce improved managerial methods at Bethlehem and his consulting contract was terminated in 1901.[45]

Taylor: The Peripatetic Philosopher

Fred and Louise Taylor were unable to have children of their own. In 1901, 17 years after their marriage, and when Fred was 45 years old, a tragedy in Savannah (Georgia) left four children of the Aiken family without parents. The Aikens were relatives of Mrs. Taylor's, and she and Fred adopted three of the children: Kempton, Robert, and Elizabeth. A fourth child, Conrad, was older and did not join the Taylor family—he later became a Pulitzer Prize–winning poet and a literary critic.[46] The Taylors and their new family moved from South Bethlehem to Germantown, Pennsylvania, while they awaited the construction of their Chestnut Hill home, Boxly, where another stage in Taylor's career would begin.

At Midvale and Bethlehem, Taylor demonstrated his talents as an inventor and mechanical engineer. He developed and patented a steel hammer (for forging steel plates), numerous machine tools such as grinders and boring and turning mills (lathes), and, with J. Maunsell White III, a process for cutting metal with high speed, "self-hardening" steel-cutting tools. The Taylor–White process was patented in 1900, and Taylor's share of the royalties amounted to some $50,000 before the patent was nullified in 1909.[47]

As Taylor's notoriety spread, he gained disciples, and task management was installed at other companies, including James Mapes Dodge at the Link-Belt Engineering Company, and Wilfred Lewis at the Tabor Manufacturing Company, a manufacturer of molding machines. In his spare

---

[44] Frederick W. Taylor quoted in Copley, *Taylor*, vol. 1, p. 364 and vol. 2, p. 142.

[45] It has also been noted that Taylor prompted further top-management opposition as his time studies led to a 25 percent reduction in the Bethlehem workforce, thereby, depopulating the surrounding community. As a result, Bethlehem's top managers, who owned rental houses and most of the local stores, were upset because "what was gained in the factory" was "lost in the city." See Stéphane Castonguay, "Engineering and Its Discontents: Taylorism, Unions, and Employers," *Social Epistemology* 7(3) (1993), pp. 301–302.

[46] John A. Bromer, J. Myron Johnson, and Richard P. Widdicombe, "A Conversation with Robert P. A. Taylor: Interview Conducted in Providence, Rhode Island, October 14 and 15, 1976," Chapter 2, pp. 1–3, typescript dated July, 1978, Frederick Winslow Taylor Collection, Samuel C. Williams Library, Stevens Institute of Technology, Hoboken, NJ. For details on the aforementioned tragedy, see "Killed Wife and Himself," *New York Times* (February 28, 1901), p. 1.

[47] Thomas J. Misa, *A Nation of Steel* (Baltimore, MD: Johns Hopkins University Press, 1995), pp. 197–198, 204–205. For White's unsung contribution to the Taylor-White process, see Christopher P. Neck and Arthur G. Bedeian, "Frederick W. Taylor, J. Maunsell White III, and the Matthew Effect: The Rest of the Story," *Journal of Management History* 2(1) (1996), pp. 20–25. See also Charles D. Wrege, Ronald G. Greenwood, and Ti Hsu, "Frederick W. Taylor's Early Work at Bethlehem Steel Company: First Phase; 1898–1899 – Some Insights," *Canal History and Technology Proceedings*, 12 (1993), pp. 102–138; *Idem,* "Frederick W. Taylor's Work at Bethlehem Steel, Phase II, The Discovery of High-Speed Tool Steel, 1898, Was It An Accident?," *Canal History and Technology Proceedings*, 13 (1994), pp. 115–161; *Idem,* "Frederick W. Taylor's at Bethlehem Steel, Phase III: Sale of the "Taylor-White' Patent and the Initiation of the High Speed Steel Patent Suit: 1902–1905," *Canal History and Technology Proceedings*, 14 (1995), pp. 105–127; *Idem,* "Frederick W. Taylor at Bethlehem Steel Company, Phase IV: The High-Speed Steel Patent Suit, 1906–1908," *Canal History and Technology Proceedings*, 15 (1993), pp. 125–164; and Charles D. Wrege, Ronald G. Greenwood, and Regina Ebert Greenwood, "A New Method of Discovering Primary Management History: Two Examples Where 'Little Things Mean a Lot'," *Journal of Management History*, 1997, 3(1), pp. 59–92.

time, Taylor landscaped and renovated Boxly, developed new mixtures for soils to improve golf greens, and designed golf clubs. He received a patent for a putter with a Y shaft, experimented with lengths and thicknesses of golf-club shafts, and spent a great deal of time on the links, or, more euphemistically, in experimentation. He had taken up golf at age 40 (in 1896), and his skills developed rapidly; he played to an eight handicap and won the men's championship at the Philadelphia Country Club in 1902, 1903, and 1905.[48]

In 1906, Taylor was elected president of the ASME. His fame was growing, and those who were to spread Taylor's message increased in numbers. Henry-Louis Le Chatelier, H. King Hathaway, Morris L. Cooke, Frank B. Gilbreth, and others we will discuss were joining the earlier followers Gantt, Barth, and Thompson.

Asked to teach a course at what was to become the Harvard University Graduate School of Business Administration, Taylor refused, saying that task management could be learned only in practice. Professor Edwin Gay, soon to be dean of the school, told Taylor that the course on scientific management would be taught with or without him, period. Taylor succumbed, although he was never entirely happy about teaching his system in a classroom. Taylor was not against business education, but believed that experience was the only way to learn his methods. His Harvard lectures began in 1909 and were given each winter through 1914.[49] Taylor never accepted a penny of reimbursement for his lectures, not even for traveling expenses.

The Eastern Rate Case

Taylor also found task management getting some extraordinary free publicity. The Boston lawyer Louis D. Brandeis, later an Associate U.S. Supreme Court Justice, was becoming known in the early twentieth century as "the people's lawyer."[50] In 1910, when a group of railways operating north of the Ohio and Potomac rivers and east of the Mississippi (known collectively as the Eastern railroads) asked the Interstate Commerce Commission (ICC) for a hike in freight rates to cover investments in permanent improvements such as stations, tunnels, and bridges.[51] Brandeis took up the cause of the shippers (banded together as the Commercial Organizations of the Atlantic Seaboard) who would be affected by the proposed increase. In doing so, he brought about an unusual series of hearings, known as the Eastern Rate Case, which thrust Taylor's task management into the public eye.

Earlier in 1910, Cooke and Taylor had submitted a paper, "The Philosophy of Management," to the ASME Meeting Committee. Cooke recalled Taylor had used the phrase "scientific management" in his Boxly talks and in a paper "Shop Management" he delivered at the 1903 ASME meeting, and suggested that Taylor consider changing the title of their paper to "The Principles of Scientific Management."[52] Taylor responded positively: "As to the title our paper . . . 'The Principles of Scientific Management' sounds less bombastic and pretentious. I am afraid the word 'philosophy' in the title will tend to make the thing sound rather high-falutin."[53]

---

[48] Shannon G. Taylor and Arthur G. Bedeian, "From Boardroom to Bunker: How Fred Taylor Changed the Game of Golf Forever," *Management & Organizational History*, 2(3) (2007), pp. 195–218. Taylor was an avid sportsman who also participated in baseball, rowing, skating, gymnastics, cricket, and croquet. See *idem*, "The Fred Taylor Baseball Myth: A Son Goes to Bat for His Father." *Journal of Management History* 14(3) (2008), pp. 294–298.

[49] Frederick W. Taylor, "An Outline of the Organization of a Manufacturing Establishment under Modern Scientific or Task Management," a lecture given at Harvard University, Boston, 1909–1914. Reprinted in Sasaki Tsuneo and Daniel A. Wren, ed., *Intellectual Legacy of Management Theory*, ser. 2, pt. 2, vol. 2 (London; Pickering and Chatto, 2002), pp. 259–303.

[50] Oscar Kraines, "Brandeis and Scientific Management," *Publications of the American Jewish Historical Society* 41(1) (September 1951), pp. 41–60.

[51] On this point, see Keith D. Revell, *Building Gotham: Civic Culture and Public Policy in New York City, 1898–1938* (Baltimore, MD: Johns Hopkins University Press, 2003), pp. 64–69.

[52] Letter from Morris L. Cooke to Frederick W. Taylor, March 27, 1910. Frederick Winslow Taylor Collection, Samuel C. Williams Library, Stevens Institute of Technology, Hoboken, NJ.

[53] Letter from Taylor to Cooke, March 29, 1910, Frederick Winslow Taylor Collection, Samuel C. Williams Library, Stevens Institute of Technology, Hoboken, NJ.

The ICC began public hearings on August 15, 1910, at the Waldorf-Astoria Hotel in New York City. As the shippers' counsel, Brandeis recalled his previous work in 1903 for the W. H. McElwain Company of Boston, a shoe manufacturer that professed to being guided by Taylor's efficiency methods.[54] Brandeis subsequently read Taylor's 1903 ASME paper and "studied the series of articles by Harrington Emerson in the *American Engineer and Railroad Journal* in 1906 on the application efficiency methods in the locomotive repair shops of the Atchison, Topeka, and Santa Fe Railroad" in preparing his brief in the Eastern Rate Case.[55]

In October, Brandeis visited Taylor at the home of Taylor's mother-in-law, Mrs. Edward A. Spooner, in Plymouth, Massachusetts. He subsequently requested a list of "all the different kinds of businesses into which scientific management had (to a greater or less extent) been introduced."[56] Taylor responded with a list of "the various kinds of work to which the principles of scientific management have been applied."[57] On November 1, James Mapes Dodge gave Brandeis a tour of the Link-Belt Company, one of the better known applications of Taylor's ideas.[58] Brandeis subsequently met with Cooke, who reported to Taylor: "I dined with him [Brandeis] Tuesday [November 8] and explained to him the situation in regard to scientific management in those establishments with which I am familiar. He asked me to testify, and I declined, on the ground of being too busy."[59]

Thus, Brandeis was well acquainted with the phrase "scientific management" when on November 20 he met with a group of Taylor followers and prospective Eastern Rate Case witnesses at the Great Northern Hotel in New York City. Henry v. Riper Scheel was present at the meeting and noted Brandeis "repeatedly used the term 'scientific management' and this established the appellation as standard thereafter."[60] In a later correspondence with Horace B. Drury, Brandeis, however, noted:

> The term "scientific management" was not adopted as synonymous with the Taylor system, but as expressing the fundamental conception of the new movement, to which Mr. Taylor's contribution was of course greater than any other.
>
> It seemed to me important that all differences between the various advocates of efficiency should be eliminated, and some term be adopted to express the new idea which was common to them all; and

---

[54] Horace B. Drury, *Scientific Management: A History and Criticism* (New York: Columbia University, 1915), p. 17 references Brandeis's retainer with the W. H. McElwain Company. Edward L. Prescott, McElwain Company Treasurer, discussed the manufacturer's experiences with Taylor's methods at the Amos Tuck Conference in 1911. See *Addresses and Discussion at the Conference on Scientific Management Held October 12, 13, 14 Nineteen Hundred Eleven*, Hanover, NH, Dartmouth Press, 1911, pp. 204–214.

[55] Oscar Kraines, "Brandeis' Philosophy of Scientific Management," *Western Political Quarterly*, vol. 13(1), March, 1960, p. 192.

[56] Letter from Louis D. Brandeis to Taylor, October 26, 1910, Item 098J001, Frederick W. Taylor Digital Collection, Samuel C. Williams Library, Stevens Institute of Technology, Hoboken, NJ. Accessible at http://stevens.cdmhost.com/cdm/compound object/collection/p4100coll1/id/472/rec/1

[57] Letter from Taylor to Brandeis, November 4, 1910, Item 098J004, Frederick W. Taylor Digital Collection, Samuel C. Williams Library, Stevens Institute of Technology, Hoboken, NJ. Accessible at http://stevens.cdmhost.com/cdm/compoundobject/collection/p4100coll1/id/478/rec/36

[58] Letter from James Mapes Dodge to Taylor, November 3, 1910, Item 098J007, Frederick W. Taylor Digital Collection, Samuel C. Williams Library, Stevens Institute of Technology, Hoboken, NJ Frederick W. Taylor Digital Collection. Accessible at http://stevens.cdmhost.com/cdm/singleitem/collection/p4100coll1/id/481/rec/1

[59] Letter from Morris L. Cooke to Taylor, November 10, 1910, Item 098J011, Frederick W. Taylor Digital Collection, Samuel C. Williams Library, Stevens Institute of Technology, Hoboken, NJ. Accessible at http://stevens.cdmhost.com/cdm/compound object/collection/p4100coll1/id/512/rec/1

[60] Henry van Riper Scheel, "Some Reflections of Henry Laurence Gantt," *Journal of Industrial Engineering*, 12 (May–June, 1961), p. 221. In addition to Scheel and Brandeis, the meeting was attended by Gantt, Gilbreth, and Robert T. Kent. It should be noted that U.S. Navy Commander Holden A. Evans used the term "scientific management" in *The American Machinist* 3 months before this October 1910 meeting. In doing so, he suggested that the term was already in general use: "The term 'scientific management' is now generally accepted as referring to the type of management advocated by Fred W. Taylor and those who have been associated with him." See Evans, "Scientific Factory Management," *American Machinist* 33 (June 16, 1910), p. 1108. For more on Evans, who in his own words "had become a worshiper at the Taylor shrine," see his *One Man's Fight for a Better Navy* (New York: Dodd, Mead & Company), p. 182.

I asked all who were to be witnesses to agree on this subject. Several names, like "Taylor System", "Functional Management", "Shop Management" and "Efficiency" were proposed. It seemed to me that the only term which would properly describe the movement and also appeal to the imagination, was "Scientific Management", and as I recall it all present were ultimately unanimous in the adoption of that term.[61]

At the hearings, H. King Hathaway testified that scientific management had increased workers' wages at the Tabor Manufacturing Company; Dodge gave evidence of progress at the Link-Belt Company; and Frank B. Gilbreth vouched that scientific management could be used in a union shop. It was Harrington Emerson's November 22 testimony, however, that sensationalized the hearings. Emerson had developed "standard unit costs" for the Atchison, Topeka & Santa Fe Railroad; comparing the costs of other railroads with these standards, he estimated that by adopting Taylor's methods the railroads could annually eliminate $240 million in labor costs and cut $60 million in materials and maintenance expenses.[62] His calculations were complex, overlooked differences among various railroads, never examined the question of whether Taylor's methods could be applied to all shipping, and may have been presented for effect. Regardless of these potential limitations, Emerson's testimony stunned the popular press and was reported in the next morning's papers.[63] When Taylor was asked about Emerson's $300 million annual savings, he replied:

I believe we can save a million dollars a day, just as he said we can, but the reports of these hearings in Washington were not quite fair enough to say that it can't be done all at once. It would take four or five years.[64]

The phrase "scientific management" caught on with the press and overnight Taylor gained worldwide audience. The hearings, with the decision going against the railroads on the basis that investments in permanent improvements could not be considered as operating expenses for setting freights rates, concluded that it was too early to judge the merits of scientific management.[65] Nevertheless, the resulting widespread publicity popularized Taylor's ideas. Within 24 hours, scientific management, earlier an obscure technology developed by a relatively unknown engineer, became international news. Although Taylor had not testified, most of Brandeis's witnesses identified him to be their teacher. Taylor became a national hero overnight. Newspaper and magazines published dozens of articles about his work. This publicity and the publication of Taylor's

---

[61] Letter from Brandeis to Horace B. Drury, January 13, 1914, reprinted in Louis D. Brandeis, *Letters of Louis D. Brandeis*, vol. 3, eds, Melvin I. Urofsky and David W. Levy (Albany, NY: State University of New York, 1973), pp. 240–241.

[62] *Evidence Taken by the Interstate Commerce Commission in the Matter of Proposal Advances in Freight Rates by Carriers*, Senate Document 725, 61st Cong., 3rd sess., vol. 4 (Washington, DC: U.S. Government Printing Office, 1911), pp. 2829–2830, 2836. See also Louis D. Brandeis, *Scientific Management and Railroads: Being part of a Brief Submitted to the Interstate Commerce Commission* (New York: Engineering Magazine, 1911), pp. 83–86.

[63] See, for example "All Scoff at Brandeis: Officials Say Railroads Are Economically Managed," *New York Times* (November 23, 1910), p. 4 and "Invite Brandeis to Manage Their Roads: Westerners Wire Lawyer to Name His Salary if He Can Save $300,000,000," *New York Times* (November 24, 1910), p. 8. See also "Railways Can Save $300,000,000 a Year," *New York Times* (November 16, 1910), p. 10.

[64] Frederick W. Taylor, "The Conservation of Human Effort," *City Club Bulletin* [City Club of Philadelphia] 4(1) (January 18, 1911), pp. 35–36.

[65] Having lost their 1910–1911 bid for a hike in freight rates, the Eastern Railroads filed a new second petition on May 14, 1913, asking for an average five per cent increase. Rather than representing either the railroads or shippers, Brandeis was retained, as special counsel, by the ICC "to undertake the task of seeing all sides and angles of the case are presented of record." Letter from James S. Harlan (ICC Commissioner) to Brandeis, August 15, 1913, reprinted in *Nomination of Louis D. Brandeis: Hearings on the Nomination of Louis D. Brandeis to be an Associate Justice of the Supreme Court of the United States before the Subcommittee of the Senate Commission on the Judiciary*, 64th Congress, 1st Session (1916), p. 158. The railroads' second petition for a rate advance was partially approved with Brandeis's concurrence. See "Willard Cheered by Rate Decision," *New York Times* (December 31, 1914), p. 13.

book *The Principles of Scientific Management*, in 1911, gave a new impetus to his campaign for efficiency. Within 2 years of publication, his book was translated into French, German, Dutch, Swedish, Russian, Italian, Spanish, and Japanese. Conferences were held and societies formed to study Taylor's work.

On the other hand, labor unions, especially the machinists' union and various railway brotherhoods, opposed all aspects of Taylor's methods, especially time study. Labor leaders characterized Taylor's piece-rate pay plan as a return to "sweat shop" exploitation. Moreover, they feared Taylor's more efficient methods would lead to layoffs of unnecessary workers. Organized labor had struggled long and hard to grow its membership, and it instinctively assumed that anything new originating in management was for ownership's advantage and labor's disadvantage. Taylor tried to counter labor opposition by expressing support for unions:

> We welcome the cooperation of the unions and will pay them for their cooperation; we welcome it and want it. We want their help. . . . I never look for the unions to go out. I am heartily in favor of combinations of men. I do not look for a great modification in the principles of unions as they now exist; they are of necessity largely now fighting organizations; I look for educational institutions, for mutual and helpful institutions; I look for great modifications, but never for the abolition of them. I simply look for a change, that the union shall conform itself to this new idea, the idea of a standard that is over all of us, and a set of laws that will be over all sides.[66]

Picking up on this theme shortly before his death, Taylor called for unions and management to join together in achieving better wages and working conditions. To this end, he stated: "Any company that has any sense at all would be delighted to have the union appoint an expert and the company would be willing to pay the wages." To this, he added:

> If the unions will take up the education of their members, it will be a step in the right direction. They will have to take this step before we can co-operate with them. Instead of preparing for war they must try to promote working conditions which render possible higher wages.
>
> The unions have done an immense amount of good. Unions have made better working conditions. They have stopped great injustices in the trades and for that they deserve commendation. Because a man points out that they are doing a few things that are wrong it does not mean that he does not tolerate anything that they are doing.[67]

Because Taylor firmly believed that his methods were objective, he never fully comprehended organized labor's hostility toward scientific management. Moreover, he pointed out that efficient methods such as those he proposed had historically increased employment, not reduced it. Nevertheless, for a company to introduce scientific management was to invite labor trouble.

Watertown and the Congressional Investigation

The 1910 ICC hearings thrust Fred Taylor and scientific management into the limelight, but there were also unanticipated repercussions. At the time of the hearings, Taylor was introducing his methods at the Brooklyn Navy Yard and at the U.S. Army's Ordnance Department. Despite repeated attempts, his efforts at the Navy Yard were largely unsuccessful, as the naval bureaucracy

---

[66] *Industrial Relations, Final Report and Testimony Submitted to Congress by the Commission on Industrial Relations*, vol. 1 (Washington, DC: U.S. Government Printing Office, 1916), pp. 789 and 810.
[67] Frederick W. Taylor, "Scientific Management and Labor Unions," *Bulletin of the Society to Promote the Science of Management* 1(1) (December 1914), p. 3.

rejected his methods.[68] In contrast, Major General William Crozier, Chief of the U.S. Army's Ordnance Department, had read Taylor's work and saw its applicability to military arsenals.[69] In early 1911, Crozier selected the arsenals at Watertown, Massachusetts, and Rock Island, Illinois, as sites to test Taylor's methods. In protest, James O'Connell, president of the International Association of Machinists (IAM), in a circular sent to all IAM lodges, railed against time studies, saying they reduced workers to virtual slavery.[70] The IAM was especially objected to rewarding workers based on output, as it believed doing so fostered a rivalry that pitted young against old, with the latter seen as expendable. The IAM opposed Taylor's methods in both governmental and nongovernmental applications.

Taylor advised Crozier to install scientific management at Watertown despite the resistance at Rock Island, but cautioned him to do so carefully, step by step, including first sounding out worker sentiments in each department. Barth attempted to follow Taylor's advice, but trouble started when Dwight V. Merrick, who was assisting Barth, began to use a stopwatch to time the procedures used by the arsenal's molders, who casted the molds used to make shell casings. One of the molders refused to allow Merrick to time his work, citing "the organization" (the IAM) as the reason for his refusal. Lt. Colonel Charles B. Wheeler, the arsenal's commanding officer, explained to the worker why the stopwatch timing was necessary. The worker again refused and was discharged for "refusal to obey orders."[71] In sympathy, the arsenal's other molders likewise refused. In August, 1911, the first strike opposing the installation of scientific management occurred at the Watertown Arsenal. Taylor attributed the strike to a mistake in tactics: the sentiments of the molders had not been examined, nor had they been briefed on the purposes of the time study. Taylor did not fault the molders or the IAM, but blamed a premature attempt to time various jobs without following his recommendation to consult workers first before beginning any time studies. Moreover, as was Taylor's practice prior to conducting any time studies, the arsenal had not yet been reorganized following his methods. The molders returned to work after 1 week and offered no further resistance.

After the strike, however, the IAM petitioned Congress to investigate the arsenal workers' complaints alleging inferior working conditions and humiliating treatment.[72] As a consequence, the U.S. House of Representatives appointed a special committee to investigate what it called "the Taylor system." The committee consisted of William B. Wilson, a former official of the United Mine Workers Union, who had joined the union at the age of 11, then chair of the House Labor Committee and later Secretary of Labor under President Woodrow Wilson; William C. Redfield, a manufacturer who later became Secretary of Commerce under Wilson; and John Q. Tilson, the only Republican member, as an umpire.

The hearings began in October 1911 and lasted through February 1912. Taylor spent 12 hours, scattered over 4 days, testifying before the committee. As Copley stated, "Terrorism was in the air," as organized labor set out to harass Taylor.[73] The hearing transcripts illustrate the hostility and sharpness in both questions and answers. For example, following a series of questions and discussion about the effect of scientific management on worker displacement, the following clash erupted over Taylor's definition of a "first-class man":

---

[68] Peter B. Petersen, "Fighting for a Better Navy: An Attempt at Scientific Management (1905–1912)," *Journal of Management* 16(1) (March 1990), pp. 151–166.

[69] *Idem*, "The Pioneering Efforts of Major General William Crozier (1855–1942) in the Field of Management," *Journal of Management* 15(3), 1989, pp. 503–516.

[70] James O'Connell, "Official Circular No. 12," Office of the International President, International Association of Machinists, April 26, 1911, Washington, DC. Reprinted in *Hearings to Investigate the Taylor System*, vol. 2, pp. 1222–1223.

[71] Copley, *Taylor*, vol. 2, p. 344.

[72] Hugh G. J. Aitken, *Scientific Management in Action: Taylorism at Watertown Arsenal, 1908–1915* (Princeton, NJ: Princeton University Press, 1985).

[73] Copley, *Taylor*, vol. 2, p. 347.

THE CHAIRMAN [MR. WILSON]. Is it not true that a man who is not a good workman and who may not be responsible for the fact that he is not a good workman, has to live as well as the man who is a good workman?

MR. TAYLOR. Not as well as the other workman; otherwise, that would imply that all those in the world were entitled to live equally well whether they worked or whether they were idle, and that certainly is not the case. Not as well.

THE CHAIRMAN. Under scientific management, then, you propose that because a man is not in the first class as a workman that there is no place in the world for him—if he is not in the first class in some particular line that this must be destroyed and removed?

MR. TAYLOR. Mr. Chairman, would it not be well for me to describe what I mean by a "first-class" workman. I have written a good deal about "first-class" workmen in my books, and I find there is quite a general misapprehension as to the use of that term "first-class."

THE CHAIRMAN. Before you come to a definition of what you consider a "first-class" workman I would like to have your concept of how you are going to take care, under your scientific management, of a man who is not a "first-class" workman in some particular line?

MR. TAYLOR. I can not [sic] answer that question until I define what I mean by "first-class." You and I may have a totally different idea as to the meaning of these words, and therefore I suggest that you allow me to state what I mean.

THE CHAIRMAN. The very fact that you specify "first-class" would indicate that in your mind you would have some other class than "first-class."

MR. TAYLOR. If you will allow me to define it I think I can make it clear.

THE CHAIRMAN. You said a "first-class" workman can be taken care of under normal conditions. That is what you have already said. Now, the other class that is in your mind, other than "first-class," how does your system propose to take care of them?

MR. TAYLOR. Mr. Chairman, I can not [sic] answer that question. I cannot answer any question relating to "first-class" workmen until you know my definition of that term, because I have used these words technically throughout my paper, and I am not willing to answer a question you put about "first-class" workmen with the assumption that my answer applies to all I have said in my book.

THE CHAIRMAN. You yourself injected the term "first-class" by saying that you did not know of a condition in normal times when a "first-class" workman could not find employment.

MR. TAYLOR. I do not think I used that term "first-class."

Mr. REDFIELD. Mr. Chairman, the witness has now four times, I think, said that until he is allowed to define what he means by "first-class" no answer can be given, because he means one thing by the words "first-class" and he thinks that you mean another thing.

THE CHAIRMAN. My question has nothing whatever to do with the definition of the words "first-class." It has to do with the other class than "first-class" not with "first-class." A definition of "first-class" will in no manner contribute to a proper reply to my question, because I am not asking about "first-class," but the other than "first-class" workmen.

MR. TAYLOR. I can not [sic] describe the others until I have described what I mean by "first-class."

Mr. REDFIELD. As I was saying when I was interrupted, the witness had stated that he cannot answer the question for the reason that the language that the chairman uses, namely, the words "first-class" do not mean the same thing in the Chairman's mind that they mean in the witness's mind, and he asks the privilege of defining what they do mean, so that the language shall be mutually intelligible. Now, it seems to me, and I think it is good law and entirely proper, that the witness ought to be permitted to define his meaning; and then if, after his definition is made, there is any misunderstanding, we can proceed.[74]

Then committee chairman Wilson, Redfield, and Tilson engaged in a spirited discussion of whether or not Taylor should be allowed to define his terms; Redfield and Tilson prevailed, and Taylor proceeded to explain his use of the term "first-class" and concluded:

> . . . among every class of workmen we have some balky workmen – I do not mean men who are unable to work, but men who, physically well able to work, are simply lazy, and who through no amount of teaching and instructing and through no amount of kindly treatment, can be brought into the "first class." That is the man whom I call "second class." They have the physical possibility of being "first class," but they obstinately refuse to do so.
>
> Now, Mr. Chairman, I am ready to answer your question, having clearly in mind that I have these two types of "second-class" men in view; the one which is physically able to do the work, but who refused to do it—and the other who is not physically or mentally fitted to do that particular job. These are the two types of "second-class" men.
>
> THE CHAIRMAN. Then, how does scientific management propose to take care of men who are not "first-class" men in any particular line of work?
>
> MR. TAYLOR. I give it up.
>
> THE CHAIRMAN. Scientific management has no place for such men?
>
> MR. TAYLOR. Scientific management has no use for a bird that can sing and won't sing.
>
> THE CHAIRMAN. I am not speaking about birds at all.
>
> MR. TAYLOR. No man who can work and won't work has any place under scientific management.
>
> THE CHAIRMAN. It is not a question of a man who can work and won't work; it is a question of a man who is not a "first class" man in any one particular line, according to your own definition.
>
> MR. TAYLOR. I do not know of any such line of work. For each man some line can be found in which he is first class.[75]

In another instance, Taylor was being questioned by John R. O'Leary (third vice president of the International Molders' Union of North America) on fines that had been levied against workers at Midvale Steel:

> MR. O'LEARY. Did I understand you to say that you had the permission and cooperation of the men in putting in that system?
>
> MR. TAYLOR. Yes . . . they ran it, invested the funds, took care of the sick; they furnished the doctor and the nurse. . . .
>
> MR. O'LEARY. What did they charge the men who were injured, for the doctor?
>
> MR. TAYLOR. Not a cent. The services were all free.
>
> MR. O'LEARY. Are you aware that there have been many suits instituted against the Midvale Steel Company to recover those fines, and that they were recovered?

---

[74] *Hearings to Investigate the Taylor System*, vol. 3, pp. 1452–1453.
[75] *Ibid.*, vol. 3, pp. 1455–1456.

MR. TAYLOR. No; I am not aware of it.

MR. O'LEARY. Are you aware that men are fined a dollar for going to the urinal?

MR. TAYLOR. I have not the slightest idea that is true. Who ever [sic] said that told an untruth. Nothing of that kind was done while I was there.[76]

No support for O'Leary's charges ever appeared in any other testimony. As Ida M. Tarbell, one of the leading "muckrakers" of her day, declared:

> One of the most sportsmanlike exhibits the country ever saw was Mr. Taylor's willingness to subject himself to the heckling and the badgering of labour leaders, congressmen, and investigators of all degrees of misunderstanding, suspicion and ill will. To a man of his temperament and highly trained intellect, who had given a quarter of a century of the hardest kind of toil to develop useful truths, the kind of questioning to which he was sometimes subjected must have been maddening.[77]

Coming from Tarbell, this was quite a compliment. Baited, insulted, and made to appear a beast, Taylor staggered from the stand at the close of his testimony. Taylor's pride was sorely wounded, his lifework reviled before a congressional committee. At one point, it appeared as if Taylor and his organized-labor opponents would come to blows. The ensuing exchange was so heated that it was struck from the record.[78] There was no victory for anyone in the committee's final report. Phrased in political double-talk, the report said that it was too early "to determine with accuracy their [Taylor's and other scientific management systems'] effect on the health and pay of employees and their effect on wages and labor cost."[79] The committee found no evidence to support abuses of workers or any need for remedial legislation. It did refer to possible abuses, perhaps as a bone for opponents, but presented no evidence that they had occurred.

Despite recommending that no legislation was needed, the congressional representatives from the Watertown and Rock Island districts succeeded in passing a House resolution to prevent the use of time-measuring devices and performance incentives in any military installation.[80] In considering the 1914–1915 military appropriation bill, however, a heated debate occurred in the U.S. Senate. Among the pro-rider anti-Taylor advocates was Senator Henry Cabot Lodge, a descendant of the early Massachusetts textile tycoons, who spoke of ending "the days of slavery" brought about by men such as Taylor who thought it "profitable to work the slaves to the last possible point and let them die."[81] Such demagoguery clearly indicated his ignorance of what Taylor was attempting. The rider failed in the Senate, but was restored in conference between the two chambers. Legislation prohibiting the use of federal funds for time-study with "a stopwatch or other time-measuring device" stayed in effect from 1916 until 1949.[82] It should be noted that there was never a strike at any company at which Taylor was personally in charge nor had any workers operating under his system found it desirable to unionize.

---

[76] *Ibid.*, vol. 1, pp. 745–746.

[77] Ida M. Tarbell, *New Ideals in Business: An Account of Their Practice and Their Effects upon Men and Profits* (New York: Macmillan, 1916), p. 315.

[78] Copley, *Taylor*, vol. 2, p. 348.

[79] *Hearings to Investigate the Taylor System*, vol. 3, p. 1930.

[80] U.S. House of Representatives, Labor Committee, Hearings on House Resolution 8662, *A Bill to Prevent the Use of Stop Watch or Other Time-Measuring Devices on Government Work and the Payment of Premiums or Bonuses to Government Employees* (Washington, DC: Government Printing Office, 1914).

[81] Senator Henry Cabot Lodge, February 23, 1915, *Congressional Record Containing the Proceedings and Debates of the Sixty-Third Congress*, Third Session, vol. 52, pt. 5 (Washington, DC: Government Printing Office, 1915), p. 4352. Mary Barnett Gilson, an early employment counselor and later lecturer at the University of Chicago, called Senator Lodge an "exhibitionist" who tilted at windmills. See Gilson, *What's Past Is Prologue* (New York: Harper & Brothers, 1940), p. 55.

[82] Milton J. Nadworny, *Scientific Management and the Unions: 1900–1923* (Cambridge, MA: Harvard University Press, 1955), pp. 82 and 103.

The Mental Revolution

Taylor believed that labor and management should strive to find common ground. He wrote that "Scientific management . . . has for its very foundation the firm conviction that the true interests of the two [employers and employees] are one and the same; that prosperity for the employer cannot exist through a long term of years unless it is accompanied by the prosperity for the employé, and *vice versa*; and that it is possible to give the workman what he most wants – high wages – and the employer what he wants – a low cost – for his manufactures."[83] Taylor declared "The principal object of management should be to secure the maximum prosperity for the employer, coupled with the maximum prosperity for each employee."[84] To make this a reality, he called for a "mental revolution" where "both sides take their eyes off the division of surplus . . . and together turn their attention toward increasing the size of the surplus."[85] Thus, as envisioned by Taylor, the concerns of labor and management should be based on a "mutuality of interest." In brief, he advocated a congruency between the goals of employee and employer such that there would be "justice for all . . . parties through impartial scientific investigation of all elements of the problem."[86] In his words: "It is safe to say no system or scheme of management should be considered which does not in the long run give satisfaction to both employer and employee, which does not make it apparent that their best interest are mutual, and which does not bring about such thorough and hearty cooperation that they can pull together instead of apart."[87] Taylor recognized that self-proclaimed "efficiency experts" were giving scientific management a black eye. He warned "the mechanism of management must not be mistaken for its essence, or underlying philosophy."[88] This philosophy, reflecting a mutuality of interests, had four basic principles:

First. The development of a true science.

Second. The scientific selection of the workman.

Third. His scientific education and development.

Fourth. Intimate friendly cooperation between the management and the men.[89]

For Taylor, no single element constituted scientific management. Rather it was a combination of elements, which could be summarized as follows:

Science, not rule of thumb.

Harmony, not discord.

Cooperation, not individualism.

Maximum output, in place of restricted output.

The development of each man to his greatest efficiency and prosperity. [90]

---

[83] Taylor, *Principles of Scientific Management*, p. 10.
[84] *Ibid.*, p. 9. See also Chris Nyland, "Taylorism and the Mutual-Gains Strategy," *Industrial Relations* 37(4) (October 1998), pp. 519–542.
[85] *Hearings to Investigate the Taylor System*, vol. 3, p. 1387.
[86] Taylor, *Principles of Scientific Management*, p. 139.
[87] Taylor, *Shop Management*, p. 21.
[88] Taylor, *Principles of Scientific Management*, p. 128.
[89] *Ibid.*, p. 130n.
[90] *Ibid.*, p. 140.

Taylor's ideas aroused much interest. Unfortunately, many imitators used his name, but short-circuited his methods, promising they could produce the same results in half the time. Taylor deplored these fakers, properly fearing that they promised quick panaceas without grasping the fundamental attitudes that had to be changed and the necessity of gaining workers' acceptance of his methods. Taylor made a marked distinction between "true" scientific management and the efficiency craze that had suddenly emerged. True scientific management required a "mental revolution" on the part of employers and employees, which came about from mutual respect over a period of time and not from the mechanical adoption of purported efficiency devices. At the congressional hearings following the Watertown Arsenal strike, Taylor tried to clarify first what scientific management was by explaining what it was not:

> Scientific management is not any efficiency device, not a device of any kind for securing efficiency; nor is it any bunch or group of efficiency devices. It is not a new system of figuring costs; it is not a new scheme of paying men; it is not a piecework system; it is not a bonus system; it is not a premium system; it is no scheme for paying men; it is not holding a stop watch on a man and writing things down about him; it is not time study; it is not motion study nor an analysis of the movements of men; it is not the printing and ruling and unloading of a ton of blanks on a set of men and saying, "Here's your system; go use it." It is not divided foremanship or functional foremanship; it is not any of the devices which the average man calls to mind when scientific management is spoken of. The average man thinks of one or more of these things when he hears the words "scientific management" mentioned, but scientific management is not any of these devices. I am not sneering at cost-keeping systems, at time study, at functional foremanship, nor at any new and improved scheme of paying men, nor at any efficiency devices, if they are really devices that make for efficiency. I believe in them; but what I am emphasizing is that these devices in whole or in part are not scientific management, they are useful adjuncts to scientific management, so are they also useful adjuncts of other systems of management.
>
> Now, in its essence, scientific management involves a complete mental revolution on the part of the workingman engaged in any particular establishment or industry – a complete mental revolution on the part of these men as to their duties toward their work, toward their fellow men, and toward their employers. And it involves the equally complete mental revolution on the part of those on the management's side – the foreman, the superintendent, the owner of the business, the board of directors – a complete mental revolution on their part as to their duties toward their fellow workers in the management, toward their workmen, and toward all of their daily problems. And without this complete mental revolution on both sides scientific management does not exist.
>
> That is the essence of scientific management, this great mental revolution.[91]

Taylor believed that labor-union leaders were the principal opponents of his methods, not the unions' rank-and-file members. He was convinced that there was a conspiracy among union leaders to oppose scientific management. On April 26, 1914, speaking at a joint meeting of the executive boards of the Wisconsin State Federation of Labor and Milwaukee Federated Trades Council, Taylor presented the case for time study, improved work methods, and rewarding workers based on output. Nels P. Alifas, president of IAM's District #44 (Navy Yards and Arsenals), was invited to respond to Taylor's comments. Alifas had been a machinist during the 1911 Rock Island Arsenal strike and had also testified at the 1911–1912 *Hearings to Investigate the Taylor System*. He stated the IAM's position:

> Some people may wonder why we should object to a time study. . . . The objection is that in the past one of the means by which an employee has been able to keep his head above water and prevent being oppressed by the employer has been that the employer didn't know just exactly what the employee

---

[91] *Hearings to Investigate the Taylor System*, p. 1387.

could do. The only way that the workman has been able to retain time enough in which to do the work with the speed with which he thinks he ought to do it, has been to keep the employer somewhat in ignorance of exactly the time needed. The people of the United States have a right to say we want to work only so fast. We don't want to work as fast as we are able to. We want to work as fast as we think it's comfortable for us to work. . . . We are trying to regulate our work so as to make it an auxiliary to our lives and be benefited thereby.[92]

Taylor made repeated offers to Samuel Gompers, president of the American Federation of Labor, to visit plants using his methods and to get the facts for himself; Gompers refused.[93] In Taylor's view, organized labor's philosophy and that of scientific management were in direct opposition. Whereas labor unions stood "for war, for enmity," scientific management encouraged a "mutuality of interests."[94] To Gompers, "more, more, more" meant labor's gains came from employers' pockets; for Taylor, "more" came to everyone through improved productivity.[95] True, by searching for technological breakthroughs, scientific management made it possible to get more output for the same amount of input and, thus, higher profits. At the same time, working with better technology and work methods, scientifically selected and trained workers naturally produce more output per hour. In a competitive labor market, the demand for these more productive workers increases, driving up their wages. As Taylor reasoned, both employers and employees have a mutuality of interests in increasing a company's productive efficiency so it will be able to provide one of them higher wages and the other higher profits. If the company fails, everyone loses. Taylor considered his inability to convince labor to accept scientific management to be his greatest failure.[96]

Taylor and the Human Factor

In response to the charges that scientific management was cold and impersonal and disregarded the human factor, Taylor wrote about systems and people: "No system can do away with the need of real men. Both system and good men are needed, and after introducing the best system, success will be in proportion to the ability, consistency, and respected authority of the management."[97] Taylor well understood he was dealing with human needs as well as materials and machines. Writing in *Shop Management*, he quoted from his 1895 ASME paper "Piece-Rate System":

> No system of management, however good, should be applied in a wooden way. The proper personal relations should always be maintained between the employers and men; and even the prejudices of the workmen should be considered in dealing with them.

---

[92] Frederick W. Taylor and Nels P. Alifas, "Scientific Shop Management" (Milwaukee, WI: Milwaukee State Federation of Labor, 1914) in John R. Commons, ed., *Trade Unionism and Labor Problems*, 2nd ser. (Boston, MA: Ginn, 1921), pp. 148–149. For more on the Taylor-Alifas exchange, see "Report of Frank J. Weber," *Proceedings of the Twenty-second Annual Convention of the Wisconsin State Federation of Labor* (Milwaukee, WI, 1914), pp. 29–30. Further details regarding Alifas's views on scientific management, or what he considered "merely a name for an ingenious set of oppressive practices," are available at U.S. House of Representatives, Labor Committee, *Method of Directing the Work of Government Employees: Hearings Before the Committee on Labor, Sixty-fourth Congress, First Session on H.R. 8665, a Bill to Regulate the Method of Directing the Work of Government Employees. March 30, 31, April 1 and 4, 1916* (Washington, DC: Government Printing Office), p. 203.

[93] Copley, *Taylor*, vol. 2, pp. 403–404. In his testimony before the committee to investigate the Taylor System, Gompers categorically denied the existence of soldiering and labor resistance. *Hearings to Investigate the Taylor System*, p. 27. Gompers's biographer, Philip Taft, has suggested that Gompers was not unalterably opposed to scientific management, but yielded to the influence of IAM president William H. Johnson because the machinists were the largest and most powerful affiliate in the American Federation of Labor. See Philip Taft, *The A. F. of L. in the Time of Gompers* (New York: Harper & Brothers, 1957), pp. 299–300.

[94] Copley, *Taylor*, vol. 2, p. 407.

[95] Robert F. Hoxie, "President Gompers and the Labor Vote," *Journal of Political Economy* 16(10) (December 1908), p. 694.

[96] Trombley, *The Life and Times of a Happy Liberal*, p. 258.

[97] Taylor, *Shop Management*, p. 148. See also *idem*, "A Piece-Rate System," pp. 880–881.

The employer who goes through his works with kid gloves on, and is never known to dirty his hands or clothes, and who either talks to his men in a condescending or patronizing way, or else not at all, has no chance whatever of ascertaining their real thoughts or feelings.

Above all it is desirable that men should be talked to on their own level by those who are over them. Each man should be encouraged to discuss any trouble which he may have, either in the works or outside, with those over him. Men would far rather even be blamed by their bosses, especially if the "tearing out" has a touch of human nature and feeling in it, than to be passed by day after day without a word, and with no more notice than if they were part of the machinery.

The opportunity which each man should have of airing his mind freely, and having it out with his employers, is a safety-valve; and if the superintendents are reasonable men, and listen to and treat with respect what their men have to say, there is absolutely no reason for labor unions and strikes.

It is not the large charities (however generous they may be) that are needed or appreciated by workmen so much as small acts of personal kindness and sympathy, which establish a bond of friendly feeling between them and their employers.

The moral effect of this system on the men is marked. The feeling that substantial justice is being done them renders them on the whole much more manly, straightforward, and truthful. They work more cheerfully, and are more obliging to one another and their employers. They are not soured, as under the old system, by brooding over the injustice done them; and their spare minutes are not spent to the same extent in criticising their employers.[98]

On resistance to change:

Through generations of bitter experiences working men as a class have learned to look upon all change as antagonistic to their best interests. They do not ask the object of the change, but oppose it simply as *change*. The first changes, therefore, should be such as to allay the suspicions of the men and convince them by actual contact that the reforms are after all rather harmless and are only such as will ultimately be of benefit to all concerned.[99]

Taylor believed that it took 4–5 years to fully install his methods, as evidenced by his response to Emerson's testimony (above). Scientific management was not an overnight panacea. Its implementation required diligence and an understanding of Taylor's philosophy to be successful. Even then, it was not a cure-all:

Scientific management fundamentally consists of certain broad principles, a certain philosophy, which can be applied in many ways. . . . It is not here claimed that any single panacea exists for all of the troubles of the working people or of employers. . . . No system of management, no single expedient within the control of any man or any set of men can insure continuous prosperity to either workmen or employers.[100]

In 1915, three weeks before his death, Taylor spoke to the Cleveland Advertising Club:

Scientific management at every step has been an evolution, not a theory. In all cases the practice has preceded the theory. . . . All the men that I know of who are connected with scientific management are ready to abandon any scheme, any theory, in favor of anything else that can be found this is better. There is nothing in scientific management that is fixed.[101]

[98] *Idem, Shop Management,* pp. 184–185.

[99] *Ibid.,* p. 137.

[100] *Ibid.,* pp. 28–29. Taylor made a similar statement in his presentation at the first conference on scientific management: Frederick W. Taylor, "The Principles of Scientific Management," in *Scientific Management: First Conference at the Amos Tuck School,* p. 54.

[101] *Idem,* "The Principles of Scientific Management," *Bulletin of the Taylor Society* 2(5) (December 1916), p. 15. Address before the Cleveland Advertising Club, March 3, 1915, published posthumously.

In recognizing that there was never only "one best way," Taylor realized that management should continually strive to improve managerial practices through scientific investigation. Worried by the declining health of his wife, bedeviled by organized labor's antagonism, and frustrated by imitators who used his name, but short-circuited his methods and disdained his underlying philosophy, Taylor's last days were nigh. In a drafty railcar drawing room, while returning from a speaking trip, he became ill. He died from pneumonia on March 21, 1915, one day after his 59th birthday.[102] His headstone at the West Laurel Hill Cemetery, Philadelphia, bears this inscription: "*Frederick W. Taylor, 1856–1915, Father of Scientific Management.*"

SUMMARY

Frederick W. Taylor was a central figure in the development of management thought. Entering the U.S. industrial scene at a time of transition from entrepreneur-owner small- and medium-sized firms to large-scale, fully integrated corporations run by professional managers, Taylor gave a push and provided credibility to the belief that management is an independent science and discipline. The engineers of the day, having opened the door to efficient resource utilization, turned to technical subjects and left it to Taylor and others to promote what would come to be known as *scientific management*. Characterized by advancing technology, market growth, labor unrest, and a lack of managerial knowledge, U.S. companies of all sizes and in all industries were eager to learn better methods to manufacture and market products. To meet this need, Taylor provided a voice, a spirit that captured the public's imagination, including the army and navy, business leaders, government reformers, farmers, the legal and medical professions, church workers, club women, home economists, educators, and academics.[103] In an ironic twist, although Taylor's efforts at the Brooklyn Navy Yard were generally unsuccessful, in 1943, the U.S. Maritime Commission recognized his service by naming a World War II Liberty Ship in his honor.[104]

Although Taylor died over 100 years ago, he is still considered to be "the most influential business guru of the twentieth century."[105] In a contemporary review of his ideas, Locke concluded that "Taylor's track record is remarkable . . . *most of his insights are still valid today.*"[106] In the eyes of many, however, Taylor was a divisive person. His biographer wrote that he was not "the possessor of a nature that ordinarily would be called lovable" and acknowledged that "most of the men with whom I talked about Fred Taylor and his work either spoke of him personally with significant reserve or denounced him with bitterness which sometimes was really remarkable in its intensity."[107] Taylor was sometimes dogmatic and expressed himself in terms that made him an easy target for contemporary social critics. He once remarked, for example, that the first requirement of a pig-iron handler is that he be so dull that he resemble an ox and that an "intelligent gorilla," if properly trained, would be better suited to the job.[108] Arguably, his point was intended to illustrate that savings could come from carefully examining even menial jobs requiring only physical labor, and to emphasize that there was nothing special about the fact that some workers were suited to this kind of job and others were not.[109] His choice of analogies, however, was less than diplomatic, and such references were understandably ill received. Taylor, however, clearly understood that "the working man" had "the same feelings, the same motives, the same ambitions, the same failings, the same virtues" as "men

[102] Karen Pennar and Christopher Farrell, "Micromanaging from the Grave," *Business Week* (May 15, 1995, p. 34) reported that Frederick W. Taylor was "micromanaging from the grave" with a gift of $10 million to the Stevens Institute of Technology. Rather than coming from Taylor, the gift came from his son, Robert P. A. Taylor, and was given in the name of his father.

[103] Samuel Haber, *Efficiency and Uplift: Scientific Management in the Progressive Era, 1890–1920* (Chicago, IL; University of Chicago Press, 1964), pp. 51–74.

[104] "5 Ships to be Named for Noted Engineers," *New York Times* (December 5, 1943), p. 67.

[105] Geoffrey Colvin, "Managing the End of an Era," *Fortune* (March 6, 2000), p. F-8. See also Arthur G. Bedeian and Daniel A. Wren, "Most Influential Management Books of the 20th Century," *Organizational Dynamics* 29 (2001), pp. 221–225; Daniel A. Wren and Robert D. Hay, "Management Historians and Business Historians: Differing Perceptions of Pioneering Contributions," *Academy of Management Journal* 20 (1977), pp. 470–475.

[106] Edwin A. Locke, "The Ideas of Frederick W. Taylor: An Evaluation," *Academy of Management Review* 7 (1982), pp. 22–23.

[107] Frank Barkley Copley, "Frederick W. Taylor, Revolutionist," *The Outlook* 111 (September 1, 1915), p. 41.

[108] Taylor, *Principles of Scientific Management*, pp. 40 and 59.

[109] Lyndall F. Urwick, "The Truth about 'Schmidt': Reflections of Col. Lyndall F. Urwick," *Working Paper Series*, 3, No. 1, Management History Division, Academy of Management, 1978, pp. 8–9, 12. Reprinted in Arthur G. Bedeian, ed., *Evolution of Management Thought*, vol. 1 (London: Routledge, 2012), pp. 252–271.

who are not workmen" and that their wants are the same. That is, both want "a high salary and the chance for advancement."[110] Whereas Taylor could be short and sharp with "workingmen," he was, perhaps, even less diplomatic with businessmen who could not grasp his "mental revolution." "A shoe manufacturer once questioned the need of giving workers a bonus of from 35 to 50 percent for maintaining standards; in his opinion 20 percent was plenty. 'Well,' said Taylor, peering at him over his spectacles, 'you are a damn hog.'"[111]

As Nelson has observed, social scientists of every stripe have set up Taylor as a "straw man," emblematic of a hierarchical, authoritarian style of management that caused decades of labor strife, forgetting that scientific management "was a commitment to knowledge, reason and continuous attention to detail that was equally antithetical to old-fashioned empiricism and to new-fashioned panaceas."[112] Responding in his own defense, Taylor explained that he viewed his efforts as a means for bettering the lives of working people and that

> It ought to be perfectly evident to any man that no other human being would devote the whole of his life and spend every cent of his surplus income for the purpose of producing higher dividends for a lot of companies in which he has not the slightest interest. . . . I have devoted nearly all my time and money to furthering the cause of Scientific Management. This is done entirely with the idea of getting better wages for the workmen – of developing the workmen under our system to make them all higher class men – to better educate them – to help them to live better lives, and, above all, to be more happy and contented.[113]

A true appreciation of Taylor's efforts acknowledges that the customs of his time differ from those of today. Moreover, it recognizes Taylor's ideals, including the belief that the concerns of employee and employer should be based on a "mutuality of interests," were well ahead of his time. Taylor's work was, and still remains, revolutionary. The original seed he sowed has spread and multiplied a million fold. It has extended from the mechanical operations on which he focused at the beginning of his career into activities such as employee selection and training, job design, inventory control, and wage and salary administration. Further, Taylor's methods began an economic revolution that not only enabled industrial workers in the developed world to earn middle-class wages and achieve middle-class status, but also has lifted countless millions of the developing world's poor out of poverty and has turned cities such as Tokyo, Hong Kong, Dubai, and Beijing into economic hubs that rival New York, London, and Paris. Of equal significance, the application of scientific management has assisted many of the world's underdeveloped and poverty-stricken countries to become world-class competitors within a single generation.[114]

Taylor's efforts also produced a change in the way managers regarded themselves. The old "rule-of-thumb" and "seat-of-the-pants" images were replaced by "an attitude of questioning, of research, of careful investigation . . . of seeking exact knowledge and then shaping action on the discovered facts."[115] Scientific management was to be a tool for increased productivity, greater purchasing power, and a higher standard of living. With regard to the latter, the legacy of scientific management has spread to all aspects of modern life, including public policy, art, and literature.[116]

On balance, Taylor left an indelible mark on his age and ours. His emphasis on efficiency remains a prevailing value of contemporary management.[117] He was not alone, but was joined by others who would apply, adapt, and refine. Taylor, however, was the lodestar that guided all those who have since followed in his footsteps to bring professional management to the workplace and replace opinion with fact.

[110] Frederick W. Taylor, "The Working Man," a lecture given at Harvard University, Boston, 1909–1914. Reprinted in Ernest Dale, ed., *Readings in Management: Landmarks and New Frontiers*, 3rd. ed. (New York: McGraw-Hill, 1975), pp. 100, 102.

[111] Trombley, *The Life and Times of a Happy Liberal*, p. 9.

[112] Daniel Nelson, "Epilogue," in *idem*, ed., *A Mental Revolution: Scientific Management since Taylor* (Columbus, OH: Ohio State University Press, 1992), p. 239.

[113] Copley, *Taylor*, vol. 2, pp. 237–238.

[114] Peter F. Drucker, "The New Productivity Challenge," *Harvard Business Review* 67(6) (November–December), 1991, p. 71 and *idem*, "The Coming Rediscovery of Scientific Management," *Conference Board Record* 13(6) (June 1976), p. 26.

[115] Majority Report of Sub-Committee on Administration, "The Present State of the Art of Industrial Management," *Transactions of the American Society of Mechanical Engineers* 34 (1912), p. 1137.

[116] Richard G. Olson, *Scientism and Technocracy: The Legacy of Scientific Management* (Lanham, MD: Lexington Books, 2016).

[117] Daniel A. Wren, "The Centennial of Frederick W. Taylor's *The Principles of Scientific Management*: A Retrospective Commentary," *Journal of Business and Management* 17(1) (2011), pp.11–22.

Spreading the Gospel of Efficiency

chapter

8

Space and time rarely allow the full measure of a person and that person's work. This is true of Frederick W. Taylor and also applies to those who joined with him in propagating scientific management. The present focuses on six individuals who rallied around Taylor and were prominent in the embryonic days of the scientific-management movement: Carl G. Barth, Henry L. Gantt, Frank B. and Lillian M. Gilbreth, Harrington Emerson, and Morris L. Cooke. These individuals were at the vanguard in spreading the gospel of efficiency.

The Most Orthodox: Carl G. Barth

Of all the disciples in the forefront of the scientific-management movement, Carl Georg Lange Barth (1860–1939) was the most orthodox. Born in Christiana (now Oslo), Norway, Barth received his early education in the Lillehammer public schools. He attended the Royal Norwegian Navy's Technical School at Horten, graduating with honors in 1876, when only 16 years old.

Carl G. Barth. Frederick W. Taylor, "The Principles of Scientific Management," *American Magazine* 71(5) (March 1911), p. 574.

Barth then began a civilian apprenticeship as a machinist, first serving as a blacksmith's helper and then, in turn, as a lathe and slotting machine operator in the boiler shop at the Karljohansvern navy yard. His mathematical skills were soon recognized, however, and he was appointed an assistant instructor in mathematics and office assistant to the superintendent at the Technical School, earning less than 3 cents an hour. In 1881, Barth immigrated to the United States in the hope of higher pay. His first job was with William Sellers & Company (Philadelphia, Pennsylvania), a leading machine-tool manufacturer, where he began as a draftsman earning $2 a day. As Barth's talents were again quickly evident, his salary was soon raised to $20 a week. Barth worked at Sellers for 13 years (1881–1895, except for 1891, spent with Arthur Faulkenau Machine Company as engineer and chief draftsman) and rose to the position of chief machine designer. Beginning in 1882, he concurrently taught mechanical drawing in the evening school at the Franklin Institute (Philadelphia) for 6 years.[1] For a time he then gave private mathematics lessons, even running an evening school of his own teaching mechanical drawing. Beginning in 1895, Barth worked for 2 years as engineer and chief draftsman with Rankin & Fritsch Foundry & Machine Company at St. Louis. He subsequently worked temporarily at the St. Louis Water Commission as a machine designer and then for a year-and-a-half at the International Correspondence Schools (Scranton, Pennsylvania), revising a paper on machine design for its International Library of Technology and preparing monthly articles with titles such as "Designing of a Pin Joint" and "Cone Pulleys and Back Gearing" for its *Home Study Magazine*.

In 1899–1900, Barth was an instructor teaching manual training and mathematics at the Ethical Culture Schools of New York, a private academy in that is now known as Fieldston, when Wilfred Lewis, a former associate at William Sellers and Company, suggested he might be of assistance to Fred Taylor, who was searching for someone to handle complex mathematical problems in his metal-cutting experiments at the Bethlehem Iron Works. Barth ultimately joined Taylor at Bethlehem in late 1899. His first assignment was to help Henry L. Gantt with mathematical problems associated with cutting metals that had plagued Taylor since his early days at Midvale Steel. Barth's solution was a circular logarithmic slide rule that gave near instantaneous solutions for the interrelation of depth of cut, machine speed, and material feed.[2] Taylor credited Barth's extraordinary analytic ability with eliminating rule-of-thumb procedures in determining the one best combination of machine speeds, material feeds, and tools for cutting metals.

During the remainder of his life, Taylor relied on Barth more than anyone for aid in developing new engineering methods. Barth assisted Taylor in the pioneering installations of scientific management at the Tabor Manufacturing Company, the Link-Belt Engineering Company, Fairbanks Scales, Yale & Towne Manufacturing Company, and later at the Watertown Arsenal. He also helped George D. Babcock install scientific management at the Franklin Motor Car Company (1908–1912) and, thus, was a pioneer in the rationalizing the automobile industry. In the days before the moving assembly line, component parts were brought to stationary work areas for

---

[1] Biographical data are from "Testimony of Carl G. Barth, of Philadelphia, PA," *Hearings before Special Committee of the House of Representatives to Investigate the Taylor and Other Systems of Shop Management under Authority of House Resolution 90* (Washington, DC: U.S. Government Printing Office, 1912) vol. 3, pp. 1539–1543. See also Florence M. Manning, "Carl G. Barth: A Sketch," Master's Thesis, University of California, Berkeley, 1927; *idem,* "Carl G. Barth, 1860–1930: A Sketch," *Norwegian-American Studies and Records* 13 (1943), pp. 114–132; and Kenneth Bjork, *Saga in Steel and Concrete: Norwegian Engineers in America* (Northfield, MN: Norwegian- American Historical Association, 1947), pp. 278–312.
[2] Carl G. Barth, "Supplement to Frederick W. Taylor's 'On the Art of Cutting Metals' – I," *Industrial Management* 58(3) (September 1919), pp. 169–175.

fabrication. Franklin made three models of cars—touring, runabout, and sedan—and relied on a sales forecast to determine which models to produce, when, and in what quantities. One-hundred cars were produced per month in lots, or batches. Franklin was unprofitable due to high manufacturing costs and rampant labor turnover (425 percent). After Barth finished installing scientific management, Franklin was producing 45 cars per day, wages were up 90 percent, labor turnover was less than 50 percent, and it was profitable.[3] Between 1908 and 1913, the Ford Motor Company would perfect the moving assembly line for the mass production of automobiles to replace the small-batch assembly methods of the past (see Chapter 9).

Barth lectured on scientific management at the University of Chicago (1914–1916) and at Harvard University (1911–1916 and 1919–1922) and was "exceedingly proud of being accused of being Mr. Taylor's most orthodox disciple."[4] He resisted any tampering with Taylor's methods and later maintained that only those who had worked directly with Taylor fully understood the task-management system. Barth's contribution to management thought resided in his faithful execution of Taylor's methods. He was patient and accurate in his experiments and analyses. Whereas he may not have possessed Taylor's imagination, Barth performed a bulk of the technical work necessary for developing scientific management. In this respect, Taylor and Barth complemented each other in temperament and skills. Barth conducted his later consulting management work in conjunction with his son, J. Christian Barth, under the firm name of Carl G. Barth & Son.

Charting Other Paths: Henry L. Gantt

Henry Laurence Gantt (1861–1919) was born into a prosperous Calvert County, Maryland, farm family. When the War Between the States left the family destitute, Gantt learned at an early age the meaning of hard work, the demands of frugal living, and the self-discipline required to make one's way in the world.[5] He received his preparatory education at the McDonogh School at Owings Mills, Maryland. McDonogh was founded in 1872 as a "school farm" for "poor boys of good character." Gantt graduated with distinction from Johns Hopkins University in 1880, when only 19 years old. In the next 3 years, Gantt taught natural science and mechanics at McDonogh and earned a mechanical engineering degree from the Stevens Institute of Technology. He then became a draftsman for Poole and Hunt, an engineering firm located in Baltimore. In 1886 Barth returned to his teaching post at McDonogh. He joined the Midvale Steel Company in 1887 as an assistant in the engineering department.

Henry L. Gantt. Courtesy of Peter B. Petersen.

Here the 26-year-old Gantt met and began to work with a man who would have a significant influence on his future career, Fred Taylor.

Taylor and Gantt were an unusual team: they shared a common interest in science as a means of improving management methods and developed a deep mutual admiration for each other's work. Gantt grasped the essence of Taylor's work and became one of his leading disciples.

---

[3] George D. Babcock, *The Taylor System in Franklin Management: Application and Results* (New York: Engineering Magazine, 1917).

[4] Carl G. Barth, "Discussion," on "The Present State of the Art of Industrial Management: Majority and Minority Report of Sub-Committee on Administration," *Transactions of the American Society of Mechanical Engineers* 34 (1912), p. 1204.

[5] Biographical data are from Leon P. Alford, *Henry L. Gantt: Leader in Industry* (New York: American Society of Mechanical Engineers, 1934). See also Alex W. Rathe, *Gantt on Management* (New York: American Management Association, 1961); Peter B. Petersen, "A Further Insight into the Life of Henry L. Gantt: The Papers of Duncan Lyle," in Dennis F. Ray, ed., *Proceedings of the Southern Management Association* (1984), pp. 198–200.

He collaborated with Taylor at Midvale, followed him to the Simonds Rolling Machine Company to become superintendent, and joined him again at Bethlehem. In 1901, Gantt became a "consulting industrial engineer" on his own, and, although he espoused the tenets of scientific management throughout his life, he later expanded his concern to the nation's overall economic growth. During his lifetime, he published over 150 papers and three major books; made numerous presentations before the American Society of Mechanical Engineers (becoming vice president in 1914); patented more than a dozen inventions; lectured at universities, including Stevens, Columbia, Harvard, and Yale; and became one of the first successful management consultants.

The Task and Bonus System

Gantt's initial ideas on machines, tools, and methods were a direct outgrowth of his association with Taylor. The influence of Taylor's ideas on a mutuality of interests between employees and employers, scientifically selecting employees, appropriate performance incentives, detailed task instructions, and more is reflected in Gantt's early work. Gantt recognized that the workingman, "a human unit in a living organization," was the most important component in any successful undertaking. He believed that if business was to reflect society's values and serve social purposes, worker exploitation could not be tolerated. In his words, "the only healthy industrial condition is that in which the employer has the best men obtainable for his work, and the workman feels that his labor is being sold at the highest market price."[6]

On this road to high wages and low costs, Gantt developed a task and bonus system of wage payments that was simpler than Taylor's differential piece-rate pay plan. His views on organized labor paralleled Taylor's, but he was more persuasive and philosophical in expressing them:

> If the amount of wealth in the world were fixed, the struggle for the possession of that wealth would necessarily cause antagonism; but, [because] . . . the amount of wealth is not fixed, but constantly increasing, the fact that one man has become wealthy does not necessarily mean that someone else has become poorer, but may mean quite the reverse, especially if the first is a producer of wealth. . . . As long . . . as one party – no matter which – tries to get all it can of the new wealth, regardless of the rights of the other, conflicts will continue.[7]

To Gantt, the "more, more, more" of organized labor was an antagonistic force unless it cooperated in producing more for the mutual benefit of both labor and management. He was not convinced that the differential piece-rate pay plan favored by Taylor would secure worker cooperation.[8] Gantt's "task work with a bonus" system guaranteed a day wage and paid a daily bonus of 50 cents if workers completed their assigned tasks. Gantt later discovered, however, that this arrangement offered little incentive for additional efforts beyond the minimum required to receive each day's bonus. To overcome this shortcoming, he modified his task and bonus system to pay workers if a task was completed in less than a predetermined standard time. A worker could, thus, receive 4 hours' pay for doing a 3-hour job in less than 3 hours.[9]

In extending his task and bonus system, Gantt adapted a suggestion by the superintendent of the Bethlehem machine shop, Edgar P. Earle, to give first-line supervisors a bonus for each of their workers who reached the standard time set for their daily tasks, plus an extra bonus based on the bonuses earned by the workers being supervised. Thus, if 9 of 10 workers in a department completed their assigned tasks within the predetermined standard time, their supervisor

---

[6] Henry L. Gantt, *Work, Wages, and Profits*, 2nd ed. (New York: Engineering Magazine, 1916), p. 33.
[7] *Ibid.*, p. 55.
[8] Alford, *Gantt*, pp. 85–106.
[9] *Ibid.*, p. 165. For a detailed explanation and the computations necessary for implementing Gantt's "task and with a bonus" system, see Charles W. Lytle, *Wage Incentive Methods* (New York: Ronald Press, 1942), pp. 185–200.

would receive 10 cents per worker, or $0.90; if all ten met the standard, the first-line supervisor would receive 15 cents per worker, or $1.50. Gantt viewed this extra bonus as a way to encourage supervisors to teach and help workers improve their performance. He knew the importance of education from his days as a teacher and felt that "task work with a bonus" would shift first-line supervisors from drivers to leaders.[10] Gantt was convinced that force could not be the basis for leadership, and believed that increased productivity could only be achieved through knowledge. Like Taylor, Gantt encountered more resistance from first-line supervisors concerned with protecting their authority than from the workers they supervised. For Gantt, all the elements within an enterprise must come together to achieve efficient performance. Further, he maintained that workplace rewards should be equitably distributed according to each participant's contributions.

The Habits of Industry

As a consulting industrial engineer, Gantt would serve some 50 clients, including American Locomotive Company, Robins Conveying Belt Company, and Brighton Mills, before his death in 1919. Taylor would occasionally recommend Gantt for jobs requiring an engineer-manager. Sayles Bleachery, a textile dye plant located in Lincoln, Rhode Island, was one of Gantt's early clients. Despite patenting three different machines to aid in finishing cotton cloth, Gantt encountered resistance from both management and labor. Ultimately, the workers in a folding room went out on strike. They objected to Gantt's plant reorganization, asked for a 10 percent increase in wages, and struck when it was refused. The strike spread and Gantt had to hire and train replacement workers. This experience forced Gantt to rethink how to best train workers; from then on he considered intensive employee training to be an essential management responsibility.

In training employees, Gantt felt that supervisors should do more than improve worker skills and knowledge; he added an ingredient to training called the "habits of industry." These habits were *industriousness* and *cooperation*, which would facilitate the acquisition of all other knowledge. Gantt felt that, as a result of doing their work promptly and to the best of their ability, workers would experience pride in the quality and quantity of output they produced.[11] As an example, he cited a group of women who formed a society of "bonus producers," with membership open only to those who consistently earned a daily bonus. To Gantt, this was the ideal in labor–management relations. Gantt believed, however, that such relations could only occur after management had created a proper atmosphere of cooperation and trust. The result would be win–win: higher wages for employees and increased profit (due to lower costs) for employers.

Graphic Aids to Management

Gantt was less inclined toward painstaking experiments than either Taylor or Barth. Eventually, he turned to graphic methods for recording and conveying operating information. One of his earliest graphic portrayals involved using horizontal bars to compare planned and actual performance. The bars on the graph provided performance feedback to both management and workers, as shortfalls ("exceptions") were clearly highlighted for further action. Gantt expanded his graphical portrayals to include charts showing daily output, production costs, output per machine and worker in comparison with original planning estimates and losses due to idle machinery.[12]

---

[10] Henry L. Gantt, *Industrial Leadership* (New Haven, CT: Yale University Press, 1916), p. 85.
[11] *Idem, Work, Wages, and Profits*, p. 154.
[12] Peter B. Petersen, "The Evolution of the Gantt Chart and Its Relevance Today," *Journal of Managerial Issues* 3(2) (Summer 1991), pp. 131–155.

Gantt's major breakthrough in charting came, however, when serving as a dollar-a-year consultant to the Department of the Army during World War I (1914–1918).[13] The conversion of U.S. industry to wartime production did not come quickly or smoothly. The United States had the productive capacity, but the coordination of private industrial efforts with government agencies was haphazard. Plants were scattered all over the nation, shipments were late, warehouses crowded or disorganized, and the military utilized its resources poorly. Gantt had had some contact with governmental work before the war. In 1911, with Charles Day and Harrington Emerson, he was asked by Secretary of the Navy George von L. Meyer to serve as a civilian board to study inefficiency at the navy yards in New York City, Boston, Philadelphia, Norfolk, Portsmouth, Mare Island, and Puget Sound. The board concluded that if work at the sites visited was "fully standardized and planned," costs could be reduced by one-half.[14] Its efforts went for naught, however, when Secretary Meyer's attempt to introduce scientific management in the navy's ship-yards was met with stern resistance from line officers.[15] Just prior to the war, Gantt had also served as a consultant to General William Crozier, head of the U.S. Army's Ordnance Department.[16] Crozier, impressed by Gantt's graphic displays, developed a series of progress and performance charts to aid in managing army arsenals. When Gantt gave up his consulting work to aid in the war effort, he puzzled over how to track the huge amount of defense work being performed at so many different sites. Scheduling was especially crucial, and the information necessary to plan and coordinate private contractors' efforts with those of government agencies was lacking. Gantt spent three months trying to solve this puzzle before realizing that "We have all been wrong in scheduling on a basis of *quantities*. The essential element in the situation is *time*, and this should be the basis in laying out any program."[17]

Gantt's solution was a bar chart for planning and coordinating work. Although numerous variations were developed, the essence of what came to be known as a Gantt Progress Chart is to show how work is to be routed and scheduled, through various operations, to completion. By updating progress on a Gantt Chart, one can see at a glance the activities that are behind schedule, on time, and ahead of schedule. For example, a manager can see from the Gantt chart in Figure 8.1 that Operation 1 is behind schedule. Corrective action can now be taken to move the project ahead. In addition, Gantt Charts facilitate the coordination of activities and the scheduling of labor.

Applying his newfound solution at the army's Frankford Arsenal, Gantt developed a means of scheduling and coordinating munitions production and supply between private contractors and army arsenals. At the height of the war, German submarines were sinking merchant vessels more rapidly than they could be replaced. Together with fellow consultants Harrington Emerson and Walter N. Polakov, Gantt worked with the Emergency Fleet Corporation to overcome this short-fall. "On the day of the Armistice, the United States had 341 shipyards, 350,000 shipyard work-ers, and had had 1,284 launchings."[18] Wallace Clark, a member of Gantt's consulting firm who will enter our story shortly, was Director of the U.S. Shipping Board's Scheduling Section. He used Gantt charts to route and monitor about 12,000 ships. Improved scheduling reduced the

[13] For a discussion of Gantt's contributions to the War Industries Board in World War I, see Kyle Bruce, "Scientific Management and the American Planning Experience of WWI: The Case of the War Industries Board," *History of Economics Review* 23 (Winter 1995), pp. 37–60.

[14] "Navy Yard System Is Declared Faulty," *New York Times* (March 9, 1912), p. 16.

[15] Peter B. Petersen, "Fighting for a Better Navy: An Attempt at Scientific Management (1805–1912)," *Journal of Management* 16(1) (March 1990), p. 159. For background into the politics surrounding Myer's decision, including Fred Taylor's meeting with President Howard Taft at the White House to offer his services to personally train Naval Constructor Holden A. Evans for introducing scientific management in the nation's navy yards, see his *One Man's Fight for a Better Navy* (New York: Dodd, Mead & Company), pp. 251–259.

[16] *Idem*, "The Pioneering Efforts of Major General William Crozier (1855–1942) in the Field of Management," *Journal of Management* 15(3) (September 1989), pp. 503–516.

[17] Alford, *Gantt*, p. 207.

[18] *Ibid.*, p. 199.

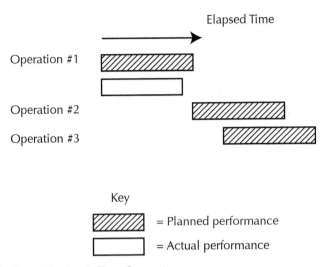

FIGURE 8.1 A Simplification of the Gantt Chart Concept.

inactive and unavailable ship times from 4 to 2 weeks.[19] World War I took a measurable turn for the better as a result of Gantt's contributions. The productive might of the United States was brought to fruition as arsenals and shipyards boomed. Surely this must have provided some consolation for the man whose efforts to improve the management of navy shipyards had been spurned so few years before. Gantt's and Emerson's wartime efforts were honored in 1943, when the U.S. Maritime Commission named Liberty Ships in their honor.[20]

Gantt never patented his bar charts nor profited from them. He was, however, awarded the Distinguished Civilian Service Medal "for meritorious service to the government of the United States." Wallace Clark popularized the Gantt chart in a book that has been translated into eight languages.[21] Gantt charts formed the basis for the Union of Soviet Socialist Republic's first Five-Year Plan in 1928 and were used in the 1930s to build the Hoover Dam.[22] All subsequent graphic project controls drew their inspiration from Gantt's bar-chart concept; the modern variation became the Program Evaluation and Review Technique (PERT), a computerized, more intricate scheme for planning and controlling both time and costs.

Gantt: The Later Years

As early as 1916, Gantt widened his views on industry and the role of industrial engineers. In particular, he deplored the failure of U.S. industrial leadership, which, in his opinion, was caused by individual advancement based on favoritism rather than ability. Gantt argued for a "new" era in which the industrial engineer, not the financier or the labor activist, would lead an industrial democracy based on equality of opportunity. He believed that only industrial engineers could cope with the complexities of wealth creation and, thus, should lead the United States with a concern not for profits, but for productive efficiency. Gantt was influenced by Thorstein B. Veblen's criticism of laissez-faire economics and the role of big business in shaping modern society.[23]

---

[19] Daniel A. Wren, "Implementing the Gantt Chart in Europe and Britain: The Contributions of Wallace Clark," *Journal of Management History* 21(3) (2015), pp. 309–327.

[20] "5 Ships to Be Named for Noted Engineers," *New York Times* (December 5, 1943), p. 67.

[21] Wallace Clark, *The Gantt Chart: A Working Tool of Management* (New York: Ronald Press, 1922).

[22] For further information on the worldwide impact of Wallace Clark's work, see Pearl Franklin Clark, *Challenge of the American Know-How* (New York: Hillary House, 1957).

[23] Alford, *Gantt*, p. 264.

He saw a conflict between business executives and engineers, with business executives defending the status quo and engineers as championing progress. Gantt was also impressed by the views of New York City writer and newspaperman Charles Ferguson, who "wanted to reconcile the traditional ideals of individualism and freewheeling opportunity with the increasing need for cooperation and social control."[24]

In late 1916, Gantt formed the New Machine, an organization whose membership was comprised of engineers and other sympathetic reformers seeking to acquire political as well as economic power.[25] The New Machine operated on the premise that engineers would form Ferguson's "aristocracy of the capable" and do the heavy thinking for the masses. It called for President Woodrow Wilson to transfer "control of the huge and delicate apparatus [i.e., industry] into the hands of those who understand its operation," to establish bureaus for better placement of employees, and to set up "public service banks" to extend credit on the basis of ability and personality rather than property.[26]

Gantt soon lost his concern for mere factory matters and sought broader areas for reform. He attacked the profit system, and on this point he appears to have been largely influenced by world events. In January 1917, the Bolsheviks overthrew Czar Nicholas II, and violent bloodshed swept Russia. Eugene Debs, a founder of the International Labor Union and the Industrial Workers of the World (IWW), as well as five-time Socialist Party of America candidate for U.S. President, was something of a folk hero; there had been Communist uprisings in Bavaria and Hungary; the Wobblies (as IWW members were known) were provoking labor unrest; and many people were firmly convinced that the Bolsheviks were about to overturn society. In the preface to his last book, published in 1919, Gantt wrote:

> The attempt which extreme radicals all over the world are making to get control of both the political and business systems on the theory that they would make the industrial and business serve the community, is a real danger so long as our present system does not accomplish that end. . . . [T]o resume our advance toward the development of an unconquerable democratic civilization, we must purge our economic system of all autocratic practices of whatever kind, and return to the democratic principle of rendering service, which was the basis of its wonderful growth.[27]

Gantt believed that businesses had a social responsibility to incorporate community service in their activities. He argued that *"the business system must accept its social responsibility and devote itself primarily to service, or the community will ultimately make the attempt to take it over in order to operate it in* [the community's] *own interest."*[28] To this end, he further contended that "the engineer, who is a man of few opinions and many facts, few words and many deeds, should be accorded the economic leadership which is his proper place in our economic system."[29] In November 1919, Gantt was stricken with a "digestive disturbance" and died at age 58.[30]

---

[24] Robert D. Cuff, "Woodrow Wilson's Missionary to American Business, 1914–1915: A Note," *Business History Review* 43(4) (Winter 1969), p. 546.

[25] Peter B. Petersen, "Henry Gantt and the New Machine (1916–1919)," in Jack A. Pearce II and Richard B. Robinson, Jr., eds., *Proceedings of the Annual Meeting of the Academy of Management* (1986), pp. 128–132. See also *idem,* "Correspondence from Henry L. Gantt to an Old Friend Reveals New Information about Gantt," *Journal of Management* 12(3) (Fall 1986), pp. 339–350; *idem,* "Henry Gantt's Last Hurrah," unpublished paper presented at the annual meeting of the Academy of Management, San Antonio, TX, August 16, 2011.

[26] Alford, *Gantt*, pp. 269–277.

[27] Henry L. Gantt, *Organizing for Work* (New York: Harcourt Brace Jovanovich, 1919), pp. iv–v.

[28] *Ibid.*, p. 15.

[29] *Ibid.*, p. 20.

[30] For commemorative comments by Gantt's colleagues Harrington Emerson, Walter N. Polakov, and Wallace Clark, see "Henry Laurence Gantt: In Appreciation," *Industrial Management* 58(6) (December 1919), pp. 488–491. See also Peter B. Petersen, "The Followers of Henry L. Gantt (1861–1919)," in Dorothy P. Moore, ed., *Proceedings of the Annual Meeting of the Academy of Management* (1993), pp. 174–178.

With Gantt's death, the New Machine lost its champion and was disbanded. Gantt did not live to see the direction that management thought would take in the 1920s and afterward. Rather than engineers providing the economic leadership advocated by the New Machine, "the business system" would turn to improved human-resource practices, labor–management cooperation, better employee-representation plans, and, overall, an enhanced understanding of the human factor at work. Given his concern for the "working man," Gantt would have been pleased. In 1929, the Institute of Management and ASME posthumously awarded Gantt the first Henry Laurence Gantt Medal—"For his humanizing influence upon industrial management and for invention of the Gantt chart."

Partners for Life: The Gilbreths

Frank Bunker Gilbreth (1868–1924) and his wife Lillian Moeller Gilbreth (1878–1972) were contemporaries of Fred Taylor and part of the small band of original scientific-management pioneers.[31] Their accomplishments still stand out for their fervor and devotion to a single goal: eliminating waste and discovering the "one best way." It was the Gilbreths' contention that of the various ways doing a task, only one was the best, and it was their job to find it. This ideal became their credo and religion, and they did everything in their power to end the tragedy, as they saw it, of the enormous waste taking place everywhere—in government, in industry, in homes, and in personal lives. The Gilbreths viewed their quest for the "one best way" as the means by which individuals could maximize their full potential, benefiting both themselves and society.

The Gilbreth Family at their summer home in Nantucket, 1923—Left to right: Frank (Sr.), Frank (Jr.), Bill, Fred, Dan, Jane, Lil, Martha, Ernestine, Anne, and Lillian M. Gilbreth. Provided by Ernestine Gilbreth Carey. Bettman/Getty Images.

[31] Biographical data are from Edna Yost, *Frank and Lillian Gilbreth: Partners for Life* (New Brunswick, NJ: Rutgers University Press, 1949); Laurel D. Graham, *Managing on Her Own: Dr. Lillian Gilbreth and Women's Work in the Interwar Era* (Norcross, GA: Engineering & Management Press, 1998); Jane Lancaster, *Making Time" Lillian Moller Gilbreth* – A Life Beyond "Cheaper by the Dozen" (Boston, MA: Northeastern University Press, 2004); and Julie Des Jardins, *Lillian Gilbreth: Redefining Domesticity* (Boulder, CO: Westview Press, 2013). See also Lillian M. Gilbreth, *As I Remember* (Norcross, GA: Engineering and Management Press, 1998). Originally written in 1941.

Frank was the son of a Fairfield, Maine, hardware merchant. He learned the virtues of frugality and thrift characteristic of New England Puritanism at an early age. When he was 3 years old, his father died, and his family relocated to Andover, Massachusetts. In 1878, the family moved to Boston, where Frank was educated at Rice Primary School and English High School, graduating in 1885. Although he had passed the Massachusetts Institute of Technology entrance exam, Frank was unwilling to attend college while his mother ran a boardinghouse to support him and his two sisters. He was urged to take up bricklaying by his Sunday-school teacher, Renton Whidden, who offered Frank the impressive pay of $3 a day. Frank needed the money and took the job. To learn his new job, Frank studied other bricklayers as they went about their work. He found they performed their task in three ways: They used one set of motions when working deliberatively but slowly, a second when working rapidly, and a third when trying to teach an apprentice. It was this simple observation that led to the first precepts of *motion study*. For, as Frank reasoned, if one set of motions was right, then the other two must be wrong.[32]

Frank was determined to learn to lay bricks the "right" way. At first, he was Whidden's slowest apprentice, but he soon began developing his own ideas. Designing his own scaffolds and work methods for everything from mortar consistency to trowel usage, he cut the motions required to lay a brick from 18 to 6. Within a year, he was faster than any of his coworkers. A journeyman was expected to lay 175 bricks an hour. Frank could easily lay 350 bricks. In all, by age 20, he could draw journeyman's pay in more than 50 trades.

Several years later (1910), Frank testified before the Interstate Commerce Commission in the Eastern Rate Case. He explained his new science of bricklaying as follows:

> Bricks have been laid the same way for 4,000 years. The first thing a man does is to bend down and pick up a brick. Taylor pointed out that the average brick weighs ten pounds, the average weight of a man above his waist is 100 pounds. Instead of bending down and raising this double load, the bricklayer could have an adjustable shelf built so that the bricks would be ready to his hand. A boy could keep these shelves at the right height. When the man gets the brick in his hand, he tests it with his trowel. If anything, this is more stupid than stopping to pick up his material. If the brick is bad he discards it, but in the process it has been carried up perhaps six stories, and must be carted down again. Moreover, it consumes the time of a $5-a-day man when a $6-a-week boy could do the testing on the ground. The next thing the bricklayer does is to turn the brick over to get its face. More waste: more work of the $6 boy. Next what does the bricklayer do? He puts his brick down on the mortar and begins to tap it down with his trowel. What does this tapping do? It gives the brick a little additional weight so it will sink into the mortar. If anything this is more stupid than any of the others. For we know the weight of the brick and it would be a simple matter in industrial physics to have the mortar mixed so that just that weight will press it down into the right layer. And the results? Instead of having eighteen motions in the laying of a brick, we have only six. And the men put on the work to try to lay 2,700 with apparently no more effort than they laid a thousand before.[33]

Nothing Succeeds Like . . .

By 1895, Frank had begun his own construction business in Boston with *speed work* as its motto. To assure that cost arrangements would be satisfactory to his customers, Frank designed a Cost-Plus-A-Fixed-Sum Contract. Before long, Frank's work spread from Maine to New Mexico and

---

[32] Lillian M. Gilbreth, *The Quest for the One Best Way* (New York: Society of Industrial Engineers, 1924), p. 16.

[33] Frank B. Gilbreth quoted in Paul U. Kellogg, "A National Hearing for Scientific Management," *The Survey* 25 (December 3, 1910), pp. 411–412. This testimony does not appear *ad verbum* in the official 10-volume *Evidence Taken by the Interstate Commerce Commission in the Matter of Proposal Advances in Freight Rates by Carriers*, Senate Document 725, 61st Cong., 3rd sess. (Washington, DC: U.S. Government Printing Office, 1911).

from London to Berlin. At one time he employed up to 10,000 men. He even maintained an office in London, performing work for the Admiralty and War Office.

To keep track of all the work his company was doing, Frank ordered weekly photographs showing the progress of each job. These were supplemented by daily correspondence and an array of supporting forms. The Gilbreth Company constructed dams, houses, factories, canals, skyscrapers, and even whole towns (e.g., Woodland, Maine). Much work was performed in San Francisco following the 1906 earthquake and fire.

Frank's reputation for record-setting performances drew increasing attention. One of his most famous—and least conventional—practices was to start moving construction materials toward a job site even before a contract was awarded. Then, once the contract was signed, he would startle the public by beginning work within hours. Frank soon became one of the best-known building contractors in the world.

As Frank's ideas gained prominence, they also gained acceptance. Persuaded that a system that was not in writing was unworthy of the name, he set out to put his ideas into book form.[34] Working in conjunction with Lillie, he published *Field System* and *Concrete System* in 1908, and followed with *Bricklaying System* (1909), *Motion Study* (1911), *Fatigue Study* (1916), and *Applied Motion Study* (1917).

The Field System was an accounting system without a set of books. It was designed to aid construction contractors by showing operating costs, costs related to estimates, and the total cost of a job each Saturday up to the previous Thursday. No bookkeepers were needed, and because original memoranda or receipts were filed, there was no general ledger. Frank developed other facets of the field system and provided detailed instructions for its use, even including a rule about no smoking on the job and the admonition that whistle blasts at starting and quitting time should not be over 4 seconds long. He demonstrated the value of involving workers in making improvements by establishing a suggestion program, including a $10 first prize each month for the best idea on how to increase efficiency, give better service to customers, or secure additional construction work. Included in the field system were provisions for photographing working conditions at the time of any accident for use in lawsuits or other claims. Though Frank's advice was quite detailed and largely only applicable to construction, it was indicative of his desire to rationalize work.

The Concrete System contained detailed advice for concrete contractors.[35] Frank wrote here too of motivating workers, including contests between work groups to finish a wall or build concrete pillars. *The Bricklaying System* was also technical, but brought forth a facet of study new to Frank. His original concern was with the training of apprentices, and Frank saw the wastefulness of hand-me-down instruction from experienced workers. For example, he proposed first finding the best way of laying bricks through motion study, followed by instruction, and insisted that an emphasis be placed on learning the right way to lay bricks before maximum output was expected of a new bricklayer. At a record pace, some of Frank's workers could individually lay 3,000 bricks per day.[36] This early work was but a prelude to his later in-depth analysis of motions and fatigue. In this connection, Frank devised a system for classifying hand motions into 17 basic divisions called *therbligs* (*Gilbreth* spelled backward with the *th* transposed).[37]

As Frank's contacts grew, his interests broadened. Through membership in ASME, he met Taylor and other leaders of the new scientific-management movement—men like Barth and Gantt.

[34] Gilbreth, *Quest for the One Best Way*, p. 22.
[35] Jane Morley, "Frank Bunker Gilbreth's Concrete System," *Concrete International: Designed Construction*, 12 (November 1990), pp. 57–62.
[36] Leland W. Peck, "A High Record in Bricklaying Attained by Novel Methods," *Engineering News* 62 (August 5, 1909), pp. 152–154.
[37] Frank B. Gilbreth and Lillian M. Gilbreth, "Classifying the Elements of Work: Methods of Analyzing Work into Seventeen Subdivisions," *Management and Administration* 8(2) (August 1924), pp. 151–154 and 8(3) (September 1924), pp. 295–298.

And So, into Scientific Management

By 1912, Frank had completely given up the construction business and began devoting his full attention to management consulting. With the same single-minded focus he had given to bricklaying, he now studied the emerging scientific-management field. More and more convinced that "the greatest waste in the world comes from needless, ill-directed, and ineffective motions,"[38] Frank sought new methods of discovering that waste and eliminating it. In 1892, he was the first to use motion-picture cameras to analyze a worker's motions. He put roller skates on messengers in a Montgomery Ward office to reduce their fatigue and increase delivery speed. At the suggestion of Jacob M. Dickinson, former Secretary of War, he tried to develop a better method of picking cotton.[39] He observed 150 appendectomies to find the "one best way" to remove an appendix. In conjunction with Lillie, Frank authored papers such as "The Application of Scientific Management to the Work of the Nurse," "Motion-Study in Surgery," and "Scientific Management in the Hospital."[40] At one point, he even studied the motions of epileptics.[41] And with the same dedication, working now with Walter Camp, Frank filmed and analyzed the swings of golf champions such as Gil Nichols and James "Long Jim" Barnes. Nor was the national pastime exempt from his studies. In 1913, he filmed and analyzed a baseball game between the Phillies and the Giants at the Polo Grounds.[42] Frank's many industrial clients included Eastman Kodak, Lever Brothers, Pierce Arrow Motor Cars, and U.S. Rubber.

Frank's use of a motion-picture camera to study motions was a major contribution to the field of scientific management. Initially, he and Lillie filmed a worker going through his work-cycle against a background of 4-inch squares. Then they would run the film forward and backward to study the worker's motions. They called this "micromotion study." Subsequently, they conceived the idea of attaching small electric lights to the worker's body so that by filming the worker in motion they would be able to obtain a continuous white tracing of the worker's movements. They called this a *cyclegraph*. To reproduce the time required for each movement they created a *chronocyclegraph* showing, instead of a continuous white tracing, a series of dashes, with the pattern of dashes—bunched up (where the movement had been slowest) or spread out at greater intervals elsewhere—giving an indication of the time occupied in a worker's separate movements. As a further refinement, they employed a stereoscopic camera to see a worker's movements in three dimensions. They called this a *stereochronocyclegraph*. Finally, they developed a special clock or, *microchronometer*, to show correct time to one-thousandth of a minute.[43]

Despite the connotations of *speed work*, Frank remained something of an idealist. It is said that "nothing ever aroused his temper more than a selfish employer who wanted to adopt all the latest things in management in his plant, but wanted to hog all the savings himself and not share with his workers."[44] In contrast to the "blacklists" of the period, Frank instituted a "white list"

[38] Frank B. Gilbreth and Lillian M. Gilbreth, "Motion Study and Time Study Instruments of Precision," *Transactions, International Engineering Congress*, 1915, vol. 2 (San Francisco, CA: 1916), p. 473.

[39] "Efficiency Expert Will Lecture on Waste of Effort," *New Orleans Times-Picayune* (April 17, 1916), p. 5.

[40] For more on the Gilbreths' pioneering work in the medical field, see Charles D. Wrege, "The Efficient Management of Hospitals: Pioneer Work of Ernest Codman, Robert Dickinson, and Frank Gilbreth, 1910–1918" in Richard C. Huseman, ed., *Proceedings of the Annual Meeting of the Academy of Management* (1980), pp. 114–118; *idem*, "Medical Men and Scientific Management: A Forgotten Chapter in Management History," *Review of Business and Economic Research* 18(3) (Spring 1983), pp. 32–47; and Caitjan Gainty, "'Going After the High-Brows': Frank Gilbreth and the Surgical Subject, 1912–1917," *Representations* 118(1) (Spring 2012), pp. 1–27.

[41] Frank B. Gilbreth, "Discussion," on "Job Specification — Job Analysis." *Proceedings, Annual Convention, Industrial Relations Association of America* (Newark, NJ, 1920), pp. 206–207

[42] Arthur G. Bedeian, "Frank B. Gilbreth, Walter C. Camp, and the World of Sports," *Management & Organizational History* 7(4) (November 2012), pp. 319–335.

[43] Bruce Kaiper, "The Cyclegraph and Work Motion Model," in Lew Thomas and Peter D'Agostino, eds., *Still Photography: The Problematic Model* (San Francisco, CA: NFS Press, 1981), pp. 57–63.

[44] Frank B. Gilbreth, Jr. *Time Out for Happiness* (New York: Thomas Y. Crowell Company, 1970), p. 140. See also Arthur G. Bedeian, "Finding the "One Best Way'," *Conference Board Record* 13(6) (June 1976), pp. 38–39.

designed to provide rewards for workers who had performed well. In an effort to develop the skills of the men who worked for him, Frank developed "a three-position plan" of promotion.[45] Under the plan, each man should perform his own job, as well as train the man below him to be his successor and to learn the next higher position to which he might be promoted. These efforts were part of his goal of developing employees to their fullest potential. As Frank put it, "We want to find the highest task a man can perform permanently, year after year, and thrive, and be happy. A man wants to do more than get fat, he wants to be happy."[46]

Frank's efforts paralleled what Taylor was attempting, although they differed in terminology. Taylor called his work "time study," and Frank dubbed his "motion study." In practice, they shared the same objective: eliminating unnecessary motions to increase efficiency. Unlike Taylor, though, Frank maintained that the stopwatch was not the essence of his system. In one of the many amusing anecdotes about the Gilbreths in *Cheaper by the Dozen*, his son, Frank, Jr., and daughter, Ernestine, wrote that Frank, however, was fascinated with time and always the efficiency expert at home and on the job. He buttoned his vest from the bottom up, instead of top down, because the former took only 3 seconds and the latter took 7. He used two shaving brushes (one in each hand) to lather his face and found that he could reduce shaving time by 17 seconds. He similarly tried shaving with two razors, found that he could reduce the total shaving time by 44 seconds, but gave up this idea because it took 2 minutes to bandage each nick and cut. His children suggested that it was the two lost minutes that bothered him and not the nicks and cuts.[47]

Support for the Scientific-Management Movement

Frank was one of the scientific-management movement's most fervent advocates. Taylor devoted 8 pages of *The Principles of Scientific Management* to Frank's motion studies of bricklayers. In 1911, Taylor asked Frank and Lillie to write responses to all the letters he had received after the serialized publication of *The Principles of Scientific Management* in *The American Magazine*. The magazine refused to print the responses; it was fearful that doing so would offend its subscribers. Aware of the publicity Taylor's work was generating, D. Van Nostrand Company agreed to publish the responses in book form, but only if Lillie's name did not appear on the cover, as it did not want it known that Frank's heretofore undisclosed coauthor was a woman. The Gilbreths agreed and, furthermore, declined any royalties so that the book could be sold at a lower price and, thus, have as wide a circulation as possible.[48] The Gilbreths' responses became the basis for Frank's (actually ghostwritten by Lillie) *Primer of Scientific Management*. In the 103-page *Primer*, Frank posed common questions about scientific management and provided answers in an effort to explain Taylor's workplace philosophy. The following questions and responses are illustrative examples:

> **Does [Scientific Management] not make machines out of men?**
> Is a good boxer, or fencer, or golf player a machine? . . . He certainly approaches closely the 100 per cent mark of perfection from the standpoint of the experts in motion study. It is not nearly so important to decide whether or not he is a machine as to decide whether or not it is desirable to have a man trained as near perfection as possible. . . .

---

[45] Frank B. Gilbreth and Lillian M. Gilbreth, "The Three Position Plan of Promotion," *Iron Age* (November 4, 1915), pp. 1657–1659 and *idem*, "The Three Position Plan of Promotion," *Annals of the American Academy of Political and Social Science* 65 (May), pp. 289–296.

[46] Frank B. Gilbreth quoted in Milton J. Nadworny, "Frank and Lillian Gilbreth and Industrial Relations," *Journal of Industrial Engineering* 13(2) (May 1962), p. 122.

[47] Frank B. Gilbreth, Jr., and Ernestine Gilbreth Carey, *Cheaper by the Dozen* (New York: Crowell, 1948), p. 3.

Does not the monotony of the highly specialized subdivision of work cause the men to become insane?

No, he will not become insane, for if his brain is of such an order that his work does not stimulate it to its highest degree, then he will be promoted, for under Scientific Management each man is specially trained to occupy that place that is the highest that he is capable. . . .

Does not the "speed boss" speed up the men to a point that is injurious to their health?

"Speed boss," like "task," is an unfortunate name . . . the "speed boss" does not tell the men how fast they shall make their motions . . . [but he does] tell the men at what speeds their machines shall run. . . .

If Scientific Management is a good thing for the workers, why do the labor leaders all oppose it?

They do not all oppose it. Some oppose it for the simple reason that they do not understand it; the others have visions that Scientific Management is something that will reduce the value of their jobs,—and all are afraid, because of the bad treatment that workmen as a whole have had in the past, that Scientific Management is simply a new "confidence game," presented in a more attractive manner than ever before . . . they simply cannot imagine Dr. Taylor or any other practical man working for their interests unless there is a "come-back" somewhere.[49]

Frank also observed that Taylor's ideas and scientific management should not be confused with what Henry Ford was doing with assembly-line production. He had toured a Ford assembly plant and was totally without sympathy for how jobs were designed:

At the Ford plant he [Frank] saw men at benches too low for them, men stretching farther than their normal reach, men in uncomfortable positions as they put on rear wheels, and much other evidence of making workers adjust to the line rather than making the line conform to the best needs of human beings. Management claimed that people adjusted to these things and did not mind, just as contractors kept saying that bricklayers did not mind stooping for bricks.[50]

Although Frank had been one of Taylor's most devout disciples, beginning in 1912, the two became increasingly estranged.[51] This was partially due to Taylor's reluctance to consider motion study separate from time study and doubts Taylor harbored about whether Frank possessed the patience required to spend the 4–5 years Taylor felt necessary to successfully introduce his methods in any setting. Taylor was also concerned that Frank was becoming increasingly identified with his name in the mind of the general public, regardless of his own personal reservations regarding Frank's qualifications.[52] Their final break came in 1914 when Taylor received a complaint from Milton C. Herrmann at Herrmann, Aukam & Company, a New Jersey handkerchief-manufacturing

[48] Brian C. Price, *One Best Way: Frank and Lillian Gilbreth's Transformation of Scientific Management, 1885–1940* (Unpublished dissertation, Purdue University, West Lafayette, IN, 1987), p. 141. See also *idem*, "Frank and Lillian Gilbreth and the Motion Study Controversy, 1907–1930," in David Nelson, ed., *A Mental Revolution: Scientific Management since Taylor* (Columbus, OH: Ohio State University Press, 1991), pp. 58–76; Carol Carlson Dean, "*Primer of Scientific Management* by Frank B. Gilbreth: A Response to Publication of Taylor's *Principles* in *The American Magazine*," 3(1) (1997), pp. 31–41.

[49] Frank B. Gilbreth, *Primer of Scientific Management* (New York: D. Van Nostrand, 1912), pp. 49, 53–54, 65, 87–88.

[50] Yost, *Frank and Lillian Gilbreth*, p. 246.

[51] See Milton Nadworny, "Frederick Taylor and Frank Gilbreth – Competition in Scientific Management," *Business History Review* 21(1) (Spring 1957), pp. 23–34; Daniel Nelson, *Frederick W. Taylor and the Rise of Scientific Management* (Madison, WI: University of Wisconsin Press, 1980), pp. 131–136.

[52] Hugo J. Kijne, "Time and Motion Study: Beyond the Taylor-Gilbreth Controversy," in J.-Spender and Hugo J. Kijne, eds., *Scientific Management: Frederick Winslow Taylor's Gift to the World?* (Boston, MA: Kluwer Academic), p. 69.

company. Herrmann alleged that Frank had overcharged and that inferior assistants had been assigned in Frank's place while he was on another job in Germany. Taylor wrote Gilbreth concerning Herrmann's complaints, ending his letter with "Is there anything that you wish me to do in this matter?"[53] Subsequently, Taylor dined with the Gilbreths at their home, received an autographed copy of Lillie's book *The Psychology of Management*, and the Herrmann, Aukam matter was discussed further. We do not know the course of that evening, but H. King Hathaway took over the consulting work at Herrmann, Aukam. Frank was understandably bitter. In the ensuing years, the Gilbreths went their own way, concentrating their efforts on motion, skill, and fatigue problems.

The First Lady of Management

In his move away from the Taylor system, Frank was increasingly aided by Lillie, the daughter of a German-born sugar refiner, who spent her early years in Oakland, California. She had attended the University of California, Berkeley, majoring in English and modern languages. A Phi Beta Kappa graduate in 1900, she was the first woman to give the university's commencement-day address. After receiving an M.A. degree in English literature, she began work toward a Ph.D. degree in psychology. She interrupted her studies in mid-1903 for a trip abroad and, upon arriving in Boston prior to embarking, was introduced to Frank. Shortly after her return from Europe, he proposed marriage and a dozen children, which by his calculation was the most efficient number.[54] Lillie and Frank married in 1904. After their marriage, Lillie changed her academic interests to industrial psychology, for she thought that this field would best complement Frank's work. Combining marriage and an ever-growing family with assisting in Frank's work, Lillie continued to do research on her thesis "The Psychology of Management" and submitted it in 1912. The University of California accepted the thesis but informed her that she would have to return to campus for a year of residency before her Ph.D. degree could be granted. Lillie had been led to believe that this requirement would be waived in her case, but university officials were steadfast. Frank was furious and began looking for a publisher for what was to have been Lillie's thesis, one of the first contributions of its kind. *Industrial Engineering and The Engineering Digest* published the thesis in serial form (May 1912–May 1913), and it was eventually published in book form by Sturgis & Walton, but only after she agreed that her name would appear as L. M. Gilbreth and that no publicity would be given to the fact that the author was a woman.[55] Eventually, the university authorities agreed that Lillie could spend her residency in any college that granted advanced degrees in industrial psychology or management. Such institutions were scarce at that time, but Frank found that Brown University was planning to offer a Ph.D. degree in educational psychology with an emphasis in applied management. At Brown, Lillian wrote a

Lillian M. Gilbreth. Courtesy of the Ronald G. Greenwood Collection, University Archives, Alvin Sherman Library, Nova Southeastern, Fort Lauderdale, FL.

---

53 Frederick W. Taylor to Frank B. Gilbreth, March 11, 1914, Taylor Collection, file 59A.

54 For more on Gilbreth family life, see Arthur G. Bedeian and Shannon G. Taylor, "The *Übermensch* Meets the "One Best Way": Barbara S. Burks, the Gilbreth Family, and the Eugenics Movement," *Journal of Management History* 15(2) (2009), pp. 216–221.

55 Lillian M. Gilbreth, *The Psychology of Management: The Function of the Mind in Determining, Teaching and Installing Methods of Least Waste* (New York: Sturgis & Walton, 1914). Originally serialized in *Industrial Engineering and The Engineering Digest*, May through December 1912 and January through May 1913.

new dissertation "Some Aspects of Eliminating Waste in Teaching," finally completing her Ph.D. degree requirements in 1915.[56]

Lillie brought a human element into scientific management through her training, insight, and concern for worker welfare. In *The Psychology of Management*, she defined her topic as "the effect of the mind that is directing work upon that work which is directed, and the effect of this undirected and directed work upon the mind of the worker."[57] Heretofore, management had been considered an area in which no one could hope to succeed who had not inherited the "knack." The prevailing belief, reflected in Thomas Carlyle's famous quote "The History of the world is but the Biography of great men," was that leaders were born and not made.[58] In contrast, with the advent of scientific management, it became possible to base management on "laws" and study it in the classroom. Lillie would observe: Successful management "lies on the *man*, not on the *work*."[59] Scientific management provided a means to make the most of people's efforts. As Taylor explained:

> In the past the prevailing idea has been well expressed in the saying that "Captains of industry are born, not made"; and the theory has been that if one could get the right man, methods could be safely left to him. In the future it will be appreciated that our leaders must be trained right as well as born right, and that no great man can (with the old system of personal management) hope to compete with a number of ordinary men who have been properly organized so as efficiently to cooperate.[60]

Lillie characterized three historical styles of management: *traditional*, *transitory*, and *scientific*. Traditional management was the driver, or Marquis of Queensbury, style that followed the unitary line of command and was typified by centralized authority. Lillie adopted the prizefighting term "Marquis of Queensbury" because she felt that it embodied the physical and mental contest waged between workers and managers "according to the rules of the game." Transitory management referred to all forms in the interim stage between the traditional and the installation of scientific management. Scientific management, or the Taylor plan of management, described the goal toward which all firms should strive.

Lillie compared and contrasted these three styles of management according to how they affected individuality, functionalization, measurement, analysis and synthesis, standardization, records and programs, teaching, performance incentives, and welfare. On individuality, she noted that psychologists up to that time had been largely concerned with the psychology of crowds. Comparatively little work had been done on the psychology of individuals. Under traditional management, individuality was stifled by the power of a central figure; under scientific management, it became a fundamental principle in selection, performance incentives, and overall consideration of worker welfare, that is, "general wellbeing, mental, physical, moral and financial."[61] The objective of scientific management was to develop each worker to the fullest potential by strengthening personal traits, special abilities, and skills. Its focus was on how management could develop workers for their mutual benefit, not on workers' use and exploitation, as under the Marquis of Queensbury type of management.

Functionalization promoted worker welfare by improving skills through specialization, enabling greater pride in output and higher wages; measurement ensured that workers received the product of their labors; standardization improved morale and prevented workers from becoming a machine; and teaching overcame fear and instilled pride and confidence in workers. Traditional

---

[56] Ronald G. Greenwood, Charles D. Wrege, and Regina A. Greenwood, "Newly Discovered Gilbreth Manuscript," in Kae H. Chung, ed., *Proceedings of the Annual Meeting of the Academy of Management* (1983), p. 111.

[57] Gilbreth, *The Psychology of Management*, p. 1.

[58] Thomas Carlyle, *Heroes, Hero Worship and the Heroic in History* (London: Chapman and Hall, 1840), p. 27.

[59] Gilbreth, *The Psychology of Management*, p. 3.

[60] Frederick W. Taylor, *The Principles of Scientific Management* (New York: Harper & Brothers, 1911), pp. 6–7.

[61] Gilbreth, *The Psychology of Management*, p. 30.

management relied solely on rewards and punishment, whereas scientific management attempted to enlist worker cooperation. The rewards under scientific management differed because they were predetermined (ensuring against fear of rate cutting), prompt (rather than delayed under profit sharing), and personal (in the sense that workers were rewarded for their efforts and not by their class of work). With scientific management, workers gained "mental poise and security" rather than the anxiety created by traditional management. Concerning welfare, scientific management promoted regular work, encouraged good personal habits, and fostered the physical, mental, moral, and financial development of workers.

Lillie fully intended to become a practicing psychologist. She soon found, however, she was devoting most of her time to rearing the 12 Gilbreth children. The scientific management of the Gilbreth family and their Montclair, New Jersey, home was immortalized in the best-selling books and movies, *Cheaper by the Dozen* and *Belles on Their Toes*, as well as in the later novel, *Time Out for Happiness*.[62]

On June 14, 1924, tragedy struck the Gilbreths. Three days before they were to sail to Europe to attend the First World Power Conference (June 30–July 1, 1924) in London and the First International Management Congress in Prague, Czechoslovakia (July 20–24, 1924), Frank died of a heart attack while talking to Lillie from a telephone booth at the Lackawanna Railroad Depot in Montclair. A family meeting was held, and Lillie decided to fulfill the Gilbreths' European commitments. She sailed for London 5 days later. At the World Power Conference, she spoke on Frank's behalf.[63] In Prague, Lillie presided at a session on Education, participated in various activities of the U.S. delegation, attended a memorial service in Frank's honor, and was made a member of the Masaryk Academy of Labor, the highest scientific honor in Czechoslovakia.[64]

Returning to Montclair, Lillie was determined to continue Frank's work. She became president of Gilbreth, Inc., and in the fall of 1924 joined the faculty at Purdue University as a lecturer. In 1935 she was made a professor of management in the Purdue School of Mechanical Engineering, the first woman to hold such an appointment.

A strong psychological thread ran through all of Lillie's work, and she made contributions in areas such as the application of management and motion-study techniques to the home (e.g., to ease access and save time: refrigerators with features for eggs, milk, and butter, and to minimize movements and fatigue; a foot-pedal trash can; and shelves, sinks, and tables at a proper height),[65] the rehabilitation of the disabled,[66] the use of leisure time to create "happiness minutes,"[67] and the design and marketing of products to women consumers.[68] As a result of Frank's service as an Army Major during World War I, he and Lillie had become interested in how to use motion study to design jobs to retrain soldiers, especially amputees, so they could resume a productive life after the war. They developed devices to assist the disabled, such as a typewriter for a one-armed

[62] Frank B. Gilbreth, Jr., and Ernestine Gilbreth Carey, *Cheaper by the Dozen* (New York: Crowell, 1948); Frank B. Gilbreth, Jr. and Ernestine Gilbreth Carey, *Belles on Their Toes* (New York: Crowell, 1950); Frank B. Gilbreth, Jr., *Time Out for Happiness* (New York: Crowell, 1970).

[63] For Lillie's review of papers presented at the conference, see Lillian M. Gilbreth, "A Review of the Papers Presented before the First World Power Conference," *American Machinist* 61(6) (August 7, 1924), p. 222.

[64] International Management Congress, *Report of the Proceedings of the First International Management Congress in Prague (PIMCO)*, July 20–24, 1924 (Prague, Czechoslovakia: Institute for the Technical Management of Industry, Masaryk Academy of Work, 1925), pp. 29, 53–54, 102–103, 110.

[65] Anne M. Perusek, "The First Lady of Management," *SWE* [Society of Women Engineers] *Magazine* 46(1) (January–February, 2000), p. 88.

[66] See J. Michael Gotcher, "Assisting the Handicapped: The Pioneering Efforts of Frank and Lillian Gilbreth," *Journal of Management* 18(1) (March 1992), pp. 5–13; Franz T. Lohrke, "Motion Study for the Blinded" A Review of the Gilbreths' Work with the Visually Handicapped," *International Journal of Public Administration* 16(5) (1993), pp. 667–682.

[67] Mario Krenn, "From Scientific Management to Homemaking: Lillian M Gilbreth's Contributions to the Development of Management Thought," *Management & Organizational History* 6(2) (May 2011), pp. 145–161.

[68] Laurel D. Graham, "Lillian Gilbreth's Psychologically Enriched Scientific Management of Women Consumers," *Journal of Historical Research in Marketing* 5(3) (2013), pp. 351–369.

typist, and Lillie worked with the General Electric Company to redesign home appliances for disabled homemakers.[69] The Gilbreths were among those who lobbied Congress to pass the War Risk Insurance Act for disabled veterans. Later, this act served to pioneer legislation for those who were not war casualties, but needed vocational rehabilitation.[70]

Lillie also contributed to healing the rift between Frank's *motion* study and Taylor's *time* study. In 1921, years after Taylor's death, the Gilbreths issued an "indictment" of time study in the *Bulletin of the Taylor Society*. They attacked Taylor's followers (Carl G. Barth, Dwight V. Merrick, and Sanford E. Thompson) for continuing to promote stopwatch study because of their interest in selling time devices, forms, and books about time study. Further, they argued that time study was less precise, therefore less scientific, whereas motion study provided absolutely accurate times and the "one best way."[71] The attack was probably unnecessary. After Taylor's death, his followers began to recognize that, to overcome union resistance, they needed to address the widespread belief that time study was synonymous with "speed work." Following Frank's death, Lillie wrote in the *Bulletin of the Taylor Society* that time study and motion study were complementary and the stop watch was used by the Gilbreths' protégés when it was appropriate, but filmed studies were more accurate and useful.[72]

Moving out further from Frank's shadow, Lillie went on to pioneer in the field now known as human-resource management. She was keenly interested in the scientific selection, placement, and training of workers. Always progressive in her thinking, she displayed a deep appreciation of the human factor in industry. As early as 1914, she wrote that scientific management is "built on the basic principle of recognition of the individual, not only as an economic unit but also as a personality, with all the idiosyncrasies that distinguish a person."[73] Whereas much of Lillie's work is now taken for granted, it was far in advance of its time. More than 50 years ago, she publicly urged an end to discrimination in both hiring and retention of workers over 40.[74] Convinced that programs to hire and train "older" workers were simply "good business," she called for research to measure comparative job performance by age. In the larger public arena, Lillie served under Presidents Hoover, Roosevelt, Eisenhower, Kennedy, and Johnson on committees dealing with civil defense, war production, aging, and rehabilitation of the physically disabled.

In addition to teaching at Purdue University and lecturing throughout the world, Lillie taught at the University of Wisconsin at Madison; Rutgers University at New Brunswick; and Newark College of Engineering. The Gilbreth Medal, named for both Frank and Lillian, was awarded to Lillie in 1931—the only female recipient to date; she was also the only woman to receive the coveted Gantt Gold Medal (1944) and the only woman to be awarded the prestigious Comite Internationale de l'Organisation Scientifique (CIOS) Gold Medal (1954). The recipient of 22 honorary degrees, she was the first woman to be named an honorary member of the ASME (1926), as well as the first elected to the National Academy of Engineering (1965). In 1987, she

---

[69] Lillian M. Gilbreth, *The Home-Maker and Her Job* (New York: Appleton-Century-Crofts, 1927); and *idem, Management in the Home: Happier Living through Saving Time and Energy* (New York: Dodd, Mead, 1955). See also Elspeth H. Brown, "The Prosthetics of Management: Motion Study, Photography, and the Industrialized Body in World War I America," in Katherine Ott, David Serlin, and Stephen Mihm, eds., *Artificial Pasts, Practical Lives: Modern Histories of Prosthetics* (New York: NYU Press, 2002), pp. 249–281; Nicholas Sammonds, "Picture This: Lillian Gilbreth's Industrial Cinema for the Home," *Camera Obscura* 21(3, 63) (December 2006), pp. 102–133.

[70] Daniel A. Wren and Ronald G. Greenwood, *Management Innovators: The People and Ideas That Have Shaped Modern Business* (New York: Oxford University Press, 1998), p. 146. Like Taylor, Gantt, and Emerson, Frank was also honored by the U.S. Maritime Commission in 1943 with a Liberty Ship named in his honor, see "5 Ships to be Named for Noted Engineers," *New York Times* (December 5, 1943), p. 67.

[71] Frank B. and Lillian M. Gilbreth, "An Indictment of Stop-Watch Time Study," *Bulletin of the Taylor Society* 6(3) (June 1921), pp. 99–108. See also the discussion that followed the Gilbreths' paper (pp. 109–135).

[72] Lillian M. Gilbreth, "The Relations of Time and Motion Study," *Bulletin of the Taylor Society* 13(3) (June 1928), pp. 126–128.

[73] *Idem, Psychology of Management*, pp. 18–19.

[74] Lillian M. Gilbreth, "Scrapped at Forty," *The Survey* 62(7) (July 1, 1929), pp. 402–403; *idem*, "Hiring and Firing: Shall the Calendar Measure Length of Service?" *Factory and Industrial Management* 79(2) (February 1930), pp. 310–311.

was honored when the U.S. Postal Service issued a stamp to commemorate her achievements. Is there any doubt about why she has been called the First Lady of Management?

The Gilbreths were a formidable team. He an engineer and she a psychologist, they pooled their talents in search of the "one best way." Their interests ranged widely. They made contributions to materials handling and work methods, to the study of motions and fatigue, to empower the disabled, and to modern human-resource management. The impact of their contributions continues today. Indeed, the configurations for the crew compartment, crew seats, and instrument panel of the National Aeronautical and Space Administration's Apollo command and service modules were designed using techniques pioneered by Frank and Lillian Gilbreth.[75]

Efficiency through Organization: Harrington Emerson

Harrington Emerson (1853–1931) was born in Trenton, New Jersey, and educated at private schools in Paris, Munich, Siena, and Athens.[76] His father was a Professor of Political Economy who taught at various European universities, and he was a grandson of Samuel D. Ingraham, Secretary of the Treasury under President Andrew Jackson. He earned an engineering degree from the Royal Polytechnic (Munich) in 1875. Returning to the United States in 1876, he taught modern languages at the University of Nebraska (Lincoln) until 1882, when he was dismissed because he favored allowing students and faculty greater freedom in their personal behavior and advocated removing religion from classroom instruction.[77] After holding a succession of jobs, he established the Emerson Institute (later the Emerson Efficiency Engineers) at New York City in 1901. Emerson was symbolic of the new breed of "efficiency engineers" (a term he coined) who were bringing innovative methods

Harrington Emerson. Bain Collection / Library of Congress.

of time and cost savings to U.S. industry. The nation's first big business, the railroads, was showing signs of wear and tear. Locomotive and railcar repair and maintenance shops were a bottleneck that kept rolling stock from rolling. Emerson began as a troubleshooter for the general manager of the Burlington Railroad and in 1904 became a consultant to the Atchison, Topeka, & Santa Fe Railroad. He standardized materials and tools, centralized production scheduling and routing, instituted time study, and introduced a performance incentive plan. After two years, output was up 57 percent, costs were down 36 percent, and the average pay of Santa Fe workers was up 14.5 percent. In spite of conflict with unionized shop workers (who lost the struggle), Emerson's efforts were praised as an example of what scientific management could do for the nation's railroads.[78]

---

[75] Norman J. Ryker, Jr., "Man-Equipment Task System for Apollo," in *The Frank Gilbreth Centennial* (New York: American Society of Mechanical Engineers, 1969), pp. 4–36.

[76] For further biographical data, see Edward J. Mehren, "Harrington Emerson's Place in Industrial Engineering," *Society of Industrial Engineers Bulletin* 13(7) (June–July 1931), pp. 4–8; Sidney Brooks, "Harrington Emerson: Some Glimpses of His Life," *Society of Industrial Engineers Bulletin* 13(7) (June–July 1931), pp. 9–11. See also Morgan L Witzel, ed., *The Biographical Dictionary of Management*, vol. 1 (Bristol, England: Thoemmes Press, 2001), pp. 276–282.

[77] William F. Muhs, "Harrington Emerson as Professor," unpublished paper presented at the annual meeting of the Academy of Management, Detroit, Mich., August 11, 1980, p. 4.

[78] Carl Graves, "Applying Scientific Management Principles to Railroad Repair Shops – The Santa Fe Experience, 1904–1918," in Jeremy Atack, ed., *Business and Economic History*, 2nd ser., vol. 1 (1981), pp. 276–282.

By 1925, Emerson's reputation had spread to Germany, Japan, Britain, India, Kenya, and Uganda. His innovations enabled railroads (including the London underground) to reduce costs, minimize operating downtime, and decrease capital requirements by standardizing methods, materials, and equipment.[79] Success on the Santa Fe and other railroads created opportunities for Emerson's firm to apply his ideas to a cross section of companies in multiple industries and to municipalities such as Seattle, Milwaukee, and New York. Though Emerson used many of Taylor's methods, in soliciting clients, he "emphasized his flexibility and deviation from Taylor's more rigid prescriptions."[80]

Like the Gilbreths, waste and inefficiency were the twin evils that Emerson saw pervading the entire U.S. industrial system. His experience had shown that railroad repair shops averaged 50 percent efficiency and that preventable labor and material wastes were costing the railroad industry $300 million annually (hence his well-publicized Eastern Rate Case testimony of savings equaling $1 million a day).[81] Emerson believed that national prosperity was not a function of either an abundance or a lack of natural resources, but rather the "ambition, the desire for success and wealth" of a nation's workers[82]. In Emerson's view, the United States possessed abundant resources and an ambitious workforce, which had led to its rise as a world industrial power, yet it was losing its advantage due to inefficient use of resources. Emerson was convinced that the resulting waste could only be reduced by the proper organization of men, machines, and materials.

Line and Staff Organization

Taylor's "functional foremanship" did not appeal to Emerson. He agreed with Taylor that the specialized knowledge of staff members was necessary, but differed in how best to use this expertise. Influenced by his European education, Emerson admired Count Helmuth Karl Bernhard Graf von Moltke who, from 1857 to 1888, had modernized the Prussian army's General Staff.[83] The logic behind Moltke's modernization was straightforward. Each subject vital to military efforts was to be studied to perfection by a separate staff specialist who, with other specialists, would form a supreme general staff to advise the nation's field marshals on all matters pertaining to the Prussian army.

Emerson sought to apply Moltke's staff logic to the workplace. His goal was to achieve a "complete parallelism between line and staff, so that every member of the line can at any time have the benefit of staff knowledge and staff assistance."[84] As envisioned by Emerson, each firm was to have a chief-of-staff serving over four major subdivisions: the first to plan, direct, and advise on the well-being of employees; the second to plan, direct, and advise on structures, machines, tools, and other equipment; the third to plan, direct, and advise on materials, including their purchase, custody, issue, and handling; and the fourth to plan, direct, and advise on methods and conditions, including standards, records, and accounting. Staff knowledge and advice were to be available to every member of the line: "It is the business of staff, not to accomplish work, but to set up standards and ideals, so that the line may work more efficiently."[85] The distinction between Emerson's line and staff organization and Taylor's functional foremanship is, thus,

[79] Mark Aldrich, "On the Track of Efficiency: Scientific Management Comes to Railroad Shops, 1900–1930," *Business History Review* 84(3) (Autumn, 2010), pp. 501–526.

[80] James P. Quigel, Jr. *The Business of Selling Efficiency: Harrington Emerson and the Emerson Efficiency Engineers, 1900–1990* (Unpublished dissertation, Pennsylvania State University, State College, PA, 1992), pp. 301, 421.

[81] Harrington Emerson, "Preventable Waste and Losses on Railroads," *Railroad Age* 45 (June 5, 1908), p. 12.

[82] Harrington Emerson, *Efficiency as a Basis for Operations and Wages* (New York: Engineering Magazine, 1911), p. 37. Originally serialized in *The Engineering Magazine*, July, 1908, through March, 1909.

[83] *Ibid.*, pp. 64–66. After the unification of the German Empire in 1871 Prussian General Staff's title was changed to "Great General Staff." Karl von Clausewitz commented on the Prussian Army's General Staff as early as 1793. Karl von Clausewitz, *On War* (New York: Random House, 1943), p. 489. Originally published in 1832.

[84] Emerson, *Efficiency as a Basis for Operations and Wages*, p. 69.

[85] *Ibid.*, p. 112.

apparent: Instead of giving one person the responsibility and authority over each workplace function, Emerson left supervision and authority to line managers, who then accessed staff for specialized knowledge and advice. This shift maintained the advantages of specialized knowledge and facilitated coordination without the disadvantages associated with violating the unity of command principle.

Principles of Efficiency

Ironically, Emerson's efficiency work was somewhat overshadowed by the press coverage Taylor's task-management system received following the Eastern Rate Case hearings. Subsequent to the hearings, Emerson published *Twelve Principles of Efficiency*, which became another landmark in the history of management thought. A chapter was devoted to each of the eponymous principles; broadly conceived, the first five concerned relations with people and the remainder concerned methods, institutions, and systems. The principles were considered to be interdependent and when coordinated to form a basis for building a management system. In the book's preface, Emerson stated his basic premise: "It is not labor, not capital, not land, which has created modern wealth or is creating it today. It is ideas that create wealth, and what is wanted is more ideas – more uncovering of natural reservoirs, and less labor and capital and land per unit of production."[86]

No modern author could state the contemporary challenges facing today's global organizations more cogently. For Emerson, "ideas" were the dominant force for eliminating waste and assuring national prosperity. He saw his 12 principles as instruments for this purpose and the line-staff form of organization as essential for enabling managers to access specialized knowledge and advice. To Emerson "defective organization" was "the industrial hookworm disease."[87] With respect to Emerson's 12 principles of efficiency: The first principle was "clearly defined ideals." This principle made explicit the need for agreement among employees and employers on workplace goals ("ideals") and the importance of everyone pulling in a "straight line." Emerson hoped to reduce conflict, vagueness, uncertainty, and the aimlessness that arose when people did not understand or share a common purpose. The second principle, common sense, exhorted managers to take a larger view of problems and to seek special knowledge and advice wherever they may be found. All employees who had something of value to contribute were encouraged to participate in problem solving.[88] The third principle, competent counsel, was related to the second principle, in that, it pertained to assembling an experienced and knowledgeable staff. Discipline became the fourth principle and provided for obedience and adherence to workplace rules. It was a foundation for the other 11 principles and prevented anarchy. The fifth and final principle pertaining to people was the fair deal. Peace, harmony, and high performance were dependent on fairness in all employee–employer relations. Rather than being patronizing or altruistic, the employee–employer relationship was to be based on mutual advantage.

The seven principles pertaining to workplace methods were more mechanistic and largely self-explanatory: "reliable, immediate, accurate, and permanent records" (information and accounting systems); "dispatching" (planning and routing of work); "standards and schedules" (methods and time for tasks); "standardized conditions"; "standardized operations"; "written standard practice instructions"; and "efficiency reward" (rewards proportionate to efficiency). Each principle was liberally sprinkled with examples from Emerson's consulting experience and formed a thorough, though often redundant, statement of his workplace philosophy.

---

[86] Harrington Emerson, *The Twelve Principles of Efficiency* (New York: Engineering Magazine, 1913), p. x.

[87] *Ibid.*, p. 29. Originally serialized in *The Engineering Magazine*, June, 1910, through September, 1911.

[88] William F. Muhs, "Worker Participation in the Progressive Era: An Assessment by Harrington Emerson," *Academy of Management Review* 7(1) (January 1982), pp. 99–102.

Emerson's Efficiency Engineering and Practice

Emerson made other contributions in cost accounting, in using Hollerith tabulating machines for accounting records, and in setting standards for judging worker and shop efficiency. In cost accounting, Emerson made a clear distinction between historical cost accounting (descriptive) and "the new cost accounting," which estimated what costs should be after waste was eliminated and before work commenced. Although others had written about cost-accounting standards, Emerson appears to have been the first to develop a system of standardized costs for more accurately assessing relative efficiencies in materials and services.[89] G. Charter Harrison took Emerson's ideas and installed the first full-fledged standard cost-accounting system in the Boss Manufacturing Company, Kewanee, Illinois, in 1911. At that time, Boss Manufacturing was the nation's largest maker of work gloves and boots.[90] As early as 1920 Emerson was using Gantt graphics in standard costing to measure and monitor expenses.

Emerson also devised an incentive plan that paid workers a 20 percent bonus for 100 percent efficiency; above 100 percent efficiency, workers received their standard wages for time saved plus a 20 percent bonus for the time worked. For example, at 100 percent efficiency, the bonus was 20 cents per one dollar of wages; at 120 percent efficiency, the bonus was 40 cents per one dollar of wages (i.e., 40 cents = 20 cents for bonus and 20 cents for working 20 percent more efficiently).[91] In practice, scheduling and staff specialists had a more lasting effect on productivity than incentive bonuses, which contributed to worker unrest and "tended to favor skilled workers but [were] limited by inaccurate time studies."[92] Emerson's experiences with performance bonuses met similar resistance as encountered by other scientific management consultants. On the Baltimore & Ohio Railroad, Emerson found 99 percent employee turnover and recognized the waste in hiring, training, and other costs. The B&O's experience was typical in the 1900–1919 period, when annual labor-turnover rates in the United States exceeded 100%.[93]

Emerson's consulting firm was a seedbed for others who became distinguished consultants and executives. These included Earl K Wennerlund, later a vice-president of production at General Motors; Charles E. Knoeppel, who would form his own consulting firm, C. E. Knoeppel and Company, Industrial Engineers, and develop the "profit graph," a forerunner to the breakeven chart; and Herbert N. Casson, who would take efficiency methods and scientific management to Great Britain.[94] In 1925, following a series of disagreements with his partners, Emerson resigned from the firm he founded. Originally called Emerson Engineers, even though none of the members of the association were engineers, the firm later took the name Emerson Consultants.

Emerson has been called the "high priest of efficiency" for his efforts to eliminate waste in industry.[95] He testified before the Special Committee of the House of Representatives to Investigate the Taylor and Other Efficiency Systems (1911–1912); helped found the Efficiency

---

[89] Emerson, *The Twelve Principles of Efficiency*, pp. 167–201; and *idem*, "Standardization and Labor Efficiency in Railroad Shops," *Engineering Magazine* 33(5) (August 1907), pp. 783–786.

[90] David Solomons, "Retrospective: Costing Pioneers, Some Links with the Past," *Accounting Historians Journal* 21(2) (December, 1994), pp. 135–149.

[91] Emerson, *Efficiency as a Basis for Operations and Wages*, pp. 193–196.

[92] Quigel, "The Business of Selling Efficiency," p. 424; Aldrich, "On the Track of Efficiency," p. 525.

[93] Laura Owen, "History of Labor Turnover in the U.S.," *EH Net Encyclopedia*, ed., Robert Whaples, April 29, 2004. http://eh .net/encyclopedia/history-of-labor-turnover-in-the-u-s/

[94] William F. Muhs, "The Emerson Engineers: A Look at One of the First Management Consulting Firms in the U.S.," in John A. Pearce II and Richard B. Robinson, Jr., eds., *Proceedings of the Annual Meeting of the Academy of Management* (1986), pp. 123–127. For insights into the life and work of Herbert N. Casson and Charles E. Knoeppel, see Morgan L Witzel, ed., *The Biographical Dictionary of Management*, vol. 1 (Bristol, England: Thoemmes Press, 2001), pp. 137–144 and pp. 539–540, respectively.

[95] [W. Jerome Arnold] "Famous Firsts: High Priest of Efficiency," *Business Week*, June 22, 1963, pp. 100, 104.

Society (1912); served on the Federated American Engineering Societies' Committee on the Elimination of Waste in Industry (1921); and was instrumental in the founding of the Association of Management Consulting Firms (1929). His contributions were unique in advocating a line-staff form of organization, developing standards for use in cost accounting, and anticipating the need for employment specialists. His testimony at the Eastern Rate Case hearings brought the scientific-management movement to the world's attention.

The Gospel in Public-Sector Organizations: Morris L. Cooke

While Taylor, Barth, the Gilbreths, Gantt, and Emerson were eliminating waste and inefficiency in industry, Morris Llewellyn Cooke (1872–1960) was extending the gospel of efficiency to public-sector organizations. Cooke attended Lehigh Preparatory School and then Lehigh University in Bethlehem, Pennsylvania, graduating in 1895 with a degree in mechanical engineering. After an apprenticeship at Cramp's Shipyard (Philadelphia), he worked in various companies in the surrounding area. Long before he had met or heard of Fred Taylor, he was applying a "questioning method" to the waste he saw all around him. As scientific management gained notoriety, Cooke became an avid defender of Taylor's methods. Cooke eventually met Taylor and evidently impressed him, as Taylor asked Cooke to join a committee Taylor was forming to apply scientific management to the ASME's offices. Taylor, who was then ASME president, personally financed the study and paid Cooke's salary; during the year-and-a-half study their friendship grew. Cooke soon became an insider in the scientific-management movement.

Distrustful of the so-called new breed of "efficiency engineers," Taylor only recommended four men, all who had worked under his direction, as competent to introduce his methods: Barth,

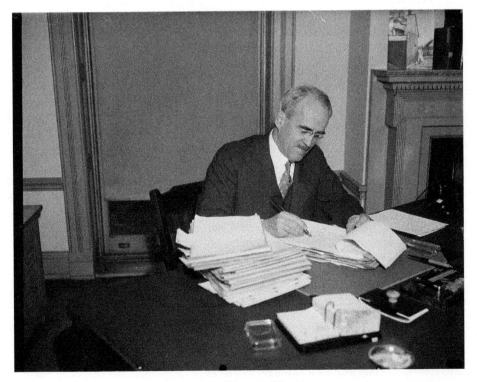

Morris L. Cooke. Harris & Ewing Collection / Library of Congress.

Gantt, Horace King Hathaway, and Cooke.[96] Known as a friend of labor, Cooke once saw a sign at a factory gate reading, "Hands Entrance." In response, he asked: "Where do the heads and hearts enter?"—the sign was promptly removed.[97] Perhaps Cooke was being flippant, but he made his point—scientific management called for more than hands.

In 1909, Henry S. Pritchett, President, Carnegie Foundation for the Advancement of Teaching, asked Taylor to recommend someone to conduct an economic study of higher education to determine if the best use was being made of university faculty and facilities. Taylor recommended Cooke. The resulting report was a bombshell in the academic world.[98] Cooke visited physics departments at nine universities, as they were believed representative of university teaching and research, in general. In his final report, Cooke attempted something that few were eager to attempt: measure the cost of inputs relative to outputs in teaching and research.

His findings were quite upsetting: inbreeding (an institution hiring its own graduates) was widespread; managerial practices were even worse than those in industry; committee management was a curse; departments enjoyed excessive autonomy, which worked against university-wide coordination of course offerings and scheduling; pay was based on seniority not merit; and life tenure for professors protected the unfit, who should be retired. Cooke believed that professors should spend more time in teaching and research, leaving administration to specialists rather than faculty committees. Assistants should be used more widely, allowing higher priced talent to undertake more complex assignments, and the costs of teaching and research should be more closely controlled by a university's central administration. Cooke concluded that "there are very few, if any, of the broader principles of management which obtain generally in the industrial and commercial world which are not more or less applicable to the college field, and so far as he discovered no one of them is now generally observed."[99] Initial reactions to the report were predictable: Richard C. Maclaurin, president of the Massachusetts Institute of Technology, asked how Isaac Newton's 14 years of research on his theory of gravitation would have fared if Cooke's ideas were implemented. He felt a focus on efficiency distracted from a university's fundamental purpose, would lead to higher administrative overhead, and that Cooke's report was "written from the point of view of the man who is used to report on the efficiency of a glue factory or soap works."[100] Nonetheless, as Kanigel notes, the effects of Cooke's report "are felt today, as any college professor who's ever filled out a state-mandated faculty productivity form can attest."[101]

The Boxly Talks

Throughout this period, Taylor continued to give his famous talks at Boxly, his Chestnut Hill, Pennsylvania, home. Always interested in improving his presentation, Taylor asked Cooke to analyze his standard talk with an eye to improving its flow and content. A stenographer was hired to transcribe Taylor's June 4, 1907, lecture. It was also suggested that a transcription of Taylor's remarks might provide a basis for Cooke to write a book about the Taylor system. In prefacing his comments, Taylor assured his audiences that task management (his preferred term before scientific management became popular) was superior to previous ideas: "I want to try to convince you that the task idea, because that is what is back of everything we do, is overwhelmingly better than [ordinary management] in its practical results."[102]

---

[96] Frank B. Copley, *Frederick W. Taylor: Father of Scientific Management* (New York: Harper & Brothers, 1923) vol. 2, p. 357.

[97] Kenneth E. Trombley, *The Life and Times of a Happy Liberal: A Biography of Morris Llewellyn Cooke* (New York: Harper & Brothers, 1954), p. 10.

[98] Morris L. Cooke, *Academic and Industrial Efficiency* (New York: Carnegie Foundation for the Advancement of Teaching Bulletin No. 5, 1910).

[99] *Idem* quoted in "Scores Management of Our Universities," *New York Times* (December 19, 1910), p. 1.

[100] Richard C. Maclaurin, "Educational and Industrial Efficiency," *Science*, Series 2, 33(838) (January 20, 1911), p. 101.

[101] Robert Kanigel, *One Best Way: Frederick Winslow Taylor and the Enigma of Efficiency* (New York: Viking, 1997), p. 490.

[102] "Report of a Lecture by and Questions put to Mr. F. W. Taylor: A Transcript," *Journal of Management History* 1(1) (1995), p. 8.

Taylor's 2-hour talk, plus a question-and-answer period, was strongly worded and included his well-worn pig-iron-handling anecdote. When Taylor read the stenographic transcription, he was surprised at what he had actually said and responded, "Did I say that?"[103] He vowed to be more careful in the future about what he said and how he spoke about task management.

After Cooke acquired a copy of a Boxly talk transcription, he told Taylor that he did, indeed, intend to write a book about the Taylor system, tentatively titled *Industrial Management*, to enable people to more fully understand Taylor's methods. In the course of events, Cooke's intended book was not published but, according to Wrege and Stotka, became Taylor's *The Principles of Scientific Management*. In Wrege and Stotka's eyes, Taylor "attached his name to someone else's work," and Cooke "created a classic."[104] Was the "Father of Scientific Management" a plagiarist? Or, was this a mutual agreement between Taylor and Cooke to promote Taylor's ideas? The story is convoluted, but it merits examination.

The basis for Cooke's *Industrial Management* was Taylor's Boxly talk, which Cooke was to improve. In 1907, Cooke wrote Taylor that he intended "to edit 'Industrial Management' . . . because I think to write a popular exposition of the Taylor System will be a thing worthwhile."[105] At one point, while Cooke was "boiling down the Boxly talks," he and Taylor were to be coauthors. Cooke edited an initial manuscript that he had prepared, rewrote 31 pages of Taylor's 62-page Boxly talk, and added 43 pages from other sources. The resulting Cooke manuscript was never published, but 69 pages of *Industrial Management* (which began with the stenographer's transcription of Taylor's talk) were incorporated into Taylor's *The Principles of Scientific Management*.[106] On this basis, Wrege and Stotka concluded that Cooke "created the classic" and that "Taylor's use of Cooke's manuscript is merely an example of [Taylor's] tendency to publish, under his own name, material written by others."[107]

Is there another side to this story? On the *Industrial Management* manuscript he was preparing, Cooke printed this comment:

> . . . this chapter [Chapter 2] is very largely a recital of Mr. Taylor's personal experiences in the development of scientific management, and as such has been written by himself in the first person.[108]

Cooke told Taylor that he would forgo any profits from *Industrial Management,* but Taylor responded that he would assign all royalties from *The Principles of Scientific Management* to Cooke. The archives of Harper & Brothers, Taylor's publisher, indicate that $3,207.05 in royalties was paid to Cooke from June 1911 (the month *The Principles of Scientific Management* was published) until the last quarter of 1913.[109] According to Dean:

> . . . the royalty money was likely a minor matter to both Taylor and Cooke. Neither of them needed the royalty money, as suggested by the fact that Cooke was making nearly $50,000 a year through Taylor [from consulting referrals] – considerable sum considering the time. The royalty payment to Cooke was likely a mere gesture on Taylor's part for Cooke's contribution to Taylor's "principles."[110]

---

[103] Copley, *Taylor*, vol. 2, p. 284.

[104] Charles D. Wrege and Anne Marie Stotka, "Cooke Creates a Classic: The Story behind F. W. Taylor's *Principles of Scientific Management*," *Academy of Management Review* 3(4) (October 1978), pp. 736–749.

[105] *Ibid.*, p. 738.

[106] Wrege and Greenwood, *Taylor*, p. 182.

[107] Wrege and Stotka, p. 749.

[108] *Ibid.*, pp. 746–747. The Cooke manuscript is preserved in the Charles D. Wrege Research Papers Regarding History of Management #5618. Kheel Center for Labor-Management Documentation and Archives, Cornell University Library, Collection Number: 5930 mf.

[109] *Archives of Harper & Brothers (1817–1914)*. Reels 31 and 32 of microfilm published by permission of Harper & Row and the Butler Library, Columbia University. Index compiled by Christopher Feeney, University Press, Cambridge, 1982. We are indebted to Carol Carlson (Dean) Gunn for a photocopy of this material.

[110] Carol Carlson Dean, "The Principles of Scientific Management by Fred Taylor: Exposures in Print beyond the Private Printing," *Journal of Management History* 3(1) (1997), pp. 11–12.

A reasonable conclusion is that Cooke contributed to, but did not write, *The Principles of Scientific Management*. He edited and enriched Taylor's Boxly talks and duly received royalties for his efforts. It was an arrangement agreed upon and fulfilled, indicating the solid relationship that existed between Taylor and Cooke.

Public Administration

In addition to working closely with Taylor and consulting with various businesses, Cooke also became involved in public administration. In 1911, Rudolf Blankenburg, a reform candidate, was elected Mayor of Philadelphia. He asked Taylor to become the city's Director of Public Works. Citing his failing health, Taylor recommended Cooke for the job. Cooke had been itching for civic reform ever since, as a poll watcher, a machine politician had bullied him. He found the Department of Public Works honeycombed with corruption. Cooke insisted that government be nonpolitical and use science and technology for the public good.

In 4 years, as Public Works Director, Cooke saved the city over $1 million in garbage-collection costs, achieved a $1.25 million reduction in utility rates, fired 1,000 inefficient workers, established pension and benefit funds, opened channels of communication for workers and managers, and moved municipal administration from smoke-filled rooms into the sunshine. Although he was unable to apply time study or incentive pay, Cooke revamped budgeting procedures, hired numerous experts to replace political favorites, advocated hiring a professional city manager, and sought to replace committees with individuals who had responsibility and authority. In his book *Our Cities Awake: Notes on Municipal Activities and Administration*, Cooke called for cooperation and full workplace participation by employees at all levels:

> Here then is a work in which we can all have a hand, a work which will always be ineffectually done if it is confined to well-educated and highly trained men at the top . . . administrative leadership will in the future more and more consist in getting the largest possible number "into the play" – in having the great body of employees increasingly critical in their judgments about both their own work and the work which is going on around them.[111]

After serving in the Blankenburg administration, Cooke opened his own consulting firm in 1916. Like other scientific-management pioneers, he contributed his knowledge to the War Department during World War I, serving as executive assistant to the United States Shipping Board. Always concerned with gaining the cooperation of labor, he became increasingly interested in the growing post-war national labor movement. He became a friend and advisor to Samuel Gompers, president of the American Federation of Labor. Cooke saw a need to bring labor and management together in a time of mutual antagonism.[112]

In his 1928 Presidential Address to the Taylor Society, Cooke expressed doubts about "company unions" not freely established by their members: "Certainly no grouping of workers where the urge for organization does not originate with the workers themselves would be expected to hold their interest."[113] He believed that insistence on "management prerogatives" and "labor intransigence" must give way to cooperation. Cooke held that labor was just as responsible for production as management and stressed that improved productivity was an effective barrier

---

[111] Morris L. Cooke, *Our Cities Awake: Notes on Municipal Activities and Administration* (Garden City. NJ: Doubleday, Page: 1918), p. 98.

[112] For more on Cooke's involvement with Gompers see Chris Nyland, "Taylorism and the Mutual-Gains Strategy," *Industrial Relations* 37(4) (October 1998), pp. 519–542.

[113] Morris L. Cooke, "Some Observations on Workers' Organizations," *Bulletin of the Taylor Society* 14(1) (February 1929), p. 7. "Company unions" were outlawed in the United States by the 1935 National Labor Relations Act (the Wagner Act), 29 *U.S.C.* §8(a)(2). Cooke's contact with labor leaders was extensive. For details, see Sanford M. Jacoby, "Union-Management Cooperation in the United States: Lessons from the 1920s," *Industrial and Labor Relations Review* 37(1) (October 1983), pp. 20–24.

against unemployment and low wages. In this last book, coauthored with Philip Murray, Cooke advised management to "tap labor's brains," by which he meant actively involving labor in determining workplace procedures and policies for increasing the output and distribution of goods and services.[114] Murray was one of the most important labor leaders of the era: the first president of the Steel Workers Organizing Committee (SWOC), the first president of the United Steelworkers of America (USWA), and the longest-serving president of the Congress of Industrial Organizations (CIO).

During the administration of Franklin D. Roosevelt, Cooke held numerous positions, chief among them being Director of the Rural Electrification Administration (1935–1937). In 1950, President Harry S. Truman appointed Cooke chairman of the President's Water Resources Policy Commission. When Cooke was asked by his biographer to list his lifetime accomplishments, he replied:

1. Rural Electrification

2. Inexpensive electricity in our homes

3. Progress in labor-management relations

4. Conservation of our land and water

5. Scientific management in industry[115]

To this, Cooke's biographer added another accomplishment: "service to government." On balance, "Cooke's interest lay in the broader social and political implications of scientific management."[116] He worked to further cooperation between labor and management and favored increased worker participation in management decision making. If scientific management was to make headway in the twentieth century, it required someone like Cooke to open new vistas in public administration and to gain the support of the U.S. labor movement.

SUMMARY

A movement's adolescence is analogous to the developmental transition between childhood and adulthood, replete with growth, rebellion, and a search for an identity. From Taylor's early work at Midvale and Bethlehem to the maturity of in the 1920s, the scientific-management movement's search for a meaningful identity is reflected in the lives of the individuals examined in this chapter. Carl G. Barth was the true believer who remained faithful to Taylor's orthodoxy. Henry L. Gantt began under Taylor's guidance, contributed significantly, and then developed his own unique ideas. The Gilbreths combined motion study with Taylor's time study, studied fatigue, and emphasized the psychology of scientific management. Harrington Emerson embraced the efficiency movement while rejecting Taylor's "functional foremanship" and differential piece-rate plan. Morris L. Cooke, nurtured by Taylor, introduced scientific management to public administration and sought a rapprochement between management and organized labor. These individuals led the vanguard in spreading the gospel of efficiency in the early days of the scientific-management movement. As we will see, however, changing times would bring new challenges.

---

[114] Morris L. Cooke and Philip Murray, *Organized Labor and Production: Next Steps in Industrial Democracy* (New York: Harper & Brothers, 1940), p. 211. As for the actual authorship of this book, see: Jean Christie, *Morris Llewellyn Cooke: Progressive Engineer* (New York: Garland Publishing, 1983), p. 244n. Originally an unpublished dissertation, Columbia University, New York, NY.

[115] Trombley, *Cooke*, p. 249.

[116] Edwin T. Layton, Jr. *The Revolt of the Engineers: Social Responsibility and the American Engineering Profession* (Baltimore, MD: Johns Hopkins University Press, 1986), p. 157.

chapter

9

The Human Factor: Preparing the Way

Scientific management was born and nurtured in an era that emphasized science as a way of life and living. As noted in Chapter 7, in the first decade of the twentieth century, President Theodore Roosevelt and others voiced concern about depletion of the United States' natural resources. This concern was preliminary to a larger question of national efficiency and the misuse of both physical and human resources. One manifestation of this concern was an apprehension regarding the efficiency of "industrial and manufacturing establishments," in general, and, in particular, the "men . . . working in these establishments." For Fred Taylor and the band of scientific-management pioneers that had gathered around him, the "blundering" methods used by management were "ill-directed" and responsible for an untold waste in human effort.[1] Their solution to eliminating this waste was carefully selecting and developing "first-class" workers. Simply stated, their goal was to put "The Right Man in the Right Place." This chapter examines how modern personnel management (or as we know it today, "human-resource management") grew out of "welfare work," on the one hand, and scientific management, on the other.[2] Even more broadly inspired

---

[1] Frederick W. Taylor, *The Principles of Scientific Management* (New York: Harper & Brothers, 1911), pp. 5–8.
[2] Henry Eilbirt, "The Development of Personnel Management in the United States," *Business History Review* 33(3) (Autumn 1959), pp. 345–364. See also Guy Alchon, "'The World We Seek as Christians': Mary van Kleeck, Philanthropy, and Early Social Science Initiatives," in Theresa Richardson and Donald Fisher, eds., *The Development of the Social Sciences in the United States and Canada: The Role of Philanthropy* (Stamford, CT: Ablex, 1999), pp. 59–73.

social forces were also at work during the same period, and these are also examined as they affected industrial psychology, industrial sociology, and industrial relations. Together, these forces set the stage for later developments in labor–management relations, the human-relations school of management, and, eventually, the field of organizational behavior.

Personnel Management: A Dual Heritage

Modern personnel management has a dual heritage. This heritage may be traced to the 1880s and the near simultaneous emergence of the scientific management and Social Gospel movements. Scientific management originated from an engineering philosophy that focused on the need for the "strictest economy in the use of workers."[3] In contrast, the roots of the Social Gospel movement reside in religion and philanthropy, and the desire to improve "the general tenor of American living and the standards of the poor and unfortunate."[4]

Personnel as Welfare Work

Paternalism, whether by state, church, or business, is as old as civilization. The feudal system of the Middle Ages (see Chapter 2) was based on paternalistic ideals, and many early factory owners, such as Robert Owen, sought to ameliorate the anguish of working life and to "elevate" their employees by providing recreational activities, dancing lessons, meals, housing, education, sanitation, and so on. The Waltham System for textile manufacturing, popular in the early 1800s, had paternalistic overtones as mill owners looked after employees' education, housing, and morals (see Chapter 5). The 1832 McLane Report on *Manufactures in the United States* found the typical firm to be family owned with relatively few employees.[5] Thus, at this stage of the United States' industrial growth, firms were smaller and usually owner managed. The rapid growth of the U.S. economy in the latter third of the nineteenth century, however, created unprecedented accumulations of physical and human resources in plants, factories, and mills. This rapid growth moved the means of production from small workshops and homes to factories, where it was possible to manufacture products on a grand scale. It also changed relations between owner-managers and their employees. The Social Gospel movement emerged in the 1880s as a counterpoint to Social Darwinism (see Chapter 6). Social Gospel proponents felt a duty to reform social and economic conditions. Rather than wait for a gradual improvement in the quality of life found in poorer neighborhoods, they argued for immediate action in improving personnel-administration and industrial-relations policies. In large measure, the responses of the era's owner-managers built on the familial traditions of the past, as expressed through "industrial betterment" or "welfare work."[6]

Drawing on the Social Gospel movement, the first "welfare-work office" was established at the National Cash Register Company in 1897. NCR's founder and president, John H. Patterson,

---

[3] Ordway Tead and Henry C. Metcalf, *Personnel Administration: Its Principles and Practices* (New York: McGraw-Hill, 1920), p. 27.

[4] Eilbirt, "Development of Personnel Management," p. 348.

[5] U.S. Congress, *Documents Relative to the Manufactures in the United States, Collected and Transmitted to the House of Representatives, in Compliance with a Resolution of Jan. 19, 1832* by the Secretary of the Treasury [McLane Report], 22nd Congress, 1st Session, H. R. Document 308, 2 vols. (Washington, DC: Printed by Duff Green, 1833).

[6] Edwin E. Witte, *The Evolution of Managerial Ideas in Industrial Relations*, Bulletin 27 (Ithaca, NY: New York State School of Industrial and Labor Relations, Cornell University, 1954). See also Homer J. Hagedorn, "A Note on the Motivation of Personnel Management: Industrial Welfare 1885–1910," *Explorations in Entrepreneurial History* 10(3–4) (April 1958), pp. 134–139; Oscar W. Nestor, *A History of Personnel Administration, 1890–1910* (Unpublished dissertation, University of Pennsylvania, 1954), released in book form by Garland Press, New York, 1986.

appointed Lena H. Tracy to be the firm's first welfare director.[7] Likewise, Joseph Bancroft and Sons appointed a welfare secretary in 1899, the H. J. Heinz Company employed a social secretary in 1902, the Colorado Fuel and Iron Company did likewise in 1901, and the International Harvester Company followed in 1903. Other welfare-work offices were established at Filene's Department Stores, the Natural Food Company, Plymouth Cordage, John B. Stetson Company, and Westinghouse Electric. Clearly, concern for employee welfare was becoming fashionable among large companies.

Employee-welfare programs were, in part, intended to counter a growing union movement, but were also motivated by the realization that "employees' productivity depended quite as much upon their environment and lives in the fourteen hours away from work as the ten hours while at work."[8] As a consequence, many welfare programs extended beyond the workplace into employees' homes and included their spouses and children. Thus, "welfare secretaries" were tasked with improving employees' lives, both off and on the job. The secretaries handled employee grievances, operated medical dispensaries, oversaw recreation and educational activities, arranged job transfers, administered dining facilities, prepared nutritious menus, and watched over the moral behavior of employees, especially unmarried females.[9] Many of the era's welfare secretaries were women with backgrounds in vocational guidance and social work. In addition to Lena H. Tracy, other women welfare secretaries included Gertrude B. Beeks at International Harvester Company, Elizabeth Briscoe at Bancroft and Sons, Florence Hughes at New Jersey Zinc, Laura Ray at Greenhut-Siegel, Aggie Dunn at H. J. Heinz, Lucy Bannister at Westinghouse, and Diana Hirschler at Filene's.[10]

The role of welfare secretaries, however, was not always clearly defined, as the experience of Henry L. Gantt (see Chapter 8) at Bancroft Mills illustrates. Bancroft's first welfare secretary, Elizabeth Briscoe, was appointed in 1902. In 1903, Bancroft experienced severe productivity problems and its owner, John Bancroft, employed Gantt as a consultant. Gantt's recommendations soon ran counter to Briscoe's welfare efforts. When Gantt, for instance, suggested dismissing inefficient employees, Briscoe objected. She insisted that all workers, inefficient or not, should be retained. Gantt argued that poor personnel selection and assignments were contributing to the productivity problem that he had been hired to solve. Gantt was able to increase productivity to some extent by improving work methods, upgrading training, and installing a bonus system in one department, but he was unable to fully implement all of his recommendations largely as a result of the opposition stemming from Briscoe's welfare efforts. When Gantt completed his consultancy, in 1909, it appeared that welfare work had won out over scientific management.[11] In later years (1911–1927), however, Bancroft melded "welfarism" and scientific management to fit its owner's Quaker beliefs about how employees should be treated while still increasing productivity. Thus, Gantt may have "lost" initially, but in the long run it was shown that welfare work

[7] See Lena Harvey Tracy, *How My Heart Sang: The Story of Pioneer Industrial Welfare Work* (New York: R. R. Smith Publisher, 1950); John H. Patterson, "Altruism and Sympathy as Factors in Works Administration," *Engineering Magazine* 20 (January 1901), pp. 577–602; and Samuel Crowther, *John H. Patterson: Pioneer in Industrial Welfare* (Garden City, NY: Doubleday, 1923).

[8] Witte, *Evolution of Managerial Ideas*, p. 8.

[9] For more on the duties of social secretaries, see William H. Tolman, *Social Engineering* (New York: McGraw, 1909), pp. 48–59. See also Stuart D. Brandes, *American Welfare Capitalism: 1880–1940* (Chicago, IL: University of Chicago Press, 1976); and Nick Mandell, *The Corporation as Family: The Gendering of Corporate Welfare, 1890–1930* (Chapel Hill, NC: University of North Carolina Press, 2002).

[10] Lee Anne G. Kryder, "Transforming Industrial Welfare Work into Modern Personnel Management: The Contributions of Gertrude B. Beeks," Paper presented at the Annual Academy of Management meeting, Dallas, August 16, 1983; Charles D. Wrege and Bernice M. Lattanzio, "Pioneers in Personnel Management: A Historical Study of the Neglected Accomplishment of Women in Personnel Management," *Working Paper Series*, Management History Division, Academy of Management, 1977.

[11] Daniel Nelson and Stuart Campbell, "Taylorism versus Welfare Work in American Industry: H. L. Gantt and the Bancrofts," *Business History Review* 46(1) (Spring 1972), pp. 1–16. Nelson and Campbell concluded that Gantt lost this battle at Bancroft; however, there is other evidence that Gantt introduced Bancroft's senior management to options they would pursue later. For this latter viewpoint, see Peter B. Petersen, "Henry Gantt's Work at Bancroft: The Option of Scientific Management," in John A. Pearce II and Richard B. Robinson, eds., *Proceedings of the Annual Meeting of the Academy of Management* (1985), pp. 134–138. For more on Briscoe's contributions, see Peter B. Petersen, "A Pioneer in Personnel," *Personnel Administrator* 33(6) (June 1988), pp. 60–64.

and scientific management could complement each other by enhancing both employee relations and productivity.

Although the time period is not precise, use of the phrase "welfare work" began to wane about 1910, to be replaced with the phrase "employment work." According to Meyer Bloomfield, who was instrumental in forming an early employment-managers association, employment work could achieve more good because "welfare work . . . often lacked analysis, self-criticism and human insight. Moreover, the good which [welfare] work could do was often vitiated by sentimentality, if not self-deception."[12] Moreover, as welfare work reached further into employees' personal lives, it became resented, with employees objecting to being told what they could or could not do on their own time and in their own homes. Although welfare secretaries and welfare-work offices are not found in today's workplace, their legacy survives in the "fringe benefits" and industrial-relations policies of contemporary human-resource programs.

Scientific Management and Personnel

At the turn of the twentieth century, at the gates of many factories across the country, unskilled workers would line up each morning and a foreman would appear to hire the day's labor. This often amounted to little more than hiring friends or the well connected, however, or even in some cases, selling jobs. As foremen had the power to hire, they also had the right to fire. Fred Taylor (see Chapter 7) denounced this practice and said worker selection should "not just leave it to the poor overworked foreman to go out and say, 'come on, what do you want? If you are cheap enough I will give you a trial.' That is the old way."[13] As early as 1903, Taylor proposed that an Employment Bureau should be part of a central Planning Department, and one of the specialized functions he identified was "shop-disciplinarian."

Taylor listed the duties of a shop-disciplinarian as selecting and discharging employees, keeping performance records, handling disciplinary problems, administering wage payments, and serving as a peacemaker.[14] Several of Taylor's earliest disciples, including Henry P. Kendall at Plimpton Press (Norwood, MA) and Richard A. Feiss at garment manufacturer Joseph & Feiss Company (Cleveland, OH), founded "employment departments."

Created in 1910, the Employment Department at Plimpton Press was managed by Jane C. Williams.[15] Succinctly stated, its purpose was to achieve savings by minimizing human costs. Williams's duties included determining job applicants' suitability, training and orienting workers, maintaining performance records, interviewing employees monthly, reviewing efficiency ratings every 6 months to determine pay increases, hearing grievances, providing a nurse in case of accident or illness, maintaining a library of popular and technical magazines and books, helping families with financial counseling, and operating a lunchroom. This was undoubtedly the most advanced employment department of its day.

Mary B. Gilson. *A History of Opheleum Fraternity: Published Upon the Occasion of the Tenth Anniversary* (Pittsburg: F. G. Wetterstein, 1913), p. 99.

---

[12] Meyer Bloomfield, "Man Management: A New Profession in the Making," *Bulletin of the Taylor Society* 6(4) (August 1921), p. 161.

[13] Frederick W. Taylor, "The Principles of Scientific Management," *Bulletin of the Taylor Society* 2(5) (December 1916), p. 17. Address before the Cleveland Advertising Club, March 3, 1915, published posthumously.

[14] *Idem,* "Shop Management," *Transactions of the American Society of Mechanical Engineers* 24 (1903), p. 1404.

[15] Jane C. Williams, "The Reduction of Labor Turnover in the Plimpton Press," *Annals of the American Academy of Political and Social Science* 71 (May 1917), pp. 71–81. For a discussion of the role played by other women in the early growth of personnel as an occupation, see Frank B. Miller and Mary Ann Coghill, "Sex and the Personnel Manager," *Industrial and Labor Relations Review* 18(1) (October 1964), pp. 32–44.

Established in 1913, the Employment and Services Department at Joseph & Feiss was the first to use a selection test in hiring new employees. As described by Mary Barnett Gilson, the department's head until that time, employee selection "was a case of trial and error, and the errors were of necessity many."[16] In justifying the cost associated with an employment department, Richard A. Feiss, a son of Julius Feiss (the "Feiss" in Joseph & Feiss), echoed Edward Atkinson's observation from over 30-years earlier (quoted in Chapter 6) that a "difference in management will alter results, in the same place, at the same time, in the use of similar machinery." Feiss explained:

> Given two establishments in the same industry, in the same locality, build for them the same buildings, equip them with the same machinery and establish for them similar methods of handling equipment and materials – and yet, in the course of time, there will be a difference in both the quantity and quality of their output. This difference in result will be caused by the difference between the two in the quality of their personnel. . . . If one of the above plants were headed by a management of the ordinary or traditional type and the other by a management which fully realized the importance of personnel and had developed an active philosophy tending toward the solution of the personal problem, the difference between the two in practical result would be so great as to be unbelievable to the uninitiated. In fact, this difference would often spell failure in the one case and success in the other.[17]

Ordway Tead dated the appearance of the modern personnel department at "about 1912," when some dozen companies had established distinct functions devoted to personnel work.[18] The first nationwide organization to deal with personnel matters was the National Association of Corporation Schools (NACS), founded in 1913. Its goal was to advance the training and education of industrial employees. By 1917, the NACS had expanded its reach to include "human relations" (meaning, employee relations). NACS was later renamed the National Association of Corporation Training (NACT). In 1922, the NACT merged with the Industrial Relations Association of America (founded in 1918 as the National Association of Employment Managers; NAEM) to form the National Personnel Association. The NAEM had grown out of a local Employment Managers Association started in 1911 by Meyer Bloomfield, then the director of the Vocational Bureau in Boston. In 1922, the NAEM merged with the Industrial Relations Association of America (IRRA) to form the National Personnel Association (NPA). In 1923, the NPA became the American Management Association.

In 1915, the first training program for employment managers was offered at Dartmouth College's Amos Tuck School of Administration and Finance. Under Harlow Person's direction, the program required preparing "a thesis which is the solution of a specific problem of management in a specific plant."[19] Through his role in the Society to Promote the Science of Management (SPSM), later renamed The Taylor Society, Person was able to promote employment management, or as it was called by the 1920s, "personnel administration," as a means for treating workers with the fairness and dignity to which they were entitled.[20]

---

[16] Mary B. Gilson, *What's Past Is Prologue* (New York: Harper & Brothers, 1940), p. 61. See also Charles D. Wrege and Ronald G. Greenwood, "Mary B. Gilson – A Historical Study of the Neglected Accomplishments of a Woman Who Pioneered in Personnel Management," in Jeremy Atack, ed., *Business and Economic History,* 2nd ser., vol. 11 (Urbana, IL: College of Commerce, University of Illinois, April 1982), pp. 35–42.

[17] Richard A. Feiss, "Personal Relationship as a Basis of Scientific Management," *Annals of the American Academy of Political and Social Science* 65 (May 1916), p. 27.

[18] Ordway Tead, "Personnel Administration," in Edwin R. A. Seligman, ed., *Encyclopedia of the Social Sciences*, vol. 12 (New York: 1934), p. 88.

[19] Harlow S. Person, "University Schools of Business and the Training of Employment Executives," *Annals of the American Academy of Political and Social Science* 65 (May 1916), p. 126.

[20] Witte, *Evolution of Managerial Ideas*, p. 9.

Despite rising professionalism, the era's personnel practices continued to reflect earlier welfare programs. For example, in March 1913, Ford Motor Company created a Sociological Department to improve employees' standard of living. It hired 100 "advisers" to visit its employees' homes to ensure that the homes were neat and clean and to verify that the employees did not abuse alcohol, that their sex lives were without tarnish, and that they used their leisure time wisely. Services of the company's legal department were free and assisted employees with everything from becoming a U.S. citizen to buying a home. The company's concern for its employees' private lives, however, lasted less than 2 years. It ended in November 1915 when Henry Ford engaged his Episcopalian pastor, the Very Reverend Samuel S. Marquis, to head the Sociological Department. Ford told Marquis, "There is too much of this snooping around in private affairs. We'll change this from a Sociology department to an Education department."[21] Thereafter, the home visits stopped, and the Ford Company turned its attention to advising and educating its employees. The company maintained a staff of 10 physicians and 100 nurses should employees become injured or sick, and pioneered in hiring disabled employees, ex-convicts, and minorities.

Faced with a tight labor market and over 370 percent annual employee turnover in his factories, on January 5, 1914, Henry Ford announced he would raise the company's minimum wage from $2.34 for 9 hours to $5.00 per 8-hour day, double the average wage in the Detroit area.[22] In addition, he announced a plan to share $10,000,000 of profits with more than 30,000 employees.[23] Over 15,000 applicants besieged Ford's Detroit factory seeking some 5,000 available jobs. Fire hoses had to be used to disperse the crowd. Three days later, with the rush of job-seekers showing no sign of abating, newspapers around the country were asked to warn workers against coming to Detroit, as the available jobs were only for Detroiters.[24] Ford saw the $5.00 a day wage as "neither charity nor wages [but] simply profit sharing." He did acknowledge, however, "[i]n a way it is a piece of efficiency engineering, too. We expect to get better work, more efficient work, as one result."[25] Indeed, Ford's unprecedented move immediately boosted assembly-line productivity and built company pride and loyalty among his workers. In 1922, at a time when the average manufacturing worker put in 47.9 hours a week,[26] the company instituted a 5-day, 40-hour week for 50,000 of its employees. Edsel Ford, Henry's son explained: "Every man needs more than one day a week for rest and recreation. . . . The Ford Company always has sought to promote [an] ideal home life for its employes. We believe that in order to live properly every man should have more time to spend with his family."[27] Following Ford's lead, the 5-day, 40-hour week soon became standard practice in other companies.

It has been estimated that from 1915 to 1920 at least 200 personnel departments were established in the United States.[28] "Present development," Tead and Metcalf wrote, in 1920, "is in the

---

[21] John R. Commons, "Henry Ford, Miracle Maker," *The Independent* 102 (May 1, 1920), p. 160. Other facets of Ford's employment policies, including hiring the handicapped, those with criminal records, minorities, and "those past middle life" are found in John R. Lee, "The So-Called Profit Sharing System in the Ford Plant," *Annals of the American Academy of Political and Social Science* 65 (May 1916), pp. 297–310.

[22] Boyd Fisher, "Methods of Reducing the Labor Turnover," *Annals of the American Academy of Political and Social Science* 65 (May 1916), pp. 144–154.

[23] "Gives $10,000,000 to 26,000 Employees," *New York Times* (January 6, 1914), p. 1.

[24] "No Jobs for Outsiders: Ford Co. Warns That 5,000 Places Are Only for Detroiters," *New York Times* (January 9, 1914), p. 1.

[25] Henry Ford quoted in "Ford Gives Reasons for Profit Sharing," *New York Times* (January 9, 1914), p. 1.

[26] Ethel B. Jones, "New Estimates of Hours of Work per Week and Hourly Earnings, 1900–1957," *Review of Economics and Statistics* 45(4) (November 1963), Table 1, p. 375.

[27] Edsel Ford quoted in "5-Day, 40-hour Week for Ford Employes," *New York Times* (March 25, 1922), p. 1. Although the Ford Company is often cited as the first major employer in the United States to introduce a 5-day work week, this innovation was introduced at Joseph & Feiss Company in 1917. See Richard A. Feiss, "Why It Paid Us to Adopt the Five-Day Week," *Factory: The Magazine of Management* 25(4) (August 15, 1920), pp. 523–526.

[28] Daniel Nelson, "'A Newly Appreciated Art:' The Development of Personnel Work at Leeds & Northrup, 1915–1923," *Business History Review* 44(4) (Winter 1970), pp. 520–535.

direction of a new science and a newly appreciated art – the science and art of personnel administration."[29] A study by the Bureau of Labor Statistics for the years 1913–1919 determined that modern employment practices reduced labor turnover, thus decreasing training and other costs, while also providing workers with more stable employment, especially in larger firms. The study found that the larger the firm, the lower the turnover rate. This was, in part, because larger firms could pay higher wages, provide better working conditions, and guarantee stable employment. They were also more likely to have a central department devoted to employee welfare.[30] Interest in improved employment practices was not confined to the United States, however. In Great Britain, for example, during the 1920s, B. Seebohm Rowntree, owner of the Cocoa Works at York, employed a sociologist in a psychological department to supervise employee education, health, canteens, housing, and recreation. Rowntree has been called the "Father of British Management."[31] Rowntree & Co. is now part of Nestlé S.A.

Interest in the potential of personnel management to increase employee productivity led to significant changes in assumptions about human behavior. For instance, Tead partially backed away from an earlier "instinct" theory of behavior he had developed as the coauthor of the first collegiate textbook in the area, *Personnel Administration: Its Principles and Practice*.[32] Tead and his coauthor (Henry C. Metcalf) concluded that instincts (i.e., inborn tendencies) still had a great deal to do with human conduct, but advances in personnel research were opening new vistas that enabled scientific employee selection, placement, and training. Writing later, Tead argued that managers should adopt a "psychological point of view" to seek "the cause and effect relations in behavior." He believed that such relations could be studied for guiding human conduct.[33] Moreover, he contended that an understanding of such relations would encourage proper work habits. Tead is remembered as being associated with Robert G. Valentine and Richard Gregg in creating the profession that was first known as "industrial counselor."[34]

In brief, the dual origins of personnel management led to a common meeting ground in the 1920s. Although the employee-welfare movement realized that productivity depended, in part, on employee attitudes and loyalty, it lacked the rigor and professionalism necessary to sustain the growth of modern organizations. Scientific management provided some of this rigor by being coupled with industrial psychology (which will be discussed next), national associations devoted to improving employee relations, and by inspiring the first college-level preparation for employment managers. Welfarism was not dead, but would continue in a less emphatic fashion in the years ahead. Scientific management, on the other hand, would find its goals and methods reshaped by the behavioral and social sciences. Together, the scientific management and Social Gospel movements paved the way for modern human-resource management.

---

[29] Tead and Metcalf, *Personnel Administration*, p. 1.

[30] Paul F. Brissenden and Emil Frankel, *Labor Turnover in Industry* (New York: Macmillan, 1922), especially pp. 54–79.

[31] Lyndall F. Urwick, "The Father of British Management," *The Manager* 30(2) (February 1962), pp. 42–43; Morgan L. Witzel, "Benjamin Seebohm Rowntree," in *idem*, ed., *The Biographical Dictionary of Management*, vol. 2 (Bristol, England: Thoemmes Press, 2001), pp. 863–865.

[32] Tead and Metcalf, *Personnel Administration: Its Principles and Practice*. See also *idem*, *Instincts in Industry: A Study of Working-Class Psychology* (London: Constable, 1919). Tead's thinking on instincts "stemmed indirectly" from Thomson J. Hudon's *The Law of Psychic Phenomena: A Systematic Study of Hypnotism, Spiritism, and Mental Therapeutics, Etc* (Chicago, IL: A. C. McClurg, 1893), among other influences. See Ordway Tead, "Ordway Tead," in Louis Finkelstein, ed., *Thirteen Americans: Their Spiritual Autobiographies* (New York: Institute of Religious and Social Studies, 1953), pp. 17–30.

[33] Ordway Tead, *Human Nature and Management: The Applications of Psychology to Executive Leadership* (New York: McGraw-Hill, 1929), p. 9.

[34] Richard Washburn Child, "The Human Audit," *Harper's Weekly* 61 (July 17, 1915), pp. 52–54. See also Henry P. Kendall, "The First Industrial Counselor – Robert G. Valentine, 1871–1916," *The Survey* 37 (November 25, 1916), pp. 189–190; "Labor Problems in Scientific Management," *Iron Age* 94 (December 10, 1914), pp. 1369–1372 and Charles D. Wrege, Ronald G. Greenwood, and Racquel A. Frederiks, "New Insights into the Contributions of the First Industrial Counselor: The Private Papers of Robert G. Valentine 1912–1916" in Kelly A. Vaverek, ed., *Proceedings of the Southwest Academy of Management* (1992), pp. 69–73.

Psychology and the Individual

The main flow of economic thought has in large part addressed how humans attempt to satisfy their wants and desires. Near the middle of the nineteenth century, British economist William E. Hearn advanced a then novel theory explaining how these wants and desires are one of the chief sources of human action:

> Food, drink, air and warmth are the most urgent of [our] necessities [which] . . . man shares with all other animals. . . . The satisfaction, therefore, of his primary appetites is imperative upon man . . . first in the degree of their intensity . . . and the first which he attempts to satisfy. . . . Man is able not merely to satisfy his primary wants, but to devise means for their better and more complete gratification. . . . Thus the comparative range of human wants is rapidly increased . . . as the attempt to satisfy the primary appetites thus gives rise to new desires . . . [and] when they have acquired such comforts they are pained at their loss, but their acquisition does not prevent them from continuing to desire a further increase.[35]

Katherine M. H. Blackford.
The Business Philosopher: The Magazine of Practical Business Building 6(11) (November 1910), p. 638.

This anticipation (by some four score years) of a hierarchy of human needs (see Chapter 15) and the premise that once a lower level need is satisfied higher level needs are pursued was not a result of an empirical investigation, but rather observation and logical deduction. Before the advent of scientific management, psychology was based on such introspective, armchair, or deductive bases. Pseudosciences, such as astrology, physiognomy, phrenology, and graphology, were commonly used by managers seeking to select employees based on the movement and position of stars in the heavens, employees' physical characteristics such as bumps on their skulls, and their handwriting.[36]

Even in reputable consulting firms such as Emerson Efficiency Engineers, Katherine H. M. Blackford (who claimed to be a physician) emphasized "character analysis" as an aid in selecting employees. She based her claims on two "laws":

FIRST, *Human bodies vary in nine ways*: Color, Form, Size, Structure, Texture, Consistency, Proportion, Expression, Condition.

SECOND, *Men's characters vary in accordance with the way their bodies vary in these nine particulars.*[37]

To illustrate the nature of Blackford's beliefs, which at the time were considered by many to be scientific, she maintained, for example, that "Some work requires positive energy, the driving power to get things done, some requires a slow, enduring pace. If a man has high cheekbones and a nose which is convex when seen in profile, he has this positive energy. If he also has a high forehead and a large head and is a man of fine texture, he can best use his energy in mental work.

---

[35] William E. Hearn, *Plutology, or the Theory of the Efforts to Satisfy Human Wants* (Melbourne, Australia: G. Robertson, 1863), pp. 12–15.

[36] See Mary H. Booth, *How to Read Character in Handwriting* (Philadelphia, PA: John C. Winston, 1910); Gerald E. Fosbroke, *Character Reading through Analysis of the Features* (New York: G. P. Putnam's Sons, 1914).

[37] Katherine M. H. Blackford, "The Science of Character Analysis – What It Is and What It will Do For You" quoted in Arturo F. Ratti, "Secrets of the Psyche," *American Mercury* 19 (February 1930), p. 140. See also Katherine M. H. Blackford and Arthur Newcomb, *Analyzing Character: The New Science of Judging Men; Misfits in Business, the Home and Social Life* (New York: Blackford, 1916); *idem, The Job, The Man, The Boss* (New York: Doubleday, 1916).

If his forehead is low, his shoulders broad, his waist small and his texture coarse, he is best suited for physical work."[38] By the 1920s, Blackford's character analysis had given way to new models of employee selection as successive studies discredited her assertion that there was a correlation between physical characteristics and "the right job."[39]

Toward Scientific Psychology

Elsewhere, psychology was escaping its introspective, pseudoscience beginnings. When Wilhelm Wundt opened the world's first psychological laboratory in 1879 at the University of Leipzig (Germany), scientific methods took hold in psychology. Wundt did not entirely abandon introspection, but began to examine human behavior through controlled experiments. As the founder of experimental psychology, Wundt opened the way for applied psychology, and later, through the work of his students, the field of industrial psychology, which survives to this day under the name "industrial-organizational psychology." Wundt sought to understand "psychological man" by identifying the constituent parts of human consciousness. His own observations of human behavior, combined with the emergence of the psychoanalytical theories of Sigmund Freud, soon led Wundt to an instinct-based explanation for behavior and thought. Concluding that people are not rational, but controlled by innate (i.e., inborn) instincts, Wundt believed that by understanding "instinctive actions," the secrets of the hitherto unexplored mind could be revealed.[40] In the ensuing years, economist Thorstein B. Veblen would identify three positive human instincts: sense of workmanship, parental bent, and idle curiosity (which promote the collective welfare of society), and three negative human instincts: pecuniary interests, emulation, and predation (which negate the collective welfare of society and promote individualism). Others during this period created more encompassing lists of human instincts. Ordway Tead, for instance, delineated 10, including sex, self-assertion, pugnacity, and play. William James, the "Father of American Psychology," identified 37 different instincts, including anger, love, curiosity, and sociability.[41]

The disparities and disagreements among these competing lists of instincts soon proved that this approach was futile, and instinct theory was dismissed as an oversimplified basis for explaining behavior. The variability noted in attempts to identify a set of universal human instincts, however, led to recognition of the psychological differences between individuals. In the same way that Fred Taylor had recognized the importance of employee selection in matching the right man to the right job, psychologists came to understand that a science of human behavior required the study of individuals and not their innate instincts. It is here that applied psychologists formed an alliance with scientific management. In time, "instinct theory" gave rise to trait theories of leadership (see Chapter 15), which held that human behavior, in interaction with one's environment, is determined by personal characteristics and, hence, people are causal agents in their own lives.

The Birth of Industrial Psychology

Scientific management gave industrial psychology its scope and direction. Echoing the scientific-management ethos, the earliest objective of industrial psychology was to promote "the maximum *efficiency* of the individual in industry" and "his optimum *adjustment* . . . in the industrial

---

[38] Katherine M. H. Blackford quoted in Floyd Taylor, "What Do Your Hands Tell?" *Popular Mechanics* 47(1) (January 1927), pp. 21–22.

[39] For a full critique of the "Blackford Employment Plan," see Elspeth H. Brown, *The Corporate Eye: Photography and the Rationalization of American Commercial Culture 1884–1929* (Baltimore, MA: Johns Hopkins University Press, 2005), pp. 23–64. Originally prepared as a dissertation, Yale University, New Haven, CT, 2002.

[40] The notion that that people are not rational, but controlled by innate (i.e., inborn) instincts, may be traced to Charles Darwin who wrote that "the very essence of an instinct is that it is followed independently of reason." See Charles Darwin, *The Descent of Man, and Selection in Relation to Sex*, vol. 1 (New York: D. Appleton and Company, 1872, pp. 95–96).

[41] Thorstein Veblen, *The Instinct of Workmanship, and the State of the Industrial Arts* (New York: B. W. Huebsch, 1914), pp. 1–37; William James, *The Principles of Psychology*, vol. 2 (New York: H. Holt, 1890), pp. 383–441; Tead, *Instincts in Industry*, p. 11. For more on Veblen's notion of "good" and "bad" instincts, see Phillip A. O'Hara, "Thorstein Veblen's Theory of Collective Wealth, Instincts and Property Relations," *History of Economic Ideas* 7(3) (1999), pp. 153–179.

situation."[42] Whereas engineers studied mechanical efficiency and industrial psychologists studied human efficiency, their goal was the same—eliminating waste and inefficiency while maximizing employee satisfaction.

Hugo Münsterberg (1863–1916) is generally credited with the establishment of industrial psychology. Münsterberg recognized Fred Taylor as "the brilliant originator of the scientific management movement," saying that Taylor had "introduced most valuable suggestions which the industrial world cannot ignore."[43] In promoting industrial psychology, Münsterberg drew on Taylor's work and stressed the importance of using genuine scientific methods to achieve workplace efficiency. Münsterberg, however, did not fail to appreciate the social implications of industrial psychology. As he explained:

> We must not forget that the increase of industrial efficiency by future psychological adaption and the improvement of the psychophysical conditions is not only in the interest of the employers, but still more of the employees; their working time can be reduced, their wages increased, their level of life raised. And above all, still more important than naked commercial profit on both sides, is the cultural gain which will come to the total economic life of the nation, as soon as every one can be brought to the place where his best energies may be unfolded and his greatest personal satisfaction secured. The economic experimental psychology offers no more inspiring idea than this adjustment of work and psyche by which mental dissatisfaction in the work, mental depression and discouragement, may be replaced in our social community by overflowing joy and perfect inner harmony.[44]

Born in Danzig (Germany) and educated in Wundt's University of Leipzig laboratory, Münsterberg was enticed to join the Harvard University faculty by William James. His interests were far ranging, including the application of psychological principles to crime detection, education, law, morality, industry, art, and philosophy.[45] To lay a broader foundation for scientific management, he met with President Woodrow Wilson, Secretary of Commerce William C. Redfield, and Secretary of Labor William B. Wilson to encourage them to create a government bureau dedicated to applying scientific research to the psychological problems of industry. Interest in scientific management was high, and Münsterberg sought to place the study of workplace behavior in the hands of qualified scientists and at the forefront of the nation's consciousness. According to Münsterberg, "While today the greatest care is devoted to the problems of material and equipment, all questions of the mind . . . like fatigue, monotony, interest, learning . . . joy in work . . . reward . . . and many similar mental states are dealt with by laymen without any scientific understanding."[46]

Even though the government bureau Münsterberg sought never materialized, his applied research interests grew. In attempting to understand "business life," he once again echoed Taylor in seeking answers to three primary questions:

> We ask how we can find the men whose mental qualities make them best fitted for the work which they have to do; secondly, under what psychological conditions we can secure the greatest and most satisfactory output from every man; and finally how we can produce most completely the influences on human minds which are desired in the interests of business. In other words, we ask how to find the best possible work, and how to secure the best possible effects.[47]

---

[42] Morris S. Viteles, *Industrial Psychology* (New York: W. W. Norton, 1932), p. 4.

[43] Hugo Münsterberg, *Psychology and Industrial Efficiency* (Boston: Houghton Mifflin, 1913), pp. 166, 50. Originally published in 1912.

[44] *Ibid.*, pp. 308–309.

[45] Jeremy T. Blatter, "Screening the Psychological Laboratory: Hugo Münsterberg, Psychotechnics, and the Cinema," *Science in Context* 28(1) (2015), pp. 53–76.

[46] Margaret Münsterberg, *Hugo Münsterberg: His Life and Work* (New York: Appleton-Century-Crofts, 1922), p. 250. See also Merle J. Moskowitz, Hugo Münsterberg: A Study in the History of Applied Psychology, *American Psychologist* 32(10) (October 1977), pp. 824–842; Frank J. Landy, "Hugo Münsterberg: Victim or Visionary?" *Journal of Applied Psychology* 77(6) (December 1992), pp. 787–802; Jutta Spillman and Lothar Spillman, "The Rise and Fall of Hugo Münsterberg," *Journal of the History of the Behavioral Sciences* 29(4) (October 1993), pp. 322–338; and Erik J. Porfeli, "Hugo Münsterberg and the Origins of Vocational Guidance," *Career Development Quarterly* 57(3) (March 2009), pp. 225–236.

[47] Münsterberg, *Psychology and Industrial Efficiency*, pp. 23–24.

The direction of Münsterberg's work was directly linked to Taylor's vision for scientific management and contained three broad parts: (1) "The Best Possible Man"; (2) "The Best Possible Work"; and (3) "The Best Possible Effect." Part 1 was a study of job demands and the necessity of identifying the men whose mental qualities made them best fit to meet those demands. Part 2 sought to determine the psychological conditions under which the greatest and most satisfactory output could be achieved. Part 3 examined how to influence human needs in a manner consistent with the interests of business. For each of these objectives, Münsterberg outlined definite proposals relating to the use of tests in worker selection, the application of research on learning in employee training, and the study of psychological techniques to increase workers' ethical and aesthetic motives. To illustrate his proposals, Münsterberg drew on evidence gathered from studies he had conducted on trolley-car motormen, telephone operators, and merchant-marine officers.

Münsterberg answered Taylor's call for studies that would provide insights into the "motives that influence men." The spirit of scientific management was readily apparent in Münsterberg's focus on individuals, his emphasis on efficiency, and his awareness of the social benefits to be derived from applying the scientific method to investigate workplace behavior. Moreover, Münsterberg's notoriety stimulated popular interest in applying psychology to everyday life. This growing interest led to the founding of *The Journal of Applied Psychology* in 1917. Among those who followed in Münsterberg's footsteps were Charles S. Myers, who pioneered industrial psychology in Great Britain; Walter D. Scott, who devised personnel classification tests for the U.S. Army during World War I; Cecil A. Mace, who performed the first experiments in goal setting as a motivational technique; Walter Van Dyke Bingham, whose Division of Applied Psychology at the Carnegie Institute of Technology led to the creation of the Bureau of Personnel Research and the first psychological consulting service for industry; Morris S. Viteles, whose textbook became the "bible of industrial psychology;" and more.[48] It was Münsterberg, though, who blazed the way by defining the goals and terrain of industrial psychology.

The Social Person Era: Theory, Research, and Practice

Scientific management shaped its times and in turn was shaped by them. It provided the rationale for personnel management, industrial psychology, and institutional labor economics (to be discussed shortly). Another set of forces, only related to scientific management in time, would apply Christian ideas to society as a whole, including the everyday world of work. And, so it was, the late nineteenth century also marked the dawning of the "social person" era.

The Antecedents of Industrial Sociology

As recounted earlier, the Social Gospel movement emerged as a counterpoint to Social Darwinism. Chapter 6 discussed the reforms sought by Richard T. Ely, a founder of the Christian Social Union, and of Washington Gladden. Social Gospel proponents (predominantly Protestant,

[48] See Geoff Bunn, "'A Flair for Organization': Charles Myers and the Establishment of Psychology in Britain," *History & Philosophy of Psychology* 3(1) (2001), pp. 1–13; Edmund C. Lynch, "Walter Dill Scott: Pioneer Industrial Psychologist," *Business History Review* 42(2) (Summer 1968), pp. 147–170; Paula Phillips Carson, Kerry D. Carson, and Ronald B. Heady, "Cecil Alec Mace: The Man who Discovered Goal-Setting," *International Journal of Public Administration* 17(9) (January 1994), pp. 1679–1708; Michelle P. Kraus, *Walter Van Dyke Bingham and the Bureau of Personnel Research* (Unpublished dissertation, Carnegie Mellon University, 1982, released in book form by Garland Press, New York, 1986; Morris S. Viteles, "Morris S. Viteles," in Edwin G. Boring and Gardner Lindzey, eds., *The History of Psychology in Autobiography,* vol. 5 (New York: Appleton-Century-Crofts, 1967), pp. 417–449; *idem,* Industrial Psychology: Reminiscences of an Academic Moonlighter," in Theophile S. Krawiec, ed., *The Psychologists: Autobiographies of Distinguished Living Psychologists* (New York: Oxford University Press, 1974), pp. 440–500. See also Peter B. Petersen, "Early Beginnings: Occupational Safety Management 1925–1935," *Journal of Managerial Issues* 11(4) (Winter 1990), pp. 382–405, Jesús F. Salgado, "Some Landmarks of 100 Years of Scientific Personnel Selection at the Beginning of the New Century," *International Journal of Selection and Assessment* 9(1–2) (March/June, 2001), pp. 3–8 and Ben Shepherd, "Psychology and the Great War, 1914–1918," *The Psychologist* 28(11) (November 2015), pp. 944–946.

but also Roman Catholic and Jewish) felt that they had a duty to reform social and economic conditions, especially in the workplace. Another proponent in the Social Gospel movement was C. Whiting Williams (1878–1975). Born into a relatively prosperous family, Williams was educated at Oberlin College, graduating in 1899. He held various positions before being named vice president and director of personnel for the Hydraulic Pressed Steel Company (Cleveland, Ohio) in 1918. He resigned from this position after only a year because he felt he did not know enough about workers and their lives to be a personnel director. As the Social Gospel movement was based on direct involvement in social and political action, Williams shed his white collar and headed out disguised as a worker to study industrial conditions firsthand.[49] He felt the only way to gain an intimate familiarity with workers' daily lives was to participate and observe at the same time. He explained: "men's actions spring rather from their feelings than their thoughts, and people cannot be interviewed for their feelings."[50] His first job was in a steel mill, cleaning out open-hearth furnaces so they could be rebricked and refired. It was hot, dirty work; the daily shifts were 12 hours long; and the pay was 45 cents per

Whiting Williams. Whiting Williams, *What's On the Worker's Mind* (New York: Charles Scriber's Sons, 1920), frontispiece.

hour, with time-and-a-half for work over 8 hours a day. This was Williams's introduction to workers' lives on the job. Over a period of 7 months, he labored in coal mines, a railroad round-house, a shipyard, and an oil refinery, as well as in various steel mills.

According to Williams, the workers' prayer was, "Give us this day our daily job," because a job meant "bread": the opportunity to provide sustenance for the workers and their families. He discovered that all workers—including managers—measured their individual worth and their value to society in terms of their jobs. Jobs influenced workers' social standing, and how they earned their living determined where and how they and their families lived. Without jobs, people were isolated not only economically but also from their community and society at large: "[the worker's] vision of himself, his friends, his employer, and the whole of this world to come is circumscribed by his job."[51] Work was thus central to workers' lifestyles, friends, where they lived, how they spent their leisure time, and how they felt about themselves. "This vital connection between job status and social status means that the problem of effective relations with the worker inside the factory cannot be successfully separated from the whole problem of general social relations outside [the factory]."[52] Williams's appreciation of work as not only important for economic support, but also for social and psychological well-being. He was well ahead of other theorists who were just beginning to view the workplace as part of a broader social system in which work provides a sense of fulfillment and happiness, as well as a source of identity and self-worth. In his 1918 monograph, Williams was among the first to discuss "what every worker wants" in a job.[53]

Within factories, Williams observed the operations of a job hierarchy that had little or nothing to do with pay, but rather emphasized the nature of an individual's work. While working in a steel mill, he was promoted to millwright's helper. His pay was now 2 cents per hour more, but his

[49] Daniel A. Wren, *White Collar Hobo: The Travels of Whiting Williams* (Ames, IA: Iowa State University Press, 1987).

[50] Whiting Williams, *What's on the Worker's Mind? By One Who Put on Overalls to Find Out* (New York: Charles Scribner's Sons, 1920), p. vi.

[51] *Idem*, "What the Worker Works For," *Collier's* 66(6) (August 7, 1920), p. 8.

[52] *Idem*, "Theory of Industrial Conduct and Leadership," *Harvard Business Review* 1(3) (April 1923), p. 326.

[53] *Idem*, *Human Relations in Industry* (Washington, DC: U.S. Department of Labor, 1918). See also *idem*, "What Every Worker Wants," in Herbert J. Chruden and Arthur W. Sherman, Jr., eds., *Readings in Personnel Management* (Cincinnati, OH: South-Western, 1961), pp. 239–250.

former fellow shovelers envied him, not because of the pay increase, but because the nature of his job had changed from the dirty, hot work of a shoveler to a cleaner, more pleasant work of an assistant to a skilled worker. This made Williams skeptical about the notion that people would necessarily work harder if they were given more money. He recognized that social status is conferred by one's occupation or the type of work one performs:

> We give the dollar altogether too great an importance when we consider it the cause . . . of men's industry. . . . The dollar is merely an especially convenient and simple means for facilitating the measurement of a man's distance from the cipher of insignificance among his fellows. . . . Beyond a certain point . . . the increase of wages is . . . quite likely to lessen as to increase effort.[54]

Williams's perspective was unique, in that he viewed earnings as a means of social comparison—that is, the pay a worker received was considered not in absolute terms, but relative to what others received. Using the dollar as a unit of self-evaluation facilitated understanding a person's "distance from the cipher of insignificance" among others. This did not mean that money was unimportant, but it carried social value that might enhance or deflate how people viewed themselves relative to others. Hence, incentive plans that ignored this fact were less than effective as motivators. The mainspring of workers' lives was the "wish to enjoy the feeling of [their] worth as persons among other persons."[55] Togetherness in thinking, feeling, and being part of a group was important to workers because they drew their social status, security, and concept of self-worth from their peers. They chose to get along with one another not because they could not always find another job, but because they could not always move from their respective communities. From their employer, and especially their supervisor, they expected recognition and treatment conducive to preserving self-worth. It was not the paternalistic clubs, cafeterias, and recreation activities that won worker loyalty, but successful relations with their supervisors as representatives of management. Williams recommended an Eleventh Commandment, "Thou Shalt Not Take Thy Neighbor for Granted," and urged management to change from appeals to fear to appeals to "hope and surety of reward." Latent in Williams's study of workers' daily lives was Charles H. Cooley's "looking-glass self," (the idea that the self arises reflectively in reaction to the opinions of others) and the realization that one's self is embedded in one's work group as a primary social unit of importance.[56]

Other findings from Williams's "shirt-sleeve empiricism" included the following: (1) workers restricted output ("stringing out the job") because they perceived scarce job opportunities, and employers tended to hire and lay off indiscriminately; (2) unions arose out of workers' desire for job security, and unions would not have made much progress if employers had evidenced concern for this desire; (3) long factory hours (e.g., 12-hour shifts in steel mills) made both workers and supervisors grouchy and tired, causing interpersonal conflict; and (4) workers listened to radical agitators because employers failed to speak "of the plans and purposes, the aims and ideals – the character – of his employer, the company."[57] Williams made a career of lecturing, consulting, and writing of his experiences as a worker. Over the years, he resumed his worker's disguise to also study strikers and strikebreakers, unemployment, and labor–management relations in Great Britain and continental Europe.

Despite his pioneering work in the discipline that today is called industrial sociology, Williams's efforts were not widely recognized. Rather, the roots of industrial sociology are

---

[54] *Idem, What's on the Worker's Mind*, p. 323.

[55] *Idem, Mainsprings of Men* (New York: Charles Scribner's Sons, 1925), p. 147. Originally serialized in *Scribner's Magazine* 73 (January through April 1923).

[56] Charles H. Cooley, *Human Nature and the Social Order* (New York: Charles Scribner's Sons, 1902), p. 152.

[57] Williams, *What's on the Worker's Mind*, p. 289.

traditionally traced to the Hawthorne studies (see Chapter 13).[58] There are, perhaps, several reasons why Williams's work was largely overlooked. One reason is that it was simply overshadowed by the era's fascination with scientific management. Muldoon notes, however, that it would be incorrect to think that contemporaries were unfamiliar with Williams's findings. Instead, he contends that Williams's work, limited to his own personal encounters, was considered highly subjective and, therefore, unscientific.[59] This may explain why Williams's books were rarely reviewed or cited in the scholarly journals of the period. Moreover, as a relatively new discipline, sociology was striving to become more respected. The prestige enjoyed by sociologists affiliated with leading universities provided a mantle of legitimacy that Williams's work lacked.

Sociological Foundations

The study of sociology began in the late nineteenth century as an outgrowth of its parent discipline, philosophy, rather than as an applied area of study. The ideas of Max Weber, Emilé Durkheim, and Vilfredo Pareto would shape the thoughts of management writers in later years. In Chapter 10, we will discuss how Weber's scholarly efforts contributed to economics and sociology and a theory of bureaucracy. Durkheim divided societal solidarity into two primary types: *mechanical*, or those dominated by and having a collective consciousness, and *organic*, characterized by the division of labor and specialization and societal interdependence. According to Durkheim, mechanical societies were bound together by friendliness, neighborliness, and kinship. A lack of such solidarity in organic societies, however, led to anomie, or "normlessness," that could be restored only by a new "collective consciousness" that required social collaboration and self-sacrifice to a group in order to restore solidarity.[60] In Durkheim's anomie, Elton Mayo (see Chapter 13) would find a new prescription for social solidarity in work groups.

Pareto recognized that society is made up of interdependent parts that comprise what he called a "social system." He understood that the state of a society could be analyzed both at a particular time and with regard to the successive transformations that it underwent within a period of time, as it sought equilibrium among their varied parts. As we will see in coming chapters, Pareto's ideas might have remained just so much gibberish without the work of Lawrence J. Henderson, a Harvard University physiologist, who influenced a number of scholars such as Talcott Parsons, George Homans, Elton Mayo, Fritz Roethlisberger, and Chester Barnard through a seminar Henderson conducted that was known as the "Pareto Circle."[61]

Some Early Empirical Investigations

Before Whiting Williams undertook his own brand of "shirt-sleeve empiricism," there had been other studies on workers' daily lives. Two of these studies merit brief mention because of their unique insights and international perspectives. Anticipating Williams by some 25 years, in 1891, Paul Göehre, a young theology student and later General Secretary of the Evangelical-Social Congress, worked for 4 months pretending to be an apprentice in a Chemnitz (Germany)

---

[58] Daniel A. Wren, "Industrial Sociology: A Revised View of Its Antecedents," *Journal of the History of the Behavioral Sciences* 21(4) (October 1985), pp. 311–320. See also Steven R. Cohen, "From Industrial Democracy to Professional Adjustment," *Theory and Society*, 12(1) (January 1983), pp. 47–67; Mark Pittenger, "'What's on the Worker's Mind': Class Passing and the Study of the Industrial Workplace in the 1920s," *Journal of the History of the Behavioral Sciences* 39(2) (Spring 2003), pp. 143–161.

[59] Jeffrey Muldoon, "The Hawthorne Legacy: A Reassessment of the Impact of the Hawthorne Studies on Management Scholarship, 1930–1958," *Journal of Management History* 18(1) (2012), pp. 105–119.

[60] Emilé Durkheim, *The Division of Labor in Society*, trans. George Simpson (New York: Free Press, 1947). Originally published in 1893.

[61] Barbara S. Heyl, "The Harvard 'Pareto Circle.'" *Journal of the History of the Behavioral Sciences* 4(4) (October 1968), pp. 316–334.

machine-making factory to see why workers were attracted to Social Democracy, an ideology that advocated a peaceful transition from capitalism to socialism.[62] Göehre observed that workers took more pride in producing a complete unit of work rather than an unidentifiable fragment, higher productivity occurred when supervisors instilled a feeling of group interdependence and teamwork, and there were informal group pressures for adherence to norms. Lower morale and reduced efficiency resulted when workers were isolated and did not feel part of a broader "community of labour." Göehre's findings presaged research on the relationship between job-design and productivity that first appeared in the 1940s (see Chapter 15).

In an equally prescient effort, in 1924 and 1926, Belgian psychologist Hendrik de Man asked 78 "wage workers and salaried employees of both sexes from various parts of Germany," who were attending lectures he gave at the University of Frankfurt-on-Main, to complete a detailed questionnaire "concerning their own feelings about their daily work."[63] Based on the completed questionnaire, he concluded that there was a natural impulse in people to find "joy in work." As explained by De Man, this impulse reflected a desire for activity, play, constructiveness, curiosity, self-assertion, and a longing for "mastery" (power). Inhibitive factors that contributed to "distaste for work" derived from job elements such as detail work, monotony, reduction of worker initiative, fatigue, and poor working conditions; and in "social hindrances," like a sense of dependency, unjust wage systems, speedups, insecurity of livelihood, and lack of social solidarity. De Man's main conclusion that a worker's mental attitude toward work is a mix of "pleasurable and unpleasurable elements" is remarkably similar to that of Frederick I. Herzberg's later two-factor theory of job satisfaction (see Chapter 20), published some 30 years later. Much like Herzberg, De Man felt that work itself was a motivator and that management's job was to remove the "hindrances" that prevented employees from finding joy in work. In this regard, De Man believed that "it is psychologically impossible to deprive any kind of work of all its positive emotional elements," and human beings will find a "certain scope for initiative which can satisfy after a fashion the instinct for play and the creative impulse" in any assigned work.[64]

The "Democratization of the Workplace"

Theory and research into various aspects of industrial life steadily advanced during the first two decades of the twentieth century. Inspired by the spirit of democracy enshrined in President Abraham Lincoln's immortal words, "[A] government of the people, by the people, for the people,"[65] there were also advances directly involving labor–management relations and they were most evident in the trade-union movement and the changing nature of union–management cooperation.

The Trade-Union Movement

The year 1886 was marked by several momentous events. While Henry R. Towne was encouraging engineers to think in economic terms, the American Federation of Labor (AFL) was being formed under the presidency of Samuel B. Gompers. The AFL was a federation of craft unions that would succeed where the Knights of Labor and the National Labor Union had failed

---

[62] Paul Göehre, *Three Months in a Workshop: A Practical Study*, trans. A. B. Carr [pseudonym of Elizabeth Nelson Fairchild] (London: Swan Sonnenschein, 1895). Originally published in 1891. See also Richard J. Whiting, "Historical Search in Human Relations," *Academy of Management Journal* 7(1) (March 1964), pp. 45–53.
[63] Hendrik de Man, *Joy in Work*, trans. Eden and Cedar Paul (London: G. Allen & Unwin, 1929), p. 9. Originally published in 1927.
[64] *Idem, The Psychology of Socialism*, trans. Eden and Cedar Paul (London: G. Allen & Unwin, 1928), p. 9. Translated from the second edition originally published in 1927.
[65] Abraham Lincoln, "Gettysburg Address," delivered November 19, 1863, Gettysburg, PA, pp. 2–3. Available at http://americanhistory.si.edu/documentsgallery/exhibitions/gettysburg_address_1.html#

(see Chapter 6). Also of note in the same year was the publication of Richard T. Ely's *The Labor Movement in America*. As Ely explained, this volume was intended to be a clarion call "to protect and advance the interest of the great mass of the working classes" by uniting in associations to bargain collectively with employers.[66]

Although at one time associated with the Social Gospel movement, Ely's ideas regarding the role of labor incorporated both Christian and socialist elements. He advocated independent worker associations and public ownership of the nation's railway, gas, electric, telephone, and telegraph industries. Ely would later reverse his views regarding converting private property to public use and operation, but continued to see capitalist employers as a separate social class.[67] He insisted, however, that neither socialism nor communism could advance the cause of labor more than workers forming voluntary associations to negotiate with employers.

Prior to the publicity scientific management received following the 1910 Eastern Rate Case, organized labor had paid scant attention to Fred Taylor and his followers. In 1912, following on the heels of the 1911 House of Representatives investigation into the Taylor system, Congress created a Commission on Industrial Relations to "inquire into the general condition of labor in the principal industries of the United States."[68] One member of the commission, John R. Commons, was Ely's former pupil and University of Wisconsin colleague. Commons was a central figure in institutional labor economics, which emphasized the employment relationship in broad social and legal terms rather than the labor market view of neoclassical economics. As an advocate for social justice, and someone who believed that carefully crafted legislation could create social change, Commons had taken an early position that the "clever devices of compensation"—formulated by Taylor, Gantt, Emerson, and others—divided workers and forced job negotiations between an employer and individual employees.[69] He felt strongly that workers needed to organize and bargain collectively to offset employers' economic strength.

As a member of the Commission on Industrial Relations, Commons had the opportunity to meet with Taylor and "came to realize that improved methods of management and personnel administration were yet another valuable approach to solving labor problems and improving industrial relations."[70] After visiting various factories that had implemented Taylor's methods, Commons concluded that scientific management and labor could cooperate, but only under certain circumstances. Plimpton Press, one of the most scientifically managed companies Commons visited, was unionized, but experienced little labor–management conflict. In contrast, the Joseph and Feiss Company, another model Taylor installation, was not unionized, but was managed so well that Commons felt a union was unnecessary. In Commons's judgment, however, such companies were rare. Indeed, he believed that some 75 to 90 percent of the nation's employers were so backward that "only the big stick of unionism or legislation" could assure worker interests were protected.[71]

In his book *Industrial Goodwill*, Commons wrote of the need for workers to unionize so that they would have a "voice" in workplace governance. He called on employers to view workers as "human resources," in which parents, taxpayers, and the nation had made a significant investment.[72] Although Commons openly admired Taylor, he felt that scientific management cut across

---

[66] Richard T. Ely, *The Labor Movement in America*, new ed. (New York: Thomas Y. Crowell, 1886), p. 92.

[67] Idem, *Social Aspects of Christianity, and Other Essays* (New York: T. Y. Crowell, 1889), pp. 72–78; and *idem, Ground Under Our Feet: An Autobiography* (New York: Macmillan, 1938), pp. 251–252.

[68] *Final Report of the Commission on Industrial Relations*, Senate Document no. 415, 64th Cong., 1st sess. (Washington, DC: U.S. Government Printing Office, 1916), vol. 1, p. 3.

[69] John R. Commons, "Organized Labor's Attitude Toward Industrial Efficiency," *American Economic Review* 1(3) (September 1911), pp. 463–472.

[70] Bruce E. Kaufman, "The Role of Economics and Industrial Relations in the Development of the Field of Personnel/Human Resource Management," *Management Decision* 40(10) (2002), p. 970.

[71] John R. Commons, "The Opportunity of Management," in John R. Commons, Willis Wisler, Alfred P. Haake, Otto F. Carpenter, Jennie McMullin Turner, Ethel B. Dietrich, Jean Davis, Malcolm Sharp, and John A. Commons *Industrial Government* (New York: Macmillan, 1921), p. 263.

[72] Idem, *Industrial Goodwill* (New York: McGraw-Hill, 1919), pp. 129–130.

"the solidarity of labor," placed job knowledge in the hands of employers rather than workers, and had the "defects of autocracy."[73] In his autobiography, Commons explained, "I was trying to save Capitalism by making it good. . . . I wanted also to make trade unions as good as the best of them that I knew."[74]

Based on his work with the Commission on Industrial Relations and his contact with Taylor, Commons took a broad view of labor–management relations. He was concerned with the greater strength of employers relative to employees. In response to the imbalance of individual workers bargaining alone, he sought to strengthen labor by advocating industrial goodwill, sound managerial practices, and government legislation and oversight. In time, Commons would come to be considered the "Father of Industrial Relations."[75] Other prominent economists who also played a role in expanding personnel management to include industrial relations were luminaries such as Senator Paul H. Douglas (Illinois) and Harvard University professor Sumner H. Slichter.[76]

Practitioners and consultants were also influential in reshaping industrial relations, especially in the post–World War I period. The philosophy of the AFL, as represented by Samuel B. Gompers, was to achieve gains for labor through power rather than cooperation.[77] Organized labor during this period viewed scientific management as autocratic, because it forced employees to depend on an employer's conception of fairness. Employees had no voice in setting standards, determining wage rates, or deciding other work-related issues. When asked what organized labor wanted, Gompers simply replied: "more, more, and then more."[78]

The Changing Nature of Union–Management Cooperation

To understand the eventual union–management cooperation that was achieved following Fred Taylor's death in 1915, it is necessary to reach back to the Social Gospel movement, which espoused industrial betterment and sought to resolve labor unrest through associations such as the National Civic Federation (NCF), formed in 1900.[79] The NCF sought to mediate disputes, educate the public about labor–management relations, and improve industrial relations by demonstrating that labor and management had mutual interests. The era's most prominent call for improved labor–management relations came from President Woodrow Wilson who, in his May 20, 1919, Annual Message to Congress, declared that there "must be the genuine democratization of industry, based upon a full recognition of the right of those who work, in whatever rank, to participate in some organic way in every decision which directly affects their welfare or the part they are to play in industry."[80] During the Great War, President Wilson's National War Labor Board, established in 1918, also furthered many of organized labor's goals: for example, it

---

[73] *Ibid.*, pp. 18–19.

[74] John R. Commons, *Myself* (New York: Macmillan, 1934), p. 143.

[75] Bruce E. Kaufman, *The Origins and Evolution of the Field of Industrial Relations in the United States* (Ithaca, NY: ILR Press, 1993); *idem*, "John R. Commons: His Contributions to the Founding and Early Development of the Field of Personnel/ HRM", *Proceedings of the 50th Annual Meeting Industrial Relations Research Association* (Madison, WI: IRRA, 1998), pp. 328–341.

[76] *Idem*, "Personnel/Human Resource Management: Its Roots as Applied Economics," in Roger E. Backhouse and Jeff Biddle, eds., *Toward a History of Applied Economics* (Durham, NC: Duke University Press, 2000), pp. 229–256; *idem*, "Human Resources and Industrial Relations: Commonalities and Differences," *Human Resource Management Review* 11(4) (Winter 2001), pp. 339–374; *idem*, The Theory and Practice of Strategic HRM and Participative Management: Antecedents in Early Industrial Relations," *Human Resource Management Review* 11(4) (Winter 2001), pp. 505–533.

[77] Jean Trepp McKelvey, *AFL Attitudes toward Production: 1900–1932* (Ithaca, NY: New York State School of Industrial and Labor Relations, Cornell University, 1952), pp. 6–11.

[78] Samuel Gompers quoted in Florence Thorne, *Samuel Gompers: American Statesman* (New York: Greenwood, 1969), p. 41.

[79] Marguerite Green, *The National Civic Federation and the American Labor Movement, 1900–1925* (Washington, DC: Catholic University Press, 1956).

[80] Woodrow Wilson, *The Papers of Woodrow Wilson: May 10–31, 1919: May 10–31, 1919*, vol. 59, ed. Andrew S. Link (Princeton, NJ: Princeton University Press, 1988), p. 291. Wilson had been a student of Richard Ely's at Johns Hopkins University. See Ely, *Ground under Our Feet*, pp. 108–119.

prohibited employers from engaging in antiunion activities, required time-and-one-half pay for work over 8 hours per day, established the principle of shop committees elected by employees to confer with management regarding grievances, proposed the principle of a "living wage" for all workers (in practice, this became an early minimum wage), acknowledged the right of women to receive equal pay for equal work, and provided mediation and conciliation services to settle unresolved disputes.[81]

During the Wilson administration (1912–1920), almost one-and-a-half million workers were added to union rolls. The economic, social, and political tides, however, soon began to shift. A short, steep economic depression in 1920–1921 weakened unions by reducing their membership as employment plummeted; further, companies were becoming more benevolent; management was waging intense drives for "open shops," in which workers were not required to join or financially support a union as a condition of hiring or continued employment; and government and the courts were growing hostile to union organizers' aggressive tactics. As noted in Chapter 8, there was also a concern that "radicals" and Bolsheviks, who had seized power in Russia during 1917, were gaining a foothold in the union movement. The general public reacted with alarm.[82] Union membership suffered, declining from around 5 million in 1920 to 3.5 million in 1921. In response to the resulting loss in bargaining power, unions had little choice, but to become less confrontational and more cooperative.

Under the leadership of Daniel Willard, president of the Baltimore and Ohio Railroad, and Bert M. Jewell, president of the AFL's Railway Employees' Department, a model plan for labor–management cooperation was developed following what came to be known as the Great Railroad Strike of 1922. The strike prompted an anguished outcry as nationwide rail travel was halted. In the aftermath of the strike, some firms moved to in-house unions, thus ousting the AFL. Recognizing that the momentum of the pro-union Wilson years had been lost, the AFL gave its support to several joint labor–management initiatives to improve productivity and, departing from earlier policies, agreed to the linking of wages to productivity increases.[83]

In coming years, successful union–management cooperation could be found in the clothing trades and railroads. The clothing unions, under the stewardship of Sidney Hillman, were among the first segments of organized labor to agree to cooperate in implementing scientific management. Hillman was head of the Amalgamated Clothing Workers of America and a key figure in the founding of the Congress of Industrial Organizations. The railroads also developed extensive plans for cooperation, first on the Baltimore and Ohio and then later on the Chesapeake & Ohio, the Chicago and North Western, the Canadian National Railways, and others.[84] In each instance, the railway unions implicitly accepted scientific management and participated through joint union–management shop committees in improving work routing and scheduling, hiring practices, and job analysis.

When William F. Green was elected AFL president in 1924, scientific management gained even greater acceptance. At its 1925 convention, the AFL "declared unreservedly for a policy of cooperation with progressive management in the elimination of industrial waste." Scientific management was to be supported to the extent that it "first, recognizes the right of workers to organize into responsible trade unions; second, is just as much concerned with the welfare of the human

---

[81] Valerie Jean Conner, *The National War Labor Board* (Chapel Hill, NC: University of North Carolina Press, 1983). The seeds planted by the National War Labor Board would bear fruit for more than half a century through legislation such as the Fair Labor Standards Act (FLSA; 1938), the National Labor Relations Act (1947), and the Equal Pay Act (1968), an amendment to FLSA.

[82] Sanford M. Jacoby, Union-Management Cooperation in the United States: Lessons from the 1920s," *Industrial and Labor Relations Review* 37(1) (October 1983), p. 22.

[83] *Ibid.*, p. 24.

[84] Otto S. Beyer, Jr., "Experiences with Coöperation between Labor and Management in the Railway Industry," in *Wertheim Lectures on Industrial Relations, 1928* by Otto S. Beyer, Jr., Joseph H. Willits, John P. Frey, William M. Leiserson, John R. Commons, Elton Mayo, and Frank W. Taussig (Cambridge, MA: Harvard University Press, 1929), pp. 3–31.

being engaged in manufacture as with the increased production of material goods; third, recognizes the potential value of trade unions as a constructive factor in production, and, fourth, is willing to participate in the setting up of joint union–management cooperative machinery directed to increases productivity with these conditions." It soon, thereafter, began articulating a set of what was to grow to be 16 principles of "progressive management." These were published in 1930 under the title "Labor's Principles of Scientific Management."[85] In an effort to further labor and management cooperation, the AFL made its engineering service and educational department available to employers.[86] The goal of both units was to demonstrate how union–management cooperation could lead to increased employer profits, as well as improved worker benefits. This "new unionism," with its recognition of what Fred Taylor had earlier termed a "mutuality of interests," completed a cycle in labor–management relations. Both labor and management now accepted scientific management.

Employee Representation Plans

Whereas union–management cooperation plans involved organized labor, the idea of employee representation and participation through shop councils and committees emerged as another approach for achieving industrial cooperation. The roots of the employee representation movement were in part a continuation of the industrial-betterment movement, in part, a hope for a restoration of the prewar open-shop days when unions had little influence and, in part, an outgrowth of the old Social Gospel theme that labor and management could coexist peacefully if they recognized their common purpose. In the waning days of his term of office, President Wilson had appointed two industrial commissions to investigate the unusual number of industrial conflicts that had occurred in 1919. One of the commissions, vice-chaired by Herbert Hoover, endorsed the idea of workers being represented through employee-elected shop councils. These councils would give workers a choice to be represented without having to join a union and pay dues. Hoover disagreed with the unionists who felt that shop councils were antiunion. He felt that shop councils provided an alternative for workers who wished a voice and a choice in the nation's economic system.[87]

John R. Commons and 8 of his University of Wisconsin colleagues studied 30 employee-elected shop councils from July to September 1919, including those at Filene's Department Store, the Dennison Manufacturing Company, the Ford Motor Company, the White Motor Company, and the Joseph and Feiss Company. One colleague praised Joseph and Feiss Company as "the greatest experimental laboratory of industrial psychology that we have found in America."[88] Another noted that the White Motor Company required all foremen and executives to spend 1 hour each day exercising in the company's gymnasium. She observed that doing so "gets them acquainted with each other undressed; it keeps them in splendid physique; and it keeps them from indigestion and getting cross and sour with their workmen."[89] The results of this experiment in managerial exercise to improve labor–management relations were not recorded.

The employee representation plan at the Dennison Manufacturing Company was perhaps more typical of attempts at worker involvement. In 1911, Dennison Manufacturing initiated an

---

[85] Geoffrey C. Brown, "Labor's Principles of Scientific Management," *The American Federationist* 37(2) (February 1930), pp. 194–195.

[86] *Idem*, "What the Union Offers the South," *The American Federationist* 37(9) (September 1930), pp. 1068–1073. See also Rexford Guy Tugwell, *Industry's Coming of Age* (New York: Harcourt, Brace, 1927), p. 41; Tom Tippett, *When Southern Labor Stirs*. (New York: Jonathan Cape & Harrison Smith, 1931), p. 183.

[87] Robert H. Zieger, "Herbert Hoover, the Wage-Earner, and the 'New Economic System.' 1919–1929," in Ellis W. Hawley, ed., *Herbert Hoover as Secretary of Commerce* (Iowa City, IA: University of Iowa Press, 1981), pp. 84–85, 96–98.

[88] Alfred P. Haake, "The Measurement of Motives," in Commons, *Industrial Government* Commons *et al.*, *Industrial Government*, p. 46. See also Richard A. Feiss, "Personal Relationship as a Basis for Scientific Management," *Annals of the American Academy of Political and Social Science* 65 (May 1916), pp. 27–56.

[89] Jennie McMullin Turner, "Thinking and Planning," in Commons, *Industrial Government*, p. 11.

Employees' Industrial Partnership Plan to share in company profits through a stock-dividend plan. Five years later, it established the country's first company-sponsored unemployment compensation fund to stabilize employment and provide worker security. It formed a works committee in 1919.[90]

During the same period, the Russell Sage Foundation, under the direction of Mary van Kleeck, sponsored numerous studies of employee-representation plans that typically reported lower labor turnover, mutual employee and employer prosperity, more effective grievance handling, and a voice for workers.[91] By 1924, some 814 employee representation plans were in existence covering over 1.5 million workers.[92] Despite union opposition to these so-called "company unions," these plans prepared the way for the idea that workers could meaningfully participate in designing the nature of work in addition to doing their jobs. Admittedly, some plans were no doubt used to forestall unionization. For this reason, the National Labor Relations Act (the Wagner Act) outlawed employee representation plans in 1935. Such plans were seen as being a form of company unions, wherein representatives could not bargain as equals (because they generally lacked the ability to sign legally enforceable agreements) and the right to strike was not recognized.

When Slichter retrospectively examined labor policies in the 1920s, he wondered why employers did not take advantage of the surplus of labor following the World War I to exploit workers. The now largely forgotten 1920–1921 economic depression had created a buyer's market for labor. Employers had an oversupply of workers from whom to choose, yet the era was marked by an increase in employee benefits. Employee turnover was low, employment-stabilization policies had increased job security, real wages rose 11 percent, 300 companies had some form of employee stock-ownership plan, 370 companies provided industrial-pension plans, and more progress had been made in labor–management relations among nonunion than union shops. Indeed, union membership was down 30 percent. Instead, Slichter noted, employers had created "industrial goodwill" with group-insurance plans, loans for and encouragement of home ownership, and provided paid vacations.[93] The 1920s was a prosperous decade for employee and employer alike.

SUMMARY

The dual heritage of modern personnel management may be traced to the early 1880s and the near simultaneous emergence of the scientific management and Social Gospel movements. Whereas scientific management originated from an engineering philosophy that focused on the need for the "strictest economy in the use of workers," Social Gospel proponents strived to improve "the general tenor of American living and the standards of the poor and unfortunate." Scientific management inspired psychologists and sociologists to become involved in the study of workplace dynamics. With advances in understanding the relationship between work and workers' lives on and off the job, there were also advances involving labor–management relations. These advances were most evident in the trade-union movement and the changing nature of union–management cooperation. The path ahead was opening for further progress in understanding people at work.

[90] W. Jack Duncan and C. Ray Gullett, "Henry Sturgis Dennison: The Manager and the Social Critic, *Journal of Business Research* 2(2) (April 1974), pp. 133–143. See also Kyle Bruce, "Activist Manager: The Enduring Contribution of Henry S. Dennison to Management and Organization Studies," *Journal of Management History* 21(2) (2015), pp. 143–171.

[91] See, for example, Ben M. Selekman's study of the Partnership Plan at Dutchess Bleachery Inc., Wappingers Falls, NY: *Sharing Management with the Worker* (New York: Russell Sage Foundation, 1924).

[92] Harold B. Butler, *Industrial Relations in the U.S.* (Geneva: International Labor Office, 1927), pp. 84–105.

[93] Sumner H. Slichter, "The Current Labor Policies of American Industries," *Quarterly Journal of Economics* 43(3) (May 1929), pp. 393–435. See also Robert F. Foerster and Else H. Dietel, *Employee Stock Ownership in the United States* (Princeton, NJ: Princeton University Press, 1926).

History rarely provides a full measure of individuals during their own lifetime. Epitaphs are often prematurely written, and succeeding events bring newfound appreciation to previously unrecognized accomplishments. Such is the case with two individuals whose contributions are the focus of this chapter. Both lived during the late nineteenth and early twentieth centuries; both wrote during the scientific-management era; both were Europeans; and both made lasting contributions to the evolution of management thought. One was a practicing manager and the other an academician; one was trained in the physical sciences, the other in the social sciences; and neither was accorded the full measure of his contributions until some decades after his death. Henri Fayol, a French manager-engineer, and Max Weber, a German economist-sociologist, addressed the fundamental issue of how organizations should be structured. Both Fayol and Weber sought to combine theory with practice. Their ideas have influenced succeeding generations of managers and scholars and, even today, continue to significantly impact managerial thinking.

Henri Fayol: The Man and His Career

Jules Henri Fayol (1841–1925) was born in Constantinople (now Istanbul, Turkey). His father, a noncommissioned artillery officer was an engineer fulfilling his military-service obligation in a cannon factory under an agreement between the French and Turkish governments.[1] André and Eugénie Cantin Fayol, Henri's parents, returned to France after André completed his military service. The family resided in La Voulte-sur-Rhône, where Andre headed a workshop at Pouzin. Henri received his elementary education at the École Sainte Jeanne-d'Arc and, subsequently, graduated from the Lycée de Lyon (now the Lycée Ampère) at Valence in 1858. He then entered l'Escole des mines de Saint-Étienne (at age 17) to become a mining engineer. After graduating in 1860, he went to work at the Commentry coalfield in central France. Société Boigues, Rambourg et Cie, a limited partnership (*société en commandité*), owned the coalfield and steel mills at Fourchambault and Torteron, a forge at d'Imphy, foundries at Fourchambault and Montluçon, and an iron mine at Berry. Following the death of several partners in 1874, Société Boigues, Rambourg was reorganized as Société Commentry-Fourchambault and Decazeville (popularly known as Comambault), a joint-stock company (*société ànonyme*).[2]

Henri Fayol, 1900. *La Société de Commentry-Fourchambault et Decazeville, 1854–1954.* Paris: Brodard et Taupin, 1954, p. 160.

From 1860 until 1866, Fayol worked as a mining engineer, conducting geological research, advancing a new theory about the formation of coal-bearing strata, and developing new methods for fighting underground mine fires. His efforts were rewarded with a promotion to manager of the Commentry coalfield at age 25; 6 years later, he was placed in charge of several colliers. In 1888, Comambault was in dire financial straits: no dividends had been paid since 1885, its Fourchambault and Montluçon foundries were operating at a loss, and its coal deposits at Commentry and Montvicq were nearing depletion. This same year, Fayol was named Comambault's managing director (chief executive officer) and charged with revitalizing its operations. He closed the foundry at Fourchambault and centralized production at Montlucon to gain economies of scale and acquired new coal deposits at Brassac and Decazeville and iron reserves at Joudreville. With the assistance of Joseph Carlioz, who was in charge of Comambault's commercial department, Fayol expanded Comambault's operations backward to mine coal and iron ore and forward to smelt the iron into steel and to sell both mined coal and raw steel.[3] Fayol established research facilities to advance Comambault's technical capabilities; entered into alliances with or acquired other firms; opened new mills to broaden Comambault's geographical base; hired staff specialists in research, manufacturing, and selling; and, to gain a competitive advantage, repositioned Comambault as a supplier of specialty steels.

Through his training was in engineering, Fayol realized that managing a geographically dispersed company with 10,000 employees required skills other than those he had studied. He viewed management as more than devising systems and methods for increasing throughput (as it had been for scientific management). For Fayol, management involved all the activities

[1] For biographical details on Fayol's life, see Amédée Fayol, "Henri Fayol (1841–1925): Ingénieur, Géologue, Administrateur" ["*Engineer. Geologist, Manager*"], *La Nature: Revue des Sciences et de Leurs Applications* No. 3144 (September 15, 1947), pp. 303-304; John D. Breeze, "Harvest from the Archives: The Search for Fayol and Carlioz," *Journal of Management* 11(1) (Spring 1985), pp. 43–47; Tsuneo Sasaki, "Henri Fayol's Family Relationships," *Journal of Management History* 1(3) (1995), pp. 13–20; idem, "The Comambault Company Revisited," *Journal of Economics* (College of Economics, Nihon University, Tokyo, Japan) 68 (January 1999), pp. 33–50; Jean-louis Peaucelle and Cameron Guthrie, *Henri Fayol, The Manager* (London: Pickering & Chatto, 2015). See also John D. Breeze and Arthur G. Bedeian, *The Administrative Writings of Henri Fayol: A Bibliographic Investigation*, 2nd ed. (Monticello, IL: Vance, 1988).
[2] Tsuneo Sasaki, "Fayol and Comambault," *Enterprises et Histoire*, No. 34 (December 2003), pp. 8–28; idem, "The Comambault Company Revisited," *Journal of Economics* (College of Economics, Nihon University, Tokyo, Japan) 68 (January 1999), pp. 113–128. Reprinted in Sasaki and Wren, *Henri Fayol and the Process School*, series 3 of the *Intellectual Legacy of Management Theory* (London: Pickering and Chatto, 2004).
[3] John D. Breeze, "Administration and Organization of the Commercial Function by J. Carlioz," in Kae H. Chung, ed., *Proceedings of the Annual Meeting of the Academy of Management* (1982), pp. 112–116.

associated with producing, distributing, and selling a product. A manager needed to be able to formulate plans, organize plants and equipment, deal with people, and much more. Engineering school had never taught such skills.[4]

From his experiences as a general manager, Fayol began to develop his own ideas about managing. "Fayol drew his theory from his everyday practice of management, with a concern for theorizing such as that of the scientist who knows that a theory, if it is true, corresponds to a large number of practical cases . . . His theory becomes clearer when it is confronted by the facts and it gains depth and flexibility when we consider how Fayol acted as a manager."[5] Beginning in his early days as a mining engineer at the Commentry coalfields, Fayol had kept notes on events that had affected mine output. For example, as early as 1861, he observed that all work had to be stopped because a draft horse working in the St. Edmund mine fell and broke its leg. A replacement horse could not be secured in the absence of the mine's manager, as the livery stable-keeper had no authority to act on his own.[6] Fayol's resolution of this impasse was not a result of his technical training, but the managerial insight that responsibility and authority must be co-equal or delays and disorder would result. Foreshadowing modern thinking on work groups, Fayol organized miners into self-selected teams. This increased group cohesiveness and, in turn, reduced employee turnover. Moreover, work-group output increased as the teams refused to accept inferior members. Anticipating the job-redesign movement by some 50 years (see Chapter 15), Fayol also recognized that some jobs could be enlarged to relieve monotony and enhance skill levels. When managing at Commentry, he returned the responsibility for reinforcing mine tunnels (so that a tunnel's walls and roof would not collapse) to the miners rather than using timbering crews.[7]

Speaking in Saint Etienne on June 16, 1908, at the 50th anniversary (*Cinquantenaire*) of the Société de l'Industrie Minerale's founding, Fayol expressed his belief: "All the employees in an enterprise . . . participate to a greater or lesser degree in the administrative function . . . [and] all have occasion to exercise their administrative faculties and to be noticed for them. [Those] who are particularly talented, can climb steadily from the lowest rung to the highest levels of the hierarchy in . . . an organization."[8] In this simple statement, Fayol was beginning to distinguish between managerial ability and technical knowledge. He noted that the effect of management on business activities was not fully understood and that technical expertise "can be completely destroyed by defective administrative procedures." Fayol further observed that "a leader who is a good administrator but technically mediocre is generally much more useful to the enterprise than if he were a brilliant technician but a mediocre administrator." Thus, according to Fayol, a firm's performance depended more on its leaders' managerial ability than on technical abilities. In this same address, Fayol also presented an early list of management principles, including unity of command, hierarchical transmission of orders, separation of powers among distinct departments, and centralization/decentralization. In addition to these and other principles, Fayol spoke of *prévoyance* ("foresight"), the act of forecasting, planning, and budgeting. He also stressed the value of organization charts, meetings and reports, and an accurate and rapid accounting system.[9] Although Fayol's Société de l'Industrie Minérale address revealed advances in his thinking, it lacked the depth and conceptual clarity of his yet-to-come *magnum opus*.

---

[4] Norman M. Pearson, "Fayolism as the Necessary Complement to Taylorism," *American Political Sciences Review* 39(1) (February 1945), p. 73.

[5] Peaucelle and Guthrie, *Henri Fayol, The Manager*, p. 1. See also Daniel A. Wren, "Henri Fayol: Learning from Experience," *Journal of Management History* 1(3) (1995), pp. 5–12.

[6] Henri Fayol, diary entry of July 29, 1898, in Frédéric Blancpain, ed., "Les Cahiers Inédits d'Henri Fayol," *Bulletin de l'Institute International d'Administration Publique* 28/29 (1973), p. 23.

[7] Donald Reid, "Fayol: From Experience to Theory," *Journal of Management History* 1(3) (1995), pp. 21–36.

[8] Henri Fayol, "L'Exposé des Principes Généraux d'Administration," in Daniel A. Wren, Arthur G. Bedeian, and John D. Breeze, "The Foundations of Henri Fayol's Administrative Theory," *Management Decision* 40(9) (2002), p. 911.

[9] *Ibid.*, p. 910, pp. 912–916. For a full treatment of Fayol's contributions to contemporary accounting, see Lee D. Parker and Philip Ritson, "Accounting's Latent Classicism: Revisiting Classical Management Origins," *Abacus* 47(2) 2011, pp. 234–265.

Fayol's masterpiece, *Administration Industrielle et Générale*, was first published in the *Bulletin de la Société de l'Industrie Minérale* in 1916.[10] Republished in book form the next year by H. Dunod et E. Pinat, Éditeurs,[11] it was known throughout France as "a catechism for the chief executive's education."[12] Fayolisme became as firmly entrenched in French management thinking as Taylorism had become in the United States. From 1918 to his death in 1925, Fayol presided over the meetings of the Centre d'Etudes Administratives, a group he formed to promote Fayolisme. In 1926, the Centre merged with the Henry le Chatelier's Conference de l'Organisation Française to form the still active Comité National de l'Organisation Française.[13] This merger brought together France's two main professional management associations.

World War I initially slowed dissemination of Fayol's ideas beyond France. It was almost 4 decades before his originality was appreciated outside a small circle of scholars in Europe and Great Britain.[14] Early interpretations contrasted Fayol's and Taylor's work. Whereas Taylor approached the study of management from the workshop or technical level, Fayol approached it from the viewpoint of upper level administration. Fayol's emphasis on administrative management reflected his more than 50 years' experience as an industrial mining executive. Be that as it may, Fayol insisted that his work complemented Taylor's thinking, in that both he and Taylor sought to improve managerial practice.

The Need for Management Theory

Fayol noted in his earlier writings that managerial ability was essential for an enterprise's success. If managerial ability was important, however, then why did schools and universities neglect managerial training to focus exclusively on teaching technical skills? The answer, according to Fayol, was the absence of management theory. Fayol defined theory as "a collection of principles, rules, methods, and procedures tried and checked by general experience."[15] Writing from his years of experience, he noted that many managers theorized, but in practice there existed many managerial contradictions and little systematic reflection. Fayol believed that a lack of theory made it more difficult to teach and practice management because managers' experiences were localized and not easily understood by other managers or students of management.

Every enterprise required management: "Be it a case of commerce, industry, politics, religion, war, or philanthropy, in every concern there is a management function to be performed."[16] Thus, like Charles Dupin (see Chapter 4), Fayol felt that management required special study apart from technical matters and could be taught in schools and universities as theory was developed and codified.

---

[10] Henri Fayol, "Administration Industrielle et Générale," [*General and Industrial Administration*] *Bulletin de la Société de l'Industrie Minérale*, 5th series, 10(3) (1916), pp. 5–162. See also Bennett H. Brough, "The Mining and Metallurgical Congress at St Etienne," *Journal of the Iron and Steel Institute* 76(1) (1908), pp. 203–208.

[11] Available online at http://bibnum-stendhal.upmf-grenoble.fr/files/original/77990.pdf

[12] Charles de Fréminville, "Henri Fayol: A Great Engineer, A Great Scientist, and A Great Management Leader," *Bulletin of the Taylor Society* 12(1) (February 1927), p. 304.

[13] John D. Breeze, "Henri Fayol's Centre for Administrative Studies," *Journal of Management History* 1(3) (1995), pp. 37–62.

[14] See Henri Fayol, *Industrial and General Administration*, trans. John A. Coubrough (Geneva: International Management Institute, 1930); *idem*, "The Administrative Theory of the State," trans. Sarah Greer, in Luther Gulick and Lyndall Urwick, eds., *Papers on the Science of Administration* (New York: Institute of Public Administration, Columbia University, 1937), pp. 99–114; and *idem*, *General and Industrial Management*, trans. Constance Storrs (London: Sir Isaac Pitman and Sons, 1949).

[15] *Idem*, *General and Industrial Management*, trans. Storrs, p. 15. Except where specifically noted, the Storrs translation will be referenced, as it is the most readily available English translation.

[16] *Ibid.*, p. 41.

Managerial ability, according to Fayol, depended on certain qualities and knowledge:

- Physical qualities: health, vigor, address [literally, manner of behaving]

- Mental qualities: ability to understand and learn, judgment, mental vigor, and adaptability

- Moral qualities: energy, firmness, willingness to accept responsibility, initiative, loyalty, tact, dignity

- General education: general acquaintance with matters not belonging exclusively to the function performed

- Special knowledge: that peculiar to the function, be it technical, commercial, financial, managerial, and so on

- Experience: knowledge arising from the work proper; the recollection of lessons a person has derived from things.[17]

Fayol even diagrammed what he believed to be the relative importance of technical and managerial abilities for employees with different levels of authority. As he explained, at the worker level, technical ability was most important; but as individuals moved up the "scalar chain," the relative importance of managerial ability increases, whereas the need for technical ability decreases. The need for managerial ability was more urgent at higher levels of an organization. Ability in commercial, financial, security, and accounting matters also diminishes in importance as a manager's authority increases. As for differences in firm size, Fayol contended that managers of small firms need relatively more technical ability than their counterparts in larger firms, where managerial rather than technical ability is required at higher levels.

In summary, Fayol held that all employees, from foremen to work superintendents, should receive some managerial training. He believed schools and universities did not teach management because it was thought that experience was the only way to acquire managerial skill. Recognizing that most higher managers have "neither the time nor inclination for writing,"[18] Fayol used his experiences and observations to propose a body of knowledge that included principles as guides to thinking and practice and elements or functions that compose a manager's job. His goal was to begin a general discussion from which a theory of management might emanate.

The Principles of Management

Fayol recognized that the term "principles" is often misunderstood. To some observers, it suggests an unquestioned or rigid way of doing things, on the order of laws in the physical sciences. For this reason, Fayol was careful to explain what he meant by "principles":

> For preference I shall adopt the term principles whilst dissociating it from any suggestion of rigidity, for there is nothing rigid or absolute in management affairs, it is all a question of proportion. Seldom do we have to apply the same principle twice in identical conditions; allowance must be made for different and changing circumstances. . . .
>
> Therefore principles are flexible and capable of adaptation to every need; it is a matter of knowing how to make use of them, which is a difficult art requiring intelligence, experience, decision and proportion. Compounded of tact and experience, proportion is one of the foremost attributes of the manager.[19]

---

[17] *Ibid.*, p. 7.
[18] *Ibid.*, p. 15.
[19] *Ibid.*, p. 19.

Moreover, Fayol stressed that in advancing a list of principles he was not suggesting that the list was inclusive. Other principles could be identified. The principles he chose to review were simply those he had found most useful in his own career. The 14 principles on which Fayol concentrated were as follows:

- Division of work

- Authority

- Discipline

- Unity of command

- Unity of direction

- Subordination of individual interests to the general interest

- Remuneration

- Centralization

- Scalar chain (line of authority)

- Order

- Equity

- Stability of tenure of personnel

- Initiative

- *Esprit de corps.*

Division of work is the well-known idea of assigning separate tasks to individual specialists with the intent of producing "more and better work with the same effort." Fayol recognized that division of labor leads to heighten expertise, which increases productivity. He also noted that, as a result of the specialization that derives from the division of work, tasks are performed more quickly because employees do not lose time shifting from one activity to another. Nevertheless, Fayol appreciated that benefits derived from dividing work must be balanced against obvious disadvantages such as boredom and monotony. As he unequivocally stated, "division of work has its limits which experience and a sense of proportion teach us may not be exceeded."[20]

Authority was defined as "the right to give orders and the power to exact obedience." Fayol distinguished between the formal authority managers held by virtue of office or rank and personal authority, which was "compounded of intelligence, experience, moral worth, ability to lead, past services, etc."[21] Well ahead of modern-day scholars, Fayol recognized that savvy managers complement their official authority with personal authority. He further realized that authority and responsibility are corollaries in the sense that wherever authority is exercised, responsibility arises. Fayol stated the classic case for authority being commensurate with responsibility. This principle appears throughout the management literature.

Discipline is essentially respect and obedience between a firm and its employees. Fayol felt that discipline was vital for a smoothly functioning and prosperous firm. He viewed "defects in discipline" to be a result of ineptitude on the part of a firm's managers. Discipline came from placing knowledgeable managers at all levels of authority, workplace agreements that are satisfactory to both managers and employees, and the judicious use of employee sanctions.

---

[20] *Ibid.*, p. 20.
[21] *Ibid.*, p. 21.

Unity of command was expressed as follows: "For any action whatsoever an employee should receive orders from one superior only."[22] Just as the Biblical injunction (*Matthew* 6:24) advises: "No one can serve two masters." To Fayol, dual command was a threat to authority, discipline, and stability.

Unity of direction means "one head and one plan for a group of activities having the same objective."[23] It provides the coordination necessary for focusing a firm's efforts. Unity of direction comes from a sound organization structure and is essential to "unity of action."

Subordination of individual interests to the general interest is a plea to abolish "ignorance, ambition, selfishness, laziness, weakness and all human passions."[24] As viewed by Fayol, the placing of an individual's or group's interests over a firm's general welfare would inevitably lead to conflict among participants. Fayol's observations in this respect represent an early expression of what modern agency theory refers to as "opportunism," meaning a form of self-interested behavior (see Chapter 19). Fayol recognized that individuals or groups who serve only themselves are harmful to the interests of their fellow employees and the interest of firms in general.

Remuneration deals with day wages, piece rates, bonuses, and profit sharing. Fayol concluded that appropriate employee remuneration depends on many factors. In general, however, a firm's method of payment should be fair, should motivate by rewarding successful performance, and should not lead to excessive over-payment. Fayol also acknowledged nonfinancial incentives (such as housing and food) as a form of remuneration.

Centralization is a principle that Fayol felt was always present to a greater or lesser extent and, thus, belonged to the "natural order." His discussion of centralization as a question of proportion unique to each firm, and his appreciation of the distortion that occurs as information is serially transmitted along a scalar chain, continue to offer valuable insights for contemporary managers:

> Centralization is not a system of management good or bad of itself, capable of being adopted or discarded at the whim of managers or of circumstances; it is always present to a greater or less extent. The question of centralization or decentralization is a simple question of proportion, it is a matter of finding the optimum degree for the particular concern. In small firms, where the manager's orders go directly to subordinates, there is absolute centralization; in large concerns, where a long scalar chain is interposed between manager and lower grades, orders and counter-information, too, have to go through a series of intermediaries. Each employee, intentionally or unintentionally, puts something of himself into the transmission and execution of orders and of information received, too. He does not operate merely as a cog in a machine. What appropriate share of initiative may be left to intermediaries depends on the personal character of the manager, on his moral worth, on the reliability of his subordinates, and also on the condition of the business. The degree of centralization must vary according to different cases. The objective to pursue is the optimum utilization of all faculties of the personnel.[25]

Scalar chain refers to "the chain of superiors ranging from the ultimate authority to the lowest ranks."[26] As Fayol explained, this path shows a firm's line of authority and the links through which communications are transmitted from the top to the bottom of a firm and back. To counter possible communication delays caused by the unity-of-command principle, Fayol developed what is referred to as the "gang plank." The gang plank allows communications to cross lines of authority. Thus, Foreman F desiring to communicate a message to Foreman P could do so directly without reporting upward (F through E to A) and having the message in turn transmitted downward to P. The gang plank (see Figure 10.1) permits lateral communication through the shortest path and avoids overburdening a firm's scalar chain.

---

[22] *Ibid.*, p. 24.
[23] *Ibid.*, p. 25.
[24] *Ibid.*, p. 26.
[25] *Ibid.*, p. 33.
[26] *Ibid.*, p. 34.

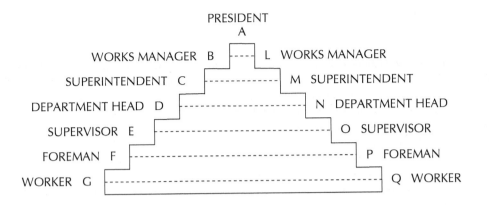

FIGURE 10.1 Fayol's Gangplank.

Order, with regard to material things, ensures, in the same words used by James W. See (see Chapter 16) "A place for everything and everything in its place." As Fayol noted, the same may be said for people, "The right man in the right place." The objective of *material order* is to avoid wasting resources. Fayol recognized that *social order* requires good organization and good selection and, by necessity, a need to balance a firm's human requirements with its available resources. Fayol considered ambition, nepotism, favoritism, or merely ignorance resulting in unnecessary positions, or positions filled with incompetent employees, to be the enemies of social order.

Equity, as envisioned by Fayol, results from a combination of kindliness and justice. As such, equity provides a basis for dealing with employees and instilling devotion and loyalty. Fayol took care to distinguish between equity and equality and, in doing so, anticipated modern equity theory (see Chapter 20). Recognizing the difficulty invoked by instilling a sense of equity at all levels of a firm, Fayol—no doubt reflecting on his personal experience—observed that in dealing with employees' desire for equity, "the head of the business must frequently summon up his highest faculties."[27]

Fayol's 12th principle, *stability of tenure of personnel,* sought to provide for orderly human-resource staffing and establishing provisions to assure that a firm's employees possessed the requisite abilities for the work to be performed. Fayol appreciated that it took time to develop the necessary skills to perform at a superior level. He also recognized that it took time for a manager and a group of employees to develop into a high performing team. In particular, managers must make a concerted effort to know their employees and inspire their confidence. From his own experience, Fayol knew this could be a lengthy undertaking.

Initiative, as a principle, exhorted employees to display zeal and energy in all endeavors. Fayol observed "thinking out a plan and ensuring its success is . . . one of the most powerful stimulants of human endeavour . . . and . . . [this] is want is called initiative." Fayol considered the "freedom to propose and execute" to be key aspects of initiative that were essential to subordinate satisfaction. As Fayol thus realized, "The initiative of all, added to that of the manager, and supplementing it if need be, represents a great source of strength for businesses."[28]

Finally, *esprit de corps* stressed building harmony and unity within a firm. Fayol warned against sowing dissension among subordinates. Calling once again on his years of experience as a manager, he understood that "real talent is needed to co-ordinate effort, encourage keenness, use each man's abilities, and reward each one's merit without arousing jealousies and disturbing harmonious relations." Quoting the Aesopian proverb "union is strength," Fayol advised: "Dividing

---

[27] *Ibid.*, p. 38.
[28] *Ibid.*, p. 39.

enemy forces to weaken them is clever, but dividing one's own team is a grave sin against the business."[29]

As Fayol explained, his principles were intended as guides to theory and practice and were not meant to be an exhaustive in scope, nor rigidly applied. The factory system of production that developed during the Industrial Revolution (see Chapter 3) reflected many of these principles in practice. Fayol, however, was the first person to formulate a set of general management principles.

The Elements of Management

Fayol is also credited with being the first person to identify and describe the elements or functions that compose a manager's job. He labeled the elements: planning, organizing, command, coordination, and control. Taken together, these five elements represent what is often referred to as "the management process."

Planning

Fayol recognized that planning, by defining a firm's objectives, set the stage for the other elements of a manager's job. At various times, he used the French *prévoyance* (anticipation or foresight) instead of *préparer* (to plan) when discussing this function. To Fayol, managing meant looking ahead, and foresight was an essential element of managing. As described by Fayol, a firm's plan of action represented "the result envisaged" and should rest on (1) a firm's resources, including buildings, tools, materials, employees, sales outlets, and public relations; (2) the nature of work in process; and (3) future trends in a firm's business activities that cannot be predetermined. In modern terms, Fayol was describing a rudimentary strategic audit that assesses a firm's present capabilities and strengths and scans the surrounding environment to anticipate future marketplace opportunities.

Fayol also understood the importance of what modern authorities call "contingency planning." Fayol's 30-year career as managing director was characterized by numerous technological, political, social, and economic changes that required recurring adjustments. "By constantly looking to the future, Henri Fayol promoted the idea of a lasting enterprise, renewing her assets as those on hand eroded. The profits made at the Commentry mine financed investments in the company's future, reinforcing its position in the mining and steel industries that would continue growing for another half century."[30] He observed:

> One cannot anticipate with precision everything which will happen over a longer period but one can minimize uncertainty and carry out one's program as a result . . . any long-term program should be susceptible to being changed according to the variety, complexity and instability of events. Like any living object the industrial enterprise undergoes continuing transformations: the personnel, the tooling, the methods, even the goals of the association change; the program must without ceasing be kept, as far as possible, in harmony with the environment.[31]

In commenting on the advantages and shortcomings of the forecasting system he used at Comambault, Fayol underscored the benefit of involving a firm's managers in anticipating a firm's future. In doing so, he showed an early appreciation of what would become known as "participative management":

> The study of resources, future possibilities, and means to be used for attaining the objective call for contributions from all departmental heads within the framework of their mandate, each one brings to

[29] *Ibid.*, p. 40. The moral of Aesop's fable "The Old Man and His Sons" is more generally rendered "Unity is strength." See *Three Hundred and Fifty Aesop's Fables*, trans. by George Fyler Townsend (Chicago, IL: Belford, Clarke & Co, 1884), p. 267.
[30] Peaucelle and Guthrie, *Henri Fayol, The Manager*, pp. 52–53.
[31] Henri Fayol, "L'Exposé des Principes Généraux d'Administration," reproduced and translated in Wren, Bedeian, and Breeze, "The Foundations of Henri Fayol's Administrative Theory," p. 915.

this study the contribution of his experience together with recognition of the responsibility which will fall upon him in executing the plan.[32]

Such participation ensured that no resource was neglected and promoted managers' interest in a firm's future success. Furthermore, Fayol realized that lower echelon managers would give increased attention to planning because they would be more committed to executing what they themselves had planned. Fayol saw that a good plan of action would facilitate the efficient use of a firm's resources and, in doing so, would possess certain characteristics: unity (one overall plan followed by specific plans for each supporting activity); continuity (incorporate both short-range and long-range plans); flexibility (be capable of adjusting to unexpected events); and precision (eliminate as many uncertainties as possible). Considering these characteristics, Fayol advised that firms establish a series of separate plans that would together constitute one overall plan for obtaining their objectives. Thus, he recommended that daily, weekly, monthly, annual, 5-year, and 10-year forecasts (or plans) be prepared and redrafted as time passed or as conditions changed.

Fayol's stress on long-range planning was a unique contribution to management thought, and his ideas are as important today as they were for his own time. He also offered innovative insights into planning on a national scale. The French government planned and budgeted on an annual basis with little or no regard for long-term development; the result was hand-to-mouth operations and a lack of fiscal responsibility on the part of government ministers. Fayol attributed the ministers' failure to develop long-term forecasts on the fact that ministers "come and go" and, thus, "have no time to acquire professional competence, business experience and managerial capacity indispensable to the drawing up of a plan."[33] For this reason, he argued for an increase in ministerial tenure to hold ministers to their work and to give them a sense of moral responsibility for the future of France.

Organizing

Organizing is the second element or function that Fayol identified as being part of a manager's job. For Fayol, organizing meant providing a firm with everything it needed to achieve its objectives. This included the classical factors of production: land, labor, and materials. Later writers divided Fayol's organizing element into two separate functions: organizing and staffing (human-resource management). According to Fayol, it was the duty of a firm's managers to ensure that its "human and material organization is consistent with [its] objectives, resources, and requirements."[34] In this regard, a firm's managers should provide unity of direction, define duties clearly, encourage initiative and responsibility, harmonize activities and coordinate efforts, and resist "excess of regulation, red tape, and paper control."[35] Fayol appreciated that structure should not be an end in itself, ignoring the human factor:

> [T]o create a useful organization it is not enough to group people [into departments] and distribute duties; there must be knowledge of how to adapt the organic whole to requirements, how to find essential personnel and put each where he can be of most service. . . . Of two organizations similar in appearance, one may be excellent the other bad, depending on the personal qualities of those who compose them.[36]

Thus, like Edward Atkinson and the Marshalls before him (see Chapter 6), Fayol realized it was people, not structure, that made the difference between the success or failure of two otherwise similar firms. In retrospect, Fayol anticipated today's contingency approach to management (see Chapter 20).

---

[32] *Idem, General and Industrial Management*, p. 48.
[33] *Ibid.*, p. 52.
[34] *Ibid.*, p. 53.
[35] *Ibid.*, p. 54.
[36] *Ibid.*, p. 57.

Fayol noted that the successive layers of authority that compose an organization (the so-called "organizational pyramid") are a product of functional and scalar growth. "Functional growth" relates to the horizontal structure of a firm, in that employees are added to perform functional duties as a firm's work load expands. In contrast, "scalar growth" is vertical, caused by the need to add layers of supervision to coordinate various activities divided among departments. Fayol described what happens to a firm's structure as its work force increases. As an illustration he considered what occurs relative to functional and scalar growth in a firm where 15 employees report to each first-line supervisor and, in turn, each group of four supervisors is under the direction of a higher level supervisor or manager. In such a situation, every 60 employees required 4 supervisors, and these 4 supervisors required 1 common manager.

This illustrated how a hierarchy developed, but in practice Fayol "had to adapt to a number of other considerations, including the cooperation between specialized technical functions and a large number of other units in other hierarchies."[37] He realized that there is a natural limit to the number of subordinates that a manager can effectively supervise, termed "the span of control," but this number was not formula driven and, in practice, adjustments were sometimes necessary.

On the subject of staff employees, Fayol visualized a group of individuals who had the "strength, knowledge, and time" to assist line managers by acting as an "extension of a manager's personality." Staff employees were to take orders only from a firm's general manager and to "subserve" line managers in dealing with daily obligations such as correspondence, interviews, conferences, as well as assisting in harmonizing current and future plans. Based on his own experience as an executive, Fayol believed that line managers generally had neither time nor energy to focus on long-term strategy. Staff employees, freed of daily pressures associated with running a department, could "search for improvements" in work methods, identify developing changes in immediate business conditions, and consider longer term trends.[38]

Fayol reviewed the differences between his recommendations for utilizing staff employees and Taylor's functional foremanship. Fayol agreed with Taylor's goal, providing specialized assistance, but disagreed with the means. Functional foremanship negated the unity of command principle, and to Fayol this was treading on dangerous ground. Order must be maintained, and for Fayol this was possible only if no subordinate reported to more than one superior: "So . . . let us treasure the old type of organization in which unity of command is honoured. It can, after all, be easily reconciled . . . with [staff] assistance given to superintendents and foremen."[39] In extending his comments, Fayol expressed the opinion that organization charts, showing all the positions in a firm and their relationships to one another, aided in maintaining the unity of command principle throughout a firm. He observed that, compared to lengthy written descriptions, organization charts enabled managers to more easily grasp a firm's "organic whole." Unfortunately, Fayol's thoughts on organizing were not published until recently.[40]

Focusing on what he referred to as the "body corporate," Fayol viewed employee selection and training to be vital for determining a firm's fate. He considered selecting capable employees to be among "the most important and most difficult of business activities." Noting that the consequences of poor selection are "commensurate with the rank of the employee," Fayol advised that the length of time devoted to choosing an employee should increase with the level of the position being filled. On balance, like Taylor, Fayol's treatment of evaluating a firm's employees was limited, reflecting the rudimentary practices of the day. Training, in contrast,

---

[37] Peaucelle and Guthrie, *Henri Fayol, The Manager*, p. 63.

[38] *Ibid.*, p. 63.

[39] *Ibid.*, p. 70.

[40] See Jean-Louis Peaucelle, *Henri Fayol, Inventeur des Outils des Gestion: Textes Originaux et Recherches Actuelles* (Paris: Economica, 2003). See also Fayol's previously unpublished typescript "Personal Observations and Experiments" in Peaucelle and Guthrie, *Henri Fayol, The Manager*, pp. 183–221.

was dealt with at length, primarily because Fayol had an ulterior motive. As previously discussed, Fayol called for less technical training of young engineers and increasing attention to the elements of management. In Fayol's view, contemporary education in French schools was based on two illusions "that the value of engineers and industrial leaders comprises technical ability almost exclusively [and] bears a direct relationship to the number of years devoted to the subject of mathematics."[41] Fayol believed that the latter "illusion" was just as "dire" as the former, but would likely prove harder to dispel: "Long personal experience has taught me that the use of *higher* mathematics counts for nothing in managing businesses."[42] Basic mathematics helped train the mind, but further study should be devoted to management rather than more math. Fayol sought balance and advised young engineers to study workmen, "their behaviour, character, abilities, work, and even their personal interests."[43] Indeed, Fayol thought that everyone should study the elements of management, for they were necessary in the workshop as well as in the home.

Command, Coordination, and Control

Having been formed, Fayol reasoned that a firm must be set into motion. He viewed this as the "mission of command," as spread among a firm's managers. Fayol used the French *commander* (to command) as well as *diriger* (to direct) in his writing. Because "command" has a more specific meaning in English, perhaps the most representative translation of this third element of management would be "to direct or to supervise." Fayol felt that it was every manager's duty to "get the optimum return from all employees" and that doing so required certain personal qualities and principles of management. Fayol held that managers should:

- have a thorough knowledge of their employees
- eliminate incompetent employees
- be well versed in the agreements binding a firm and its employees
- set a good example for others
- conduct periodic audits of a firms' performance
- confer with their assistants as a group to provide for unity of direction and the focusing of effort
- avoid becoming engrossed in detail
- strive at making unity, energy, initiative, and loyalty prevail among all employees.[44]

In a diary entry dated July 29, 1898, Fayol wrote: "In business administration, the question of [managing] people represents more than one-half of the problem."[45] As a young manager, Fayol had built effective work teams in the Commentry mines, discontinued paternalistic practices such as monitoring employee church attendance, closed company-owned stores in areas where local merchants were present, and demonstrated other people-management skills that led to his promotions. With his experience that people represent more than one-half the challenge managers face, Fayol learned that communication skills were crucial. He saw conferring with assistants to be important for establishing and maintaining clear communications. His admonition to avoid being engrossed in detail was not antithetical to keeping informed, but rather meant

---

[41] Fayol, *General and Industrial Management*, pp. 83–84.
[42] *Ibid.*, p. 84. By "higher mathematics" Fayol meant "special mathematics," such as differential and integral calculus.
[43] *Ibid.*, p. 91.
[44] *Ibid.*, pp. 97–98.
[45] *Idem*, in Blancpain, "Les Cahiers Inédits d'Henri Fayol," p. 24.

to be a warning not to neglect large problems while lavishing attention on picayune matters. Further reflecting an appreciation of the human element, Fayol believed that to encourage initiative, managers should allow subordinates "the maximum share of activity consistent with their position and capability, even at the cost of some mistakes."[46] Moreover, Fayol felt that authority should be delegated downward to develop employees' abilities and to avoid "drying up initiative and loyalty."

Coordination was Fayol's fourth element or function of management. By coordination, Fayol meant "to harmonize all the activities of a concern so as to facilitate its working, and its success."[47] Later writers have stressed the necessity of coordination in all elements of management rather than treating it as a separate element. To Fayol, coordination required balancing expenses with revenues, equipment maintenance with meeting production goals, and sales against production. The functions of planning and organizing facilitated coordination by specifying duties, establishing schedules, and focusing responsibilities on furthering a firm's objectives. Command instilled initiative, and conferences with assistants and subordinates provided a clearinghouse for airing problems, progress, and plans. Fayol recommended that line managers use staff employees to enhance coordination, but warned that their use did not replace line managers' direct responsibility for achieving a firm's objectives.

Control, Fayol's final element of management, consisted of "verifying whether everything occurs in conformity with the plan adopted, the instructions issued, and the principles established."[48] Fayol's *contrôler* was a positive view of monitoring plans and performance to gauge and verify a firm's progress toward achieving its goals. Control was to be applied to people, objects, and activities, and its objective was to identify errors so as to correct them and prevent their recurrence. The accounting function played a key role in the information system with regard to collecting and disseminating information for internal decision-making and external reporting. Effective control should be based on prompt action, followed by sanctions, if necessary. Fayol saw control as having an integrative effect on the other elements of management because it could be used to stimulate better planning, simplify and strengthen a firm's organization structure, enhance the directing of employees, and facilitate coordination. In effect, control completed a cycle of activities that could then be improved as the management process continued.

A Final Note

Fayol's orientation was that of a top-level executive. He believed that "The responsibility of general management is to conduct the enterprise toward its objective by making optimum use of available resources. It is the executive authority, it draws up the plan of action, selects personnel, determines performance, ensures and controls the execution of all activities."[49] Fayol assumed the top management position when Commentry-Fourchambault et Decazeville was headed for bankruptcy and restored it to prosperity in a period characterized by economic, social, political, and technological change. For all intents and purposes, Fayol was a strategist before that term became popular.[50] The familiar ring of Fayol's ideas suggests how thoroughly they have penetrated current managerial thinking. Whereas many of them may seem relatively self-evident today, they were revolutionary when first advanced. They remain important not only because of Fayol's

---

[46] *Idem, General and Industrial Management*, pp. 102–103.

[47] *Ibid.*, p. 103.

[48] *Ibid.*, p. 107. In *Henri Fayol, The Manager*, p. 260, Peaucelle and Guthrie suggest "to verify" is a more accurate translation.

[49] *Ibid.*, pp. 61–62; see also p. 6.

[50] Daniel A. Wren, "Henri Fayol as Strategist: A Nineteenth Century Corporate Turnaround," *Management Decision* 39 (2001), pp. 475–487. See also Lee D. Parker and Philip A. Ritson, "Revisiting Fayol: Anticipating Contemporary Management," *British Journal of Management* 16(3) (September 2005), pp. 175–194; Daniel A. Wren, "The Influence of Henri Fayol on Management Theory and Education in North America," *Enterprises et Histoire*, No. 34 (December) (2003), pp. 98–107.

influence on succeeding generations of managers, but also because of the continuing validity of his work. As a keen observer of management practice has noted: "Whether they admit it or not, it's obvious most managers today are fundamentally Fayolists."[51] For this reason, Fayol is known as the "Father of Modern Management." By the time of his death in 1925, Fayol had been awarded the Delesse Prize of the French Academy of Sciences, the Gold Medal of the Société d'Encouragement pour l'Industrie Nationale of France, the Gold Medal and Medal of Honor of the Société de l'Industrie Minerale, and been named a Chevalier (Knight) of the Légion d'honneur and a Commander of the Order of the Crown (Romania).

Bureaucracy: Max Weber

The life and work of Karl Emil Maximilian "Max" Weber (1864–1920) ran chronologically parallel to those of Henri Fayol and Fred Taylor. Born in Erfurt, Prussia, to a life of affluence in a family with social and political connections, Weber (pronounced *Vay-ber*) was an intellectual of the first degree, with far-ranging interests in sociology, religion, economics, and political science. While in the final stages of preparing his epochal study, *The Protestant Ethic and the Spirit of Capitalism*,[52] on why capitalism flourished in certain parts of seventeenth- and eighteenth-century Europe and not others (see Chapter 2), Weber had an opportunity to visit the United States, which he considered the most capitalistic of all nations. Weber was invited by his former University of Freiburg colleague Hugo Münsterberg (see Chapter 9) to attend the International Congress of Arts and Sciences, which was being held in conjunction with the 1904 St. Louis World's Fair. He presented a paper at the congress titled "The Relations of the Rural Community to Other Branches of Social Sciences."[53] Weber combined attending the congress with a stop in New York City to do some further research at Columbia University and the New York Public Libraries, and a short stay with relatives in Mount Airy (North Carolina). Further, curious to see firsthand how the spirit of capitalism abounded in the United States, Weber also took time to visit several cities, including Philadelphia, Washington (DC), Baltimore, Boston, Chicago, New Orleans, and Tuskegee (Alabama), as well as the Muskogee Indian Territory in Oklahoma.[54]

Max Weber, circa 1896–1897. Private CollectionArchives Charmet/Bridgeman Images. Marianne Weber, *Max Weber: A Biography*, trans. and ed. Harry Zohn (New Brunswick, NJ: Transaction Publishers, 1988), p. 347. Originally published in 1926.

The economic developments he observed were different from those in Germany. As documented in the McLane Report (Chapter 5), U.S. manufacturing and marketing had grown from small stores and owner-managed businesses to large professionally managed firms that were bound together by an intercontinental network of communication and transportation. In Germany,

[51] [W. Jerome Arnold], "Famous Firsts: Discoveries from Looking Inward," *Business Week* (June 6, 1964), p. 152.

[52] Max Weber, *The Protestant Ethic and the Spirit of Capitalism*, trans. Talcott Parsons (London: Allen & Unwin, 1930). Originally published in 1904.

[53] *Idem*, "The Relations of the Rural Community to Other Branches of Social Science," Carl W. Seidenadel, trans., in Howard J. Rogers, ed., *Congress of Arts and Science, Universal Exposition*, St. Louis, vol. 7. (Boston, MA: Houghton, Mifflin, 1906), pp. 725–746.

[54] Henry W. Brann, "Max Weber and the United States," *Southwestern Social Science Quarterly* 25(2) (June 1944), pp. 18–30. See also Larry G. Keeter, "Max Weber's Visit to North Carolina," *Journal of the History of Sociology*," 3(2) (Spring 1981), pp. 108–114; Lawrence A. Scaff, "Remnants of Romanticism: Max Weber in Oklahoma and Indian Territory," *Journal of Classical Sociology* 5(1) (2005), pp. 53–72, and *idem*, *Max Weber in America* (Princeton, NJ: Princeton University Press, 2011).

large-scale firms had been developed only in chemicals, metals, and complex industrial machine-goods.[55] In these industries, cartels had been formed to control prices and ration markets. Antitrust laws limited this practice in the United States, but German cartels could operate without fear of either government intervention or threat of competition. In contrast to Germany, a "spirit of capitalism" in the United States encouraged innovation and competition.

Bureaucracy as the Ideal

Primarily prescriptive in nature, Weber's writings strike an interesting contrast with the practitioner-oriented recommendations offered by Taylor and Fayol. Weber's major contribution was an outline of the characteristics of what he termed "bureaucracy," that is, government by bureaus (German *Büro*).[56] In reviewing Weber's work, it is important to emphasize four points:

1. Weber did not use the term *bureaucracy* in the disparaging, emotionally tinged sense of red tape, endless lines, and rule-encumbered inefficiency. Rather, he used it as a noncritical label referring to what he regarded as the most modern and efficient method of organizing yet developed. In Weber's words,

   Experience tends universally to show that the purely bureaucratic type of administrative organization – that is, the monocratic variety of bureaucracy – is, from a purely technical point of view, capable of attaining the highest degree of efficiency and is in this sense formally the most rational known means of carrying out imperative control over human beings. It is superior to any other form in precision, in stability, in the stringency of its discipline, and in its reliability. It thus makes possible a particularly high degree of calculability of results for the heads of the organization and for those acting in relation to it. It is finally superior both in intensive efficiency and in the scope of its operations and is formally capable of application to all kinds of administrative tasks.[57]

   What is not often understood is that bureaucracy developed as a reaction against the personal subjugation and cruelty, as well as the capricious and subjective judgments, of earlier administrative systems (such as monarchies and dictatorships) in which the lives and fortunes of all were completely dependent upon the whims of a despot whose only law was his own wish. For this reason, the benefits Weber attributed to bureaucracy can perhaps best be understood when compared to the alternatives it replaced. "Thus, for example, tax farming, whereby local collectors worked for a percentage of the take, was displaced by bureaucracies staffed with full-time salaried officials; inside contracting, whereby owners of equipment and materials contracted with foremen for labor, gave way to modern hierarchies."[58] Compared to the administrative practices that preceded them, the efficiencies attributed to bureaucracies become understandable.

   The world observed by Weber was decidedly unjust. It was dominated by class consciousness and nepotism. To be a military officer or an official in government or industry presupposed an aristocratic birth. In Weber's view, this was a ridiculous waste of human resources that ran counter to his belief that the working class could produce leaders as well as followers. Bureaucracy, with its emphasis on legal authority (see below), was intended to put an end to the exploitation of the masses and to assure equal opportunity and treatment for all.

---

[55] Alfred D. Chandler, Jr., "The Emergence of Managerial Capitalism," *Business History Review* 58(4) (Winter 1984), pp. 498–501.

[56] The word "bureaucracy" was coined by Frenchman Vincent de Gournay in 1745. See Fred Riggs, "Shifting Meanings of the Term 'Bureaucracy'," *International Social Science Journal* 31(4) (November 1979), pp. 563–584.

[57] Max Weber, *The Theory of Social and Economic Organization*, trans. A. M. Henderson and Talcott Parsons, ed. Talcott Parsons (New York: Free Press, 1947), p. 337. Originally published in 1922.

[58] Marshall W. Meyer, "Organizational Structure as Signaling," *Pacific Sociological Review* 22(4) (October 1979), p. 484.

2. To Weber, bureaucracy was an idealized form that did not exist in reality.[59] It was an intellectual construct to be used for broad historical comparisons of the relative performance of different administrative structures. In this regard Weber's bureaucratic model is hypothetical rather that factual. It is not meant to be a working model nor is it meant to correspond to reality.

3. Weber's ideal bureaucracy is based on *legal* authority as contrasted with that which rests on either *tradition* (custom) or *charisma* ("the gift of grace").[60] As developed by Weber, legal authority stems from rules and other controls that govern an undertaking in pursuit of specific goals. Managers are given the authority to interpret and enforce these rules and other controls by virtue of their position. Obedience is not owed to a person but to the impersonal authority of an office. Thus, authority adheres to specific positions rather than to individuals. This is necessary if authority is to outlast the tenure of individual officeholders. Familiar examples of legal authority structures are the military, politically elected offices, government bureaus, colleges or universities, and business firms (especially those above a certain size).

4. The need Weber identified for efficient organizing is inherently culture-free. Reliance on rationality and legalism, the idea of equality of citizens and the vast services offered in a modern state make some form of expert administration inevitable. In addition, the increasing size of firms, advanced technology, and the global marketplace make bureaucracy unavoidable. Thus, bureaucracy in government was followed by an increase in the bureaucracy of business corporations, trade unions, churches, service groups, and voluntary associations. Today, *all* undertakings of any size in any culture are bureaucratic to some degree.

The Advantages of Bureaucracy

Weber identified the essential characteristics of his "ideal" bureaucracy and believed that specific advantages would accrue to undertakings that embodied them. These characteristics and sample advantages include the following:

- *Division of labor*. Labor is divided so that authority and responsibility are clearly defined.

  Advantage—Efficiency will increase through specialization.

- *Managerial hierarchy*. Offices or positions are organized in a hierarchy of authority.

  Advantage—A clear chain of command will develop from the highest to the lowest level of an organization (Fayol's scalar chain principle), defining different levels of authority, and thus individual discretion, as well as enabling better communication.

- *Formal selection*. All employees are selected on the basis of technical qualifications demonstrated by formal examination, education, or training.

  Advantage—Employees will be hired and promoted based on merit and expertise, thus, benefiting both them and their employer.

- *Career orientation*. Although a measure of flexibility is attained by electing higher level officials who presumably express the will of an electorate (e.g., a body of citizens or a board of

---

[59] Max Weber, *The Methodology of the Social Sciences*, ed. and trans. Edward A. Shils and Henry H. Finch (Glencoe, IL: Free Press, 1949), p. 90. Originally published from 1914 to 1917.
[60] *Idem*, *The Theory of Social and Economic Organization*, p. 328. See also Max Weber, "The Three Types of Legitimate Rule," trans. Hans Gerth, *Berkeley Journal of Sociology* 4(1) (Summer 1958), pp. 1–11. Originally published in 1922.

directors), employees are career professionals rather than "politicians." They work for fixed salaries and pursue "careers" within their respective fields.

> Advantage—The hiring of "career" professionals will assure the performance of assigned duties without regard for extraneous pressures, as well as assure a continuity of operations across election cycles.

- *Formal rules and other controls.* All employees are subject to formal rules and other controls regarding the performance of their duties.

> Advantage—Efficiency will increase as formal rules and other controls relating to employee performance are enforced.

- *Impersonality.* Rules and other controls are impersonal and uniformly applied in all cases.

> Advantage—When rules and other controls are applied impersonally and uniformly, involvement with personalities and personal preferences is avoided. Subordinates are thereby protected from arbitrary actions of their superiors. Moreover, when rules are fixed and announced beforehand, it is possible to foresee how authority (coercive and otherwise) will be used in given circumstances and to plan on the basis of this knowledge.[61]

The Disadvantages of Bureaucracy

Although Weber considered bureaucracy to be the most efficient means of organizing, both his own experience and subsequent research have shown that it often results in certain disadvantages. These include the following:

- Bureaucracies are bent on self-preservation and the advancement of their members above all else. Changes that might, for instance, increase efficiency and innovation, and, thereby, put jobs at risk are seldom willingly embraced. When programs fail to produce intended results, they are continued with the justification all that is needed is a larger budget, more rules, and increased power to gain success. As a consequence, bureaucracies may become bloated and more an impediment than a solution to a program's problems. This may especially be the case in government bureaucracies where change-inhibiting bureaucrats do not have to respond to the economics of supply and demand or have to manage a payroll and budget as if their livelihoods were at stake, and their success in producing results is not constantly monitored.

- Rules and other controls may take on a significance of their own and, as a consequence, become ends in themselves. Employees, for example, may accuse budget personnel of being more interested in applying rules and regulations than achieving a firm's primary goals. Furthermore, whereas rules fixed and announced beforehand do enhance the predictability of outcomes, they also increase complexity after a certain point, thereby amplifying the likelihood of errors.

- Extreme devotion to rules and other controls may lead to situations in which past decisions are blindly repeated without appreciation or concern for changed conditions. Such "bureaucratic rigidity" leads to managers being compensated for doing what they are told and not for thinking. The result is "rule by rules" rather than common sense.

- Whereas delegation of authority to lower levels may increase operational effectiveness, it may also encourage an emphasis on subunit rather than overall goals, thereby prompting subunit conflict and decreasing effectiveness. A typical example can be found in many universities

---

[61] *Idem, From Max Weber: Essays in Sociology*, ed. and trans. Hans H. Gerth and C. Wright Mills (New York: Oxford University Press, 1946), pp. 329–333. Originally published from 1906 to 1924.

where conflicts over which department is going to offer what courses often result in unnecessary duplication of courses across departments, as well as the needless expenditure of resources.

- Though rules and other controls are intended to counter worker apathy, they may actually contribute to it by defining unacceptable behavior and, thus, specifying a minimum level of acceptable performance. That is, it is possible, once rules have been defined, for employees to *remain* apathetic, for they now know just how *little* they can do and still remain secure. This is commonly known as "working to the rules," because what is not covered by rules is by definition not an employee's responsibility. Within an educational setting, statements such as "all students must attend at least 50 percent of the classes during a term to pass" or "the minimum requirement for graduation is a C average on all course work undertaken" are illustrations of this phenomenon in that they clearly define *minimum* levels of acceptable behavior. Unfortunately, a typical administrative response in such circumstances is to enact additional rules (such as mandatory class attendance) and, in turn, further aggravate an already poor situation. Unless care is taken such a situation may result in a "vicious circle of bureaucracy," wherein rules beget more rules. Furthermore, once employees discover the appeasing effect of working to the rules, they may push for even more rules to further restrict management's power and protect their own prerogatives, power, and jobs. Therefore, rules may be functional in one sense, but in another (unintended) sense they permit employee involvement without requiring emotional commitment.

Despite these and other criticisms, bureaucracy is a central feature in modern societies. It is thus important to realize that the disadvantages just outlined are not necessarily inherent in bureaucracy per se. As envisioned by Weber, the bureaucratic model is both rational and efficient. Gaining its benefits, however, requires learning enough about its characteristics to avoid being controlled by them.

Though many of us may feel that we live in a bureaucratic world of baffling rules and other controls, we should not forget that bureaucracy also makes it possible for us to get potable water instantly, place an international telephone call in seconds, and have a package delivered a continent away overnight. Indeed, almost all the benefits we take for granted in today's society—modern medicine, modern science, modern industry—rest upon a bureaucratic foundation. In this respect, Weber's ideas have stood the test of time remarkably well. His pioneering work, like that of Fayol, has stimulated a wealth of research into the management process and remains a landmark in the evolution of management thought. In recognition of his contributions in developing the tenets of bureaucracy, Weber is known as the "Father of Organization Theory." Weber's goal was not perfection, but systematization—moving managerial practice and organizational design toward more logical ways of operating. Weber's work on bureaucracy remained largely unknown to English-speaking audiences until it began to be translated in the late 1920s. Like Fayol, Weber had to wait until cultural conditions created the need to think in theoretical terms. As firms grew in size and complexity, the search for a theory of organizations led researchers and practitioners to Max Weber and his bureaucratic model.

SUMMARY

The emergence of the management process and organization theory took place in two forms: Fayol's identification of the principles and elements of management and Weber's search for an ideal way of organizing. From different backgrounds and perspectives, both Fayol and Weber attempted to develop methods for managing large-scale organizations. Fayol stressed education for management rather than technical training and the importance of planning, organizing, command, coordination, and control. Weber sought to replace authority based on tradition and charisma with legal authority and to proscribe an impersonal and merit basis for selecting, hiring, and promoting employees. Both Weber and Fayol had history's misfortune of being overshadowed by others and having to wait until after their deaths to receive proper credit for their roles in the ongoing evolution of management thought.

Scientific Management in Theory and Practice

Whereas Taylor and his contemporaries provided the early impetus for the scientific-management movement, several other individuals helped shepherd it to maturity. Their efforts took place along various dimensions. First, following the urging of Henry R. Towne and Henri Fayol, there was an increased recognition of the need to establish college curricula to formalize the study of scientific management, as well as to undertake efforts to educate practicing managers in properly applying its principles. Second, as the scientific-management movement grew in the United States, it sparked attention in other parts of the world, including Western and Eastern Europe, Japan, China, and Australia. Finally, moving beyond scientific management's emphasis on the shop floor, it became apparent that rather than uniformly applying a traditional military command-and-control style of organizing, firms should be organized based on their individual goals and the unique demands of their specific industries.

The Study and Practice of Scientific Management

The Wharton School of Finance and Economy, established at the University of Pennsylvania in 1881, was the world's first successful undergraduate school of business. It was founded by Joseph Wharton, a philanthropist and industrialist in Philadelphia who had built an industrial empire focusing on metallurgy, running both the Bethlehem Steel Corporation and the American Nickel Company. It was not until 17 years later (1898) that the second and third schools of business were begun at the University of Chicago and the University of California at Berkeley. The Amos Tuck School of Administration and Finance at Dartmouth College, established in 1900, was the first graduate school of business administration; the second graduate school of business was formed in 1908 at Harvard University. Dartmouth was the first institution to offer what is known today as a Master of Business Administration (MBA) degree. Despite Taylor's belief that aspiring managers had to live their calling and learn through years of shop-floor experience, the benefits of studying general management as a formal discipline were quickly recognized.[1]

Education for Industrial Management

Exactly when management per se first became an academic subject is impossible to determine.[2] Towne's 1886 ASME paper, in which he observed that the study of management was wholly unorganized, had no medium for the exchange of experience, and was without professional associations (see Chapter 6), was clearly a landmark in calling for a remedy to what he recognized as an untenable situation.[3] An engineer, John Richards used his experiences for a series of 10 lectures on "works administration" at Stanford University in 1895–1896.[4] Dexter Kimball, dean of Cornell University's Sibley College of Engineering, credited Taylor's 1903 ASME paper on shop management with inspiring his own course in works administration. Offered for the first time in the spring term of the 1904–1905 academic year, the course addressed the economic basis of "modern" production. Kimball's 1913 textbook *Principles of Industrial Organization* grew out of his course notes.[5] The course applied scientific management to plant location, equipment policies, production control, labor compensation, and much more. Kimball stressed the need for scientific management, noting that "as industrial enterprises have grown in magnitude, as processes have become more refined and competition keener the problems of organization have steadily grown in importance."[6] Two particularly noteworthy early courses in "scientific shop management" were initiated at the University of Missouri's School of Engineering in 1909–1910. Together, the courses covered topics such as functional foremanship, time studies, "training in the principles of handling men," "the building up and preservation of an organization," and the "selection and training of officers."[7]

---

[1] Frederick W. Taylor, "Why Manufactures Dislike College Students," in Henry S. Munroe, Arthur L. Williston, and Henry H. Norris, eds., *Proceedings of the Seventeenth Annual Meeting of the Society for the Promotion of Engineering Education* 17 (1910), pp.79–92.

[2] John F. Mee, "Management Teaching in Historical Perspective," *Southern Journal of Business* 7(2) (May 1972), pp. 21–29. See also Daniel Nelson, "Scientific Management and the Transformation of University Business Education," in *idem*, ed., *A Mental Revolution: Scientific Management since Taylor* (Columbus, OH: Ohio State University Press, 1992), pp. 77–101.

[3] Henry R. Towne, "The Engineer as an Economist," *Transactions of the American Society of Mechanical Engineers* 7 (1886), pp. 428–429.

[4] Richard J. Whiting, "John Richards – California Pioneer of Management Thought," *California Management Review* 6(2) (Winter 1963), pp. 35–38.

[5] Dexter S. Kimball, *I Remember* (New York: McGraw-Hill, 1953), p. 85.

[6] *Idem, Principles of Industrial Organization* (New York: McGraw-Hill, 1913).

[7] H. Wade Hibbard and Herbert S. Philbrick, "Teaching of Scientific Shop Management, with Use of Engineering School Shops as the Laboratory," William G. Raymond, Arthur N. Talbot, and Henry H. Norris, eds., *Proceedings of the Nineteenth Annual Meeting Society for the Promotion of Engineering Education* 19 (1911) (Ithaca, NY: 1912), pp. 91–92.

Edwin F. Gay, first dean of the Harvard Business School, questioned what could be learned in college that was practical and read Taylor's *Shop Management* on the advice of Wallace Sabine, Dean of Harvard's School of Applied Science. Subsequently, Gay attended one of Taylor's Boxly lectures, toured local plants that applied Taylor's principles, and invited Taylor to speak to the Harvard Business School students. Harvard's "Industrial Management" course began in 1908; Taylor gave two lectures in Spring, 1909 and would lecture annually until 1914. C. Bertrand Thompson, "an educator, a missionary of the gospel," assumed responsibility for "Industrial Management" in 1911 and arranged lectures by Taylor and other scientific-management stalwarts. Thompson compiled the most extensive bibliography of scientific management for that period, served an apprenticeship studying with Taylor and his disciplines, and did much to further the scientific-management movement in academia and industry.[8] Thompson's Harvard affiliation, and the notion that management was a discipline amenable to scientific methods of inquiry, gave credibility to its formal study among those who opposed business education as being too vocational for college students. By 1913, scientific management was being taught either in engineering or business schools at the Carnegie Institute of Technology, Cornell, Dartmouth, Harvard, Northwestern (which began teaching personnel management in 1912), Ohio State University, Pennsylvania State University, University of Pittsburgh, and University of Wisconsin.[9]

With a growing appreciation and emphasis on scientific management among engineers, in particular, and the general public, more widely, the ASME experienced an identity crisis: Was its purpose to further mechanical engineering, or was it to become an outlet for ideas about performance incentives, cost accounting, and other facets of sound management? The ASME refused to publish Taylor's book *The Principles of Scientific Management* in its official journal due to disagreements within the society over its appropriateness and interest to its membership. As a result, Taylor had the book privately printed and distributed.[10] By 1919, however, 4 years after Taylor's death, the ASME recognized industrial engineering as a legitimate subject for study and created a Management Division in 1920.[11] By 1922, this was the ASME's largest division. Industrial engineering and industrial management became continuing threads in collegiate education, as the work of Taylor, the Gilbreths, Henry L. Gantt, and others led to research in ergonomics, or the study of human factors related to the design of jobs to maximize the efficiency and quality of employees' work.

Dartmouth's Tuck School led the way for those pursuing graduate-level studies; by 1910 the Dartmouth catalog listed a course in business management. As dean of the Tuck School, Harlow S. Person hosted the first scientific management conference in the United States.[12] As president of the Taylor Society (successor to the Society to Promote the Science of Management), Person's efforts broadened interest in scientific management. He extended the Society's membership and

[8] Daniel A. Wren, Regina Ebert Greenwood, Julia Kurtz Teahen, and Arthur G. Bedeian, "C. Bertrand Thompson and Management Consulting in Europe, 1917–1934," *Journal of Management History* 21(1), pp.15–39. See also C. Bertrand Thompson, ed., *Scientific Management: A Collection of the More Significant Articles Describing the Taylor System of Management* (Cambridge, MA: Harvard University Press, 1914) and *idem, The Theory and Practice of Scientific Management* (Boston, MA: Houghton Mifflin, 1917).

[9] Daniel Nelson, "Scientific Management and the Transformation of University Business Education," in Daniel Nelson, ed., *A Mental Revolution: Scientific Management since Taylor* (Columbus, OH: Ohio State University Press, 1992), pp. 77–101. For more on early scientific-management education at Harvard University, and especially the role of Henry H. Farquhar, see Hindy L. Schachter, "Frederick Winslow Taylor, Henry Hallowell Farquhar, and the Dilemma of Relating Management Education to Organizational Practice," *Journal of Management History* 22(2) (2016), pp. 199–213.

[10] Carol Carlson Dean, *The Principles of Scientific Management by Frederick W. Taylor: The Private Printing," *Journal of Management History* 3(1) (1997), pp. 18–30.

[11] Mikiyoshi Hirose, "The Attitude of the American Society of Mechanical Engineers toward Management: Suggestions for a Revised Interpretation," *Kansai University Review of Economics and Business* 25 (1–2) (September 1996), pp. 125–148.

[12] *Addresses and Discussions at the Conference on Scientific Management held October 12, 13, 14, Nineteen Hundred and Eleven* (Hanover, NH: Amos Tuck School of Administration and Finance, Dartmouth College, 1912).

range of interests and took an expansive view of business education. Person worked to dissipate the notion that scientific management was merely the use of a stopwatch. In Person's view, educators should emphasize the philosophy underlying scientific management and focus on developing creative leadership in industry. Person also recognized the value of involving social scientists in the study of management. He believed that management and labor were so closely entwined in daily activities that they failed to see larger relationships; however, social scientists would be able to take a larger, more objective view of workplace dynamics to chart a future course of action for research and practice.[13]

Leon P. Alford was another among the early group contributing to management education.[14] Alford was trained as an electrical engineer, worked in industry, and became editor-in-chief of the influential journals *American Machinist, Industrial Engineering, Management Engineering,* and *Manufacturing Industries*. He also edited a number of early management handbooks. Management historians have not generally acknowledged his role in management education; nevertheless, his influence as a journal editor, as a member of various professional committees, and as an author was substantial.[15] Among Alford's early writings was an attempt to provide another interpretation of science in management. Writing with Englishman A. Hamilton Church, he deplored the term "scientific management" because it implied that there was "a science rather than an art of management."[16]

The weakness of the Taylor approach, in Alford and Church's view, was that it superseded the art of leadership by substituting an "elaborate mechanism" or system. They did not mean that the mechanism was useless, but rather that it overlooked the dynamic possibilities of effective leadership. Alford thought that Taylor's so-called "principles" were too mechanical. To remedy this problem, he (and Church) proposed three broad principles: (1) the systematic use of experience; (2) the economic control of effort; and (3) the promotion of personal effectiveness. The first principle emphasized both personal experiences of executives and scientific studies; the second was based on the subprinciples of division of labor, coordination, conservation (least effort expended to a given end), and remuneration; and the third stressed personal rewards, developing contented workers, and promoting the workers' physical and mental health. As Church was later to explain, "the real objective of the new science . . . is not to throw the square pegs out of the round holes, but to gently shepherd the round pegs towards the round holes, and the square pegs towards the square holes."[17] From these three broad principles, Alford and Church believed that a truly scientific basis for the art of management could be discovered.

Alford's call for art plus science in management was a reflection of his admiration for Gantt, about whom he prepared an excellent biography (see Chapter 8). In the style of Gantt, Alford pleaded for industrial engineers to become involved in community service and foster improved relations between employers and employees. Alford continued to stress these themes as a member of the American Engineering Council and contributed to the better-known reports of this group, including *Waste in Industry* (1921), *The Twelve Hour Shift* (1922), and *Safety and Production* (1928).

---

[13] Harlow S. Person, "The Manager, the Workman and the Social Scientist," *Bulletin of the Taylor Society* 3(1) (February 1917), pp. 1–7.

[14] William J. Jaffe, *L. P. Alford and the Evolution of Modern Industrial Management* (New York: New York University Press, 1957).

[15] Leon P. Alford, ed., *Management's Handbook* (New York: Ronald Press, 1924); and later, *idem,* ed., *Cost and Production Handbook* (New York: Ronald Press, 1934) and coedited with John R. Bangs *Production Handbook* (New York: Ronald Press, 1944). See also Alford, *Laws of Management Applied to Manufacturing* (New York: Ronald Press, 1928) and *Principles of Industrial Management* (New York: Ronald Press, 1940).

[16] A. Hamilton Church and Leon P. Alford, "The Principles of Management," *American Machinist* 36(22) (May 30, 1912), pp. 857–861.

[17] A. Hamilton Church, *The Science and Practice of Management* (New York: Engineering Magazine, 1914), p. 227.

The International Scientific-Management Movement

France and Britain

Whereas the Industrial Revolution began in Great Britain and spread to the United States, the scientific-management movement began in the United States and would be shaped by context and culture in other nations. As early as 1907, Taylor was in touch with Henry Le Chatelier professor at the Sorbonne, regarding metal cutting, time study, and Le Chatelier's efforts to introduce scientific management in France.[18] Taylor's *Shop Management* was translated by Leon Descroix and published in Le Chatelier's *Revue de Métallurgie* in 1907.[19] When Fred and Louise Taylor visited Europe in 1912, and again in 1913, Le Chatelier introduced Taylor to industrialists Louis Renault, a founder of the automobile company Société Renault Frères, and Edouard and André Michelin, founders of the Michelin Tire Company (Compagnie Générale des Établissements Michelin). The Michelin brothers stopped short of applying Taylor's principles before World War I, but afterward applied scientific management in its workshops and formed the Comité Michelin to promote Taylorism in France.[20]

Renault, had previously visited Taylor at Boxly and was told to expect 3 to 5 years to successfully implement Taylor's ideas.[21] Under competitive pressure from the Ford Motor Company and German automobile manufacturers, Renault sought a "quick-fix" and employed an untrained engineer, George de Ram, to conduct time studies among employees at his Billancourt plant.[22] Piece rates were subsequently cut, and a strike ensued in December 1912. Renault compromised by loosening expected output by 20 percent, but another strike ensued in February 1913. The strike turned into a lockout and, after 6 weeks, a Renault victory.[23] Following the 1913 strike, Taylor wrote Le Chatelier: "If a man [Renault] deliberately goes against the experience of men who know what they are talking about, and refuses to follow advice given in a kind but unmistakable way, it seems to me that he deserves to get into trouble."[24]

Charles de Fréminville, a former chief engineer of the Paris-Orléans railroad, learned of scientific management through Le Chatelier's translations of Taylor's writings and became a second leading French proponent of *Taylorisme*.[25] He attempted to apply scientific management to the French manufacturer Panhard et Levassor, a pioneer in the automobile industry. Panhard and Levassor's managers resisted de Fréminville's efforts or simply took those parts of scientific management they felt would lead to quick returns at little cost. Fréminville did not lose interest, however; as noted in Chapter 10, he and Le Chatelier helped merge Fayol's Centre d'Etudes Administratives with the Conference de l'Organisation Française to form the still active Comité National de l'Organisation Française.

---

[18] Ralph E. Oesper, "The Scientific Career of Henry Louis Le Chatelier," *Journal of Chemical Education* 8(3) (March 1931), p. 456.

[19] George G. Humphreys, *Taylorism in France, 1904–1920: The Impact of Scientific Management on Factory Relations and Society* (New York: Garland, 1986), p. 59. Originally an unpublished dissertation, University of Oklahoma, Norman, OK, 984.

[20] Francesca Tesi, "Michelin et le Taylorisme" [*Michelin and Taylorism*], *Histoire, Économie, et Société* 27(3) (September, 2008) pp. 111–126; *idem*, "The Application of Taylorism in France: The Role of the Michelin Family in the Rationalization of French Work," *Business and Economic History On-line* 7 (New Series), 2009, pp. 1–22.

[21] Patrick Fridenson, "*Un tournant taylorien de la société française (1904–1918)*" [*"A Taylorian Turning Point in French Society"*], *Annales, Histoire, Sciences Sociales* 42(5) (Sept.–Oct., 1987), p. 1042.

[22] Georges de Ram, "Sur Essai D'Application du Système Taylor: Dans un Grand Atelier de Mécanique Français" ["A Test of the Taylor System in a Large French Works"], *Revue de Métallurgie* 6(9) (September 1909), pp. 929–930.

[23] Gary S. Cross, *A Quest for Time: The Reduction of Work in Britain and France, 1840–1940* (Berkeley, CA: University of California Press, 1989), p. 107.

[24] Frederick W. Taylor to Henry le Chatelier, March 20 1913, *Frederick Winslow Taylor Collection* (Correspondence Series), Special Collections, Samuel C. Williams Library, Stevens Institute of Technology, Hoboken, NJ.

[25] Lyndall Urwick and Edward F. L. Brech, *The Making of Scientific Management: Thirteen Pioneers*, vol. 1 (London: Sir Isaac Pitman & Sons, 1951), pp. 105–111.

During World War I, scientific management made greater headway when Georges Clemenceau, the then French Minister of War, ordered that all military plants adopt Taylor's principles.[26] In response, Bertrand Thompson and de Fréminville implemented Taylor's methods in the marine engineering facilities at Châlons-sur-Marne, Guérigny, and Clermont-Ferrand. The French Minister of Marine, Georges Leygues, issued instructions that the same methods be introduced in the Arsenal at Touls.[27] The initial French experience with scientific management, however, was less than positive: managers seized the methods and forgot the "mental revolution." In general, as had happened to Taylor's disgust in the United States, managers perverted what Taylor had described as scientific management.[28] Although the French used the term *Taylorisme* to refer to *l'organisation scientifique du travail*, in reality, the application of Taylor's principles fell far short of ideal.

"Taylorism" was first introduced in England at Joseph Hopkinson & Company, a valve manufacturer, in 1905.[29] According to Urwick and Brech, "the Taylor doctrine" was not well received by the British. Taylor had engendered a measure of bitterness with British manufacturers over patent rights for the processing of high-speed steel, and organized labor also opposed his methods.[30] Whitson, however, found that British engineering journals cited Taylor's work fairly frequently and, often, positively.[31] In counterpoint, a 1911 editorial appeared in the trade journal *The Engineer*: "We do not hesitate to say that Taylorism is inhuman. As it dehumanizes the man, for it endeavours to remove the only distinction that makes him better than a machine – his intelligence."[32]

Manufacturers also held conflicting views: Hans Renold Co., a chain-making firm, introduced scientific management in 1908.[33] Renold met with Taylor in the United States on three occasions, and was impressed with the application of Taylor's methods at the Link-Belt Company. Renold and his son, Charles, were able to implement scientific management successfully, but one authority has suggested that their example "did not appear to make scientific management any more widely accepted [in Britain]."[34] Edward Cadbury, head of the eponymous chocolate firm, was critical of scientific management's methods and treatments of workers, but Rowlinson concluded Cadbury was out of touch with the firm's shop-level practice that used the essential elements of "scientific management."[35]

Germany, Austria, Poland, and Russia

In Imperial Germany, a strong engineering tradition provided favorable conditions for the introduction of Taylorism. Taylor's work was translated into German as early as 1907, and any number of German consultants claimed to apply his principles. Frank B. Gilbreth had consulting

---

[26] Clemenceau's February 26, 1918, order is reprinted at "Taylor Methods in French Industries," *Bulletin of the Taylor Society* 4(3) (June 1919), pp. 29–35.

[27] Devinat, *Scientific Management in Europe*. p. 237.

[28] Humphreys, *Taylorism in France*, p. 105.

[29] Angelo Pichierri, "Diffusion and Crisis of Scientific Management in European Industry," in Salvador Giner and Margaret Scotford Archer, eds., *Contemporary Europe: Social Structures and Cultural Patterns* (London: Routledge & Kegan Paul, 1978), p. 58.

[30] Urwick and Brech, *The Making of Scientific Management*, p. 111. See also Steven Kreis, *The Diffusion of an Idea; A History of Scientific Management in Britain, 1890–1945* (Unpublished dissertation, University of Missouri, Columbia, MO, 1990).

[31] Kevin Whitson, "The Reception of Scientific Management by British Engineers, 1890–1914," *Business History Review* 71(2) (Summer 1997), pp. 207–229. Also see *idem*, Scientific Management and Production management Practice in Britain between the Wars," *Historical Studies in Industrial Relations*, No. 1 (March 1996), pp. 47–75.

[32] "Taylorism," *The Engineer* 111 (May 19, 1911), p. 520. See also "Taylorism Again," *The Engineer* 113 (April 12, 1912), p. 382.

[33] Trevor Boyns, "Hans and Charles Renold: Entrepreneurs in the Introduction of Scientific Management Techniques in Britain," *Management Decision* 39(9) (2001), pp. 719–728.

[34] Edward F .L. Brech, *The Evolution of Modern Management*, vol. 2: *Productivity in Perspective, 1914–1974* (Bristol: Thoemmes Press, 2002), p. 30.

[35] Michael Rowlinson, "The Early Application of Scientific Management by Cadbury," *Business History* 3(4) (October 1988), pp. 384, 391.

assignments in Germany, and Henry L. Gantt accompanied a group of touring ASME members to Germany in 1913. Time study was used at Friedrich Krupp AG in 1910, with a 25 percent reduction in labor costs.[36] In what was called the *rationalization movement*, a few other firms such as Siemens, Borsig, Orsam, and Bosch attempted to apply Taylor's principles. The trade-union response was largely negative, as evidenced by strikes at Bosch in 1912 and 1913. After World War I, Germany took a nationalistic approach to scientific management by creating the Reichskuratorium für Wirtschaftlichkeit (RKW; roughly, The National Board of Efficiency). The state-funded RKW was a clearinghouse for German academic and industry specialists to study and promote industrial efficiency during the interwar years of the Weimar Republic.[37] When Adolf Hitler and the National Socialists came to power, labor unions were disbanded and the RKW was used to control industrial practices. War, depression, and fascism shaped the course of scientific management in Germany.

In Austria, Taylorism was first publically discussed in 1914 at the Österreichischer Ingenieurund Architektenverein (Organization of Austrian Engineers and Architects). Discussions of Taylorism in both Germany and Austria were soon interrupted when the guns of August 1914 sounded the beginning of World War I.[38] Following the war, however, these discussions resumed as *Taylor–Zeitschrift*, a journal devoted to Taylorism was published in Austria from 1920 to 1929.[39]

In 1896, the Russian-educated Polish engineer, Karol Adamiecki, developed a form of graphical analysis known as a "harmonogram" to solve production bottlenecks. Harmonograms enabled simultaneously charting several complicated operations, and, thus, promoting their systematic arrangement. Adamiecki's harmonograms had elements of Henry L. Gantt's charts but, were also similar to a Program Evaluation and Review Technique (PERT) workflow network.[40] Harmonograms were used in some Polish and Russian rolling mills, but their widespread adoption was hindered by the sociopolitical ideology of Russia's anticapitalistic Communist regime. Adamiecki's work was not translated into English during his lifetime, but he became a leading figure in the European scientific-management movement by establishing the Polish Institute of Scientific Management at Warsaw in 1923, presenting a paper at the first international management conference in Prague, and being actively involved in the International Labor Organization (ILO) and the Comité Internationale de l'Organisation Scientifique (CIOS).

Following the 1917 Bolshevik revolution, which overthrew the Provisional Government that had toppled Russia's last czar, Nicholas II, Communist Party founder Vladimir I. Lenin advocated

[36] Bruce Kogut and David Parkinson, "The Diffusion of American Organizing Principles to Europe," in Bruce Kogut, ed., *Country Competitiveness: Technology and the Organizing of Work* (New York: Oxford University Press, 1993), pp. 184–187.

[37] J. Ronald Shearer, "*The Reichskuratorium für Wirtschaftlichkeit*: Fordism and Organized Capitalism in Germany, 1918–1945," *Business History Review* 71(4) (Winter 1971), pp. 569–602.

[38] Mary Nolan, *Visions of Modernity: American Business and the Modernization of Germany* (New York: Oxford University Press, 1994), pp. 41–44.

[39] André Pfoertner, "The Americanization of Austrian Business" in Günter Bischof and Anton Pelinka, eds., *The Americanization/Westernization of Austria* (New Brunswick, NJ: Transaction Publishers, 2004), p. 63.

[40] John Mee, "History of Management," *Advanced Management-Office Executive* 1(10) (October 1962), pp. 28–29. See also Theodore Limperg and Lyndall F. Urwick, "Charles Adamiecki (1866–1933)," *Bulletin of the International Management Institute* 3(1) (January, 1929), pp. 102–103; Arthur G. Bedeian, "The Writings of Karol Adamiecki: A Reflection," upublished paper presented at the annual meeting of the Academy of Management, Minneapolis, MN, August 20, 1974; Edward R. Marsh, "The Harmonogram of Karol Adamiecki," *Academy of Management Journal* 18(2) (June 1975), pp. 358–364; Zdzislaw P. Weslolowski, "The Polish Contribution to the Development of Scientific management," in Jeffrey C. Susbauber, ed., *Proceedings of the Annual Meeting of the Academy of Management* (1978), pp. 12–16, and Bart J. Debicki, "Forgotten Contributions to Scientific Management: Work and Ideas of Karol Adamiecki," *Journal of Management History* 21(1), 2015, pp. 40–67.

the use of scientific-management principles to systematize Russian industry. In Lenin's view, scientific management was the most progressive means to achieve economic advancement.[41]

Lenin's goal was to show how society would benefit if workers controlled the means of production. In 1920, Alexsei K. Gastev, a leading proponent of scientific management, became the founder and director of the Institute of Labor in Moscow. The Institute of Labor merged with the Institute for the Experimental Study of Live Labor to form the Central Institute of Labor in 1921. Gastev came into conflict with Platon M. Kerzhentsev, leader of the Council on Scientific Management, who charged that Gastev wanted to deprive "the mass of workers, in a purely Taylorist fashion, of initiative and organized participation in rationalization."[42] Although numerous conferences were held, institutes established, and attempts made to implement "the Taylor System," only few improvements were made because of the Communist Party's distrust of capitalism.[43] Ideology prevailed. In 1938, Gastev was charged with "counter-revolutionary terrorist activity" and executed the next year. Productivity remained low and the idea of "super-workmen" arose. Alexei Grigorevich Stakhanov, in particular, became nationally known for his extraordinary performance in mining coal. Working at the Tsentralnaya-Irmino mine located at the Donbass province in Ukraine (then a constituent republic within the Union of Soviet Socialist Republics), Stakhanov and his crew's purported output (102 tons in 5 hours and 45 minutes) was, indeed, extraordinary—more than 14 times his daily 7 ton quota—and he was hailed as an example for others.[44] True or not, this achievement was so remarkable that Stakhanov's photo appeared in the United States on the December 16, 1935, cover of *Time* magazine.[45] Higher productivity was expected to come from the selflessness of hard work and devotion to the Soviet Union rather than job analysis and improved work methods. By one account, however, "Stakhanovites" were "ostracized by their fellow workers for raising output quotes."[46]

After Lenin's death in 1924, his successor, Joseph Stalin sought to undertake a program of national economic planning. To assist in this effort, Stalin hired one of Henry L. Gantt's disciples, Walter N. Polakov, as a consultant. Born at Luga, Russia, in 1879, Polakov earned a degree in Mechanical Engineering at Dresden's Royal Institute of Technology in 1902 and did advanced graduate work in psychology and industrial hygiene at the University of Moscow. After working for the Tula Locomotive Works and as Chief Engineer and Naval Instructor in the Russian Department of Navigation and Harbors, he immigrated with his wife to the United States in 1906. He was well known as an expert in power-plant management. Polakov prepared an appendix titled

---

[41] Vladimir I. Lenin, "The Urgent Problems of the Soviet Union," *Pravda* (April 28, 1918), pp. 3–5. (Abstracted in "What Lenine Said About the 'Taylor Society'," *Bulletin of the Taylor Society*, 4(3) (June 1919), pp. 35–38). Lenin's 1918 sentiments regarding scientific management stand in stark contrast to his earlier views. See, for example, his "Taylor's System: The Enslavement of Man to the Machine," *Put' Pravdy* No. 35 (March 13, 1914), p. 1, trans. Bernard Isaacs and Joe Fineberg in Lenin, *Collected Works: December 1913–August 1914*, vol. 20 (Moscow: Progress Publishers, 1972), pp. 152–154. Also see Judith A. Merkle, *Management and Ideology: The Legacy of the International Management Movement* (Berkeley, CA: University of California Press), pp. 103–135; Andrey A. Semenov, "The Origin of Scientific Management Systems in Russia," Report No. 6, Graduate School of Management, St. Petersburg State University, 2010, and Mikhail Grachev and Boris Rakitsky, "Historic Horizons of Frederick Taylor's Scientific Management," *Journal of Management History* 19(4) 2013, pp. 512–527.

[42] Platon M. Kerzhentsev quoted in Kendall E. Bailes, "Alexei Gastev and the Soviet Controversy Over Taylorism, 1918–1924," *Soviet Studies* 29(3) (July 1977), p. 390. See also Mark R. Beissinger, *Scientific Management, Socialist Discipline, and Soviet Power* (Cambridge, MA: Harvard University Press, 1988), p. 54.

[43] Daniel A. Wren and Arthur G. Bedeian, "The Taylorization of Lenin: Rhetoric or Reality?" *International Journal of Social Economics* 31(3) (2004), pp. 287–299. See also Zenovia A. Sochor, "Soviet Taylorism Revisited," *Soviet Studies* 38(2) (April 1981), pp. 246–264; Mikhail Grachev and Boris Rakitsky, "Historic Horizons of Frederick Taylor's Scientific Management," *Journal of Management History* 19(4) (2013), pp. 512–527.

[44] Arthur G. Bedeian and Carl R. Phillips, "Scientific Management and Stakhanovism in the Soviet Union: A Historical Perspective," *International Journal of Social Economics* 17(10) (1990), pp. 28–35.

[45] The accompanying story is titled "Heroes of Labor," *Time* 26(25) (December 16, 1935), pp. 25, 28.

[46] Victor Kravchenko, *I Choose Freedom: The Personal and Political Life of a Soviet Official* (New York: Charles Scribner's Sons, 1946), pp. 187–205, 298–302.

Walter N. Polakov. "Walter N. Polakov, Student of Industrial Relations," *Popular Science Monthly* 98(1) (January 1921), p. 22.

"The Measurement of Human Work" for Wallace Clark's book *The Gantt Chart: A Working Tool of Management*.[47] He subsequently worked as an independent consultant in the Soviet Union from December 1929 to May 1931 using Gantt charts to plan and control industrial output, so that the goals of the Soviet Union's Five-Year Plans, first announced in 1928, could be achieved. Polakov's efforts in introducing Gantt charts to the Soviet Union were "warmly recommended" for all factories by the Soviet Supreme Council of the National Economy.[48] According to Polakov, the Soviet Five-Year Plans were "impressive achievements" despite assorted shortfalls, and Gantt charts were part of this success.[49]

Scientific Management in Other European Nations

Taylorism was also imported into other European nations, where its success varied from one setting to another.[50] The leaders of the scientific-management movement in Czechoslovakia were Tomáš G. Masaryk and Edvard Beneš, both of whom would serve as their country's president.[51] In Italy, economic conditions mediated against the wide introduction of scientific management in all but the largest firms such as Olivetti, the typewriter manufacturer, and automotive companies Fiat and Magneti Marelli.[52] The founder of the Italian Communist Party, Antonio Gramsci, was critical of scientific management for destroying worker autonomy.[53] The Ente Nazionale Italiano per l'Organizzazione Scientifica del Lavoro (Italian National Organization of Scientific Work), founded in 1926, actively published information on scientific management.

Taylorism was introduced into Sweden in 1912 by Gustav Axel Jæderholm. Taylor's *The Principles of Scientific Management* was translated into Swedish in 1913, with a foreword by Erik August Forsberg, who taught at the Royal Institute of Technology in Stockholm. Forsberg had previously introduced Taylor's methods as Technical Director at AB Separator, a company now known as Alfa Laval.[54] *The Principles of Scientific Management* was available in Finnish in 1914 and, according to Jacob de Julin, quickly became "the gospel of practically every progressive plant in Finland."[55] The 3-month Bolshevik uprising in 1918, with its accompanying looting and destruction of industrial plants, however, slowed the country's introduction of Taylor's principles.

---

[47] Walter N. Polakov, "The Measurement of Human Work," in Wallace Clark, *The Gantt Chart: A Working Tool of Management* (New York: Ronald Press, 1922), pp. 150–157.

[48] Daniel A. Wren, "Scientific Management in the U.S.S.R., with Particular Reference to the Contribution of Walter N. Polakov," *Academy of Management Review* 5 (January 1980), pp. 1–11; Diana J. Kelly, "Marxist Manager amidst the Progressives: Walter N. Polakov and the Taylor Society," *Journal of Industrial History* 6 (2) (November 2004), pp. 61–75; *idem*, (2016) The Scientific Manager and the FBI: The Surveillance of Walter Polakov in the 1940s, *American Communist History* 14(1) (2016), pp. 1–23; and *idem*, "Perceptions of Taylorism and a Marxist Scientific Manager, *Journal of Management History* 22(3) (2016), pp. 341–362.

[49] Walter N. Polakov, "The Gantt Chart in Russia," *American Machinist* 75 (August 13, 1931), pp. 261–264.

[50] Frank B. Gilbreth and Lillian M. Gilbreth, "Scientific Management in Other Countries than the United States," *Bulletin of the Taylor Society* 9(3) (June 1924), pp. 132–142.

[51] John Mihalasky, "Scientific Management in Central Eastern Europe – Czechoslovakia, Hungary, and Poland," in J.-C. Spender and Hugo J. Kijne, eds., *Scientific Management: Frederick Winslow Taylor's Gift to the World?* (Boston, MA: Kluwer, 1996), pp. 133–162.

[52] Perry R. Willson, *The Clockwork Factory: Women and Work in Fascist Italy* (Oxford, England: Clarendon Press, 1993), p. 41.

[53] Antoinette S. Phillips and Arthur G. Bedeian, "Understanding Antonio Gramsci's Ambiguous Legacy," *International Journal of Social Economics* 17(10) (1990), pp. 36–41.

[54] Esbjorn Segelod and Leif Carlsson, "The Emergence of Uniform Principles of Cost Accounting in Sweden 1900–1936," *Accounting, Business & Financial History* 20(3) (November, 2010), pp. 327–363. See also Nils Runeby, "Americanism, Taylorism and Social Integration," *Scandinavian Journal of History* 3(1–4) (1978), pp. 21–46.

[55] Jacob de Julin, "American Industrial Methods in Finland," *Industrial Management* 58(1) (July, 1919), p. 51.

Norwegian industrialist Joakim Lehmkuhl introduced scientific management to his home country in 1920 with the publication of his book *Rationel arbeidsledelse* (*Rational Labor Management*). Scientific management, however, did not gain a foothold in Norway until the 1950s.[56] Scientific management came to Denmark in 1905, with its introduction at NKT's cable factory in Middelfart.[57] It did not spread widely, however, as the economy was primarily comprised of small- and medium-sized firms in which employer–employee relations were marked by co-operation and negotiation.[58] The same seems to be the case with the Netherlands. Although H. J. Hendrikse translated *Shop Management* in 1909 and *The Principles of Scientific Management* in 1913, and Theo van der Waerden's *Het Taylorstelsel met eene inleiding over stukloon en moderne loonsystemen* [*The Taylor System with an Introduction to Modern and Piecework Wage Systems*] was published in 1916, Taylorism did not reach its "heyday" until after World War II.[59] Meanwhile, a Spanish translation of Taylor's *Shop Management* appeared in 1914.[60] Although initially received with enthusiasm, scientific management was seen by Spanish intellectuals as coercive and as destroying employee initiative. Others simply questioned if Taylorism could fulfill its claims.[61]

Formalizing Scientific Management in Europe

European interest widened scientific management's frontiers along separate, yet related, paths. In 1924, the First International Congress on Scientific Management was held in Prague; among those attending from the United States were Harlow Person, representing the Taylor Society, and Lillian M. Gilbreth, representing her husband Frank (see Chapter 8). The International Committee of Scientific Management (Le Comité International de l'Organisation Scientifique, known as CIOS) was formed in 1925 to continue exchanging ideas about management. Subsequent CIOS meetings were held in Brussels (1925), Rome (1927), Paris (1929), Amsterdam (1932), London (1935), and Washington, DC (1938). The 1941 meeting, to be held in Berlin, was cancelled due to World War II. CIOS would not resume its work until after the war.[62]

Beginning in the 1920s, the Twentieth Century Fund, endowed by the Boston department-store owner Edward A. Filene and the Rockefeller Foundation, sought to promote improved management, particularly scientific management, in European industry, which was rebuilding following World War I. The International Management Institute (IMI), a spin-off from the Geneva-based ILO, was formed in 1927 to gather research about better management practices. Frenchman Paul Devinat, former chief of the IMI Employers' Organisation Service, was appointed the IMI's first director.[63] Englishman Lt. Colonel Lyndall F. Urwick, whom we will discuss shortly, succeeded Devant in 1928. The IMI experienced difficulties contending with national employer groups, the threat of war, the rise of fascism in Europe, and a subsequent worldwide economic depression that undercut its funding. The IMI ceased its activities in January 1934, when the Twentieth Century fund withdrew its financial support.[64]

[56] Francis Sejersted and Madeleine B. Adams, *The Age of Social Democracy: Norway and Sweden in the Twentieth Century* (Princeton, NJ: Princeton University Press), p. 45.

[57] Jørgen Burchardt, "Introduktion af nye ledelsesformer – da Scientific Management kom til Danmark 1905–1920," *Tidsskrift for Arbejdsliv* 3(2) (2001), pp. 69–90. See also *idem*, "Introduction of New Management Concepts: When Scientific Management Came to Europe," Unpublished paper presented at the 2009 Business History Conference, Milan, Italy, June 13, 2009.

[58] Frans Bévort, John Storm Pedersen, and Jon Sundo, "Denmark," in Ingrid Brunstein, ed., *Human Resource Management in Western Europe* (Berlin: Walter de Gruyter, 1995), p. 31.

[59] Wiemer Salverda, Maarten van Klaveren, and Marc van der Meer, "The Debate in the Netherlands on Low Pay," in *idem*, eds., *Low-Wage Work in the Netherlands, 1900–1930* (New York: Russell Sage Foundation), p. 26. See also Erik S. A. Bloemen, *Scientific Management in Nederland 1900–1930* (Amsterdam: Nederlandsch Economisch-Historisch Archief, 1988).

[60] Frederick W. Taylor, *La Dirección de los Talleres: Estudio Sobre la Organizatción del Trabajo* [*The Direction of Workshops: Study of the Orgniazation of Work*]. trans. Eduardo Lozano (Barcelona: Libreria de Feliu y Susana, 1914).

[61] Mauro F. Guillén, *Models of Management* (Chicago, IL: University of Chicago Press, 1994), pp. 158–159.

[62] Erik Bloeman, "The Movement for Scientific Management in Europe between the Wars," in J.-C. Spender and Hugo J. Kijne, eds., *Scientific Management: Frederick Winslow Taylor's Gift to the World?* (Boston, MA: Kluwer, 1996), pp. 111–131.

[63] Charles D. Wrege, Ronald G. Greenwood, and Sakae Hata, "The International Management Institute and Political Opposition to its Efforts in Europe, 1925–1934," *Business and Economic History*, 2nd series 16 (1987), pp. 249–265.

[64] Trevor Boyns, "Lyndall Urwick at the International Management Institute, Geneva, 1928–1934: Right Job, Wrong Man?" Paper presented at the European Business History Association, 11th Annual Conference, Geneva, 13–15 September 2007.

Formalizing scientific management as an academic subject seems to have been hindered by the belief that management could be learned best by experience. In Germany, Taylor had followers among certain industrialists and in technical societies, but he had little impact on institutions of higher education. Kieser noted the study of business economics (*Betriebswirtschaftslehre*), law, foreign languages, bookkeeping, and business letter writing were taught, but these efforts offered "nothing like a theory of management."[65] In France, scientific management took hold in its oldest technical university the Conservatoire des Arts et Métiers (CNAM), founded in 1794. CNAM's Director, Jules Amar applied Taylor's principles to the physiology of work and organized courses on scientific management for Bertrand Thompson.[66] CNAM's faculty discussed formal courses on "*Taylorisme*," but did not reach a consensus until 1929 when a chair for *l'organisation scientifique du travail* was given to Louis Danty-Lafrance. Danty-Lafrance became a leading authority on scientific management and CNAM "became the main body in French higher education for the spread of Taylor's thinking and practice, to be joined by the Institut d'Études Supérieures des Techniques de l'Organisation (IESTO) in 1955."[67]

Japan, China, and Australia

The Meiji Restoration, in 1868, marked the transition of Japan from a feudal society to a capitalist economy. Industrialization came slowly, however; in 1870, more than 80 percent of the Japanese population was employed in agriculture and less than 5 percent in manufacturing. Industry, dominated by family firms with a small number of employees, was generally technologically backward and lacked modern-management methods.[68]

Japan's first introduction to Taylorism appears to have occurred in late 1911 with the publication of a series of articles by journalist Ikeda Tōshirō in the newspaper *Sakigake shinbun*.[69] Ikeda had become interested in Taylorism while in the United States at the time of the 1910–1911 Eastern Rate Case. Given the popularity of his articles, Ikeda elaborated on Taylor's ideas in a privately printed booklet, *Mueki no tesuu habuku hiketsu* (*The Secrets of Eliminating Useless Labor*) in 1913, which is said to have sold some 1.5 million copies. In a similar coincidence, Hoshino Yukinori, director of Japan's Kajima Bank, was in the United States when Taylor's book *The Principles of Scientific Management* was published in 1911. Hoshino obtained permission to translate the book, which was distributed throughout Japan in 1913 as *Gakujutsu Genron Kanri-ho* (*The Principles of Scientific Supervisory Methods*).[70] Landing in fertile soil, the scientific-management movement grew rapidly. Earlier, in 1912, Yōichi Ueno, a leading Japanese teacher, author, and consultant had published a paper "On Efficiency," which described the work of Taylor, Frank B. Gilbreth, and Bertrand Thompson. Ueno translated many of Taylor's articles, attended international conferences and, in 1922, was the founding president of the Sangyo Noritsu Kenkyusho (Institute of Industrial Efficiency). He helped form a Japanese branch of the Taylor Society in 1925 and the Nihon Noritsu Rengokai (Japanese Federation of Management Associations) in 1927. In 1931, the Nihon Noritsu Rengokai and the Nihon Kogyo Kyokai

[65] Alfred Kieser, "The Americanization of Academic Management Education in Germany," *Journal of Management Inquiry* 13(2) (June 2004), p. 92.

[66] Jules Amar, *The Human Motor, or, The Scientific Foundations of Labour and Industry*, trans. Elise P. Butterworth and George E. Wright (London: G. Routledge, 1920). Originally published in 1914.

[67] Jean-Louis Peaucelle and Cameron Guthrie, "The Private Life of Henri Fayol and His Motivation to Build a Management Science," *Journal of Management History* 18(4) (2012), p. 481.

[68] Koji Taira, "Factory Legislation and Management Modernization during Japan's Industrialization, 1886–1916," *Business History Review* 44(1) (Spring 1970), pp. 84–109.

[69] William M. Tsutsui, *Manufacturing Ideology: Scientific Management in Twentieth-Century Japan* (Princeton, NJ: Princeton University Press, 1998), pp. 18–19.

[70] Toshikazu Nakase, "The Introduction of Scientific Management in Japan and Its Characteristics – Case Studies of Companies in the Sumitomo Zaibatsu," in Keiichiro Nakagawa, ed., *Labor and Management* (Toronto: University of Toronto Press, 1979), pp. 171–202.

(Japanese Industrial Association) combined to form the Nihon Noritsu Kyokai (Japanese Management Association). Ueno is known as the "Father of Japanese Administrative Science."[71]

In Japanese industry, the most advanced scientific-management application occurred at the Hyōgo Factory of the Kanegafuchi (Kanebō) Cotton Textile Company. Kanebō manager Sanji Mutō had studied in the United States and saw no inherent conflict between a firm paying high wages and earning high profits.[72] Like Taylor and Gantt, Mutō not only began paying more to attract better employees, but also began to train employees and improve factory supervision and organization. Mutō eventually became president of Kanebō, one of Japan's leading textile firms. He and other scientific-management advocates understood that productivity is the link between high wages and high profits, and that productivity is achieved through technology, capital, and improved work methods. What many popular writers call "Japanese-style management" is not a recent phenomenon, but a direct result of scientific management's introduction into Japan during the late Meiji period.[73] Under the influence of scholars such as Ueno and practitioners such as Mutō, scientific management provided the basis for modernizing Japanese industry.

Following the successful October 1911 revolution that overturned the Qing Dynasty, interest in scientific management increased among Chinese engineers, industrialists, government officials, and academics. Scientific management was introduced to China by Mu Xiangyu.[74] Also known as Mu Ouchu or H(siang) Y(ueh) Moh, Mu, who earned a BS degree in agriculture from the University of Illinois in 1913, and a MS degree in cotton planting and manufacturing from Texas A&M University in 1914, became aware of Taylor's work through his classes. While at Texas A&M, he wrote Taylor for permission to translate *The Principles of Scientific Management* into Chinese.[75] Mu returned to China in 1914 and a year later organized the Teh Dah Cotton Spinning Company in Shanghai. His Chinese translation, with Dong Dongsu, appeared in 1916. Dong's name, however, does not appear on the book's title page as translator. He is, however, acknowledged in the book's preface. The Mu-Dong translation was first serialized in the Shanghai journal *Zhonghua Shi Ye Jie*. Mu went on to open two additional cotton mills and in 1920 established the Chinese Cotton Goods Exchange. In 1921, he founded the Chinese Industrial Bank of Shanghai. Mu subsequently served in various government roles, including Vice Minister of the Ministry of Industry, Commerce and Labour.[76] By the 1920s, various Chinese firms were experimenting with Taylor's methods. It was not until 1930, however, that the

Mu Xiangyu. Isaac F. Marcosson, "The Changing East: The Industrialization of China," *The Saturday Evening Post* 195(19) (November 4, 1922), p. 18.

---

[71] Ronald G. Greenwood and Robert H. Ross, "Early American Influence on Japanese Management Philosophy: The Scientific Management Movement in Japan," in Sang M. Lee and Gary Schwendiman, eds., *Management by Japanese Systems* (New York: Praeger, 1982), pp. 43–54. See also William M. Tsutsui, "The Way of Efficiency: Ueno Yōichi and Scientific Management in Twentieth-Century Japan," *Modern Asian Studies* 35(2) (April 2001), pp. 441–467 and Tamotsu Nishizawa, "Business Studies and Management Education in Japan's Economic Development," in Rolv Petter Amdam, ed., *Management, Education and Competitiveness: Europe, Japan and the United States* (Oxon, England: Routledge, 1996), pp. 96–110.

[72] Taira, "Factory Legislation," pp. 103–105. See also M. T. Vaziri, Joe Won Lee, and Joseph L. Krieger, "Onda Moku: The True Pioneer of Management through Respect for Humanity," *Leadership and Organization Development Journal* 9(1) (1988), pp. 3–7.

[73] Balázs Vaszkun and William M. Tsutsui, "A Modern History of Japanese Management Thought," *Journal of Management History* 18(4) (2012), pp. 368–385.

[74] In Chinese, names are sequenced last name, first name. Mu is, thus, Xiangyu's surname.

[75] Hsiang Y. Moh to Frederick W. Taylor, April 23, 1914; Taylor to Moh, May 4, 1914; Moh to Taylor. May 15, 1914. Frederick Winslow Taylor Collection, Samuel C. Williams Library, Stevens Institute of Technology, Hoboken, NJ.

[76] Mu's career is profiled in Isaac F. Marcosson, "The Changing East: The Industrialization of China," *Saturday Evening Post* 195 (November 4, 1922), pp. 18–19, 116–118, 121–122.

Chinese Management Association (Zhongguo gongshang guanli xiehui) was formed.[77] In recognition of his pioneering role in introducing scientific management to his home country, Mu is known as "the Father of Modern Chinese Management."[78]

The first applications of Taylor's principles in Australia occurred in the early 1920s, with Pearson Law and Company (later Pelaco), a clothing manufacturer, and the New South Wales Railways as examples.[79] Later in the decade, scientific management was introduced in Australia by the subsidiaries of multinational corporations such as General Motors Corporation, Goodyear Tire & Rubber Co., and Standard Telephones & Cables. Taska has documented how scientific management spread to Australian educational practices, "resulting in the dissemination of a [single] managerial culture which is still relevant today."[80] Based on a wider analysis of scientific management's adoption, Taska has concluded that "the diffusion of scientific management in different national contexts depended on two interrelated preconditions: a relatively fluid class structure, which gave professionals opportunities for social mobility and an integrated educational system, which provided the credentials to support such mobility" and that "these were precisely the conditions that existed in Australia during the early decades of the twentieth century, where leading Australian professionals, public administrators and educators were increasingly drawn to American ideas on industrial reform."[81]

And Beyond

Records in the Taylor Collection at the Stevens Institute of Technology detailing the early dissemination and translation of Taylor's *Shop Management* and *The Principles of Scientific Management* are at best incomplete. Both volumes appeared in various formats and venues throughout the world. Translated by Ramón Alvarez Martinez in 1911 with the title *Principios del Manejo Cientifico*, *The Principles of Scientific Management* was published in Mexico in a private edition by Adolfo Prieto for use by the Compañía Fundidora de Fierro ye Acero de Monterrey. Henri Simsons, the Latvian government's representative in London, contacted Taylor in 1912 for permission to translate *The Principles of Scientific Management* into Lettish.[82] Similarly, William L. Church, a President - Ambursen Hydraulic Construction Company (Boston, MA), wrote Taylor in 1911 on behalf of the New England Esperanto Association to inquire about the possibility of translating *The Principles of Scientific Management* into Esperanto, "the universal language."[83] Whether the Church translation ever appeared in print is unknown.

In reviewing the spread of scientific management in both the United States and throughout the world, a key point should be kept in mind. As Dunford explains, "It is important not to confuse the existence of scientific management as a form of rhetoric with its existence as a concrete practice."[84] He further notes that evidence for the extent to which scientific management was truly applied in Australia as claimed is sparse. Take the New South Wales railway workers as a case in point. The workers struck to protest the introduction of a "card system" that was considered application of scientific involved recording on a card how long it took each worker to perform individual jobs. Needless to say, neither Taylor nor any of his followers would have considered this to be an example

---

[77] Stephen L. Morgan, "Transfer of Taylorist Ideas to China, 1910–1930s," *Journal of Management History* 12(4) (2006), pp. 408–424.

[78] Chunhong Yan, *Zhongguo jin dai shi ye jia* (Beijing: Beijing ke xue ji shu chu ban she, 1995).

[79] Chris Wright. "Taylorism Reconsidered: The Impact of Scientific Management within the Australian Workplace," *Labour History*, No. 64 (May 1993), p. 39.

[80] Lucy Taksa, "The Cultural Diffusion of Scientific Management: The United States and New South Wales," *Journal of Industrial Relations* 37(3) (September, 1995), pp. 427–461.

[81] *Idem*, "Uniting Management and Education in Pursuit of Efficiency: F.W. Taylor's Training Reform Legacy," *Economic and Labour Relations Review* 17(2) (April 2007), p. 133.

[82] Frederick W. Taylor, *Frederika Vinslova Teilora Zinātniskās Rīcības Principi* [*Frederick Winslow Taylor's Principles of Scientific Management*], trans. Henri Simsons (Rigâ: Apgahdajis A. Gulbis, 1912).

[83] William L Church to Frederick W. Taylor, June 19, 1911; Taylor to Church, June 22, 1911; Church to Taylor, June 26, 1911, *Frederick Winslow Taylor Collection* (Box 63, Folder 3), Special Collections, Samuel C. Williams Library, Stevens Institute of Technology, Hoboken, NJ.

[84] Richard Dunford, "Scientific Management in Australia: A Discussion Paper," *Labour & Industry* 1(3) (October 1988), p. 506.

of Taylor's methods. From years of consulting in Europe, Bertrand Thompson would have agreed with Dunford's assessment in noting that there was "a large group of shameless fakers, mostly unemployed bookkeepers, who solicited clients from house to house and got quite a number of them at bargain rates."[85] Thompson stated that he had even "seen the installation of an adding machine, or even of a telephone, referred to as 'Taylorization.'"[86] In instances such as the New South Wales railway strike, it seems that worker "hostility to Taylorism was based more on the fear of what could be done with [Taylor's] techniques than what had actually been done."[87]

Scientific Management in Industrial Practice

The international practice of scientific management is evident in the work of Bertrand Thompson's and Wallace Clark's consulting firms throughout Europe. Thompson's "Taylor-Thompson System" adapted Taylor's ideas to fit the situations he faced, particularly in working with labor unions. For example, he joined with union representatives in a successful installation in General Electric's plant at Nancy, France, but declined to work at its German plant because its labor contract prohibited employee bonus payments. Thompson's firm was a model for others, and he left behind a cadre of trained consultants, including Suzanne Garcin-Guynet, the first female management consultant in France.[88]

Wallace Clark worked for Henry L. Gantt's consulting firm and, after Gantt's death, became the foremost promoter of his ideas. Clark demonstrated the versatility of Gantt charts in sales, personnel, production, finance and budgeting. His work was successful in all but a few instances, such as in the Soviet Union where he refused to follow Polakov's work believing that "political conditions" would prevail over thorough study and implementation.[89] Trained by Taylor and Gantt, Thompson and Clark provided a better understanding of the practice of scientific management in an international setting.

In the United States, companies such as the Plimpton Press, Link-Belt, Joseph & Feiss, and Tabor Manufacturing were considered model scientific-management installations. Henry P. Kendall, manager of the Plimpton Press (Norwood, Massachusetts), was an early promoter of scientific management in the printing industry. He thought that industrial plants could become efficient by being viewed as systems comprised of interacting parts, but (like Person) a greater long-run effect could be achieved only if the scientific-management philosophy was fully accepted by all parties.[90] Plimpton Press also developed an advanced employment department, which centralized hiring, disciplining, and discharging. Plimpton Press's employment manager, Jane C. Williams, credited scientific management with reducing labor turnover from 186 percent in 1912 to 13 percent in 1916.[91] James Mapes Dodge (1852–1915) pioneered the link-belt conveyor, which became the basis for later belt assembly-line operations, and the Link-Belt Company (Philadelphia, Pennsylvania) was a showcase installation for Taylor's methods.[92]

Wilfred Lewis, president of the Tabor Manufacturing Company (Philadelphia, Pennsylvania), a machine-tool producer, was an authority on gearing and an advocate of metric reform. At Tabor,

[85] C. Thompson, "The Taylor System in Europe," *Advanced Management: Quarterly Journal* 5(4) (October–December 1940), p. 173.

[86] *Ibid.*, p. 172.

[87] *Dunford, "Scientific Management in Australia: A Discussion Paper,"* p. 507.

[88] Daniel A. Wren, Regina A. Greenwood, Julia Teahen, and Arthur G. Bedeian, "C. Bertrand Thompson and Management Consulting in Europe, 1917–1934," *Journal of Management History* 21(1) (2015), pp. 15–39.

[89] Daniel A. Wren, "Implementing the Gantt Chart in Europe and Britain: The Contributions of Wallace Clark," *Journal of Management History* 21(3) (2015), pp. 309–327.

[90] Henry P. Kendall, "Unsystematized, Systematized, and Scientific Management," in Thompson, ed., *Scientific Management,* pp. 103–131.

[91] Jane C. Williams, "The Reduction of Labor Turnover in the Plimpton Press," *Annals of the American Academy of Political and Social Science* 71 (May 1917), pp. 71–81.

[92] See George P. Torrence, *James Mapes Dodge* (New York: Newcomen Society of North America, 1950); James M. Dodge, "A History of the Introduction of a System of Shop Management" in Thompson, ed., *Scientific Management,* pp. 226–231.

Taylor's principles were credited with increasing output 250 percent.[93] King Hathaway, general manager of Tabor Manufacturing, advocated careful planning before installing Taylor's methods, including an extensive program of educating workers and supervisors as to the principles and purposes of scientific management. At Joseph & Feiss Company (Cleveland, Ohio), Richard A. Feiss recognized the merits of scientific management in the labor-intensive clothing industry. Feiss implemented time-and-motion study, provided bonuses for performance and attendance, installed a planning department to smooth work flows, and employed an orthopedic surgeon to design chairs and tables for worker comfort, reduced fatigue, and efficiency. Mary B. Gilson, who headed the Joseph & Feiss Employment and Service Department, championed employment testing, proper selection and placement, promoting women to supervisory positions, and other advanced practices that made her the era's best known and most influential personnel manager.[94] At Joseph & Feiss, Taylor's methods were combined with the best ideas emerging in the nascent personnel-management movement.

Bertrand Thompson noted that an increase in the "stability of payroll" was one of the many benefits of scientific management in practice.[95] He was referring to employment stabilization through improved production planning, employee selection and placement, and job training. Scientific management sought to reduce costs, and labor turnover was a major expense. General Electric's Magnus Alexander conducted the first reported statistical analysis of labor turnover was a major expense.[96] He found that, in 1912, for 12 GE factories, 22,031 employees were new unnecessary hires, amounting to a turnover rate greater than 55 percent. The attrition was estimated to cost $831,030, which included the expense of hiring and training, as well as reduced production while new hires were learning their jobs. Joseph Willits, an instructor at the renamed Wharton School of Finance and Commerce, replicated Alexander's study in a group of Philadelphia textile mills. He found turnover rates ranging from 50 to 100 percent, and, occasionally, rates that even reached 500 percent.[97] Willits recommended improvements in employee selection and placement, employee training, and wage incentives to bolster employee retention. In brief, Taylor's search for "first-class workers" and Münsterberg's search for the "best possible worker for the best possible effect" both contributed to lower labor turnover and stabilized employment. Labor turnover carried a high cost, both for employees and employers, and scientific management sought to eliminate such wastefulness.

The Hoxie Report

Organized labor's opposition to scientific management found further voice in an investigation conducted under the auspices of the U.S. Commission on Industrial Relations.[98] The investigation's purpose was to examine the competing claims of organized labor and scientific-management advocates regarding working conditions under the Taylor system. The investigation was conducted under the direction of Robert F. Hoxie, an associate professor of political economy at the University of Chicago. He was assisted by former U.S. Commissioner of Indian Affairs and

---

[93] Wilfred Lewis, "An Object Lesson in Efficiency," in Thompson, ed., *Scientific Management*, pp. 232–241. See also H. K. Hathaway, "Wilfred Lewis," *Bulletin of the Taylor Society* 15(1) (February 1930), pp. 45–46.

[94] David J. Goldberg, "Richard A. Feiss, Mary Barnett Gilson, and Scientific Management at Joseph & Feiss, 1909–1925," in Daniel Nelson, ed., *A Mental Revolution: Scientific Management since Taylor* (Columbus, OH: Ohio State University Press, 1992), pp. 40–57.

[95] C. Bertrand Thompson, *The Taylor System of Scientific Management* (New York: A. W. Shaw, 1917), p. 27.

[96] Magnus W. Alexander, "Hiring and Firing: Its Economic Waste and How to Avoid It," *Annals of the American Academy of Political and Social Science* 65 (May 1916), pp. 128–144. See also Kyle Bruce, "Magnus Alexander, The Economists and Labour Turnover," *Business History* 47(4) (October 2005), pp. 493–510.

[97] Joseph H. Willits, "The Labor Turn-Over and the Humanizing of Industry," *Annals of the American Academy of Political and Social Science* 61 (September 1915), pp. 127–137.

[98] This section draws on Chris Nyland, "Taylorism, John R. Commons and the Hoxie Report," *Journal of Economic Issues* 30(4) (December 1996), pp. 985–1016.

"industrial counselor" Robert G. Valentine, the then chairman of the Massachusetts Minimum Wage Commission (see Chapter 9), representing "employing management in general" and John P. Frey, editor of the *International Molders' Journal*, representing organized labor. Over the period January to April 1915, some or all of the investigators inspected 30 industrial plants that had adopted, in whole or part, scientific management.[99]

An early inkling of the controversy that was to follow occurred when Hoxie insisted on making no distinction between the theory and the practice of scientific management. To Hoxie, scientific management was what was practiced by any firm if that firm called it "scientific"; to Taylor, scientific management ceased to exist if the principles and philosophy he had established were violated in practice. Hoxie's logic did not impress Taylor, and this undoubtedly led to Taylor's unfavorable opinion of a report Hoxie prepared detailing the investigators' findings. Taylor's numerous objections to Hoxie's claims are detailed in an appendix attached to the Hoxie report.[100]

The Hoxie report described a marked degree of diversity among the 30 plants inspected. The investigators found that the precepts of scientific management were often violated in practice. They disclosed that many so-called "efficiency experts" who promised quick returns did not have "the ability or the willingness to install scientific management in accordance with the Taylor formula and ideals."[101] Functional foremanship was discovered to have few adherents in practice. Some plants tried using functional foremen, but soon returned to the old-style, line type of organization. In a third area of inquiry, the investigators established that little or no progress was being made with respect to scientifically selecting workers. "Labor heads," an early designation for employment or personnel managers, were poorly trained and of "doubtful experience and capacity."[102]

Instruction and training of workers was another area in which practice fell far short of theory. Learning proceeded by trial-and-error, as trained instructors were scarce, and instruction, more often than not, focused on attaining a level of output rather than teaching employees how to do quality work. Despite these shortfalls, the Hoxie report concluded that training practices in scientific management plants were generally better than those that could be found elsewhere in industry. A fifth area of concern, and of greater criticism, was the use of time study and task setting. Standards and performance incentives were often established after only a cursory inquiry. This led to inaccuracies and injustices. In general, time-study men were poorly trained and inexperienced, and often set rates based on management's desires rather than true scientific inquiry and observation. Piece-rate pay plans also came under close scrutiny. The investigators found no pure adoptions of the Taylor, Gantt, or Emerson piece-rate pay plans. The Midvale differential piece-rate plan, used briefly by Taylor, was infrequently encountered, and most plans were modifications of the Gantt and Emerson plans.

On a broader plane, the Hoxie report tried to reconcile Taylor's view with that of unions regarding industrial democracy. Taylor maintained that scientific management was the essence of industrial democracy. His argument hinged upon harmony and a mutuality of interest between labor and management. Employees were rewarded on the basis of their effort; discipline fell under scientifically derived laws and not under autocratic, driving management; and protests were to be handled by reliance upon scientific inquiry and mutual resolution. According to the union view, however, scientific management monopolized knowledge and power in the hands of management by denying workers a voice in setting work standards, determining wage rates, and

---

[99] Robert F. Hoxie, *Scientific Management and Labor* (New York: Appleton-Century-Crofts, 1915), p. 4.

[100] *Ibid.*, Frederick W. Taylor, "Appendix II: The Labor Claims of Scientific Managment According to Mr. Frederick W. Taylor," pp. 140–149. Gantt in Appendix III (pp. 150–151) and Emerson in Appendix IV (pp. 152–168) also filed statements taking exception to Hoxie's claims. The three statements do not present a unified theory of the scientific-management movement, but do agree on its fundamental aims.

[101] *Ibid.*, p. 29.

[102] *Ibid.*, p. 32.

establishing conditions of employment. Moreover, it introduced a spirit of mutual suspicion among employees and destroyed the solidarity and cooperative spirit of labor by emphasizing individual employees. Furthermore, it weakened, the protection that unions gave employees, and, in turn, stymied the labor movement.

Siding with labor, the Hoxie investigators concluded that industrial democracy could come only through the collective-bargaining process. They saw no possibility for an enlightened management, and seemed dedicated to the proposition that the interests of labor and management were inalterably opposed for all times and in all places. In addition, they found no evidence of union officials or union members resisting workplace improvements. On this count, their examination was less than equitable. They, however, accused management of seeking shortcuts to efficiency, faulted Taylor for trying to generalize his machine-shop experience to all types and sizes of firms, and denounced "efficiency experts" that were guilty of selling patent-medicine panaceas to employers who were eager to improve employee performance.

Those who criticize are also open to criticism. What can be said about the methods the investigators used to reach their conclusions? Hoxie, as well as Frey and Valentine, made numerous attempts to be fair to Taylor by acknowledging that practice fell far short of theory. Their predilections toward organized labor, however, resulted in a demonstrable bias. In this regard, there is evidence that their methods were less than meticulous. Gilson, at Joseph & Feiss Company, one of the plants included in the study, wrote that when Hoxie and Frey visited, they held a brief interview with Richard Feiss and some of his managers, took a few notes, but never visited the plant's work floor. They promised to return to see working conditions in the plant, but never did.[103] If this encounter was characteristic of the investigators' conduct at the other plants they visited, one must conclude that the investigators were less than forthright. It is unfortunate that those charged with conducting a thorough study of scientific management in its early days did so with closed minds and hasty feet.

Nyland noted that the Hoxie report was "heavily skewed" toward organized labor's position and, as a consequence, "the Taylorists were charged publicly with a great many crimes, found innocent of none and guilty of many."[104] A pro-labor bias was also evident in the selection of Robert Valentine to represent "employing management in general." Although, Valentine considered himself an impartial labor expert who could bring workers and management together, he also believed that government should be used to protect workers from the negative effects of industrialization.[105] Taylor objected to Valentine's appointment given Valentine's lack of business experience and unfamiliarity with scientific management. In previous testimony before the U.S. Commission on Industrial Relations, Valentine had admitted his only experience with scientific management was, "I have run into it on the slant in a number of places . . . a half dozen cases." When asked whether employees should participate if "any efficiency system" was introduced, he responded, "I not only think the individual should participate, but I think he should participate as a part of a union."[106] In effect, scientific management was without a representative in the Hoxie–Valentine–Frey investigation.

When John Frey reminisced for a Columbia University oral history project, he admitted "when he and Hoxie came across evidence that did not support the claims of the AFL [American Federation of Labor], he reworked the data until it confirmed his preconceived

---

[103] Mary B. Gilson, *What's Past Is Prologue* (New York: Harper & Brothers, 1940), p. 93.

[104] Nyland, "Taylorism, John R. Commons and the Hoxie Report," p. 1007.

[105] Brad Snyder, *The House of Truth: A Washington Political Salon and the Foundations of American Liberalism* (New York: Oxford University Press, 2017), pp. 63–64. See also Ordway Tead, "Industrial Counselor, A New Profession," *The Independent* 88 (3548) (December 4, 1916), pp. 393–395.

[106] *Industrial Relations, Final Report and Testimony Submitted to Congress by the Commission on Industrial Relations*, Vol. 1 (Washington, DC: U.S. Government Printing Office, 1916), p. 853.

ideas."[107] Frey also had unfavorable memories of Valentine, who "didn't care to come" to plant visits, their meetings, and of Hoxie, who Frey viewed as someone who "knew little of practical matters" and "even less about work, workers, and industry."[108]

John R. Commons, a member of the Commission on Industrial Relations, recalled two other events that shaped the Commission's work. Charles McCarthy, the Commission's director of research and a Taylor supporter, was charged with overseeing the Hoxie-led investigation. The Commission's chair, Frank P. Walsh, a labor attorney from Kansas City, Missouri, soon found reasons to disagree with McCarthy and dismissed him. In a second event, "in the midst of his investigation of Scientific Management," Walsh then proceeded to reassign or discharge anyone employed by Commons.[109] Hoxie was among those terminated. This explains why the Hoxie report was never released by the Commission, but was independently published in 1915. Upon its publication, the Hoxie report was harshly reviewed by both the academic community and scientific-management advocates. British economist Charles W. Mixter commented that "irrespective of its intent the effect of [Hoxie's] book as a whole will be to multiply misconceptions and misunderstandings with regard to the scientific management practice."[110] Barth, Hathaway, Gantt, Sanford E. Thompson, and others expressed extreme displeasure at the Hoxie report's "critical attitude" and what Barth, for one, considered false statements. Barth was especially upset that the investigators had judged "scientific management by the work done by numerous mediocre or fake workers in the business, instead of by that of the real leaders, and the basing of so many of their arguments on the results of the work."[111] Hoxie and his colleagues had botched an unprecedented opportunity to examine the relations between organized labor and scientific management and purposefully misled generations of scholars about their findings.

The Thompson and Nelson Studies

The findings of two other inquiries—one conducted during the height of the scientific management movement and another conducted more recently—of organizations employing "the Taylor system of scientific management" contrast with the manner and method of the Hoxie report. Bertrand Thompson studied 172 "definitely known" applications of scientific management in 80 types of organizations, including factories, municipal governments, department stores, and publishing houses. One hundred and forty-nine of the applications were in factories. In 113 factories, the applications had progressed far enough to permit a summary analysis. Of these, 59 were judged complete successes, 20 partially successful, and 34 failures. Thompson attributed the failures to "the personality of the consulting engineers and . . . the personality of the managements."[112] Failures by consulting engineers were due largely to their "inexperience and incompetence," whereas management failures were attributed to hasty installations, impatience with the initial pace of results, dissension within a factory's management group, and factors completely outside the control of management (e.g., the prevailing business cycle). With one exception, no failure was attributed to difficulties with workmen.[113]

---

[107] John P. Frey, *Reminiscences of John Phillip Frey*. Interview conducted December 22, 1954, Washington, D.C. (New York: Columbia University Oral History Collection, Columbia University, 1953), p. 290. For Frey's contemporaneous account of the Hoxie-Valentine-Frey investigation, see *idem, Scientific Management and Labor* (New York: Efficiency Society, 1916) or "Scientific Management and Labor," *American Federationist* 23(4) (April 1916), pp. 257–268 and (May 1916), pp. 358–368.

[108] *Ibid.*, pp. 287–288.

[109] John R. Commons, *Myself* (New York: Macmillan, 1934), pp. 176–177.

[110] Charles W. Mixter, [Review of the book *Scientific Management and Labor*], *American Economic Review* 6 (June 1916), p. 376.

[111] See the comments on Horace B. Drury's "Scientific Management and Progress" *Bulletin of the Taylor Society* 2(4) (November 1916), pp. 1–10 and 3(1) February 1917, pp. 7–22.

[112] Thompson, *The Taylor System of Scientific Management*, p. 13.

[113] C. Bertrand Thompson, *The Theory and Practice of Management* (Boston, MA: Houghton Mifflin, 1917), pp. 100–101.

Thompson was aware of the Hoxie report and commented on the inclusion of plants that were not truly scientifically managed:

> If the system in the plant was developed by Mr. Taylor personally, or by any of his assistants or co-workers while associated with him, then the Taylor system may be held responsible for the results; otherwise not.
>
> When this qualification is kept in mind, an impartial investigator must admit that, from the viewpoint of the employer, the employee or the public, the Taylor system is a demonstrated success.[114]

In a second study, Daniel Nelson investigated 29 applications of scientific management, each directed by one of Taylor's closest followers. Although variations occurred, Nelson found a pattern of "general adherence to Taylor's ideas."[115] The two ideas that were least likely to have been introduced were the differential piece rate (even Taylor had embraced the Gantt plan) and functional foremanship. Nelson also noted a "strong positive correlation" between scientific management and industrial efficiency. Except for heat-using industries such as beverages, petroleum refining, and chemicals, scientific management was "associated with growth, not stagnation."[116] Scientific management was used mostly in batch-assembly (job shop) and labor-intensive nonassembly operations. In more capital-intensive industries (such as smelting primary metals) scientific management was less likely to be applied. In the automobile industry, scientific management was practice before the acceptance of Henry Ford's assembly line, but not afterward (see Chapter 12). Barth and George Babcock were successful at the Franklin Motor Car Company, for example, but once the moving assembly-line and mass-production techniques came to the auto industry, scientific management methods were less useful.[117]

Nelson noted that scientific management was seen as a "partial solution to the labor problem," meaning a partial solution to finding a "scientific" basis for performance incentives.[118] It was organized labor's view that scientific management "tends to eliminate skilled crafts . . . degrades the skilled worker . . . [and] displaces skilled workers and forces them into competition with the less skilled."[119] The belief that skilled labor would be displaced by workplace improvements is as old as the Luddites who protested the introduction of water-power to replace hand-loom weavers (see Chapter 3). In the case of scientific management, however, it was not machinery but improved work processes that threatened organized labor. Later writers, such as David Montgomery and Harry Braverman, have perpetuated the notion that scientific management "deskilled" or dumbed-down jobs as a means of decreasing management's dependence on skilled labor.[120]

What is the evidence for such claims? If scientific management deskilled jobs, we would expect a decline in the number of craft workers and an increase in the number of unskilled laborers in the United States from 1900 to 1930. U.S. Census Bureau data indicate, however, that the number of "craftsmen and kindred workers," excluding foremen, increased 72 percent from 1900

---

[114] *Thompson, The Taylor System of Scientific Management*, pp. 13, 25.
[115] Daniel Nelson, "Scientific Management, Systematic Management, and Labor, 1880–1915," *Business History Review* 48(4) (Winter 1974), p. 500. Also see *idem*, "Industrial Engineering and the Industrial Enterprise, 1890–1940," in Naomi R. Lamoreaux and Daniel M. G. Raff, eds., *Coordination and Information: Historical Perspectives on the Organization of Enterprise* (Chicago, IL: University of Chicago Press, 1995), pp. 35–50.
[116] Daniel Nelson, "Taylorism," *Proceedings of the International Colloquium on Taylorism* (Paris: Éditions la Découverte, 1984), pp. 55–57.
[117] Charles B. Gordy, *Scientific Management in the Automobile Industry* (Unpublished dissertation, University of Michigan, Ann Arbor, MI, 1929), pp. 5–7.
[118] Nelson, "Scientific Management, Systematic Management, and Labor, 1880–1915," p. 479.
[119] Hoxie, *Scientific Management and Labor*, p. 16.
[120] David Montgomery, *The Fall of the House of Labor: The Workplace, the State and American Labor Activism, 1865–1925* (Cambridge, England: Cambridge University Press, 1987), pp. 214–256; Harry Braverman, *Labor and Monopoly Capitalism* (New York: Monthly Review Press, 1974), pp. 85–168.

to 1920 (2,900,000 to 4,997,000) and 96 percent from 1900 to 1930 (2,900,000 to 5,695,000). Similarly, the number of "operative and kindred workers" (semiskilled) increased 77 percent (3,720,000 to 6,587,000) from 1900 to 1920, and 107 percent (3,720,000 to 7,691,000) from 1900 to 1930. The number of unskilled laborers, excluding farmers and miners, increased at a lesser pace: 35 percent (3,620,000 to 4,905,000) from 1900 to 1920, and 47 percent from 1900 to 1930.[121]

Sociologist Douglas Eichar took a different tack, examining blue-collar workers by skill level as a percentage of the total U.S. labor force. Craft workers were 10.5 percent of the labor force in 1900, 13 percent in 1920; semiskilled operatives increased from 12.8 percent in 1900 to 15.6 percent in 1920; and unskilled nonfarm laborers decreased from 12.5 percent in 1900 to 11.6 percent in 1920.[122] Both in absolute numbers and as a percentage of the U.S. work force, the number of skilled craft and semiskilled operatives increased while the number of unskilled laborers increased at a far slower pace. The claim that scientific management deskilled the general labor force is a myth that needs to be put to rest.

In summary, scientific management became an international movement in the first two decades of the twentieth century. In his assessment of organizations applying scientific management, Bertrand Thompson cautioned that a key distinction between the "Taylor system" and the "Taylor spirit" must be kept in mind. Thompson observed that "the System has served and should continue to be made to serve as a symbol, or if you like, an ideal and a model without which principles tend to dissipate into an ever less intense influence and 'spirit,' as has to a large extent already occurred."[123] Thompson's observation continues to be true today as the "spirit" of Taylor's principles still influence modern industry throughout the world.

Emerging General Management

Although scientific management as a way of thinking dominated the last part of the nineteenth century and the early part of the twentieth century, at the same time, there were indications that a broader conception of management was emerging. In large part, this broadening was grounded in scientific management and an extension of the need to systematize the increasing number of large-scale enterprises. Scientific management was a response to the growth of large-scale enterprises and the need to examine and refine managerial practices. It inspired other disciplines, such as public administration, office management, marketing, and accounting, to search for improved methods; encouraged an interest in the theory and practice of organization design; provided a basis for the study of business policy; and spawned a philosophy of management.

The Impact of Scientific Management on Other Disciplines

Stimulated by scientific management, other disciplines began to search for efficiency through science. William H. Leffingwell applied the principles of scientific management to office management.[124] The University of Chicago's Leonard D. White picked up where Morris L. Cooke left off and made numerous contributions to public administration. White was the first to teach public administration in the classroom and also pioneered in personnel management for government

---

[121] *Historical Statistics of the United States: Colonial Times to 1970*, pt. I (Washington, DC: Bureau of the Census, 1975), pp. 139–142.

[122] Douglas M. Eichar, *Occupation and Class Consciousness in America* (New York: Greenwood, 1989), p. 47.

[123] Thompson, "The Taylor System in Europe," p. 172.

[124] William Henry Leffingwell, *Scientific Office Management* (Chicago, IL: A. W. Shaw, 1917).

agencies.[125] Ralph Starr Butler, Louis D. H. Weld, Paul T. Cherington, and Paul D. Converse and others expanded scientific management to marketing.[126]

Accounting saw the development of standard costing in Emerson's and Taylor's use of the railroad system of accounts. Through a combination of ideas associated with economic analysis in engineering and accounting, managers were first exposed to contingencies in financial planning and control. The relationships among the volume of production, fixed costs, variable costs, sales, and profits had long been a vexing managerial conundrum. An engineer, Henry Hess, developed a "crossover" chart in 1903, which showed the relationship among these variables.[127] In the chart, the "crossover point" is the point where total costs equaled total revenues; that is, the point where losses turned to profits. Walter Rautenstrauch, a professor at Columbia University, coined the phrase "break-even point" in 1922 to describe the same set of relationships.[128] In the same year, John H. Williams, an accountant, popularized the idea of a "flexible budget," showing how management could plan and control at various levels of output.[129] Taken together, these advances enabled managers to better forecast, control, and account for unforeseen marketplace developments.

James O. McKinsey pioneered in using budgets as planning and controlling aids. McKinsey, like Taylor, deplored traditional postmortem uses of accounting. Rather than treating accounting as an end in itself, he viewed budgets as an aid in making operational decisions. For McKinsey, a budget was not a set of figures, but a way of assigning responsibility and measuring performance.[130] As a former professor at the University of Chicago, and later as a senior partner of McKinsey and Co., McKinsey was also influential in the early days of the American Management Association (AMA). The AMA was founded in 1923 as a somewhat adult extension university for practicing managers. Its objective was to broaden the study of management to encompass not only production control and personnel administration, but also to include sales, financial, and other facets of management. Slowly, but undeniably, management education was beginning to shift from an emphasis on shop-floor routines toward a broader view that covered all areas of business.

Early Organization Theory

During the 1920s, the study of organizations primarily focused on designing formal authority–activity relationships among individuals and departments. The early factory system, based on the division of labor, required the coordination of effort, and the grouping of activities into departments satisfied this requirement. As we have noted, most firms were family-owned and -managed, with few employees. They relied on personal supervision to coordinate different activities. The first large-scale enterprises in the United States (and the world) were the railroads. In 1896, Englishman Joseph Slater Lewis authored a "handbook for the use of manufacturers, directors,

[125] Leonard D. White, *Introduction to the Study of Public Administration* (New York: Macmillan, 1926); *idem, The City Manager* (Chicago, IL: University of Chicago Press, 1927).

[126] For the extent of the influence of scientific management on these and other pioneers, see Joseph C. Seibert, "Marketing's Role in Scientific Management," in Robert L. Clewett, ed., *Marketing's Role in Scientific Management* (Chicago, IL: American Marketing Association, 1957), pp. 1–3; Robert Bartels, *The Development of Marketing Thought* (Homewood, IL: Irwin, 1962), and 2nd ed., published as *The History of Marketing Thought* (Columbus, OH: Grid, Inc., 1976); and Paul D. Converse, *The Beginnings of Marketing Thought in the United States* (Austin, TX: Bureau of Business Research, University of Texas, 1959).

[127] Henry Hess, "Manufacturing: Capital, Costs, Profits, and Dividends," *Engineering Magazine* 26 (December 1903), pp. 367–379.

[128] Walter Rautenstrauch, "The Budget as a Means of Industrial Control," *Chemical & Metallurgical Engineering* 27(9) (August 30, 1922), pp. 411–416.

[129] John Howell Williams, *The Flexible Budget* (New York: McGraw-Hill, 1934).

[130] James O. McKinsey, *Budgeting* (New York: Ronald Press, 1922); *Organization* (New York: Ronald Press, 1922); *Budgetary Control* (New York: Ronald Press, 1922); and *Managerial Accounting* (Chicago, IL: University of Chicago Press, 1924). See also William B. Wolf, *Management and Consulting: An Introduction to James O. McKinsey* (Ithaca, NY: Cornell University Press, 1978).

auditors, engineers, managers, secretaries, accountants, cashiers, estimate clerks, prime cost clerks, bookkeepers, draughtsmen, students, pupils, etc." interested in guidance for organizing their firms on "sound commercial lines."[131] It has been referred to as the "first significant book on management in English."[132] With each of these developments, there was a growing recognition that new organization forms were necessary to coordinate the activities of large-scale enterprises that were unprecedented in size and scope.

In 1909, Russell Robb gave a series of lectures on "organization" at the newly formed Harvard Business School. In the lectures, Robb argued that rather than uniformly applying a traditional military command-and-control style of organizing, firms should be organized based on their individual goals and the unique demands of their specific industries. Robb anticipated modern contingency theorists when he noted that "all organizations will differ somewhat from each other, because the objects, the results that are sought, and the way these results must be attained, are different . . . there is no 'royal road,' no formula that, once learned, may be applied in all cases with the assurance that the result will be perfect harmony, efficiency, and economy, and a sure path to the main purpose in view."[133] Thus, the goals pursued differed, as did the means (today we might say "strategy") to attain those goals, resulting in different organizing styles and no one way to organize. Based on this premise, Robb believed that business objectives differed from those of the military and, therefore, different styles of organizing were required. Much could be learned from the military style of organizing as related to fixing responsibility and authority, clearly defining duties and channels of communication, and providing for order and discipline. The military, however, stressed a degree of control unnecessary in business. Robb maintained that because large business enterprises demanded an extensive division of labor, they required greater coordination among their constituent elements than did their military counterparts. Business success was not based on obedience, but on economy of effort; therefore, the manner of organizing had to be different. More emphasis had to be placed on employee selection and training, workplace processes had to be arranged to achieve maximum efficiency, and managers had to be aware that a "great factor in organization is 'system,' the mechanism of the whole."[134] In taking a systems perspective, Robb's lectures were truly remarkable for the time, predating what would become known in the early 1950s as "general systems theory" (see Chapter 21).

Scientific Management at DuPont and General Motors

No story is more fascinating to management historians than the emergence of large-scale enterprises. Scientific management played a part in the development of two industrial giants—DuPont and General Motors. As noted in Chapter 7, in 1896 Taylor had worked closely with Johnson Company's founder Tom L. Johnson; Arthur J. Moxham, who worked in the company's comptroller's office; and T. Coleman du Pont, company general manager, in developing a system to monitor the cost of raw materials. In 1902, cousins Pierre, Coleman, and Alfred I. du Pont purchased E. I. du Pont de Nemours and Company, after the demise of its president Eugene I. du Pont, to keep the powder company in family hands. Being familiar with Taylor's work at the Johnson Company and its Steel Motor Works and Lorain Steel Railway subsidiaries, the du

---

[131] Joseph Slater Lewis, *The Commercial Organisation of Factories: A Handbook for the Use of Manufacturers, Directors, Auditors, Engineers, Managers, Secretaries, Accountants, Cashiers, Estimate Clerks, Prime Cost Clerks, Bookkeepers, Draughtsmen, Students, Pupils, etc.* (London: E. & F. N. Spon Books, 1896).

[132] Joseph A. Litterer, *The Emergence of Systematic Management as Shown by the Literature of Management from 1870 to 1900* (unpublished dissertation, University of Illinois, Urbana, IL, 1959), p. 248, released in book form by Garland Press, New York, 1986.

[133] Russell Robb, *Lectures on Organization* (Privately printed, 1910), pp. 3, 14. Further insights into Robb's life and writings may be found in Edmund R. Gray and Hyler I. Bracey, "Russell Robb: Management Pioneer," *SAM Advanced Management Journal* 35(2) (April 1970), pp. 71–76.

[134] Robb, *Lectures on Organization*, p. 173.

Ponts, and especially Pierre as president, sought to broaden Taylor's cost-accounting system to include a measure of overall company performance. Toward this end, as early as 1903, the DuPont Company used "return on investment" (ROI; the ratio between net profit and total capital invest-ment).[135] Pierre is credited with implementing the financial, opera-tional, and managerial techniques necessary to turn the DuPont Company into one of the world's largest multidivisional enterprises. In doing so, he emulated the cost-accounting system Taylor developed at the Johnson Company and its subsidiaries.[136] The influence of Harrington Emerson is similarly evident in the DuPont Company's early development. The company's general man-ager, Hamilton M. Barksdale, created a line and staff structure that closely followed Emerson's recommendations. Reflecting the systems perspective introduced by Russell Robb, Barksdale also developed uniform objectives and policies for DuPont's divisions and decentralized author-ity to the division level.[137]

Donaldson Brown, Barksdale's cousin, was another key figure in the DuPont Company's early years. Brown developed a formula to measure the performance of each department within the company. The formula ($R = T \times P$, where R is the rate of return on capital invested, T the rate of turnover on invested capital, and P the percentage of profit on sales) also provides a means of comparing performance across departments.[138] Brown also created the famous DuPont Chart System, which was used for corporate decision-making for over one-half century before new information technologies emerged for the presentation of financial data.[139]

The nascent General Motors Corporation, founded in 1908, adapted the multidivisional struc-ture developed at DuPont. William C. Durant created General Motors (GM) from a collection of motorcar and parts producers. The combination was unwieldy, and, in 1920, General Motors was saved from financial ruin by an infusion of du Pont family money. Durant resigned, and Pierre du Pont came out of semiretirement to become GM's president. Pierre made at least two key staffing decisions: he brought Donaldson Brown to General Motors and he handpicked Alfred P. Sloan, Jr., to be his successor. Sloan took over the GM reins in 1923. He centralized administration and decentralized operations, grouping together those that had a common relationship. By decentral-izing operations and centrally coordinating control, GM's various product divisions (e.g., Chevrolet, Buick, Pontiac, and Cadillac) could more quickly respond to their market-sector com-petition. This multidivisional ("M-form") structure enabled GM to more efficiently integrate an increasing number of specialized skills by grouping together all the employees necessary to pro-duce an individual product.[140] With an M-form structure, each major product division is adminis-tered through a separate and semiautonomous division. Each division operates as a mini-company, with its own departments for production, marketing, finance, and so on. Decentralizing into

[135] H. Thomas Johnson, "Management Accounting in an Early Integrated Industry: E. I. Du Pont de Nemours Powder Company, 1903–1912," *Business History Review* 49(2) (Summer 1975), p. 189.

[136] Alfred D. Chandler, Jr., and Stephen Salisbury, *Pierre S. du Pont and the Making of the Modern Corporation* (New York: Harper & Row, 1971), p. xxi.

[137] Ernest Dale, *The Great Organizers* (New York: McGraw-Hill, 1960). See also Ernest Dale and Charles Meloy, "Hamilton McFarland Barksdale and the Du Pont Contributions to Scientific Management," *Business History Review* 36(2) (Summer 1962), pp. 127–152.

[138] F. Donaldson Brown, *Some Reminiscences of an Industrialist* (Unpublished manuscript, Hagley Museum and Library, Wilmington, DE, 1957), pp. 26–28. See also: Ernest Dale, Regina S. Greenwood, and Ronald G. Greenwood, "Donaldson Brown: GM's Pioneer Management Theorist and Practitioner," in Richard C. Huseman, ed., *Proceedings of the Annual Meeting of the Academy of Management* (August 1980), pp. 119–123.

[139] American Management Association, *How the Du Pont Organization Appraises Its Performance: A Chart System for Forecasting, Measuring and Reporting the Financial Results of Operations,* Financial Management Series, no. 94 (New York: American Management Association, 1950). See also JoAnne Yates, "Graphs as a Managerial Tool: A Case Study of Du Pont's Use of Graphs in the Early Twentieth Century," *Journal of Business Communication* 22(1) (Winter 1985), pp. 5–33.

[140] The development General Motors is examined by, among others, Alfred D. Chandler, Jr., ed., *Giant Enterprise: Ford, General Motors and the Automobile Industry* (New York: Harcourt Brace & World, 1964); Peter Drucker, *The Concept of the Corporation* (New York: John Day Company, 1946); and Alfred P. Sloan, Jr., *My Years with General Motors* (New York: Doubleday & Company, 1963).

product divisions also made it possible to use Brown's $R = T \times P$ formula for measuring and comparing performance across divisions.

Drawing on his knowledge of Taylor's cost-accounting system, Pierre du Pont developed a measure of overall company performance. He went on to build both DuPont and General Motors into two of the world's largest and most successful companies. Taylor and, in turn, scientific management, thus, played a role in creating what is today known as the "modern corporation."

Business Policy

As the notion of general management was emerging during the 1920s, the idea of collegiate schools of business began to spread rapidly. Economics, once called Moral Philosophy and later Political Economy, was the womb that nurtured emerging business subjects. Thus, Towne's call for the "engineer as an economist" found fulfillment not in the ASME but in nascent schools of business. Their rapid growth resulted in the formation of the Association of Collegiate Schools of Business (ACSB; the present-day American Assembly of Collegiate Schools of Business) in 1916. By 1926–1927, the ACSB had 38 members offering courses in accounting, economics, finance, marketing, commercial law, transportation, statistics, physical environment, social control and ethics, production, personnel, and labor.[141]

Although education for business grew rapidly in the first quarter of the twentieth century, there were few efforts among educators to integrate course offerings to provide a general overview of a manager's job. Arch W. Shaw, publisher of *System* magazine (now *Bloomberg Businessweek*), which was devoted to "output and profit increasing methods put to use in leading factories," was a notable exception. In 1908, Shaw lectured at Northwestern University's new School of Commerce, and in 1910 he spoke at Harvard University's Graduate School of Business Administration. While at Harvard, he became familiar with the problem method of instruction, which had grown out of the interrogative Socratic Method of teaching law developed in the 1870s by Christopher C. Langdell at the Harvard Law School. During the 1911–1912 academic year, Shaw taught a business-policy course at Harvard based on the problem, or case, method. The course was "to deal with top-management problems, and it also aimed at integrating subjects that the students had studied in their first year."[142] Shaw invited business executives to attend his classes and described a challenge confronting their companies; his students were required to prepare reports with policy recommendations on how to address each challenge, which were then presented to the executives. Despite Shaw's unique approach, only two schools (Harvard and the University of Michigan) required the study of business policy in 1925, and it was not until 1959 that a capstone course (now generally known as "Business Strategy") became a requirement in AACSB accredited schools.

A. Hamilton Church, discussed above in connection with his mentor Leon P. Alford, was more in the mainstream of management thought during the scientific-management era. Church began his career in Great Britain, became a consultant on cost-accounting systems, and moved to the United States at the turn of the century. Tutored by Joseph Slater Lewis (mentioned above), Church sought a more general approach to the study of management than that offered by Taylor.[143] He became interested in a broadened view of management after studying the allocation of overhead costs, that is, those costs (such as management salaries) that are difficult to attribute to any one product or activity. For Church, every industrial undertaking consisted of two elements: (1) the determinative element, which fixed a firm's manufacturing and distribution policies; and

---

[141] Frances Ruml, "The Formative Period of Higher Commercial Education in American Universities," *Journal of Business* 1(2) (April 1928), pp. 253–254.

[142] Melvin T. Copeland, "The Genesis of the Case Method in Business Instruction," in M. P. McNair, ed., *The Case Method at the Harvard Business School* (New York: McGraw-Hill, 1954), p. 26.

[143] Joseph A. Litterer, "Alexander Hamilton Church and the Development of Modern Management," *Business History Review* 35(2) (Summer 1961), p. 214.

(2) the administrative element, which took a firm's policies as determined and gave them practical expression through buying, manufacturing, and selling.[144] In modern parlance, Church was describing *policy formulation* (the determinative element) and *implementation* (the administrative element).[145] As Church explained, in making these two elements operational, managers used two fundamental "instruments": *analysis*, consisting of cost accounting, time-and-motion study, routing, machine layout, and planning; and *synthesis*, combining workers, functions, machines, and all activities effectively to achieve some useful result. In brief, managers *analyzed* to find better ways and then *coordinated* (synthesized) activities.

In Church's mind, Taylor's work only focused on a limited aspect of a manager's job. Church believed that managers should be concerned with a firm's overall efficiency. He incorporated a general-management viewpoint in his books and articles, and emphasized the challenge of managing a firm's departments in relation to one another and to a firm as a whole. Writing in *The Making of an Executive*, Church stopped short of formulating a general-management process as had Fayol, but nevertheless provided early insights into policy formulation and implementation.[146]

Whereas the work of Taylor and his contemporaries reflected a set of values or beliefs, an Englishman, Oliver Sheldon, was the first to lay claim to developing an explicit philosophy of management. Sheldon began and ended his business career at the Cocoa Works at York, a British chocolate-manufacturing company headed by B. Seebohm Rowntree and now part of Nestlé UK. Sheldon was undoubtedly familiar with Gantt's view that businesses had a social responsibility to incorporate community service in their activities. Sheldon believed that managers "should devise a philosophy of management, a code of principles, scientifically determined and generally accepted, to act as a guide, by reason of its foundation upon ultimate things, for the daily practice of the[ir] profession."[147]

Sheldon encouraged managers to develop common motives, common ends, a common creed, and a common fund of knowledge. The basic premise of his philosophy of management, like that of Gantt, was community service:

> Industry exists to provide the commodities and services which are necessary for the good life of the community, in whatever volume they are required. These commodities and services must be furnished at the lowest prices compatible with an adequate standard of quality, and distributed in such a way as directly or indirectly to promote the highest ends of the community.[148]

In Sheldon's thinking, combining scientific management's emphasis on efficiency with community service was the responsibility of all managers. Toward this end, Sheldon held that managers must adopt three principles: (1) "the policies, conditions, and methods of industry shall conduce to communal well-being"; (2) "management shall endeavor to interpret the highest moral sanction of the community as a whole" in applying social justice to industrial practice; and (3) "management . . . [shall] take the initiative . . . in raising the general ethical standard and conception of social justice."[149] It was Sheldon's belief that in applying these principles that managers must consider both human *and* technical efficiency. He endorsed scientific methods of work analysis, but with due consideration being given to developing human potential to the greatest extent possible. Per Sheldon's philosophy, the economic basis of service, the dual emphasis on human and technical efficiency, and the responsibility of managers to provide social justice would all lead to a mutually beneficial "science of industrial management."

[144] Alexander H. Church, *The Science and Practice of Management* (New York: Engineering Magazine, 1914), pp. 1–2.

[145] Mariann Jelinek, "Toward Systematic Management: Alexander Hamilton Church," *Business History Review* 54(1) (Spring 1980), p. 72.

[146] Alexander H. Church, *The Making of an Executive* (Scranton, PA: International Textbook Company, 1923).

[147] Oliver Sheldon, *The Philosophy of Management* (London: Sir Isaac Pitman and Sons, 1923), p. 284.

[148] *Ibid.*, p. 285.

[149] *Ibid.* , pp. 285–286.

SUMMARY

Scientific management was a significant force influencing (1) the formal study of management; (2) the practice of management in the United States, a majority of the nations in Western and Eastern Europe, and Japan, China, and Australia; (3) early organization theory; (4) applications in other business disciplines; (5) the creation of a general business-policy course; and (6) an explicit philosophy of management. The original seed planted by Taylor provided the crucial impetus, but it took the efforts of many to spread the scientific-management message. In practice, scientific management did not always run true to its founder's ideals: organized labor resisted it as a threat to its autonomy; its methods were adapted in different countries, but without preserving its spirit; and, much too often, firms of all types grasped its techniques and forgot its philosophy. Yet scientific management was not a failure. Growing out of the need to systematize business practices, it gave a voice to efficiency, purpose to practice, and content to theory. Its youth was robust, its maturity was fruitful, and it spawned intellectual descendants throughout the world who still write about, study, and practice its teachings. Scientific management reflected the *zeitgeist* of its times and prepared the way for subsequent developments in the evolution of management thought.

Scientific Management in Retrospect

The scientific-management movement can only be fully understood in the context of the world within which it was created. Following Fred Taylor's death in 1915, a web of economic, technological, social, and political forces transformed scientific management as it became a global phenomenon. Although we will consider these forces separately for expository purposes, in reality, they were inextricably intertwined. With the unfolding of the twentieth century, each of these forces was perpetuated and reinforced by aspects of the broader cultural landscape, in general, and by the developing field of management, in particular.

Alfred D. Chandler noted that the "initial expansion and accumulation of resources" that marked the growth of "Big Business" in the United States was complete by the beginning of World War I (see Chapter 6). With unprecedented challenges of managing large-scale enterprises, the need for rationalization or full use of resources became apparent. As described by Chandler, the early twentieth century faced two basic challenges: (1) improving production techniques and processes to achieve economies of scale so as to reduce the per-unit cost of production or distribution, and (2) improving planning, coordination, and performance assessment.[1]

The emergence of these twin challenges marked what Chandler identified as a second phase in the growth of Big Business: the rationalization or full use of resources. The scientific-management movement hit its initial stride as this phase was gaining interesting national attention. The opening line in Taylor's *The Principles of Scientific Management* quotes President Theodore Roosevelt's 1908 call for "the conservation of our natural resources" as a means of increasing "national efficiency."[2] Roosevelt considered the application of scientific management

---

[1] Alfred D. Chandler, Jr., *Strategy and Structure: Chapters in the History of the Industrial Enterprise* (Cambridge, MA: MIT Press, 1962), pp. 386–390.

[2] Theodore Roosevelt, "Address by the President," in *Proceedings of a Conference of the Governors in the White House*, Washington, DC, May 13–15, 1908. Newton C. Blanchard, James Franklin Fort, James O. Davidson, John C. Cutler, and Martin F. Ansel, eds., (Washington, DC: Government Printing Office, 1909), p. 12.

to the conservation of the nation's natural resources an act of patriotism.[3] In response to Roosevelt's call, Taylor listed three reasons for writing his book:

First. To point out, through a series of simple illustrations, the great loss which the whole country is suffering through inefficiency in almost all of our daily acts.

Second. To try to convince the reader that the remedy for this inefficiency lies in systematic management, rather than in searching for some unusual or extraordinary man.

Third. To prove that the best management is a true science resting upon clearly defined laws, rules, and principles, as a foundation. And further to show that the fundamental principles of scientific management are applicable to all kinds of human activities, from our simplest individual acts to the work of our great corporations, which call for the most elaborate cooperation. And, briefly, through a series of illustrations, to convince the reader that whenever these principles are correctly applied, results must follow which are truly astounding.[4]

As the twentieth century unfolded, people became intrigued with the promise of a better and more efficient world. This chapter considers the economic, technological, social, and political forces that transformed scientific management as it sought to eliminate waste and preserve the world's material resources.

The Economic Environment: From the Farm to the Factory

The impact of industrial growth on the world's economic environment was an initial force that transformed scientific management as it became a global phenomenon. As the United States became an industrialized nation, millions of jobs were created. Thousands of people left their farms in search of a new life. In 1800, agriculture was the primary livelihood of 90 percent of the population in the United States; by 1900, 33 percent were engaged in farming and by 1929, 20 percent. The transformation of the United States from a rural, agricultural nation into an industrialized power represents one of the most dramatic changes in world history. The typical citizen who awakened on the morning of January 1, 1901, saw little change between the old and the new centuries, yet the change was there. The United States was now the world's leading industrial nation and had moved into a new economic era.

Thousands of immigrants from Europe and Asia also left their homes to improve their lives by migrating to the United States. In contrast with other industrialized nations such as Britain, France, Germany, Italy, and Japan, the population of the United States in the late nineteenth and early twentieth centuries was very diverse and growing more so. Immigrants or their children composed more than 80 percent of the population in New York City, Chicago, Milwaukee, and Detroit. By 1900, there were more Italian-Americans in New York City than in any city in Italy except Rome; more residents of Polish descent in Chicago than in Warsaw; and by 1920 more people of Irish ancestry had immigrated to the United States than the total remaining on the Emerald Isle.[5]

---

[3] Henry Beach Needham, "Roosevelt on *Efficiency in Business*: 'Scientific Management is the application of the Conversation Principle to Production' [An Interview with Theodore Roosevelt]," *System: The Magazine of Business* 19(6) (June 1911), p. 586.

[4] Frederick W. Taylor, *The Principles of Scientific Management* (New York: Harper & Brothers, 1911), p. 7.

[5] Thomas K. McCraw, "American Capitalism," in idem, ed., *Creating Modern Capitalism* (Cambridge, MA: Harvard University Press, 1997), p. 307.

These individuals and many, many more were responding to Emma Lazarus's famous words, inscribed on the Statute of Liberty in New York harbor: "Give me your tired, your poor, your huddled masses yearning to breathe free . . . I lift my lamp beside the golden door!"[6]

By 1910, 48 percent of the workers employed in mining, 31.9 percent in manufacturing, and 26.3 percent in transportation were born outside the United States.[7] In 1913, Ford Motor's Highland Park (Michigan) plant had a workforce of 71 percent foreign-born workers from 22 different national groups. The majority of these workers hailed from southern and eastern Europe, but nationalities from all across the world were represented, including Armenians, Austro-Hungarians, Canadians, Croatians, Danes, English, Frenchmen, Germans, Hollanders, Irish, Italians, Japanese, Lithuanians, Poles, Russians, Rumanians, Sicilians, Scotch, Serbians, and Turks.[8] Safety bulletins were issued in 42 different languages.[9] As such a large percentage of its workers could not speak English, the company started the Ford English School in 1914. In addition to English, students were taught civics, mathematics, and history, and educated on virtues such as thriftiness, cleanliness, good manners, and timeliness.

Contrary to what might be expected, the large influx of immigrant labor from the 1880s to 1920s did not result in lower wages. As noted in Chapter 6, daily wages and annual earnings in manufacturing increased 59 percent between 1860 and 1890, and real wages (the purchasing power of the workers' incomes) increased 60 percent from 1860 to 1890 (1.6 percent compounded annually).[10] In addition, the average number of hours worked per week started to decrease: in 1890, the average industrial workweek was 60 hours; in 1910, 55 hours, and in 1920, 50 hours.[11] At roughly the same time, the number of worker hours input per unit of output dropped from an index number of 74 in 1919 to 42 in 1929 (1899 = 100), for a gain in efficiency of 43 percent.[12]

The economies of scope and scale associated with Big Business demanded an even sharper focus on managerial talent. Large accumulations of resources were needed to meet the demands of mass markets and mass distribution. As firms grew, a new breed of professional managers was replacing the owner-entrepreneurs who built the first wave of the modern corporation. The personalized, informal structures of the family business inevitably yielded to the logic of growth. No longer could owner-entrepreneurs personally supervise all of a firm's activities. Technology demanded specialized knowledge, and staff departments were added to handle personnel, engineering, production, purchasing, legal affairs, and other ancillary activities. Melman found that between 1899 and 1929, the percent of employees in management relative to those in production almost doubled (9.9 percent in 1899 to 18.5 percent in 1929), and between 1929 and 1947 increased from 18.5 to 22.2 percent.[13]

---

[6] Emma Lazarus, "The New Colossus," November 2, 1883. Available online at http://www.mcny.org/story/new-colossus. See also "In Memory of Emma Lazarus," *New York Times* (May 6, 1903), p. 9.

[7] Sumner H. Slichter, "The Current Labor Policies of American Industries," *Quarterly Journal of Economics* 43(3) (May 1929), p. 394.

[8] "Automobile Trade Notes," *New York Times* (November 15, 1914), p. 6. See also Allan Nevins (with the collaboration of Frank Ernest Hill), *Ford: The Times, the Man, the Company* (New York: Charles Scribner's Sons, 1954), p. 648; Joyce Shaw Peterson. *American Automobile Workers, 1900–1933* (Albany, NY: State University of New York Press, 1987), p. 17.

[9] Robert A. Shaw, "Discussion," *Proceedings of the National Safety Council*, Sixth Annual Safety Congress, New York City, September 12, 1917 (Chicago, IL: The Council, 1917), pp. 236–237. See also Horace Lucien Arnold and Fay Leone Faurote, *Ford Methods and the Ford Shops* (New York: Engineering Magazine, 1915), pp. 56, 59.

[10] Ross M. Robertson, *History of the American Economy,* 3rd ed. (New York: Harcourt Brace Jovanovich, 1973), pp. 379–380.

[11] Edgar W. Martin, *The Standard of Living in 1860* (Chicago, IL: Chicago University Press, 1942), p. 220.

[12] U.S. Dept. of Commerce, Bureau of the Census, *Historical Statistics of the United States: Colonial Times to 1970* (Washington, DC: U.S. Government Printing Office, 1975), pt. 1, p. 162.

[13] Seymour Melman, "The Rise of Administrative Overhead in the Manufacturing Industries of the United States, 1899–1947," *Oxford Economic Papers* 3(1) (February 1951), pp. 66–68, 91. Melman used the U.S. Census of Manufactures' definition of management as salaried employees (i.e., line and staff) and others as wage earners.

Technology: Opening New Horizons

Technology, a second force that transformed scientific management as it became a global phenomenon, opened new horizons in business. President Calvin Coolidge captured the spirit of the era in a January 17, 1925, address to the American Society of Newspaper Editors:

> After all, the chief business of the American people is business. They are profoundly concerned with producing, buying, selling, investing, and prospering in the world. . . . Wealth is a product of industry, ambition, character, and untiring effort. . . . So long as wealth is made the means and not the end, we need not greatly fear it.[14]

The U.S. economy came of age in this period as unprecedented inventions improved the nation's standard of living. In Chapter 6, we saw how developments in transportation and communication spurred the initial growth of U.S. enterprises in the years following the War Between the States. As the twentieth century dawned, a whole series of technological advancements capitalized on one another, spurring further economic growth. Open-hearth steelmaking superseded the Bessemer process by 1900. Orville Wright would never have flown at Kitty Hawk (North Carolina) in 1903, if German Karl Benz had not perfected the first workable internal combustion engine. By 1908, developments in "cracking" oil molecules during refining yielded richer fuels for automobiles and aircraft. Research at E.I. du Pont de Nemours & Co. led to discoveries in synthetic materials. Charles F. Kettering eliminated the dangerous hand crank required to start early automobiles when he developed an electric self-starter. Lee De Forest and Guglielmo Marconi pioneered the vacuum tube and radio. The Panama Canal (1914) connected the Atlantic and Pacific Oceans. The technological breakthroughs of this period were as astounding to our ancestors as those of today are to our generation. Never before had the human condition been transformed so completely. Adult stature and life expectancy drastically improved due to technological breakthroughs. For instance, the spread of mechanical refrigeration put an end to the "spring sickness" that typically followed winters in which people did not have green vegetables to consume. As a result of this and other advances, for a male born in Massachusetts in 1860, the life expectancy was 46.4 years and 47.3 years for a female.[15] By 1930, in the U.S. general population, a male's life expectancy had increased to 58.1 and a female's to 61.6 years.[16]

Developments in power generation also deserve a mention. Heretofore, water wheels, horses, and coal had been the primary energy sources for the engines of industry. Although coal continued to dominate, newfound oil deposits were soon to reshape the U.S. energy base. Of even greater impact, on October 10, 1879, Thomas A. Edison created a cotton filament for the incandescent light bulb. He built the nation's first central power plant at New York City in 1882. By 1920, one-third of the country's industrial power came from electricity and half of urban homes were electrified. In rural areas, 98 percent of the homes still relied on kerosene lamps and candles, but not for long.

The automobile was another technological advancement that brought about substantial economic and social change during this period. The automobile gave people a new mobility—a freedom of movement that led to the growth of satellite communities. In 1900, there were 8,000 registered automobiles in the United States. By 1930, there were 26.8 million cars on the road. As noted in Chapter 8, between 1908 and 1913, the Ford Motor Company perfected the moving assembly line to mass produce automobiles. The results were impressive: in 1910 (pre-assembly

---

[14] Calvin Coolidge, "The Press under a Free Government," address before the American Society of Newspaper Editors, Washington, DC, January 17, 1925; reprinted in Calvin Coolidge, *Foundations of the Republic: Speeches and Addresses* (New York: Charles Scribner's Sons, 1926), pp. 187–188.

[15] Maris A. Vinovskis, "Mortality Rates and Trends in Massachusetts before 1860," *Journal of Economic History* 32(1) (March 1972), Table 9, p. 211.

[16] Elizabeth Arias, "United States Life Tables, 2004," *National Vital Statistics Reports* 65(9) (December 28, 2007), p. 35.

line), 2,773 workers produced 18,664 autos (6.73 per worker); in 1914 (post-assembly line) 248,307 autos were produced by 12,880 workers (19.28 per worker).[17] Prices were driven downward as productivity increased: in 1908 and 1910 a fully equipped Model T touring car cost $950; $490 in 1914; and $360 in 1916.[18]

It should be noted that despite the claim that "Fordism" was an extension of Taylor's methods,[19] Taylor's closest associates were adamant that Taylor's ideas should not be confused with Ford's mass production. In addition to Frank Gilbreth's comments regarding the distinction between scientific management and assembly-line conditions at Ford (reported in Chapter 8), according to Harlow S. Person (Managing Director of the Taylor Society), Taylor was "never sympathetic" to mass production with its "unregulated development." Moreover, in further comments, Person made it clear that scientific management differed from "efficiency engineering," a term Taylor hated, and, which his "apostles" considered a "bastard perversion" of Taylor's methods.[20] Although it has been suggested that Ford's engineers "had doubtlessly caught some of Taylor's ideas . . . [and] kept in touch with the ideas of men like Taylor,"[21] there is no record of either Taylor or the four engineers authorized to implement his methods (Carl G. Barth, Henry L. Gantt, H. King Hathaway, and Morris L. Cooke)[22] ever advising Henry Ford or the Ford Motor Company. Beyond this, when asked directly, Henry Ford denied "any dependence upon scientific management," claiming to have acted wholly on his own inspiration.[23]

Information technology in the spirit of Henry V. Poor's definition of information as "recorded communication" (see Chapter 5) was also evolving. Smaller firms could rely on informal communications, account books, and face-to-face exchanges to track business affairs. As firms grew in size, however, adding levels of authority, the transmission of communications from the top to the bottom of a firm and back could be disastrously lengthy. Whereas Fayol's gang plank allowed communications to cross lines of authority (see Chapter 10), more formal systems of gathering, recording, and maintaining information were developed. As mentioned in Chapter 6, Christopher L. Sholes sold his typewriter patent to E. Remington & Sons in 1873. Demand for the typewriter, however, languished until the late nineteenth century when expanding businesses created a need for prompt and legible correspondence. Vertical file cabinets facilitated arranging correspondence and records. The A. B. Dick Company licensed the rights to Thomas A. Edison's "multiplying letters" device for making duplicate copies of letters and introduced it throughout the world, calling it a "mimeograph" machine. Pneumatic tubes were designed and installed in factories and retail stores to send money, receipts, and other papers from floor to floor and between departments.[24] Long before Nike, the first "shoosh" was the sound of information transmitted via a pneumatic tube.

The revolution in information technology had an unintended effect: it shifted clerical work from men to women and created office jobs as an alternative to factory labor for women. In 1880, less than 5 percent of clerical workers in the United States were women. By 1900, women comprised over 30 percent. Male clerks who wrote letters and other documents by hand using pen

---

[17] Nevins, *Ford: The Times, the Man, the Company*, pp. 644, 648.

[18] Karel Williams, Colin Haslam, and John Williams, "Ford versus 'Fordism': The Beginning of Mass Production?" *Work, Employment & Society* 6(4) (December 1992), p. 519.

[19] For a discussion that considers "Fordism" to be an outgrowth of Taylor's methods see Ed Andrew, *Closing the Iron Cage: The Scientific Management of Work and Leisure* (Montréal: Black Rose Books, 1981), p. 98.

[20] Mark Sullivan, *Our Times: The United States 1900–1925*, vol. 4: *The War Begins, 1909–1914* (New York: Charles Scribner's Sons, 1932), p. 76n.

[21] Daniel Nelson, "Scientific Management, Systematic Management, and Labor, 1880–1915," *Business History Review* 48(4) (Winter 1974), pp. 489–490.

[22] Kenneth E. Trombley, *The Life and Times of a Happy Liberal: A Biography of Morris Llewellyn Cooke* (New York: Harper & Brothers, 1954), p. 9.

[23] Horace Lucien Arnold and Fay Leone Faurote, *Ford Methods and the Ford Shops* (New York: Engineering Magazine Company, 1915), p. 20.

[24] For more on these and other similar developments during this era, see JoAnne Yates, *Control through Communication: The Rise of System in American Management* (Baltimore, MD: Johns Hopkins University Press, 1989).

and ink were largely replaced by female typists and stenographers. At the same time, other women entered formerly all-male offices as cashiers, bookkeepers, and secretaries using new devices such as the mimeograph, Dictaphone, cash register, adding machine, and stenotype.[25] In brief, advancing technology was reshaping the nature of work by increasing the number of skilled and semiskilled jobs, creating alternative employment opportunities for women, and substituting capital (i.e., plant and equipment) for labor.

The Social Environment: From Achievement to Affiliation

A third force that transformed scientific management as it became a global phenomenon was most evident in the changing values and cultural fabric of the era's social environment. Between 1868 and 1900, Horatio Alger, Jr., wrote more than 100 books for boys with piquant titles such as *Bound to Rise*, *Luck and Pluck*, *Sink or Swim*, and *Tom, the Bootblack*. At least 20 million copies were sold, and "Horatio Alger" became synonymous with "rags to riches" success. The typical plot involved a poor, young man who overcame poverty and hardship to achieve economic standing by diligence, honesty, perseverance, and thrift. Quite often he was befriended by a benefactor who recognized his latent talents and assisted him in reaching the pinnacle of the financial world. The heroes in Alger's books were a personification of David C. McClelland's "high achiever", who exhibited the self-control, hard work, and orderly life associated with Max Weber's Protestant ethic (see Chapter 2).[26] They learned in the school of hard knocks; no formal schooling could prepare them for success in business. Charles M. Schwab, a protégé of steel-magnate Andrew Carnegie (see Chapter 6), stated the case:

> [I]f the college man thinks that his education gives him a higher social status, he is riding for a fall. Some college men . . . have pride in their mental attainments that is almost arrogance. Employers find it difficult to control, guide, and train such men. Their spirit of superiority bars the path of progress.[27]

Early scientific-management theory rested on fundamental values such as rewards for individual performance, as well as the classical virtue of enlightened self-interest. Utilitarianism, also in vogue during this era, held that all behavior stemmed from the pursuit of personal pleasure and avoidance of pain.[28] It assumed that individuals, acting in their own self-interest, made rational decisions about what pleasures or pains to seek or avoid. The notion that workers, like all other human beings, act in their own self-interest, gave rise to the imaginary figure, "economic man" or *homo economicus*, who always acts rationally to maximize his welfare.[29] In the period leading up to the scientific-management era, *homo economicus* was generally assumed to be motivated solely by money. Before Taylor, however, piece-rate incentive plans had largely failed because management had all too often either failed to properly set performance standards or engaged in rate-cutting when earnings were judged to be too high. Neither practice was in management's self-interest because it only encouraged workers to engage in systematic soldiering. As envisioned by Taylor, the principal object of management was to secure the maximum prosperity

---

[25] Elyce J. Rotella, "The Transformation of the American Office: Changes in Employment and Technology," *Journal of Economic History* 41(1) (March 1981), pp. 51–57. Also see Angel Kwolek-Folland, *Engendering Business: Men and Women in the Corporate Office, 1870–1930* (Baltimore, MD: Johns Hopkins University Press, 1994), pp. 4–6.

[26] David C. McClelland, *The Achieving Society* (Princeton, NJ: Van Nostrand, 1961).

[27] Charles M. Schwab, "The College Man in Business," in Alta Gwinn. Saunders and Hubert Le Sourd Creek, eds., *The Literature of Business* (New York: Harper & Brothers, 1920), p. 5.

[28] Jeremy Bentham, *An Introduction to the Principles of Morals and Legislation* (London: Printed for T. Payne and Son, 1789). Originally published in 1780.

[29] The term *"homo economicus"* or "dollar-hunting animal" was coined by Charles S. Devas in *The Groundwork of Economics* (London: Longmans, Green, & Co, 1883), p. 27.

for both employers and employees. The "mental revolution" that Taylor called for recognized a congruency between the goals of employee and employer. There would be justice for all based on the impartial scientific determination of a "fair day's work." In brief, the ideals of scientific management were compatible with the era's prevailing values such as rewards for individual performance and the classical virtue of enlightened self-interest.

Cultural Thought: The Collision Effect

Changes in cultural thought are always difficult to pinpoint. As the twentieth century unfolded, the scientific-management movement slowly incorporated new dimensions that affected the course of management thought. Two disparate yet strangely congenial dimensions, in particular, were coming together to mark a new era in U.S. cultural thinking: (1) the closing of the Western frontier and (2) the Social Gospel movement and its successor, Progressivism. With regard to the closing of the Western frontier, historian Frederick Jackson Turner identified four cultural forces that were reshaping economic, social, and political ideals in the United States during this period: (1) "the exhaustion of the supply of free land and the closing of the movement of Western advance as an effective factor in American development"; (2) "the concentration of capital in the control of fundamental industries as to make a new epoch in the economic development of the United States"; (3) "expansion of the United States politically and commercially into lands beyond the seas"; and (4) the division of political parties on "issues that involve the question of Socialism."[30] According to Jackson, the U.S. West typified the ideals of individualism, freedom to rise on one's own initiative, and political and economic democracy. Whenever labor-market outcomes or social conditions became too oppressive, the West provided an avenue of escape. Jackson believed that when the safety valve offered by the Western frontier closed, new institutional arrangements were necessary to maintain the nation's cultural qualities.

Scott labeled this era in U.S. history the "period of collision."[31] He believed that, unless tempered, the inevitable clash of the forces Turner identified as reshaping U.S. ideals would have eventually led to the nation's cultural degeneration, as people were drawn into inescapable proximity and interdependency. He dubbed this degeneration the "collision effect." Rather than leading to chaos, Scott argued that, with the closing of the Western frontier, its ideals were replaced by a new value system he called the "social ethic." This ethic substituted human collaboration for human competition and took "groups," as distinct from their individual members, as its primary focus. This had a profound effect on management thought. In retrospect, by stressing the mutuality of employee–employer interests coupled with the belief that each individual should be given the highest and most interesting work for which he was fit, scientific management bridged the gap between the social ethic's emphasis on human collaboration and the individualism on which the United States had been founded and the West personified. Though neither known nor regarded as a social philosopher, Fred Taylor and other scientific-management advocates fully appreciated the changes occurring in the U.S. social environment and saw scientific management as a means for securing the maximum prosperity for both employers and employees.

The Social Gospel

The Social Gospel movement and its successor, Progressivism, was a second dimension that marked a new era in U.S. cultural thinking. As noted in Chapter 6 and discussed further in Chapter 9, the Social Gospel movement emerged in the late nineteenth century as a counterpoint

---

[30] Frederick Jackson Turner, *The Frontier in American History* (New York: H. Holt and Company, 1920), pp. 244–247.
[31] William G. Scott, *The Social Ethic in Management Literature* (Atlanta, GA: Bureau of Business and Economic Research, Georgia State College of Business Administration, 1959), p. 9.

to Social Darwinism. Social Gospel proponents (predominantly Protestant, but also Roman Catholic and Jewish) felt a duty to reform social and economic conditions, especially in the workplace. Rather than wait for a gradual improvement in the quality of life found in poorer neighborhoods, they argued for immediate action in improving personnel-administration and industrial-relations policies. They shaped the field of personnel management by appealing for profit sharing, the right to organize unions, workplace arbitration, worker cooperatives, legislation governing the hiring and firing of employees, the employment of women and children, and workplace sanitation. The Social Gospel movement was an antecedent of industrial sociology and was a predecessor of Progressivism.

For Social Gospel proponents, labor unions (in particular) were instruments of social and economic reform. Robert G. Valentine, discussed in Chapter 11 in connection with the Hoxie Report, envisioned the eventual replacement of labor unions and labor–management conflict by enlightened "industrial counselors" who were not advocates of either side, but would put their own ideas forward in the interest of employers, employees, *and* the general public.[32] Some of the era's "share in the management" plans involved union consent and cooperation, whereas others gave employees a voice and a choice through various types of employee representation plans. Valentine viewed such plans as part of an evolution toward true industrial democracy that began with the first welfare-work offices established in the late 1890s by forward-thinking companies such as the National Cash Register Company and Joseph Bancroft and Sons, as discussed in Chapter 9. In retrospect, these early efforts were an uneven mixture of philanthropy, humanitarianism, and business acumen.

Scientific management complemented the work of Social Gospel proponents by linking efficiency and morality. For Taylor, hard work led to morality and well-being; for Social Gospel proponents, morality and well-being yielded hard work. This reciprocity between hard work and morality was the core of the romance linking later Progressives and scientific management (as discussed below).

Uplift through efficiency was in vogue among Social Gospel proponents who pursued efficiency virtually in all aspects of U.S. society. Popular books and manuals on efficiency in the home, in education, in conserving natural resources, in religion, and in industry abounded.[33] Taylor even penned a foreword to Mary Pattison's *Principles of Domestic Engineering or the What, Why and How of a Home*, a book he believed to be "the first work in the field of household or domestic engineering."[34] Members of this new field predicted that scientific management would revolutionize the "*home* of the future," releasing women from the drudgery of housework and free them to assume an equal role in society.[35] Taylor's principles held an unprecedented grip on the U.S. psyche.

This cultural fascination with efficiency, however, was soon to wane. By the 1920s, the gospel of uplift through efficiency was ebbing as U.S. factories poured forth an abundance of goods.

---

[32] Robert G. Valentine, "Scientific Management and Organized Labor," *Bulletin of the Society to Promote the Science of Management* 1(2) (January 1915), pp. 3–9. See also idem, "The Progressive Relation between Efficiency and Consent," *Bulletin of the Society to Promote the Science of Management* 2(1) (January 1916), pp. 7–20.

[33] Among others, see Joseph M. Rice, *Scientific Management in Education* (New York: Hinds, Noble and Eldredge, 1914); Ernest J. Dennen, *The Sunday School under Scientific Management* (Milwaukee, WI: Young Churchman Co., 1914); Eugene M. Camp, *Christ's Economy: Scientific Management of Men and Things in Relation to God and His Cause* (New York: Seabury Society, 1916); Samuel P. Hays, *Conservation and the Gospel of Efficiency* (Cambridge, MA: Harvard University Press, 1959); Samuel Haber, *Efficiency and Uplift: Scientific Management in the Progressive Era 1890–1920* (Chicago, IL: University of Chicago Press, 1964); and Raymond E. Callahan, *Education and the Cult of Efficiency* (Chicago, IL: University of Chicago Press, 1962).

[34] Frederick W. Taylor, "Foreword," in Mary Pattison, *Principles of Domestic Engineering or the What, Why and How of a Home* (New York: Trow Press, 1915), p. 17.

[35] Mary Pattison, *Principles of Domestic Engineering*, p. 149. Pattison, who conducted motion studies of housekeeping chores at her Experimental Housekeeping Station at Colonia, New Jersey, was also influenced by, but, in turn, influenced the work of the Gilbreths. See Charles D. Wrege, "Untold Gilbreth Stories," *The Quest* [Newsletter of the Gilbreth Network] 2(2) (Summer 1998), p. 1.

Prosperity reigned, and a new gospel of consumption emerged, with a heavy emphasis on the importance of everyone being part of the "middle class." Whiting Williams, Elton Mayo, Mary Parker Follett, and others we have or will discuss were beginning to stress the benefits of an egalitarian work place in which human progress is best achieved through groups that interact, participate, and communicate. Personnel departments advocated welfare programs and worker happiness as both social and business assets (see Chapter 9). The need for affiliation was rising, there was security in group membership, and people were becoming more conscious of social relations and less concerned with maximizing individual gain. The Western frontier was closed, Horatio Alger's self-made man was increasingly seen as a myth, and new social values were replacing the promise of individual freedom on which the nation was founded. The seeds were sown for the Social Person Era, the next topic in our study on the evolution of management thought.

The Political Environment: The Advent of Progressivism

Changes in the U.S. political environment represent a fourth force that transformed scientific management as it became a global phenomenon. The most evident change occurred in the role of government in business. The task of government and political institutions throughout time has primarily revolved around two basic themes: (1) the need to balance protecting one person's rights against violating another person's rights, and (2) the need to limit the power of government in order to protect individual rights. Political theorists, such as Niccolò di Bernado dei Machiavelli and Thomas Hobbes, saw a central role for government in connection with the first theme; Jean Jacques Rousseau and John Locke sought a system of balances through which individuals could check excesses of government power in regard to the second theme (see Chapter 2). Constitutional or representative government—the philosophy of Rousseau and Locke made manifest in United States' founding documents—makes consent of the governed the source of all legitimate authority. In the late nineteenth century, the United States was seeking to perfect democracy. In striving to do so, the "collision effect" prompted an outpouring of legislation to change the relationship between individuals and government, as well as between businesses and government. Founded on a belief in a government with limited powers, the right to own private property, individual liberty, and business operating without excessive regulation, the United States encountered imbalances among the ideals and reality of a growing economic democracy.

Scientific Management and the Progressives

The political articulation of the Social Gospel was found in its successor, Progressivism. The so-called Progressive movement attempted to mitigate the perils of the "collision effect" by providing a broader base for democracy. It is a strange quirk of history that Taylor has never been considered progressive by modern critics, yet his work and philosophy eventually became embedded in Progressive thought. Whereas the roots of the Social Gospel movement as expressed in its call for "industrial betterment" or welfare programs lie in religion and philanthropy, Progressivism was "urban, middle-class, and nationwide."[36] For the era's Progressives, the central challenge was restoring equality of opportunity by replacing government interventions that benefited large-scale capital with programs that favored individuals with little or no wealth.[37] The Progressives sought to enfranchise women, elect U.S. senators by direct popular vote, establish a minimum wage, enact worker compensation laws, encourage trade unions, and enact a federal income tax.

[36] Richard Hofstadter, *The Age of Reform: From Bryan to F. D. R.* (New York: Alfred Knopf, 1955), p. 131.
[37] Eric F. Goldman, *Rendezvous with Destiny: A History of Modern American Reform* (New York: Alfred Knopf, 1952), p. 59.

Scientific management attracted the Progressive movement's attention at the 1910 Eastern Rate Case hearings. Louis Brandeis, a leading Progressive, helped popularize the catchy title ("scientific management") that made efficiency synonymous with morality and social order.[38] The shippers (banded together as the Commercial Organizations of the Atlantic Seaboard) could be spared a freight-rate increase, and the public a hike in prices, if the principles of scientific management were applied to the nation's railroads. In the mind of Progressives, everyone would benefit, as lower costs would also allow higher wages; all that was needed was for business to embrace Taylor's methods. It was here that the Progressives' romance with scientific management was consummated. Whereas some of the era's reformers, like socialist Eugene Debs, wanted to replace the whole free-market system, more moderate Progressives like Louis Brandeis and journalist Walter Lippman thought that efficiency through science and leadership by professional experts would bring social order and harmony. Each envisioned a new era that would remove commerce from the "cesspool of commercialism" and turn business executives into "industrial statesmen."[39] The appeal of scientific management was that it offered leadership by expertise and science and, hence, would rise above class prejudice and overcome rule by drive and whim. High wages for employees and low costs for employers were possible by applying Taylor's principles. Scientific management made the interests of employers and employees congruent. Labor–management conflict was, thus, unnecessary.

Business and the Progressives

The era's biggest change in the relations between government and business in the United States came in 1901 following the assassination of President William McKinley and succession of Theodore Roosevelt to the presidency. Roosevelt's Progressive inclinations initially gave business leaders and financial markets little reason for concern. His first annual message to Congress balanced his Progressive beliefs with a pro-business stance.[40] In 1902, however, the U.S. Justice Department (under President Roosevelt) brought suit to dissolve the Northern Securities Company by invoking the Sherman Antitrust Act that had been passed in 1890. This direct blow at Northern Securities, a trust formed by J. Pierpont Morgan, Edward H. Harriman, and their associates to control the Northern Pacific Railway, the Great Northern Railway, and the Chicago, Burlington and Quincy Railroad, opened a new chapter in government–business relations. The Justice Department subsequently filed similar suits against the Beef Trust (1905), the Standard Oil Company of New Jersey (1906), and the American Tobacco Company (1907). Roosevelt also initiated new legislation regulating railroads (Elkins Act, 1903, and Hepburn Act, 1906) and the telephone, telegraph, and wireless industries (Mann-Elkins Act, 1910). Other federal legislation sought to limit working hours and regulate female and child labor. The Clayton Antitrust Act (1914) and the Federal Trade Commission Act (1914) strengthened the Sherman Act. The Federal Reserve Act (1913) created a more elastic currency and weakened the hold of New York City banks over cash and reserves. In 1913, the U.S. Congress passed the Underwood-Simmons Tariff Act, which imposed a one-percent tax on personal incomes over $3,000 and a surtax up to six-percent on incomes in excess of $500,000.

Changes in the U.S. political environment during the early scientific-management era introduced a new balance in the powers of business and government. Though Taylor's forays into the political arena, especially his experience with the Interstate Commerce Commission (1910) and

[38] David Savino, "Louis D. Brandeis and His Role Promoting Scientific Management as a Progressive Movement," *Journal of Management History* 15(1) (2009), pp. 38–49.
[39] Walter Lippman, *Drift and Mastery: An Attempt to Diagnose the Current Unrest* (New York: Mitchell Kennerley, 1914), pp. 8, 328. See also Louis Brandeis, *Business - A Profession* (Boston MA: Small, Baynard & Company, 1914).
[40] Theodore Roosevelt, "First Annual Message to Congress," December 3, 1901. Available at http://americanhistory.si.edu/documentsgallery/exhibitions/

Commission on Industrial Relations (1915), were less than satisfactory, he persisted in seeking to replace management by privilege with management by science. Joining with Theodore Roosevelt and other like-minded conservationists, he also sought to eliminate waste and preserve the world's human and physical resources.

SUMMARY OF PART II

Figure 12.1 provides a synopsis of the scientific-management era. Scientific management was not an invention; it was a synthesis, a stage in evolving management thought. Charles Babbage could lay a valid claim to the formation of a rational, systematic approach to management, but it was Frederick W. Taylor who gave systematic management a voice. Taylor was the *deus ex machina*, the unexpected power who suddenly became the focal point for an idea.

Scientific management was more than time and motion study; it was a much deeper philosophy of managing human and physical resources in a technologically advanced world where people were achieving unprecedented domain over their environment. The Industrial Revolution had provided the impetus; Taylor provided the synthesis. As people gained greater control over their lives and experienced a heretofore unimaginable standard of living, they pursued a vision of human prosperity in the fullest

FIGURE 12.1 Synopsis of the Scientific-Management Era.

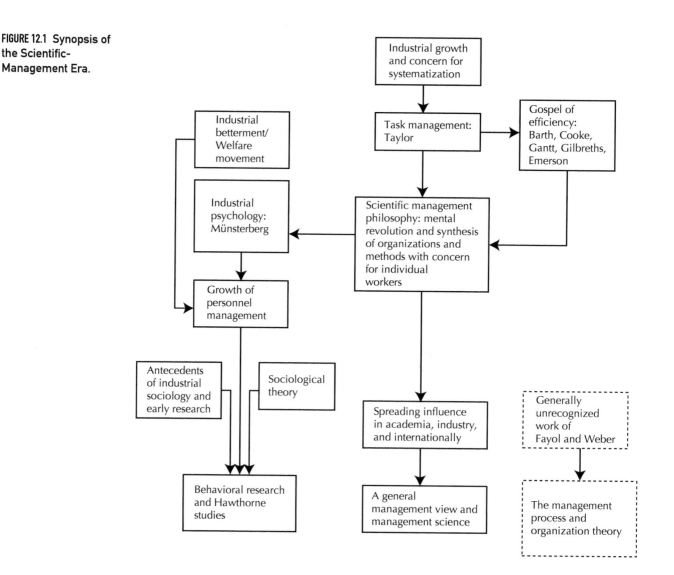

meaning of the term. Taylor had an idea, a great idea, on how that might be done—by a mental revolution on the part of all parties, founded on science and not whim, and leading to harmony and cooperation. Perhaps he was idealistic, even Utopian, but it would be wrong to fault Taylor for seeking the promise of industrial harmony, individual betterment, and greater national productivity.

Those who followed in Taylor's footsteps diverged from his orthodoxy as an interacting web of economic, technological, social, and political forces transformed scientific management as it became a global phenomenon. Some left large footprints, whereas others only paused long enough to leave small and blurred tracks. All reflected, however, the imprint of Taylor's search for rationality in a changing and more industrialized world.

Two of Taylor's contemporaries, Fayol and Weber, were to achieve acclaim only in more modern times.

The question to what extent the person makes the times rather than vice versa has been debated throughout history. Taylor and his disciples were the products of an era that in economic terms sought the rationalization or full use of resources, in social terms sanctioned individual reward and effort, and in political terms encouraged uplift through efficiency. In turn, they were instrumental in giving voice to a movement that sought greater material prosperity and industrial harmony. Scientific management was the offspring of its culture and, in turn, sired a new era of industrial, social, and political vigor. The efforts of Taylor and his disciples still shape our lives today.

The Social Person Era

part

3

Eras in management thought never begin and end neatly in any particular year. Just as in a musical performance, there is a blending of movements as themes shift among major and minor keys. The notion of a "social-person era" reflects more of an emerging philosophy than a call for managerial action. Although rooted late in the scientific-management era, it did not receive any large degree of recognition until the 1930s. It was dominated by the belief that employee satisfaction and productivity were dependent on favorable social interactions among employees and between employees and their supervisors; therefore, the key to efficiency and workplace harmony was supportive human relations. Part 3 begins by examining the Hawthorne studies, which served to give academic credence to the human-relations movement. The lives and thoughts of two individuals—Mary P. Follett and Chester I. Barnard—who significantly contributed to our understanding of authority and responsibility, the need to coordinate effort, conflict resolution, and how to structure and design organizations for maximum effectiveness and efficiency are discussed. Next, the growth and refinement of the human-relations movement as it moved through micro and macro phases, from roughly 1930 into the early 1950s, are reviewed. Part 3 concludes with a look at human relations in theory and practice and a consideration of the economic, social, technological, and political environments of the social-person era.

The Hawthorne Studies

No studies in the history of management thought have received so much publicity, so many different interpretations, so much praise, and yet so much criticism, as those begun in 1924 at the former Hawthorne (Cicero, Illinois) Works of the Western Electric Company, the supply arm of AT&T. Colloquially referred to by local residents simply as "Western," the Hawthorne Works manufactured telephones and switchboards. The Hawthorne studies spanned an 8-year period and dramatically revealed previously unappreciated patterns of employee behavior. Perhaps the most significant feature of the studies was that, for the first time, resources comparable to those commonly devoted to research in the physical sciences were devoted to the human element in management, thereby counterbalancing the shop floor-industrial engineering orientation common to the earlier scientific-management era. Referred to as the "Hawthorne Studies," this research had a profound effect upon the so-called "human-relations" movement.

At the time of the studies, the 113-acre Hawthorne Works employed some 40,000 people 6 days a week in nearly every trade and profession.[1] Many employees were either first- or second-generation local residents of Czech, Hungarian, or Polish origin. Hawthorne was noted for its enlightened human-resource policies and generous employee benefits. It sponsored athletic, recreational, and social programs; operated a variety store offering merchandise at discounted prices; and sponsored an evening school. It maintained an employee building and loan association, a noncontributory benefit plan, a savings plan, and an employee stock-purchase program. It also operated a company restaurant, several cafeterias, and numerous lunch counters where employees could purchase meals at cost. Employee morale was thought to be high and there had

---

[1] For more on the particular "context" in which the Hawthorne studies were conducted, see John S. Hassard, "Rethinking the Hawthorne Studies: The Western Electric Research in Its Social, Political and Historical Context," *Human Relations* 65(11) (2012), pp. 1431–1461.

been no labor unrest. As Hawthorne was virtually AT&T's sole supplier of telephone apparatus, there was intense pressure to meet production schedules and, thus, to avoid any form of work stoppage.[2]

The Hawthorne Studies Begin

Illumination Study (1924–1927)

Initiated in collaboration with the National Research Council's Committee on Industrial Lighting, what became known as the Illumination Study (funded by the General Electric Company) was conducted under the direction of Dugald C. Jackson, a professor of electrical engineering at the Massachusetts Institute of Technology (MIT), assisted by his colleagues Joseph W. Barker and Vannevar Bush.[3] Thomas Edison, inventor of the electric light bulb, was the Committee's honorary chairman. The study's original intent was to investigate the relationship between variations in workplace lighting and employee productivity. Based on prior research, it had been hypothesized that as the total intensity of illumination was increased, employee productivity would increase.[4] In the winter of 1924, the MIT researchers investigated existing lighting conditions and performance in Western's punch press, coil winding, and relay-assembly departments to establish an initial baseline from which potential changes in employee productivity (i.e., output) could be measured over time. The level of illumination was then varied in each department, with the result that "output bobbed up and down without direct relation to illumination."[5]

In the summer of 1925, the researchers selected two groups of coil-winding operators, who were equal in experience and performance, for further study. Coil winding consists of turning a fine wire evenly in layers around a piece of soft iron. When an electric current is sent through the wire, the iron becomes a magnet that attracts iron and steel. The wire-wound magnet is called a "coil." One set of coil winders was designated the variable group (i.e., the level of lighting to be varied) and the other the control group (no changes in lighting to be made). The groups were placed in two different buildings that were away from their regular department. The researchers systematically modified the level of illumination in the building housing the variable group. This time, however, regardless of whether the lighting was brighter, dimmer, or constant, output generally increased. Other modifications in the level of illumination also yielded unanticipated and seemingly contradictory results. In one instance, Homer Hibarger, a Western employee, studied two operators and gradually reduced the light intensity to the equivalent of ordinary moonlight (0.06 footcandles) and output still increased. Ladialas "Wanda" Beilfus, one of the operators, recalled:

> Geri [Geraldine Sirchio] . . . was with me. We were taken to a small room. Mr. Hibarger was there with us, but it wasn't that bad. The lighting was a little darker but we could see what we were doing. . . . They found out even with the bad lighting we did just as well.[6]

---

[2] Joseph M. Juran, "Early SQC: A Historical Supplement," *Quality Progress* 30(9) (September 1997), p. 74.

[3] Dugald C. Jackson, "Lighting in Industry," *Journal of the Franklin Institute* 205(3) (March 1928), pp. 285–303; and Joseph W. Barker, "Technique of Economic Studies of Lighting in Industry," *Transactions of the Illuminating Engineering Society* 23 (1928), pp. 174–188. See also Charles D. Wrege and Ronald G. Greenwood, "Dugald C. Jackson: The Forgotten First Director of the Hawthorne Studies," unpublished manuscript, Charles D. Wrege Research Papers, 1925–2013, Box 3, Folder 31, Kheel Center for Labor-Management Documentation and Archives, Cornell University and on Vannevar Bush, the cover story, "Yankee Scientist," *Time* 43(14) (April 3, 1944), pp. 52–57. As Director, U.S. Office of Scientific Research and Development during World War II, Bush was a central figure in organizing scientific and engineering talent to develop the atomic bomb, microwave radar, mass produced antibiotics, and other technologies crucial to the Allied victory.

[4] Total intensity of illumination consisted of artificial and natural illumination. The General Electric Company funded the Illumination Study because it was interested in research that would convince its customers to use artificial illumination in conjunction with natural illumination and, thereby, increase sales of lamps, fixtures, and wiring.

[5] Charles E. Snow, "Research on Industrial Illumination: A Discussion of the Relation of Illumination Intensity to Productive Efficiency." *Tech Engineering News* 8(7) (November 1927), p. 272.

[6] Wanda Beilfus (née Blazejak) quoted in Alfred A. Bolton, "Relay Assembly Testroom Participants Remember: Hawthorne a Half Century Later," *International Journal of Public Administration* 17(2) (1994), p. 377.

In April 1927, the Illumination Study was abandoned. Two conclusions seemed obvious: (1) illumination was only one of many factors affecting employee output, and (2) no simple cause-and-effect relationship existed between illumination and employee productivity. It was, thus, recognized that other factors would have to be investigated, and that better experimental controls would be necessary in future studies. In preparing a report on the study's findings, Charles E. Snow, a MIT graduate student Jackson selected as the field engineer to run the Illumination Study, concluded that there were too many factors at play to definitely establish that illumination was directly related to employee productivity. Snow acknowledged that, whereas many of these factors could be controlled or eliminated, the "one great stumbling block remaining is the problem of the psychology of the human individual."[7] At this juncture, it would have been easy to move on to other pursuits. Hibarger, however, intrigued by the unanticipated and seemingly contradictory results, felt the study should be continued. George Pennock, Superintendent of Inspection, and Clarence Stoll, Works Manager, agreed. With their support, Hibarger designed and conducted a second study.

Relay-Assembly Test-Room Study (1927–1932)

In early 1927, a second study was begun in an effort to further investigate the puzzling results of the Illumination Study, with the goal of determining the effects of working conditions (e.g., rest breaks, workday length, company-provided mid-morning lunches, and method of payment) on employee productivity. This phase of the Hawthorne studies, known as the Relay-Assembly Test-Room study, lasted 5 years. The original study participants were five relay assemblers (Adeline Bogotowicz; Irene Rybacki; Theresa Layman; Wanda Beilfus, who had participated in the Illumination Study; and Anna Haug), one layout operator (Bea Stedry), who supplied the assemblers with parts, and Hibarger, who served as the test room's initial observer. On the following page is a photograph of the relay assemblers at their work bench. The trays opposite each assembler contain parts for assembly. In front of each assemble is a jig used in assembling the relays. Stedry, the layout operator, is on the far left. Hibarger is seated facing the assemblers on the left, out of the picture.[8]

The number of assemblers participating in the study was limited by the capability of a recording device that would punch a hole in a telegraph tape each time an assembler dropped a completed relay down a collection chute. The telegraph tape had only five channels, thus limiting the number of assemblers that could be included in the study. Hibarger's role as observer was to record the principal events in the room hour by hour and to create and maintain a friendly atmosphere. The work involved repetitively assembling telephone relays. The relays weighed a few ounces, consisting of a coil, armature, contact-springs, and insulators held in position by several machine screws. They required approximately 1 minute to assemble. How the study participants were selected offers a glimpse of work life in the late 1920s. Frank Platenka, the regular relay-assembly department supervisor, told Wanda Beilfus there was going to be a study and asked her to "pick out girls who I felt would not be married soon" and who would like to work on a special room to be used for a study.[9] The assemblers were invited to Pennock's office "where the plan and objectives of the study were explained . . . [and] they readily consented to take part in the study."[10]

The assemblers were observed in their regular department (without their knowledge) for 2 weeks prior to moving to a special test room, where work conditions could be more closely controlled.[11] Additionally, careful measurements were made of factors such as pulse rate, blood

---

[7] Snow, "Research on Industrial Illumination," p. 282.

[8] T. North Whitehead, "Social Relationships in the Factory: A Study of an Industrial Group," *The Human Factor* 9(11) (November 1935), p. 383.

[9] Ladialas "Wanda" Beilfus quoted in Bolton, "Relay Assembly Test Room Participants Remember," p. 361.

[10] Claire E. Turner, "Test Room Studies in Employee Effectiveness," *American Journal of Public Health* 23(6) (June 1933), pp. 577–584.

[11] Much of the following section is based on the seminal research of Charles D. Wrege, *Facts and Fallacies of Hawthorne: A Historical Study of the Origins, Procedures, and Results of the Hawthorne Illumination Tests and Their Influence on the Hawthorne Studies*, 3 vols. (unpublished dissertation, New York University, NY, 1961), released in book form (2 vols.) by Garland Press, New York, 1986. See also Ronald G. Greenwood, Alfred A. Bolton, and Regina A. Greenwood, "Hawthorne a Half Century Later: Relay Assembly Participants Remember," *Journal of Management* 9(2) (Fall 1983), pp. 217–231.

Relay-Assembly Test-Room Participants, circa 1928: (left to right) Beatrice Stedry (layout operator), Anna Haug (operator #5), Wanda "Lottie" Beilfus (operator #4), Theresa Layman (operator #3), Geraldine Sirchio (operator #2), and Mary Volango (operator #1). Ronald G. Greenwood Collection, courtesy of Regina A. Greenwood. University Archives, Alvin Sherman Library, Nova Southeastern, Fort Lauderdale, FL.

pressure, blood condition ratings, and vascular skin reactions, as well as general weather conditions and test-room temperature and humidity. Every 6 weeks the assemblers were given a complete medical examination to track their health and menstrual cycles. Records were kept of the amount of sleep each assembler had had the previous night, what food she had eaten, recreations, home conditions, and other outside influences. Unlike their regular department, the assemblers were allowed to talk and to leave their workbenches whenever they wished. The assemblers had no supervisor, as they would have had in a regular department. At most, Hibarger exercised a quasi-supervisory function. After about 6 weeks, the assemblers were placed on an incentive plan that tied their pay to the performance of their small group. The assemblers were told to work at a "comfortable pace." They were also assured that they would not suffer financially, but rather have the opportunity to make more money than they had in the relay-assembly department. Thus, the researchers reported that "we were able to easily convince the operators that any gains in output would be returned entirely to them and we were thus reasonably assured of their cooperation."[12]

During the first seven periods of the study (April 25, 1927, to January 21, 1928), various working conditions were changed to determine the effect, if any, on productivity. Two 5-minute rest periods were introduced, followed by two 10-minute rests, then six 5-minute rests, and later a lunch was provided in Western's employee restaurant. Whenever a change was planned, its purpose was explained to the assemblers and their comments solicited. Changes that did not meet their approval were abandoned. The most surprising finding during this time was that the

---

[12] Western Electric Company, "An Investigation of Rest Pauses, Working Conditions, and Industrial Efficiency," supplementary program report as of May 11, 1929, p. 144. Reproduced in Fritz J. Roethlisberger, Hawthorne Study Records, Microtext Collection, University of Wisconsin – Milwaukee Library, Milwaukee, WI, 1977.

assemblers' productivity "tended in general to increase no matter what changes in working conditions were introduced."[13] There was an emerging concern, however, about the behavior and production of Adeline Bogotowicz and Irene Rybacki. Hibarger had evidence that Bogotowicz was restricting output (she and Rybacki were consistently the lowest producers); and Theresa Layman, who sat at a workbench closest to Bogotowicz, said that Bogotowicz and Rybacki talked only to each other and refused to talk with others. Rybacki and Bogotowicz were dismissed from the test room and returned to the regular relay-assembly department. The reasons offered for their dismissal were "lack of co-operation," "poor output," and "talking problem."[14] An undated Hawthorne report, however, noted that Rybacki had been cooperative when the study began and became antagonistic only after her health declined. Medical tests revealed that Irene was severely anemic: she received medical treatment and was given a 2-week paid leave. She was able to recover her health and return to work in the regular relay-assembly department.[15]

Bogotowicz's and Rybacki's positions in the test room were assigned to Mary Volango and Geraldine "Geri" Sirchio (who also participated in the Illumination Study), two experienced relay assemblers. Output in period eight went up as soon as Sirchio and Volango arrived, exceeding any previous level achieved by the original five assemblers. Sirchio became the work group's informal leader, and although output would vary from one period to the next, the trend continued upward, exceeding previous peak levels. Then, in period 12, over a year after the study started, rest periods were removed, the workday and workweek were returned to their original length, and the assemblers again had to furnish their own lunches. Total output went up as the workweek increased to 5½ days (48 hours), but hourly output declined. Rest periods were reinstated in period 13 and weekly and hourly output reached an all-time high.

It was clear to Pennock, Hibarger, and others that something unusual was happening. Pennock visited MIT, his alma mater, in the winter of 1927 to seek professional advice. MIT's President Julius A. Stratton recommended that Pennock seek out Clair E. Turner, a MIT professor of biology and public health. Turner soon joined the study as a consultant. At Turner's suggestion, fatigue, health habits, and mental attitudes were explored as potential explanations for the assemblers' enhanced productivity.[16] Turner was able to establish that reduced fatigue as a result of rest periods was not the cause of the assemblers' increased output. The rest periods, however, gave the assemblers more opportunities for social interaction. Mental attitudes, more than anything else, seemed to explain the increase. In order of importance, Turner attributed the assemblers' increased output to (1) working in a small group, (2) a less restrictive and friendlier

[13] George A. Pennock, "Industrial Research at Hawthorne: An Experimental Investigation of Rest Periods, Working Conditions and Other Influences," *Personnel Journal* 8(5) (February 1930), p. 297.

[14] T. North Whitehead, *The Industrial Worker: A Statistical Study of Human Relations in a Group of Manual Workers*, vol. 1 (Cambridge, MA: Harvard University Press, 1938), p. 117; Fritz J. Roethlisberger and William J. Dickson (with the collaboration of Harold A. Wright), *Management and the Worker: An Account of a Research Program Conducted by the Western Electric Company, Hawthorne Works, Chicago* (Cambridge, MA: Harvard University Press, 1939), p. 53. In a historical aside, the Roethlisberger and Dickson's 1939 book should not be confused with either the earlier or the similarly titled book by George F. Johnson *et al. The Management and the Worker* (Chicago, IL: A. W. Shaw Company, 1920) or Roethlisberger and Dickson's preliminary report on the Hawthorne studies *Management and the Worker: Technical vs. Social Organization in an Industrial Plant* (Boston, MA: Bureau of Business Research, Graduate School of Business Administration, Harvard University, 1934). According to Richard Trahair, George F. F. Lombard recalled that Roethlisberger and Dickson's 1939 full report, which drew on department reports prepared by various Hawthorne managers, was delayed as the manuscript "sat on the lawyer's desk at Western Electric for years because at the time the company did not want it known that so much money had been spent during the Depression on personnel matters, and that perhaps if it were known, shareholders would want to know why" (Richard C. S. Trahair to Charles D. Wrege, personal communication, dated March 4, 2011).

[15] "Explanation of Removal of Two Operators," no date. Reproduced on Reel 3, Box 5, Folder 2, of the Microfilmed Records of the Industrial Relations Experiment Carried Out by the Western Electric Company at the Hawthorne Works, Hawthorne, IL. Hawthorne Studies Collection, Baker Library, Harvard University Business School, Boston, MA.

[16] Claire E. Turner, *I Remember –* (New York: Vantage Press, 1974), pp. 83–87; Charles D. Wrege, "Solving Mayo's Mystery: The First Complete Account of the Origin of the Hawthorne Studies—The Forgotten Contributions of C. E. Snow and H. Hibarger," in Robert L Taylor, Michael J. O'Donnell, Robert A. Zawacki, and Donald D. Warwick, eds., *Proceedings of the Annual Meeting of the Academy of Management* (1976), pp. 12–16.

supervisory style, (3) increased earnings, (4) the novelty of being a study participant, and (5) the attention given to the assemblers by company officials and the researchers.[17]

Pennock was the first to note the influence of supervisory style on the assemblers' productivity. The assemblers were aware they were producing more in the test room than they did in the regular relay-assembly department, and they said the increase had occurred without any conscious effort on their part. They offered two explanations. First, "it was fun" working in the test room. They enjoyed being the center of attention. Second, the new supervisory style, or more accurately, the absence of the old supervisory style, allowed them to work freely without anxiety. For example, in the test room, as noted, the women were allowed to talk with one another, whereas in their regular department, conversation was forbidden. Hibarger's efforts to create a friendly atmosphere in the test room resulted in the women receiving a great deal of considerate and personal attention. In short, the test-room supervision was more thoughtful and less authoritarian than the supervision style the assemblers had previously experienced, and the atmosphere was freer and less anxiety provoking. This was in dramatic contrast to the atmosphere created by the regular relay-assembly room supervisor, Frank Platenka. As one of the operators, Theresa Layman, explained: "[W]e were more relaxed. We didn't see the boss [Platenka], didn't hear him . . . he was mean. He died; I didn't even go to see him." Another operator, Wanda Beilfus added, "It [the test room] was just family, you know, real friendly."[18] Turner summed up the results: "[There was] a fundamental change in supervision . . . no group chief . . . but instead a 'friendly observer' . . . . Discipline was secured through leadership and understanding. . . . An *esprit de corps* grew up within the group."[19]

At this point, style of supervision and the assemblers' *esprit de corps* or group spirit (which we note was one of Fayol's 14 principles of management; see Chapter 10) were believed to explain the increases in productivity. One other factor, the assemblers' performance-incentive plan, was believed to contribute, but had not yet been examined empirically. Because the assemblers were paid on the output of 5 rather than 100 or more assemblers, their pay was tied more closely to their own individual effort. The average wage of the assemblers before going into the test room was $16 per week; in the test room, their average weekly earnings ranged from $28 to $50. Could this boost in wages possibly explain the increase in output?

To test this possibility, two new study groups were formed: a group of five relay assemblers and a group of five operators splitting mica, which was used as an insulator (Figure 13.1). For their first 9 weeks together, the relay assemblers were placed on a performance-incentive plan (the same as that used earlier in the relay-assembly test room) that tied their pay to the performance of their small group. Initially, total output went up, leveled off (for all but one assembler whose output decreased), and then remained constant at a new higher level (112.6 percent over an established output base of 100 percent). After returning to the performance-incentive plan used in the regular relay-assembly department for a period of 7 weeks, the assemblers' performance dropped to 96.2 percent of the established output base. The mica splitters had always been on an individual piece-rate plan. After being moved to a special observation room, the mica splitters' rest periods and length of workday were varied, as had been done earlier in the relay-assembly test room. Changes in the mica splitters' output were similarly recorded. The mica splitters were studied for 14 months, and their average hourly output rose 15 percent.

Although the relay assemblers' output had gone up in both studies, except when they were returned to the group performance-incentive plan used in the regular relay-assembly department, Turner was hesitant to solely attribute the increase to the different pay schemes: "[the] changed pay incentive may have been one factor in increasing output but it certainly was not the

[17] Turner, "Test Room Studies," p. 583.
[18] Greenwood, Bolton, and Greenwood, "Hawthorne," pp. 222, 224.
[19] Turner, "Test Room Studies," p. 579.

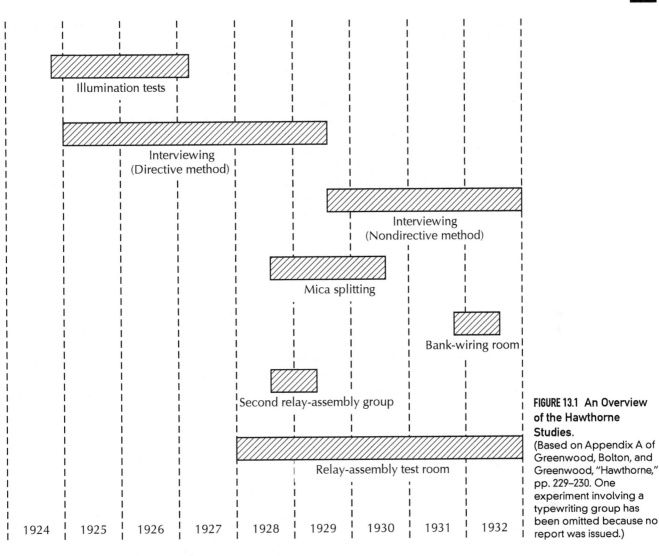

Illumination tests

Interviewing
(Directive method)

Interviewing
(Nondirective method)

Mica splitting

Bank-wiring room

Second relay-assembly group

Relay-assembly test room

1924   1925   1926   1927   1928   1929   1930   1931   1932

FIGURE 13.1 An Overview of the Hawthorne Studies. (Based on Appendix A of Greenwood, Bolton, and Greenwood, "Hawthorne," pp. 229–230. One experiment involving a typewriting group has been omitted because no report was issued.)

only factor."[20] An interim report dated May 1929 summarized the results of all three studies: output of the assemblers was up from 35 to 50 percent; fatigue reduction was not a factor in this increased output; pay "was a factor of the appreciable importance in increasing output"; and the workers were more "content" owing to the "pleasanter, freer, and happier working conditions" caused by the "considerate supervision."[21]

The Interviewing Program (1925–1932)

During the Illumination Study, Charles Snow and Homer Hibarger had begun interviewing Western employees to gain insights into employee–supervisor relations.[22] They used questionnaire items such as: "How is your general health?" "Are you happy on the job?" "Are you influenced

---

[20] *Ibid*, p. 582.
[21] Western Electric Company, "Investigation," pp. 126–128.
[22] William J. Dickson, "The Hawthorne Plan of Personnel Counseling," *American Journal of Orthopsychiatry* 15(2) (April 1945), pp. 343–347; Scott Highhouse, "The Brief History of Personnel Counseling in Industrial-Organizational Psychology," *Journal of Vocational Behavior* 55(3) (December 1999), pp. 318–336.

by any pressure from your working associates?" Because these items could be answered "yes" or "no," they were limited in the information they collected. Clearly, another approach was needed if they were to gain any useful insights into employee–supervisor relations.

In October, 1927, T. K. Stevenson, Western's personnel director, had heard Harvard University professor Elton Mayo speak on "What Psychology Can Do for Industry in the Next Ten Years." Stevenson spoke with Mayo after the speech about the relay-assembly test-room study results and suggested that he visit the Hawthorne Plant.[23] An Australian who earned a Bachelor of Arts degree in logic and philosophy from the University of Adelaide, Mayo had made unsuccessful attempts to study medicine at the Universities of Adelaide and Edinburgh. In 1911, he became a lecturer teaching moral philosophy at the University of Queensland.[24] While in Scotland, he had participated as a research associate in a study of psychopathology, the scientific investigation of mental disorders; this experience served as an early basis for his work as an industrial researcher.

In 1922, Mayo immigrated to the United States. Soon after arriving, he became a research associate at the University of Pennsylvania's Wharton School of Finance and Commerce and, subsequently, received a Laura Spelman Rockefeller Memorial Fund Fellowship to study "Individual Industrial Efficiency." In his research on industrial unrest in Australia, Mayo had found that personal difficulties experienced in the workplace could not be explained by any one factor, but must be dealt with in what he called "the psychology of the total situation."[25] This was a Gestalt concept that formed the basis for Mayo's view of organizations as social systems and recognition that knowing the parts is not equivalent to knowing the whole. Moreover, this concept highlighted how, in addition to knowing how each part of a social system functions, it is necessary to foresee how their interactions could produce unanticipated consequences. In a study remarkably similar to the original goal of the Hawthorne researchers, Mayo followed the conventional wisdom of the time and sought a relationship between working conditions and employee output at Continental Mills, a wool textile mill near Philadelphia (Pennsylvania).[26] By introducing rest periods, Mayo was able to reduce employee turnover in the mill's mule-spinning department from 250 to 5 percent, and to improve man-hour efficiency. The rest periods, in Mayo's terms, reduced employees' "pessimistic reveries," hence improving their morale and productivity. By "pessimistic reveries," Mayo meant a specific state of consciousness in which melancholic preoccupations or thoughts are uppermost in an individual's mind and completely overshadow everything else.[27] Mayo considered employee reveries to be a form of mild mental illness or psychopathology encouraged by industrial society.[28] Mayo's research at Continental Mills attracted the attention of Wallace B. Donham, dean of Harvard's Graduate School of Business, to which, in 1926, Mayo was appointed an associate professor of industrial research.

---

[23] Richard Gillespie, *Manufacturing Knowledge: A History of the Hawthorne Experiments* (Cambridge, England: Cambridge University Press, 1991), p. 70. See also Richard C. S. Trahair and Kyle D. Bruce, "Human Relations and Management Consulting: Elton Mayo and Eric Trist," in Matthias Kipping and Timothy Clark, eds., *Oxford Handbook of Management Consulting* (Oxford: Oxford University Press), p. 57.

[24] For a biography of Mayo's life, see Richard C. S. Trahair, *The Humanist Temper: The Life and Work of Elton Mayo* (New Brunswick, NJ: Transaction Books, 1984). See also Lyndall F. Urwick, "Elton Mayo – His Life and Work," in *Papers and Proceedings XIIth International Congress of Scientific Management* (Melbourne: CIOS, 1960), n. p. Reprinted in Arthur G. Bedeian, ed., *Evolution of Management Thought*, vol. 3 (London: Routledge, 2012), pp. 113–136.

[25] Elton Mayo, "The Basis of Industrial Psychology: The Psychology of the Total Situation Is Basic to a Psychology of Management," *Bulletin of the Taylor Society* 9(6) (December 1924), pp. 249–259. See also Elton Mayo, "The Irrational Factor in Human Behavior: The 'Night-Mind' in Industry," *Annals of the American Academy of Political and Social Science* 110 (November 1923), pp. 117–130. For more on Mayo's research on industrial unrest in Australia, see Helen Bourke, "Industrial Unrest as Social Pathology: The Australian Writings of Elton Mayo," *Australian Historical Studies* 20(79) (1982), pp. 217–233.

[26] Elton Mayo, "Revery and Industrial Fatigue," *Personnel Journal* 8 (December 1924), pp. 273–281. See also Robert L. Duffus, "Satisfactory Rest Periods Solve Labor Turnover," *New York Times*, November 16, 1924, p. X8.

[27] George C. Homans, "Report of the Committee," in National Research Council, Committee on Work in Industry, *Fatigue of Workers: Its Relation to Industrial Production* (New York: Reinhold, 1941), p. 71.

[28] Mark A. Griffin, Frank J. Landy, and Lisa Mayocchi, "Australian Influences on Elton Mayo: The Construct of Revery in Industrial Society," *History of Psychology* 5(4) (November 2002), pp. 356–375.

Mayo first visited the Hawthorne plant for 2 days in 1928 and 4 days in 1929, and became more deeply involved in 1930. The 1929 visit, however, was critical for the interviewing program. Mayo felt that "a remarkable change of mental attitude in the group" was the key factor in explaining the Hawthorne puzzle. In his opinion, the relay assemblers had become a social unit, had liked the increased attention they received, and had developed a great deal of pride in being associated with the different studies. According to Mayo, "The most significant change that the Western Electric Company introduced into its 'test room' bore only a casual relation to the experimental changes. What the Company actually did for the group was to reconstruct entirely its whole industrial situation."[29]

To understand a group's "total situation," Mayo felt that a conversational, or nondirective, approach should be used in the interview program. The basic premise of this approach was that a "new" supervisory role was necessary. This role would be one of openness, concern, and willingness to listen. For instance, the Hawthorne researchers had noted that the relay assemblers were "apprehensive of authority," but once the researchers had shown more concern with the assemblers' personal needs, the assemblers lost their shyness and fear, and talked more freely to company officials and observers. Moreover, the assemblers developed a greater zest for work and formed personal friendships, both on and off the job. They began seeing one another socially after working hours, attending parties in one another's homes, and going to the theater together. In sum, the assemblers became a cohesive group that stressed loyalty and cooperation. This seemed to improve their *esprit de corps* and to be closely associated with a friendlier supervisory style, both of which increased productivity. This presumed link between supervision, group spirit, and productivity became the foundation of the so-called "human-relations movement."

Using the nondirective technique Mayo recommended, the Hawthorne interview program allowed employees to express their feelings more freely. An interviewer's job was to keep employees talking, and the average length of employee interviews increased from 30 to 90 minutes. In later follow-up interviews, employees expressed the opinion that working conditions had improved (although they had not changed) and that wages were better (even though the wage scale was the same). In brief the opportunity to let off steam made the employees feel better about their total work situation even though it remained the same.

The complaints gathered in the interviews were thoroughly investigated and found generally to be irrelevant to actual facts. This separation of fact and sentiment led the researchers to distinguish between the *manifest* (material) and *latent* (psychological) content of a complaint. For example, one employee interviewed was preoccupied with the noise, temperature, and fumes in his department. Further examination revealed that his latent concern was the fact that his brother had recently died of pneumonia and the interviewee feared that his own health might be impaired. In another case, complaints about a low piece rate were traced to an employee's concern for medical bills arising from his wife's illness. In essence, "Certain complaints were no longer treated as facts in themselves but as symptoms or indicators of personal or social situations which needed to be explored."[30] From the researchers' viewpoint, workers' preoccupation with personal concerns inhibited their performance, a conclusion that, as noted, Mayo had called "pessimistic reveries" in his early research. The outcome of the interviewing program was supervisory training in the need to listen and understand employees' personal concerns. Supervisors were trained to be interviewers, to listen rather than to talk, and "to exclude from their personal contacts with employees any moral admonition, advice, or emotion."[31]

[29] Elton Mayo, *The Human Problems of an Industrial Civilization* (New York: Macmillan, 1933), p. 73.
[30] Roethlisberger and Dickson, *Management and the Worker*, p. 269.
[31] *Ibid.*, p. 323.

Use of this nondirective interviewing technique enabled supervisors to handle employees' personal concerns more intelligently, to locate factors adversely affecting employee performance, and to remove the events or factors in employees' social or physical environment that were adversely influencing their lives. The "new" supervisor was to be more people-oriented, more concerned, less aloof, and skilled in handling social and personal situations. The product of this human-relations style of management was to be better employee morale, fewer pessimistic reveries, and improved output.

Bank-Wiring Observation Room Study (1931–1932)

Clair Turner wrote Mark L. Putnam, chief of Western's Industrial Research Division, in late 1930 that the mica-splitting study was not yielding useful information and suggested that "we would do well to substitute a test room study group of men" to gain additional insights into what factors influence group output.[32] It was subsequently decided that the entire Bank-Wiring Department would be studied as a "group." The plan for the proposed study, however, took a different turn because of objections by the department's supervisor, Henry S. Wolff, and his fellow supervisors in other departments. They were concerned that the purpose of the proposed study was to increase output, as had happened in the relay-assembly test room, and that this would reflect unfavorably upon the supervisors and current output. William J. Dickson, chief of Hawthorne's employee-relations research department, summarized the supervisors' sentiments:

> They felt that those girls [in the relay-assembly test room] had been given special inducements in the form of a special gang rate, the ordinary production difficulties had been carefully eliminated, and that the operators had been petted and babied along from the start. "Of course," they said, "anybody could get production that way, only we [bank-wiring supervisors] can't get away with things like that."[33]

To overcome the supervisors' concerns, a number of changes were made in the plan for the proposed study: A group of bank-wiring room operators would be segregated in a special area for observation, but visitors would not be allowed; employee earnings would be based on their output as a group, factored into the output of the operators remaining in the regular bank-wiring department; the operators' supervisor would remain the same, and an observer working with the researchers would be kept in the background rather than being "friendly and supportive," as Hibarger had been with the relay assemblers; and workplace layout and procedures would remain constant. In effect, the only similarities to the relay test room would be placing the operators in a separate area and the presence of an observer.

The operators selected for the study were a group of 14 men—9 wiremen, 3 solder men, and 2 inspectors—engaged in assembling terminal banks for use in telephone exchanges. It was clear from early findings that the men constituted a complex social group with well-established norms and a common body of sentiments beyond that formally required by their job. They had their own conception of a "fair day's work" and prevailed as a group upon one another not to exceed this

---

[32] Claire E. Turner to M. L. Putnam, October 13, 1930. Reproduced on Reel 7, Box 17, Folder 3, of the Microfilmed Records of the Industrial Relations Experiment Carried Out by the Western Electric Company at the Hawthorne Works, Hawthorne, IL. Hawthorne Studies Collection, Baker Library, Harvard University Business School, Boston, MA. Although Turner planned these studies, the primary investigator was W. Lloyd Warner, a Harvard University anthropologist who moved to the University of Chicago in 1935. See Dietrich Herzog, *Klassengesellschaft ohne Klassenkonflikt: Eine Studie über William Lloyd Warner und die Entwicklung der neuen amerikanischen Stratifikationsforschung* [*Class Society Without Class Conflict: A Study on William Lloyd Warner and the Development of New American Stratification Research*] (Berlin: Duncker & Humblot, 1965).

[33] William J. Dickson, "Procedure in Establishing Bank Wiring Test Room," undated, but circa mid-July, 1931. Reproduced on Reel 3, Box 7, Folder 1, p.3, of the Microfilmed Records of the Industrial Relations Experiment Carried Out by the Western Electric Company at the Hawthorne Works, Hawthorne, IL. Hawthorne Studies Collection, Baker Library, Harvard University Business School, Boston, MA.

level of output.[34] Operators who exceeded the agreed-upon rate were known as "rate-busters." The operators feared that those who could not keep up with the pace of "rate-busters" would be "bawled out." They also were worried that if the rate-busters' output was adopted as a daily output standard, the *bogey* or "the level of performance which could be sustained by an expert operator at maximum efficiency" would be increased, and they would find themselves having to work harder for the same amount of pay.[35] At the same time, the men strongly believed that an operator's output should not fall too far below the group norm. If it did, an operator was known as a "rate chiseler." Additionally, the operators held that no one should ever say or do anything that would injure a fellow operator. If he did, he was a "squealer." The operators engaged in several practices that violated company policies. For instance, although it was forbidden, the operators frequently traded jobs. There also was a great deal of informal helping among operators, which was also against company policy. Thus, it was important that no one squeal on a fellow operator. Finally, the operators felt that a person should not attempt to maintain social distance. For example, if someone was an inspector, he should not act like one.[36]

The bank-wiring room operators had developed various methods for enforcing their norms. Pressure was executed through subtle forms of ridicule, sarcasm, and *binging*, a practice whereby one operator expressed displeasure with the actions of another by hitting him as hard as possible on the upper arm. Exceeding the accepted output norm would elicit such chastisement, along with taunts of "Speed King" or "The Slave." The virtue of these practices did not lie in the resulting physical pain experienced by an operator, but rather in the mental hurt that came from knowing that one's coworkers disapproved of his behavior.

Discovery of the bank-wiring room operators' "informal organization" and their restriction of output surprised the Hawthorne researchers. Fred Taylor was keenly aware of systematic soldiering and work group pressures; Whiting Williams had recounted his own experiences concerning informal workplace relationships and attitudes; and Stanley Mathewson had made an extensive study of pressures leading to employee restriction of output.[37] Despite the experiences of others, the researchers found it noteworthy that "attention had been called to the fact that social groups in shop departments were capable of exercising very strong control over the work behavior of their individual members."[38] Output restriction was news to the researchers because they claimed to have been "unaware of its implications for management practice and employee satisfaction."[39] Knowledge builds on knowledge, and the failure of the researchers to learn from prior writings on informal-group behavior is a fault that was roundly criticized,[40] although it should not detract from the significance of their findings.

What explained the difference in output between the relay assemblers and the bank-wiring room operators? In the former case, the employees had increased productivity, but in the latter, output restriction was the norm. Both groups included observers working with researchers, but their roles were different. In the relay-assembly study, the observer took the assemblers into his confidence, asked for their suggestions, and encouraged them to participate in decisions affecting their welfare. In the bank-wiring room, however, the observer merely watched while the operators engaged in the same informal behavior they had practiced in the past. The Hawthorne

---

[34] For more on the use of performance incentives at Hawthorne, see Stanley S. Homes, *Extra Incentive Wage Plans Used by the Hawthorne Works of the Western Electric Company, Inc.*, Production Executives' Series, No. 17 (New York: American Management Association, 1925).

[35] William F. Hosford, "Wage Incentive Applications in the Western Electric Company," *N. A. C. A. Bulletin* 12(21) (July 1, 1931), p. 1769.

[36] Roethlisberger and Dickson, *Management and the Worker*, p. 522.

[37] Stanley B. Mathewson, *Restriction of Output among Unorganized Workers* (New York: Viking Press, 1931).

[38] Roethlisberger and Dickson, *Management and the Worker*, p. 379.

[39] *Ibid.*, p. 380.

[40] Mary B. Gilson, [Review of the book *Management and the Worker*]. *American Journal of Sociology* 46(1) (July 1940), pp. 98–101.

researchers' eventual explanation for the output differences would add ammunition to their arguments for a new style of supervision. In explaining the bank-wiring operators' behavior, additional insights for understanding organizations as social systems would be forthcoming.

The Hawthorne researchers found that informal work groups perform two functions: (1) they protect group members from coworker behavior that may be regarded as inappropriate, such as rate busting and chiseling; and (2) they protect employees from employers who would attempt to raise output standards, cut pay rates, or challenge a work group's norms. Informal groups are, in effect, instruments used by employees to control one another's activities and sentiments, as well as to provide protection from the actions of their employers. As discovered in the Hawthorne interview program, in studying group behavior, facts had to be separated from sentiments. To this end, the Hawthorne researchers began to explore the "facts" as perceived by employees, in contrast to company practices as seen by upper management. In regard to output restriction, the researchers concluded that fears of an economic depression and layoffs were not reasons for evading work, because employees restricted output in both good and bad economic times. Restriction was actually detrimental to employees, because it increased unit costs and could, therefore, lead to a decrease in pay rates, an increase in required output, or the introduction of new technology to offset higher costs. Because Western had a long record of enlightened workplace polices and generous employee benefits, the researchers considered the employees' belief that restricting output was in their best interests to be "non-logical," based on a misconception of reality.

Having concluded that mismanagement or general economic conditions were unrelated to informal groups norms, the researchers sought an explanation by viewing the bank-wiring room as part of a larger organization-wide social system, influenced by group sentiments and activities. The researchers reasoned that employees viewed interactions with extra-departmental personnel, such as efficiency experts and other staff members, as disturbing because their actions could impinge on the employees' welfare. These staff members tended to follow the "logic of efficiency," according to which maximizing goods and minimizing costs is the ultimate argument for doing things. Not surprisingly, employees perceived this approach as interfering with their autonomy. Further, supervisors (as a class) represented authority and, thus, possessed power to discipline employees in an effort to enhance output. Recognizing that employees were apprehensive of such authority, the researchers reckoned that employees resisted supervisory attempts to force their behavior into an efficiency mold. Again, the researchers concluded that this was non-logical behavior on the employees' part, but stressed that supervisors and other managers must recognize this phenomenon and take into account employee sentiments when workplace changes are introduced. The Hawthorne researchers thus admonished managers to view every organization as a social system. As they understood, a strict logic of efficiency in administering a technical system would inevitably fail because it omitted the non-logical sentiments of an organization's social system.

Organizations as Social Systems

The work of his Harvard colleague Lawrence J. Henderson and the Italian economist Vilfredo Pareto influenced Elton Mayo's thinking on organizations as social systems. Although Mayo was never a full-fledged Paretian, he did accept many of Pareto's ideas.[41] By contrast, Mayo's student, Fritz J. Roethlisberger, was closer in his general philosophy to Paretian thinking, especially about the structure of social systems. Roethlisberger received an A.B. degree from Columbia University in 1921 and a B.S. from the MIT in 1922. From 1922 to 1924, he was engaged in industrial

---

[41] See, especially, Vilfredo Pareto, *The Mind and Society*, vol. 4: *The General Form of Society*, Trans. Arthur Livingston (New York: Harcourt, Brace and Company, 1935). Originally published in 1916.

practice as a chemical engineer; he then returned to Harvard in 1925 to pursue an M.A. degree. He later joined Harvard's industrial research department and soon became involved in the Hawthorne research.[42]

Roethlisberger and William J. Dickson prepared the most widely read report of the Hawthorne studies, *Management and the Worker*. In this report, the influence of Paretian thinking is clearly evident, especially regarding the structure of social systems. According to Roethlisberger and Dickson, the technical needs for efficiency and economic rate of return should be viewed as inter-related with a concern for the human element found in every organization. Employees have physical needs, but they also have personal needs. These needs arise from early social conditioning and persist in relations with coworkers and other workplace participants. Roethlisberger and Dickson recognized that events and objects in a work environment "cannot be treated as things in themselves. Instead they have to be interpreted as carriers of social value."[43] For example, a physical desk has no social significance; but if individuals who have desks supervise others, then a desk becomes a status symbol and a carrier of social value. Other items, such as type of clothing, age, gender, and seniority, can also take on social significance. Roethlisberger and Dickson concluded that because individuals are not governed by facts and logic, sentiments about events and objects in a work environment must be considered when dealing with employees, and with people in general.

Roethlisberger and Dickson recognized that when an organization's formal structure (with its rules, policies, and procedures) clashes with norms of its members' informal groups, there will invariably be trade-offs and conflict. They stressed, however, that such informal groups should not be viewed as "bad," but as an inevitable aspect of the social system within a formal organization. Viewing an organization as a social system enables managers to balance the "logic of efficiency" demanded by formal rules, policies, and procedures and the "logic of sentiments" that is the basis for informal groups.[44] Thus, Roethlisberger and Dickson held that managers must strive to achieve equilibrium between an organization's technical and human requirements. It, thus, follows that, in order to survive, an organization must secure its economic goals in such a way that "individuals through contributing services to this common purpose obtain personal satisfaction that makes them willing to cooperate."[45]

In short, the outcome of the Hawthorne studies was a call for an additional set of managerial skills. Technical skills alone were insufficient to cope with the employee sentiments and behavior discovered at Hawthorne. A second set of skills was required: first, diagnostic skills in understanding human behavior, and second, interpersonal skills in counseling, motivating, leading, and communicating with employees. The economic logic of efficiency must be balanced with an appreciation for the full-range of employee sentiments.

Human Relations, Leadership, and Motivation

Over the intervening years, interpreting what happened at Hawthorne has become part of an evolving story. In particular, a phenomenon known as the *Hawthorne Effect* has long been part of social-science folklore. As noted above, one of the early explanations offered for the relay

---

[42] Fritz. J. Roethlisberger, *The Elusive Phenomena*. George F. F. Lombard, ed., (Cambridge, MA: Harvard University Press, 1977). See also George F. F. Lombard, ed., *The Contributions of F. J. Roethlisberger to Management Theory and Practice* (Cambridge, MA: Graduate School of Business, Harvard University, 1976).

[43] Roethlisberger and Dickson, *Management and the Worker*, p. 557.

[44] *Ibid.*, pp. 556–564. "Logic of sentiments" is actually a contradiction because Roethlisberger and Dickson concluded that sentiments were "non-logical."

[45] *Ibid.*, p. 569. The authors acknowledged their indebtedness to Chester I. Barnard (who is discussed in the next chapter) for this distinction.

assemblers' increased output was the increased attention they received. The researchers removed the assemblers from their regular department, placed them in a test room, and assumed a new supervisory style. The use of less stringent controls created a new social situation for the relay assemblers. The assemblers were advised and consulted about changes, their views were listened to sympathetically, and their physical and mental health became matters of great concern to the researchers and company officials. As they progressed, the Hawthorne Studies became less of a controlled investigation, and more a series of exercises in creating a social environment that encouraged employees to freely air their concerns, and to establish new interpersonal bonds with each other and with their supervisors.

The relay assemblers, in particular, felt they were part of something special and showed a great deal of pride in being associated with the different studies. Viewed psychologically, the assemblers had become ego-involved in their work. These changes have prompted the charge that the researchers' actions—indeed, their very presence—altered the situation they hoped to investigate and, thus, tainted their findings. In particular, it has been suggested that the increase in assemblers' productivity was a result of being singled out and made to feel important. Variously defined, the central idea behind the "Hawthorne effect," a term coined by Harvard-trained psychologist John R. P. French, is that changes in participants' behavior during the course of a study may be "related only to the special social position and social treatment they received" rather than a hypothesized cause or influence.[46] As a consequence, this "specialness" becomes "confounded with the independent variable under study, with a subsequent facilitating effect on the dependent variable, thus leading to ambiguous results."[47] Mayo recognized this phenomenon early on, writing: "Apparently the greater personal interest, together with the release from dominating supervision, was far more important than wage incentive, length of working day, rest periods, and similar factors" in explaining the assemblers' behavior.[48] As Roethlisberger further acknowledged, "If a human being is being experimented upon, he is likely to know it. Therefore, his attitudes toward the experiment and the experimenters become very important factors in determining his responses to the situation."[49]

Was there a Hawthorne Effect that biased the studies' results? Did the rise in the relay assemblers' output occur because they were being observed and had gained near celebrity status? Theresa Layman, one of the relay assemblers, recalled, "No, we kept working. It didn't matter who watched us or who talked with us." Donald Chipman, who succeeded Hibarger as the test room's observer, recalled, "I agree . . . early in the study it had some bearing but . . . that just wore off."[50] Clair Turner stated, "We at first thought that the novelty of test room conditions might be partly responsible for increased output but the continuing increase in production over a four-year period suggests it was not of great importance."[51] A survey of industrial/organizational and organizational behavior textbooks has concluded: "mythical beliefs among students about the Hawthorne Studies . . . [and] the Hawthorne Effect [are] probably an unfortunate tradition."[52] Although the Hawthorne Effect is widely referenced, there remains considerable doubt that being observed had any continuing impact on participants' performance.[53]

---

[46] John. R. P. French, Jr., "Field Experiments: Changing Group Productivity," in James G. Miller, ed., *Experiments in Social Process: A Symposium on Social Psychology* (New York: McGraw-Hill, 1950), p. 82.

[47] Desmond L. Cook, "The Hawthorne Effect in Educational Research," *Phi Delta Kappan* 44(3) (December 1962), p. 118. Italics omitted.

[48] Elton Mayo, "Psychology and Industry: The Problem of Working Together," in Walter V. Bingham, ed., *Psychology Today: Lectures and Study Manual* (Chicago, IL: University of Chicago Press, 1932), Appendix, p. 23.

[49] Fritz J. Roethlisberger, *Management and Morale* (Cambridge, MA: Harvard University Press, 1942), p. 14.

[50] Greenwood, Bolton, and Greenwood, "Hawthorne," p. 223.

[51] Turner, "Test Room Studies," p. 584.

[52] Ryan Olson, Jessica Verley, Lindsey Santos, and Coresta Salas, "What We Teach Students about the Hawthorne Studies: A Review of Content within a Sample of Introductory I-O and OB Textbooks," *The Industrial-Organizational Psychologist* 41(3) (January 2004), pp. 34–35. See also Charles D. Wrege and Arthur G. Bedeian, ". . . thumbs down for the Hawthorne effect," *The Psychologist* 21(11) (November 2008), p. 990.

[53] Stephen R. G. Jones, "Was There a Hawthorne Effect?" *American Journal of Sociology* 98(3) (November 1992), pp. 451–468.

Human Relations and Human Collaboration

As the economic depression that followed the October 1929 Wall Street stock-market crash (see Chapter 18) deepened, hours of work at Hawthorne were reduced and the original relay-assembly test-room study was discontinued. With the passage of time, Mayo changed his interpretation of what happened at Hawthorne.[54] As early as October 1931, he began to emphasize the need for "effective collaboration" and a restoration of "social solidarity" in a changing world that left people without stability, purpose, or norms. When Mayo began to elaborate on his social philosophy, he gained a wider audience. Both academics and business leaders were attracted to his view that employee unrest and political dissidence were symptoms of psychopathology caused by an unsuitable work environment. By contrast, the views of Clair Turner, who had been more involved at Hawthorne on a day-to-day basis, became less influential in explaining the studies' results. Thus, MIT's star waned, and Harvard's waxed. As Roethlisberger recalled, "Mayo was an adventurer in the realm of ideas . . . the [Hawthorne] data were not his; the results were not his; but the interpretations of what the results meant and the new questions and hypotheses that emerged from them were his."[55]

Mayo's education and experiences suggest the basis for his emerging interpretation of human behavior. As noted, for a short time Mayo studied medicine, and though he never received a medical degree, he developed an interest in psychopathology. At that time, individuals such as Jean-Martin Charcot, a French neurologist; Carl G. Jung, a Swiss psychiatrist; Pierre M. F. Janet, a French psychologist; and Sigmund Freud, the Austrian originator of psychoanalysis were in the vanguard of analyzing psychopathological thought. The works of Janet especially intrigued Mayo. His last book was devoted to a critique of Janet's theories of obsessive thinking.[56] Janet believed that obsessive thinking was the primary mental disorder among trauma patients. Freudians called this compulsion. Mayo viewed Janet's theories of obsessive thinking and Freud's views on compulsive disorders to be complementary.[57] The essence of Mayo's obsession-compulsion interpretation was that individuals were incapacitated by their obsessions to such a degree that they were inflexible in their responses to life, including their personal, social, and workplace behavior. With respect to work, Mayo maintained that obsessions reduced an individual's general life satisfaction, which then led to decreased productivity and increased turnover and absenteeism.

Although Mayo never once concluded that any large number of Hawthorne employees suffered from severe trauma sufferers, he did think that the company's interview program had demonstrated that minimal levels of obsession (or preoccupation) existed in the sense that "conditions of work tended in some way to prevent rather than facilitate a satisfactory personal adaptation."[58] In Mayo's view, some employees are unable to find satisfactory outlets for expressing personal concerns and dissatisfactions in their work life. He believed that blockage resulted in "pessimistic reveries" and preoccupations with personal concerns at a latent level, which are manifest as an apprehension of authority, output restriction, and a variety of other behaviors that reduce morale and productivity. Mayo contended that the technical requirements necessary for people to work together cause a sense of personal futility, which leads to social maladjustment and, eventually, to obsessive, irrational behavior. As he explained:

> Human collaboration in work, in primitive and developed societies, has always depended for its perpetuation upon the evolution of a non-logical social code which regulates the relations between persons and their attitudes to one another. Insistence upon a merely economic logic of

---

[54] Trahair, *Humanist Temper*, p. 254.

[55] Roethlisberger, *Elusive Phenomena*, pp. 50–51.

[56] Elton Mayo, *Some Notes on the Psychology of Pierre Janet* (Cambridge, MA: Harvard University Press, 1948). See also Yeh Hsueh, "The Hawthorne Experiments and the Introduction of Jean Piaget in American Industrial Psychology, 1929–1932." *History of Psychology* 5(2) (May 2002), pp. 163–189.

[57] Mayo, *Human Problems of an Industrial Civilization*, pp. 107–110.

[58] *Ibid.*, p. 114.

production . . . interferes with the development of such a code and consequently gives rise in the group to a sense of human defeat. This human defeat results in the formation of a social code at a lower level and in opposition to the economic logic. One of its symptoms is "restriction."[59]

Based on the belief that the technical requirements necessary for people to work together cause a sense of personal futility, which leads to social maladjustment and, eventually, to obsessive, irrational behavior, Mayo and Roethlisberger formed the philosophical rationale for the human-relations movement. The movement's goal was the restoration of a social code to facilitate effective human collaboration in both work and life by balancing an organization's economic goals and its employees' personal needs.

Anomie and Social Disorganization

Mayo borrowed Émile Durkheim's term *anomie* (from the Greek word meaning "without norms") as a basis for his thinking about effective workplace collaboration.[60] Durkheim used the term to refer to a sense of normlessness that leads some individuals to feel disconnected from society.[61] According to Durkheim, in traditional societies, individuals interacted within a close-knit community that shared common sentiments and values. There was a social solidarity, built around family and kinship, which gave individuals (who often performed the same job throughout their lives) a work identity as well as a personal identity in their social life. The onset of the Industrial Revolution destroyed this solidarity through a greater division of labor, increased social and physical mobility, and the growth of large-scale organizations in which the manner of dealing with interpersonal relations shifted from a personal to an impersonal base. The result was a normless and rootless mode of life in which individual identities were lost along with the social bonds that gave continuity and purpose to human existence. This led to personal and social disorganization and a general overall sense of futility, defeat, and disillusionment. Social inventions to cope with industrial changes had not kept pace with technological developments. Thus, the rapid economic growth experienced by the United States both before and after the turn of the century had disturbed "communal integrity."

Mayo argued that an increasingly technically oriented society placed undue emphasis on engineering and yielded a technological interpretation for the meaning of work, in the sense that achievement was based on a logic of efficiency. The social needs of individuals were pushed into the background, thereby reducing their "capacity for collaboration in work."[62] An emphasis on a logic of efficiency stifled individuals' desire for group approval, social satisfaction, and social purpose gained through communal life. Drawing on Pareto's concept of an economic *élite*, composed of property owners and entrepreneurs, Mayo championed the creation of an administrative or managerial *élite* that was not only technically oriented but who also understood human nature.[63] He hoped that this *élite* would restore a social code to facilitate effective human collaboration in both work and life by balancing an organization's economic goals and its employees' personal needs. As envisioned by Mayo, managers could aid in accomplishing this goal by receiving training in the human and social aspects of workplace behavior, developing listening and counseling skills, and recognizing and understanding the non-logical social code that regulates the relation between persons and their attitudes to one another. The difficulty, as Mayo perceived it, was that managers thought the answer to effective human collaboration resided solely in technical efficiency, when in fact the challenges they faced were also social and human.

---

[59] *Ibid.*, pp. 120–121.
[60] *Ibid.*, p. 129.
[61] Émile Durkheim, *Le suicide: étude de sociologie* [*Suicide: A Sociological Study*] (Paris: F. Alcan, 1897), p. 363.
[62] Mayo, *Human Problems of an Industrial Civilization*, p. 166.
[63] *Ibid.*, p. 177.

Developing the Human-Relations-Oriented Manager

Elton Mayo and Fred Taylor espoused the same goal: collaboration and cooperation in industry. Although the means they advocated differed, they both believed the employee–employer relationship should be mutually beneficial. Mayo, however, went further in arguing that the notion of unitary authority from a central source (be it government, church, or industrial leaders) should be abandoned. Drawing heavily from Chester I. Barnard (see Chapter 14), Mayo concluded that authority used in securing cooperation should be based on human-relations skills rather than on technical skill or expertise. The human-relations-oriented manager would act as an investigator of employee sentiments so as to further collaborative efforts for achieving mutual goals. Because people spent so much time in groups and derived much of their satisfaction from working together, Mayo felt that managers should focus on maintaining group integrity and social solidarity. Groups were the universal solvent, and it was a manager's task to find the universal container.

First-line supervisors, management's most immediate contact with operative employees, played a particularly crucial role in maintaining group integrity and social solidarity. In the bank-wiring observation room, for example, the work-group supervisor did not try to force operators to wire 7,312 terminals a day (the "bogey"), but accepted the average of 6,000–6,600. The supervisor's dilemma was explained in an interim program report:

> In such circumstances the first line supervisor finds himself in a conflict situation. He can do either of two things; uphold the system of ideas common to management and attempt by driving or other methods to enforce them, or take the side of the workmen and conceal the true situation from his superiors. In the test room the Group Chief has seen fit to side with the workmen, and perhaps rightly. It is quite likely that by opposing them he would only aggravate the situation.[64]

Roethlisberger described first-line supervisors ("foremen") as standing in the middle of "two contrasting worlds," subject to conflicting pressures from other managers above and operative employees below.[65] As such, they are necessarily disadvantaged in securing the employee–employer collaboration Mayo envisioned. The situation, as Mayo perceived it, is worse when supervisors believe in a strict logic of efficiency, failing to recognize that the challenges they face are also social and human. Mayo believed that the answer to preparing managers (at all levels) for their new human-relations role was twofold: train them (1) to understand their subordinates' nonlogical sentiments and (2) how to maintain an equilibrium between an organization's economic goals and its employees' personal needs. For Mayo, achieving this equilibrium was the key to workplace effectiveness. This was the new leadership, one that balanced the economic logic of efficiency with an appreciation for the full range of employee sentiments. Later research conducted at the University of Michigan and at Ohio State University would confirm that effective leadership combines a concern for both production and people (see Chapter 15).

Human Relations and Motivation

As we will see in Chapter 17, how the human-relations-oriented manager motivated people became a controversial subject. Early reports of the Hawthorne studies gave some credence to the conclusion that changing to a small-group incentive payment plan was one factor in explaining

---

[64] Arthur C. Moore and William J. Dickson, "Report on Bank Wiring Test Group for the Period November 9, 1931 to March 18, 1932," March 21, 1932. Reproduced on Reel 3, Box 7, Folder 3, of the Microfilmed Records of the Industrial Relations Experiment Carried Out by the Western Electric Company at the Hawthorne Works, Hawthorne, IL. Hawthorne Studies Collection, Baker Library, Harvard University Business School, Boston, MA.

[65] Fritz J. Roethlisberger, "The Foreman: Master and Victim of Double Talk," *Harvard Business Review* 23(3) (Spring 1945), p. 290.

the increased output in the relay-assembly test room. Mark L. Putnam, chief of Western's Industrial Research Division, told *Business Week* that pay was the number one concern expressed by Hawthorne employees during interviews in 1930.[66] When the assemblers were asked what they liked in the relay-assembly test room, one responded, "*We made more money in the Test Room.*"[67] A November 12, 1930, memo to Mayo from his Harvard colleague Richard S. Meriam underscores this point: "Economic and financial factors are of considerable importance in the test room. The employees are anxious for high earnings. The test room has apparently removed the doubt in the employees' minds that the company would permit them to make very high earnings."[68] The evidence regarding economic incentives and output at Hawthorne was available, but the published results took on an alternative interpretation.[69]

There is evidence that Mayo's writings and, in turn, his influence on Roethlisberger and Dickson in preparing the most widely read report on the Hawthorne studies resulted in a different interpretation of what happened at Hawthorne. An early indication of Mayo's view is revealed in a memo written by Roethlisberger in which he reported that there appeared to be a significant relationship between physiological factors and output. According to Roethlisberger, this made Mayo very happy because "it looked as if the organization of the girls in the test room was more conditioned by biological factors rather than anything as naive as economic incentive. As this fits in with what Mayo has been saying for the last five years we were very pleased."[70]

In *Management and the Worker*, Roethlisberger and Dickson state that the "efficacy of the wage incentive was so dependent on its relation to other factors that it was impossible to consider it as in itself having an independent effect on the individual."[71] That is, pay for performance was only one factor that could not be addressed separately. As time went on, Roethlisberger mentioned other factors that explained human motivation:

> Whether or not a person is going to give his services whole-heartedly to a group depends, in good part, on the way he feels about his job, his fellow workers, and supervisors . . . [a person wants] . . . social recognition . . . tangible evidence of . . . social importance . . . the feeling of security that comes not so much from the amount of money we have in the bank as from being an accepted member of a group.[72]

Still later it appears that the notion of the "economic man" was discarded:

> Far from being the prime and sole mover of human activity in business, economic interest has run far behind in the list of incentives that make men willing to work . . . man at work is a social creature as well as an "economic man." He has personal and social as well as economic needs. Work provides him with a way of life as well as a means of livelihood . . . As we discarded the notion of "economic man," we began to question the concept of business organization as merely a logical organization of operations for the efficient production of goods.[73]

[66] "Human Factor in Production Subject of Unique Research," *Business Week,* January 21, 1931, p. 16.

[67] Greenwood, Bolton, and Greenwood, "Hawthorne," p. 220.

[68] Richard S. Meriam to Elton Mayo, November 12, 1930, Elton Mayo Papers, Folder 3, Baker Library, Graduate School of Business Administration, Harvard University, Boston. Quoted in Charles D. Wrege, "Review of 'Why the Hawthorne Myth Dies Hard: A Case Study of Class Bias in Psychology'," addressed to William Bevan (Editor, *American Psychologist*), August 1, 1979, p. 15, Charles D. Wrege Research Papers, 1925–2013, Box 4, Folder 23, Kheel Center for Labor-Management Documentation and Archives, Cornell University.

[69] See, for example, Stuart Chase, "What Makes the Worker Like to Work?" *Reader's Digest* 38 (February 1941), pp. 15–20.

[70] Fritz J. Roethlisberger to Emily Osborne, April 5, 1932, F. J. Roethlisberger Papers, Folder 1, Baker Library, Graduate School of Business Administration, Harvard University, Boston, quoted in Richard Gillespie, *Manufacturing Knowledge,* p. 88.

[71] Roethlisberger and Dickson, *Management and the Worker,* p. 160.

[72] Roethlisberger, *Management and Morale,* pp. 15, 24–25.

[73] Fritz J. Roethlisberger, "A 'New Look' for Management," *Worker Morale and Productivity*, General Management Series, no. 141 (New York: American Management Association, 1948), pp. 12–13, 16.

What was the human relationists' view of motivation? In early reports, employees were quoted to the effect that they worked harder because "they made more money" or that pay was their "number one" concern. As Roethlisberger and Mayo examined the Hawthorne data, however, the importance of financial incentives faded. In brief, the Hawthorne studies have been subjected to so much manipulation and misinterpretation that their actual results are clouded in myth and advocacy.[74] Mayo wanted to promote employee–employer collaboration, not pay for performance, and it would require a later generation of scholars to iterate that the social person supplemented, but did not supplant, economic man.

SUMMARY

In addition to challenging many prevailing assumptions of the day, the Hawthorne studies immeasurably increased our knowledge and understanding of employee attitudes and motivations.[75] As a result of the Hawthorne studies,

- It became clear that employees are not motivated solely by money. The importance of personal and social factors in motivation and employee attitudes (toward every aspect of their work) was revealed.

- The importance of individual attitudes in determining employee behavior became undeniable.

- The significance of effective supervision in maintaining employee job satisfaction and productivity became indisputable.

The Hawthorne studies were an intellectual gold mine, forever altering the landscape of management theory and practice. Their contribution to the growth and development of the human-relations approach can hardly be overstated. As though responding to Taylor's plea for a "study of the motives which influence men" (see Chapter 7), the Hawthorne researchers systematically explored the nature and content of the human element found in every organization. By testing hypothetical assertions about the basis of work rather than allowing their unquestioned acceptance, the Hawthorne researchers pioneered a course of investigation that is still being pursued today. Critics note that, by current standards, the Hawthorne studies were unscientific; that is, many of the Hawthorne researchers' conclusions did not necessarily follow from the available evidence. These and other criticisms will be considered in Chapter 17.

---

[74] Lyle Yorks and David A. Whitsett, "Hawthorne, Topeka, and the Issue of Science versus Advocacy in Organizational Behavior," *Academy of Management Review* 10(1) (January 1985), pp. 21–30.
[75] William J. Dickinson, "Hawthorne Experiments," in Carl Heyel, ed., *The Encyclopedia of Management*, 2nd. ed. (New York: Van Nostrand Reinhold, 1973), p. 301.

The Search for Organizational Integration

Interest in organizations as social systems was stimulated by the Hawthorne Studies and would continue to grow as the social-person era unfolded. This chapter discusses the lives and thoughts of two individuals who, though separated in time, significantly contributed to our understanding of authority and responsibility, the need to coordinate effort, conflict resolution, and how to design organizations for maximum effectiveness and efficiency. One was a political philosopher turned business sage who never met a payroll in her life; the other, a telephone-company executive whose hobbies were classical piano and the works of Johann Sebastian Bach. Together, they were integrators who bridged the scientific-management and the social-person eras.

Mary P. Follett: The Political Philosopher

Born in Quincy, Massachusetts, in 1868, Mary Parker Follett had a difficult early life. Her father, an alcoholic, died young; her mother was inclined to social rather than practical matters.[1] A respectable inheritance from her maternal grandfather provided sustenance, while Follett

---

[1] The definitive biography of Follett is Joan C. Tonn, *Mary P. Follett: Creating Democracy, Transforming Management* (New Haven, CT: Yale University Press, 2003).

found intellectual uplift in reading and education. She attended Thayer Academy, a preparatory school for college-bound students located in Braintree, Massachusetts. At Thayer, she found a mentor in Anna Boynton Thompson, her history teacher. Thompson introduced Follett to the German Idealist School of Philosophy, including the works of Johann Fichte and Georg W. F. Hegel. Later Follett would tell classical scholar F. Melian Stawell:

> One of these [businessmen] gave me in a nutshell the threads of a tangle he had with his employees. He wanted me to straighten it out. I answered him straight out of Fichte: he didn't know that of course, but I did, and it seemed to meet the case.[2]

After graduating from Thayer Academy in 1883, Follett continued her studies at the Harvard University Annex for female students (renamed Radcliffe College in 1894), where she expanded her interests in philosophy and history to include psychology, especially the emerging Gestalt movement, which led her to think in patterns or wholes. Thompson encouraged Follett to interrupt her studies at the Annex to attend classes at Newnham College, Cambridge University, in England, where Follett's interests extended into law, political science, and government. While at Cambridge, she continued to do research for her first book, *The Speaker of the House of Representatives*. Still considered one of the most insightful analyses of the speaker's role, the book established her reputation as a political philosopher and drew her into Boston's intellectual life.[3] Two years after the book's publication in 1896, Follett received her A.B. degree from Radcliffe College.

Mary Parker Follett. Vice President, National Community Service Association.

John Collier, "The Crisis of Democracy," *The Community Center: The Magazine of the National Community Center Association* 1(5) (June 1917), p. 1.

With academic opportunities limited for women, she spent most of her early years working with various community-service groups to provide vocational guidance, education, recreation, and job-placement assistance for the less fortunate among Boston's youth. In these largely volunteer organizations, operating with little or no formal warrant, she realized that there was a need to rethink prevailing views on authority and responsibility, organization, leadership, and conflict resolution. In observing and working with different service organizations, she gained an understanding of group dynamics and the importance of teamwork. Through her involvement with the Boston Placement Bureau, she met with an array of business leaders and became active in the Taylor Society in the period following Taylor's death. Chronologically, Follett belonged to the scientific-management era; philosophically and intellectually, she was a member of the social-person era. Her work served as a link between these eras by building on the principles of scientific management while anticipating many of the ideas that would become associated with the later human-relations movement.

The Group Principle

Reflecting the influence of Gestalt theory, the basis of Follett's thinking was the "whole man" and, in particular, the relation between "whole men" within groups. From her reading in philosophy, psychology, political science, and law, and her understanding of Fichte, about whom her mentor

---

[2] Mary P. Follett quoted in F. Melian Stawell, "Mary Parker Follett," *Newnham College Roll Letter* [Cambridge University] (1935), p. 43.
[3] Mary P. Follett, *The Speaker of the House of Representatives* (New York: Longmans, Green, 1896).

Anna Thompson had written a book,[4] Follett developed what she dubbed "the group principle." Fichte espoused a nationalism in which freedom of individuals was subordinated to group interests. He believed that individuals could not escape the influence of their social world and that, by extension, their ego belonged to a wider plurality or community of egos. Fichte further supposed the existence of a Great Ego that willed the common world in which we all live.[5]

In her second book, *The New State: Group Organization the Solution of Popular Government*, published in 1918, Follett explained that the essence of what she termed the "group principle" was to bring out individual differences and integrate them into a single whole. She quoted the sixth-century BCE Greek philosopher Heraclitus of Ephesus, who said: "Nature desires eagerly opposites and out of them it completes its harmony, not out of similars."[6] In Heraclitus's philosophy of "Everything is in flux," the Hegelian logic or dialectic of "thesis, antithesis, and synthesis" found expression. Follett was never a full Hegelian and felt those who interpreted Hegel's ideas to mean that the state was "above and beyond" individual citizens misunderstood his logic. As she further explained:

> When we say that there is the One which comes *from* the Many, this does not mean that the One is *above* the Many. The deepest truth of life is that the interrelating by which both are at the same time a-making is constant.[7]

This vague jargon of "interrelating" and "a-making" would form Follett's notion of "circular response." Building on these and other ideas, Follett challenged the prevailing political assumptions of the period. She believed that "We find the true man only through group organization. The potentialities of the individual remain potentialities until they are released by group life. Man discovers his true nature, gains his true freedom only through the group."[8]

Follett's group principle was to be the "new" psychology and renounced the established belief that individuals thought, felt, and acted independently. She held that groups and individuals come into existence simultaneously and believed that with "group-man appear group-rights."[9] This view demonstrated Follett's acceptance of the Gestalt movement, and reflected Charles H. Cooley's "looking-glass self" (the idea that the self arises reflectively in reaction to the opinions of others) and the realization that one's self is embedded in one's work group as a primary social unit of importance (see Chapter 9).[10] Using phrases such as "togetherness," "group thinking," and "the collective will," Follett sought a new society based on groups and not individuals.

Follett's underlying premise was that only through group membership could individuals find their "true self." Based on her group principle, Follett concluded that an individual's "true self is the group-self" and that "man can have no rights apart from society or independent of society or against society."[11] In opposing the notion that the purpose of government is to protect individual rights, she proposed a new concept of democracy: "Democracy then is a great spiritual force evolving itself from men, utilizing each, completing his incompleteness by weaving together all in the many-membered community life which is the true Theophany."[12]

---

[4] Anna Boynton Thompson, *The Unity of Fichte's Doctrine of Knowledge* (Boston, MA: Ginn, 1895).

[5] Henry D. Aiken, *The Age of Ideology: The Nineteenth Century Philosophers* (Boston, MA: Houghton Mifflin, 1957), pp. 54–60. Fichte was a disciple of Immanuel Kant and in his early years followed Kantian notions of rationalism and the absolutely inalienable rights of the individual. In his later years, Fichte broke with Kant, turned to nationalism and statism, and became part of the romantic revolt against reason.

[6] Mary Parker Follett, *The New State: Group Organization the Solution of Popular Government* (London: Longmans, Green, 1918), p. 34n.

[7] *Ibid.*, p. 284.

[8] *Ibid.*, p. 6.

[9] *Ibid.*, p. 137.

[10] Charles H. Cooley, *Human Nature and the Social Order* (New York: Charles Scribner's Sons, 1902), p. 152.

[11] Follett, *The New State*, p. 137.

[12] *Ibid.*, p. 161. *Theophany* is the visible manifestation of a deity to a human.

Follett felt that "the theory of government based on individual rights no longer has a place in modern political theory."[13] In its stead, a collectivistic democracy was to be built, moving in succession from small neighborhood groups to community groups, to state groups, to a national group, and, eventually, to a common international-group will, reminiscent of Fichte's Great Ego. Setting aside the issue of potential group conflicts, Follett had faith that society could grow a new "social consciousness" and that individuals could live together peaceably in what she dubbed "The World State."[14] She had little confidence in "ballot-box democracy," believing that it reflected crowd psychology and defined "right" by the sheer weight of numbers.

Conflict Resolution

In her third book, *Creative Experience*, Follett developed the idea that through conferences, discussions, and cooperation, individuals could evoke each other's latent ideas and make manifest their unity in pursuit of common goals. Relying heavily on Gestalt theory, which held that every psychological situation has a specific character apart from the absolute nature of its component parts, she felt that through group experiences individuals could achieve a greater unleashing of their creative powers.[15] As viewed by Follett, the goal of group effort was an integrative unity that transcended its component parts. In essence, she was beginning to examine the issue of potential group conflicts that she had not addressed in *The New State*. Follett believed that confronting conflicts would result in one of the following four outcomes: "(1) voluntary submission of one side; (2) struggle and the victory of one side over the other; (3) compromise; or (4) integration."[16] The first and second outcomes were clearly unacceptable because the use of force or power led to strife. Compromise was likewise futile because it postponed rather than resolved an issue and because the "truth does not lie 'between' the two sides."[17] Integration involved finding a solution that satisfied both sides without compromise or domination. One illustration of what Follett meant by integration came from a friend who was involved in the paper industry:

> At a meeting of our manufacturing committee recently the following question came up. Our paper had been six cents, and the competing firm reduced their price to five and three-quarters. We then cut to five and a half and they replied with a price of five and a quarter. The question before us then was whether or not we should make a further reduction. Part were in favor; part, against. The solution came when something quite different was suggested: that we should stand for a higher quality of paper and make an appropriate price for it.[18]

Although Follett realized integration was not an option in all instances, she felt it was a viable alternative more often than might be assumed. As Fox explains:

> She . . . insisted that although integration is not possible in every case, it *is* possible in more cases than we realize. And perhaps if it is not possible now, it will be later. . . . The important thing is to work for something better. . . . We need not be afraid of difference, but rather should welcome it as the opportunity for new social creation. She gave us a theory of human interaction that shows how the same factors that cause change also provide the means for solving the problems presented by change, a theory that tells us that the possibilities for the healthy resolution of conflict is part of the natural process of human intercourse.[19]

---

[13] *Ibid.*, p. 172.
[14] *Ibid.*, pp. 344–360.
[15] Mary P. Follett, *Creative Experience* (London: Longmans, Green: 1924), pp. 91–116.
[16] *Ibid.*, p. 156.
[17] *Ibid.*
[18] *Ibid.*, p. 158.
[19] Elliot M. Fox, "Mary Parker Follett: The Enduring Contribution," *Public Administration Review* 28(6) (November–December 1968), p. 528.

Follett's single-minded search for integrative unity, for commonality of will, and for human cooperation established her reputation as a political philosopher. By 1924, however, her interest in political science had waned, replaced by a growing fascination with the result-oriented world of business. As she noted, political science "did not seem really to come to grips with our [present] problems." In turning to the business world and business executives, Follett explained: "*There* I found hope for the future. *There* men were not theorizing or dogmatizing; they were thinking of what they had actually done and they were willing to try new ways."[20] In January 1925, Follett gave the first of a series of four lectures in New York City under the auspices of the Bureau of Personnel Administration, which was dedicated to advancing sound employer–employee relations. Beginning with these lectures, Follett made the transition from a political scientist to a business philosopher.

A Business Philosopher

Viewing management as a universal activity, Follett understood how the principles that apply in the political sphere necessarily apply to business as well. The same challenges of achieving unity of effort, defining authority and responsibility, resolving conflict, exhibiting leadership, and so on exist in both politics and business. Drawing on this understanding, Follett pushed ahead into the business world. First, from her book *Creative Experience*, she extended her thinking on "constructive conflict" and achieving unity of effort. Because domination and compromise, as methods of conflict resolution, led to strife, Follett held that integration, as a means for confronting contrasting interests, should be paramount in all business affairs. In dealing with labor, she deplored the notion of collective bargaining, because it rested on a relative balance of power and inevitably ended in compromise. Bargaining meant that there were competing interests, and in their effort to gain at each other's expense the confronting sides would likely lose sight of what they held in common. In labor–management negotiations, for example, when pro-labor or pro-management positions solidified, Follett noted that the confronting parties often failed to appreciate that they were partners in a common endeavor, for which they had joint responsibilities. She felt that collective responsibility should begin with group responsibility, wherein employees are involved as partners in shaping workplace policies. Speaking to executives at the Bureau of Personnel Administration, she explained:

> When you have made your employees feel that they are in some sense partners in the business, they do not improve the quality of their work, save waste in time and material, because of the Golden Rule, but because their interests are the same as yours.[21]

In Follett's view, this was not to be a reciprocal back-scratching arrangement, but a true feeling on the part of both labor and management that they serve a common purpose. She believed that in the past an artificial line had been drawn between those who managed and those who were managed. In reality, there was no line, and all members of an organization who accepted responsibility for work at any level contributed to what she called a "functional whole or integrative unity":

> [L]abor and capital can never be reconciled as long as labor persists in thinking that there is a capitalist point of view and capitalists that there is a labor point of view. There is not. These are imaginary wholes which must be broken up before capital and labor can cö-operate.[22]

---

[20] Mary P. Follett quoted in Lyndall F. Urwick, "Great Names in Management: Mary Parker Follett, 1868–1933," unpublished speech, University of New South Wales, Kensington, Sydney, Australia, June 14, 1967, p. 3.
[21] Mary P. Follett, "The Psychological Foundations: Business as an Integrative Unity," in Henry C. Metcalf, ed., *Scientific Foundations of Business Administration* (Baltimore, MD: Williams & Wilkins, 1926), p. 160.
[22] Follett, *Creative Experience,* pp. 167–168.

Follett's "principle of integrative unity" involves finding solutions that satisfy all parties, without domination, surrender, or compromise. It calls for confronting sides to rethink their relationship and to openly share information, to avoid win–lose quick fixes, to be creative in examining differences from multiple angles, and to see difficulties as "ours" and not "yours." To Follett, for conflict to be constructive, it required respect, understanding, talking it through, and creating win–win solutions.

Beyond viewing a business as a working unit, Follett felt that both labor and management should recognize their interrelationships with creditors, stockholders, customers, competitors, suppliers, and society in general. This wider perspective would encourage seeing society and the larger economy as working together rather than as a "congeries of separate pieces." For Follett, integration was a principle applicable to all aspects of life.

Authority, Responsibility, and Power

Follett reasoned that integration, as a principle of conduct, would be less than fully effective unless people rethought their concepts of authority, responsibility, and power. In this third area, Follett sought to develop "power-with" instead of "power-over," and "co-action" to replace consent and coercion. She realized that with both an "order giver" and an "order taker," integration would be difficult to achieve, as the notions of "boss" and "subordinate" created barriers to recognizing common interests. To overcome this difficulty, Follett proposed depersonalizing orders and shifting obedience to the "law of the situation, referring to the necessity of acting in accord with the unique requirements inherent in any situation": "One *person* should not give orders to another *person*, but both should agree to take their orders from the situation."[23] She noted that situational requirements are constantly changing, thus demanding a continual effort to maintain effective work relationships. Thus, she observed "different situations require different kinds of knowledge, and the man possessing the knowledge demanded by a certain situation tends to be in the best managed business, and other things being equal, to become the leader of the moment."[24]

In the same way that Fred Taylor sought obedience to facts determined by study rather than flawed rules of thumb, the rationale for Follett's "law of the situation" was based on facts and not title or position. In a paper for the Taylor Society, Follett put it this way: "If, then, authority is derived from function, it has little to do with hierarchy of position as such. . . . We find authority with the head of a department, with an expert . . . the dispatch clerk has more authority in dispatching work than the President . . . authority should go with knowledge and experience."[25]

Follett understood that by shifting authority to knowledge, personal confrontations could be minimized. She admired this facet of scientific management because it divorced person and situation. To Follett, the essence of good human relations was creating the feeling of working with someone rather than working under someone. In practice, this became "power-with" versus "power-over." She held that management should not exercise power over workers, nor should workers, through unions, exercise power over management. Jointly exercised power was "co-active," not coercive. Displaying a number of insights into the psychology of power, Follett rejected both the authoritarian's striving for power and Mohandas K. Gandhi's policy of peaceful noncooperation as insidious uses of power. She felt that Gandhi's noncooperation movement was still a desire for power-over because it sought to defy the British Colonial Authority to secure

---

[23] Mary P. Follett, "The Giving of Orders," in Henry C. Metcalf (ed.), *Scientific Foundations of Business Administration* (Baltimore, MD: Williams & Wilkins, 1926), p. 139. See also *idem, Creative Experience* (New York: Longmans, Green, 1924), p. 152.

[24] *Idem*, "Some Discrepancies in Leadership Theory and Practice," in Henry C. Metcalf, ed., *Business Leadership* (London: Pitman & Sons, 1930), p. 213.

[25] *Idem*, "The Illusion of Final Authority," *Bulletin of the Taylor Society* 2(6) (December 1926), p. 243.

Indian independence. Follett maintained that constructive conflict through integration could not be achieved when one or both sides to a conflict were attempting to dominate the other.

Follett believed that in all human interactions, from interpersonal conflicts to international disputes, power-over had to be reduced and obedience had to be shifted to the law of the situation. The basis for this shift would be what Follett called "circular response." By this, she meant a continuous reciprocal process based on the opportunity for confronting parties to influence each other, such that, through open interactions, over time, "power-with" could be obtained. For labor and management, power-with would come through full disclosure of costs, prices, and profits. Follett was an advocate of employee representation plans that were popular in the 1920s (see Chapter 9). Under these plans, employees elected representatives to shop or work councils; these representatives gave workers a voice in dealing with management. Follett found great promise in such plans because "management has seen that an enterprise can be more successfully run by securing the cooperation of the workers . . . . [Further] the aim of employee representation . . . should not be to share power, but to increase power . . . in all."[26] As envisioned by Follett, employee representation plans should not be a struggle over who decided what and how profits were to be divided, but a step toward achieving integration. The National Labor Relations Act (the Wagner Act), however, outlawed such plans in 1935. Employee representation plans were seen as being a form of company unions, wherein representatives could not bargain as equals (because they generally lacked the ability to sign legally enforceable agreements) and the right to strike was not recognized.

Follett thought final authority was an illusion based on a false premise of power; authority accrued to the prevailing situation, not to individuals or their positions. Likewise, she held that final responsibility was also an illusion. Responsibility was inherent in each job or workplace function and was cumulative in the sense that it was the sum of all individual and group responsibilities in a system of cross-relationships. At the individual level, a person was responsible for his work, not responsible to someone. At the departmental level, all those who contributed jointly shared responsibility for getting their jobs done. The role of a department manager was merely to interweave individual and group responsibilities. In turn, an organization's chief executive had cumulative responsibility for interweaving interdepartmental work.

Follett's thoughts on authority and responsibility were clearly iconoclastic. Traditional thinking associated with military or other organizations held that authority was power-over and rejected the idea that responsibility accrued to a final authority. Follett was nonetheless adamant. Authority resided in the situation, not a person or position. Logically then, responsibility was inherent in the work being performed and accumulated in interweaving workplace functions. This was heady material for the executives attending Follett's Bureau of Personnel Administration presentations.

The Task of Leadership

Two facets of Follett's philosophy have been explored: (1) reducing conflict through an integration of interests and the necessary corollary and (2) obeying the law of the situation. A third facet of Follett's philosophy concerned building the underlying psychological processes necessary to achieve goals through coordinating and controlling effort. Follett's view of control drew on her "principle of integrative unity." She saw that control was impossible to achieve unless there was unity and cooperation among all elements (material and people) in a given situation. In this sense, a situation was out of control when contrasting interests were not reconciled. For Follett, the basis for control resided in self-regulating and self-directing individuals and groups who recognized common interests and controlled their actions to meet agreed-upon goals.

---

[26] *Idem*, "How Is the Employee Representation Movement Remolding the Accepted Type of Business Manager?" in Henry C. Metcalf (ed.), *Business Management as a Profession* (Chicago, IL: A. W. Shaw, 1927), pp. 344, 353.

Follett recognized that managers controlled not single elements, but complex interrelationships; not persons, but situations; with the desired outcome being unity and cooperation across the full range of a prevailing situation. How was this unity and cooperation to be achieved? Follett called for a new philosophy of control that was "fact-control rather than man-control," and "correlated control" rather than "super-imposed control." She argued that each situation generated its own control because the facts of the situation and the interweaving of the many groups in the situation were what determined appropriate behavior. As most situations were too complex for centralized top-down control to function effectively, controls were to be gathered, or correlated, at many points in an organization. This interweaving and correlation was to be based on four fundamental principles of organization:

1. Co-ordination as the reciprocal relating of all the factors in a situation.

2. Co-ordination by direct contact of all the responsible people concerned.

3. Co-ordination in the early stages.

4. Co-ordination as a continuing process.[27]

Follett concluded that organization *was* control, because the purpose of organizing and coordination was to ensure controlled performance; coordination achieved unity, and unity was control. As an illustration, Follett cited a conflict between a purchasing agent and a production manager. The purchasing agent suggested acquiring somewhat inferior materials that he said would serve the purpose for which they are intended, but because they were lower priced they would save money. The production manager, however, maintained that he could not obtain satisfactory results with this material. According to Follett, if the purchasing agent and production manager had followed the principles of early and continuous coordination, they would have known each other's thinking and turned their attention to finding quality materials at a lower cost. An integration of their interests could, thus, have been achieved to their mutual satisfaction. This synthesis of interests was self-regulation through coordination to achieve integration.[28]

Follett held that leadership should not be based on power, but on the reciprocal influence of leader on follower and follower on leader in the context of the prevailing situation. A leader's primary task was defining the *purpose* of an organization; the leader "should make his co-workers see that it is not *his* purpose which is to be achieved, but a common purpose, born of the desires and the activities of the group. The best leader does not ask people to serve him, but the common end. The best leader has not followers, but men and women working with him."[29] Further, Follett maintained:

> The leader then is one who can organize the experience of the group . . . and thus get the full power of the group. The leader makes the team. This is pre-eminently the leadership quality – the ability to organize all the forces there are in an enterprise and make them serve a common purpose. Men with this ability create a group power rather than a personal power. . . . When leadership rises to genius it has the power of transforming . . . experience into power. And that is what experience is for, to be made into power. The great leader creates as well as directs power. . . . Leaders and followers are both following the invisible leader–the common purpose. The best executives put this common purpose clearly before their group.[30]

[27] *Idem*, "The Process of Control," in Luther H. Gulick and Lyndall F. Urwick, eds., *Papers on the Science of Administration* (New York: Institute of Public Administration, Columbia University, 1937), p. 161.

[28] *Ibid.*, p. 167. See also Mary P. Follett, "The Psychology of Control," in Henry C. Metcalf, ed., *Psychological Foundations of Business Management* (Chicago, IL: A. W. Shaw, 1927), p. 172.

[29] *Idem*, "Leader and Expert," in Henry C. Metcalf, ed., *Psychological Foundations of Business Management* (Chicago, IL: A. W. Shaw, 1927), p. 235.

[30] *Idem*, "The Essentials of Leadership" in Lyndall F. Urwick, ed., *Freedom and Coordination: Lectures in Business Organization* (London: Management Publications Trust, 1949), pp. 52, 55.

Follett reasoned that an organization's goals should be integrated with individual and group purposes, and this integration called for the highest caliber leaders. Such leaders did not depend on commands and obedience, but on skills in coordinating, defining purposes, and evoking responses to the law of the situation. Recognizing that mere exhortation would not bring about such leadership, Follett called for the training of executives in what she called the "capacity for organized thinking." Such thinking eschews dominating or manipulating others and recognizes a broader range of obligations leading to a profession of management that enlists knowledge for the service of others. To those who aspired to be managers, she advised:

> [M]en must prepare themselves as seriously for this profession as for any other. They must realize that they, as all professional men, are assuming grave responsibilities, that they are to take a creative part in one of the large functions of society, a part which, I believe, only trained and disciplined men can in the future hope to take with success.[31]

Follett felt that the notion of substituting a service motive for a profit motive was an oversimplification. Instead, she argued that these motives should be integrated into a larger professional motive:

> We work for profit, for service, for our own development, for the love of creating something. At any one moment, indeed, most of us are not working directly or immediately for any of these things, but to put through the job in hand in the best possible manner. . . . To come back to the professions: can we not learn a lesson from them on this very point? The professions have not given up the money motive. I do not care how often you see it stated that they have. Professional men are eager enough for large incomes; but they have other motives as well, and they are often willing to sacrifice a good slice of income for the sake of these other things. We all want the richness of life in the terms of our deepest desire. We can purify and elevate our desires, we can add to them, but there is no individual or social progress in curtailment of desires.[32]

A Final Note

Mary Follett passed away on December 18, 1933. Tonn has remarked, "Although Mary Follett's name may be obscure, her ideas are not."[33] In appreciation of her many contributions to management thought, Sir Peter Parker has declared, "People often puzzle about who is the father of management. I don't know who the father was, but I have no doubt about who was the mother."[34] Follett uncannily presaged many of today's management thinkers in advocating participative management, appreciating the benefits of teams (i.e., groups), endorsing cooperative conflict resolution, and recognizing that authority should go with knowledge.

Critics might maintain, however, that elements of Follett's business philosophy are idyllic notions of a political philosopher. The simplicity of people living and working together without coercion and compromise is nonetheless appealing. Integration, moving to a broader plane for problem solutions, would result in more creativity and imagination than are commonly witnessed in daily life. Depersonalization of authority and obedience to the law of the situation would end tyranny and autocracy. Control based on a perceived unity of purposes would improve labor–management relations.

---

[31] *Idem*, "How Must Business Management Develop in Order to Possess the Essentials of a Profession?" in Henry C. Metcalf, ed., *Business Management As a Profession* (Chicago, IL: A. W. Shaw, 1927), p. 87.

[32] *Idem*, "How Must Business Develop in Order to Become a Profession?" in Henry C. Metcalf (ed.), *Business Management As a Profession* (Chicago, IL: A. W. Shaw, 1927), pp. 101–102.

[33] Tonn, *Mary P. Follett*, p. 492.

[34] Sir Peter Parker quoted in Dana Wechsler Linden, "The Mother of Them All," *Forbes* (January 16, 1995), p. 76.

Follett's call for leaders dedicated to improving business practices through science and service has been a refrain since the earliest days of the Industrial Revolution. Her ideas on reducing conflict, obeying the law of the situation, and building the underlying psychological processes necessary to achieve goals through coordinating and controlling effort, however, were unique for their time and continue to have present-day relevance. As one of her contemporaries recalled, "Mary Follett was a gentle person, not an impressive or aggressive spellbinder, but of all the pioneers she, more than others, approached management through human values, psychology and the laboratory of collaborative work experience. The significance and originality of her contribution cannot be overrated."[35]

Chester I. Barnard: The Erudite Executive

Chester Irving Barnard was born in Malden, Massachusetts, in 1886, and educated at Mount Hermon School for Boys in Northfield, Massachusetts.[36] He personified the Horatio Alger ideal of the farm boy who made good. As a student at Harvard University, Barnard supplemented his income by tuning pianos and conducting a small dance band. He studied economics at Harvard, completing all but one degree requirement in 3 years (1906–1909). Lacking a laboratory science, he was not allowed to graduate. Even without a bachelor's degree, he did well enough to earn seven honorary doctorates for his lifelong efforts to understand the nature and purpose of organizations.

Chester I. Barnard. Courtesy of William B. Wolf.

Barnard joined the Boston office of the Statistical Department of the American Telephone and Telegraph (AT&T) system at $50 a month in 1909. Early on he became an expert in telephone rates. He later served as vice president of operations for the Bell Telephone Company of Pennsylvania. In 1927, he was named president of the New Jersey Bell Telephone Company. His commitment to making a difference in the lives of others was reflected in his public service and volunteer work. He assisted David. E. Lilienthal in developing operational policies for the U.S. Atomic Energy Commission and was a special assistant to the Secretary of the Treasury; served the New Jersey Emergency Relief Administration and the New Jersey Reformatory at Rahway; and also served as president of the Rockefeller Foundation, chairman of the National Science Foundation, president of the Bach Society of New Jersey, and founded the Newark Art Theatre. For his service as president of the United Service Organizations (USO), he was awarded the Presidential Medal of Merit. He also received the U.S. Navy's Meritorious Civilian Award. Barnard was a self-made scholar who applied the theories of the Italian economist Vilfredo F. D. Pareto (whom he read in French), Mary P. Follett, Kurt Lewin (see Chapter 15), Max Weber (whom he read in German), and the philosophy of Alfred North Whitehead to create the first in-depth analysis of organizations as cooperative systems. He was a Fellow of the American

[35] Luther H. Gulick, "Looking Backward to 1915" (Paper presented at the Eastern Academy of Management, Hartford, CT, May 13, 1977), pp. 5–6; transcript and recording, Bizzell Memorial Library, Harry W. Bass Business History Collection, University of Oklahoma Libraries, Norman, OK.

[36] Biographical data and an excellent discussion of Barnard's ideas are found in William B. Wolf, *The Basic Barnard: An Introduction to Chester I. Barnard and His Theories of Organization and Management* (Ithaca, NY: New York State School of Industrial and Labor Relations, 1974). Originally published 1968. See also *idem*, "Understanding Chester I. Barnard," *International Journal of Public Administration* 17(6) (1994), pp. 1035–1069; *idem*, *Conversations with Chester I. Barnard* (Ithaca, NY: New York State School of Industrial and Labor Relations, Cornell University 1973); and *idem* and Haruki Lino, *Philosophy for Managers: Selected Papers of Chester I. Barnard* (Tokyo: Bunshindo, 1986).

Association for the Advancement of Science and the American Academy of Arts and Sciences, as well as a director of the National Bureau of Economic Research. By the time of his death in 1961, this Harvard dropout had earned a place in history as a management scholar.

The Nature of Cooperative Systems

Barnard's best-known work, *The Functions of the Executive*, was an expansion of eight lectures sponsored by the Lowell Institute (Boston) in November and December of 1937. His explicit purpose in presenting the lectures was to develop a theory of organizations and to stimulate others to examine the nature of cooperative systems. To Barnard, the search for universals in organizations had been hampered by too much emphasis on the nature of religious and government institutions, and their differing views on the origin and character of authority. He complained that most research focused on social unrest and reform and included "practically no reference to formal organization as the concrete social process by which social action is largely accomplished." In Barnard's opinion, social failures throughout history were due to a lack of formal organization. He explained that "formal organization is that kind of coöperation among men that is conscious, deliberate, and purposeful."[37]

Barnard believed that by developing a theory of organizations, it would be possible to enhance the effectiveness and efficiency of cooperative systems. He sought to understand how to (1) adjust an organization's internal processes so as to ensure its survival; (2) examine the external forces to which an organization must readjust to maintain an equilibrium in a "continuously fluctuating environment of physical, biological, and social materials, elements, and forces"; and (3) analyze the functions performed by executives at all levels in an organization.[38] Barnard's focus on maintaining an equilibrium in an organization's internal processes while confronting external environmental forces was seen as novel compared to conventional thinking. He rejected the traditional view of organizations having fixed boundaries and as being comprised by a defined set of employees. In considering the larger environment in which an organization was situated, Barnard's analyses went beyond earlier thinking to also include investors, suppliers, customers, and others whose actions contributed to an organization although they were not its employees.[39]

Barnard's view of organizations as cooperative systems began with individuals as discrete beings; however, reminiscent of Follett's group principle, he noted that humans did not function except in interacting with other humans in social relationships. As individuals, people could choose whether or not they would enter into a specific cooperative system. They made this choice based on their motives (meaning purposes, desires, and impulses of the moment) or by considering whatever action alternatives were available. As described by Barnard, organizations, through their executive function, seek to modify individuals' motives and action alternatives through influence and control. He recognized that attempts at influence and control were not always successful in attaining the goals sought by organizations and their members. The disparity between personal motives and organizational motives led Barnard to distinguish between "effectiveness" and "efficiency." A formal system of cooperation required an objective or purpose, and, if cooperation was successful and the objective was attained, the system was effective. Barnard saw the matter of efficiency differently. He felt cooperative efficiency was the result of individual efficiencies, because individuals cooperated only to satisfy "individual motives." The efficiency of a cooperative system, then, was the degree to which an individual's motives were satisfied, and only the individual could determine whether this condition had been met.[40]

---

[37] Chester I. Barnard, *The Functions of the Executive* (Cambridge, MA: Harvard University Press, 1938), pp. 3–4.
[38] *Ibid.*, p. 6.
[39] *Idem*, "Comments on the Job of the Executive," *Harvard Business Review* 18(4) (Spring 1940), pp. 295–308.
[40] *Idem*, *Functions of the Executive*, p. 44.

As viewed by Barnard, cooperation within formal organizations afforded possibilities for expanding the power of groups beyond what individuals could accomplish alone, for example, moving a stone, producing an automobile, or constructing a bridge. Individuals cooperated to do what they could not do individually; and, when their purpose for cooperating was attained, their efforts were deemed effective. Individuals, however, also had personal motives, and the degree to which individuals continued to contribute to a formal organization was a function of the satisfaction or dissatisfaction they personally derived from their membership in an organization. If members' motives were not satisfied by a formal organization, they withheld effort or participation, and from their point of view, the organization was inefficient. Barnard contended in the final analysis that "the only measure of the efficiency of a coöperative system is its capacity to survive."[41] For Barnard, this meant that an organization must offer inducements necessary to satisfy individual motives in pursuit of group purposes to assure its continued survival. Viewed in modern-systems theory terms, a formal organization must renew its energy or import negative entropy by offering net satisfactions to contributing members. An inefficient organization cannot be effective and, therefore, cannot survive beyond its store of negative entropy. For Barnard, efficiency and effectiveness were irrevocable and universal requirements for an organization to survive.

Formal Organizations: Theory and Structure

Barnard defined an organization as "a system of consciously coördinated activities or forces of two or more persons."[42] He intended for this definition to encompass all such systems, including military, fraternal, religious, academic, business, or any organization, irrespective of variations in terms of physical or social environment, number and kinds of members, or the nature of members' activities. Barnard treated such systems "as a whole because each part is related to every other part included in it in a significant way."[43] He noted that different levels of systems existed, ranging from departments (subsystems) in a commercial firm to systems forming society as a whole. Regardless of level, Barnard held that all systems must contain three elements to survive: (1) members who are willing to cooperate; (2) a common purpose; and (3) a method of communication.[44]

As for the first of these elements, Barnard reasoned that an organization could not exist without members. Further, a willingness to cooperate to accomplish a common purpose was likewise indispensable. He recognized that the intensity and timing of this willingness would naturally fluctuate, because it was based on the satisfaction or dissatisfaction experienced or anticipated by each individual member. An organization, thus, had to provide adequate inducements, both physical and social, to offset the sacrifices individuals made by forgoing membership in alternative organizations. Barnard further reasoned that the willingness to cooperate for individual each member was the joint effect of "personal desires and reluctances" to participate; for an organization, it was the joint effect of "objective inducements offered and burdens imposed."[45] Inducing individuals to cooperate involved an "economy of incentives," which consisted of two parts: (1) offering objective incentives and (2) changing subjective attitudes through persuasion. Objective incentives were material (e.g., money), nonmaterial (e.g., prestige, power), and associational (e.g., social compatibility, participation in decision-making). Persuasion involved changing attitudes by precept, example, and appeal to individual motives.

A common purpose, the second element that Barnard believed all systems must contain to survive, was a corollary to the first required element—a willingness of members to cooperate.

---

[41] *Ibid.* p. 44.
[42] *Ibid.* p. 73.
[43] *Ibid.* p. 77.
[44] *Ibid.*, p. 82.
[45] *Ibid.*, pp. 85–86.

Barnard contended that willingness to cooperate could not be induced unless members knew what effort would be expected and what incentives they would receive as a result. This thus required that an organization inculcate in its members a common purpose or objective. Barnard believed that it was not what an organization's purpose meant personally to its members, but what they perceived the purpose to mean to the organization as a whole. As noted above, Barnard recognized that the motives of an organization and its members logically differ, and members cooperated not because their personal motives were the same as that of the organization but because of the satisfaction they experienced (or anticipated) by contributing to the organization's success in achieving its goals.

Barnard considered communication, the third element required by all systems to survive, to be the process by which common purpose and willingness to cooperate become dynamic. He felt that all interpersonal activities were based on communication. He stated that (1) "channels of communication should be definitely known"; (2) "objective authority requires a definite formal channel of communication to every member of an organization," that is, everyone must report to or be subordinate to someone; and (3) "line[s] of communication must be as direct or short as possible" to speed dissemination and reduce distortions caused by transmission through multiple channels.[46]

Having identified elements essential for a formal organization to survive, Barnard sought to do the same for informal organizations. By informal organization, he meant "the aggregate of the personal contacts and interactions and the associated groupings of people" that was not a part of nor governed by a formal organization.[47] Without structure, and often without consciously recognizing a joint purpose, informal groupings arose out of job-related contacts and, in turn, established shared attitudes, customs, and norms. Barnard noted that informal organizations often create conditions leading to formal organizations and vice versa. He believed that informal organizations served three necessary functions: (1) they are a means of communication; (2) they further cohesiveness among an organization's members; and (3) they protect informal group members' personal integrity.

The Acceptance Theory of Authority

One of Barnard's most unusual ideas related to his theory of authority. He defined authority as "the character of a communication (order) in a formal organization by virtue of which it is *accepted* by a contributor to or 'member' of the organization as governing the action he contributes." As suggested by this definition, authority had two aspects: (1) "the subjective, personal *accepting* of a communication as being authoritative" and (2) "the character in [a] communication by virtue of which it is accepted."[48] According to Barnard, the source of authority does not reside in persons of authority, or those who give orders, but in the acceptance or nonacceptance of authority by subordinates. In essence, Barnard held that the real "source of authority lies in the members of an organization, that they confer authority upon their superiors by deigning to accept and act upon commands, that they may, if they wish, decide to accept orders seriatim, and that they may withdraw conferred authority at any time by refusing to obey the commands of their superiors."[49]

Barnard's thinking in this regard was antithetical to all previous concepts of authority, which held that authority resides in "persons of authority" or "those who issue orders."[50] Whereas Follett argued for depersonalizing authority and obeying the law of the situation, Barnard held authority originated at the bottom of an organization and flowed upward. In this sense, formal authority

---

[46] *Ibid.*, pp. 175–177.
[47] *Ibid.*, p. 115.
[48] *Ibid.*, p. 163.
[49] Cyril J. O'Donnell, "The Source of Managerial Authority," *Political Science Quarterly* 67(4) (December 1952), p. 575.
[50] Barnard, *Functions of the Executive*, p. 163.

becomes real only when it is accepted as legitimate by subordinates. For Barnard, subordinates would accept a communication as legitimate if four conditions were met: (1) they understand the communication; (2) they believe the communication is consistent with an organization's purpose; (3) they believe the communication is compatible with their personal interests; and (4) they are mentally and physically able to comply with the communication.

To explain how an organization could function according to this view, Barnard contended that there is a "zone of indifference" within which employees will rarely challenge orders from their superiors. This zone of indifference might be narrow or wide, depending on the degree to which inducements outweighed the burdens and sacrifices of complying with a communication. If an employee, for instance, felt that a communication ran counter to a personal moral code, the benefit of accepting the communication would be weighed against the discomfort created by acting immorally and whether or not the accompanying organization sanctions were sufficiently strong enough to induce compliance. Some communications are accepted without deliberation, but others may require considerable thought. Such discretion would pertain to what Barnard identified as the first or subjective aspect of authority.

The second, or objective, aspect of authority that Barnard identified was more closely akin to traditional conceptions of authority. It rested on the presumption that communications were authoritative and had a "potentiality of assent" when they came from individuals in superordinate positions. In one case, a communication from a higher up might be accepted because it came from a "person of authority"; this was formal authority, or the authority of position. In another instance, a communication might be accepted because a subordinate had respect for and confidence in a superior's personal ability irrespective of the superior's rank or position; Barnard called this the "authority of leadership."

When authority of leadership was combined with authority of position, the zone of indifference became exceedingly broad. Nevertheless, Barnard stressed "the determination of authority remains with the individual."[51] In a free society, individuals always have discretion in defining what is and is not an acceptable communication. What is perhaps the most striking insight of Barnard's theory of authority is that all organizations depend on managers (as leaders) that can develop the capacity and willingness of others to follow.

The Functions of the Executive

Viewed more broadly, Barnard portrayed an executive's job as securing and maintaining the coordination essential to achieve cooperative effort. Such coordination required a system of communication that could only function if staffed by executives (meaning managers at all levels). To quote Barnard, "It might be said, then, that the function of executives is to serve as channels of communication so far as communications must pass through central positions."[52] Communication was a central value in all Barnard's writings and, undoubtedly, his views were influenced by his own experience in the AT&T system. To Barnard, executive work "is not *of* the organization, but the specialized work of *maintaining* the organization in operation. . . . The executive functions serve to maintain a system of cooperative effort. They are impersonal. The functions are not, as so frequently stated, to manage a group of persons."[53] For Barnard, on the whole, the role of the executive functions in an organization was analogous to that of the human nervous system in relation to the rest of the body: "It exists to maintain the bodily system by directing those actions which are necessary more effectively to adjust to the environment, but it can hardly be said to manage the body, a large part of whose functions are independent of it and upon which it in turn depends."[54]

---

[51] *Ibid.*, pp. 173–174.
[52] *Ibid.*, p. 215.
[53] *Ibid.*, p. 216.
[54] *Ibid.*, p. 217.

Barnard identified three essential executive functions that correspond with the three elements necessary for a system to survive: (1) to create a system of communication, (2) to secure essential services from individuals, and (3) to formulate and define an organization's purpose.[55] In creating a system of communication, Barnard believed that executives had to define individual duties, clarify lines of authority and responsibility, and consider both formal and informal means of communication. Informal communication assisted in maintaining internal communication by allowing issues to be raised and discussed without forcing decisions and overloading executive positions. By securing essential services from individuals, the second executive function, Barnard was referring to the role executives play in establishing cooperative relationships among people and eliciting their individual contributions to an organization's goals. This included recruiting employees who could work together compatibly, as well as (1) preserving morale; (2) providing positive inducements such as wages and removing negative inducements such as reducing hours or work required; and (3) maintaining deterrents such as supervision and control, inspection, education and training to ensure a cooperative system's viability.

The third executive function, formulate and define an organization's purpose, was examined above in our comments on Barnard's thoughts relating to the nature of cooperative systems. What was not previously mentioned is that Barnard viewed the delegation of authority and assignment of responsibility to be critical aspects of this function. For Barnard, delegation involved making decisions about the placement of various responsibilities and authority within a cooperative system so that individuals would know how they contributed to the ends being sought, and to the means to those ends. Decision-making had two facets: analysis, or the search for the "strategic factors" that would create a set or system of conditions necessary to accomplish an organization's purposes; and synthesis, or the recognition of interrelationships among elements or parts that compose a whole system.

Barnard borrowed the term "strategic factor" from labor economist John R. Commons to refer to those factors that limit executives in decision-making. According to Barnard, "The strategic factor is, then, the center of the environment of decision. It is the point at which choice applies. To *do* or not to do *this*, that is the question."[56] Like Fayol, Barnard saw organizations as purposeful wholes functioning in a changing environment. Barnard's insights provided the foundation for developing the business-policy course at Harvard University and for much of the terminology still used in strategic-management theory.[57]

Barnard's ruminations on the decision-making process were also a notable contribution to general management theory. He recognized that individuals are limited in their "power of choice" by "the combined effect of physical, biological, and social factors."[58] In "Mind in Everyday Affairs," an appendix to his *The Functions of the Executive,* Barnard noted there were two categories of mental processes: "logical" and "non-logical." Logical processes involved "conscious thinking which could be expressed in words, or other symbols, that is, reasoning," whereas non-logical processes were those "not capable of being expressed in words or as reasoning" and "are only made known by a judgment, decision, or action." Non-logical processes may "lie in physiological conditions or factors, or in the physical and social environment," and may not require conscious effort.[59] Barnard concluded that "both kinds [of mental processes] together are much better than either alone if the conditions permit."[60]

---

[55] *Ibid.*, pp. 217–234.

[56] *Ibid.*, p. 205.

[57] Dave McMahon and Jon C. Carr, "The Contributions of Chester Barnard to Strategic Management Theory," *Journal of Management History* 5(5) (1999), pp. 228–240; Kenneth R. Andrews, "Introduction to the 30th Anniversary Edition" of Barnard's *The Functions of the Executive* (Cambridge, MA: Harvard University Press, 1968), pp. xix–xx.

[58] Barnard, *Functions of the Executive*, p. 14.

[59] *Ibid.*, p. 302. See also Milorad M. Novicevic, Thomas J. Hench, and Daniel A. Wren, "Playing by Ear . . . in an Incessant Din of Reasons: Chester Barnard and the History of Intuition in Management Thought," *Management Decision* 40(10) (2002), pp. 992–1002.

[60] *Ibid.*, p. 306.

Barnard was clear in stating that the three essential executive functions that he had identified had no separate existence, but were "aspects of a process of organization as a whole." He labeled and defined the nature of this "executive process" as "the sensing of the organization as a whole and the total situation relevant to it."[61] This was the art of managing and involved integrating the whole with respect to an organization's internal equilibrium as well as its adjustment to external conditions. Working from the micro to the macro level, Barnard viewed all aspects of society as one large, cooperative system. Every organization had to secure members, money, and materials from its environment and could "survive only as it secures by exchange, transformation, and creation, a surplus of utilities in its own economy."[62]

Moral Leadership

For Barnard, the creative force in all organizations was moral leadership. As he explained, this meant ethical behavior that was "governed by beliefs or feelings of what is right or wrong, regardless of self-interest or immediate consequences of a decision to do or not to do specific things under particular conditions."[63] This included personal responsibility (an individual's character development); official responsibility (when acting "on behalf" of an organization); and corporate responsibility (internal to the interests of stockholders, creditors, and employees, and external to one's community and society in general). Barnard believed that executives should adhere to a moral code, demonstrate a high capacity for personal responsibility, and strive to create a moral faculty in others. He observed "[T]he endurance of organization depends upon the quality of leadership; and that quality derives from the breadth of the morality upon which it rests. . . . A low morality will not sustain leadership long, its influence quickly vanishes, it cannot produce its own succession."[64]

Coda

Chester Barnard was an erudite executive who drew on his own experiences and sociological insights to build a theory of cooperative systems. As Fritz J. Roethlisberger recalled, "[Barnard was] the one and only executive in captivity who could not only run a successful organization but could also talk intelligently about what he was up to in the process."[65] Barnard impressed not only Roethlisberger but also Elton Mayo (Roethlisberger's Harvard mentor), who moved away from viewing organizations as biological organisms to seeing organizations as cooperative social systems.[66] Barnard's thoughts on maintaining an equilibrium within cooperative systems also influenced other Hawthorne researchers (see Chapter 13) and later inspired Herbert A. Simon's work on decision-making in organizations (see Chapter 15).[67] Barnard's theory of authority, his call for moral leadership, and his identification of universal elements in both formal and informal organizations remain significant contributions to management thought.

---

[61] *Ibid.*, p. 235

[62] *Ibid.*, p. 245.

[63] Chester I. Barnard, "Elementary Conditions of Business Morals," *California Management Review* 1(1) (Fall 1958), p. 4.

[64] Barnard, *Functions of the Executive*, pp. 282–283.

[65] Fritz J. Roethlisberger, *The Elusive Phenomena: An Autobiographical Account of My Work in the Field of Organizational Behavior at the Harvard Business School.* George F. F. Lombard, ed. (Boston, MA: Division of Research, Graduate School of Business, Harvard University, 1977), p. 67.

[66] Robert T. Keller, "The Harvard 'Pareto Circle' and the Historical Development of Organization Theory," *Journal of Management* 10(2) (1984), p. 199.

[67] See William B. Wolf, "The Barnard-Simon Connection," *Journal of Management History* 1(4) (1995), pp. 88–99; Chester I. Barnard, "Foreword," in Herbert A. Simon, *Administrative Behavior: A Study of Decision-Making Processes in Administrative Organization* (New York: Macmillan, 1947), pp. ix–xii; and Ellen S. O'Connor, "New Contributions from Old Sources: Recovering Barnard's Science and Revitalizing the Carnegie School," *European Management Journal* 31(1) (February 2013), pp. 93–103.

SUMMARY

Mary P. Follett and Chester I. Barnard were bridges between the scientific-management and the social-person eras. Follett ushered in a group view of society while living and working in the scientific-management period. Barnard was a student of formal organization, yet stressed the role of informal groupings in achieving an equilibrium within a cooperative system. Both endeavored to create a spirit of cooperation and collaboration within organizations and society. Both sought to reshape previous theories of authority. Both concluded moral leadership would enhance the effectiveness of organizations and the well-being of society.

People and Organizations

This and the next chapter examine two streams of management thought that developed from about 1930 to the early 1950s. These chapter focuses on the growth and refinement of the human-relations movement as it passed through micro and macro phases. The micro phase saw an outpouring of behavioral research on topics such as group dynamics, participation in decision-making, leadership, and motivation. The macro phase witnessed a search for analytical tools and conceptual models to explain the interactions between the formal and informal processes operating within organizations. The title of this chapter, "People and Organizations," conveys the human orientation of both phases, with the structural aspects of organizations being a secondary subject of inquiry. In contrast, Chapter 16, "Organizations and People," focuses on the structure and design of organizations, with the human element placed in a relatively subordinate role.

People at Work: The Micro View

Whereas social scientists had studied workplace dynamics in the first 3 decades of the twentieth century, the 1930s and 1940s saw an unprecedented outpouring of research into "human relations at work." In contrast to the scientific-management movement that was largely dominated by engineers, the human-relations era was decidedly interdisciplinary in its focus, involving sociologists, psychologists, psychiatrists, and anthropologists. A common premise underlying the era's social-science research was the Gestalt notion that all behavior involves a "multiplier effect." That is, the behavior of group members is more than the simple sum of their individual actions. Individuals are unique due to their distinctive genetic makeup and family, social, and work experiences. When placed in interactions with other one-of-a-kind individuals, predicting the resulting outcomes is all the more difficult, if not impossible. Thus, as recognized by both Mary P. Follett and Chester I. Barnard (see Chapter 14), because of the multiplier effect, individuals within groups cannot be studied in isolation, but must be analyzed as part of a dynamic social system.

Developing Constructs for Group Analysis

Interest in the study of groups appears to have been a product of the Social Gospel movement and its emphasis on industrial betterment. In 1922, the Federal Council of the Churches of Christ in America passed a resolution creating the National Conference on the Christian Way of Life. The resolution called for an inquiry into "The Meaning of Christianity for Human Relationships, with special attention to industry, citizenship and race relations in the United States and the function of the church in social and civic affairs."[1] The conference, later called The Inquiry, led to several seminal studies into group behavior.[2] Eduard C. Lindeman joined with other educators (including John Dewey and Robert M. MacIver) to develop methods to observe and categorize group inter-actions, measure group participation, and classify the attitudes of a group's members. Lindeman was influenced by Follett's thinking on conflict resolution and "power-with" rather than "power-over." He coined the phrase "*participant observer*" to describe someone who is a study participant, but who has also been trained to be an observer – what he termed a "coöperating observer" – rather than a researcher disguised as a study participant.[3] Lindeman believed that the "interpreta-tion of an event can only be approximately correct when it is a composite of two points of view, the *outside* and the *inside*. Thus the view of the person who is a participant in the event, whose wishes and interests were in some way involved, and the view of the person who was not a participant but only an observer, or analyst, coalesce in one final synthesis."[4] Over time, the role of participant observers has changed, from what is today generally referred to as a "key informant," to that of a covert observer, such as Whiting Williams, who participated in and reported on workers' daily lives (see Chapter 9). Regrettably, Lindeman's pioneering work now seems to have been largely forgotten.

In contrast, the work of psychiatrist Jacob L. Moreno has continued to be referenced. Moreno developed a therapeutic technique, *sociometry*, which had as its purpose "a process of classification, which is calculated, among other things, to bring individuals together who are capable of harmonious inter-personal relationships, and so creating a social group which can function at the maximum efficiency and with the minimum of disruptive tendencies and processes."[5] Moreno felt the "socio-psychopathology" of a group's structure was not entirely due to chance. He, thus, believed that group structures could be studied using quantitative methods to ascertain the evolution and pattern of attitudes and interactions among a group's members. In his analyses, Moreno classified the pat-tern of attitudes and interactions that existed among group members based on three emotions: *attraction*, *repulsion*, and *indifference*. He assessed these emotions by asking group members to indicate whom from among the group they would and would not prefer to associate. Moreno then paired and ranked group members' feelings for one another using a chart he called a *sociogram*. He recognized that group-member preferences are dynamic and vary as group membership and the

[1] Charles D. Wrege and Sakae Hata, "Before Bales: Pioneer Studies in Analyzing Group Behavior: 1921–1930" (paper presented at the annual meeting of the Academy of Management, Boston, 1984), p. 2. See also Gisela Konopka, *Eduard C. Lindeman and Social Work Philosophy* (Minneapolis, MN: University of Minnesota Press, 1958), pp. 33–34.
[2] For a description of these studies, see Eduard C. Lindeman, *Social Education: An Interpretation of the Principles and Methods Developed by the Inquiry During the Years 1923–1933* (New York: New Republic, 1933).
[3] *Idem, Social Discovery: An Approach to the Study of Functional Groups* (New York: Republic Publishing Company, 1924), p. 191.
[4] John J. Hader and Eduard C. Lindeman, *Dynamic Social Research* (London: K. Paul, Trench, Trubner & Co., 1933), p. 148.
[5] William A. White, "Foreword," in Jacob L. Moreno (with the collaboration of Helen H. Jennings), *Who Shall Survive? A New Approach to Human Interrelations* (Washington, DC: Nervous and Mental Disease Publishing, 1934), p. xii. See also Jacob L. Moreno, "The Autobiography of J. L. Moreno, MD," ed., Jonathan D. Moreno, *Journal of Group Psychotherapy Psychodrama & Sociometry* 42(1–2) (Spring 1989), pp. 59–126.

challenges facing a group change. For example, in a study of "leadership structures" at the New York Training School for Girls, different pairing preferences were expressed depending on whether respondents were choosing a roommate or a workmate. Other early similar research sought to increase work-team output by sociometrically selecting team members.[6]

Moreno also developed what is known as *psychodrama* and *sociodrama*. Both techniques involve dramatic enactments of real-life situations or conflicts. Together these techniques formed a basis for remedying difficulties in individual or group relationships. Psychodrama consists of placing individuals "on stage" to act out their personal problems with the aid of other "actors" and a facilitator.[7] Once an individual's manner of dealing with others is revealed, therapy or treatment is then recommended to resolve any difficulties that may have been disclosed. Psychodrama is intended to be a cathartic experience, enabling individuals to release and relieve their innermost doubts and anxieties.

Sociodrama, an outgrowth of psychodrama, focuses on understanding relationships within groups. It is based on the assumption that groups are organized according to social and cultural roles. Group therapy is used to understand these roles and might include role-playing exercises dealing with superior–subordinate relationships, interpersonal and team relationships, gender and race issues, and so forth. Role reversal or enacting the roles of opposite social or cultural group members—for example, a white supervisor playing the role of an African-American worker—might be used to broaden role flexibility and create an understanding of others' views. In effect, sociodrama is group psychotherapy designed to reduce resentments, frustrations, and misunderstandings. Moreno's work supplemented the counseling and interpersonal relations aspects of the human-relations movement by providing techniques for studying and changing an individual's or group's behavior vis-à-vis other individuals or groups. Heretofore, psychology and psychoanalysis, both essentially concerned with the study of mental processes, had been inadequate for analyzing individual or group workplace behavior.

Group dynamics, as developed by Kurt T. Lewin, is another concept that developed during the same period in which Moreno was popularizing his sociometric methods. Indeed, there is evidence that Moreno substantially influenced Lewin's work.[8] Lewin studied at the University of Berlin under Max Wertheimer and Wolfgang Kohler, two founders of the Gestalt movement. Lewin's own thinking falls under the heading of *field theory*, which holds that group behavior is an intricate set of symbolic interactions and forces that not only affect group structure, but also modify individual behavior. From a field-theory perspective, a group is never at a steady state, but is in a continuous process of mutual adaptation that Lewin labeled "quasi–stationary equilibrium." An analogy might be that of a river flowing within its banks; it appears relatively stationary, but there is continual movement and change.

Lewin viewed behavior as a function of the interaction between a person and his or her social environment, which Lewin regarded as a dynamic "field." This is expressed in his famous formula $B = f(P, E)$, where Behavior (B) is a function of the interaction between a Person (P) and his or her Environment (E). Using terms such as "life space," "space of free movement," and "field forces," that is, tensions emanating from group pressures on an individual, Lewin investigated resistance to change and the social climate within groups. For example, Lewin and his graduate students studied groups of 10- and 11-year-old boys to determine how democratic or authoritarian behavior by the groups' adult leaders affected the groups' social climate. They concluded that authoritarian behavior on the part of a leader impaired initiative and bred hostility

---

[6] Raymond H. Van Zelst, "Sociometrically Selected Work Teams Increase Production," *Personnel Psychology* 5(3) (September 1952), pp. 175–185.

[7] Jacob L. Moreno, *Psychodrama*, vol. 1 (Boston, MA: Beacon Press, 1946), pp. 177–222.

[8] Barbara A. Wech, "The Lewin/Moreno Controversy," in Dennis R. Ray, ed., *Proceedings of the Southern Management Association* (1996), pp. 421–423. See also Pitirim Sorokin, *Fads and Foibles in Modern Sociology and Related Sciences* (Chicago, IL: Henry Regnery, 1956), pp. 5–6.

and aggressiveness, whereas leader behaviors they labeled democratic and laissez-faire were more effective in maintaining group morale and satisfaction.[9] Unfortunately, this study is often misrepresented as a study on leadership and its effect on productivity rather than on resistance to change and the social climate within groups. In reality, Ralph K. White, one of the group leaders, was quite shy and had had little experience with young boys. Ralph was supposed to be a democratic leader, but when the results for his group were discussed, Ronald Lippitt (another group leader) remarked, "This isn't democratic leadership. That is *laissez-faire*." Typical of his approach to working with graduate students, rather than discard the observations from White's group, Lewin declared, "Okay, we'll make a third group. A *laissez-faire* group." Over the years, the notion has been erroneously passed down that laissez-faire was intended as a style of leadership when in fact it was recognized as a lack of leadership.[10]

In research on changing family food habits conducted during World War II, Lewin found that changes were more easily induced through group decision-making than through lectures and individual appeals.[11] This was a new insight into introducing changes and suggested that changes are more readily accepted when people feel they have been involved in a decision to change rather than simply being asked or told to change. Lewin felt successful change included three aspects: "unfreezing" or recognizing the need for change, "moving" or modifying old ways so that new behavior patterns can be introduced, and "freezing" or establishing new behavior patterns.[12] Lewin's three phases provided a foundation for future "action research" (the purpose of which was to collaborate with group members to study their behavior) and modern organizational change and development techniques that focus on the behavior of groups as groups rather than on how groups influence the behavior of individuals.

In 1945, Lewin founded the Research Center for Group Dynamics at the Massachusetts Institute of Technology; following his death in 1947, the center was moved to the University of Michigan's Survey Research Center where Rensis Likert (pronounced *lick-urt*) and others would further the study of employee participation in decision-making and the use of group interventions to achieve changes in workplace behavior.[13] In 1947, another of Lewin's disciples, Leland P. Bradford, established the first sensitivity training (or human relations) laboratory, the National Training Laboratory, at Bethel, Maine.[14] The goal of sensitivity training is to achieve changes in behavior through "gut-level" interactions that led to increased interpersonal awareness. Like Moreno's psychodrama, sensitivity training is intended to be a cathartic experience, enabling individuals to release and relieve their innermost doubts and anxieties, as well as to see themselves as others see them.

By focusing on group interactions rather than isolated individuals, Lindeman, Moreno, and Lewin introduced new perspectives for understanding workplace behavior. This focus, reflecting a Gestalt orientation, led to further studies on introducing change, conflict resolution, group behavior, and the effects of group processes on individual behavior. On the whole, these studies emphasized the dynamic nature of individual interactions within a group setting.

---

[9] Kurt T. Lewin, Ronald Lippitt, and Ralph K. White, "Patterns of Aggressive Behavior in Experimentally Created 'Social Climates,'" *Journal of Social Psychology* 10(2) (May 1939), pp. 271–299; Ronald Lippitt and Ralph K. White, "The 'Social Climate' of Children's Groups," in Roger G. Barker, Jacob S. Kouin, and Robert F. Wright, eds., *Child Behavior and Development: A Course of Representative Studies* (New York: McGraw-Hill, 1943), pp. 485–508.

[10] Comments made by Gertrud (Mrs. Kurt) W. Lewin after the presentation of the following paper by her daughter: Miriam Lewin Papanek, "Kurt Lewin and His Contributions to Modern Management Theory," in Thad B. Green and Dennis F. Ray, eds., *Proceedings of the Annual Meeting of the Academy of Management* (1973), pp. 317–322. See also Gertrud W. Lewin quoted in William B. Wolf, "Reflections on the History of Management Thought," *Journal of Management History* 2(2) (1996), p. 8.

[11] Kurt T. Lewin, "The Dynamics of Group Action," *Educational Leadership* 1(4) (January 1944), pp. 195–200.

[12] Kurt T. Lewin, "Group Decision and Social Change," in Theodore M. Newcomb and Eugene L. Hartley, eds., *Readings in Social Psychology* (New York: Henry Holt, 1947), p. 344.

[13] "The Career of Rensis Likert: Using Science for Man – A Gentle Revolution," *ISR Newsletter* 1(9) (Winter 1971), pp. 1–7.

[14] Leland P. Bradford, *National Training Laboratories: Its History: 1947–1970* (Bethel, ME: Privately printed, 1974). See also Scott Highhouse, "A History of the T-Group and Its Early Applications in Management Development," *Group Dynamics: Theory, Research, and Practice* 6(4) (December 2002), pp. 277–290.

The Growth of Human-Relations Research and Training

The 1930s witnessed the emergence of a more favorable political climate for organized labor. The passage of the National Labor Relations Act (the Wagner Act) and the formation of the Congress of Industrial Organizations (CIO), both in 1935, brought a new emphasis on collective bargaining. Morris L. Cooke (see Chapter 8) and CIO president Philip Murray called for management to "tap labor's brains" for ideas on how to increase workplace productivity.[15] Industrial democracy, meaning in essence the workplace application of a human-relations philosophy with organized labor's support, was a common theme.[16] Accordingly, a number of university-based programs began to appear that would pave the way for the further growth of human-relations research. In 1943, the Committee on Human Relations in Industry was formed at the University of Chicago. Drawing its members from business (Burleigh Gardner), sociology (William Foote Whyte), and anthropology (W. Lloyd Warner), this committee was to characterize a new style of interdisciplinary social-science research.[17]

Industrial relations centers also came into vogue. The first such center, the New York State School of Industrial and Labor Relations, was established at Cornell University (1945); others followed, such as the Institute of Labor and Industrial Relations at the University of Illinois (1946) and the Labor-Management Center at Yale University (1947). In 1947, a group of academicians, labor leaders, and others interested in advancing the state of knowledge in personnel and industrial relations formed the Industrial Relations Research Association.

Human-relations training also gained popularity during the late 1940s. Oriented toward overcoming barriers to communication and enhancing interpersonal skills, this training was largely based on the belief that the pathway to revealing hidden employee talents resided in group-oriented techniques, such as role-playing, nondirective counseling, group-discussion methods and, eventually, sensitivity training. It was also at this time that Carl R. Rogers, a clinical psychologist at the University of Chicago, developed his nondirective counseling approach, which involved creating a comfortable atmosphere for clients by accepting their feelings, regardless of content.[18] The University of Michigan's Norman R. F. Maier was one of the foremost advocates of "group-in-action" training techniques. For Maier (pronounced *mayor*), group decision-making was

A way of controlling through leadership rather than force.

A way of group discipline through social pressure.

A way of being fair to the job and all members of a group.

Permitting the group to jell on the idea it thinks will best solve a problem.

Pooled thinking.

Cooperative problem solving.

A way of giving each person a chance to participate in things that concern him in his work situation.

A method that requires skill and a respect for other people.[19]

---

[15] Philip Murray and Morris L. Cooke, *Organized Labor and Production: Next Steps in Industrial Democracy* (New York: Harper & Brothers, 1940), p. 211.

[16] For example, see Clinton S. Golden and Harold J. Ruttenberg, *The Dynamics of Industrial Democracy* (New York: Harper & Brothers, 1942).

[17] Burleigh B. Gardner and William Foote Whyte, "Methods for the Study of Human Relations in Industry," *American Sociological Review* 11(5) (October 1946), pp. 506–512. See also David G. Moore, "The Committee in Human Relations in Industry at the University of Chicago," in Kae H. Chung, ed., *Proceedings of the Annual Meeting of the Academy of Management* (1982), pp. 117–121.

[18] Carl P. Rogers, *Counseling and Psychotherapy: Newer Concepts in Practice* (Boston, MA: Houghton Mifflin, 1942). See also Kevin T. Mahoney and David B. Baker, "Elton Mayo and Carl Rogers: A Tale of Two Techniques," *Journal of Vocational Behavior* 60(3) (June 2002), pp. 437–450.

[19] Norman R. F. Maier, *Principles of Human Relation: Applications to Management* (New York: John Wiley & Sons, 1952), p. 30.

Managers during this period were encouraged to engage in group decision-making and adapt group-oriented techniques to enhance employee commitment. Human-relations training was also introduced in business-school classrooms. An interest in sharpening students' interpersonal skills led to a plethora of textbooks dealing with "human relations at work." World War II had placed great emphasis on the need for trained managers; teamwork and group leadership were in vogue, and universities sought to fill a call for graduates capable of managing both productive and satisfied workers. Drawing on the Hawthorne studies' emphasis on the importance of socially skilled managers, enhanced by the ideas and techniques of Moreno and Lewin, and popularized by university-based centers and union involvement, human-relations research and training reached their apogee in the 1950s.

Changing Assumptions about People at Work

As noted, whereas engineers largely dominated the scientific-management movement, the human-relations era was decidedly interdisciplinary in its focus. Thence came a different perspective on the nature of employee motivation, the role of managers in eliciting employee collaboration, and the importance of employee sentiments and informal work-group activities. This new perspective challenged prevailing assumptions about people at work. Investigations in the post-Hawthorne era led to (1) a deeper understanding of employee motivation; (2) questions about benefits from division of labor; and (3) an interest in obtaining greater employee commitment to an organization's goals through employee participation in workplace decision-making.

People and Motivation

One line of thinking about why individuals are motivated to behave as they do is that all human beings have recurring needs they attempt to satisfy. *Need theory* is one of the oldest explanations for why individuals engage in particular behaviors (see Chapter 9). In 1938, Henry A. Murray identified 27 basic personality needs that individuals attempt to satisfy by their actions (i.e., behavior).[20] Three of these needs—the needs for Power, Affiliation, and Achievement—have been the focus of continuing research, including that of David C. McClelland as discussed in Chapter 2. Abraham H. Maslow built on Murray's work to develop one of the most widely recognized need theories of motivation. According to Maslow, individuals are motivated to satisfy five categories of inborn needs: physiological, safety, love, esteem, and self-actualization. Maslow held that these needs form a hierarchy of ascending importance, from low to high. He contended that a "lower" need must be relatively satisfied before the "next higher" need can motivate behavior. For example, an individual's safety needs would have to be generally satisfied before the next level of need (social) could motivate behavior. Thus, the strength of any need is determined not only by its position in the hierarchy, but also by the degree to which it and all lower needs have been satisfied. Relative satisfaction of a need, however, triggers dissatisfaction at the next highest level. This sequence of "increased satisfaction, decreased importance, increased importance of the next higher need" repeats itself until the highest level of the hierarchy (self-actualization) is reached. Maslow suggested that an individual could progress down as well as up the various need levels. If a lower level need (safety, for instance) were threatened at some later point in time, it again would become dominant and assume an important position in an individual's overall motivation.

Maslow borrowed the term "self-actualization" from Kurt Goldstein, a well-known "holistic" psychologist. Goldstein saw self-actualization as the master motive from which sprang all other

---

[20] Henry A. Murray, *Explorations in Personality: A Clinical and Experimental Study of Fifty Men of College Age* (New York: Oxford University Press, 1938), p. 145.

motives.[21] Maslow, however, treated self-actualization in a more limited fashion as emerging only after all lower level needs are relatively satisfied: "A musician must make music, an artist must paint, a poet must write, if he is to be ultimately happy. What a man *can* be, he must be . . . to become more and more what one is, to become everything that one is capable of becoming."[22] Maslow believed the drive to self-actualize was universal, but the need for self-actualization is only rarely reached and never completely fulfilled.

Behaviorism and psychoanalysis were two other widely accepted motivation theories in the mid-1900s. As Maslow moved through his career, he became disenchanted with the behaviorist view that behavior is determined by stimuli and response contingencies. Sigmund Freud was the dominant figure in psychoanalysis. His thinking largely drew on the study of neurotics or psychotics. Maslow felt that there were shortcomings in basing our understanding of human motivation on the behavior of the emotionally disturbed. He believed that psychology should emphasize the study of the whole person, including those positive values that make individuals become good, honorable, creative, heroic, and so on. Maslow's response, "humanistic psychology," was a revolt against behaviorism and psychoanalysis, creating what became known as the Third Force in psychology. The Third Force gathered momentum as other prominent psychologists agreed that previous research and thinking had largely overlooked the majority of well-adjusted individuals leading productive lives.

Maslow's later years brought rich insights into what motivates managers. In the summer of 1962, he was named a visiting fellow at Non-Linear Systems (Del Mar, California). Non-Linear Systems president Andrew Kay arranged the appointment. This was Maslow's first exposure to a large business. He kept journals that summer and later published them as a book titled *Eupsychian Management*. Eupsychian was a neologism, a new word, and meant "good psychological management," or management by competent, mentally healthy, self-actualizing individuals. Maslow felt that one way to improve mental health, in general, would be to begin in the workplace, because most people are employed. He further believed that the best managers are individuals who are psychologically healthy.[23]

Whereas Maslow focused on the satisfaction of higher level needs, human-relations training emphasized group-performance incentives, employees' social needs, and workplace collaboration. The most widely cited and enduring plan for achieving these goals was developed by Joseph N. Scanlon, a seaman, prizefighter, cost accountant, open-hearth steel worker, union organizer, and union officer.[24] At the Empire Sheet and Tin Plate Company, he worked with its managers and officials of the United Steel Worker of American (an affiliate of the CIO) to broker a plan to save workers' jobs and stave off bankruptcy. A joint labor–management committee met frequently to hear worker suggestions on cutting waste and improving productivity and profitability in return for workers sharing in the cost savings. The plan was successful in saving jobs during the Depression and the subsequent years of World War II.

During the War, Scanlon developed some "forty to fifty" successful labor–management production committees for the War Production Board. Following the War, he joined the Massachusetts Institute of Technology (MIT) faculty, where he became a colleague of Douglas McGregor. McGregor's *The Human Side*

Joseph N. Scanlon, 1955. Harry W. Bass Business History Collection Bizzell Memorial Library, University of Oklahoma, Norman, OK. Courtesy of Daniel A. Wren.

---

[21] Kurt Goldstein, *The Organism: A Holistic Approach to Biology, Derived from Pathological Data in Man* (New York: American Book Company, 1939), p.160. Originally published in 1936.

[22] Abraham H. Maslow, "A Theory of Human Motivation," *Psychological Review* 50(4) (July 1943), p. 380.

[23] *Idem, Eupsychian Management: A Journal* (Homewood, IL: Richard D. Irwin, 1965), p. 75.

[24] Daniel A. Wren, "Joseph N. Scanlon: The Man and the Plan," *Journal of Management History* 15(1) (2009), pp. 20–37.

of Enterprise devoted a chapter to the Scanlon plan as an example of "management by integration and self-control . . . a way of industrial life – a philosophy of management – which rests on assumptions entirely consistent with [McGregor's] Theory Y."[25] (Theory Y is discussed further in Chapter 20.) The heart of the Scanlon plan involved: (1) a suggestion system that sought methods and means to reduce labor costs; (2) joint labor–management committees that sought to solve production difficulties; and (3) sharing cost savings. There were no individual awards, cooperation and collaboration were stressed over competition, and everyone benefitted from the cost-saving suggestions of others. Scanlon realized firms faced different circumstances and, thus, no one plan was appropriate for all—the only essentials were labor and management's willingness to work together in seeking cost savings and sharing these savings (75 percent to labor and 25 percent to management).

The Scanlon plan appealed to labor because it could save jobs in failing firms and explicitly required union participation in committees that sought to solve production difficulties. Before his death in 1956, Scanlon successfully introduced his plan in 60 small- to medium-sized firms, including various manufacturing and nonmanufacturing industries and union and nonunion shops. Frederick Lesieur, an MIT colleague, installed the Scanlon plan in over 200 firms before his retirement in 1986.[26] Others continued this work and Scanlon's plan achieved standing among labor-relations scholars as "an organization wide gain sharing plan that seeks to provide all employees with incentives to search for ways to reduce the overall cost of goods sold."[27] Rather than becoming a management fad, Scanlon's ideas have proven their worth in combining employee participation and financial incentives.

Although the Scanlon plan was typical of the era's emphasis on human relations in the workplace, individual incentives did not pass entirely from the industrial scene. Writing in his book *Incentive Management: A New Approach to Human Relationships in Industry and Business*, James F. Lincoln appealed to employee ambition. Lincoln believed that people were trading freedom for security; they were relying on someone else (the federal government) for their well-being while pride in work, self-reliance, and other time-tested virtues were declining. In Lincoln's view, the remedy to this decline was a return to an "intelligent selfishness," in which people are rewarded based on their individual performance. As president of Lincoln Electric Company (Cleveland, Ohio), the world's largest producer of welding equipment, he pioneered a pay-for-performance incentive plan designed to motivate employees by rewarding them only for what they produced. In addition, however, all employees received an annual bonus based on their individual output, dependability, degree of cooperativeness with other employees, and company profitability. These bonuses were often almost as much as employees' yearly salaries.[28] Writing in 1951, Lincoln reported that his company had never experienced work stoppages, labor turnover was negligible, employee productivity was five times that of other U.S. manufacturers, dividends per share were continually rising, and product prices were steadily declining.[29]

When Lincoln Electric expanded overseas in the late 1980s and early 1990s, it underestimated the challenge of exporting its pay-for-performance system to other cultures with different labor

---

[25] Douglas McGregor, *The Human Side of Enterprise* (New York: McGraw-Hill, p. 110). *Time* magazine called Scanlon "the most sought-after labor-relations adviser in the U.S. today." See "The Scanlon Plan," *Time* 46(13) (September 26, 1955), p. 90.

[26] Frederick G. Lesieur, ed., *The Scanlon Plan: A Frontier in Labor-Management Cooperation* (Cambridge, MA: Cambridge Technology Press of Massachusetts Institute of Technology, 1958).

[27] Thomas A. Kochan and Paul Osterman, *The Mutual Gains Enterprise: Forging a Winning Partnership among Labor, Management, and Government* (Boston, MA: Harvard Business School Press, 1994), p. 54. For doubts about employee participation in general, see George Strauss, "Worker Participation: Some Under-Considered Issues," *Industrial Relations* 45(4) (October 2006), pp. 778–803.

[28] Lincoln Electric's 80th annual bonus in 2013 *averaged* $33,029 for "roughly 3,000 employees" in its North American Division. *Average total* earnings per worker were $87,366. www.prnewswire.com/news/the-lincoln-electric-company. Retrieved March 18, 2016. Further information on Lincoln Electric's adjustments to technological change and global operations, as well as its bonus plan's history may be found in Virginia P. Dawson, *Lincoln Electric: A History* (Cleveland, OH: Lincoln Electric Company, 1999).

[29] James F. Lincoln, *Incentive Management: A New Approach to Human Relationships in Industry and Business* (Cleveland, OH: Lincoln Electric Company, 1951), pp. 251–289.

laws, customs, and workplace values.[30] For example, under Brazilian law, bonuses awarded for 2 years were automatically considered part of an employee's permanent base salary. In France and other European countries, employees preferred more vacation time to big bonuses. European unions, in general, opposed any attempt to place employees in competition with one another to produce more. Lincoln's overseas experience is a lesson to companies from any nation seeking to globally export its domestic management practices.

Job Enlargement

In 1776, Adam Smith warned that, despite its economic advantages, division of labor could lead to dysfunctional consequences for employees in terms of "intellectual, social, and martial virtues"[31] (see Chapter 2). Almost 175 years later, social scientists and innovative companies began to take Smith's warning seriously. In 1944, at its Endicott plant (New York), the International Business Machines Corporation (IBM) began to combine the work of two or more machine operators into one job. IBM called this *job enlargement* and found that doing so led to higher product quality, less idle time for employees and machines, and "enriched" jobs by introducing skill variety and individual responsibility.[32]

Soon afterward, in a study of an automobile factory, Walker and Guest found that assembly-line employees rebelled against the anonymity of their jobs, even though they were satisfied with their pay and employment security.[33] Having met these more basic needs, the employees bridled at the repetitiveness and mechanical pacing of their conveyor belt-driven work. As a result of Walker and Guest's findings, *job enlargement* (and later *job enrichment*) assumed a new prominence in studies of workplace behavior. Job enlargement served to relieve monotony, enhance skill levels, and increase feelings of task significance among employees. Job enrichment went further by also encouraging employers to give as much responsibility to their employees as possible.

Participation in Decision-Making

A third area in which prevailing workplace assumptions were challenged during the 1940s and 1950s concerned the nature of power relations within organizations. There was a growing appeal to give employees a greater voice in workplace decisions. Operating on the premise that worker participation would yield a greater commitment to organizational goals and also further individual and group satisfaction, researchers sought to involve employees in workplace decision-making. James C. Worthy, drawing on his experiences with Sears, Roebuck and Company, argued for "flatter," less complex organizational structures that would decentralize power and authority and thereby lead to improved employee attitudes, encourage individual responsibility and initiative, and provide outlets for individual self-expression and creativity.[34] Sears, Roebuck also collaborated with the University of Chicago's Committee on Human Relations in a comprehensive study of the influence of organization structure on employee morale. Worthy's analysis of "tall" versus "flat" structures, their

---

[30] Barnaby J. Feder, "Rethinking a Model Incentive Plan: A U.S. Company Regroups After a Worker Motivation Plan Fails Abroad," *New York Times* (September 5, 1994), p. 33. See also Jordan I. Siegel and Barbara Zepp Larson, "Labor Market Institutions and Global Strategic Adaptation: Evidence from Lincoln Electric," *Management Science* 55(9) (September 2009), pp. 1527–1546.
[31] Adam Smith, *An Inquiry Into the Nature and Causes of the Wealth of Nations* (London: w. Strahan and T. Cadell in the Strand, 1776), vol. 2, bk. V, ch. 1, pp. 366–367.
[32] Charles R. Walker, "The Problem of the Repetitive Job," *Harvard Business Review* 28(3) (May 1950), pp. 54–58. See also Robert H. Guest, "Job Enlargement – A Revolution in Job Design," *Personnel Administration* 20(2) (March–April 1957), pp. 9–16.
[33] Charles R. Walker and Robert H. Guest, "The Man on the Assembly Line," *Harvard Business Review* 30(3) (May–June 1952), pp. 71–83.
[34] James C. Worthy, "Organizational Structure and Employee Morale," *American Sociological Review* 15(2) (April 1950), pp. 169–179.

James C. Worthy. Courtesy of Arthur G. Bedeian.

impact on employee behavior, and the influence of managers' assumptions on employee morale remains a landmark in advancing our understanding of workplace dynamics.[35]

William B. Given, Jr., and Charles P. McCormick were two other executives who challenged prevailing workplace assumptions. Using the catchphrase "bottom-up management," as president of the American Brake Shoe Company, Given sought to develop a program of employee participation "to release the thinking and encourage the initiative of all those down the line, so that ideas and impetus flow from the bottom up."[36] Bottom-up management involved widespread delegation of authority, considerable latitude in decision-making, a free interchange of ideas at all levels, and the corollary acceptance of the fact that managers grow by having the freedom to fail. Recognizing that a "push from the top" was occasionally needed, Given tried to confine top-down management to setting policy, clarifying goals, and providing employee training.

McCormick, president of McCormick & Company, introduced a unique model of employee participation that involved establishing a Junior Board of Directors. Part of what became known as The Multiple Management Plan, the Junior Board was used as a means of training and motivating younger managers. Junior board directors were given free access to financial and other company records, encouraged to elect their own officers, and told that "every recommendation they made for the advancement of the business would have the serious consideration of the company."[37] The Junior Board met with the McCormick & Company "senior board" once a month to submit its recommendations, which were generally accepted and acted on to a greater extent than McCormick himself had expected. In fact, McCormick attributed his company's success during the lean years of the Great Depression to the Junior Board's efforts. One example of a Junior Board recommendation involved the redesign of the company's traditional bottle for specialty extracts, which McCormick expected his older executives would wish to retain. The Junior Board conducted a market investigation, considered homemakers' ideas, and came up with a new design that was immediately accepted by the company's senior board and the marketplace. The success of the Junior Board led to the creation of two other boards. A Factory Board and a Sales Board, which operated essentially as the Junior Board for the company's production and sales departments, were established in 1933 and 1935, respectively. In McCormick's opinion, The Multiple Management Plan offered a number of advantages: (1) it opened communication channels for junior managers; (2) it involved young managers in decision-making; (3) it provided a means for identifying and developing future executives; (4) it relieved senior board members of a great deal of detailed planning and research; and (5) it provided for interlocking arrangements between various departments to coordinate and follow through on company activities.

During the 1930s and 1940s, employee participation in decision-making received greater and greater acclaim. It was viewed as democracy in action, opening communication channels, diffusing authority, and motivating employees by encouraging greater commitment to shared organizational goals.[38] Moreover, it was seen as challenging unilateral authority and as equalizing power between employees and employers.

---

[35] James C. Worthy, *Brushes with History: Recollection of a Many Favored Life* (Privately printed, 1998), pp. 84–101.

[36] William B. Given, Jr., *Bottom-Up Management: People Working Together* (New York: Harper & Brothers, 1949), pp. 3–4.

[37] Charles P. McCormick, *Multiple Management* (New York: Harper & Brothers, 1938), p. 5. See also McCormick's sequel, *The Power of People: Multiple Management Up to Date* (New York: Harper & Brothers, 1949). McCormick & Company's has continued this practice globally with "13 local Multiple Management Boards, 3 regional boards, and a global board." Letter from Jim Lynn, Corporate Communication Director, McCormick & Company, to Daniel A. Wren, October 6, 2014.

[38] See Gordon W. Allport, "The Psychology of Participation," *Psychological Review* 53(3) (May 1945), pp. 117–132.

Leadership: Combining People and Production

Kurt Lewin's experiences as a Jew who fled Nazi Germany undoubtedly influenced his thinking about leadership, resistance to change, and the social climate within groups. Lewin's work exemplified the emergence of a pro-participation and antiauthoritarian literature during the 1930s and 1940s. Contributors to this literature included Theodor W. Adorno and his associates, who made a significant impact on the leadership literature in 1950 with their book *The Authoritarian Personality*.[39] Influenced by the Nazism and fascism witnessed in World War II, Adorno and his associates tried to relate personality structure to leadership, followership, morals, prejudices, and politics. The F scale (Fascist Scale), developed as a part of the book, became an accepted instrument for analyzing leadership styles as well as followers' leader preferences.

Research, however, was beginning to challenge the idea that one leadership style was good and another bad. As early as 1945, the University of Michigan's Institute for Social Research, under the direction of Rensis Likert, began a series of studies to determine what principles and methods of leadership resulted in the highest employee productivity, least absenteeism, lowest turnover, and greatest job satisfaction. The studies focused on the operation of small work groups. The studies' primary objective was to identify leader behaviors that resulted in high levels of work-group performance and satisfaction. As a result of this effort, two relatively distinct styles of leadership were identified: (1) *job-centered*—leader behaviors oriented toward close supervision, pressure for better performance, meeting deadlines, and evaluating output, and (2) *employee-centered*—leader behaviors oriented toward human aspects of subordinate relations and developing effective work groups with high performance goals. Employee-centered leaders are concerned with employee needs, welfare, advancement, and personal growth, whereas job-centered leaders are concerned with ensuring employees meet performance standards.[40] The Michigan researchers emphasized that a hard-and-fast line could not be drawn between the two styles of leadership they had identified. Both were important to productivity. They explained their results as a matter of emphasis. Managers of high-producing groups were seen as emphasizing high productivity as *one* aspect of their jobs, but not the *only* aspect. In contrast, managers of low-producing groups were viewed as emphasizing high productivity to the exclusion of other important aspects of their job.

Likert identified four profiles of organizational characteristics: System 1—"exploitative authoritative"; System 2—"benevolent authoritative"; System 3—"consultative"; and System 4—"participative group."[41] Likert regarded System 4 to be "the ideal" state for an organization in terms of performance and maximum employee satisfaction and morale, with System 1 the least effective performance. System 2 was more effective than System 1, but less effective than System 3, and so on. System 4 involved three basic concepts: (1) the "principle of supportive relationships," (2) group decision-making and group methods of supervision, and (3) high performance goals.

Likert considered the *principle of supportive relationships* to be a guide for applying System 4. Simply stated: "*The leadership and other processes of the organization must be such as to ensure a maximum probability that in all interactions and all relationships with the organization each member will, in the light of his background, values, and expectations, view the experience as supportive and one which builds his sense of personal worth and importance.*"[42] Likert felt that this principle incorporated essential elements for the success of every organization and provided a "fundamental formula" for tapping an employee's full potential.

In his last book, Likert, writing with his wife Jane, referred to System 5 as "an even more sophisticated, complex, and effective system" that would emerge as the social sciences advanced. In System 5, a superior's hierarchical authority would be replaced with an authority of relationships.

---

[39] Theodor W. Adorno, Else Frenkel-Brunswick, David J. Levinson, and R. Nevitt Sanford (in collaboration with Betty Aron, Maria Hertz Levinson, and William Morrow), *The Authoritarian Personality* (New York: Harper & Brothers, 1950).

[40] See, for example, Rensis Likert *New Patterns of Management* (New York: McGraw-Hill, 1961), pp. 23–44.

[41] *Ibid.*, p. 223.

[42] *Ibid.* p. 103.

In case of conflict, groups would work together through overlapping memberships until a consensus is reached. Employees would be called "associates" (there would be no position titles). Leadership would involve a "shared sense of purpose." If these ideas sound familiar, it may be because Likert was a great admirer of Mary P. Follett (see Chapter 14).[43]

At about the same time the Michigan research was beginning, the Personnel Research Board of the Ohio State University began a series of studies that developed a "situational approach to leadership."[44] Conducted under the primary direction of Ralph M. Stogdill and Carroll L. Shartle, the purpose of the studies was to determine the impact of leader behavior on job performance and employee satisfaction. The studies revealed that followers perceived their leaders' behaviors to be composed of two principal dimensions: (1) *consideration*—leader behaviors oriented toward developing mutual trust, two-way communication, respect for followers' ideas, and concern for their feelings and (2) *initiating structure*—leader behaviors oriented toward structuring followers' activities for the purpose of goal attainment. Because consideration and initiating structure are independent dimensions, it is possible for a leader to be high in initiating structure and low in consideration, low in initiating structure and high in consideration, or high or low in both. Consideration is similar to the Michigan dimension of employee-centeredness and initiating structure is analogous to the Michigan dimension of job-centeredness.

Ralph M. Stogdill. Courtesy of Arthur G. Bedeian.

Although one might assume that the most effective leaders would be those who ranked high on both consideration and initiating structure, the Ohio State researchers found this is not always the case. Both dimensions are necessary for effective leadership, but it is more important for a leader to strike a balance appropriate for a particular situation than to exhibit a high degree of both types of behavior at all times. Simply stated, a leader needs to be flexible, because the proper balance of leader behaviors varies from situation to situation.

In retrospect, the Michigan and Ohio State studies added immensely to our knowledge about effective leadership. Perhaps most significantly, they showed that no single leadership style is universally effective. Moreover, the systematic methodology they introduced and the increased awareness they generated concerning effective leaders served as a springboard for the leadership research that followed. In contrast to earlier trait theories of leadership (see Chapter 9), both the Michigan and Ohio State studies showed that leaders may be best characterized by how they behave rather than by their personal traits.

People at Work: The Macro View

On the macro side of the human-relations movement, a search was underway for analytical tools and conceptual models to explain the interactions between the formal and informal processes operating within organizations. In particular, there were a number of attempts to understand the interaction of the social and technical systems occurring within organizations. The results of these efforts laid the groundwork for later developments in organization theory.

---

[43] *Idem*, "From Production- and Employee-Centeredness to Systems 1–5," *Journal of Management* 5(2) (Fall 1976), p. 151.

[44] Carroll L. Shartle, "The Early Years of the Ohio State University Leadership Studies," *Journal of Management* 5 (Fall 1979), pp. 127–134; Chester A. Schriesheim and Barbara J. Bird, "Contributions of the Ohio State Studies to the Field of Leadership," *Journal of Management* 5(3) (Fall 1979), pp. 135–145.

Organizations as Sociotechnical Systems

One of the earliest and most perceptive attempts to understand the interaction of the social and technical systems operating within organizations was an analysis of human relations in the restaurant industry by William Foote Whyte. A key concept in his analysis was job status, or the relative prestige of a job in the jobholder's eyes or in the regard of others. Restaurants are characterized by varying levels of job status, ranging from the low status of bussers, who clear dirty dishes from tables, to the relatively high status of cooks. Whyte found that a restaurant's work flow—taking customer orders, preparing the orders, and serving the orders—posed a number of human-relations challenges. For example, waiting tables was considered a low-status job. Waitresses, however, when placing customer orders, originated work for higher status cooks. Because those who initiate work for others are of higher status (managers initiate work for subordinates), Whyte discovered that conflicts were inevitable when someone in a lower status job (e.g., waitresses) initiated work for someone of higher status (e.g., cooks). Whyte reported that restaurants avoided conflict between waitresses and cooks by placing a spindle on their order counters. The spindles are wheels on a shaft. The wheel has clips on it so that the lower status waitresses can put customer orders on the wheel rather than call them out to higher status cooks. In this way, the cooks can remove and prepare customer orders under the pretext that they had not come from a lower status waitress, but from the spindle.[45] The spindles, thus, effectively served to depersonalize authority and required all to obey the "law of the situation." Mary Follett would be quite pleased.

The Tavistock Institute of Human Relations (London) was also responsible for a number of studies concerning organizations both as social systems and as a part of their broader community. Elliott Jaques (pronounced *jacks*) conducted an extensive case study of the Glacier Metal Company (London) based on Lewin's field theory and examined changes in technology as they moved through and affected work groups.[46] As part of the study, Jacques developed a theory of equitable payment and a technique for determining the time span of discretion for different jobs. Such longitudinal research into ongoing firms was (and is) rare.

Jacques's findings underscored the importance of studying organizations as interacting sociotechnical systems and were consistent with Barnard's ideas about all aspects of society being one large, cooperative system. Two of Jacques's Tavistock colleagues, Eric L. Trist and Kenneth W. Bamforth, reported a classic example of how changes in technology disrupt an organization's social system. They studied the social and technical consequences of the mechanized longwall method of mining coal as introduced in Great Britain following World War II.[47] The longwall method required breaking up established small, highly cohesiveness work groups and the substitution of specialized, larger groups working in shifts. Under the traditional shortwall method, miners had organized relatively autonomous work groups that rotated job assignments and shifts among themselves with a minimum of supervision. By contrast, with the longwall method, each miner was responsible for a single specialized task. The introduction of the longwall method resulted in a deskilling of the work performed by the miners and a loss of autonomy. This led to decreased commitment, lower productivity, and an increased sense of personal alienation. Trist and Bamforth documented how the longwall method so disrupted the miners' social structure that its advantages were essentially negated. The lesson: Technological changes will not be effective unless due consideration is given to maintaining an organization's social system.

---

[45] William Foote Whyte, *Human Relations in the Restaurant Industry* (New York: McGraw-Hill, 1948), pp. 69–76. See also idem, "The Social Structure of the Restaurant," *American Journal of Sociology* 54(4) (January 1949), pp. 302–308.

[46] Elliott Jaques, *The Changing Culture of a Factory* (London: Tavistock Publications, 1951).

[47] Eric L. Trist and Kenneth W. Bamforth, "Some Social and Technical Consequences of the Longwall Method of Coal-Getting: An Examination of the Psychological Situation and Defences of a Work Group in Relation to the Social Structure and Technological Content of the Work System," *Human Relations* 4(1) (February 1951), pp. 3–38.

New Tools for Macro Analysis

A review of the macro side of the human-relations movement would be incomplete without discussing the contributions of Carnegie Mellon University professor and Nobel laureate Herbert A. Simon. As noted in Chapter 14, Simon was greatly influenced by Chester I. Barnard's thoughts on decision-making in organizations, especially on authority, inducements, and communications. Building on Barnard's analysis of how decisions are made in organizations, Simon questioned the validity of the rational model of decision-making grounded in traditional economic theory.[48] Rather than portraying managers as completely rational decision-makers who invariably seek to maximize expected benefits (or minimize costs), Simon advanced the view that managerial (and in general) decisions are bounded by individuals' limited mental capacity and emotions, as well as by environmental factors over which they may have no control. He labeled this "bounded rationality" to reflect not only the limited capability of the humans to grasp the full complexity of decisions but also the uncertainty of future events with which they must cope.[49] Given that organizations exist in highly complex environments, in which many possible alternatives and their consequences may remain unknown, all intendedly rational behavior is inherently bounded.

As this suggests, *optimum decisions* (meaning "best possible" decisions) are almost never made—except perhaps by chance. Even if it were possible to acquire perfect knowledge of all alternatives and their consequences (assumptions of classical economic theory), it is doubtful that, given the limitations of human-information-processing, an adequate evaluation could be made. In response to this dilemma, Simon believed that humans typically reduce the complexity they confront by constructing a simplified model that encompasses only the information they feel equipped to handle. Thus, only a limited number of alternatives and a limited range of consequences are considered.

Simon further believed that once managers have identified a limited set of alternatives, they typically deviate from the demands of rationality by selecting the first alternative deemed "satisfactory" or "good enough," rather than searching for the optimum choice. That is, rather than examine all possible alternatives and attempt to rank them according to a well-ordered and stable set of preferences (as described by classical economic theory), they conduct a sequential search and settle for the first that satisfies some predetermined "aspiration level"—a subjectively defined performance goal that is a product of past organization goals, past organization performance, and past performance of comparable organizations. Thus, choices are influenced more by the order in which alternatives are examined than by the preexistence of clear guidelines for ensuring that the optimum choice is selected.

As a shorthand label for this process, Simon used the Scottish word *satisficing* (satisfying).[50] Examples of satisficing criteria include "share of market" versus "total market," "adequate profit" versus "maximum profit," and "fair price" versus "best price." Thus, satisficing is evident in a business whose managers are willing to hold to a decision alternative that results in a 25 percent rate of return on investment even if they are aware there *may* be other alternatives that *might* raise profits still higher. For practical purposes (e.g., selecting a source of raw materials), Simon stressed that it is important that satisficing not be seen as irrational. Given the limitations of human-information processing, the cost of searching for alternatives, and the uncertainty of future events, satisficing is actually sensible.

---

[48] Herbert A. Simon, *Administrative Behavior: A Study of Decision-Making Processes in Administrative Organization* (New York: Macmillan, 1945).

[49] Matteo Cristofaro, "Herbert Simon's Bounded Rationality" Its Historical Evolution in Management and Cross-fertilizing Contribution," *Journal of Management History* 23(2) 2017, pp. 170–190.

[50] Reva Brown, "Consideration of the Origin of Herbert Simon's Theory of 'Satisficing' (1935–1947)," *Management Decision* 42(10), pp. 1240–1256.

On balance, Simon rejected the basic traditional economic notion that managers are completely rational decision-makers. Whereas economists have typically focused on how managers *should* behave, Simon focused on how they *do* behave. He posited that managers do not merely seek to maximize expected benefits and that they are not completely rational. Simon's work on bounded rationality replaced the idea of the so-called "economic decision-maker" with the more realistic "managerial decision-maker."

The work of George C. Homans represented another step forward on the macro side of the human-relations movement. Homans attended Lawrence J. Henderson's Pareto seminar (the Pareto Circle) at Harvard University (see Chapter 13) and coauthored (with Boston attorney and member of the Harvard Corporation Charles P. Curtis, Jr.) an early book on Vilfredo Pareto's 1916 book *Trattato di Sociologia Generale* [*Treatise on General Sociology*] that formed the basis for his later view of organizations as social systems.[51] In *The Human Group*, Homans viewed groups as social systems that, in turn, are comprised of an external system and an internal system.[52] Homans described a group's external system consisting of forces that are determined by the nature of its particular environment. Conversely, he considered a group's internal system to be "the elaboration of group behavior that simultaneously arises out of the external system and reacts upon it," resulting in an interaction between both systems.[53] Carrying this reasoning further, Homans identified and discussed various mutually dependent elements that interact across a group's internal and external systems: (1) activities, behavior formally required of group members or that informally emerge; (2) interactions, organizationally prescribed or informally originated transactions between group members; and (3) sentiments, emotions having positive and negative values (such as like or dislike). Although Homans's treatment of groups as social systems was exceedingly broad, it provided a building block for further developments in organization theory.

Talcott Parsons, another member of Henderson's Pareto Circle, also played a major role in the early development of social-systems analysis. Parsons received his doctorate from the University of Heidelberg in sociology and economics, wrote his dissertation on Max Weber, and introduced Chester I. Barnard to Weber's views on bureaucracy. In an early work, Parsons drew together the ideas of Weber, Pareto, Alfred Marshall, and Émile Durkheim to develop a "voluntaristic theory of social action."[54] His ideas influenced Barnard's search for a theory of "cooperative systems." Parsons is especially remembered for producing a general theoretical system for the analysis of society known as "structural functionalism."[55]

SUMMARY

This is the first of two chapters examining twin streams of management thought that developed from about 1930 to the early 1950s. The current chapter focused on the growth and refinement of the human-relations movement as it passed through micro and macro phases. The micro phase saw an outpouring of behavioral research into topics such as group dynamics, group decision-making, leadership, and motivation. The macro phase witnessed a search for analytical tools and conceptual models to explain the interactions between the formal and informal processes operating within organizations. The title of this chapter, "People and Organizations," conveys the human orientation of both phases, with the structural aspects of organizations being a secondary subject of inquiry. In contrast, Chapter 16, "Organizations and People," focuses on the structure and design of organizations, with the human element placed in a relatively subordinate role.

[51] George C. Homans and Charles P. Curtis, Jr., *An Introduction to Pareto: His Sociology* (New York: Alfred A. Knopf, 1934).

[52] George C. Homans, *The Human Group* (New York: Harcourt, Brace & World, 1950).

[53] *Ibid.*, p. 109.

[54] Talcott E. F. Parsons, *The Structure of Social Action: A Study in Social Theory with Special Reference to a Group of Recent European Writers* (New York: McGraw-Hill, 1937).

[55] *Idem, The Social System* (Glencoe, IL: Free Press, 1951).

chapter 16

Organizations and People

Contemporaneous with the writings of both Mary P. Follett and Chester I. Barnard, the advent of the Western Electric studies and the outpouring of behavioral research into topics such as group dynamics, group decision-making, leadership, and motivation reviewed in Chapter 15, a complementary stream of management thought focused on the structure and design of organizations. By comparison, this second stream has been accused of ignoring the importance of human factor in achieving an organization's success.[1] In point of fact, it intentionally distinguished between "the structure of positions and the behavior of persons temporarily occupying them." In doing so, it held that "the only way in which to study organization fruitfully is to isolate it from the personalities and 'politics' of particular undertakings at a particular moment."[2] Consequently, although the human element was not entirely omitted from this second stream of management thought, it was specifically set apart for a distinct purpose: to provide an analysis independent of idiosyncratic personalities and politics. This chapter, covering the period from the roughly 1930 into the early 1950s, focuses on three aspects of the structure and design of organizations: (1) authority, coordination, span of control, and other issues relevant to the structure and design of organizations; (2) the primary responsibilities of top management; and (3) the separation of ownership and control and the transfer of property rights.

---

[1] See, for example, V. Subranabiam, "The Classical Organization Theory and Its Critics," *Public Administration* 44(4) (Winter 1966), pp. 435–446 and Thomas E. Stephenson, "The Longevity of Classical Theory," *Management International Review* 8(6) (1968), pp. 77–93.

[2] Lyndall F. Urwick, "Why the So-Called 'Classicists' Endure," *Management International Review* 11(1) (1971), p. 6.

Organizations: Structure and Design

The so-called "classicists" writing in the 1930s through the early 1950s studied the nature organizations divorced from the performance of any single person. They recognized that organizations incur obligations through the actions of individual managers and that these obligations cannot be evaded by simply pleading that a manager, who for a time occupied a position of authority, is no longer employed or has since moved on. In the classicists' view, the authority associated with a managerial position is distinct from any individual occupant. Authority is associated with positions and not particular people who are their temporary tenants. Or, as Max Weber would emphasize, "authority adheres to specific positions rather than to individuals" (see Chapter 10). The classicists examined here distinguished between designing and staffing an organization. In doing so, they studied the structure and design of organizations separately from the performance of the people staffing an organization.

James D. Mooney: Organization Theory and Practice

James D. Mooney attended the Case School of Applied Sciences (today's Case Western Reserve University), majored in mining engineering, but did not graduate. He spent 2 years searching for gold, was employed as an engineer at BF Goodrich Company, Westinghouse Electric Corporation, and Hyatt Roller Bearing Company. He served as an artillery captain during the Great War, and at its conclusion returned to Hyatt, which had been acquired by the General Motors Corporation (GM) in 1916. Some 6 years later, Mooney was appointed president of GM's fledgling Export Company.[3] As the Export Company expanded in scope, distributing an increasing variety of different automotive products, Mooney was soon faced with how to best structure its growing international operations. Responding to its overall growth as a compnay, in 1923, GM adopted an organizing plan originally developed at the Du Pont Company. Following this plan, each of GM's major product lines (Chevrolet, Buick, Pontiac, Oldsmobile, Cadillac, and so forth) was administered through a separate and semiautonomous division (see Chapter 11). The divisions operated as minicompanies with their own departments for production, marketing, finance, and so on. Such a multidivisional ("M-form") structure was, however, impractical for GM's overseas operations, which spanned 15 assembly plants serving some 70 different markets with distinct economic, political, and cultural environments. To allow units in different regions to better sense changes in market needs and adapt to varying government regulations across countries, Mooney structured the Export Company's activities geographically (based on natural, legal, political, and cultural considerations) into 6 regions with local managers, supported by staff headquartered in New York City, empowered to act in individual markets.

Intrigued by the success of this new arrangement and recognizing that "Organization is as old as human society itself,"[4] Mooney subsequently joined with Alan C. Reiley, a Columbia University historian, to trace the evolution of organized activities "down through the ages." Their intent was "to expose the *principles of organization,* as they reveal themselves in various forms of human group movement, and to help industry to protect its own growth through a greater knowledge and more conscious use of these principles."[5] Their collaboration resulted in the book

---

[3] For further biographical information on Mooney and his work at GM, see Daniel A. Wren, "James D. Mooney and General Motors' Multinational Operations, 1922–1940," *Business History Review* 87(3) (October 2013), pp. 515–543; [W. Jerome Arnold], "Drawing the Rules from History," *Business Week* (August 3, 1963), pp. 46, 51.

[4] James D. Mooney and Alan C. Reiley, *Onward Industry! The Principles of Organization and Their Significance to Modern Industry* (New York: Harper & Brothers, 1931), p. xiii. This book was later published in a more concise form under the title *The Principles of Organization* (New York: Harper & Brothers: 1939).

[5] *Ibid.*

Onward Industry!. Although both men were credited as authors, it later became evident that Mooney was responsible for the book's underlying conceptual model of organization and Reiley assumed a lesser role, primarily contributing historical examples.

In the foreword to *Onward Industry!* Mooney stated that industrial objectives could be justified only by the worthiness of their purpose. He observed that the purpose of industrial enterprises is usually defined as "profit through service." This involved justifying a service and both creating and equitably dividing profits. For Mooney, however, the "true and worthy" purpose of industrial effort was "the alleviation of human want and misery."[6] Mere productive efficiency, though necessary, in providing a service was insufficient. Equal efficiency must be realized throughout an organization, including the distribution or supplying of materials wants to those, due to poverty, who were unable to purchase them. To this end, Mooney (much like Gantt before him, see Chapter 8) felt that the application of the principles of organization could solve the problems of modern civilization.

As judged by Mooney, true efficiency requires "the efficient coordination of all relationships."[7] Further, this coordination must be based on principles of organization. Mooney viewed organization as a process and defined it as follows: "*Organization is the form of every human association for the attainment of a common purpose.*"[8] Mooney's notion of management was distinct from organization and was explained using a mind-body analogy:

> Management is the vital spark which actuates, directs, and controls the plans and procedure of organization. With management enters the personal factor, without which no body could be a living being with any directive toward a given purpose. The relation of management to organization is analogous to the relation of the psychic complex to the physical body. Our bodies are simply the means and the instrument through which the psychic force moves toward the attainment of its aims and desires.[9]

The conceptual model of organization Mooney developed consisted of three basic principles: (1) the coordinative principle; (2) the scalar principle; and (3) the functional principle. The first principle, coordination, meant "*the orderly arrangement of group effort, to provide unity of action in the pursuit of a common purpose.*"[10] The foundation for coordination was authority, "the supreme coordinating power." Authority in this sense did not imply autocracy, but as Mooney explained, "In a democracy like our own, this authority rests with the people, who exercise it through the leaders of their choice."[11] Because coordination implies working together effectively, Mooney felt every member of an organization had to understand its purpose and the "procedure" necessary to attain it, which he called its *doctrine*. Mooney explained that in a religious sense doctrine is based on faith, but for industry, it meant the attainment of "*surplus through service,*" which (as noted) should be the purpose of industrial enterprises. Mooney reasoned that the more an organization's doctrine guides its members' actions, their level of teamwork will increase, as will the accomplishment of its objectives.

The second basic principle of Mooney's conceptual model, the scalar principle, pertained to the "formal process through which [the supreme] coordinating authority operates from the top throughout the entire organized body."[12] This principle had its foundation in leadership, which was how authority entered the scalar chain. Delegation of authority allowed a superior to confer authority on a subordinate. Delegation always meant the conferring of authority, whether authority over people or authority for task performance. Conversely, authority always carried with it responsibility for accomplishing what was authorized.

The final principle of Mooney's conceptual model, the functional principle, pertained to the "*distinction between different kinds of duties.*" Functional differentiation exists in every

---

[6] *Ibid.*

[7] *Ibid.*, p. xv.

[8] *Ibid.*, p. 10.

[9] *Ibid.*, p. 13.

[10] Mooney and Reiley, *Principles of Organization*, p. 5.

[11] *Ibid.*, p. 7.

[12] *Ibid.*, p. 14.

organization to the extent that people perform different kinds of duties, such as production, sales, accounting, security, and so on. This principle can be seen in the division of labor, which creates a need for coordination. Another example of functional differentiation is the distinction between line and staff. According to Mooney, there should never be any confusion about line and staff because line represented "the authority of *man*; the staff, the authority of *ideas*."[13] Line commanded, staff advised, and Mooney envisioned no potential conflict in line-staff relations as long as this dichotomy was kept in mind.

Following Mooney's section on the principles of organization, Reiley made his major contribution to *Onward Industry!* by showing how the principles of organization evolved from military and church organization. He used historical examples from Greece, Rome, and other civilizations to illustrate applications of Mooney's three basic principles. With respect to the Roman Catholic Church, the principle of coordination found its authority in God, who delegated it to the Pope (the Bishop of Rome) as the supreme coordinating authority. The scalar principle operated via the Pope, through cardinals (who were often both line and staff), to bishops and priests and involved conferring authority on subordinates occupying an organization's lower echelons. In developing staff, the Church operated on a *compulsory staff service* principle. Under this principle, a superior had to consult elder monks even on minor matters. On matters of major importance, everyone had to be consulted. This principle did not abridge line authority, but compelled the superior to consult with others before rendering a decision. The superior could not refuse to listen. In a business, the compulsory staff principle would not protect managers from errors in judgment, but would serve to reduce errors of knowledge.

In retrospect, Mooney and Reiley's principles resembled Weber's notion of "legal authority", and his call for a clear "managerial hierarchy," and "formal rules and other controls" (see Chapter 10). Mooney and Reiley did not refer to Weber, and because Weber's work had not been translated into English at this time, it may be assumed that they independently developed their conceptual model and principles of organization. Mooney's belief that a business could only achieve its true purpose if it was structured following fundamental principles of organization was reinforced by his experiences as president of GM's Export Company and Reiley's historical examples from Greece, Rome, and other civilizations. For organization theory, Mooney and Reiley's major contribution was showing the interplay among principles assumed fundamental to any activity with an identified objective. In addiction, their belief that that the more an organization's "doctrine" guides its members' actions, their level of teamwork will increase, as will the accomplishment of its objectives was far ahead of the importance placed on socially responsible mission statements in today's corporate world.

Texts, Teachers, and Trends

Until the publication of Mooney and Reiley's *Onward Industry!* in 1931, most books on management had reflected the shop floor-industrial engineering orientation common to the earlier scientific-management era. For the most part, these books emphasized production layout, scheduling, materials handling, shop organization, production control, and other largely technique-oriented subjects. A growing interest in organization structure and design, however, was emerging. This interest was evident in Henry Dennison's book *Organization Engineering*, also published in 1931. Dennison had been a pioneer in the installation of the Taylor system in his South Framingham (Massachusetts) paper-products firm, The Dennison Manufacturing Company (today's Avery Dennison Corporation). He advocated an approach to organization design that was diametrically opposed to that proposed by Mooney and Reiley. Dennison began with the idea that the purpose of "organization engineering" was "making a success of group life." He built on the belief that "all the strength of an organization comes from its members."[14] For Dennison, the

---

[13] *Ibid.* p. 34.
[14] Henry S. Dennison, *Organization Engineering* (New York: McGraw-Hill, 1931), p. 1.

first task was to form people into groups to build teamwork. Recognizing a diversity of motives, Dennison acknowledged that leadership would be required to resolve frictions among individuals. Instead of designing an organization's structure first, Dennison argued for finding like-minded people, grouping them into teams, and then developing a total organization structure. In this sense, Dennison actually anticipated by a decade or more the work of Jacob L. Moreno and others who advocated sociometrically selected work teams (see Chapter 15).

Dennison's view of motivation was also unique:

> Four general groups of tendencies which may actuate a member of any organization are: (1) regard for his own and his family's welfare and standing; (2) liking for the work itself; (3) regard for one or more members of the organization and for their good opinion, and pleasure in working with them; and (4) respect and regard for the main purposes of the organization.[15]

Dennison believed that a person could be "actuated" by any of these four tendencies, but "only when impelled by the four combined can all of man's power be brought into steady and permanent play."[16] To this end, he anticipated the job-enlargement movement of the late 1940s by advocating the modifying of jobs so that they would provide greater employee satisfaction (see Chapter 15). He recognized the nature of informal groups and their influence on output norms and proposed nonfinancial incentives (such as social gatherings and company-sponsored family outings) that, when properly mixed with economic methods, built loyalty. Moreover, he realized that principles of organization were not "sacred in and of themselves" and an organization's structure should be flexible to "strengthen its group[s], not ossify them."[17] Dennison also recognized limits to and variations in the number of persons to whom a manager could give attention without either restricting his "field of influence" or being spread too thin. The span of control, in his view, "seldom runs beyond six to twelve people."[18]

Dennison was a progressive employer. He introduced an employee profit-sharing plan, low-interest loans for employees to purchase homes, an employee representation plan, and unemployment insurance to stabilize employees' incomes.[19] Dennison quoted Mary P. Follett on coordination and the law of the situation and she appears to have colored his view of labor–management relations.[20] Follett's influence on Dennison thinking is evident in the following remark: "The principal managerial job in any concern is the coordination, the composition, the integration of the impulses, energies, and interests of the three principal groups of human beings – the investors, the customers, the workers – keeping effective powers at a maximum, wasteful resistances at a minimum."[21] This remark underscores Dennison's (and Follett's) belief that an organization does not function based on a straight line of authority that flows from top to bottom, but rather every member has a sphere of influence given, as Follett wrote, "the necessity of acting in accord with the unique requirements inherent in any situation."[22]

Management textbooks popular during the 1930s largely continued to follow the shop floor-industrial engineering approach that had developed during the earlier scientific-management era

---

[15] *Ibid.*, pp. 63–64.

[16] *Ibid.*, p. 64.

[17] *Ibid.*, pp. 124, 126.

[18] *Ibid.*, p. 138.

[19] W. Jack Duncan, "Henry Sturgis Dennison," in Morgen L. Witzel, ed., *Biographical Dictionary of Management,* vol. 1 (Bristol, England: Thoemmes Press, 2001), pp. 233–236. See also Kyle D. Bruce "Activist Management: Henry S. Dennison's Institutionalist Economics," *Journal of Economic Issues* 40(4) (December 2006), pp. 1113–1136; *idem*, "Activist Manager: The Enduring Contribution of Henry S. Dennison to Management and Organization Studies," *Journal of Management History* 21(2) (2015), pp. 143–171.

[20] Dennison, *Organization Engineering,* pp. 100, 166.

[21] *Idem*, "Who Can Hire Management?" *Bulletin of the Taylor Society* 9(3) (June 1924), p. 110.

[22] Mary P. Follett, "The Giving of Orders," in Henry C. Metcalf, ed., *Scientific Foundations of Business Administration* (Baltimore, MD: Williams & Wilkins, 1926), p. 139.

and, thus, contributed little to the development of general management thought. Writing in *Management of an Enterprise*, C. Canby Balderston, Victor S. Karabasz, and Robert P. Brecht (all at the University of Pennsylvania) defined management as "the art and science of organizing, preparing and directing human effort applied to control the forces and to utilize the materials of nature for the benefit of man."[23] They identified the "principal elements" with which all managers must deal, regardless of the type of enterprise, as men, money, machines, and material. They applied these elements to topics such as product design; provision of physical facilities; power, heat, light, and ventilation; controlling inventories; and planning and control of production, clerical and sales operations. Organization was treated as a means of direction and control *a la* Mooney and Reiley. Together with personnel management, it was one of the few topics outside traditional shop floor-industrial engineering boundaries that Balderston, Karabasz, and Brecht addressed.

In a textbook with a similar tone, but different purpose, Edward H. Anderson and Gustav T. Schwenning outlined and described "the fundamentals underlying the process of organization for effective production."[24] The text reflects Anderson's interest in history as a means of studying management and economics, and much like Mooney and Reiley's *Onward Industry!*, contains examples from military history that illustrate the importance of organization and management strategies. After "[a] careful study of the subject," Anderson and Schwenning concluded that "there is a science of organization, and that the science is the product of evolution rather than a single theory."[25] Though they introduced few new ideas, Anderson and Schwenning's analysis and synthesis, together with an extensive bibliography, made an original contribution to the development of management thought.

On December 28, 1936, Charles L. Jamison and William N. Mitchell invited a small group of management professors to the University of Chicago's Quadrangle Club to discuss the formation of a society to "advance the philosophy of management."[26] Enough interest was evidenced for Canby Balderston to invite the group to meet at Philadelphia's Lenape Club in 1937. After similar informal meetings in 1938, 1939, and 1940, Ralph C. Davis prepared a constitution, the name "Academy of Management" was selected, officers were elected, and the Academy began formal operations in 1941. The objectives of the Academy have been stated as follows:

> The Academy is founded to foster the search for truth and the general advancement of learning through free discussion and research in the field of management. The interest of the Academy lies in the theory and practice of management . . . as it relates to the work of planning, organizing, and controlling the execution of business projects. It is also concerned with activities having to do with the forming, directing, and co-ordinating of departments and groups which are characteristic of administrative management . . . .
>
> The general objectives of the Academy shall be therefore to foster: (a) A philosophy of management that will make possible an accomplishment of the economic and social objectives of an industrial society with increasing economy and effectiveness. The public's interest must be paramount in any such philosophy, but adequate consideration must be given to the legitimate interests of Capital and Labor. (b) Greater understanding by Executive leadership of the requirements for a sound application of the scientific method to the solution of managerial problems, based on such a philosophy. (c) Wider acquaintance and closer co-operation among such persons as are interested in the development of a philosophy and science of management.[27]

---

[23] C. Canby Balderston, Victor S. Karabasz, and Robert P. Brecht, *Management of an Enterprise* (New York: Prentice-Hall, 1935), p. 4.

[24] Edward H. Anderson and Gustav T. Schwenning, *The Science of Production Organization* (New York: John Wiley & Sons, 1938), p. v.

[25] *Ibid.*

[26] Preston P. LeBreton, "A Brief History of the Academy of Management," in Paul M. Dauten, Jr., ed., *Current Issues and Emerging Concepts in Management* (Boston, MA: Houghton Mifflin, 1962), pp. 329–331.

[27] *Ibid.*, p. 330. See also Charles D. Wrege, "The Inception, Early Struggles, and Growth of the Academy of Management," in Daniel A. Wren and John A. Pearce II, eds., *Papers Dedicated to the Development of Modern Management* (Chicago, IL: Academy of Management, 1986), pp. 78–88.

Although inactive from 1942 to 1946 because of World War II, annual Academy meetings were resumed in 1947. Jamison served as the Academy's Founding president from 1936 to 1940; Brecht was president from 1941 to 1947, and Davis became president in 1948. The Academy reflected an increased awareness of the need for management education. It continues to influence the development of management thought worldwide through teaching and writing of its over 18,000 members from more than 100 countries.

A final notable textbook from this time period, *Industrial Engineering and Factory Management*, was written by Arthur G. Anderson and published in 1928.[28] Like other contemporary management textbooks, it was largely devoted to traditional shop floor-industrial engineering topics. An indication of coming trend in management thought is evident in the 1942 revision of Anderson's book retitled *Industrial Management*. Joined by Merten J. Mandeville and John M. Anderson as coauthors, the 1942 edition introduced a broader view of management's role.[29] As its authors explained, management has a responsibility to promote both economic and social progress through productive and distributive efficiency, as well as through an emphasis on human relations in business. The authors discussed the various groups—customers, stockholders, the public at large, and employees—that play a vital role in an organization's success. In doing so, they showed an awareness of a typical organization's major stakeholders and that a manager's performance is dependent on knowing how an organization influences and is influenced by its environment.

Building Blocks for Administrative Theory

In 1937, Luther H. Gulick and Lyndall F. Urwick edited a collection of papers by a number of well-known and not-so-well known management theorists and practitioners. Included were papers by James D. Mooney, Henri Fayol, Henry S. Dennison, Lawrence J. Henderson, Thomas North Whitehead, Elton Mayo, Mary P. Follett, John Lee, Vytautas A. Graicunas, and the editors themselves. The collection offered the first U.S. rendition of Henri Fayol's work, as well as a detailed demonstration by Urwick of the logical relationship between Fayol's "functions of administration" and Mooney and Reiley's principles of organization.[30] Gulick was director of Columbia University's Institute of Public Administration and had served as a member of President Franklin D. Roosevelt's Committee on Administrative Management, which attempted, without much success, to reorganize the executive branch of the federal government.[31] Gulick divided the work of chief executives into seven functional elements. He used the acronym POSDCORB (pronounced *poz-dee-korb*), representing the initials of the following activities, as shorthand for the elements:

Planning, that is working out in broad outline the things that need to be done and the methods for doing them to accomplish the purpose set for the enterprise;

Organizing, that is the establishment of the formal structure of authority through which work subdivisions are arranged, defined and co-ordinated for the defined objective;

[28] Arthur G. Anderson, *Industrial Engineering and Factory Management* (New York: Ronald Press, 1928).

[29] *Idem*, Merten J. Mandeville, and John M. Anderson, *Industrial Management* (New York: Ronald Press, 1942), p. iii.

[30] Luther H. Gulick and Lyndall F. Urwick, eds., *Papers on the Science of Administration* (New York: Institute of Public Administration, Columbia University, 1937). See also Lyndall F. Urwick, "Papers in the Science of Administration," *Academy of Management Journal* 13(1) (March 1970), pp. 361–371.

[31] *Report of the President's Committee on Administrative Management* (Washington, DC: U.S. Government Printing Office, 1935). For further information on Gulick's professional life, see Morgen L. Witzel, ed., *The Biographical Dictionary of Management*, vol. 1 (Bristol, England: Thoemmes Press, 2001), pp. 400–405.

Staffing, that is the whole personnel function of bringing in and training the staff and maintaining favorable conditions of work;

Directing, that is the continuous task of making decisions and embodying them in specific and general orders and instructions and serving as the leader of the enterprise;

Co-ordinating, that is the all important duty of interrelating the various parts of the work;

Reporting, that is keeping those to whom the executive is responsible informed as to what is going on, which thus includes keeping himself and his subordinates informed through records, research and inspection;

Budgeting, with all that goes with budgeting in the form of fiscal planning, accounting and control.[32]

Although Gulick visualized management as a universal activity, his description of the preceding elements of a chief executive's job chiefly pertained to public administration. Gulick went on to identify four basic forms of grouping activities together or what is known as of *departmentalization*: purpose, process, person or things, and place. In Gulick's scheme, there is no one most effective basis for grouping activities. If an organization is first divided at its primary level by place (i.e., geographically), the secondary level of work might be grouped by purpose, process, clientele, or even again by place. The same would be true for the third level and so on. Any decision about how to group activities had to (1) follow the *principle of homogeneity*, meaning the activities to be grouped must be compatible), (2) assure coordination, and (3) allow flexibility as an organization grew or as its objectives changed.

Lyndall F. Urwick, coeditor with Gulick of *Papers on the Science of Administration*, worked tirelessly to develop a general theory of organization and management. Educated at Oxford University, he served in Great Britain's army and government in World Wars I and II, was organizing secretary of Rowntree and Company's Cocoa Works (1920–1928), served as director of the International Management Institute in Geneva (1928–1933), and was chairman of Urwick, Orr and Partners, Ltd., management consultants, until his retirement in 1951.[33] Greatly influenced in his thinking by B. Seebohm Rowntree and Oliver Sheldon, Urwick wrote on a wide range of subjects.[34] He collaborated with Edward F. L. Brech in editing biographical sketches of scientific-management pioneers; with Henry C. Metcalf on editing Mary P. Follett's papers; with Gulick on compiling *Papers on the Science of Administration*; with Ernest Dale on line-staff relations; and with too many others to mention.[35]

Although Urwick wrote on many topics over 6 decades, his early work was heavily oriented toward developing principles of organization. In 1952, he identified 10 principles applicable to all organizations: (1) the "principle of the objective," that all organizations should be an expression

---

[32] Luther H. Gulick, "Notes on the Theory of Organization," in Gulick and Urwick, eds., *Papers on the Science of Administration*, p. 13.

[33] Henry S. Dennison, "The International Management Institute and Its Work," *Mechanical Engineering* 51(9) (July 1929), pp. 534–535; Charles D. Wrege, Ronald G. Greenwood, and Sakae Hata, "The International Management Institute and Political Opposition to Its Efforts in Europe, 1925–1934," in Jeremy Atack, ed., *Business and Economic History* (2nd series)16 (1987), pp. 249–65; and Edward F. L. Brech, Andrew Thomson, and John F. Wilson, *Lyndall Urwick, Management Pioneer: A Biography* (Oxford: Oxford University Press, 2010).

[34] On Rowntree's influence, see Lyndall F. Urwick, "The Father of British Management," *The Manager* 30(2) (February 1962), pp. 42–43.

[35] For further details, see Arthur G. Bedeian, Kismet!: A Tale of Management. In Vance F. Mitchell, Richard T. Barth, and Francis H. Mitchell, eds., *Proceedings of the Annual Meeting of the Academy of Management* (1972), pp. 134–137; Lee D. Parker and Philip Ritson, "Rage, Rage against the Dying of the Light: Lyndall Urwick's Scientific Management," *Journal of Management History* 17(4) (2011), pp. 379–396.

Lyndall F. Urwick. Courtesy of Arthur G. Bedeian.

of a purpose; (2) the "principle of correspondence," that authority and responsibility should be coequal; (3) the "principle of responsibility," that the responsibility of higher authorities for the work of subordinates is absolute; (4) "the principle of authority," that a clear line of authority should extend from the highest to the lowest level of an organization; (5) the "principle of the span of control," that no superior should supervise more than five or six direct subordinates whose work interlocks; (6) "the principle of specialization," that one's work should be limited to a single function; (7) "the principle of coordination," that the various parts of an organization should be interrelated for unity of effort; (8) "the principle of definition," that the content of each position should be clearly defined, (9) "the principle of balance," that the parts of an organization should be kept in balance, and (10) "the principle of continuity," that reorganization is a continuous process.[36]

Span of Control

Whereas Gulick and Urwick worked to develop a general theory of organization and management, Vytautas A. Graicunas's contribution to management thought was less grandiose, but nonetheless quite meaningful. His contribution to *Papers on the Science of Administration* was a mathematical proof of the logic inherent in limiting a manager's span of control from three to seven subordi-

Vytautas A. Graicunas. Courtesy of Arthur G. Bedeian.

nates. It had originally been published in the *Bulletin of the International Management Institute* (Geneva) in 1933. At the time, Urwick was the Institute's Director. Graicunas, born in Chicago in 1898, was at various times an engineer with firms in the United States and throughout Europe, as well as an associate in Hrant Pasdermadjian's Department Store Management Research Group (later the International Association of Department Stores) in Paris. He cofounded the Lithuanian Scientific Management Society at Kaunas in 1928, serving as its first chairman. In Moscow on a business trip in 1947, Graicunas was arrested by the MGB (Ministry for State Security) as he left the United States Embassy and subsequently died in prison.[37] Graicunas's ideas on the span of control were largely influenced by Urwick's "principle of the span of control." As noted, this principle held that no superior should supervise more than five or six direct subordinates whose work interlocks.

Graicunas had observed instances where managers were hampered while trying to supervise too many subordinates; he realized that this was due, in part, to their desire "to enhance their prestige and influence" by adding sections and departments to their responsibilities. Such ego bolstering could be costly from the standpoint of delays and confusion as a manager tried to simultaneously coordinate the activities

---

[36] Lyndall F. Urwick, *Notes on the Theory of Organization* (New York: American Management Association, 1952), pp. 19–20, 22–23, 51, 57–58. By 1966, Urwick's principles of organization had expanded to 12. See *idem, Organization* (The Hague: Nederlands Institut voor Efficiency, 1966), pp. 91–96.

[37] For an account of Graicunas's life, career, and demise, see Arthur G. Bedeian, "Vytautas Andrius Graicunas: A Biographical Note," *Academy of Management Journal* 17(2) (June 1974), pp. 347–349; Lyndall F. Urwick, "V. A. Graicunas and the Span of Control," *Academy of Management Journal* 17(2) (June 1974), pp. 349–354.

of an excessive number of direct reports. Graicunas noted that according to what psychologists term the "the span of attention," the number of separate factors the mind can grasp simultaneously is limited. In a majority of cases, this limit is six factors or digits. He recognized that the span of attention has an administrative counterpart—the span of control. Building on this reasoning, Graicunas demonstrated that a manager with five direct reports, who adds a sixth, increases the number of his direct single relationships by 20 percent. There are, however, direct group relationships and cross relationships that must also be considered. Rather than increasing arithmetically, these relationships increase exponentially, so that the manager adds approximately 100 percent to the coordination required among relationships. Graicunas described the situation this way:

> In almost every case the supervisor measures the burden of his responsibility by the number of direct single relationships between himself and those he supervises. But in addition there are direct group relationships and cross relationships. Thus, if Tom supervises two persons, Dick and Harry, he can speak to them as a pair. The behaviour of Dick in the presence of Harry or of Harry in the presence of Dick will vary from their behaviour when with Tom alone. Further, what Dick thinks of Harry and what Harry thinks of Dick constitute two cross relationships which Tom must keep in mind in arranging any work over which they must collaborate in his absence. . . . Thus, even in this extremely simple unit of organization, Tom must hold four to six relationships within his span of attention.[38]

According to what is known as Graicunas's Theorem, where n represents the number of subordinates, the total number of direct plus cross relationships equals:

$$F = n\left(\frac{2^n}{2} + n - 1\right)$$

n	1	2	3	4	5	6	7	8	9	10	11	12
F	1	6	18	44	100	222	490	1,080	2,376	5,210	11,374	24,708

The sharp increase beyond four subordinates denotes a rapid rise in complexity of relationships. Accordingly, in line with the psychological span of attention concept and in full agreement with Urwick's span of control principle, Graicunas concluded that the number of a manager's direct reports should be limited to a maximum of five. He conceded, however, that wider spans of control were permissible in the case of routine work at lower echelons where subordinates worked relatively independently, had little or no contact with others, and where supervisory responsibilities were less complex. At the same time, he advised that at upper levels, where responsibility was greater and often overlapped, a manager's span of control should be narrower. Graicunas also noted, "[I]t is not possible to assign comparable weights to these different varieties of relationship," indicating that he was aware that not all relationships are in effect at all times. If Dick's work did not interlock with Harry's or if their jobs were routine, then the number of operative relationships would be less and their manager's permissible span would be wider. Graicunas's formula is based on the maximum number of possible direct and cross relationships, not the number that might actually exist at a given point in time.

Toward a Top-Management Viewpoint

A second facet of the focus on the structure and design of organizations at began in the late 1930s involved a shift away from a shop-floor orientation to a larger view of executive leadership. The search for universal principles of organization was still ongoin; however, it was joined

---

[38] Vytautas A. Graicunas, "Relationship in Organization," *Bulletin of the International Management Institute* 7(3) (March 1933), p. 40.

Ralph C. Davis. Courtesy of Arthur G. Bedeian.

by an interest in the primary responsibilities of top management. This interest was accompanied by a concern over the separation of ownership and control and the transfer of property rights.

Ralph C. Davis: *Pater Familiae et Magister*

Ralph C. Davis received his mechanical engineering degree in 1916 from Cornell University. He was exposed to Dexter S. Kimball's *Principles of Industrial Organization* (1913) when he took the course for which this book was developed in the 1914–1915 semester. Kimball was dean of Cornell's Sibley College of Engineering (see Chapter 11).[39] As a result of the interest that Kimball aroused in his students, Davis "took what amounted to a 'minor' in business administration."[40] Intrigued by the shop terms his engineering professors used, Davis went on to work in either a machine shop or tool crib during every summer vacation until he graduated.[41] After passing the necessary licensure exam, Davis went on to work as a Registered Industrial Engineer for the Winchester Repeating Arms Company in 1916, where, as he put it, "I quickly discovered that I knew practically nothing about management."[42] He soon learned, however, by observing the company's president John E. Otterson, who was famous for applying scientific management at the Charleston Navy Yard in Boston, as well as from Carl G. Barth, Dwight V. Merrick, and staff members from A. Hamilton Church's consulting firm, who were all on assignment at Winchester. In 1923, following a stint conducting labor-relations studies for the Cleveland Chamber of Commerce, Davis was invited to Ohio State University to develop courses in management for the College of Commerce and Administration. He wrote his first book *The Principles of Factory Organization and Management*, in 1928, for use by his students. It followed the traditional, shop-floor orientation of similar books published around this time. Davis stated that the fundamental functions and principles of factory management were universal in their application and that certain considerations underlie good organization. As he explained:

> In developing the organization, consideration should be given to (1) the fundamental functions to be performed and their relation to one another, (2) the proper division of responsibility, (3) the definite location of responsibility, (4) the proper functioning of the system, (5) the flexibility of the organization, (6) provision for future growth, (7) personal characteristics and abilities, (8) the creation of an ideal, and (9) the quality of the leadership.[43]

In 1927, Davis was asked by General Motors to establish a department of management at the General Motors Institute (GMI; Flint, Michigan). It was at GMI (now Kettering University), from 1928 to 1930, that he was exposed to the thinking of GM executives Donaldson Brown and

---

[39] Biographical information is based on a letter from Ralph C. Davis to Arthur G. Bedeian, May 18, 1969, and on John F. Mee, "*Pater Familiae et Magister*" [The Father of the Family and Teacher], *Academy of Management Journal* 8(1) (March 1965), pp. 14–23.

[40] Letter from Ralph C. Davis to Arthur G. Bedeian, dated August 14, 1976.

[41] Letter from Ralph C. Davis to William M. Fox, dated September 19, 1958. See also William M. Fox, "The Contributions of Ralph C. Davis to the Analysis of Management Activity," paper presented at the Academy of Management Annual Meeting, August 1988, Anaheim, CA.

[42] Letter from Ralph C. Davis to Daniel A. Wren, dated, May 18, 1969.

[43] Ralph C. Davis, *The Principles of Factory Organization and Management* (New York: Harper & Brothers, 1928), p. 41.

Alfred P. Sloan, Jr., on what was to become the modern corporation (see Chapter 11). It was this exposure that led Davis to move away from his previous shop-floor approach to management and focus on the role of executives and the objectives of business. His focus was further influenced (in 1932) by John A. Coubrough's translation of Henri Fayol's *Industrial and General Administration*, a book he discovered in the Library of Congress while on a 6-month leave from Ohio State. By 1934, Davis had concluded that the executive role could be broken down into three "organic functions"—planning, organizing, and controlling.[44]

Davis's life and work illustrate the evolution of management thought over a span of more than four decades. His first 1928 book followed a traditional, shop-floor orientation; in 1934, focusing on the role of executives, he introduced the concept of organic functions of management; and in 1940, reflecting a growing interest in the primary responsibilities of top management, he identified and then related the basic factors of business to these primary functions.[45] This interest was refined in Davis's 1951 classic *The Fundamentals of Top Management*. His purpose in writing this book was to "present a fundamental statement of business objectives, policies, and general methods that govern the solution of basic business problems" from a top-management viewpoint.[46] Davis's original shop-floor orientation had completely given way to an interest in the primary responsibilities of top management.

In *The Fundamentals of Top Management,* Davis declared that management is "the function of executive leadership"; he used the terms "management" and "executive leadership" synonymously. He stressed the need for professional managers who had a sound philosophy of management with respect to the public's interest. Because business organizations are economic institutions, Davis stated that their primary mission "is to supply the public with whatever goods or services it desires at the proper time and place, in the required amounts having the desired qualities, and at a price that it is willing to pay."[47] Davis added that, in pursuing their missions, businesses must necessarily adhere to accepted standards of conduct for both political and moral reasons. He believed executive leadership to be the principal force that motivates, stimulates, and coordinates an organization in accomplishing its objectives.

Davis considered the organic functions of management to be the functions of executive leadership. Planning was the "specification of the factors, forces, effects and relationships that enter into and are required for the solution of a business problem" and provided "a basis for economical and effective action in the achievement of business objectives."[48] Organizing involved "bringing functions, physical factors, and personnel into proper relationships with one another" and was based on authority, which was "the right to plan, organize, and control the organization's activities."[49] This represented the traditional formal view of authority as the right to decide, which Davis found ultimately legitimated in organized society. For example, society upholds the right of private property; individuals exercise this right through stock ownership in a company and delegate the management of their property to the board of directors, who in turn delegate authority down through the scalar chain.

Davis defined control as "the function of constraining and regulating activities that enter into the accomplishment of an objective."[50] He broke control into eight subfunctions: routine planning, scheduling, preparation, dispatching, direction, supervision, comparison, and corrective action. In turn, Davis grouped these subfunctions into three phases of control: (1) *preliminary* control, which included routine planning, scheduling, preparation, and dispatching; (2) *concurrent* control, which included direction, supervision, comparison; and (3) *corrective action,* which

---

[44] Idem, *The Principles of Business Organization and Operation* (Columbus, OH: H. L. Hedrick, 1934), pp. 12–13.

[45] Idem, *Industrial Organization and Management* (New York: Harper & Brothers, 1940).

[46] Idem, *The Fundamentals of Top Management* (New York: Harper & Brothers, 1951), p. xix.

[47] Ibid., p. 10.

[48] Ibid., p. 43.

[49] Ibid., pp. 238, 281.

[50] Ibid., p. 663.

involved correcting variations from planned performance. Preliminary control attempts to establish advance constraints and regulations that ensure proper execution of plans; on the other hand, concurrent control operates while performance is in progress. Corrective action completes the control cycle and begins the preliminary phase again by identifying deviations and by replanning or taking other actions to prevent recurrence of performance shortfalls. Although many of his predecessors had written about control, Davis presented a much more insightful and comprehensive view of this function than had been previously rendered.

Harry Hopf: Toward the Optimum

Harry Hopf was another of this era's notable contributors to the development of management theory and practice. Like Davis, Hopf began with the precepts of Fred Taylor and concluded with a broader view of top management's role. Born in London, Hopf immigrated as a penniless youth to the United States in 1882. He would become a widely respected consultant, author, and executive.[51] Hopf began his career as a clerk in the office of a life insurance company where he became acquainted with Taylor's views on eliminating workplace inefficiencies. In applying the principles of scientific management to office work, Hopf became interested in efficiency in general, and, more specifically, in applying Taylor's principles to all types of work. He studied compensation programs for office workers and wondered why so little attention had been given to typical executive-payment schemes, such as profit sharing, stock options, and deferred compensation plans. Hopf felt that such schemes inadequately tied performance to pay, which was a conclusion Taylor had also reached about worker compensation. The conventional answer of Hopf's generation was that executives did a different kind of work, which was intangible and not subject to measurement. Not satisfied with this answer, Hopf proposed principles and standards for measuring executive work in a manner that would link performance with pay.[52] He believed that all managers should be judged (and rewarded) by the results they produced.

In discussing organization structure and design, Hopf adopted the architectural notion that form follows function; thus, structure had to follow the objectives to be sought. Otherwise, "[if] form dominates over function in organizational structure, we are bound to discover conditions of fixity and rigidity which exercise a baneful influence over accomplishment."[53] In this analogy, Hopf anticipated the dictum that "structure follows strategy," which became a guiding rule for organization theorists and business strategists in the modern era (see Chapter 20).

Hopf wrote on many other management topics: span of control, policies, coordination, and executive control, to name a few. None of his ideas were as far-reaching, however, as his concept of "optimology." It was this concept that would take Hopf beyond Taylor's shop management to a discussion of top-management responsibilities. Hopf defined the *optimum* as "that state of development of a business enterprise which tends to perpetuate an equilibrium between the factors of size, cost, and human capacity and thus to promote in the highest degree regular realization of the business objectives."[54] Much like Mooney, Hopf felt that the typical business reversed the order of priority in fulfilling its societal role: maximize earnings and thereby serve society; whereas, in contrast, he believed that a business should serve society and thereby maximize earnings. He also felt the goal of increased size was a *faux ami* (i.e., a false friend) because

---

[51] See Homer J. Hagedorn, *White Collar Management: Harry Arthur Hopf and the Rationalization of Business* (Unpublished dissertation, Harvard University, Cambridge, MA, 1955); Richard J. Vahl, *A Study of the Contributions of Harry Arthur Hopf to the Field of Management* (Unpublished master's thesis, Louisiana State University, Baton Rouge, LA, 1968); and Edmund R. Gray and Richard J. Vahl, "Harry Hopf: Management's Unheralded Giant," *Southern Journal of Business* 6(2) (April 1971), pp. 69–78.

[52] Harry A. Hopf, *Executive Compensation and Accomplishment*, Financial Management Series, no. 78 (New York: American Management Association, 1945).

[53] *Idem*, "Organization, Executive Capacity and Progress," *Advanced Management: Quarterly Journal* 11(2) (June 1946), p. 38.

[54] *Idem, Management and the Optimum* (New York: H. A. Hopf and Company, 1935), p. 5.

it caused problems of coordination: growth in size as a goal more often than not sacrificed one part to the whole, benefiting one part at the expense of another. Instead, the optimum would balance all parts and could be achieved through carefully establishing the point (or points) of equilibrium among size, cost, and human capacity. Perhaps Hopf's most significant contribution to the development of management thought was the notion that a scientific approach can be applied to determine the proper structure and design for all organizations. In doing so, he provided another step forward in developing a view of top-management responsibilities.

Analyzing Top Management

Whereas the Great Depression of the 1930s dampened economic activity worldwide, World War II mobilized vast productive capabilities, and the postwar period found managers challenged by new demands. With an unprecedented increase in international trade, executives were faced with the challenge of managing operations on a larger scale than ever before. Management scholars turned their attention to research and writing to meet this challenge.

Searching for corporate excellence is not a new idea. One prewar study that was a model for future similar investigations attempted to find practical answers to dilemmas of organization and control faced by top management. In this study, top management included three groups of executives: (1) boards of directors, (2) general managers responsible for a business as a whole, and (3) divisional managers responsible for major departments, divisions, or subsidiaries. The study's authors found that only about half their sample of 31 industrial corporations prepared detailed plans for periods up to a year in advance. Further, few had developed a system of integrated plans or developed long-range objectives. The authors reported that "one of the greatest needs observed during the course of this study is for more adequate planning and clarification of future objectives, both near-term and long-range." They traced this failing to inadequate structural arrangements in which jurisdictions, responsibilities, and relationships were ill defined, staff departments were poorly conceived and coordinated, and committees, the bane of all executive work, were poorly designed and used for the wrong tasks. In staffing, the authors found that "many companies" left provisions for the development and succession of key management personnel "largely to providence."[55] Control practices brought little solace; only one-half of the corporations used budgets as a means of planning and, subsequently, for measuring "overall results of efforts." This pioneering study was an important contribution to the development of management thought because it empirically confirmed that managers performed the same functions (viz., planning, organizing, and controlling) previous authors such as Fayol and Davis had identified based on personal observation and logical reasoning.

Jackson Martindell was perhaps the first to devise a system for analyzing the quality of a company's top management. Martindell was a security analyst who had successfully managed an investment-counseling firm in the 1920s. When the Wall Street stock market crashed in 1929 (see Chapter 18) and the Great Depression ensued, Martindell looked back on the investment criteria he had used as a security analyst to see if any had correctly predicted which companies were better able to weather the economic downturn. He found one answer for why some companies prevailed and others failed: "excellent management."[56] From that point forward, Martindell

---

[55] Paul E. Holden, Lounsbury S. Fish, and Hubert L. Smith, *Top Management Organization and Control: A Research Study of the Management Policies and Practices of Thirty-One Leading Industrial Corporations* (Stanford, CA: Stanford University Press, 1941), pp. 4–8. In a follow-up study of 15 leading corporations, many improvements in managerial practices were noted, especially with respect to long-range planning, executive development, and management information systems. See Paul E. Holden, Carlton A. Pederson, and Gayton E. Germane, *Top Management: A Research Study of the Management Policies and Practices of Fifteen Leading Industrial Corporations* (New York: McGraw-Hill, 1968).

[56] Jackson Martindell, *The Scientific Appraisal of Management: A Study of the Business Practices of Well-Managed Companies* (New York: Harper & Brothers, 1950).

began a search for the factors that typified "Excellently Managed Companies." The result was a management audit that evaluated the performance of companies across 10 criteria:

1. The economic function of a company

2. The organizational structure of a company

3. The health of a company's earnings growth

4. The fairness of a company's practices to stockholders

5. A company's research and development practices

6. The value contributed by a company's board of directors

7. A company's fiscal policies

8. A company's productive efficiency

9. A company's sales organization

10. The abilities of a company's executives.

Martindell's method of evaluation consisted of awarding points on each of the 10 criteria, summing these points for an overall performance rating, and then comparing the excellence of any particular company with the scores obtained from companies in similar industries. Although Martindell's approach to conducting a management audit is of doubtful validity, it contributed to the development of management thought by identifying criteria that could be used to judge a company's overall performance and, by implication, the quality of its top management in comparison to its competition.

Ownership and Control

At the outset of the Great Depression, Adolf A. Berle, Jr., a lawyer, and Gardiner C. Means, an economist, criticized the executives of large corporations for losing sight of whose interests they served: the corporations' shareholders. Citing Adam Smith's warning about those who managed "other people's money" being less vigilant than if they were managing their own funds (see Chapter 2), Berle and Means, noting the concentration of capital and economic power in large corporations, argued that the owners of corporate stock (shareholders) only nominally controlled the use of their property. Whereas Smith felt that ownership and control should be combined, resulting in joint risk Berle and Means found corporate managers and directors rarely held an appreciable amount of stock in the corporations they managed. They characterized corporate managers and directors as "economic autocrats" who formed "a controlling group" that "may hold the power to divert profit into their pockets."[57] As a result, Berle and Means believed that, in most instances, shareholders had little sway over the corporations they owned, having surrendered control to professional managers. Although Berle and Means offered no clear solution to this separation of ownership and control, they revived Smith's earlier concerns and prepared the way for later work in corporate governance and agency issues (see Chapter 19).

Berle and Means's concern found further expression in a study of 155 corporations conducted by economist Robert A. Gordon.[58] Focusing on the direction and coordination of large corporations in the United States, Gordon also noted the separation of ownership and management and

---

[57] Adolf A. Berle, Jr. and Gardiner C. Means, *The Modern Corporation and Private Property* (New York: Macmillan, 1934), pp. 124, 333.

[58] Robert A. Gordon, *Business Leadership in the Large Corporation* (Washington, DC: Brookings Institution, 1945), pp. 317–352.

that, further, many industries were dominated by a small number of competitors or, in some instances, by a single corporation. Consequently, he stressed the need for the "professionalization of management." In Gordon's view, the era of profiting by managing one's own investments had passed and had been succeeded by a new period in which salaried or so-called professional managers were hired by corporate boards of directors. He argued that the hiring of professional managers led to a decline in the profit motive, greater inflexibility, and increased bureaucracy. Gordon saw dangers in this increased insulation of managers from owners, especially with respect to the possibility that a self-perpetuating oligarchy of executives might place its own interests above those of a corporation's stakeholders. Gordon's answer to this dilemma was a call for professional managers who were responsive to the needs of all a corporation's constituents.

Invisible and Visible Hands

In Chapters 3 and 6, we noted that economists Jean-Baptiste Say, Edward Atkinson, and Alfred and Mary P. Marshall considered management to be a fourth factor of production. The Marshalls, in particular, observed that the earnings of management were different from profit returned to owners. In doing so, they recognized the role of managers in efficiently allocating a firm's resources. In contrast, other economists have focused on what occurs in the broader environment or marketplace surrounding a firm, largely ignoring what happens between the acquisition of inputs (factors of production) and the sale of outputs (goods and services subsequently produced or provided). Two separate yet compatible developments in the 1930s would have a substantial impact on the evolution of management thought. Modern scholars, however, would only come to fully appreciate these developments years later.

Writing in 1934, John R. Commons noted that *transactions* were the smallest unit of analysis in the transfer of property rights. In Commons's view, transactions were not the exchange of commodities, but transfers of future ownership that must be negotiated "before labor can produce, or consumers can consume, or commodities be physically delivered to other persons."[59] He identified three types of ownership transfers: "bargaining," "managerial," and "rationing." *Bargaining transactions* derive from a market of willing buyers and willing sellers who negotiate the transfer, not of commodities, but of ownership rights. *Managerial transactions* occur between a superior–subordinate, such as employer–employee, where authority is used to give orders and direct the work of others. Managerial and bargaining transactions resemble one another because employees are free to negotiate regarding wages and hours of work. *Rationing transactions* involve a "collective superior," including legislatures, criminal courts, or commercial arbitrator, all of which ration outcomes such as wealth or justice to subordinate others without bargaining and without managing, which is left to a superior.[60] For whatever reason, Commons's views on the ownership and transfer of property rights lay relatively dormant until scholars discovered their inherent power some 2 decades in the future.

English born and educated Ronald H. Coase approached the question of transactions and the ownership and transfer of property rights from a different perspective. Coase had been introduced to Adam Smith's view that the "invisible hand" of the marketplace would ensure the efficient allocation of available resources. A trip to the United States in 1931–1932 to discover why its industries were structured in so many different ways led Coarse to pose a follow-up question: If markets are so efficient in allocating resources, why do business firms exist? Why isn't everything left to the invisible hand of the marketplace? While still a 21-year-old undergraduate student at the University of London, Coarse wrote a paper in 1931 that would be published in 1937

[59] John R. Common, *Institutional Economics: Its Place in Political Economy* (New York: Macmillan, 1934), p. 58.
[60] *Ibid.*, pp. 55–74.

titled "The Nature of the Firm." The paper would become a classic contribution to understanding the workings of business firms vis-à-vis the marketplace and be cited by the Royal Swedish Academy of Sciences in awarding Coase the 1991 Alfred Nobel Memorial Prize in Economic Sciences. In the paper, Coase asked:

> . . . in view of the fact that it is usually argued that co-ordination will be done by the price mechanism, why is such organization necessary? . . . . Outside the firm, price movements direct production, which is co-ordinated through a series of exchange transactions on the market. Within a firm, these market transactions are eliminated and in place of the complicated market structure with exchange transactions is substituted the entrepreneur-co-ordinator, who directs production. It is clear that these are alternative methods of co-ordinating production.[61]

Coase, thus, realized that firms exist because hiring employees, negotiating prices, and enforcing contracts are time-consuming marketplace activities that incur heavy transactions costs that would be reduced if a firm could coordinate its exchange transactions. With few exceptions, economists had engaged in "blackboard calculations" that failed to view firms as agents that sought to engage in exchange transactions at a cost lower than that associated with market forces. Simply stated, firms exist because they are a means for entrepreneurs to lower their transaction costs. The young Coase did not pursue this line of thinking until years later. In accepting his Nobel Prize, he commented: "[I]t is a strange experience to be praised in my eighties for work I did in my twenties."[62] In Chapter 19, we will see how Coase's ideas reentered management theory and were used to explain how the "visible hand" of management is typically more efficient in allocating resources than the "invisible hand" of the marketplace. Finally, we should note that, though Coase's theory of "the firm" is framed as a theory of a single firm, it is meant to be a theory of all firms.

SUMMARY

Whereas human-relations theorists sought greater productivity and satisfaction based on social solidarity and collaboration, the contributors to the development of management thought discussed in this chapter were more concerned with the structure and design of organizations to reach essentially the same ends. These contributors reasoned that people worked more productively and are more satisfied when they know what is expected of them. Hence, they emphasized organization structure and design as means to both employee satisfaction and productivity. Their efforts were characterized by a search for principles of organization and, eventually, by a quest for broader principles of management. Mooney and Reiley deduced principles for achieving an organization's true purpose, thereby alleviating "human want and misery"; Dennison favored forming people into groups to build teamwork; and Gulick,

Urwick, Graicunas, and others advocated formalizing relationships to make coordination easier and, thus, reduce confusion and foster predictability.

A shop-floor and industrial engineering orientation existed for much of the period from the advent of the Great Depression to the early 1950s. The various books of Ralph C. Davis personified the shift in management thinking toward a broader top-management viewpoint. Gulick and Urwick brought Henri Fayol to the fore, and Urwick, in turn, attempted to develop a general theory of organization and management. Hopf applied the scientific approach to designing firms, and others displayed concern over the separation of corporate ownership and control. Finally, as will be noted in Chapter 19, what would become known as "transaction-cost economics" first emerged with the writings of Commons and Coase.

---

[61] Ronald H. Coase, "The Nature of the Firm," *Economica* 4(16) (November 1937), p. 388.

[62] *Idem*, "1991 Nobel Lecture: The Institutional Structure of Production," in Oliver E. Williamson and Sidney G. Winter, eds., *The Nature of the Firm: Origins, Evolution, and Development* (New York: Oxford University Press, 1993), p. 231.

Human Relations in Theory and Practice

What began as an investigation of the relationship between variations in workplace lighting and employee productivity at the Hawthorne plant of Western Electric forever altered the landscape of management theory and practice. Whereas the human-relations movement embodied by the Hawthorne studies had historical precedents, for some, it represented a different approach for improving employer–employee relations. In addition to examining the impact of the human-relations movement on theory and practice, including its extensions and applications, this chapter critically reviews the premises, research methods, and results of the Hawthorne studies.

The Impact of Human Relations on Theory and Practice

Like scientific management, the human-relations movement bore fruit from seeds that had been planted much earlier and nurtured in many places. The roots of concern for people in organizations may be traced to humanists of the Italian Renaissance in the late fourteenth century who questioned the Roman Catholic Church's monolithic authority, the accompanying breakup of rigid social structures, and the subsequent rediscovery of the individual as the primary unit of analysis in the study of human behavior. Throughout the preceding pages, varying views and assumptions about people vis-à-vis organizations have been examined. Robert Owen admonished factory owners to pay as much attention to their "vital machines" (their workers) as to their physical machines. Fred Taylor, concerned with the initiative of individual workers, understood he was dealing with humans as well as material and machinery and called for studies that would provide insights into the "motives that influence men."[1] Hugo Münsterberg answered this call. Viewing the workplace as part of a broader social system in which work provides a sense of fulfillment and happiness, as well as a source of identity and self-worth. Whiting Williams extended the meaning of employee relations to include human relations. As he explained, by improving human relations at every level of an organization, all parties—workers, managers, and the public—would benefit: "The coming together of factory management and factory man for the development of both will do more than humanize and justify this factory age."[2] From these varied beginnings, the human-relations movement would spread and dominate a period in management thought.

---

[1] Frederick W. Taylor, *The Principles of Scientific Management* (New York: Harper & Brothers, 1911), p. 119.
[2] Whiting Williams, *Human Relations in Industry* (Washington, DC: U.S. Department of Labor, 1918), pp. 9–10.

Applying and Extending Human Relations

In the years following the Hawthorne studies, the human-relations movement took on an interpersonal and open systems bent as other individuals and institutions applied and extended its findings. As recounted in Chapter 15, the Committee on Human Relations in Industry was formed in 1943. An interdisciplinary group, its members were drawn from business (Burleigh Gardner), sociology (William Foote Whyte), and anthropology (W. Lloyd Warner).[3] In 1945, Lewin founded the Research Center for Group Dynamics at the Massachusetts Institute of Technology; following his demise, the center was moved to the University of Michigan, where Rensis Likert and others would further the study of employee participation in decision-making and the use of group interventions to achieve changes in workplace behavior.[4] In 1947, another of Lewin's disciples, Leland P. Bradford, established the first sensitivity training (or human relations) laboratory, the National Training Laboratory, at Bethel, Maine.[5] Elliott Jaques's case study of the Glacier Metal Company (London) underscored the importance of studying organizations as interacting sociotechnical systems.[6] His Tavistock colleagues, Eric L. Trist and Kenneth W. Bamforth, documented how changes in technology can disrupt an organization's social system.[7]

Hawthorne Revisited

As noted in Chapter 13, the Hawthorne studies were an intellectual gold mine. Although unlike Taylorism, they did not inspire any investigating commissions, congressional inquiries, or confrontations such as occurred at the Watertown Arsenal, critics have relentlessly examined the studies' premises, methods, and results. Among early critics, Landsberger critiqued four separate areas: the Hawthorne researchers' (1) view of society as characterized by anomie, social disorganization, and conflict; (2) managerial view of work and workers; (3) disregard of other alternatives for accommodating industrial conflict, such as collective bargaining; and (4) failure to take labor unions into account as a method of building social solidarity.[8] Since Landsberger's critique, other criticisms have been voiced.[9] The following comments will expand on Landberger's critique with respect to the Hawthorne researchers' (1) premises about an industrial society and (2) methods and data interpretation.

Premises of an Industrial Society

Elton Mayo and Fritz J. Roethlisberger, the two principal Hawthorne researchers, both began with a view of industrial society characterized by *anomie* (from the Greek word meaning "without norms"). As noted in Chapter 13, Mayo viewed anomie as leading to social disorganization in both personal lives and communities and to a general overall sense of personal futility, defeat, and

---

[3] Burleigh B. Gardner and William Foote Whyte, "Methods for the Study of Human Relations in Industry," *American Sociological Review* 11(5) (October 1946), pp. 506–512. See also David G. Moore, "The Committee in Human Relations in Industry at the University of Chicago," in Kae H. Chung, ed., *Proceedings of the Annual Meeting of the Academy of Management* (1982), pp. 117–121.

[4] "The Career of Rensis Likert: Using Science for Man – A Gentle Revolution," *ISR Newsletter* 1(9) (Winter 1971), pp. 1–7.

[5] Leland P. Bradford, *National Training Laboratories: Its History: 1947–1970* (Bethel, ME: Privately printed, 1974). See also Scott Highhouse, "A History of the T-Group and Its Early Applications in Management Development," *Group Dynamics: Theory, Research, and Practice* 6(4) (December 2002), pp. 277–290.

[6] Elliott Jaques, *The Changing Culture of a Factory* (London: Tavistock Publications, 1951).

[7] Eric L. Trist and Kenneth W. Bamforth, "Some Social and Technical Consequences of the Longwall Method of Coal-Getting: An Examination of the Psychological Situation and Defences of a Work Group in Relation to the Social Structure and Technological Content of the Work System," *Human Relations* 4(1) (February 1951), pp. 3–38.

[8] Henry A. Landsberger, *Hawthorne Revisited: Management and the Worker, Its Critics, and Developments in Human Relations in Industry* (Ithaca, NY: New York State School of Industrial and Labor Relations, Cornell University, 1958), pp. 29–30.

[9] For a review of other criticisms, see Jeffrey Muldoon, "The Hawthorne Studies: An Analysis of Critical Perspectives, 1936–1958," *Journal of Management History* 23(1) (2017), pp. 74–94.

disillusionment. Mayo further believed that people, bound up in their "pessimistic reveries," needed constructive outlets for their latent fears and frustrations. Industrial societies, though making giant strides in technological progress, had created a cultural lag by diminishing the importance of collaborative social skills. Mayo's recommended response was to emphasize small-group interactions and to view people as embedded in a larger social system. Critics have questioned Mayo's view of industrial society. For example, Bell charged that Mayo and the other Hawthorne researchers took the goal of increasing worker productivity as given and considered themselves to be social engineers, who managed not people, but a social system intended to "adjust" workers to the demands of their jobs. According to Bell, to think that contented workers were productive workers was to equate human behavior with "cow sociology"; that is, just as contented cows give more milk, contented and satisfied workers would produce more. In Bell's opinion, the interviewers at Hawthorne were "ambulatory confessors" and represented a new method of workplace control. When workers exposed their innermost doubts and fears, they were more susceptible to managerial manipulation. The socially skilled supervisor could move from using authority to elicit desired behavior to psychological manipulation "as a means of exercising dominion."[10] Workers, relieved of pessimistic reveries by cathartic moments in the personnel counseling program Mayo advocated, would feel better and forget all other distractions. Bell recalled a folktale to make this point:

> A peasant complains to his priest that his little hut is horribly overcrowded. The priest advises him to move his cow into the house, the next week to take in his sheep, and the next week his horse. The peasant now complains even more bitterly about his lot. Then the priest advises him to let out the cow, the next week the sheep, and the next week the horse. At the end the peasant gratefully thanks the priest for lightening his burdensome life.[11]

A second criticism was that Hawthorne researchers presented a naive view of industrial conflict. According to critics, Mayo assumed that labor and management could resolve their differences in the public interest, when, in fact, society was much more complex in terms of conflict between classes and interest groups. Critics maintained that tension and conflict were inevitable in every society and, to an extent, even necessary. The goal should not be to eliminate tension and conflict, but to provide healthy outlets for their resolution.[12] Mayo's notion of a conflict-free state of equilibrium was a worthy goal, but considered too idealistic. Unfortunately, the Hawthorne researchers, like Taylor and his followers, attracted faddists and saw perversions of their original intentions. These faddists often concluded that the goal of the human-relations movement was to keep everyone happy in a conflict-free state of equilibrium with resultant labor–management bliss. When bliss was attained, higher productivity was the corollary. As Fox put it:

> Among the guilty are the "human relationists" with an inadequate concept of human relations, who mistakenly preach participation, permissiveness, and democracy for all, and those employers who confuse popularity with managerial effectiveness and misinterpret the Golden Rule in dealing with their subordinates. . . . Many mistakenly regard it [human relations] as an "end" toward which the organization shall endeavor rather than as what it should be – a "means" for achieving the organization's primary service objectives.[13]

Fox held that the regard for human relations as an end rather than a means misled managers to think that a conflict-free state and worker contentment would automatically lead to a company's

[10] Daniel Bell, *Work and Its Discontents: The Cult of Efficiency in America* (Boston, MA: Beacon Press, 1956), pp. 25–28.

[11] *Ibid.*, p. 26.

[12] Landsberger, *Hawthorne Revisited*, pp. 30–35.

[13] William M. Fox, "When Human Relations May Succeed and the Company Fail," *California Management Review* 8(3) (Spring 1966), p. 19.

success. He warned that human relations could not be substituted for well-defined goals, policies, and high performance standards necessary for achieving an organization's goals. Or, as McNair saw it, managers needed more than listening and human-relations skills to be effective to ensure a company's success. In teaching human relations as a separate skill, McNair saw the dangers of compartmentalizing knowledge when it should be an integral part of all managerial development, whether in marketing, management, or whatever. In essence, McNair concluded: "It is not that the human relations concept is wrong; it is simply that we have blown it up too big and have placed too much emphasis on teaching human relations as such at the collegiate and early graduate level. . . . Let's treat people like people, but let's not make a big production of it."[14]

Knowles also called for a better mix of managerial skills, but one that would avoid the evangelism and mysticism that so often characterized human-relations training. Too often human relationists seem to believe that only human relations could "save Western civilization from impending doom."[15] For social philosophers such as Émile Durkheim (and Mayo), advancing technology and specialization resulting from the division of labor destroyed social cohesiveness and a loss of pride in one's work. Increased interpersonal competition and concern for material things destroyed primary groups, caused status anxiety, and created obsessive-compulsive reactions. The answer to the impending doom was an evangelical zeal by human-relations advocates to downplay material acquisitiveness, rebuild primary groups (the family), and teach people to again love one another. The world could be saved by a sense of belonging, and people could once more find contentment by losing themselves in some larger entity. This mystical overtone, reflecting the Gestalt psychology of the totality, attributed collective wisdom to groups that could not be found in individuals. It was not the logic of efficiency, but the illogic of sentiments that would save the world from the brink. The moral uplift of scientific management had been efficiency; for the human-relations advocates, it was belonging and solidarity.

Research Methods and Data Interpretation

The scientific and methodical standards of today are admittedly much more rigorous than those in use at the time the Hawthorne studies were conducted. In the ensuing years, the Hawthorne researchers have been criticized for their research methods and data interpretation. In particular, they have been assailed for not randomly selecting participants, their small sample sizes, and their failure to control various study conditions.[16] As Kompler correctly notes, however:

> Historical studies must be understood in their "at that time" scientific and societal context. . . . Therefore, it would neither be fair nor correct to judge the Hawthorne studies by the scientific and methodological standards of today. Much of today's standard expertise (experimental and quasi-experimental designs, multivariate analyses, theories on work motivation, and group performance) was not available to these pioneers.[17]

Criticisms relating to the Hawthorne researchers' failure to use random selection to draw representative samples seem especially unjust. Whereas the Hawthorne studies were begun in

---

[14] Malcolm P. McNair, "Thinking Ahead: What Price Human Relations?" *Harvard Business Review* 35(2) (March–April 1957), p. 39.

[15] William H. Knowles, "Human Relations in Industry: Research and Concepts," *California Management Review* 1(1) (Fall 1958), p. 99.

[16] For example, see Michael Argyle, "The Relay Assembly Test Room in Retrospect," *Occupational Psychology* 27(2) (April 1953), pp. 98–103; J. Scott Armstrong, "The Ombudsman: Management Folklore and Management Science – On Portfolio Planning, Escalation Bias, and Such," *Interfaces* 26(4) (July–August 1996), pp. 25–55.

[17] Michael A. J. Kompler, "The 'Hawthorne Effect' Is a Myth, but What Keeps the Story Going?" *Scandinavian Journal of Work, Environment & Health* 32(5) (October 2006), p. 410.

1927, the earliest documented use of true randomization in the social sciences was published in 1928.[18]

Moving beyond methodology to data interpretation, as noted in Chapter 13, critics have suggested that performance incentives may have accounted for the output increases that occurred throughout the Hawthorne studies. Sykes, for example, has contended that human-relations advocates believed that money does not motivate behavior, when in fact the Hawthorne results, in his opinion, lead to the opposite conclusion.[19] Carey similarly criticized the Hawthorne researchers for downplaying the importance of money as a motivator in increasing output and overemphasizing the significance of "friendly supervision" in maintaining employee job satisfaction and productivity.[20] As he noted, the Hawthorne researchers selected "cooperative" workers who were willing to participate in the studies. Second, two assemblers from the original relay-assembly group "were removed for a lack of cooperation, which would have otherwise necessitated greatly increased disciplinary measures."[21] In analyzing the relay-assembly test-room production records, Carey found that output did not increase until the two removed assemblers were replaced with "more cooperative" assemblers. Was this "friendly supervision" or the use of negative sanctions to increase output? In Carey's view, the results of the Hawthorne studies showed that performance incentives and "managerial discipline" were responsible for higher output.

Franke and Kaul likewise challenged the Hawthorne researchers' data interpretation. Reanalyzing the data relay-assembly test-room study, they claimed that "three variables—managerial discipline, the economic adversity of the depression, and time set aside for rest"—explained most of the variance in employee output.[22] Thus, they concluded that it was not supervisory style or performance incentives, but the use of discipline, the larger economic environment, and relief from fatigue that led to increased output. In rebuttal, Schlaifer alleged that Franke and Kaul had improperly analyzed the relay-assembly test-room study data. He further contended that "managerial discipline" in the test room was not harsh, as it simply involved sending two operators back to their original department. Schlaifer reanalyzed the relay-assembly test-room study data to show that the "passage of time" was sufficient to explain increased output, which he concluded was "in all respects consistent with the conclusions reached by the original researchers."[23] Toelle confirmed Schlaifer's findings and further criticized Franke and Kaul's analysis for treating the relay-assembly test-room operators as one group, when there were actually two groups: the first group of five included the two operators who were later removed; the second group comprised the original three operators, plus the two replacements. Toelle found that if the groups were analyzed separately, the passage of time accounted for over 91 percent of the total variance in their output.[24]

What did happen at Hawthorne? What can 20/20 hindsight tell us about the methods and conclusions of the Hawthorne researchers? First, they did make statements that could be interpreted as rejecting the imaginary economic man, or *homo economicus*, who is generally assumed to be motivated solely by money. For example, Sykes quoted Roethlisberger and Dickson as concluding that "none of the results . . . [substantiated] the theory that the worker is primarily motivated by

[18] Louise Forsetlund, Iain Chalmers, and Arild Bjørndal, "When Was Random Allocation First Used to Generate Comparison Groups in Experiments to Assess the Effects of Social Interventions?" *Economics of Innovations and New Technology* 16(5) (July 2007), pp. 371–384. For further historical background, see Peter Gundelach, "Bringing Things Together: Developing the Sample Survey as Practice in the Late Nineteenth Century," *Journal of the History of the Behavioral Sciences* 33(1) (Winter 2017), pp. 71–89.
[19] Andrew J. M. Sykes, "Economic Interest and the Hawthorne Researchers," *Human Relations* 18(3) (August 1965), p. 253.
[20] Alex Carey, "The Hawthorne Studies: A Radical Criticism," *American Sociological Review* 32(3) (June 1967), p. 410.
[21] T. North Whitehead, *The Industrial Worker*, vol. 1 (Cambridge, MA: Harvard University Press, 1938), p. 118. In *The Human Problems of an Industrial Civilization* (New York: Macmillan, 1933), Mayo stated that they "dropped out" (p. 56).
[22] Richard H. Franke and James D. Kaul, "The Hawthorne Experiments: First Statistical Interpretation," *American Sociological Review* 43(5) (October 1978), p. 636.
[23] Robert Schlaifer, "The Relay Assembly Test Room: An Alternative Statistical Interpretation," *American Sociological Review* 45(6) (December 1980), p. 1005.
[24] Richard Toelle, "Research Notes Concerning Franke and Kaul's Interpretation of the Hawthorne Experiments," unpublished paper, University of Oklahoma, Norman, 1982.

economic interest." Sykes did not, however, quote the following sentences: "The evidence indicated that the efficacy of a wage incentive is so dependent on its relation to other factors that it is impossible to separate it out as a thing in itself having an independent effect."[25] Thus, performance incentives should not be excluded from an explanation for increased output, but should be viewed as part of a larger, more complex equation. As Shepard commented, Roethlisberger and Dickson saw performance and nonfinancial incentives as "carriers of social value" rather than as absolute explanations of employee behavior and motivation.[26] In short, the "social man" supplemented, but did not supplant, *homo economicus.*

Second, Schlaifer's finding that the "passage of time" was sufficient to explain increased output in the relay-assembly test-room suggests that trust is an important factor in building human relationships and that it took time for trust to develop between the Hawthorne researchers and study participants. Interviews with the surviving relay-group members and observer-supervisor Don Chipman indicated that a rapport did develop during the studies.[27] By contrast, in situations where a friendly and respectful relationship did not develop, such as in the bank-wiring room, productivity did not increase.

Third, there is what has become known as the "science versus advocacy" distinction.[28] It is difficult, if not impossible, for researchers to exclude personal values from their investigations. In the case of Hawthorne, Roethlisberger wrote: "Mayo was an adventurer in the realm of ideas . . . the [Hawthorne] data were not his; the results were not his; but what the results meant . . . were his."[29] If Mayo's conclusions went beyond the Hawthorne data, he was speaking as an advocate, not as a scientist, leading to further criticism. Gillespie claimed that the Hawthorne findings were "manufactured" by Mayo and his colleagues because "in Mayo's hands, the Hawthorne experiments provided the experimental data on which he could base his political and social theory."[30] An awareness of such "investigator effects" is important in understanding when a researcher's personal orientation and data interpretation begin to blur.[31]

Finally, Hassard has claimed that the findings Hawthorne studies were not "enlightened" new revelations, but were used by Mayo to promote his social philosophy for an industrial society.[32] In this regard, Bruce and Nyland have argued that Mayo's interpretation of the Hawthorne results not only reflected his "preformed personal views," but also the influence of John D. Rockefeller, Jr., (Mayo's "financial and professional benefactor") and "other conservative business leaders" who were interested "in fending off the Bolshevik threat of socialism" as represented by organized labor.[33] Both of these criticisms were voiced when Roethlisberger and Dickson's account of

---

[25] Roethlisberger and Dickson, *Management and the Worker* (Cambridge, MA: Harvard University Press, 1939), pp. 575–576; a similar statement appears on p. 185.

[26] Jon M. Shepard, "On Alex Carey's Radical Criticism of the Hawthorne Studies," *Academy of Management Journal* 14(1) (March 1971), pp. 23–32.

[27] Alfred A. Bolton, "Relay Assembly Test Room Participants Remember: Hawthorne a Half Century Later," *International Journal of Public Administration* 17(2) (1994), p. 372.

[28] Lyle Yorks and David A. Whitsett, "Hawthorne, Topeka, and the Issue of Science versus Advocacy in Organizational Behavior," *Academy of Management Review* 10(1) (January 1985), pp. 21–30.

[29] Fritz J. Roethlisberger, *The Elusive Phenomena,* ed., George F. F. Lombard (Boston, MA: Division of Research, Graduate School of Business Administration, Harvard University, 1977), pp. 50–51. See also William Dowling, "Interview with Fritz J. Rothlisberger," *Organizational Dynamics* 1(2) (Autumn 1972), 31–45.

[30] Richard Gillespie, *Manufacturing Knowledge: A History of the Hawthorne Experiments* (New York: Cambridge University Press, 1991), p. 181.

[31] Naomi Weiner-Levy and Ariela Popper-Giveon, "The Absent, the Hidden and the Obscured: Reflections on 'Dark Matter' in Qualitative Research," *Quality & Quantity* 47(4) (June 2013), p. 2180.

[32] John Hassard, "Rethinking the Hawthorne Studies: The Western Electric Research in Its Social, Political, and Historical Context," *Human Relations* 65(11) (November 2012), pp. 1431–1461.

[33] Kyle Bruce and Chris Nyland, "Elton Mayo and the Deification of Human Relations," *Organization Studies* 32(3) (March 2011), pp. 390, 391. The Hawthorne Studies received funding under a grant from the Rockefeller Foundation to the Harvard University Committee on Industrial Hazards. The Harvard group, however, always referred to itself as the Committee on Industrial *Physiology.* For details, see Jason Oakes, "Alliances in Human Biology: The Harvard Committee on Industrial Physiology, 1929–1939," *Journal of the History of Biology* 48(3) (August 2015), pp. 365–390. Mayo received personal funds from John D. Rockefeller, Jr. On this point, see Martin Bulmer, and Joan Bulmer, "Philanthropy and Social Sciences in the 1920s: Beardsley Ruml and the Laura Spelman Rockefeller Memorial, 1922–1929," *Minerva* 19(3) (September 1981), p. 383.

the Hawthorne studies *Management and the Worker* was first published. For example, as evidence of the Hawthorne researchers' pro-management and antilabor bias, Mary B. Gilson noted: "In all the more than six hundred pages describing the Western Electric experiment . . . no reference is made to organized labor except a short statement, unindexed, that it was so seldom mentioned by any workers that it was not considered sufficiently important to discuss."[34] Although Gilson acknowledged that, in his Preface to *Management and the Worker*, Mayo "modestly states that the authors . . . do not claim that the enlightenment that many collaborators of the scheme got from their researches was 'either very extensive or very profound,'" she attacked the Hawthorne researchers for "discovering the obvious," and concluded that Mayo's claim "[t]hat what they learned was 'novel and unexpected' seems to me an acknowledgment of inexperience in the field of industrial practice."[35]

Although *Management and the Worker* makes no reference to organized labor, it seems unfair to conclude that this constituted an antilabor bias.[36] Until 1935, the dominant labor organizations in the United States were the American Federation of Labor, which consisted of skilled workers, and the brotherhoods that represented various groups of railroad employees. As will be seen in Chapter 18, the passage of the National Labor Relations (Wagner) Act in 1935 provided the legislative basis for a spurt in union membership from a turn-of-the-decade 3.5 million to almost 9 million by 1939.

Given that the Hawthorne studies concluded in 1932, before organized labor made its great strides, it should not be surprising to find little mention of unions in *Management and the Worker*. Mayo and his colleagues did not draw any distinction between union–management relations and human relations, thus suggesting that in both union and nonunion employment there was an equal need for human-relations-oriented supervisors. This said, human-relations thought entered a revisionist period in the 1950s with an emphasis on "industrial human relations." Just as Morris L. Cooke tried to bring about a rapprochement between scientific management and organized labor (see Chapter 8), post-Hawthorne scholars quickly brought unions into the human-relations picture. Industrial sociologists, in particular, studied the relationship between organized labor and management. Reflecting a social-systems orientation, they focused on the economic dimensions of employee–employer relations within a more encompassing societal complex.[37]

A basic assumption that appeared to prevail in this revisionist period was that there was an inherent conflict between labor and management with respect to dividing the surpluses created by an advanced technological society. Increased industrial conflict was, in fact, a reality. A comparison of work stoppages and their causes for the period 1920 to 1929 with the decade of the 1930s evidences dramatic differences. The 1920s, characterized by employee-representation plans and union–management cooperation, showed a steady decline in work stoppages, whereas in the 1930s this trend was reversed. Of 14,256 work stoppages during the 1920s, 51 percent were due to wages and hours of work and 21 percent were the result of union organizing drives. From 1930 to 1934, stoppages associated with union organizing attempts increased to 34 percent, but wages and hours still accounted for 51 percent of the disruptions. For the remainder of the 1930s,

---

[34] Mary B. Gilson, [Review of *Management and the Worker*], *American Journal of Sociology* 46(1) (July 1940), p. 100. See also Ordway Tead, [*Review of Social Problems of an Industrial Civilization*], *Survey Graphic* 35(5) (May 1946), p. 179.

[35] Gilson, *op. cit.*, p. 101. The Mayo quotes appear on p. xii in *Management and the Worker*. For a discussion of Mayo's response that Gilson was "insane," see Chris Nyland and Kyle Bruce, "Democracy or Seduction? The Demonization of Scientific Management and the Deification of Human Relations," in Nelson Lichtenstein and Elizabeth Tandy Shemer, eds., *The Right and Labor in America: Politics, Ideology, and Imagination* (Philadelphia, PA: University of Pennsylvania Press, 2016), p. 72.

[36] It should be noted that an independent union, which was previously a company union, did exist at the Hawthorne Works. George C. Homans, "Report of the Committee," in Committee on Work in Industry of the National Research Council, *Fatigue of Workers: Its Relation to Industrial Production* (New York: Reinhold Publishing Corporation, 1941), p. 113.

[37] Examples of this way of thinking may be found in Eugene V. Schneider, *Industrial Sociology* (New York: McGraw-Hill, 1957); and Delbert C. Miller and William H. Form, *Industrial Sociology: An Introduction to the Sociology of Work* (New York: Harper & Brothers, 1951). A historical perspective is provided by Bruce E. Kaufman, *The Origins & Evolution of the Field of Industrial Relations in the United States* (Ithaca, NY: ILR Press, Cornell University, 1993), pp. 75–102.

however, and following the passage of the Wagner Act, a reversal occurred. Of the 14,290 work stoppages from 1935 to 1939, 31 percent concerned wages and hours and 53 percent were due to union organizing efforts.[38] To many scholars writing during this period, the answer to industrial conflict resided not in human-relations training per se, but in overcoming the contrasting interests and ideologies of management and labor, usually meaning organized workers. It was largely believed that industrial harmony would come through collective bargaining and the efforts of professional industrial-relations specialists.

In addition to bringing unions into the picture, the human-relations textbooks of the 1940s and early 1950s typically held that the feelings of people were more important than organization charts, rules, and directives. Human relations were based on intangibles, not on hard, scientific investigation, and there were no final answers; that is, nothing is positive or fixed in solutions to human complexities. In general, these early texts emphasized feelings, sentiments, and collaboration.[39] They were heuristic rather than specific or systematic, encouraging students to investigate and discover for themselves what worked, rather than prescribing solutions. In brief, the human-relations ethos led to a revisionist period that considered organized labor. The Hawthorne researchers were not antiunion per se, but reflected the limited influence of organized labor during the 1920s and early 1930s. Whether organized or not, it was the individual worker who was the center of attention for management's understanding and application of human-relations skills.

SUMMARY

The foregoing criticisms suggest that answering the question "What happened at Hawthorne?" may be difficult, if not, impossible. In his autobiography, Roethlisberger cautioned that the Hawthorne findings "have been so often restated and misstated that it [*Management and the Worker*] has a life of its own . . . human relations was first and foremost an *investigatory and diagnostic tool*. It was not a model of what an organization should be; it was a conceptual scheme for finding out what the relations in a *particular organization at a particular place and time* were, not what they should be."[40] Nonetheless, the Hawthorne studies were an important step in advancing the idea of improving human relations in all types of settings. Its emphasis on human relations was not new. Indeed, Elton Mayo recognized his work as "an extension of that begun by the pioneer [Taylor]."[41] Although Mayo's name is closely connected with the human-relations movement, he was but one person in a cast of many who were responsible for its growth. If George Pennock, Clair Turner, and others at Western Electric had faltered, Mayo's

efforts would have been for naught. After 1931, Mayo became more of an advocate and less of a scientific researcher, and the Hawthorne studies achieved a life of their own as expounded in Mayo's social philosophy for an industrial society. As the facts became clouded with ideological overtones, it became easier and easier to misperceive, misquote, and misinterpret what really occurred at the Hawthorne Works of the Western Electric Company.

In retrospect, certain conclusions stand out: (1) human relations was intended as a tool for understanding workplace behavior rather than as an end in itself; (2) trust was crucial in building the interpersonal relationships that provided for melding the interests of Hawthorne's managers and operative employees; (3) performance and nonfinancial incentives played a role in productivity gains, but these incentives could not explain all the Hawthorne results; and (4) care should be taken to avoid going beyond or selectively extracting data from the Hawthorne results to support one's "preformed" beliefs.

---

[38] U.S. Department of Commerce, Bureau of the Census, *Historical Statistics of the United States: Colonial Times to 1970* (Washington, DC: U.S. Government Printing Office, 1974), pt. 1, p. 179.
[39] For example, see Schuyler D. Hoslett, ed., *Human Factors in Management* (Parkville, MO: Park College Press, 1946); Burleigh B. Gardner and David G. Moore, *Human Relations in Industry* (Homewood, IL: Richard D. Irwin, Inc., 1955).
[40] Roethlisberger, *Elusive Phenomena*, pp. 305, 311.
[41] Elton Mayo, "The Basis of Industrial Psychology," *Bulletin of the Taylor Society* 9(6) (December, 1924), p. 258.

The Social-Person Era in Retrospect

Understanding the ideas of individuals in the context of their own times not only offers the possibility of "learning from history," but also the prospect of gaining a better appreciation of the cumulative impact of the past on the present.[1] As argued in the preceding pages, the evolution of management thought forms a more coherent picture when viewed in its changing cultural milieu of economic, technological, social, and political forces. Within its cultural context, scientific management found its *raison d'être* in the economic necessities of large-scale organizations, in the social sanction of individual achievement and the moral uplift of efficiency, and in a concern for national productivity and the conservation of resources. In contrast, the Social-Person Era—from the advent of the Hawthorne studies to the early 1950s—was an age in which individual hopes were dashed on the reefs of economic misfortune, technological collisions, social maladies, and political shifts heralding a transformation in traditional relationships. Though treated independently here, the forces underlying this transformation interacted to form the cultural context of the Social-Person Era.

The Economic Environment: From Depression to Prosperity

Like the Duke of Gloucester in Shakespeare's *Richard III*, the 1929 Wall Street stock-market crash found the Winter of Its Discontent in earlier days. The 1920s were prosperous, characterized by falling prices, a near doubling of industrial productivity, and a 53 percent rise in the real earnings

---

[1] Arthur G. Bedeian, "Exploring the Past," *Journal of Management History* 4(1) (1998), pp. 4–15.

for nonfarm workers.[2] Mass-production technology held costs down and increased the purchasing power of the U.S. dollar. An end to this prosperity came on October 29, 1929, known in the United States as Black Tuesday.[3] The most dramatic decline of stock prices in U.S. history wiped out $14 billion of wealth and marked the beginning of the Great Depression. By November 13, 1929, the market had lost some $30 billion in value. For more than a decade afterward, the Great Depression substantially changed life in the United States. In 1929, 48 million people were employed, and only about 1.5 million (3.2 percent) were unemployed. Unemployment peaked at 12,830,000 (24.9 percent) in 1933, dropping below 8 million only once (1937) in the following decade.[4] Using "Darby-corrected" figures, that is, following today's practice of counting those employed by state or federal relief agencies or working for the government on relief projects (building roads, dams, sidewalks and other infrastructure) as employed, unemployment rates in the late 1930s declined, suggesting that contracyclical government work put people to work.[5] Despite state and federal attempts to create jobs, businesses failed, incomes dropped, homes were lost, family savings were wiped out, and, worst of all, national morale was at an all-time low. Gone was the optimism of prosperity and promise of material wealth; the old guideposts apparently had failed, as "rags to riches" became the "midnight pumpkin." Recovery from the economic morass was painfully slow, but socially and psychologically, it was even slower. Feeling inept in adjusting to economic deprivation, people turned to state and federal governments for assistance.

Attempts at Economic Recovery

In November 1929, President Herbert Hoover asked for labor–management cooperation in reducing employee work hours as an alternative to layoffs. Doing so would reduce individual employee's total weekly wages, but was considered better than no work at all. To provide an example to railroad unions of how this hardship should be shared and to gain support for a 10 percent reduction in employee wages, Daniel Willard, president of the Baltimore & Ohio Railroad, cut his own salary 40 percent, from $150,000 to $60,000 per year.[6]

In the early days of the Great Depression, labor and management responded positively to such appeals, as forward-looking policies initiated during the 1920s provided employees with a cushion against a loss in work and wages. Company-sponsored thrift plans, for instance, gave employees some savings to fall back on to get through the hard times. Employee stock-ownership plans had been a mixed blessing: as stock prices soared in the late 1920s, some employees had sold their stock and entered into the general orgy of stock-market speculation only to later regret doing so; other employees had held on to their stocks and had seen them plummet in value, also with regret. By necessity, there was a change in attitude about women working outside the home, as increasing numbers of women entered the labor force to bolster family income.

In his 1941 State of the Union address, President Franklin D. Roosevelt promised his countrymen freedom from fear and want.[7] Hoover had previously used the Reconstruction Finance Corporation, established in 1932, to pump federal funds into state and local governments, as well as to loan money to banks, mortgage associations, railroads, and other businesses. Roosevelt went much further, however, endorsing the "New Economics" touted by Cambridge University professor John Maynard Keynes. In contrast to the Protestant ethic that emphasized frugality,

---

[2] Stanley Lebergott, *The Americans: An Economic Record* (New York: W. W. Norton, 1984), pp.390 (Table 2.4), 434–435 (Table 33.3).

[3] Maury Klein, "The Stock Market Crash of 1929: A Review Article," *Business History Review* 75(2) (Summer 2001), pp. 325–351.

[4] U.S. Department of Commerce, Bureau of the Census, *Historical Statistics of the United States: Colonial Times to 1970* (Washington, DC: U.S. Government Printing Office, 1974), pt. 1, p. 135.

[5] Michael R. Darby, "Three-and-a-Half Million U.S. Employees Have Been Mislaid: Or, an Explanation of Unemployment, 1934–1941," *Journal of Political Economy* 84(1) (February 1976), pp. 1–16.

[6] John N. Ingham, *Biographical Dictionary of American Business Leaders,* vol. 4 (Westport, CT: Greenwood, 1983), p. 1634.

[7] Franklin D. Roosevelt, State of the Union Address," January 6, 1941, Washington, DC. Accessible at http://voicesofdemocracy.umd.edu/fdr-the-four-freedoms-speech-text/

thrift, and hard work, Keynes held that savings withheld from consumption could lead to dislocation and underutilization of economic resources. Therefore, the federal government should intervene and, as explained by Hoover, "prime the economic pump" to stimulate consumption and, in turn, economic recovery.[8]

Although Keynes held that government spending contributed to recovery, economist Milton Friedman later maintained that proper monetary action by the Federal Reserve System would have prevented contraction of the money supply and allayed the Great Depression.[9] Disagreeing with both Keynes and Friedman, Robert L. Heilbroner concluded that the massive increase in gross domestic product and decline in unemployment associated with World War II ended the Depression, not government pump priming.[10] Economists may fuss and fume about proper remedial actions, but in reality "what might have been" is a matter for other historians. The fact is that the federal government became ever more involved in the nation's economic life; though capitalism was preserved, with ownership and management remaining in private hands, regulatory power became increasingly lodged in the hands of government officials. An emerging view tied corporate actions more closely than ever to the public interest, with concomitant calls for "economic statesmanship" on the part of business figures and attacks on "unjust" corporate concentrations of wealth and marketplace power.

Big Business

Whereas the years running up to the Great Depression were a period of vigorous economic growth, somehow "Big Business" was alleged to be the primary culprit responsible for the nation's economic ills.[11] In response, it was argued that public policy should come from the grassroots up to counterbalance corporate concentrations of wealth and economic power. Believing that there was a privileged elite of top earners who controlled a disproportionate share of the nation's wealth, critics sought to reduce income inequality and restore the influence of those at the base of the economic pyramid. Kenneth E. Boulding warned that the growing presence of larger and more economically powerful organizations—including labor unions, trade associations, trusts, governmental agencies, but especially corporations—risked a potential moral conflict between an aristocratic society and a political democracy based on fellowship and social equality.[12] Echoing Berle and Means's earlier claim that the ascendancy of professional managers as a result of the broad spread of public ownership in the 1920s had severed corporate control from corporate ownership (see Chapter 16), James Burnham foretold a bleak future where a ruling managerial elite (neither capitalist nor socialist) would control society's means of production and distribution for its own selfish interests. He labeled this new type of exploitative society "managerialism." In this transformed world, an elite of highly credentialed managers who possessed technical skills would dominate economic relations, politics, and culture through corporate and government bureaucracies. As reasoned by Burnham, increasing technical complexity and the need to coordinate mass phenomena—mass production, mass consumption, mass political movements, mass education, mass labor, mass armies and so on—make a "ruling class" of technocratic managers a necessity. Burnham warned that these "managers will exploit the rest of society . . . , their rights belonging to them not as individuals but through their position of actual

[8] Herbert Hoover, "Consequences to Liberty of Regimentation," *Saturday Evening Post* 207(11) (1934), p. 85.

[9] Milton Friedman and Anna J. Schwartz, *The Great Contraction: 1929–1933* (Princeton, NJ: Princeton University Press, 1965).

[10] Robert L. Heilbroner, *The Making of Economic Society* (Englewood Cliffs, NJ: Prentice- Hall, 1962). Although Darby-corrected data indicate that federal and state projects lessened unemployment, a substantial decline in percentage of unemployed is not apparent until the onset of World War II. See Darby, "Three-and-a-Half Million U.S. Employees Have Been Mislaid," p. 8.

[11] Gene Smiley, "The U.S. Economy in the 1920s," *EH Net Encyclopedia*, ed., Robert Whaples, June 29, 2004. https://eh.net/encyclopedia/the-u-s-economy-in-the-1920s/

[12] Kenneth E. Boulding, *The Organizational Revolution: A Study of the Ethics of Economic Organization* (New York: Harper & Brothers, 1953).

directing responsibility which they occupy.[13] Burnham joined a growing line of critics, dating back to Adam Smith (see Chapter 2), who doubted the motives of those who managed other people's property and money.

Although the Depression delayed industrial growth, mobilization for World War II created both technological and managerial advancements. Vast productive resources had been marshalled, training within industry had created a deeper pool of employee talent, consumer products had been rationed, worker earnings were high, and the postwar years found the United States with a pent-up demand for products and services. With demand outrunning productive ability, the nation did not experience an anticipated postwar business slump. The war effort had created new products, new technologies, new markets, and a more highly skilled, broader-based labor force. Soon, management thought was in transition, shifting from a wartime production orientation to a renewed interest in general management theory as businesses grew at home and abroad. The postwar prosperity and expansion provided palpable impetus for the further evolution of management thinking.

Seeds of Change: The New Technologies

Writing following the outbreak of World War II, Joseph A. Schumpeter was pessimistic about the future of capitalism. He saw innovations in new products, new methods of production, new markets, the use of new raw materials, or new forms of organization as essential to economic growth and human progress. As Schumpeter explained, innovation "incessantly revolutionizes the economic structure *from within,* incessantly destroying the old one, incessantly creating a new [economic structure]."[14] "Creative Destruction," as he called this process, sometimes occurred in rushes with intervening lulls, but was nevertheless incessant. In Schumpeter's account, it is the entrepreneur who gives birth to innovation that drives economic growth. Driven by the need to innovate to stay competitive, entrepreneurs propel a nation's economic progress.

In transportation, automobiles were miraculous inventions, but their use was initially limited by a lack of paved roads. Enabling legislation in 1926 provided for a "national" highway—U.S. Route 66, which began on the shores of Lake Michigan in Chicago, sloped westward across Illinois and Missouri, crossed the Great Plains and deserts of the southwest, and terminated on the shores of the Pacific Ocean at Santa Monica, California. All 2000 miles were paved by 1938. In 1947, only 44 years after Orville Wright's piloted the first powered airplane, Charles E. "Chuck" Yeager broke the sound barrier in a jet-powered test plane, the X-1, at the speed of 640 miles per hour; 66 years before the first moon landing, Charles Lindbergh soloed the Atlantic Ocean in 1927; Igor Sikorsky perfected the first helicopter in 1943; long-range guided missiles developed in World War II became useful in later years for exploring space and launching communication satellites; microwave radar initially used solely for air defense by the Allied Powers in World War II was adapted for postwar air-traffic control and, ultimately, everyday microwave ovens. Travel was expedited by innovative aircraft manufacturers such as Boeing, Lockheed, and McDonnell Douglas, who supplied new airlines such as Delta, American, and Pan American. Piston engines, soon replaced by jet turbines, extended long-distance passenger travel from highways and railways to skyways, spurring demand for travel to global destinations.

In communication and entertainment, radios were becoming a household staple. The first Rose Bowl football game was broadcast in 1927; by 1930, 12 million households owned a radio. RCA provided the first glimpse of television at the 1939 World's Fair in New York City; 15 years

---

[13] James Burnham, *The Managerial Revolution: What is Happening in the World* (New York: John Day Company, 1941), p. 126. See also Patricia Genoe McLaren, "James Burnham, *The Managerial Revolution*, and the Development of Management Theory in Post-War America," *Management & Organizational History* 6(4) (2001), pp. 411–423; Julius Krein, "James Burnham's Managerial Elite," *American Affairs* 1(1) (Spring 2017), pp. 120–151.

[14] Joseph A. Schumpeter, *Capitalism, Socialism, and Democracy* (New York: Harper & Brothers, 1942), p. 83. See also Timothy S. Kiessling, "Entrepreneurship and Innovation: Austrian School of Economics to Schumpeter to Drucker to Now," *Journal of Applied Management and Entrepreneurship* 9(1) (January 2004), pp. 80–92.

later, one-half of the American homes wired for electricity had television sets; and someday, it was hoped The Ed Sullivan Show could be seen in color. Ampex pioneered the first video-tape recorder, a three-quarter-inch band of ribbon to preserve television images; reel-to-reel magnetic tape recorders could preserve voices and music. In 1926, General Electric (GE) invented the first practical device for recording sound on film for Hollywood movies, and motion pictures became a growth industry. True to Schumpeter's notion of creative destruction, Western Electric soon pioneered groundbreaking technological advances to replace GE as the leading provider of sound recording and reproducing equipment.

Alan Turing, aware of Charles Babbage's idea of a general-purpose calculating machine, developed a special-purpose computer that broke the German signal code during World War II. This was only the beginning of a revival of interest in computing machinery. Remington-Rand, IBM, Minneapolis-Honeywell, RCA, and others began making general-purpose computers. The Electronic Numerical Integrator and Computer (ENIAC), used to calculate artillery firing tables for the U.S. Army's Ballistic Research Laboratory, was 8 feet long, 8 feet high, and 3 feet deep, contained 18,000 vacuum tubes, 1,500 relays, 70,000 resisters, 7,200 diodes, 10,000 capacitors, weighed 27 tons, and required an air-conditioned room to avoid meltdowns. To have suggested in 1950 that someday people would walk about carrying a combination tablet, personal computer, and smartphone would have been considered outlandish. In another instance of creative destruction, in 1947, Bell Laboratories invented the first solid-state transistors, replacing vacuum tubes in most applications, and in the process transforming the computer industry. Modern society, in general, was further transformed in 1959 when the first integrated circuits (microchips) were patented by Texas Instruments. Integrated circuits are used today in virtually all electronic equipment, including mobile phones, automobiles, and home appliances.

Dry-copying or electrophotography was another technological innovation. Developed in 1938 by Chester Carlson, it would be almost a decade before the Haloid Photographic Company (later renamed Xerox) negotiated commercial rights to this new process for making copies at the touch of a button. Medical breakthroughs, beginning in the mid-1920s and extending into the 1950s, were astounding: Jonas Salk developed the first polio vaccine; the World Health Organization announced that smallpox had been eradicated; and Alexander Fleming's serendipitous discovery of penicillin ignited research into antibiotics. Even further in the future, Rosalind Franklin and Maurice Wilkins's X-ray of the molecule called deoxyribonucleic acid (DNA) helix became increasingly relevant when James Watson and Francis Crick realized it consisted of a double helix and offered a clue in understanding the building blocks of life.

Developments in the public sector also led to further innovation. The Manhattan Project, under the leadership of the United States with the support of the United Kingdom and Canada, produced the first nuclear weapons during World War II. The 1930s provided a building boom in civic infrastructure that no decade has surpassed: dams such as the Hoover, Bonneville, Grand Coulee, and Shasta for hydroelectric power, irrigation, and recreation; and bridges such as the George Washington, the Golden Gate, the San Francisco–Oakland spans, and the Huey P. Long Bridge over the Mississippi River at New Orleans. The Tennessee Valley Authority (TVA) dams along the Tennessee River provided electricity for economic expansion and household use. Morris L. Cooke headed the Rural Electrification Authority, which brought electricity to non-urban dwellers. As electrical supplies increased, the home-appliance industry blossomed: electric vacuum sweepers, food freezers, refrigerators, stoves, washing machines, clothes dryers, and more.

The Social Environment: The Social Ethic and the Organization Man

The economic temper of the Social-Person Era shaped the nation's dominant social values. Attitudes and aspirations are the founts of human strength, and the crushing economic burden of the Great Depression was for many a violation of the previously held precepts of abundance and success for everyone. The 1920s had brought Madison Avenue to Peoria and Dubuque, and U.S. productivity presaged more than the Republican Party's 1928 campaign promise of "A chicken in every pot and a car in every backyard."[15] What happened to social relationships and the assumptions that guided people's behavior in the troubled 1930s? Broadly viewed, two fairly distinct developments were reshaping the nation's social values: (1) a decline of the tenets of the Protestant ethic and the rise of a social ethic, and (2) a decline in the level of esteem afforded those engaged in business.

Shifting Social Values

Robert and Helen Lynd, in their famous study of the typical U.S. city of the late 1920s (later identified as Muncie, Indiana), found a split in the social values of an average working-class citizen and the typical white-collar employee. For an average wage-earner, economic motives were primary: "This dominance of the dollar appears in the apparently growing tendency among younger working class men to swap a problematic future for immediate 'big money.'"[16] Whereas an average wage-earner measured social status by financial standing and tended to hold to the traditional virtues of individualism, including a declining interest in belonging to organized labor, white-collar employees viewed their place in society differently and held contrasting values. The Lynds noted a decline in individualism among white-collar employees and a rapidly increasing conformity and need to belong. In a follow-up study conducted in Muncie during the Great Depression, however, the Lynds found that "the heightening of insecurity during the depression has brought with it greater insistence upon conformity and a sharpening of latent issues" on the part of both groups.[17] Average wage-earners were now turning to unions for collective action. Their white-collar brethren were conforming to the demands of corporate life as salaried managers. This resulted in a sharpening of class distinctions and engendered social bitterness. The Great Depression had brought about a shift in social values for both the average wage-earner and the typical white-collar employee.

After the 1929 Wall Street stock-market crash, of what value were the Protestant-ethic virtues of frugality, thrift, and hard work? Apparently nearly everyone had been affected in some way by Black Tuesday—the loss of a job here, a savings account there, or even one's home or farm. The Great Depression struck the virtuous as well as the prodigal, the tycoon as well as the tyro, and the energetic as well as the feckless. People found their own fortunes intertwined with those of others in a pattern that defied reason or justice. "As time went on there was a continuing disposition among Americans young and old to look with a cynical eye upon the old Horatio Alger formula for success; to be dubious about talking chances for ambition's sake; to look with a favorable eye upon a safe if unadventurous job, social insurance plans, pension plans. They had learned from bitter experience to crave security."[18]

This craving for security, this turning inward of people to others who shared the same tribulations, was passed from parents to their children, and on to, in some instances, another generation or more. Perhaps people have a natural predilection to form groups when faced with threatening circumstances—when these circumstances assume a major cultural impact possibly people become more group-oriented. The presence of others facing similar trials may offer a psychological sense of comfort or security under threatening or frustrating conditions. Erich Fromm has

---

[15] "A Chicken *for* Every Pot," Campaign ad accessible at https://www.docsteach.org/documents/document/a-chicken-in-every-pot-political-ad-and-rebuttal-article-in-new-york-times

[16] Robert S. Lynd and Helen M. Lynd, *Middletown: A Study in American Culture* (New York: Harcourt, Brace and Company, 1929), p. 81.

[17] *Idem, Middletown in Transition: A Study in Cultural Conflicts* (New York: Harcourt, Brace and Company, 1937), p. 427.

[18] Frederick Lewis Allen, *The Big Change: America Transforms Itself, 1900–1950* (New York: Harper & Row, 1952), p. 149.

noted the desire of people to escape the loneliness of standing alone. In Fascist Germany, to escape their loneliness, people turned to an authoritarian regime that made their decisions for them and gave them a sense of identity, however evil. According to Fromm, this need to belong also pervaded U.S. industrial life during the 1930s, and individuals more frequently than not were willing to give up self to conform to group norms. Whereas the Protestant Reformation and the Industrial Revolution drove people from the shadows of medieval life, enabling them to find freedom in the spiritual, political, and economic spheres of society, industrialization created new threats to these newfound liberties.[19] Perhaps people felt alone in pure laissez-faire capitalism and needed something larger than themselves—God, the Nation, the Company, the Union, or whatever—with which to identify and find strength.

The conditions of the troubled 1930s may have compounded this desire for group membership as a source of strength. McClelland found in his studies of people's motives that the "need for achievement" increased in the United States from 1800 to 1890, but decreased thereafter. The trade-off between the need for achievement and the "need for affiliation" took a dramatic shift between 1925 and 1950. In 1925, the need for affiliation was primarily a familial concern; by 1950, affiliation had become an alternative for economic achievement. By that time, people were showing more concern for affiliation and less concern for achievement.[20]

David Riesman and his associates furnished additional evidence relating to this era's change in social values, noting a shift in society from an "inner-directed" to "other-directed" culture. The inner-directed person represented the era's laissez-faire capitalism and emphasized self-direction and control. The other-directed person was characterized by high social mobility and by an emphasis on consumption rather than production, and on getting along and being accepted by others as the key to achievement. Riesman called the inner-directed character of the scientific-management period "job-minded" and the other-directed person of human-relations era "people-minded."[21] For Riesman, the shift from "invisible hand to glad hand" actually began about 1900. Up until that time, individualism had been the dominant social value. After 1900, the closing of the nation's frontier meant that those seeking opportunity and freedom in the West could no longer do so. Restrictions on immigration reduced the flow of settlers eager to move west and start anew on free land rather than live in industrial tenements. The loss of the frontier diluted the value of individualism and allowed "groupism" or the social nature of humans to prevail. The inner-directed person persisted for a period after 1900, but the nation's social character had shifted. In the main, people had little choice but to live where they were, being unable to use the frontier as a safety valve. Most of the pressing challenges of production began to disappear. The new challenges that arose in the modern industrial world were challenges with people. With the expanding size and increase in corporate ownership, employee–employer relationships became less personal, as the engaged style of the small-business owner was replaced with the bureaucratic style of the professional manager. The hands-on touch of an owner-manager was lost, only to be replaced with directives from technically trained specialists. Social competence, influencing others, began to assume a new importance, and technical skills were less valued.

This shift in the nation's culture led to the rise of groupism and the social person. Self-proclaimed "progressive" educators sought to remake classroom instruction, emphasizing the skills, habits, and values necessary to function within social groups, and to replace parents as the primary agents in teaching their children with respect to societal norms. Getting along and being accepted were more important than individual accomplishments in defining one's self and aspirations. People were judged by what others thought of them, not by what they thought of themselves.

---

[19] Erich S. Fromm, *Escape from Freedom* (New York: Holt, Rinehart & Winston, 1941), pp. 7–10.

[20] David C. McClelland, *The Achieving Society* (Princeton, NJ: Van Nostrand, 1961), pp. 166–167 and *idem,* "Business Drive and National Achievement," *Harvard Business Review* 40(4) (July–August, 1962), p. 110.

[21] David Riesman (with the collaboration of Nathan Glazer and Reuel Denney), *The Lonely Crowd: A Study in Changing American Character* (New Haven, CT: Yale University Press, 1950), pp. 19–40, 151.

A "Confusion of Souls"

Although industrialization had not necessarily made people less religious, they found they could more easily segment their lives into religious and nonreligious spheres. When God smiled on frugality, thrift, and hard work, people found comfort in combining secular drives with spiritual grace. For one authority, the Great Depression caused a spiritual "confusion of souls" and a crisis for the Protestant ethic.[22] Self-help had failed, and the notion of the self-made success was no longer seen as the foundation of economic order. Charity became a public rather than a private concern, and the Protestant-ethic virtues of frugality, thrift, and hard work fell into disfavor. From this confusion and crisis, the moral order needed to take on new dimensions.

Two books in particular answered the nation's thirst for moral advice and direction. Both are among the most popular books in publishing history. Almost from its initial debut in 1937, Dale Carnegie's *How to Win Friends and Influence People* was an immediate bestseller, with 250,000 copies sold in the first 3 months following its publication.[23] Emphasizing the importance of human relations, Carnegie maintained that success in life could be achieved by (1) making others feel important through a sincere appreciation of their efforts; (2) making a good first impression; (3) winning people to one's way of thinking by letting others do the talking and being sympathetic, with the caveat, "never tell a man he is wrong"; and (4) changing people by praising good traits and giving the offender the opportunity to save face. Although Roethlisberger and Dickson's full report on the Hawthorne studies, *Management and the Worker*, had not been published at the time, Carnegie's advice for succeeding bore a striking resemblance to the rules laid down for supervisors in interviewing employees (see Chapter 13). A second book that offered the nation moral advice and direction was the Reverend Dr. Norman Vincent Peale's *The Power of Positive Thinking*.[24] In contrast to Carnegie's "getting along" approach, Peale "counseled readers that they could achieve better results in life by dwelling exclusively on optimistic interpretations of their circumstances" and believed it was an affront to God to have a low opinion of oneself.[25] Despite coming under criticism for their reliance on anecdotes and unsourced testimonials, both books were hugely popular with contemporary lay readers and garner sales even today.

These positive thinkers stressed two ways to move from a "confusion of souls" to a "clarity of minds": drawing on the inward power of faith and gaining personal strength by winning the cooperation of others through personal magnetism. The social ethic of the times deemphasized achievement by rugged individualism, as the Protestant ethic had seemingly run its course. This new ethic was others-oriented, with moral uplift coming not from efficiency but from getting along with others. For the most part, the social person was conceived, born, and nurtured in these trying times. People sought comfort in groups, solace in association, and fulfillment in affiliation.

The Social Ethic

A second facet necessary to understand the Social-Person Era relates to the image of business executives as reflected in poplar literature. Admittedly, the fictional "bad guy" business executive portrayed in literature (and film) may or may not be a true reflection of society's view of

---

[22] Donald Meyer, *The Positive Thinkers: A Study of the American Quest for Health, Wealth and Personal Power from Mary Baker Eddy to Norman Vincent Peale* (Garden City, NY: Doubleday, 1965), pp. 233–237.

[23] Dale Carnegie, *How to Win Friends and Influence People* (New York: Simon and Schuster, 1937).

[24] Norman Vincent Peale, *The Power of Positive Thinking* (New York: Prentice-Hall, 1952).

[25] Barton Swaim, [Review of *Surge of Piety: Norman Vincent Peale and the Remaking of American Religious Life*], *Wall Street Journal* (December 27, 2016), p. A15.

life behind closed corporate doors. Nonetheless, after surveying over 100 novels, Kavesh has warned that the fictional business executive is generally portrayed as flawed and cynical.[26] Although it would be wrong to blame Big Business for the Great Depression, it is evident that business figures are all too often blamed for society's materialistic ills and are among Hollywood's favorite villains.[27] The 1920s had canonized business moguls as heroes and symbols of both prosperity and the good life; when times turned turbulent, was it unfair to heap blame on the "bankster" who "robbed" people of their homes and savings?

Scott has noted that the literature of the 1930s and 1940s was characterized by a disillusionment with individualism and a plea for "humanitarianism and collectivism in the form of proletarian fiction."[28] The heroes and heroines of the early twentieth century vanished to be replaced by a "they" who did things without reason and were beyond the control of mere mortals. "They" represented power, machines, and unidentified forces, not individual managers who could be held responsible for their actions. Corporations were monsters of oppression that destroyed people and their lives piece by piece. Examples of such novels include John Steinbeck's *Grapes of Wrath* and Nathanael West's *A Cool Million: The Dismantling of Lemuel Pitkin*.[29] For Steinbeck, it was not individuals, but "they" who exploited the Joads, defenseless tenant farmers escaping from Dust-Bowl Oklahoma, to the point of starving. A satire of the Horatio Alger "myth," West's hero is caught between the depravities of international bankers and world revolutionists, who slowly destroyed his spirit and quest for success.

As the 1940s and 1950s unfolded, business executives (as well as managers at all levels in general) were depicted in popular literature and film more and more as what became known as "organization men" who subscribed to a social ethic rather than individual initiative.[30] Doing so offered security, and a manager became a hero not because of "great or daring deeds, but because he tolerates grinding mediocrity and conformity."[31] In John P. Marquand's *The Point of No Return*, Ernst Pawel's *From the Dark Tower*, and Sloan Wilson's *The Man in the Gray Flannel Suit*, the emphasis is on conformity and the futility of rebelling against organizations as social systems.[32] The reference point in the social ethic was the group and the collective nature of people seeking collaborative social solidarity. This reference point may also be discerned in the work of Mary P. Follett, Elton Mayo, and others who emphasized group responsibility and collective will. The management literature of the late 1940s and 1950s stressed teamwork, employee participation, group decision-making, small rather than large groups, committee management, and democratic leadership.

At the same time that many of the era's intellectuals sought to denigrate the importance of business, others idealized the agrarian lifestyle characterized by small farms and self-sufficiency. To be big was to be bad, and to live in an urban rather than rural society was a sign of decline. Why did intellectuals idealize agriculture and sully business? Kavesh has noted that "the growth of cities is the history of business: the big businessman is the symbol of the city, and the city became the symbol of degradation."[33]

---

[26] Robert A. Kavesh, *Businessmen in Fiction: The Capitalist and Executive in American Novels* (Hanover, NH: Amos Tuck School of Business Administration, Dartmouth College, 1955), p. 11.

[27] Rachel Dodes, "Hollywood's Favorite Villain," *Wall Street Journal* (October 14, 2011), p. D1.

[28] William G. Scott, *The Social Ethic in Management Literature* (Atlanta, GA: Bureau of Business and Economic Research, Georgia State College of Business Administration, 1959), p. 47

[29] John Steinbeck, *The Grapes of Wrath* (New York: Modern Library, 1940) and Nathanael West, *A Cool Million: The Dismantling of Lemuel Pitkin* (New York: Covici, Friede, Publishers, 1934).

[30] The term "organization man" was coined by William H. Whyte in his book *The Organization Man* (New York: Simon and Schuster, 1956). Parts of this book were originally published in *Fortune* magazine.

[31] Scott, *The Social Ethic in Management Literature*, p. 50.

[32] John P. Marquand, *Point of No Return* (Boston, MA: Little, Brown, 1949); Ernst Pawel, *From the Dark Tower* (New York: Macmillan, 1957); Sloan Wilson, *The Man in the Gray Flannel Suit* (New York: Simon and Schuster, 1955).

[33] Kavesh, *Businessmen in Fiction*, p. 6.

Baritz suggests that Mayo was one of those who were committed to an "Agrarian Golden Age":

> [Mayo] believed that there was a mystical but direct relationship between farming and truth. . . . An industrial society, by definition, could not be virtuous, for as men lost sight of the soil they lost sight of nature; and in so doing, they lost sight of the meaning of life and fell victim to the glossy gadgetry of modern industrialism. For Mayo, then, the problem of the modern factory was clear: how to make possible the re-creation of Agrarian Virtue, Agrarian Loyalty, and the Agrarian Sense of Community in the twentieth century's world of skyscrapers and subways, of smoke and steam?[34]

As noted in Chapter 13, for Mayo, the answer was to rebuild "social solidarity" and "effective collaboration" through small groups. Once the communal integrity of agrarian life was reestablished, people could cope with the evils of urban life, deskilling of work, and anomic depersonalization of factory routines. Mayo, influenced by Émile Durkheim, saw evils in industrial life much as Robert Owen had seen them in the early nineteenth century. Whereas Durkheim admonished people to unselfishly love one another, and Owen built industrial communes, Mayo accepted the parameters of industrialization and tried to rebuild people's interpersonal relations within a social framework. The gloom of the Great Depression, the horror of World War II, and the threat of the atomic bomb may have caused Mayo to harken back to an Agrarian Golden Age in which people could find stability, purpose, and established norms in small groups.

The Political Environment: FDR's Pledge

As the nation's economic cycle went from prosperity to depression and the social environment reflected increasing needs for affiliation, it reimagined the role for government in individual and business affairs. No other period in U.S. history has witnessed a political administration begin in such dire times, endure for such a long period, and cope with as many adversities as the tenure of President Franklin D. Roosevelt (FDR). Scion of a patrician family, cousin of former president Theodore Roosevelt, and paralyzed from the waist down by polio, Roosevelt brought hope to a nation in the depths of despair. In his 1932 acceptance speech for the Democratic presidential nomination, Roosevelt addressed the problems of the Great Depression, promising: "I pledge you, I pledge myself, to a new deal for the American people."[35] This pledge became the slogan of his election campaign and the name for his administration's legislative programs.

The New Deal

FDR saw as his first task restoring confidence to a stricken nation. In his Inaugural Address he declared: "The only thing we have to fear is fear itself."[36] In the next 105 days, he issued executive orders and shepherded legislation through the U.S. Congress that created agencies and public-works programs such as the Agricultural Adjustment Administration (AAA), Civilian Conservation Corps (CCC), Securities and Exchange Commission (SEC), TVA, Home Owners Loan Corporation (HOLC), Federal Emergency Relief Act, Railway Reorganization Act, Federal Deposit Insurance Corporation (FDIC), and National Industrial Recovery Act (NIRA). The day of an activist, alphabet-soup government had arrived.

Whereas some viewed the New Deal as "creeping socialism" and prophesied the end of capitalism, others saw this legislation and these new programs as necessary to smooth out the nation's

---

[34] Loren Baritz, *The Servants of Power: A History of the Use of Social Science in American Industry* (Middletown, CT: Wesleyan University Press, 1960), p. 111.

[35] Franklin D. Roosevelt, "Address Accepting the Presidential Nomination at the Democratic National Convention in Chicago," July 2, 1932. Available at http://www.presidency.ucsb.edu/ws/?pid=75174

[36] *Idem*, "Inaugural Address of the President," Washington, DC, March 4, 1933, p. 1. Available at https://www.archives.gov/education/lessons/fdr-inaugural/images/address-1.gif

business cycle. Capitalism endured as the prevailing economic system, but critics charged that the New Deal had started the nation on the road to socialism and even totalitarianism. A hands-off approach to economic policy, allowing markets to regulate themselves based on what Adam Smith called the "invisible hand," was now over. As Rexford G. Tugwell (an economist who was part of FDR's first "Brain Trust") observed, the idyllic days of business doing what it willed were gone and it would have to recognize unions, democratize industry by encouraging participation, and, above all, keep in mind, in the words of Jeremy Bentham, "the greatest good for the greatest number."[37] Tugwell felt that business had failed to provide security for the nation's wage-earners and that government should act aggressively to alleviate widespread poverty and unemployment. Roosevelt's administration responded by supporting the Social Security Act (1935), which provided for old-age assistance; the Fair Labor Standards Act (1938), which established a guaranteed minimum hourly wage of 25 cents and a maximum workweek of 44 hours for certain workers; and the Railroad Unemployment Insurance Act (1938), which restored lost wages due to unemployment or illness. These and other acts marked a pronounced shift from Adam Smith's "invisible hand" to Riesman's "glad hand," from private to public charity, and from the Protestant ethic to the social ethic.

Augmenting the Position of Labor

During the Roosevelt years, the federal government became more deeply involved in the nation's economic life than earlier Progressives (see Chapter 12) could have possibly envisioned. Of all the changes introduced by the New Deal, none had a more immediate significance for business than the newfound legitimacy enjoyed by labor unions. The 1930s witnessed the first real successes at organizing workers on a national scale by industry rather than by craft. Previous attempts to organize all workers, regardless of their profession or skill level, had met with limited success—William Sylvis's National Labor Union (see Chapter 6) and Terence V. Powderly's Noble Order of the Knights of Labor had failed in the nineteenth century. The American Federation of Labor (AFL), a federation of craft workers formed in 1886, and numerous railroad brotherhoods, beginning as early as 1863, had demonstrated that unions could be successful when workers held common skills. There had been some successful industrial unions (such as those of the garment, millinery, and coal industries), but they were typically small relative to craft unions in which all members belonged to the same profession. For example, almost 60 percent of the nation's union members in 1929 were in the building trades (919,000 members) or in transportation (892,000 members) and for the most part affiliated with the AFL or the rail brotherhoods. The largest industrial unions were in mining (271,000 members) and garments and millinery (218,000).[38]

The political climate of the 1930s created the opportunity for industrial unionism to flourish. The first significant piece of legislation, the Federal Anti-Injunction Act of 1932, more commonly known as the Norris–LaGuardia Act, was passed during President Hoover's administration. For all practical purposes, it completely divested federal courts of injunctive powers in cases growing out of a labor dispute. In 1933, Congress passed the National Industrial Recovery Act (NIRA), the first in a series of New Deal legislative acts intended to lift the nation out of the Great Depression. Section 7a of the NIRA, in similar but stronger language than that of the Norris–LaGuardia Act, specifically guaranteed that "employees shall have the right to organize and bargain collectively through representatives of their own choosing . . . free from interference, restraint, or coercion of employers . . . ."[39]

---

[37] Jeremy Bentham, *An Introduction to the Principles of Morals and Legislation*, New ed. (London: Printed for W. Pickering, 1823), p. 9n. Originally published in 1780.

[38] U.S. Department of Commerce, Bureau of the Census, *Historical Statistics of the United States*, pt. 1, p. 178.

[39] National Industrial Recovery Act, Title I, Sec. 7a, 1933. Available at https://www.ourdocuments.gov/doc.php?doc=66

When the U.S. Supreme Court declared the NIRA unconstitutional in 1935 (*United States v. A. L. A. Schechter Poultry Corporation*[40]), Congress quickly replaced it with a law that was even more pro-organized labor. The National Labor Relations Act (NLRA), more commonly known as the Wagner Act, guaranteed employees "the right to self-organization, to form, join, or assist labor organization, to bargain collectively through representatives of their own choosing, and to engage in concerted activities for the purpose of collective bargaining."[41] In addition, it placed specific restrictions on employers' conduct intended to discourage workplace unionization. The NLRA established a National Labor Relations Board (NLRB) that was granted the authority not only to issue cease-and-desist letters to employers to halt purported restriction violations, but also to determine appropriate bargaining units and conduct representation elections. The NLRB also limited the scope of nonunion employee-representation plans. Organized labor bitterly opposed such plans, seeing them as "company unions" that hindered their organizing efforts. In 1938, the U.S. Supreme Court ruled that these plans were employer dominated and violated the National Labor Relations Act (*NLRB v. Pennsylvania Greyhound Lines*[42]). Thus, ended one era in labor–management relations, while yet another began.[43]

The passage of the Wagner Act marked a critical turning point in labor–management relations. John L. Lewis, president of the United Mine Workers, led the fight for industrial unionism within the AFL. Rebuffed, Lewis formed the Committee for Industrial Organization (known after 1938 as the Congress of Industrial Organizations; CIO), whose purpose was to bring workers into unions regardless of their profession or skill level. The newly founded CIO enjoyed almost instant success and was able to claim nearly 4 million members by 1937. While the CIO prospered, the AFL did as well—almost doubling its membership from 2,126,000 in 1933 to 4,000,000 in 1939. With the passage of favorable New Deal legislation, total union membership spurted from a turn-of-the-decade 3.5 million (6.8 percent of the total labor force) to almost 9 million (15.8 percent) by 1939.[43]

Labor unions gained substantial political power during the 1930s. The pro-union stance of the Roosevelt administration was an attempt to equalize collective-bargaining power. It meshed with calls for teamwork, employee participation, group decision-making, and democratic leadership in the workplace. During World War II, labor and management joined together to keep the wheels of industry turning, and their differences were temporarily laid aside. The National War Labor Board, created to minimize labor unrest that might stall the war effort, generally favored the interests of workers. Numerous labor strikes following the war highlighted unfair union practices, resulting in the passage of the Labor–Management Relations Act (Taft–Hartley Act). Passed in 1947, the act placed restrictions on unions similar to those already imposed on employers. The Taft–Hartley Act sought to equalize the balance of power that formerly favored unions.

On the whole, not only had the nation's labor–management relations changed throughout the Social-Person Era, but so had government involvement in the nation's marketplace. This involvement threw into relief the nature of the Progressive-Conservative divide that continues to this day. Contrary to the notion that public policy should come from the grassroots up to counterbalance corporate concentrations of wealth and economic power, Roosevelt's Progressivism maintained that government experts should manage the nation's economic affairs to ensure equal outcomes. Conservatives, however, believed that individuals should be free to make their own investment decisions and, in consequence, take risks in competitive markets that may lead to unequal economic outcomes. This suggests that some inequality is good for a nation's economy as it provides an incentive to hard work and encourages innovation, which (per Schumpeter's account) propels a nation's economic progress.

---

[40] *A. L. A. Schechter Poultry Corp. v. United States*, 295 U.S. 495 (1935).

[41] National Labor Relations Act, Title 29, Chapter 7, Subchapter II, United States Code, 1935. Available at https://www.nlrb.gov/resources/national-labor-relations-act

[42] *National Labor Relations Board v. Pennsylvania Greyhound Lines, Inc., et al.* 303 U.S. 261 (58 S. Ct. 571, 82 L.Ed. 831) (1938).

[43] C. Ray Gullett and Edmund R. Gray, "The Impact of Employee Representation Plans upon the Development of Management-Worker Relations in the United States," *Marquette Business Review* 20(1) (Fall 1976), pp. 85–101.

[44] U.S. Department of Commerce, Bureau of the Census, *Historical Statistics of the United States,* pt. 1, p. 178.

SUMMARY OF PART III

Figure 18.1 depicts major landmarks in the Social-Person Era. Scientific management was the dominant theme in the 1920s. Sociologists and social psychologists popularized behaviorism in the mid-1900s. Mary P. Follett, though chronologically belonging to the scientific-management era, served as an intellectual bridge to the emerging group approach to managing. The Hawthorne studies brought the human-relations movement to the forefront and led to a further interest in groups and sociotechnical systems. The heirs of Frederick W. Taylor and scientific management focused on organization structure and design as a means of ensuring efficiency and effectiveness.

The Hawthorne studies, beginning before but enduring through the early days of the Great Depression, brought about a shift in emphasis, including (1) an increased concern for people along with production, (2) exhortations to increase the fulfillment of employee needs, (3) the use of economic incentives as but one

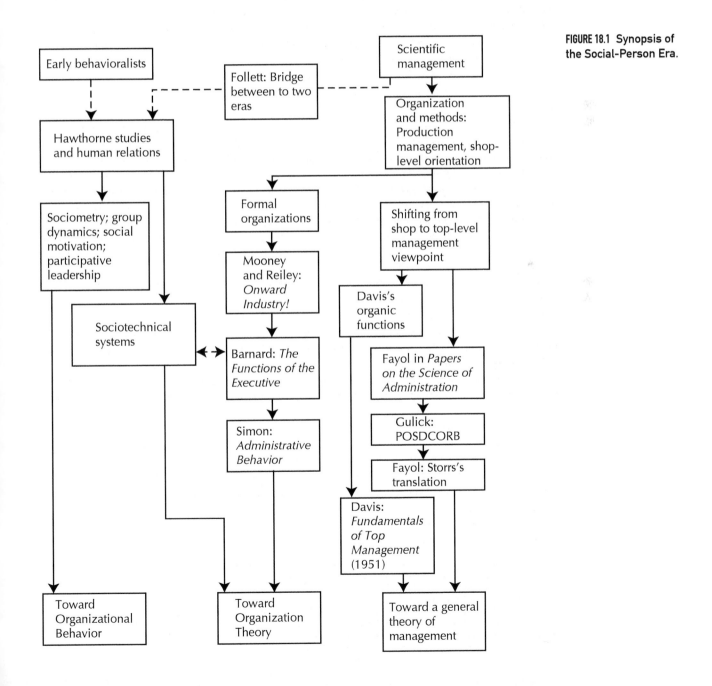

FIGURE 18.1 Synopsis of the Social-Person Era.

element in motivating employees, and (4) a greater concern for the illogic of sentiments than the logic of efficiency. The human-relations movement and the research that followed reflected several basic themes that were products of the prevailing cultural environment: (1) calls for social skills rather than technical skills; (2) an emphasis on rebuilding people's sense of belonging through small groups and social solidarity; and (3) a concern for balancing the power labor and management.

Post-Hawthorne research assumed two separate yet complementary approaches. Micro researchers studied people in groups, postulated a hierarchy of human needs, and viewed leadership as interactive and situational phenomenon. Macro researchers sought to understand and bring about an integration of an organization's formal operating systems with its informal system of sentiments, activities, and interactions. These approaches would define the fields of Organizational Behavior and Organization Theory in the Modern Era of Management.

Chronologically paralleling these developments in the human-relations movement, the descendants of scientific management offered a different set of solutions to the vexing problems of the Great Depression. Largely shop-management oriented at the beginning, this branch of management thought also began to assume new dimensions. On the one hand, sound organization structure and design were offered as one way to achieve effectiveness and efficiency. Mooney and Reiley urged *Onward Industry!* and Chester I. Barnard presented a sociological study of an organization's formal and informal systems. Alongside this branch, the elements of a top-level management viewpoint began to appear in the work of Ralph C. Davis, the translation of Henri Fayol's administrative theory in Luther Gulick and Lyndall F. Urwick's *Papers on the Science Administration*, and Urwick's efforts to synthesize a set of management principles.

Culturally, management thought in the Social-Person Era was shaped by the Great Depression, which redefined the role of government in individual and business affairs. No longer would the Protestant-ethic virtues of frugality, thrift, and hard work be seen of unquestioned value. If you were down, the government helped you up; if you lost your savings in a bank failure, the government would reimburse you; if you had saved nothing for retirement, the government would provide a pension, and so on through a host of social programs to take some of the sting out of life. Further economic growth was retarded by the Depression, and the postwar boom created a need for a new view of top-level management. The Protestant ethic and the need for achievement, though they did not disappear entirely, declined in significance as people sought comfort in groups, solace in association, and fulfillment in affiliation. People, not production, were a manager's main concern. A newfound legitimacy for labor unions brought success at organizing workers on a national scale by industry rather than by craft, introducing a consideration in managerial decision-making. It was out of this age of confusion, trauma, and diversity that the Modern Era in Management was about to begin.

Moving Onward: The Near Present

Nestled between the knowns of yesterday and the unknowns of tomorrow, the present is the twilight of history. As the zoom lens of history often leaves the near present out of focus, the historian's most difficult task is to step away from the current day and place more recent developments into perspective. In that the more recent management literature is too extensive for an in-depth analysis, we must be content to sketch the broad outlines of management thought in the post–World War II economic-expansion period and highlight major trends as companies sought to compete in an emerging global culture.

Part 4 begins by reviewing the years following World War II when a renewed interest in general management theory occurred as businesses grew at home and abroad, fostering a need for more broadly educated managers. It then focuses on the emergence of a new generation of scholars devoted to the study of what became known as "organizational behavior." It also traces the transformation of personnel management as a field into, first, human-resource management and, then, strategic human-resource management, and recounts the debate beginning at roughly the same time among organization theorists concerning the effect of technology and strategy on an organization's structure and management processes in changing environments. It then recounts the continued quest for science in management leading into the Information Age. Part 4 concludes with a consideration of the ongoing globalization of business and how competing in international markets with contrasting cultural values and institutions has influenced the evolution of management thought.

Management Theory and Practice

Technological changes and the proliferation of multinational enterprises (MNEs) in the period following World War II led to a reevaluation of management education, a renewed interest in understanding the nature of managerial work, and the formulation of business strategies to compete at home and abroad. It was concluded that management education programs were not equipping their graduates with the intellectual skills and knowledge necessary to succeed in an ever more complex and interrelated world. Others noted the lack of relevance and growing divide between management theory and practice. Inquiries into the nature of managerial work would challenge established orthodoxies and business strategists faced unprecedented challenges and opportunities in developed and emerging nations. If any one factor explained the concern for improved management theory and practice, it would be the need for more broadly educated managers who could enhance a firm's performance in a rapidly changing worldwide marketplace.

The Renaissance of General Management

Although the practice of management is rooted in antiquity it has only been within the last century that managers have begun to systematically reflect on their experiences and observations to sort out and identify those managerial practices that seemed to work better than others. These better practices were called "principles," but more closely resembled guides to managerial thought and action than scientific facts. The impetus for codifying those managerial practices that worked better (i.e., principles) into a theory was the desire to transmit knowledge more coherently to those who aspired to become successful managers. Those who first tilled the topsoil of this landscape were primarily practitioners. Owen, McCallum, Taylor, Gantt, Fayol, and Barnard are only a few examples of the practitioners who distilled their experiences and observations for the benefit of others.

If not the first, Henri Fayol was one of the initial practitioners to advance a formal statement of management principles. He believed that a lack of theory made it more difficult to teach management because managers' experiences were localized and not easily understood by other managers or students of management. Fayol defined theory as "a collection of principles, rules, methods, and procedures tried and checked by general experience."[1] As outlined in Chapter 10, he used his experiences and observations as an executive to identify the elements or functions that compose a manager's job. Fayol noted, however: "there is nothing rigid or absolute in management affairs," expecting new theories to emerge and be tested in the crucible of real-world experience.[2]

Principles of Management and the Functions of Management

As has been recounted, Fayol's work only received widespread recognition outside France following World War II. Like Max Weber, a full appreciation of Fayol's contributions to the evolution of management thought had to wait until cultural conditions created the need to think in theoretical terms. To wit, the post–World War II economic expansion and Constance Storrs's translation of Fayol's *General and Industrial Management* from its original French into English unleashed a

William H. Newman. Courtesy of Arthur G. Bedeian.

renewed interest in Fayol's ideas about managing and spawned numerous "principles and process" university textbooks for teaching management. One of the earliest of these textbooks was authored by William H. Newman. Based on course material first produced in 1948 titled "Principles of Management," Newman's *Administrative Action: The Techniques of Organization and Management* was published in 1951. Newman defined *administration* as "the guidance, leadership, and control of the efforts of a group of individuals toward some common goal."[3] The book's main headings were Planning, Organizing, Assembling Resources, Directing, and Controlling.

Though Newman's description of administration resembles Fayol's "elements of management," he recalled that he was then "unacquainted" with Fayol's work. He was instead influenced by the thinking of Fred Taylor, Chester I. Barnard, Ralph C. Davis, and his Columbia University colleague Luther H. Gulick,

---

[1] Henri Fayol, *General and Industrial Management,* trans. Constance Storrs (London: Sir Isaac Pitman and Sons, 1949), p. 15.
[2] *Ibid.*, p. 19.
[3] William H. Newman, *Administrative Action: The Techniques of Organization and Management* (Englewood Cliffs, NJ: Prentice Hall, 1951), p. 1.

among others.[4] Much like Fayol, Newman noted the importance of objectives in shaping the character of an organization. He felt that an organization's basic objectives should define its place or niche in an industry, define its social philosophy as a business "citizen," and establish an organization's general managerial philosophy.[5]

A second influential university textbook from the same era was authored by Northwestern University professor George R. Terry and simply titled *Principles of Management.* He considered management to be "the activity which plans, organizes, and controls the operations of the basic elements of men, materials, machines, methods, money, and markets, providing direction and coordination, and giving leadership to human efforts, so as to achieve the sought objectives of the enterprise."[6] Terry viewed management as a "vital process" that included planning, organizing, directing, coordinating, controlling, and leading. He defined a principle as "a fundamental statement providing a guide to action," and his principles, like Fayol's, were not meant to be rigid or absolute.

An indication of the growing recognition during this period of the importance of teaching management as a body of knowledge in nonbusiness settings came with the publication of Air Force Manual 25-1, *The Management Process.*[7] This manual identified five managerial functions: planning, organizing, coordinating, directing, and controlling. Objectives—or missions, in the military sense,—were considered the foundation of all managerial activity.

Writing in their book *Principles of Management: An Analysis of Managerial Functions,* Harold D. Koontz and Cyril J. O'Donnell defined management as "the function of getting things done through others."[8] According to Koontz and O'Donnell, managers were known by the basic managerial functions they performed: planning, organizing, staffing, directing, and controlling. They stressed that each of these functions promoted internal coordination. Coordination, however, was not a separate function, but was the result of effectively utilizing the five basic functions that all managers perform. Koontz and O'Donnell identified a number of management principles, including "the principle of parity of authority and responsibility," "the principle of unity of command," and "the principle of strategic factors." The Koontz and O'Donnell text became an enduring, integral part of the search for a systematic body of management knowledge.

Fayol's influence was apparent in all of these texts, as each viewed management as a process, or set of ongoing activities, replete with guiding principles. Although the names used to identify the various functions composing the "management process" varied across texts, they all largely followed the same framework laid out by Fayol decades ago. Likewise, all considered management to be a distinct intellectual pursuit that could be distilled into principles and, hence, a general theory of management.

Peter F. Drucker and the Practice of Management

Peter F. Drucker, one of the twentieth century's most influential management thinkers, titled his autobiography *Adventures of a Bystander,* which was anything but an accurate description of his life and work.[9] Drucker achieved prominence through his writings and consulting, and made significant contributions to management practice. Largely influenced by economist

---

[4] *Idem,* "The Takeoff," in Arthur G. Bedeian (ed.), *Management Laureates: A Collection of Autobiographical Essays,* vol. 2 (Greenwich, CT: JAI Press, 1993), p. 385.
[5] *Idem,* "Basic Objectives Which Shape the Character of the Company," *Journal of Business of the University of Chicago* 26(4) (October 1953), pp. 211–223.
[6] George R. Terry, *Principles of Management* (Homewood, IL: Richard D. Irwin, 1953), p. 3.
[7] U.S. Air Force, *The Management Process,* Air Force Manual 25-1 (Washington, DC: U.S. Government Printing Office, 1954).
[8] Harold D. Koontz and Cyril J. O'Donnell, *Principles of Management: An Analysis of Managerial Functions* (New York: McGraw-Hill, 1955), pp. v, 3.
[9] Peter F. Drucker, *Adventures of a Bystander* (New York: Harper Collins, 1991).

Peter F. Drucker. Courtesy of The Drucker Institute at Claremont Graduate University.

Joseph A. Schumpeter (see Chapter 18), a fellow Austrian, Drucker viewed free-market, capitalist economies as being in a constant state of creation, growth, stagnation, and decline. What kept an organization from failing was the ability of its managers (echoing Schumpeter) to give birth to innovations in new products, new methods of production, new markets, the use of new raw materials, or new forms of organization that drive economic growth.

Drucker stressed that managers should establish objectives in each area vital to an organization's existence. He identified eight "key-result areas": market standing (measured against a market's potential); innovation (in products and services, or in improving how these products and services were made or delivered); productivity (a yardstick for "constant improvement"); physical and financial resources (defining needs, planning, and acquiring); profitability (for rate of return on investment); manager performance and development ("management-by-objectives" and self-control); worker performance and attitude (employee relations); and public responsibility (participating "responsibly in society").[10] In setting objectives, managers had to first ask the "right questions": What is our business? Who is our customer? What do our customers buy? What is the value of our business to our customers? What will our business be? And what should it be?[11]

Although other authors had written about the need for establishing objectives, Drucker was the first to coin the phrase "management-by-objectives" (MBO). According to Drucker, "A manager's job should be based on a task to be performed in order to attain the company's objectives. . . . [T]he manager should be directed and controlled by the objectives of performance rather than by his boss."[12] Management-by-objectives was to replace management-by-drive, and control was to be self-control rather than control from above. Knowing a company's objectives, and those of each of its departments, managers could direct their own activities:

> The only principle that can do this is management by objectives and self-control. . . . It substitutes for control from outside the stricter, more exacting and more effective control from the inside. It motivates the manager to action not because somebody tells him to do something . . . but because the objective needs of his task demand it.[13]

Although Drucker popularized MBO, it was implemented by GE Vice President Harold F. Smiddy.[14] Drucker maintained that MBO was not new, having been practiced earlier at General Motors by Alfred P. Sloan, and at DuPont by Pierre du Pont and Donaldson Brown. Whatever the case, Ronald G. Greenwood concluded, "it took Drucker to put it all together, think through the underlying philosophy, and then explain and advocate it in a form others could use."[15]

For Drucker, 90 percent of managerial work is generic, working with and through people to lead in such a manner that they are able to use their individual strengths and knowledge productively. The remaining 10 percent varies according to the mission, culture, history, and vocabulary of any specific type of organization, whether for profit or not-for-profit.[16] Drucker complemented Fayol by further stressing the need to set objectives and emphasizing the value of participative

[10] *Idem, The Practice of Management* (New York: Harper & Row, 1954), pp. 63–84.

[11] *Ibid.*, pp. 49–61.

[12] *Ibid.*, p. 137.

[13] *Ibid.*

[14] For more on the relationship between Drucker and Smiddy, see Ronald G. Greenwood, "Harold F. Smiddy: Manager by Inspiration and Persuasion," in Richard C. Huseman, ed., *Proceedings of the Annual Academy of Management Meeting* (1979), pp. 12–16.

[15] Ronald G. Greenwood, "Management by Objectives: As Developed by Peter Drucker, Assisted by Harold Smiddy," *Academy of Management Review* 6(2) (April 1981), p. 230.

[16] Peter F. Drucker, *Management Challenges for the 21st Century* (New York: Harper Business, 1999).

goal-setting, and the existential necessity of an organization to give birth to innovations in new products, new methods of production, new markets, the use of new raw materials, or new forms of organization that drive economic growth.

Management Education: Challenges and Consequences

In 1959, two reports appeared that would have a significant impact on management education. Unlike Morris L. Cooke's study for the Carnegie Foundation for the Advancement of Teaching in 1910 (see Chapter 8), educators took these new reports seriously. The world's largest philanthropy, the Ford Foundation, commissioned the first report, by Robert A. Gordon and James E. Howell.[17] The second report, by Frank C. Pierson, was sponsored by the Carnegie Corporation.[18] Although the authors of the two reports exchanged some of their findings, they reached their conclusions independently; both reports were sharp indictments of collegiate business education in the United States, noting that schools of business administration were in a state of turmoil with little agreement on what should be taught and how. The reports concluded that by adhering to outdated methods of education, the nation's business schools were not preparing competent, imaginative, flexible managers for an ever-changing economy. Courses overemphasized training for specific jobs, rather than preparing broadly educated graduates with the range of intellectual skills required for a successful business career.

The reports advised that the path to preparing managers for the future resided in changing the content of the typical business-school curriculum. More stress needed to be placed on providing a general education, especially in the humanities and liberal arts, mathematics, and the behavioral and social sciences. The call for more mathematics and behavioral sciences led to an influx of specialists in these areas—including industrial engineers, operations-research analysts, communication theorists, psychologists, and sociologists—into business schools.[19] For management education, in particular, Gordon and Howell noted at least four areas that required strengthening: (1) managerial problem-solving through the scientific method and quantitative analysis, (2) organization theory, (3) management principles, and (4) human relations.[20] They recommended that these four areas be integrated into a sequence of courses, rather than covering each area separately. Toward this end, Gordon and Howell further recommended that Business Policy serve as a capstone course that delivered an integrative experience for all business-school majors. Finally, they called for business-school faculty to engage in original research so as to increase the sum of knowledge available to their students. Given that many business school faculty taught mostly from their own experiences rather than a shared knowledge base, critics claimed that collegiate business instruction was more akin to learning a trade than acquiring an education. Whereas other academic disciplines had adopted the German model of higher education (with its emphasis on research) as far back as the late 1870s,[21] it was only after the Gordon and Howell and Pierson reports were released that the imperative to "publish or perish" began to take hold in the nation's premier business schools, and tenure and promotions were made contingent upon establishing a national reputation based on peer-reviewed publications appearing in scientific journals. Not coincidentally, it was also during this period that developing a lengthy publication record took precedence in business schools over undergraduate teaching.[22] It was at this time, too, that the quality and extent of faculty research became increasingly emphasized by the (then titled) American Assembly of Collegiate Schools of Business, the agency charged with accrediting university business programs.

---

[17] Robert A. Gordon and James E. Howell, *Higher Education for Business* (New York: Columbia University Press, 1959). See also Francis X. Sutton, "The Ford Foundation: The Early Years," *Dædalus* 116(1) (Winter 1987), p. 52.

[18] Frank C. Pierson, *The Education of American Businessmen: A Study of University-College Programs in Business Administration* (New York: McGraw-Hill, 1959).

[19] William P. Bottom, "Organizing Intelligence: Development of Behavioral Science and the Research Based Model of Business Education," *Journal of the History of the Behavioral Sciences* 45(3) (Summer 2009), pp. 253–283.

[20] Gordon and Howell, *Higher Education for Business*, pp. 179–182.

[21] Laurence R. Veysey, *The Emergence of the American University* (Chicago, IL: University of Chicago Press, 1970), p. 129.

[22] Rakesh Khurana, *From Higher Aims to Hired Hands: The Social Transformation of American Business Schools and the Unfilled Promise of Management as a Profession* (Princeton, NJ: Princeton University Press, 2010), p. 307.

Harold D. Koontz. Courtesy
of Arthur G. Bedeian

The "Management Theory Jungle"

Although the Gordon and Howell report noted that there were numerous approaches to the study of management, it was Harold D. Koontz who delineated the differences between these approaches and applied the catchy label "management theory jungle" to the their varying perspectives.[23] Koontz noted six main groups, or schools, of management thought: the *management process school* (e.g., Fayol's principles and process); the *empirical school* (e.g., case analyses/the study of experiences); the *human behavior school* (e.g., human relations/behavioral sciences); the *social system school* (e.g., sociological theory/cultural interrelationships); the *decision theory school* (e.g., economic theory/consumer choice); and the *mathematical school* (e.g., operations research/management science).

Koontz acknowledged that each school had something to offer management theory, but suggested that the student of management should not confuse content with tools. A knowledge of decision-making techniques or mathematical methods alone should not be considered sufficient preparation to be a successful manager. Preferably, each school of management thought would provide managers with useful insights that, when taken together, offered a cumulative advantage. In Koontz's account, there were many reasons for managers to be confused given the "jungle warfare" among the various schools: (1) "the semantics jungle" with varying meanings of terms such as *organization, leadership, management, decision-making,* and so on;[24] (2) problems in defining management as a body of knowledge given the varying circumstances and situations in which it was applied; and (3) the "inability or unwillingness of management theorists to understand each other" caused by disciplinary jargon and a desire to protect one's professional turf. Koontz was hopeful that the jungle could be disentangled if these problems could be resolved.

Unfortunately, revisiting the theory jungle some 20 years later, Koontz found it may have become "more dense and impenetrable," having expanded from 6 to 11 schools.[25] Koontz noted, "The management theory jungle is still with us. . . . Perhaps the most effective way [out of the jungle] would be for leading managers to take a more active role in narrowing the widening gap . . . between professional practice and our college and university business [schools]." He chastised his fellow academicians for failing to make their research more relevant to practice:

> I see too many academics forgetting what I think our job is in management, and that is to organize available knowledge; develop new knowledge, of course, but organize it in such a way that it can be useful to practicing managers to underpin management . . . I think we have to agree that management theory and science should underpin practice, otherwise why develop it?[26]

[23] Harold D. Koontz, "The Management Theory Jungle," *Journal of the Academy of Management* 4(3) (December 1961), pp. 174–188; *idem*, "Making Sense of Management Theory," *Harvard Business Review* 40(4) (July–August 1962), pp. 24–46.
[24] For an historical view of the semantics confusion, see Arthur G. Bedeian, "A Historical Review of Efforts in the Area of Management Semantics," *Academy of Management Journal* 17(1) (March 1974), pp. 101–114.
[25] For a discussion on these schools circa 1961 and 1980, see Harold D. Koontz, "The Management Theory Jungle Revisited," *Academy of Management Review* 5(2) (April 1980), pp. 175–187. See also *idem*, "Toward an Operational Theory of Management," in Melvin Zimet and Ronald G. Greenwood, eds., *The Evolving Science of Management: The Collected Papers of Harold Smiddy and Papers by Others in His Honor* (New York: American Management Associations, 1979), pp. 327–347.
[26] Harold D. Koontz quoted in Ronald G. Greenwood, "Harold Koontz: A Reminiscence," unpublished paper presented at the annual meeting of the Academy of Management, Boston, MA, August 14, 1984, pp. 5-6, Ronald G. Greenwood Collection, University Archives, Alvin Sherman Library, Nova Southeastern University, Fort Lauderdale, FL.

Management Education: The Porter–McKibbin Report

The American Assembly of Collegiate Schools of Business International sponsored a 3-year comprehensive study of management education that surveyed practitioners and academics. The authors of the report, Lyman W. Porter and Lawrence E. McKibbin, noted that a breadth in knowledge and intellectual skills is required to integrate problem-finding and problem-solving across various business functions; yet many business school faculty members lacked relevant work experience and were too narrowly educated to "appreciate the complexities and subtleties of business."[27] They recommended that, in their teaching, faculty should pay more attention to external factors, especially trends in international business; develop a greater ability to integrate knowledge across business functions; put more emphasis on interpersonal and communication skills; and nurture Ph.D. students who would have analytical sophistication, as well as "the sharpened and broadened perspective of real world work experience."[28]

In Porter and McKibbin's view, management educators needed to avoid a further proliferation of theoretical approaches, couple theory more closely with application, appreciate external factors affecting the management discipline, and study business in global settings. Writing 14 years later, Pfeffer and Fong disappointedly concluded that management research continued to have little relevance to the practice of management, placed too much emphasis on "hard" (quantitative) skills to the expense of "soft" (people) skills, and many faculty still lacked the perspective afforded by work experience.[29]

The Management Theory–Practice Divide

It has been acknowledged that management practitioners do not look to academic research for guidance nor do academics look to practitioners for research topics or to assist in interpreting research findings, thereby creating a "great divide" between theory and practice.[30] It would seem that practicing managers and management researchers have different ideologies and different values—one seeking to solve day-to-day and bottom-line challenges and the other seeking tenure, promotions, and standing among their colleagues. A study of human-resource managers documents the lack of knowledge transfer between practitioners and academics, finding less than 1 percent of practicing managers regularly consult the management literature, and 75 percent never do so.[31]

Hambrick has argued that this practice–theory gap results from the desire on the part of management educators to gain academic respectability among their peers by publishing theory-laden articles in journals with a high "impact factor" (as defined by others with similar goals). These articles contrast with those published in marketing, finance, and accounting journals where the word "theory" seldom appears.[32] The management discipline's infatuation with theory is compounded by its failure to test its theories' predictions. Kacmar and Whitfield found less than 10 percent of the citations in the *Academy of Management Journal* and the *Academy of Management Review*, widely regarded as the discipline's most prestigious journals, were to direct tests of their

---

[27] Lyman W. Porter and Lawrence E. McKibbin, *Management Education and Development: Drift or Thrust into the 21st Century?* (New York: McGraw-Hill, 1988), p. 132.

[28] *Ibid.*, p. 327.

[29] Jeffrey Pfeffer and Christina T. Fong, "The End of Business Schools? Less Success Than Meets the Eye," *Academy of Management Learning & Education* 1(1) (September 2002), p. 91.

[30] Sara L. Rynes, Kenneth G. Brown, and Amy E. Colbert, "Seven Common Misperceptions about Human Resource Practices: Research Findings versus Practitioner Beliefs," *Academy of Management Learning & Education* 18(3) (2002), p.100.

[31] Sara L. Rynes, Jean M. Bartunek, and Richard L. Daft, "Across the Great Divide: Knowledge Creation and Transfer between Practitioners and Academics," *Academy of Management Journal* 44(2) (2001), pp. 340–355.

[32] Donald C. Hambrick, "The Field of Management's Devotion to Theory: Too Much of a Good Thing?" *Academy of Management Journal* 50(6) (December 2006), pp. 1346–1352.

authors' theoretical speculations.[33] The results of a study published in 2007 suggest that the relative balance between management theory and applications in university classroom instruction had tipped in favor of the former at the expense of the latter, lending "further credibility to the notion that theories are emphasized to a greater extent than the usefulness of those theories in practice at all levels of . . . management instruction."[34]

In an effort to bridge the divide, the *Academy of Management Executive (AME)* was created in 1987 to reach a practitioner audience. Toward this end, it elicited practice-oriented submissions, provided "executive summaries" for busy readers, and sought to publish articles on topics of interest to a managerial audience. Published under various titles, *AME* was superseded by the *Academy of Management Perspectives* in 2005. The new editor stated: "the direction of *AME* will change. . . . We are interested in 'evidence-based' manuscripts that rely on research findings to address the needs of Academy members outside their areas of research."[35] This restricted focus on evidenced-management findings that "rely on research findings" contrasts with the wider view that "evidence" may also come from sources such as internal company metrics, as well as "professional experience."[36] In doing so, it notably overlooks Henri Fayol's suggestion that management principles, methods, and procedures be "tried and checked by general experience."[37]

Rousseau repeated the *Academy of Management Perspective* goal of evidence-based management in her 2005 Academy Presidential Address: "Evidence-based management [EBM] means translating principles based on best evidence into organizational practices."[38] She cited Locke and Latham's goal-setting theory (see Chapter 20) as an illustration of a sustained research program (replete with replicated findings and practical applications) to identify the principles of task motivation. Rousseau and her coauthor Sharon McCarthy later noted that similar work remains to be done: "Much like its counterparts in medicine . . . and education . . . the judgments EBM entails also consider the circumstances and ethical concerns managerial decisions involve. In contrast to medicine and education, however, EBM today is only hypothetical."[39] In this comparison, the authors noted management-education programs lacked opportunities for clinical training or lab work, or for students to gain mentoring experiences in nonclassroom settings. Moreover, they observed that students too often lack experience in reading, evaluating, and interpreting academic findings or the knowledge necessary to search for relevant information in the management literature.

What Rousseau and McCarthy noted in 2007 is still true. Evidence-based management remains "hypothetical." Following a decade of concern for closing the theory–practice divide and fulfilling the promise of EBM, Pearce and Huang examined the *Academy of Management Journal* and *Administrative Science Quarterly* and found little "actionable" research relevant to practice

---

[33] K. Michele Kacmar and J. Michael Whitfield, "An Additional Rating Method for Journal Articles in the Field of Management," *Organizational Research Methods* 3(4) (October 2000), p. 397. For a similar analysis (and similar results) of citations in *Administrative Science Quarterly*, see Gerald F. Davis and Christopher Marquis, "Prospects for Organization Theory in the Early Twenty-First Century: Institutional Fields and Mechanisms," *Organization Science* 16(4) (July–August 2005), pp. 332–343.

[34] Daniel A. Wren, Jonathon R. B. Halbesleben, and M. Ronald Buckley, "The Theory-Applications Balance in Management Pedagogy: A Longitudinal Update, *Academy of Management Learning & Education* 6(4) (December 2007), p. 490.

[35] Peter Cappelli, "From the Editor," *Academy of Management Perspectives* 19(1) (February 2005), p. 5.

[36] Eric Barends, Denise M. Rousseau, and Rob B. Briner. *Evidenced-Based Management: The Basic Principles* (Amsterdam: Center for Evidence-Based megamenu, 2014), p. 5. Accessed at https://www.cebma.org/wp-content/uploads/Evidence-Based-Practice-The-Basic-Principles-vs-Dec-2015.pdf

[37] Henri Fayol, *General and Industrial Management* (Storrs trans.), p. 15.

[38] Denise M. Rousseau, "Is There Such a Thing as Evidence-Based Management?" *Academy of Management Review* 31(2) (April 2006), p. 252.

[39] Denise M. Rousseau and Sharon McCarthy, "Educating Managers from and Evidence-Based Perspective," *Academy of Management Learning & Education* 6(1) (March 2007), p. 84. For a review of recent developments in evidence-based management, see Sara L. Rynes and Jean Bartunek, "Evidence-based Management: Foundations, Development, and Controversies and Future," *Annual Review of Organizational Psychology and Organizational Behavior* 4 (2017), pp. 235–261.

and teaching. Over the past half-century, articles in both journals had become less likely to report practical applications.[40] It would seem that, on the whole, management scholarship has produced mountains of data, but little practical knowledge.

One possibility for bridging the practice–theory gap is to form mutually beneficial partnerships involving managers and researchers. "Management researchers must take the first step. Business firms have proven they can survive and be successful without depending on scholarly management research. Researchers must demonstrate how they can add value by offering ideas that improve organizational performance."[41] A recent survey of 828 academics and 939 managers has found a number of shared interests between management researchers and practicing managers. These include reducing or eliminating pay inequality, reducing or eliminating workplace discrimination, and reducing or eliminating unethical business practices.[42] History is rife with examples of executives who, drawing on personal experience, have contributed to management understanding. For example, James C. Worthy, a Vice President at Sears, Roebuck, served in the U.S. Commerce Department in both the Franklin D. Roosevelt and the Dwight D. Eisenhower administrations, partnered with the University of Chicago Human Relations Group in conducting seminal studies of employee morale and organization structure, became a Fellow of the Academy of Management, and following his retirement was a professor at the Kellogg School of Management at Northwestern University.[43] He had a talent for combining theory and practice, and provided a vivid example of how partnerships between practicing managers and management researchers can yield practice-relevant knowledge.

What Do Managers Do?

Henri Fayol was among the first to systemically reflect on his experiences and observations in an attempt to sort out and identify what managers do and what managerial practices work better than others. Although Fayol's reflections provided a conceptual basis for teaching management, others have employed alternative approaches to analyze the nature of managerial work. In studying the CEOs of 5 middle-to-large private and semipublic organizations, Mintzberg found that their daily activities were fragmented, short-term responses rather than deliberative, analytical, and logical, as Fayol had suggested. In contrast to engaging in Fayol's "elements of management" or functions, Mintzberg concluded that the "typical" manager performs 10 different, but highly interrelated roles, that may be grouped into three categories: (1) interpersonal, (2) informational, and (3) decisional. The interpersonal role derives from a manager's formal authority and occurs when dealing with others as a *figurehead, leader,* or *liaison.* The informational role involves a manager receiving, storing, and sending information as a *monitor, disseminator,* or *spokesperson.* The decisional role arises when a manager commits an organization to action as an *entrepreneur, disturbance handler, resource allocator,* or *negotiator.*[44]

Although the notion of managers performing certain roles has an intuitive appeal, others have questioned whether Mintzberg's roles identified actually reflect the activities inherent in a typical manager's workday. Moreover, in that Mintzberg's findings were based on only 5 CEOs,

[40] Jone L. Pearce and Laura Huang, "The Decreasing Value of Our Research to Management Education," *Academy of Management Learning & Education* 11(2) (June 2012), pp. 247–262.

[41] Eric W. Ford, W. Jack Duncan, Arthur G. Bedeian, Peter M. Ginter, Matthew D. Rousculp, and Alice W. Adams, "Mitigating Risks, Visible Hands, Inevitable Disasters: Management Research that Matters to Managers," *Academy of Management Executive* 17(1) (February 2003), p. 58.

[42] George C. Banks, Jeffrey M. Pollack, Jaime E. Bochantin, Bradley L. Kirkman, Christopher E. Whelphy, and Ernest H. O'Boyle, "Management's Science-Practice Gap: A Grand Challenge for All Stakeholders," *Academy of Management Journal* 59(6) (December 2016), pp. 2205–2231.

[43] James C. Worthy, "From Practice to Theory: Odyssey of a Manager," in Arthur G. Bedeian, ed., *Management Laureates,* vol. 3(1993), pp. 375–414. See also *idem, Brushes with History: Recollections of a Many-Favored Life* (Evanston, IL: Thomson-Shore, 1998).

[44] Henry Mintzberg, *The Nature of Managerial Work* (New York: Harper & Row, 1973).

there is no reason to believe that the executives he studied represented "typical" managers. Further, critics note that Mintzberg made "no attempt to categorize the activities he observed by role; he provides no information about the amount of time his subjects spent performing each role; and he says nothing about the importance of the different roles in terms of what it takes to be an effective manager in various types of organizations."[45]

After extensive interviews and observations of managers at work, Stewart offered another view of what managers do by examining: (1) demands—what had to be done in a job; (2) constraints—internal and external limits on what could be done in a job; and (3) choices—areas in which different managers could do the same job in different ways.[46] Using staffing as an example, a manager must find and select qualified employees; in doing so a manager is restricted to a company's wage scales, the available labor supply, general economic conditions, and employment laws; and a manager must choose one job candidate over all others. In a similar study, based on observations of 15 general managers (GMs) at nine companies, Kotter found that the best GMs (1) could be very different in terms of personal characteristics and behaviors; (2) thought of themselves as generalists, yet each had a specialty that matched a specific job's demands; and (3) had a detailed knowledge of their industry's intricacies and possessed a network of cooperative working relationships.[47]

Global Studies of Managerial Work

Is a nineteenth-century theory proposed by the Managing Director of a French coal and iron firm appropriate for the mid-twentieth century? How should managers be educated and trained to succeed in a global economy? In the late 1970s, the oft-asked question "If Japan can . . . why can't we" was a wake-up call for managers (and management educators) in the United States and around the world seeking to remain globally competitive in an increasingly complex and interrelated world.

At the mid-point of the twentieth century, the United States lagged behind other nations in international business education.[48] Universities worldwide began offering Master of Business Administration programs to prepare students to be globally competent, making "MBA" an international acronym. Henri Fayol's reflections on what managers do and what managerial practices work better than others were pushed aside in favor of "modern" theories. Archer noted: "the purging of Fayol's principles from the mainstream of management thought . . . in the United States is a rather peculiar phenomenon, especially when it is considered . . . that the principles were the guiding beacons for the practice of management . . . for nearly four decades prior to the 1960s."[49] Commenting on British management theory, Smith and Boyns noted a similar turning away from Fayol's pioneering work toward an interest in observations about the nature of managerial work *a la* Mintzberg, Stewart, and Kotter: "Since 1970, the focus of management thinking has turned away from the functions of management toward trying to understand management and managing through an examination of what managers do."[50]

---

[45] Neil H. Snyder and Thomas L. Wheelen, "Managerial Roles: Mintzberg and the Management Process Theorists," in Kae Chung, ed., *Proceedings of the Annual Academy of Management Meeting* (1981), p. 249. See also Mark J. Martinko and William L. Gardner, "Beyond Structured Observation: Methodological Issues and New Directions," *Academy of Management Review* 10(4) (October 1985), pp. 676–695.

[46] Rosemary Stewart, "A Model for Understanding Managerial Jobs and Behavior," *Academy of Management Review* 7(1) (January 1982), pp. 7–13.

[47] John P. Kotter, *The General Managers* (New York: Free Press, 1982).

[48] Chuck C. Y. Kwok and Jeffrey S. Arpan, "A Comparison of International Business Education in the U. S. and European Business Schools in the 1990s," *Management International Review* 34(4) (1999), pp. 357–379.

[49] Ernest R. Archer, "Toward a Revival of the Principles of Management," *Industrial Management* 32(1) (January–February 1990), p. 19.

[50] Ian Smith and Trevor Boyns, "British Management Theory and Practice: The Impact of Henri Fayol," *Management Decision* 43(10) (2005), p. 1331.

Lubatkin and colleagues have suggested that Mintzberg's analysis of the roles managers enact raised the question whether the nature of managerial work is "universal."[51] In an effort to answer this question, they studied seven Southern and Central African nations, plus Senegal and Hungary. They concluded: "At some broad level, all managers, even those from non-western, non-industrialized, non-Anglo Saxon origins, face a similar set of administrative challenges that cause them to independently construct similar solutions, or mimic the skill activities of others."[50] In line with this conclusion, after reviewing the international-management literature, Hafsi and Farashahi also found that there is a "widespread applicability of western-based concepts of general management and organizational theories to developing countries."[52]

Mintzberg has acknowledged that "managerial work is a fundamental practice that does not change . . . some of the factors we assume to be most significant – such as national culture (for example, managing in China versus the U.S.) – may not be that significant, while others – such as the forms of organization (professional versus machine, etc.) – may be more so than previously thought."[52] He has noted that his 10 managerial roles received attention because they replaced "the tired words of 'planning, organizing, coordinating, commanding, and controlling' (all words for controlling) that had dominated the literature for the last half a century."[53] Are Fayol's reflections "tired words" or do they continue to have merit? Carroll and Gillen have argued that the managerial functions Fayol's identified "still represent the most useful way of conceptualizing the manager's job, especially for management education . . . [because they] provide clear and discrete methods of classifying the thousands of activities that managers carry out and the techniques they use in terms of the functions they perform for the achievement of organizational goals."[54]

The Changing Scene

Notions of how GMs marshal resources to accomplish a firm's objectives have changed over time. We will review these changing notions and examine why firms exist, how firms differ in resource acquisition and deployment, and why firms vary in corporate governance. In the closing pages of this chapter we will trace the post–World War II emergence of MNEs and the need to develop strategies and capabilities to sustain a competitive advantage in global markets.

From Business Policy to Strategic Management to Global Strategy

As noted in Chapter 11, the study of business policy as a separate academic subject was pioneered by Arch W. Shaw at the Harvard University Business School in 1911. He sought to develop a course for GMs that integrated knowledge across business functions. Edmund P. Learned and C. Roland Christensen were among those who followed Shaw's lead developing the now famous

---

[51] Michael Lubatkin, Momar Ndiaye, and Richard Vengroff, "The Nature of Managerial Work in Developing Countries: A Limited Test of the Universalist Hypothesis," *Journal of International Business Studies* 28(4) (4th Quarter 1997), p. 711.

[52] Taïeb Hafsi and Mehda Farashahi, "Applicability of Management Theories to Developing Countries: A Synthesis," *Management International Review* 45(4) (2005), p. 488.

[53] Henry Mintzberg, *The Nature of Managerial Work* (1973) & *Simply Managing: What Manager Do—and Can Do Better* (2013)," *M@n @gement* 18(2) (2015), p. 187.

[54] Stephen J. Carroll and Dennis J. Gillen, "Are the Classical Management Functions Useful in Describing Managerial Work?" *Academy of Management Review* 12(1) (January 1987), p. 48. See also Michael J. Fells, "Fayol Stands the Test of Time," *Journal of Management History* 6(8) (2000), pp. 345–360; David A. Lamond, "Henry Mintzberg vs. Henri Fayol: Of Lighthouses, Cubists, and the Emperor's New Clothes," *Journal of Applied Management and Entrepreneurship* 8(4) (October 2003), pp. 5–23; and *idem*, "A Matter of Style: Reconciling Henry and Henri." *Management Decision* 42(2) (2004), pp. 330–356.

Harvard Business School case-study method.[55] William H. Newman authored the first textbook on business policy, *Business Policies and Management*, published in 1940.[56] Newman recalled, "This was the first textbook on business policy ever published (Richard D. Irwin did not start publishing collections of Harvard cases until after World War II)."[57] Newman traced his interest in business policy to his years serving as an assistant to James O. McKinsey, founder of the eponymous named consulting firm (see Chapter 11). Through 10 editions, the last one simply titled *Strategy*, Newman's textbook bridged the years from general management as "business policy" to general management as "strategy."

Peter F. Drucker had established the basic conceptual framework for business policy as a discipline in 1954:

> [T]he important decisions, the decisions that really matter, are strategic. They involve either finding out what the situation is, or changing it, either finding out what the resources are or what they should be. . . . Anyone who is a manager has to make such strategic decisions, and the higher his level in the management hierarchy, the more of them he must make. . . . Among these are all decisions on business objectives and on the means to reach them. . . . [T]he important and difficult job is never to find out the right answer, it is to find the right question.[58]

In the 1960s, the Harvard business-policy group introduced SWOT analysis, a basic tool for strategic management in its classroom instruction.[59] An acronym for "strengths" and "weaknesses" (within a firm) and "opportunities" and "threats" (outside a firm), SWOT analysis is used to assess the relative attractiveness of different industries and to strategically position a company within a particular market. Kenneth R. Andrews credited Howard H. Stevenson's 1969 Harvard doctoral thesis as "making the first formal study of management practice in defining corporate strengths and weaknesses as part of the strategic planning process."[60] SWOT provides a framework for matching a firm's strengths with market opportunities while minimizing its vulnerabilities.

The 1959 Gordon and Howell report's recommendation that Business Policy serve as a capstone course delivering an integrative experience for all business-school majors further boosted interest in business policy as an academic subject. Published in 1962, Alfred D. Chandler's *Strategy and Structure* also had a profound influence on the study of business policy. "Structure follows strategy", meaning that, in effective organizations, structure is adjusted to suit strategies rather than strategies modified to match established structures— would become an enduring part of the business canon.[61] Dan E. Schendel and Charles W. Hofer rechristened "business policy," renaming it "strategic management."[62] Subsequently, the phrase "global strategy" emerged in recognition of a changing worldwide competitive environment. Competing domestically or globally raises questions about why firms exist, how firms differ in resource acquisition and deployment, and why firms vary in corporate governance.

---

[55] Edmund P. Learned, "Reflections on Leadership, Teaching, and Problem Solving Groups," in Arthur G. Bedeian ed., *Management Laureates,* vol. 2 (Greenwich, CT: JAI Press, 1993), pp. 149–175.

[56] William H. Newman, *Business Policies and Management* (Cincinnati, OH: South-Western Publishing, 1940).

[57] *Idem,* "The Takeoff," pp. 375–397.

[58] Drucker, *Practice of Management,* pp. 352–353.

[59] Pankaj Ghemawat, "Competition and Business Strategy in Historical Perspective," *Business History Review* 76(1) (Spring 2002), pp. 37–74.

[60] Kenneth R. Andrews, *The Concept of Corporate Strategy* (Homewood, IL: Dow-Jones Irwin, 1971), p. 90. See also Howard H. Stevenson, *Defining Corporate Strengths and Weaknesses: An Exploratory Study* (Unpublished dissertation, Harvard University, Boston, MA, 1969).

[61] Alfred D. Chandler, Jr., *Strategy and Structure: Chapters in the History of an American Industrial Enterprise* (Cambridge, MA: MIT Press, 1962), p. 14.

[62] Dan E. Schendel and Charles W. Hofer, eds., *Strategic Management: A New View of Business Policy and Planning* (Boston, MA: Little, Brown, 1979).

Markets and Hierarchies

As observed in Chapters 3 and 6, management, as a factor of production, provides a competitive advantage. In Chapter 16, we introduced John R. Commons's notion that *transactions* are the smallest unit of analysis in the transfer of property rights. We also discussed Ronald Coase's interest in knowing why "If markets are so efficient in allocating resources, why do business firms exist?" As noted, in his Nobel Laureate address, Coase remarked on Adam Smith's observation that barter transactions are only possible when two people coincidentally wish to exchange commodities that are mutually needed by one another.[63] Because money or currency is tradable and can be stored for future use, it eliminated not only the "double coincidence of wants," but also the costs associated with searching for a willing barter partner, and the "disutility" of having to wait until such a partner is found. In a similar effort to reduce costs, as Coarse went on to explain, at some point, someone (an entrepreneur) will create a business to engage in all or most of the transactions necessary to secure the resources required to produce a desired product. As Coase reasoned, "the operation of a market costs something and by forming an organisation and allowing some authority (an 'entrepreneur') to direct the resources, certain marketing costs are saved."[64] In this sense, to the extent that costs (in general) associated with marketplace transactions can be reduced, a firm is an alternative method of coordinating production. Such costs might be associated with locating dependable raw material suppliers, negotiating contracts, transportation charges, legal fees, and broker commissions. Firms, thus, come into existence when the cost of securing the resources necessary to produce their output is less than the cost of securing those resources on the open market.

Oliver E. Williamson extended Coase's thinking and coined the phrase "new institutional economics" to refer to the study of imperfections in markets that require a consideration of non-market factors.[65] These imperfections include laws, cultural constraints, and political systems under which firms must operate, as well as considerations such as "bounded rationality" (Herbert A. Simon's label for Barnard's limits to "the power of choice"[66]; see Chapter 14) and the need for monitoring mechanisms to thwart self-serving "opportunism"—the "effort to realize individual gains through a lack of candor or honesty in transactions."[67] Williamson's opportunism paralleled Barnard's "theory of opportunism,"[68] which Williamson described as "self-interest seeking with guile," as "even among the less opportunistic, most have their price."[69] As viewed by Coase (see Chapter 16) and Williamson, what Chandler branded the "visible hand" of management is typically more efficient in allocating resources than Adam Smith's "invisible hand" of the market because, as a basic factor of production, the authority exercised by an entrepreneur-manager can provide a competitive advantage.[70] In situations where this may not be true, firms may elect to compete in the open marketplace for necessary resources instead.

The Resource- and Knowledge-Based Theories of the Firm

In an effort to discover why firms differ, Edith T. Penrose observed, "It is the heterogeneity, and not the homogeneity, of the productive services available or potentially available from its

---

[63] Ronald H. Coase, "The Institutional Structure of Production," *American Economic Review* 82(4) (September 1992), pp. 713–719.

[64] *Idem*, "The Nature of the Firm," *Economica* 4(16) (November 1937), p. 392.

[65] Oliver E. Williamson, *Markets and Hierarchies: Analysis and Antitrust Implication: A Study in the Economics of Internal Organization* (New York: Free Press, 1975).

[66] Chester I. Barnard, *The Functions of the Executive* (Cambridge, MA: Harvard University Press, 1938), p. 14; Herbert A. Simon, *Administrative Behavior: A Study of Decision-Making Processes in Administrative Organization*, 2nd ed. (New York: Macmillan, 1957), p. xxiv; and *idem*, *Models of Man: Social and Rational* (New York: John Wiley & Sons, 1957), p. 198.

[67] Oliver E. Williamson, "Markets and Hierarchies: Some Elementary Considerations," *American Economic Review* 63(3) (June 1973), p. 317.

[68] Barnard, *The Functions of the Executive*, pp. 200–211.

[69] Oliver E. Williamson, "Transaction-Cost Economics: The Governance of Contractual Relations," *Journal of Law & Economics* 22(2) (October 1979), p. 234n.

[70] Alfred D. Chandler, *The Visible Hand: The Managerial Revolution in American Business* (Cambridge, MA: Belknap Press of the Harvard University Press, 1977).

resources that give each firm its unique character."[71] The key words here are *heterogeneity* and *resources*, as Penrose was emphasizing the competitive advantage afforded by sound management considered as a factor of production:

> [A] firm is more than an administrative unit; it is also a collection of productive resources the disposal of which between uses and over time is determined by administrative decision . . . . management tries to make the best use of the resources available . . . [and] a firm is essentially a pool of resources the utilization of which is organized in an administrative framework.[72]

She noted that a firm's resources were "inherited" from prior decisions about a firm's location, special-purpose equipment, managerial talent, and "indivisible" resources, all of which posed potential limits on future decisions.

Penrose's observations would lie fallow for a quarter century before being applied by Birger Wernerfelt in a 1984 paper, "A Resource-Based Theory of the Firm."[73] Wernerfelt reasoned: *"What a firm wants is to create a situation where its own resource position directly or indirectly makes it more difficult for others to catch up."*[74] Mergers and acquisitions, for example, provide an opportunity for a firm to gain a competitive advantage by acquiring or selling resources at its disposal. Barney has emphasized that gaining a competitive advantage in this way requires that a firm's resources be rare, valuable, not easily imitated, and nonsubstitutable.[75]

Penrose identified another means for gaining a competitive advantage that became known as the "knowledge-based view": "There is no reason to assume that the new knowledge and services [from corporate exploration and research] will be useful only in the firm's existing products; on the contrary, they may . . . provide a foundation which will give the firm an advantage in some entirely new area."[76] "Knowledge" was also inherited, as it resided in the experience, education, and intuition of a firm's human resources. Penrose used the word *entrepreneurs* to describe persons within a firm who could provide innovative knowledge about products, markets, technology, administrative processes, and opportunities. A firm could grow by "changes in the knowledge possessed."[77] She cited Schumpeter on numerous occasions regarding the role of innovation through discovery. Rather than being bound by existing knowledge, Penrose held that firms have the ability to extend their capabilities through learning. Her ideas have lasting value for firms seeking to acquire competitors for their technological prowess, or seeking to learn from other industries about new production methods or processes.

Governance and Agency Issues

Given that the quality of a firm's managers and, in turn, the authority they exercise in allocating resources is intended to provide a competitive advantage, the actions of those charged with managing a firm are critical to its long-run survival. In a corporation, shareholders elect a board of

---

[71] Edith Tilton Penrose, *The Theory of the Growth of the Firm* (New York: John Wiley & Sons, 1959), p. 75. For a precis of Penrose's life and work, see Michael H. Best and Elizabeth Garnsey, "Edith Penrose, 1914–1996," *Economic Journal* 109(453) (February 1999), pp. F187–F201.

[72] Penrose, *The Theory of the Growth of the Firm*, pp. 24, 5, 149.

[73] Birger Wernerfelt, "A Resource-Based View of the Firm," *Strategic Management Journal* 5(2) (April–June 1984), pp. 171–180. The use of the definite article "the" in referring to "growth of *the* firm" (Penrose) or "a resource-based view of *the* firm" should not be taken to suggest that there is but a single independent firm. Rather, reference here is to "a theory of all firms . . . , equivalent to a psychologist talking about a theory of the mind. Or a biologist talking about a theory of the gene." Personal communication from James G. March to Arthur G. Bedeian, April 13, 2008.

[74] *Ibid.*, p. 173.

[75] Jay B. Barney, "Firm Resources and Sustained Competitive Advantage," *Journal of Management* 17(1) (March 1991), pp. 771–792.

[76] Penrose, *Theory of the Growth of the Firm*, p. 115.

[77] *Ibid.*, pp. 76–80.

directors who, in turn, are expected to hire qualified managers to oversee its daily operations. In theory—and legally—the board and senior managers of a corporation are, thus, its are *agents* and are responsible for maximizing the wealth of its shareholders.[78] In practice, however, this is not always the case, raising questions related to corporate governance.

Adam Smith expressed concerns about the intentions of those who manage "other people's money," as discussed previously. In contrast, John Stuart Mill believed that by using pecuniary incentives the "zeal" of hired managers could be aligned with the interests of a corporation's shareholders. Mill erred, of course, as the many instances of executive rewards that have little relation with a firm's performance, shareholder returns, or pay for nonexecutives attest. Michael C. Jensen has been a perennial critic of internal control systems (such as boards of directors) for failing to deal with these and other "abuses." He has argued that board members are negligent if they have a greater allegiance to a firm's president than its shareholders, if they encourage a culture that favors consensus and frowns on dissent, if they allow a firm's president to set the agenda for board meetings and to preferentially disclose vital information to selected board members, and if the possibility of personal liability leads them to minimize risks and take measures to avoid being blamed or criticized if something goes wrong.[79] As noted, Barnard anticipated Williamson's "theory of opportunism." Fayol was also well acquainted with opportunistic behavior. He listed "subordination of individual interests to the general interest" among his 14 principles of management (see Chapter 10).

Questions of corporate governance touch on issues such as executive compensation, the inside–outside "mix" of boards of directors, executive selection and development, and top-management leadership. At the heart of these questions, though, is an even larger question: *Whose interests are being served?* The answer to this larger question, along with an understanding of why firms exist and differ in resource acquisition and deployment, also provides a framework for examining the business strategies available to multinational firms.

Multinational Enterprise and Global Strategy

Perhaps the business world's most profound accomplishment in the past 100-plus years has been its ability to move beyond two world wars, the Great Depression, a post–World War II expansion in technology, and the 2007–2008 global financial crisis to create the phenomenon called the "multinational enterprise" (MNE). Following World War II, the victorious Allies formulated plans to rebuild war-ravaged Europe. The Marshall Plan and the Organization for European Economic Cooperation (predecessor to the European Union) were initial steps toward this end. Other agencies formed to promote global economic and social recovery included the International Monetary Fund, and the General Agreement on Tariffs and Trade (predecessor to the World Trade Organization).

Regional trade alliances such as the European Union, the North American Federation Trade Agreement, and the Association of Southeast Asian Nations were also established, followed by the Organization for Economic Cooperation and Development (OECD) in 1961. OECD member nations are economically well-developed nations with higher income populations that are dedicated to political democracy and free-market economics. Global opportunities and challenges also existed in emerging nations (such as those in Asia, Latin America, Africa, and the Middle East) whose economies were underdeveloped, with lower income populations, and less political stability, thus, making international direct investment a greater risk.

---

[78] Joshua Bendickson, Jeffrey Muldoon, and Eric W. Liguori, "Agency Theory: The Times, They Are A-Changin'," *Management Decision* 54(1) (2016), pp. 174–193; Joshua Bendickson, Jeffrey Muldoon, Eric W. Liguori, and Phillip E. Davis, "Agency Theory: Background and Epistemology," *Journal of Management History* 22(4) (2016), pp. 437–449.

[79] Michael C. Jensen, "The Modern Industrial Revolution, Exit, and the Failure of Internal Control Systems," *Journal of Finance* 48(3) (July 1993), pp. 831–880.

There is an extensive literature on global strategy.[80] The history of MNEs is yet unfolding, shaped by daily developments creating opportunities and challenges. The circumstances and capabilities of firms seeking to compete in global markets will, of course, vary, as will the suitability of individual firm policies. As recounted in Chapter 15, Lincoln's overseas experience exporting its pay-for-performance system to other cultures with different labor laws, customs, and workplace values is a lesson for companies from any nation seeking to globally export their domestic management practices.

State-owned enterprises (SOEs) present a unique risk to firms seeking to compete globally. SOEs are funded and controlled by a national government. Bremmer has urged "guarded globalization" because SOEs distort marketplace economics by protecting markets at home and subsidizing domestic firms abroad. It has been suggested that SOEs may be "motivated by political objectives, rather than normal profit considerations."[81] Firms entering foreign markets where SOEs are present, thus, must face not only normal marketplace pressures, but also competitors backed by the financial and political clout of their home nations. In some developing and emerging countries, SOE prices are dictated by government fiat, and foreign competitors operate under a heavy government hand, thus, placing additional limits on their efficiency and profits. In a further complication, in that government-controlled investors cannot allocate resources as well as the open marketplace, state-run "economies quickly become less innovative and less transparent."[82] This, perhaps, explains why "SOEs under perform their private counterparts under almost any circumstance."[83] On the whole, experience suggests that SOEs all too often emulate rather than innovate, and commonly lack transparency in governance where political connections are their principal resource. The protectionism and nationalism inherent in SOEs pose a threat to market-based economic development and must be considered when deciding whether to compete in developing and emerging nations.

Strategic Leadership and "Dynamic Capabilities"

As noted, Drucker contended that what keeps an organization from failing is the ability of its managers to give birth to innovations in new products, new methods of production, new markets, the use of new raw materials, or new forms of organization that drive economic growth. Nonetheless, a firm's success is not ensured indefinitely, as its competitive advantages may quickly evaporate. In what Schumpeter (see Chapter 18) dubbed "creative destruction," innovation "incessantly revolutionizes the economic structure from within, incessantly destroying the old one, incessantly creating a new [economic structure]."[84] In situations where a firm's resources, both human and physical, cannot easily be deployed to other uses, its options for growth and learning new adopting competitive strategies may be severely limited.

In the Schumpeterian tradition, David J. Teece and his colleagues advise that firms must develop the capacity to create, extend, or modify their resources to rapidly address environmental threats. They refer to this capacity as a firm's "dynamic capability," which is enhanced by its

[80] See, for example, Michael A. Hitt, Daniel Li, and Kai Xu, "International Strategy: From Local to Global and Beyond," *Journal of World Business* 51(1) (January, 2016), pp. 58–73; Robert E. Hoskisson, Lorraine Eden, Chung Ming Lau, and Mike Wright, "Strategy in Emerging Economies," *Academy of Management Journal* 43(3) (June 2000), pp. 249–267.

[81] Organisation for Economic Co-operation and Development, "International Investment of Sovereign Wealth Funds: Are New Rules Needed?" OCED Newsletter 5(4) (October 2007), p. 4. See also Garry D. Bruton, Mike W. Peng, David Ahlstrom Ciprian V. Stan, and Kehan Xu, "State-Owned Enterprises Around the World as Hybrid Organizations," *Academy of Management Perspectives* 29(1) (February 2015), pp. 92–114; Mike W. Peng, Garry D. Bruton, Ciprian V. Stan, and Yuanyuan Huang, "Theories of the (State-Owned) Firm," *Asia Pacific Journal of Management* 33(2) (June 2016), pp. 293–317.

[82] Ian Bremmer, "The New Rules of Globalization," *Harvard Business Review* 92(1–2), (January–February, 2014), p. 103.

[83] Aldo Musacchio, Sergio G. Lazzoni, and Ruth V. Aguilera, "New Varieties of State Capitalism: Strategic and Governance Implications," *Academy of Management Perspectives* 29(1) (May 2015). p. 116.

[84] Joseph A. Schumpeter, *Capitalism, Socialism, and Democracy* (New York: Harper & Brothers, 1942), p. 83.

managers' (as a factor of production) abilities to innovate. They suggest that a firm must develop "dynamic capabilities" that allow it to

> integrate, build, and reconfigure internal and external competencies to address rapidly changing environments. Dynamic capabilities thus reflect an organization's ability to achieve new and innovative forms of competitive advantage, given path dependencies and market positions.[85]

As recounted, Penrose used the word *entrepreneurs* to describe persons within a firm who provide innovative knowledge about products, markets, technology, administrative processes, and opportunities. Teece and his colleagues consider it the responsibility of a firm's general managers to implement incentives, policies, and actions necessary to achieve change. This general-management task has been termed "strategic leadership" to distinguish the work of chief executives, directors, and other top-siders from the leadership activities of lower level managers.[86] The root word "strategy" comes from the Greek word *strategos*, meaning a military leader.[87] Moving from ancient Greece to the modern business world, the word retains much of it original meaning. As generals are charged with successfully "meeting and defeating" a country's foes, top-level managers are charged with developing and implementing plans (strategic and operational) to successfully compete in the marketplace.

The central lesson of the dynamic capabilities literature is that to safeguard its long-term survival, a firm must not only achieve its current objectives, but also engage in the continuous learning necessary for ongoing innovation and renewal. Indeed, the notion that firms who fulfill the needs and desires of the public with innovative products and services will be the most successful stands at the center of free-market capitalism. In this regard, the beauty of a free-market system – based solely on *voluntary* exchange – is that, in order to survive and prosper, Penrose's "entrepreneurs" have to make their customers "better off" at the same time. What Adam Smith wrote almost 250-years ago is still true: "It is not from the benevolence of the butcher, the brewer, or the baker that we expect our dinner, but from their regard to their own interest."[88] The success of entrepreneurs such as Google's Lawrence E. Page and Amazon's Jeffrey P. Bezos (and the downfall of the firms that Google and Amazon replaced) are just two examples that show capitalist innovation is alive, and, to survive in a competitive marketplace, firms must be open to new ideas for making their customers "better off" or risk becoming victims of Schumpeter's "creative destruction." Moreover, as Smith, thus, recognized, by entrepreneurs and customers pursuing their own self-interests, in the aggregate, a nation's overall economy and the standard of living enjoyed by its citizens (all other things being equal) will be maximized (see Chapter 2).

Whether referred to as "business policy" or rechristened "strategic management," a realization that firms are in a constant state of creation, growth, stagnation, and decline is essential in developing a general theory of management. Wisdom and experience cannot be taught, but an appreciation of management theory provides the foundation for integrating the different business functions—marketing, production, accounting, finance, and information systems—to align a firm with its economic, technological, social, and political environment and heightening its managers' innovateness.

---

[85] David J. Teece, Gary Pisano, and Amy Shuen, "Dynamic Capabilities and Strategic Management," *Strategic Management Journal* 18(7) (August 1997), p. 524. See also David J. Teece, "The Foundations of Enterprise Performance: Dynamic and Ordinary Capabilities in an (Economic) Theory of Firms," *Academy of Management Perspectives* 28(4) (November 2014), pp. 328–352.

[86] Sydney Finkelstein, Donald C. Hambrick, and Albert A. Cannella, *Strategic Leadership: Theory and Research on Executives, Top Management Teams, and Boards* (New York: Oxford University Press, 2009), p. 4.

[87] Jeffrey Bracker, "The Historical Development of the Strategic Management Concept," *Academy of Management Review* 5(2) (April 1980), p. 219.

[88] Adam Smith, *An Inquiry Into the Nature and Causes of the Wealth of Nations* (London: W. Strahan and T. Cadell in the Strand, 1776), vol. 1, bk. I, ch. 2, p. 17.

SUMMARY

The twentieth century was marked by two world wars, the Great Depression, a post–World War II reawakening in technology, a global financial crisis, and the growth of worldwide business. A renewed interest in general management theory occurred as businesses grew at home and abroad, fostering a need for more broadly educated managers. Studies of business education led to a reformulation of business-school curricula and an emphasis on creating new knowledge. This emphasis on academic research created a divide between management theory and its relevance to students and those who practiced the art of management. The United States lagged behind other nations in international business education and MBA became an international acronym.

Foundational work in business policy and, later, strategic management would evolve as the need to meet global challenges and, in turn, capitalize on worldwide opportunities in developing and emerging nations mounted. This required that firms match their capabilities with opportunities and learn to work in other nations with differing histories, institutions, and cultures. Firms, rather than markets, were deemed the better allocator of resources, but the visible hand of management posed governance and agency issues. This view of firms turned attention to general management as an entrepreneurial and integrating activity that required adapting and learning in a global competitive environment.

Organizational Behavior and Organization Theory

chapter

20

Part 3 began by examining the Hawthorne studies and the previously unappreciated patterns of employee behavior that they revealed. It then discussed the lives and thoughts of two individuals—Mary P. Follett and Chester I. Barnard—who bridged the scientific-management and the social-person eras. It next reviewed the growth and refinement of the human-relations movement as it moved through micro and macro phases, from roughly 1930 into the early 1950s and concluded with a look at human relations in theory and practice and a consideration of the economic, social, technological, and political environment of the social-person era.

Beginning in the 1950s, human relations as a movement was overtaken by the emergence of a new generation of scholars devoted to the study of what became known as "organizational behavior." Moving beyond the "feel-good" reputation of human relations, organizational-behavior researchers addressed issues such as job design, work motivation, and effective leadership in an analytical fashion. Similarly, personnel management as a field began to build a firmer empirical base and over time evolved into human-resource management (HRM) and, then, strategic human-resource management (SHRM). At about the same time, organization theorists began to debate the effect of technology on an organization's structure and explore how organizations adapt to ensure a proper "fit" between their management processes, structures, and strategies and changing environments. Midway through the second half of the twentieth century, with the expanding globalization of business following World War II, and the increasing need to manage with an appreciation of diverse cultures, there was also a growing focus on understanding differences in workplace dynamics across borders, and how different national cultures might influence the applicability of management theories and practice. This chapter reviews each of these developments.

The Human Side of Organizations

Until the 1960s, those trained in the social and behavioral sciences, such as psychologists, sociologists, and anthropologists, had little impact on general management theory. As noted in Chapter 19, the Gordon and Howell report called for a greater emphasis in business education on the behavioral and social sciences: "Of all the subjects which he might undertake formally, none is more appropriate for the businessman-to-be than human behavior. . . . The very nature of the firm and of the manager's role in the firm suggests that every person anticipating a responsible position in a modern business enterprise needs a substantial amount of knowledge about human behavior"[1] The social and behavioral sciences were seen as offering a scientific base from which more powerful analytical and conceptual tools could be developed to address the ongoing challenges of employee–employer relations.

The Transition from Human Relations to Organizational Behavior

Given their methodological training, social and behavioral scientists entering business schools following the Gordon and Howell report insisted on more rigorous research for understanding workplace relations beyond the "feel-good" reputation of human relations (see Chapter 17). This led to the emergence of a new generation of scholars devoted to the study of "organizational behavior." Among the earliest, if not the first, uses of the phrase "organizational behavior" appeared in a 1948 paper by Philip Selznick published in the *American Sociological Review*.[2] By 1953, Princeton University had initiated an organizational-behavior research program.[3] A year later, Yale University's Labor and Management Center began a publication series titled "Studies in Organizational Behavior." Its first volume was Chris Argyris's *Organization of a Bank: A Study of the Nature of Organization and the Fusion Process*, published in 1954. Argyris sought to integrate "the individual and the organization." He proposed a "personality versus organization"

[1] Robert A. Gordon and James E. Howell, *Higher Education for Business* (New York: Columbia University Press, 1959), p. 166.
[2] Philip Selznick, "Foundations of the Theory of Organization," *American Sociological Review* 13(1) (February 1948), p. 25.
[3] Organizational Behavior Section, Princeton University, *Organizational Behavior: A Report on a Research Program* (Princeton, NJ: The Author, 1953).

hypothesis based on an "immaturity-maturity" theory of human behavior.[4] According to Argyris, there was an incongruence between the demands of formal organizations (with their extreme division of labor and close oversight and control) and the needs of healthy, mature individuals. Argyris argued that from infancy to adulthood, there was a tendency for the healthy personality to develop along a continuum from immaturity to maturity by moving from being passive to being active, from dependence to independence, from a lack of awareness of self to an awareness and control over self, and so on. In Arygris's telling, when these incongruences interfered with the needs of healthy personalities and the requirements of formal organizations, individuals naturally protected themselves by using defensive reactions (such as becoming aggressive or apathetic or restricting output). All too often, managers responded by either becoming more autocratic and directive or, alternatively, turning to human relations. It was Argyris's experience, however, that many managers turned to pseudo-human relations programs to sugarcoat workplace realities rather than addressing the actual causes of employee discontent.

Argyris (together with Donald Schön) also popularized the notion of "organizational learning," which grew from his early work on individual needs and the demands of modern organizations. The question was: "Why do individuals (and groups) use—defensive reasoning—to resist organizational changes?" The answer, according to Argyris and Schön, echoed Kurt Lewin's findings on introducing change (see Chapter 15) and resided in "unfreezing" and altering individuals' "defensive reasoning" patterns, and encouraging reasoning that led to "double-loop" learning; that is, learning by doing and making corrections as needed based on information fed back from different action strategies. This was in contrast to "single-loop" learning that did not question the status quo and inhibited learning from experience.[5] Argyris and Schön's work on organizational learning added to the value of Edith T. Penrose's work regarding the knowledge-based view of the firm (see Chapter 19) and also stimulated further interest in organizational change and development.

The work of Keith Davis marked the beginning of a philosophically broader understanding of workplace interactions. Davis defined "human relations" in business as "the integration of people into a work situation in a way that motivates them to work together productively, cooperatively, and with economic, psychological, and social satisfaction."[6] He held that modern human relations really had two facets: (1) a concern with understanding, describing, and identifying causes and effects of human behavior through empirical investigation and (2) the application of this knowledge. The first facet could be termed *organizational behavior* and the second *human relations*. These facets were complementary, in that one investigates and explains, whereas the other applies the knowledge thereby made available. Davis stressed the importance of economic and psychological factors in understanding the social nature of humans and human life. In doing so, he moved the study of workplace behavior from its "feelings" base toward a search for an empirical foundation.

Theories X and Y

A social psychologist by training, with the exception of 6 years during which he served as president of Antioch College, Douglas McGregor taught in the Sloan School of Management at the Massachusetts Institute of Technology from 1937 until his death in 1964. As president of Antioch

---

[4] Chris Argyris, *Personality and Organization: The Conflict between System and the Individual* (New York: Harper & Brothers, 1957), p. 50.

[5] Chris Argyris and Donald A. Schön, *Organizational Learning II* (Reading, Mass.: Addison-Wesley, 1996). See also Argyris, "Double-Loop Learning, Teaching, and Research," *Academy of Management Learning & Education*, 1(2) (December 2002), pp. 206–218.

[6] Keith Davis, *Human Relations in Business* (New York: McGraw-Hill, 1957), p. 4.

College (1948–1954), McGregor soon found that contemporary human-relations theory was inadequate for coping with the realities of organizational life:

> It took the direct experience of becoming a line executive . . . to teach me what no amount of observation of other people could have taught.
>
> I believed, for example, that a leader could operate successfully as a kind of adviser to his organization. I thought I could avoid being a "boss." Unconsciously, I suspect, I hoped to duck the unpleasant necessity of making difficult decisions, of taking the responsibility for one course of action among many uncertain alternatives, of making mistakes and taking the consequences. I thought that maybe I could operate so that everyone would like me – that "good human relations" would eliminate all discord and disagreement.
>
> I couldn't have been more wrong. It took a couple of years, but I finally began to realize that a leader cannot avoid the exercise of authority any more than he can avoid responsibility for what happens to his organization.[7]

Based on his experience at Antioch, McGregor began to formulate a set of ideas that would have a profound influence on management education: "A manager who believes that people in general are lazy, untrustworthy, and antagonistic toward him will make very different decisions [from] a manager who regards people generally as cooperative and friendly."[8] In *The Human Side of Enterprise,* McGregor expanded on the idea that one's underlying assumptions about human nature were all-important in determining one's approach to managing. He identified two fundamental management styles: Theory X and Theory Y. Theory X represented the "traditional view of direction and control." It assumed:

1. *The average human being has an inherent dislike of work and will avoid it if he can . . . .*

2. *Because of this human characteristic of dislike of work, most people must be coerced, controlled, directed, and threatened with punishment to get them to put forth adequate effort toward the achievement of organizational objectives . . . .*

3. *The average human being prefers to be directed, wishes to avoid responsibility, has relatively little ambition, wants security above all.*[9]

In contrast, Theory Y assumed:

1. *The expenditure of physical and mental effort in work is as natural as play or rest.* The average human being does not inherently dislike work.

2. *External control and the threat of punishment are not the only means for bringing about effort toward organizational objectives. Man will exercise self-direction and self-control in the service of objectives to which he is committed.*

3. *Commitment to objectives is a function of the rewards associated with their achievement.* The most significant of such rewards, e.g., the satisfaction of ego and self-actualization needs, can be direct products of effort directed toward organizational objectives.

4. *The average human being learns, under proper conditions, not only to accept but also to seek responsibility.* Avoidance of responsibility, lack of ambition, and emphasis on security are generally consequences of experience, not inherent human characteristics.

---

[7] Douglas McGregor, "On Leadership," *Antioch Notes* 31(9) (May 1, 1954), p. 3.

[8] Douglas McGregor and Joseph N. Scanlon, *The Dewey and Almy Chemical Company and the International Chemical Workers Union* (Washington, DC: National Planning Association, 1948), p. 72.

[9] Douglas McGregor, *The Human Side of Enterprise* (New York: McGraw-Hill, 1960), pp. 33–34.

5. *The capacity to exercise a relatively high degree of imagination, ingenuity, and creativity in the solution of organizational problems is widely, not narrowly, distributed in the population.*

6. *Under the conditions of modern industrial life, the intellectual potentialities of the average human being are only partially utilized.*[10]

For McGregor, the central principle that derives from Theory Y is the importance of creating "conditions such that the members of [an] organization can achieve their own goals *best* by directing their efforts toward the success of the enterprise."[11] Managers accepting the Theory Y assumptions of human nature would not structure, control, or closely supervise the work environment. Instead, they would give their subordinates wider latitude in their work, encourage creativity, use fewer external controls, foster self-control, and motivate through the satisfaction that comes from the challenge of work itself. The use of external control would be replaced by people committed to the overall goals of their organization because they perceived that this was the best way to achieve their own goals. McGregor hoped that, in adopting Theory Y, employers and employees would join together to advance their common interests.

Human-Resource Management and Industrial Relations: The Changing Scene

The desirability of employees as willing contributors to the accomplishment of an organization's goals is, of course, not a new idea. Whereas classical economists in the seventeenth and eighteenth centuries believed that work was without intrinsic reward and, thus, employees must be coerced by extrinsic motives to perform (see Chapter 3), in the late nineteenth century, neoclassical economists began to appreciate that work was much more than a means of survival and, indeed, through productive activity people could achieve self-realization.[12] As noted in Chapter 9, at the turn of the twentieth century, at the gates of many factories across the country, unskilled workers would line up each morning and a foreman would appear to hire the day's labor. This often, however, amounted to little more than hiring friends or the well connected, or even in some cases, selling jobs. Frederick W. Taylor denounced this practice and replaced it with functional foremen, who evolved into specialists to aid in making hiring decisions (see Chapter 7). For Henri Fayol, staffing was simply part of organizing (see Chapter 10). From these rudimentary beginnings, "personnel management" gradually evolved as a standard label for advising managers about employee recruitment, selection, and so forth.

As previously outlined, early personnel-management programs borrowed from many disciplines, including industrial psychology (personnel testing), labor economics (for understanding labor market factors as they affected the supply of employees and wage rates), and industrial relations (for promoting better union–management relations). Personnel management did not, however, always receive the high regard that those in the field thought it deserved. In their report on the status of U.S. business education, Gordon and Howell charged: "Next to the course in production, perhaps more educational sins have been committed in the name of personnel management than in any other required course in the business curriculum. Personnel management is a field which has had a particularly small base of significant generalization with which to work (beyond what is important in the area of human relations), and, partly for this reason, it is an area

---

[10] *Ibid.*, pp. 47–48.
[11] *Ibid.*, p. 49.
[12] For a review of early economic theories of work, see David A. Spencer, "Work is a Four-Letter Word: The Economics of Work in Historical and Critical Perspective," *American Journal of Economics and Sociology* 70(3) (July 2011), pp. 563–586.

which has not been held in high regard in the better schools."[13] As social and behavioral scientists entered U.S. business schools, they brought their research skills to personnel management, and with the growth of industrial relations and labor–management centers, personnel management began to build a firmer empirical base.

The labor economist John R. Commons appears to have been the first to use the phrase "human resources" in an industrial context.[14] E. Wight Bakke stressed that more emphasis had to be placed on the human element to elevate its importance relative to other inputs used in the production of goods and services. The central concern of the human-resource function was not "personal happiness," but "productive work," and the belief that humans had to be integrated into the total task of every organization. Maintaining an organization's human resources, however, was the responsibility of all managers, not just those in personnel or labor-relations departments.[15] Wendell L. French seems to have been the first author to add "human resources" to the title of a personnel-management textbook.[16] The notion that an organization's human resources could be managed carried a certain dignity, and the term itself gave personnel management a new legitimacy. Beginning in the 1960s, and accelerating thereafter, federal and state laws concerning equal-employment opportunity, occupational safety and health, employment testing, compensation practices, and retirement plans gave rise to a new breed of "personnel specialists" trained in both business and law.

Whereas in the early 1900s labor economists were at the forefront of the industrial-relations movement, by the earlier 2000s they were distanced both from economics and industrial relations. As Kaufman has acknowledged, "It is common today to view the field of personnel/human resource management . . . as distinct and largely unrelated to the discipline of economics and the field of industrial relations." [17] George Strauss and Thomas A. Kochan are two notable exceptions to this trend. In his graduate studies and early career, Strauss was influenced by Douglas McGregor, Paul A. Samuelson, John R. Dunlop and others who provided a broad base of knowledge in economics, human relations, and industrial relations.[18] Over the years, Strauss has seen "the transition from human relations to organizational behavior," but has never abandoned his belief that sound labor–management relations were based on employer–employee cooperation. Kochan continues the long line of "Wisconsin School" of labor-relations scholars that includes Richard T. Ely, John R. Commons, and Selig Perlman. Similar to Strauss, Kochan sees HRM and industrial relations as complementary and views unions as a legitimate and valuable component of a democratic society, enabling labor, management, and public policymakers to forge an agenda for mutual progress and prosperity.[19]

In the 1980s and 1990s, Edith T. Penrose's resource- and knowledge-based views of the firm received belated recognition (see Chapter 19). It was suggested that HRM should be incorporated into a firm's competitive strategy and, subsequently, the label "strategic human-resource management" (SHRM) appeared frequently in the management literature. The unique goal of SHRM remains the development of employment practices that lead to high-performance work systems to achieve and sustain a competitive advantage.[20]

---

[13] Gordon and Howell, *Higher Education for Business*, p. 189.

[14] John R. Commons, *Industrial Goodwill* (New York: McGraw-Hill Book Company, 1919), pp. 129–130.

[15] E. Wight Bakke, *The Human Resources Function* (New Haven, CT: Yale University Labor-Management Center, 1958).

[16] Wendell L. French, *The Personnel Management Process: Human Resources Administration* (Boston, MA: Houghton Mifflin, 1964).

[17] Bruce E. Kaufman, "The Role of Economics and Industrial Relations in the Development of the Field of Personnel/Human Resource Management," *Management Decision* 40(10) (2002), p. 962.

[18] George Strauss, "Present at the Beginning: Some Personal Notes on OB's Early Days and Later," in Arthur G. Bedeian, ed., *Management Laureates*, vol. 3 (Greenwich, CT: JAI Press, 1993), pp. 145–190.

[19] Thomas A. Kochan, "Celebrating Work: A Job Unfinished," in Arthur G. Bedeian ed., *Management Laureates*, vol. 6 (Greenwich, CT: JAI Press, 1993), pp. 199–242.

[20] For example, see Peter Boxall and Keith Macky, "Research and Theory on High-Performance Work Systems: Progressing the High-Involvement Stream," *Human Resource Management Journal* 19(1) (January 2009), pp. 3–23 and James G. Combs, Yongmei Liu, Angela T. Hall, and David J. Ketchen, Jr., "How Much Do High-Performance Work Practices Matter?: A Meta-Analysis of Their Effects on Organizational Performance," *Personnel Psychology* 59(3) (Autumn 2006), pp. 501–528.

According to Kaufman, however, "[m]odern HRM and SHRM . . . appear to have dressed up many old ideas in new garb and claimed a new discovery for things known and practiced by earlier generations."[21] In a 3-decade review, Kaufman criticized SHRM researchers for failing to add to management science; being too focused on the internal dimension of organizations (such as strategy, organizational behavior, and psychology) to the neglect of external dimensions (such as economics and industrial/employment law); an inability to develop actionable findings; and disregarding anything outside the "Anglo-American orbit". The full benefit of SHRM remains unclear, and moving beyond a predominantly Western-based research literature will not be easy. As others have noted, the common practice of equating "culture" and "nation" is questionable, and challenges relating to a nation's history; political/religious ideologies; political, economic, and social institutions; and differing expectations cannot be ignored.[22]

Job Design

How jobs should be designed for maximum effectiveness and efficiency is a concern of long-standing interest. Plato remarked on human diversity and how this led to the assignment of different parts of a task to different individuals, or what we would call the "division of labor."[23] Although Adam Smith saw the benefits of the division of labor, he also foresaw its dysfunctional consequences.[24] Taylor, Gilbreth, and other scientific-management pioneers studied the design of workers' jobs in the hope of finding a better way to reduce fatigue and increase efficiency (see Part 2). Allan H. Mogensen pioneered the work-simplification movement in the belief that jobs could be designed so that people could work smarter, not harder.[25] As a result of Walker and Guest's study of assembly-line work, "job enlargement" as a means relieving monotony among employees caused by the division of labor assumed a new prominence (see Chapter 15).[26] The belief that management has a responsibility to make work, in general, more meaningful and personally fulfilling, also, gathered momentum.

Beginning in the late 1950s, Frederick I. Herzberg sought to discover what job-related factors motivate employees.[27] He asked employees to provide examples of times when they felt exceptionally good or exceptionally bad about their jobs. The examples were analyzed and revealed that the factors which produced job satisfaction were distinct from those that produced job dissatisfaction. That is, although an unpleasant work environment might be a reason given for job dissatisfaction, a pleasant work environment was rarely cited as a reason for job satisfaction. This finding contrasted with the traditional view that job satisfaction and job dissatisfaction were opposite ends of the same continuum. Herzberg labeled the factors that produced job satisfaction "motivators." His analysis indicated that these factors were directly related to *job content*, reflecting a

---

[21] Bruce E. Kaufman, "Strategic Human Resource Management Research in the United States: A Failing Grade after 30 Years?" *Academy of Management Perspectives* 26(2) (May 2012), p. 22.

[22] Vlad Vaiman and Chris Brewster, "How Far Do Cultural Differences Explain the Differences Between Nations?" *International Journal of Human Resource Management* 26(2) (January 2015), pp. 151–164; Timothy Kiessling and Michael Harvey, "Strategic Global Human Resource Management Research in the Twenty-First Century: An Endorsement of the Mixed-Method Research Methodology," *International Journal of Human Resource Management* 16(1) (January 2005), pp. 22–45.

[23] Plato, *The Republic of Plato,* 3rd ed. trans. by Benjamin Jowett (Oxford: Clarendon Press, 1888), p. 50. Originally published circa 380 BCE.

[24] Adam Smith, *An Inquiry Into the Nature and Causes of the Wealth of Nations* (London: W. Strahan and T. Cadell in the Strand, 1776), vol. 2, bk. V, ch. 1, pp. 366–367.

[25] Allan H. Mogensen, *Work Simplification: The Consultive Approach to Methods Improvement* (Berkeley, CA: California Personnel Management Association, 1951).

[26] Charles R. Walker and Robert H. Guest, "The Man on the Assembly Line," *Harvard Business Review* 30(3) (May–June 1952), pp. 71–83.

[27] Frederick I. Herzberg, Bernard Mausner, and Barbara B. Snyderman, *The Motivation to Work* (New York: John Wiley & Sons, 1959), p. 141.

need for personal fulfillment. Motivators included feelings achievement, recognition, the work being performed, feelings of responsibility, opportunities for advancement, and job growth. He labeled the factors that led to job dissatisfaction "hygienes" and found that they were more related to environment or setting in which work is performed, or *job context*, than to job content. Hygiene factors included company policies and administration, supervision, relations with one's peers, working conditions, pay, and job security. Based on this dichotomy, Herzberg and his colleagues concluded that only motivators produce job satisfaction, whereas hygienes merely prevent job dissatisfaction. In other words:

1. To the degree that hygienes are absent from a job, dissatisfaction will occur. When present, hygienes prevent dissatisfaction, but do not lead to satisfaction.

2. To the degree that motivators are present in a job, satisfaction will occur. When absent, motivators do not lead to dissatisfaction.

Hygienes, thus, provide a platform that must be present before satisfaction can take place. Stated more directly, employers must prevent employee job dissatisfaction by providing hygienes before they can address employee job satisfaction using motivators.

As noted in Chapter 9, Herzberg's "two-factor theory" of job satisfaction is remarkably similar to Hendrik de Man's conclusion that a worker's mental attitude toward work is a mix of "pleasurable and unpleasurable elements."[28] Despite its insights, scholars noted several difficulties with Herzberg's findings. For example, doubts have been raised about his data-collection methods. Rather than asking employees to provide examples of times when they felt exceptionally good or exceptionally bad about their jobs, researchers using techniques less susceptible to respondent bias failed to replicate his findings. In this regard, critics noted that people are more likely to credit their own achievements as reasons for job satisfaction. Similarly, they are more likely to blame poor policies or supervision for their dissatisfaction. This suggests that Herzberg's results may be due to the manner in which he gathered his data. Indeed, other investigators using different methods have obtained findings contrary to what Herzberg's theory would predict. Also, although Herzberg reported replications of his original study in countries located in Europe, Africa, the Middle East, and Asia, research conducted by other investigators has shown wide diversity in the work preferences of different people in different cultures, thus casting doubt on the cross-cultural generality of his findings.

Herzberg's research stimulated an increased interest in job design. Arthur N. Turner and Paul R. Lawrence investigated "requisite task attributes" or RTAs (namely, *task variety*, *work autonomy*, *required interaction*, *optional interaction*, *knowledge and skill required*, and *responsibility*) related to job satisfaction and attendance.[29] A significant aspect of Turner and Lawrence's research was their finding that employees from varying cultural backgrounds (small town versus urban) responded differently to high RTA jobs. A summary index of the six requisite task attributes was positively related to job satisfaction and attendance for employees in small towns and negatively related for those in urban areas.

J. Richard Hackman and Edward E. Lawler III extended Turner and Lawrence's work.[30] They identified four job characteristics, termed *core dimensions*, which could be modified to enrich jobs (see Chapter 15). The core dimensions were *skill variety*, *work autonomy*, *task identity*, and *performance feedback*. Hackman and Lawler reasoned that the more a job

---

[28] Hendrik de Man, *Joy in Work,* trans. Eden and Cedar Paul (London: G. Allen & Unwin, 1929), p. 9. Originally published in 1927.

[29] Arthur N. Turner and Paul R. Lawrence, *Industrial Jobs and the Worker: An Investigation of Response to Task Attributes* (Boston, MA: Division of Research, Graduate School of Business Administration, Harvard University, 1965).

[30] J. Richard Hackman and Edward E. Lawler III, "Employee Reactions to Job Characteristics," *Journal of Applied Psychology* 55(3) (June 1971), pp. 259–286.

contains these core dimensions, the more likely it will be to provide employees with feelings of satisfaction and motivation. In turn, higher quality performance and lower absenteeism and turnover should also be more likely. Hackman and Oldham also noted the importance of taking into account an employee's desire for personal growth through satisfaction of "higher-order needs."

Hackman would later join with Greg R. Oldham to argue that *task significance* should be considered a fifth core dimension. Hackman and Oldham urged managers to determine the quantity and quality of the different core dimensions present in the jobs they supervise. They believed that if these characteristics could be expanded, for example, by increasing the range of skills and creativity required by a job or by providing performance feedback, then employees would be more likely to find their jobs more meaningful. Recognizing that there would be large individual differences in how various employees reacted to the five core dimensions, Hackman and Oldham acknowledged that the success of this approach depended on an employee's "growth-need strength." If an employee already felt sufficiently challenged and experienced a job as meaningful, growth-need strength would be low, and further efforts to enrich a job would be less effective. Some individuals seek more freedom and challenge in their jobs, and others do not; further, some jobs can be made more meaningful, and others cannot. Thus, Hackman and Oldham did not present job design as a universal panacea for all work-related challenges: "the redesign of work is much more a *way of managing* than it is a prepackaged 'fix' for problems of employee motivation and satisfaction."[31] Their research, however, did suggest that work motivation and employee satisfaction can be increased by providing a closer match between the nature of a job and employee needs.

Work Motivation

The next two topics, work motivation and leadership, are closely related. They are discussed separately here, as they relate to job performance, only to emphasize the contributions of different individuals to our general understanding. Motivation is a central issue that pervades all aspects of employee behavior. As has been noted, "The question, 'How can I motivate my people?' has been philosophically and practically posed in many eras and many tongues."[32] Classical economics argued that because work was an irksome activity, employees had to be compelled or coerced to work hard. As detailed in Chapters 2 and 15, this line of thinking was challenged by psychologists such as Henry A. Murray, Abraham H. Maslow, and David C. McClelland. As a group, these and other psychologists were primarily focused on needs, motives, and wants in an effort to discover *what* motivates people. Maslow, for example, identified five categories of inborn needs, whereas McClelland, building on the work of Murray, gave primacy to the needs for *power*, *affiliation*, and *achievement*. It soon became apparent, however, that in applied settings, a full understanding of motivation requires an appreciation of both *what* motivates people and *how* people are motivated. With regard to the latter, three motivation theories (developed beginning in the early 1960s) that focus on *how* behavior is energized, *how* it is directed, *how* it is sustained, and *how* it is stopped generated the greatest interest: Vroom's expectancy theory, Adams's equity theory, Locke and Latham's goal-setting theory.[33]

---

[31] J. Richard Hackman and Greg R. Oldham, *Work Redesign* (Reading, MA: Addison-Wesley, 1980), p. 249. For a complete historical review of the job design literature, see Greg R. Oldham and Yitzhak Fried, "Job Design Research and Theory: Past, Present, and Future," *Organizational Behavior and Human Decision Processes* 136 (September 2016), pp. 20–35; Sharon K. Parker, Frederick P. Morgeson, and Gary Johns, "One Hundred Years of Work Design Research: Looking Back and Looking Forward," *Journal of Applied Psychology* 102(3) (March 2017), pp. 403–420.

[32] David E. Terpstra, "Theories of Motivation – Borrowing the Best," *Personnel Journal* 58(6) (June 1979), p. 376.

[33] For a 100-year review of work-motivation research, see Ruth Kanfer, Michael Frese, and Russell E. Johnson, "Motivation related to Work: A Century of Progress," *Journal of Applied Psychology* 102(3) (March 2017), pp. 338–355.

One of the most influential work motivation theories of the mid-to-late twentieth-century, expectancy theory was popularized by Victor H. Vroom.[34] Expectancy theory is based on the belief that people will act to maximize their rewards. In this respect, it holds that motivation is determined by (1) *expectancies*, or the belief that effort will be rewarded, and (2) *valences*, or the value attached to specific rewards. In brief, the motivation to behave in a certain way will be greatest when individuals believe their behavior will lead to certain outcomes (e.g., a raise or a promotion) and they place a positive value on these outcomes. Expectancy theory underscores the realization that different people have different desires and that they are likely to perceive different connections between actions and the fulfillment of these desires. In doing so, it highlights important factors (i.e., expectancies and valences) that influence behavioral intentions and suggests ways in which these factors alone and in combination can be used to predict behavior.

Championed by J. Stacy Adams, equity theory attempts to explain satisfaction with outcomes (e.g., pay, promotion opportunities, increased status) and to predict changes in behavior.[35] It defines motivation in terms of the perceived equity between the effort one puts into a job and what one receives in return, especially compared to others in similar positions. Equity theory holds that perceived inequity creates tension within a person, and this tension in turn motivates a drive to restore inequity. The greater the tension one feels, the harder one will work to restore equity and, thereby reduce the tension. According to equity theory, the "other person" an individual uses as a comparison could be one person (e.g., a coworker), a group (e.g., workers on another shift), or someone from a previous, or even hypothetical, work situation. Two points are key to understanding equity theory: (1) it emphasizes "perceived" as compared to "actual" equity; it matters little whether an individual's comparisons are based on subjective perception or objective reality, and (2) equity and equality are not the same. Equality is said to exist when one perceives the outcomes they receive as being equal to the outcomes received by another person. Equity is attained when the ratio of an individual's perceived outcomes to inputs equals the ratio of the other person's outcomes to inputs. Thus, perceived inequity may exist in either of two cases: (1) when a person judges the ratio of his or her perceived outcomes to inputs as being too low relative to another, or (2) when a person feels the ratio of his or her perceived outcomes to inputs is excessive relative to another. The notion that people seek fairness is, of course, not a new finding. It is the basis for Whiting Williams's (see Chapter 9) 1920 conclusion that the pay a worker receives is considered not in absolute terms, but relative to what others receive.[36] It is also the basis for the first-century Biblical Parable of the Laborers in the Vineyard (Matthew 20: 1–16) who, after working since sunrise, were upset at being paid the same wage as others who had been hired just one hour before the end of the day. It would seem that a desire for equity is timeless.

Goal-setting theory is primarily the work of Edwin A. Locke and Gary P. Latham. It focuses on the causal effects of developing and setting specific work goals on job performance, holding that conscious goals are the most proximal determinant of motivation.[37] The more specific a goal, the better: "produce one hundred units that will pass the quality inspection" rather than "do the best you can today." Further, difficult goals are better than easy goals—goals should challenge (but not exceed) an individual's abilities. Locke and Latham's research supports a positive relationship between goal difficulty and job performance. It further indicates that goal-setting as a motivational

---

[34] Victor H. Vroom, *Work and Motivation* (New York: John Wiley & Sons, 1964).

[35] J. Stacy Adams, "Toward an Understanding of Inequity," *Journal of Abnormal and Social Psychology* 67(5) (November 1963), pp. 422–436.

[36] Whiting Williams, *What's on the Worker's Mind? By One Who Put on Overalls to Find Out* (New York: Charles Scribner's Sons, 1920), p. 323.

[37] Edwin A. Locke and Gary P. Latham, *A Theory of Goal Setting and Task Performance* (Englewood Cliffs, NJ: Prentice Hall, 1990); and Gary P. Latham and Edwin A. Locke, "Self-Regulation through Goal Setting," *Organizational Behavior and Human Decision Processes* 50(2) (December 1991), pp. 212–247.

tool works equally well whether goals are assigned or determined by group participation. According to Locke and Latham, assigned goals work best with employees already internally motivated to perform at a high level, such as employees with a high need for achievement or high self-efficacy. In contrast, they found that when employees are familiar with and at ease with participative techniques, and when their need for achievement is lower, participative goal-setting is likely to be more effective. Locke and Latham's research also revealed that employee acceptance of goals depends on a number of factors, including the extent to which employees trust a company's managers, the fairness and difficulty of goals, and the perceived legitimacy of workplace demands. In general, 40 years of research has provided robust support for a positive relationship between goal difficulty and job performance.

Edwin A. Locke. Courtesy of Edwin A. Locke.

As Kanfer and Chen have noted: "For much of the mid- to late-20th century, expectancy-value and goal setting models dominated the work motivation literature."[38] At the same time, given an increasing integration of national markets and a growing workforce diversity throughout the world, it is apparent that research is needed to establish whether Western-based theories of motivation are applicable across nations and cultures. Geert Hofstede, for one, chided Maslow, McClelland, Herzberg, and Vroom for their Freudian inclinations about the nature of human needs and aspirations, arguing that Freudian thinking does not fit other cultural patterns.[39]

Effective Leadership

Leadership has been studied for thousands of years. In retrospect, our understanding of leadership has progressed through three phases to today's current age. The three earlier phases are generally referred to as the *trait phase*, the *behavioral phase*, and the *situational phase*. As our knowledge of leadership has been largely cumulative across time, we will discuss these phases in chronological order before commenting on the current state of leadership theory.[40]

The Trait Phase

As noted in Chapter 8, the history of the world has been shaped by the leadership of great people. Without Moses, the Jews would have remained captive in Egypt. Without Winston Churchill, the British would have succumbed to the German bombing campaign carried out by the Luftwaffe in 1940 during World War II. As we have all marveled at the achievements of certain people, it is not surprising that the first attempts to understand leadership centered on determining what specific traits make a person an effective leader. Consequently, early investigations sought to discover how people in leadership positions had attained them and

---

[38] Ruth Kanfer and Gilad Chen, "Motivation in Organizational Behavior: History, Advances and Prospects," *Organizational Behavior and Human Performance* 136 (September 2016), p. 12

[39] Geert Hofstede, "Motivation, Leadership, and Organizations: Do American Theories Apply Abroad?" *Organizational Dynamics* 9(1) (Summer 1980), pp. 50, 55.

[40] For a 100-year review of leadership research, see Robert G. Lord, David. V. Day, Stephen J. Zaccaro, Bruce J. Avolio, and Alice H. Eagly, "Leadership in Applied Psychology: Three Waves of Theory and Research," *Journal of Applied Psychology* 102(3) (March 2017), pp. 434–451.

whether these people had certain traits in common. In general, these investigations defined a trait as a distinctive physical or psychological characteristic that account's for a person's behavior.

In its pure form, the trait phase grew out of the "great-man" theory of leadership, which held that a person was born either with or without the necessary traits to be a leader; leaders were born and not made. Thus, leadership was thought to be derived from nature. Learned behavior was considered irrelevant, People such as Alexander the Great, Hannibal, and Napoleon were said to be "natural leaders" who were born to lead. It was believed they were endowed with inborn qualities that would have enabled them to be effective leaders in any situation. (Despite the examples of Joan of Arc, Elizabeth I, and Catherine the Great, women leaders were ignored.)

The great-man theory (not to be confused with "instinct theory;" see Chapter 9) held sway well into the early 1900s. As Lillian M. Gilbreth noted (see Chapter 8), scientific management challenged this view by showing that "ordinary" people who were properly trained and organized could succeed as leaders. Under the influence of Gilbreth and other early behavioralists, the great-man theory began to be reevaluated for, at least, two reasons: (1) it was contended that if there were indeed "great men," or "natural leaders," it should be possible to investigate the traits that set them apart from the masses and (2) it was believed that if these unique traits could be identified, other individuals should be able to acquire them through learning and experience. It is, perhaps, no consequence that it was during this period that groups such as the Girl Guides (1909), Boy Scouts (1910), and Girl Scouts (1912) were founded. The creed of all these groups stresses the importance of traits such as kindness, reverence, obedience, and loyalty to success in life.

This logic prompted a wave of studies to discover the traits that, if acquired, would transform followers into leaders. Between 1904 and 1948, some 125 studies were conducted in an attempt to compare traits of successful leaders with those of their unsuccessful counterparts in the hope that the unique traits of the former could be identified.[41] A wide range of what are essentially personality traits were investigated, including knowledge assertiveness, enthusiasm, persistence, self-confidence, dependability, need for achievement, and social maturity. Physical attributes such as height, weight, energy, athletic ability, and attractiveness were also studied. Overall, the results were disappointing. Though certain relationships were found, these findings were generally weak, suggesting that the relationships were likely more incidental to leadership, than central.

The Behavioral Phase

Because the study of traits offered little evidence for distinguishing leaders from followers or for making the latter into the former, researchers in the 1940s began to question the existence of unique leader traits and shifted attention instead to leader behavior. This shift marked the beginning of the behavioral phase of leadership research, which held that leaders may be best characterized by how they behave, rather than by their personal traits. Underlying this phase was the assumption that leaders utilize a particular behavioral style that causes others to follow them. The behavioral phase is, perhaps, best represented by the Ohio State University Leadership Studies, conducted under the primary direction of Ralph M. Stogdill and Carroll L. Shartle, and University of Michigan Leadership Studies conducted under the direction of Rensis Likert, both discussed at length in Chapter 15.

---

[41] Ralph M. Stogdill, "Personal Factors Associated with Leadership: A Survey of the Literature," *Journal of Psychology* 25(1) (January 1948), pp. 35–71.

The Situational Phase

In the late 1960s, it was widely acknowledged that situational differences that might influence leader effectiveness deserved greater attention. As a consequence, leadership research began to shift toward a decidedly situational perspective. In doing so, it became increasingly clear that there is no one best style of leadership. The most effective style depends on factors unique to the prevailing situation. The first situational theory to be advanced was the "contingency theory of leadership," developed by Fred E. Fiedler.[42] This theory defines leader effectiveness in terms or work group performance. It holds that work group performance depends (or is contingent) on the match between a person's leadership style and the "favorableness" of the specific situation. Fiedler identified leadership style or manner of acting in a situation using a simple measure called the "least-preferred coworker" or LPC scale. The LPC asks respondents to think of all the individuals with whom they have ever worked and, using the scale, rate the one person with whom they worked *least well*. LPC items deal with personality attributes such as "friendly-unfriendly," "rejecting-accepting," and "distant-close." People who rate their least-preferred coworker in a relatively unfavorable manner are described as "task-oriented." Conversely, people who rate their least-preferred coworker in a relatively favorable manner are described as "relationship oriented." Fiedler also identified three factors that determined a situation's "favorableness": (1) "leader–member relations," or the degree to which a group trusted, liked, or was willing to follow a leader; (2) the "task structure," or the degree to which a task assignment was ill- or well-defined; and (3) "leader position power," or the formal authority as distinct from the personal power of a leader. Fiedler concluded that, judged on group performance, leaders who are task-oriented tended to be most effective in situations that are either very favorable or very unfavorable. They are more effective in favorable situation because relationship-oriented behaviors are superfluous. They are also the most effective in unfavorable situations because at least they get the job done. It is only in moderately favorable situations that leaders who are relationship-oriented tended to be the most effective because interpersonal relations are especially important. Although Fiedler's conclusions have been criticized, his findings imply that there is no such thing as a perfect leader for every situation and that anyone can be a leader by carefully selecting those situations that match one's leadership style.

Contemporary Leadership Theories

The state of contemporary leadership research is reflected in a recent review that identified 49 different leadership approaches or theories.[43] Given the voluminous literature in this area and the constraints of time and space, we limit our comments to three of the more popular current theories of leadership: charismatic leadership theory, transformational leadership theory, and leader–member exchange theory.

Taking its name from the Greek word *charisma*, meaning "divine gift," an interest in charismatic leadership may be traced to the work of Max Weber (see Chapter 10).[44] In distinguishing among types of authority, Weber discussed not only legal and traditional authority, but also the authority that derives from the charisma of a leader. A charismatic leader gets things done by attracting followers who trust, share the vision of, often attribute mystical powers to, and offer blind obedience to the leader. A special quality, charisma reaches people on an emotional,

---

[42] Fred E. Fiedler, *A Theory of Leadership Effectiveness* (New York: McGraw-Hill, 1967).

[43] Jeremy D. Meuser, William L. Gardner, Jessica E. Dinh, Jinyu Hu, Robert C. Liden, and Robert G. Lord, "A Network Analysis of Leadership Theory: The Infancy of Integration," *Journal of Management* 42(5) (July 2016), pp. 1374–1403.

[44] Max Weber, *The Theory of Social and Economic Organization,* trans. A. M. Henderson and Talcott Parsons, ed., Talcott Parsons (New York: Free Press, 1947), p. 301. Originally published 1922.

non-rational level, motivating them to extraordinary efforts. U.S. Presidents John F. Kennedy and Ronald Reagan are frequently cited examples of charismatic leaders. Both possessed intense magnetic charm that set them apart from others. In general, it has been suggested that when a leader possesses charisma, followers perform better. In particular, charismatic leaders are seen as engendering favorable outcomes by modeling a value system for followers, exuding competence and success, articulating an inspirational goal that is ideological rather than pragmatic, exhibiting high expectations, showing confidence in followers, and arousing their motivation. Whatever the consequences, charisma is likely a complex interaction of leader and follower characteristics, together with situational factors. Critics note, however, that effective leadership does not depend on charisma. U.S. Presidents Dwight D. Eisenhower and Harry S. Truman were singularly effective leaders, but neither was especially charismatic.

Transformational leadership is a second contemporary leadership theory. In the leadership literature, charismatic and transformational leadership are often discussed interchangeably.[45] This may be explained, perhaps, by the fact that in Bernard M. Bass's model of transformational leadership, the dominant research framework, charisma is but one part of becoming a transformational leader that involves inspiring followers to adopt more challenging goals, focusing efforts, and expressing important goals in influential ways.[46] The term *transformational* with regard to a form of leadership was coined by James MacGregor Burns to describe types of political leaders.[47] Research suggests that transformational-charismatic leaders emerge at particular times, such as when an organization declines and, consequently, revitalization and a renewed vision are needed. For this reason, transformational-charismatic leaders are often described as those who bring a vision of the major changes needed in an organization's structure, culture, market, and so on. It is not always clear, however, what would happen if a charismatic-transformational leader's intentions are not socially desirable; for instance, some historical figures (Adolf Hitler comes to mind) have demonstrated a personal magnetism and have led others in blind obedience toward evil ends. Transformational-charismatic leadership research has come under increasing criticism for various reasons. Perhaps most notably is that there appears to be no clear definition of transformational-charismatic leadership, making a comparison of results from different studies impossible.[48]

Leader–member exchange theory is the third and final contemporary theory of leadership to be discussed. Most leadership theories assume that a leader behaves in much the same way toward all followers. In contrast, leader–member exchange theory holds that leadership is a one-on-one exchange in which leaders behave differently with different work group members.[49] It further holds that followers, based on the quality of their interpersonal relationships (exchanges) with a leader, form different groups: an in-group (higher quality) and an out-group (lower quality).

Insiders and outsiders experience very different work outcomes. Leader interactions with insiders resemble social transactions, with leaders and followers exchanging resources and enjoying higher levels of trust and support. In this way, leader and follower become reciprocally interdependent. In contrast, in exchanges with outsiders, leaders act as supervisors, relying on formal authority to extract follower performance. At the extreme, leader exchanges with outsiders can be very mechanistic, arising from workplace rules, policies, and procedures, rather than spontaneous interaction. Such exchanges are typically characterized by low levels of trust, interaction,

[45] Meuser *et al.* "A Network Analysis of Leadership Theory: The Infancy of Integration," p. 1383

[46] Bernard M. Bass, *Leadership and Performance beyond Expectations* (New York: Free Press, 1985).

[47] James M. Burns, *Leadership* (New York: Harper & Row, 1978).

[48] Daan Van Knippenberg and Sim Sitkin, "A Critical Assessment of Charismatic-Transformational Leadership Research: Back to the Drawing Board?" *Academy of Management Annals* 7 (2013), p. 10.

[49] George B. Graen and Terri Scandura, "Toward a Psychology of Dyadic Organizing," *Research in Organizational Behavior* 9(1987), pp. 175–208.

support, and leader-provided rewards. Research suggests that, as a consequence of such differing treatments, in-group members perform better and are more satisfied than out-group members. Leader–member exchange theory underscores the fact that leader behavior originates, in part, in followers. That is, leadership is a mutual influence process. Leaders respond differently to different followers and both leaders and followers alter their behavior depending on the performance of the other.

Like other theories of leadership, leader–member exchange theory has not escaped criticism. For example, critics have taken particular exception to various methodological aspects of how leader–member exchanges are measured. Whereas leader–member exchange theory has been extended to investigate individual differences such as gender, Avolio and colleagues note that one promising area for future research would be to explore the implications of national culture on the development and quality of leader–member relationships and the resulting influence on workplace outcomes such as job satisfaction and performance.[50]

Attempts to summarize the evolution of leadership theory and research can be bewildering. After reviewing some 3,000 studies, in 1974, Ralph M. Stogdill observed: "Four decades of research on leadership have produced a bewildering mass of findings. . . . The endless accumulation of empirical data has not produced an integrated understanding of leadership."[51] Four decades would pass and Gary A. Yukl would similarly lament: "Thousands of studies on leader behavior and its effects have been conducted over the past half century, but the bewildering variety of behavior constructs used for this research makes it difficult to compare and integrate the findings."[52] To address this need, Yukl offered a hierarchical taxonomy of leadership behaviors comprised of four meta-categories and 15 components to interpret the results of leadership studies. The meta-categories resemble developments in the leadership literature over the past 60 or so years: (1) task-oriented behaviors, (2) relations-oriented behaviors, (3) change-oriented behaviors, and (4) external leadership behaviors. The component behaviors reflect task-oriented functions such as planning, clarifying, and monitoring operations; the relations-oriented activities are supporting, developing, recognizing, and empowering; the change-oriented behaviors involve advocating change, envisioning change, encouraging innovation, and facilitating collective learning; and the external-change behaviors are networking, representing, and external monitoring. The extent to which the meta-categories and component leadership behaviors in Yukl's taxonomy would be germane across cultures is, at yet, unknown. With this in mind, the next section reviews management research conducted in a non-Western context. In particular, we will consider Geert Hofstede's research on cultural differences in work-related values and the cross-cultural studies of Project GLOBE (Global Leadership and Organizational Behavioral Effectiveness).

Managing Across Borders

Geert Hofstede was among the first researchers to question the global applicability of Western-based theories of management, with their stress on market processes, emphasis on individuals, and focus on managers rather than workers. As noted above, he criticized Maslow, McClelland, Herzberg, and Vroom for their Freudian inclinations about the nature of human needs and aspirations, arguing that Freudian thinking did not fit other cultural patterns. Support for Hofstede's contention that Western-based theories of management were culturally limited evolved from a

---

[50] Bruce Avolio, Fred Walumbwa, and Todd J. Weber, "Leadership: Current Theories, Research, and Future Directions," *Annual Review of Psychology* 60 (2009), p. 434.

[51] Ralph M. Stogdill, *Handbook of Leadership: A Survey of Theory and Research* (New York: Free Press, 1974), p. xvii.

[52] Gary A. Yukl, "Effective Leadership Behavior: What We Know and What Questions Need More Attention," *Academy of Management Perspectives* 26(4) (November 2012), p. 66.

project he began in the early 1960s for the "HERMES" corporation (later revealed to be IBM).[53] Drawing on data collected in 53 countries and regions, he identified four basic societal-level work-related values (i.e., dimensions) across which different cultures could be compared: power-distance, uncertainty avoidance, individualism–collectivism, and masculinity–femininity. *Power-distance* relates to a culture's acceptance of hierarchy and relates to societal expectations about the degree of power inequality that is considered acceptable. In contrast to cultures where power differences are seen as acceptable, in those where equality is valued, participative management and joint decision-making are likely to be viewed more favorably. *Uncertainty avoidance* concerns a culture's tolerance of ambiguity and uncertainty. In cultures where structured interactions are preferred over unstructured processes, seniority-based systems, for example, would likely be valued over performance-based outcomes. *Individualism–collectivism* refers to the tendency within a culture to act as an individual or as a member of a group. In high-collectivism cultures rewarding teamwork rather than individual would likely to be viewed more favorably. *Masculinity–femininity* reflects a culture's preference for social differentiation between men and women. In a masculine culture that emphasizes the differences between the sexes, assertive competitive workplace behavior would likely be seen as more acceptable than in a feminine culture that valued quality of life and social relations.

When combined, Hofstede reported that these four dimensions explained some 50 percent of the cross-cultural differences in employees' work-related values. The remaining differences were country-specific. Hofstede found the United States to be below average on uncertainty avoidance (that is, more willing to take risks), whereas Japan was high on this dimension; Japan was high on masculinity, the Netherlands, low; France showed greater power distance (less equality) and somewhat more femininity; Asian countries appeared to be more long-term oriented, the United States less so. Hofstede and Bond later identified a fifth basic dimension: long-term versus short-term orientation, to account for certain Confucian influences in Eastern nations.[54] Labeled "Confucian Dynamism," this dimension reflects a future-minded perseverance in hard work and thrift, relationships ordered by status, and a "sense of shame." High Confucian Dynamism was found in Hong Kong, Taiwan, Japan, and South Korea (there were no data from the People's Republic of China) and in certain non-Confucian nations (such as Brazil and India).

As one example that work-related values influence the applicability of different management practices, Schuler and Rogocsky reported that the acceptability of compensation schemes varies across nations.[55] They found that compensation schemes based on seniority are more likely to be found in cultures where there are lower levels of uncertainty avoidance, whereas compensation practices based on individual performance are more prevalent in individualist cultures where there is a willingness to take risks. They further found that in cultures deemed "feminine," compensation practices that take employees' personal and social needs into consideration are more common than in "masculine" cultures; and employee-ownership plans (e.g., stock option plans) are more widespread in cultures with higher levels of individualism, lower levels of uncertainty avoidance, and high levels of power distance. As a second example, according to Greenberg, whereas a concern for justice is universal across cultures, justice standards are "highly particularistic," reflecting different internalized norms and values.[56] In highly individualistic cultures, such

[53] Geert Hofstede, *Culture's Consequences: International Differences in Work-Related Values* (London: Sage, 1980); *idem, Culture's Consequences: Comparing Values, Behavior, Institutions, and Organizations across Nations* (Thousand Oaks, CA: Sage, 2001).

[54] Geert Hofstede and Michael H. Bond, "The Confucian Connection: From Cultural Roots to Economic Growth," *Organizational Dynamics* 16(4) (Summer 1988), pp. 5–21.

[55] Randall S. Schuler and Nicolai Rogocsky, "Understanding Compensation Practice Variations across Firms: The Impact of National Culture," *Journal of International Business Studies* 29(1) (First Quarter 1998), pp. 159–177.

[56] Jerald Greenberg, "Studying Organizational Justice Cross-Culturally: Fundamental Challenges," *International Journal of Conflict Management* 12(4) (2001), p. 370.

as the United States, equity is preferred over equality. This contrasts with both the Netherlands, where people favor equality, and India, where people favor distributing outcomes according to needs. As a final example, Erez has observed that Quality Control Circles, as practiced in Japan, and autonomous work groups, such as implemented in Sweden, are less likely to be accepted in the United States due to cultural expectations relating to work autonomy and performance feedback.[57]

In discussing his research findings, Hofstede was clear that he did not mean to suggest that the five dimensions he studied were the only cultural values of importance and he stressed that his results only describe gross cultural differences and cannot be interpreted to apply to specific individuals. These limitations aside, Hofstede opened a door to an appreciation for international differences in work-related values and underscored that "the very theories . . . by which we derive our ideas and practices are cultural creations and can be so culture bound that while useful in the originating culture, they are rendered irrelevant or at least not very useful when transferred to other cultures."[58]

Project GLOBE

Robert J. House was the senior member of a team of more than 200 researchers in a cross-cultural study of societal culture and organizational behavior known as Project Global Leadership and Organizational Behavior Effectiveness (GLOBE).[59] Begun in the early 1990s, GLOBE's 25-plus-year study of 17,300 middle managers in 950 organizations in 62 societies is a long-term program to discover differences in societal-level work-related cultural values or dimensions that influence leader–follower behavior and relationships. The GLOBE Project has retained both Hofstede's power-distance and uncertainty-avoidance dimensions (relabeled long-term orientation to future orientation), and split his individualism–collectivism dimension into institutional-level collectivism (organizational and societal) and in-group collectivism (individual cohesiveness in their organizations/families). Hofstede's masculinity–femininity dimensions were expanded to include assertiveness, gender egalitarianism, humane orientation (the degree to which the group rewards others for caring, fairness, altruism, and so on), and performance orientation (the degree to which members of a collective reward individuals for performance improvement and excellence).

The GLOBE Project researchers identified 6 higher order global leadership dimensions comprised of various primary dimensions: *Charismatic/Value-Based Leadership* (including the primary dimensions: visionary, inspirational, integrity); *Team-Oriented Leadership* (including the primary dimensions: collaborative team orientation, team integrator, diplomatic); *Participative Leadership* (primary dimensions: nonparticipative, autocratic); *Humane-Oriented Leadership* (primary dimensions: modesty and humane orientation); *Autonomous Leadership* (a single dimension consisting of individualistic independence, autonomous, and unique attributes); and *Self-Protective Leadership* (including the primary dimensions: self-centered, conflict inducer, face saver oriented).[60] The researchers clustered the societies they studied by the degree to which they were *similar* in preference for each leader dimension and categorized them into higher,

[57] Miriam Erez, "Culture and Job Design," *Journal of Organizational Behavior* 31(2–3) (January 2010), pp. 389–400.

[58] Laura M. Milner, Dale Fodness, and Mark W. Speece, "Hofstede's Research on Cross-Cultural Work-Related Values: Implications for Consumer Behavior," *European Advances in Consumer Research* 1 (1993), p. 73.

[59] Robert J. House and Mansour Javidan, "Overview of GLOBE," in Robert J. House, Paul J. Hanges, Mansour Javidan, Peter W. Dorfman, and Vipin Gupta, eds., *Leadership, Culture, and Organizations: The GLOBE Study of 62 Societies* (London: Sage, 2004), pp. 11–16. See also Jagdeep S. Chhokar, Felix C. Brodbeck, and Robert J. House, eds., *Culture and Leadership across the World: The GLOBE Book of In-Depth Studies of 25 Societies* (Rahweh, NJ: Lawrence Erlbaum Associates, 2007).

[60] Peter W. Dorfman, Mansour Javidan, Paul Hanges, Ali Dastmalchian, and Robert A. House, "GLOBE: A Twenty Year Journey into the Intriguing World of Culture and Leadership," *Journal of World Business* 47(4) (October 2012), pp. 504–518.

middle, and lower groups based on the extent to which each dimension contributed to outstanding leadership. For example, charismatic/value-based leaders were preferred in countries such as the United States, Brazil, India, and Germany. Humane-oriented leaders were preferred in countries such as China, Egypt, and Japan. Autonomous leaders were preferred in countries such Russia, Egypt, and Germany. Leadership attributes such as "trustworthy, just, and honest" were found to be "universally desirable." Conversely, leadership attributes such as "irritable" and "ruthless" were found to be universally undesirable. There was, however, agreement that "in all cultures, leader team orientation and the communication of vision, values, and confidence in followers are reported to be highly effective leader behaviors."[61]

To their surprise, the GLOBE Project researchers concluded that national culture does not predict chief executive officer (CEO) leadership behaviors. Rather, they found CEO behavior to be associated with the extent to which CEOs act in accordance with a society's expectations for leaders. In this regard, the "fit" between what a society expects of its leaders and their behavior was found to be critical to CEOs' success. For example, in countries such as Germany, Brazil, and the United States where societal expectations endorse participative qualities, leaders who exhibit these attributes were found to be more effective, eliciting a high degree of commitment and effort among their followers.

Whereas the notion that there are leaders who can be successful across cultures is appealing, Hofstede's research and the GLOBE Project indicate that there are substantial differences in the attributes that managers need to be effective in different cultures. In brief, culture matters. A broad set of experiences and competencies is necessary for a manager to be a global leader. The GLOBE Project remains one of the most ambitious cross-cultural studies of leadership ever undertaken.

Organization Theory: A Continuing Venture

Whereas European scholars such as Vilfredo Pareto, Émile Durkheim, and Max Weber made major contributions to understanding the nature of organizations in the early 1900s, organization theory took an Anglo-American turn in the latter half of the twentieth century.

Aston Studies: Workflow Integration and Production Continuity[62]

Beginning in the 1960s, a number of English researchers, known as the Aston Group, began an ambitious study of the relationship between a firm's structure and technology. Under the direction of Derek Pugh and David Hickson, they studied the structural and technological characteristics of 52 firms located in Birmingham (England) and focused on two major facets of what they termed operation technology, meaning the equipping and sequencing of activities in a workflow.[63] These facets were workflow integration and production continuity. In contrast to Joan Woodward's earlier work, which concluded that a firm's success is directly related to a proper match between its technology and certain organizational characteristics,[64] they found only a weak relationship between workflow integration and various structural variables. In an attempt to

---

[61] Robert J. House, "Illustrative Examples of GLOBE Findings," in House, Hanges, Javidan, et al., p. 7.

[62] The remainder of this section draws on Arthur G. Bedeian and Raymond F. Zammuto, *Organizations: Theory and Design* (Hinsdale, IL: Dryden Press, 1991).

[63] David J. Hickson, Derek S. Pugh, and Diane Phessey, "Operations Technology and Organization Structure: An Empirical Appraisal," *Administrative Science Quarterly* 14(3) (September 1969), pp. 394–395.

[64] Joan Woodward, *Management and Technology* (London: Her Majesty's Stationery Office, 1958) and *idem, Industrial Organization: Theory and Practice* (London: Oxford University Press, 1965).

reconcile this result with Woodward's conclusions, the researchers found that organization size moderated the relationship between technology and structure, which led them to conclude that her findings were valid only for smaller organizations. This, the researchers believed, was contrary to the situation in larger organizations where "managers and administrators are buffered from the technology itself by the specialized departments, standard procedures, and formalized paperwork that size brings with it." An organization's size, not its technology, was therefore the primary determinant of organization structure.[65]

Thompson: Technological Interdependence

James D. Thompson offered an alternative view of technology, incorporating the notion of *technological interdependence*.[66] Thompson's work focused on how organizations cope with uncertainties created by a manager's cognitive limits and by events and influences that managers cannot control or predict. He developed a classification of three technologies—mediating, long-linked, and intensive—based on the mechanisms used to coordinate different types of workflow interdependence. Generally, the greater the problem-solving behavior required by a workflow, the more extensive the coordinating mechanism required to satisfy coordination needs.

Mediating technology entails the joining of independent clients or customers where subunits within an organization may not directly interact, but are interdependent and must perform adequately or other subunits falter: such as post offices, auction houses, and computer dating services. Typified by the mass-production assembly line, *long-linked technology* is characterized by the *sequential interdependence* of tasks or operations. The procedures necessary to complete a good or service are highly uniform and must be performed in a specified serial order, such as in relay teams and meat-packing firms. *Intensive technology* is characterized by *reciprocal interdependence* and exemplified by the use of a variety of different technologies and skills required to produce a good. The selection, mix, and sequence of techniques and skills used to produce a good at one stage of production are contingent on feedback from earlier production stages. Thus, the sequence of operations required to produce a good or service cannot be predetermined, such as with military combat teams, mental-health centers, basketball squads, and certain research and development projects. Of the various technological typologies that have been developed, Thompson's is generally considered to be the richest conceptually and has the advantage of being applicable to a wide variety of manufacturing and service organizations.

Contingency Theory

Contingency theory was developed in the late 1950s through 1960s as an outgrowth of the application of systems theory (see Chapter 21) to the social and behavioral sciences. Contingency theorists examined whether some organization designs fit different environmental conditions better than others, and concluded that managers should choose the design that best fits a firm's environment. A study by Tom Burns and George M. Stalker was the first major attempt to identify the types of organization structures and managerial practices appropriate for different environmental conditions.[67] Reminiscent of a metaphor used by Émile Durkheim to differentiate two modes for maintaining social order (i.e., "organic solidarity" and "mechanical solidarity"),[68]

[65] David J. Hickson, Derek S. Pugh, and Diane Phessey, "Operations Technology and Organization Structure: An Empirical Appraisal," *Administrative Science Quarterly* 14(3) (September 1969), pp. 394–395.

[66] James D. Thompson, *Organizations in Action* (New York: McGraw-Hill, 1967), pp. 15–18.

[67] Tom Burns and George M. Stalker, *The Management of Innovation* (London: Tavistock Publications, 1961), p. 5.

[68] Émile Durkheim, *The Division of Labor in Society*, trans. George Simpson (Glencoe, IL: Free Press, 1933), pp. 70, 105. Originally published in 1893.

Burns and Stalker identified two "divergent systems of management practice": *organic* and *mechanistic*. In organic systems, structure is flexible, tasks are loosely defined, and communication resembles consultation rather than order giving. Organic systems are especially appropriate for changing environments in which novel problems continually arise. In contrast, organizations with mechanistic systems are characterized by distinct functional specialties, precisely defined tasks and responsibilities, and a well-defined chain of command. Mechanistic systems, containing many bureaucratic elements, are particularly appropriate for stable environments. Burns and Stalker viewed organic and mechanistic systems as ideal types defining two ends of a continuum. They suggested that few, if any, management systems are purely mechanistic or purely organic; most combine characteristics of both. In addition, no part of their research indicated that one system is superior to the other. Rather, the nature of an organization's environment determines which system is appropriate.

Organizations and Their Environments

Paul R. Lawrence and Jay W. Lorsch built on Burns and Stalker's findings and studied 10 U.S. firms experiencing various levels of economic effectiveness in three different industry environments: plastics, consumer foods, and the container industry. The plastics industry was chosen because, at the time, it operated in a dynamic environment characterized by high rates of technological and scientific innovation and by rapidly changing customer needs and preferences. The container industry, on the other hand, had a stable environment, where customer needs were predictable and technical requirements were constant. Finally, the consumer foods industry environment was of intermediate stability, characterized by a moderate rate of change—slower than the plastics industry but faster than the container industry.

Lawrence and Lorsch argued that as an organization's environment becomes more complex and uncertain, it tends to differentiate into subunits. This structural differentiation leads to difference in subunit goals and structure, time perspectives, and interpersonal orientations, reflecting the task and environmental uncertainties with which each unit copes. They found that it is more difficult to integrate functional subunits' efforts as differentiation increases. *Integration* was "the process of achieving unity of effort among various subsystems in the accomplishment of [an] organization's tasks."[69] Perhaps most important, Lawrence and Lorsch reported that more economically effective organizations in each industry, with one exception, exhibited a higher degree of integration. A higher degree of differentiation was needed to deal with diverse and uncertain environmental demands and needed a matching degree of integration to achieve effective performance.

Consistent with Burns and Stalker's results, Lawrence and Lorsch's study implies that there is no universal best way to design an organization. The specific design of an organization and its subunits must "fit" its environment. Successful organizations are those able to diagnose and meet environmental requirements for differentiation and integration. Thus, appropriate patterns of structure vary, and they are contingent on the relationship between an organization and its environment.

Strategic Choice

John Child coined the term "strategic choice" and argued that contingency theory was in error "because it fails to give due attention to the agency of choice by whoever have the power to direct

---

[69] Paul W. Lawrence and Jay W. Lorsch, "Differentiation and Integration in Complex Organizations," *Administrative Science Quarterly* 12(1) (June 1967), pp. 3–4.

[an] organization."[70] Through strategy formulation and implementation, a management team can take steps to define and manipulate their organization's domains, thereby choosing to ignore or restrain environmental effects that might require modification of existing structural arrangements. In commenting further, Child noted: "In view of these essentially strategic and political factors, environmental conditions cannot be regarded as a direct source of variation in organizational structure, as open systems [contingency] theorists often imply."[71]

Resource-Dependence Theory

Jeffrey Pfeffer and Gerald R. Salancik advanced a resource-dependence theory of organization–environment relations.[72] They argued that most organizations are unable to internally generate all the resources necessary for their operations and, as a result, must enter into transactions with (and depend on) other organizations to obtain them. Relying on other resource suppliers creates uncertainty for an organization's managers. Managers, however, can reduce this uncertainty through their transactions with other organizations in a number of ways. For example, they can alter patterns of environmental dependence through mergers, diversification, and vertical integration; or through arrangements such as joint ventures, interlocking directorates, trade associations, coalitions, and cartels; or through promoting government regulations that increase barriers to entry, mandate price supports, limit foreign competition, and so on. Managers may likewise use the legal system to change an organization's environment, for example, by engaging in antitrust suits. Overall, strategic choice and the resource-dependence model direct attention to the many ways managers take deliberate actions to shape their organizations' environments.

Population Ecology

In the late 1970s, a more environmentally based approach to the study of organization–environment relations, known as *population ecology*, was proposed by Michael T. Hannan and John Freeman.[73] Population ecologists are interested in the processes that generate organizational diversity, and in how the diversity of organizational forms within industries and societies changes in response to long-term environmental pressures. Drawing heavily from the biological ecology literature, Hannan and Freeman suggested looking at changes in organizational populations rather than studying individual organizations to examine organizational adaptation. They stated that adaptation to changing environmental conditions takes place primarily through the creation of populations with new forms that replace existing populations. The reason, they proposed, is that there are strong inertial forces (such as sunk costs in plant, equipment, and personnel) in existing organizations that make it difficult for them to change.[74] Because existing organizations change slowly, new organizations taking advantage of emerging environmental opportunities have an opening to gain a foothold in an industry. The result, as Hannan and Freeman suggested, is that adaptation to environmental change occurs through the failure and replacement of existing organizations by new ones better suited to altered environmental conditions. A shortcoming of

---

[70] John Child, "Organizational Structure, Environment, and Performance: The Role of Strategic Choice," *Sociology* 6(1) (January 1972), p. 3.

[71] *Ibid.*, p. 10.

[72] Jeffrey Pfeffer and Gerald R. Salancik, *The External Control of Organizations: A Resource Dependence Perspective* (New York: Harper & Row, 1978).

[73] Michael T. Hannan and John Freeman, "The Population Ecology of Organizations," *American Journal of Sociology* 82(5) (March 1977), pp. 929–963.

[74] *Idem*, "Structural Inertia and Organizational Change," *American Sociological Review* 49(2) (April 1984), pp. 155–156.

this perspective, however, is that it fails to account for changes in the population of organizations such as occurred with the rise of new firms and industries in areas like biotechnology, pharmaceuticals, and information technology—changes that occurred several years after the authors stated their thesis. Nevertheless, the notion of firms and industries as changing populations is an interesting view of the dynamic competitive arena.

It is important to understand that these differences in perspective are more a matter of beliefs about how environment–strategy–structure alignment occurs than the nature of this alignment. Contingency theorists, strategic-choice advocates, and population ecologists largely agree about the patterns of organizational design that fit different environmental conditions. These approaches complement each other and, by viewing them together, they provide a richer understanding of the relationship between structure, strategy, and environment.

In the years since the Aston Studies, numerous theories have been advanced, multinational enterprise has flourished, we have learned more about other nations, and information and communication technologies have evolved. Some, however, feel relatively little progress has been made in designing organization structures for achieving and sustaining a competitive advantage. Donaldson found organization theory "fragmented . . . [of] an anti-management quality . . . [and] long on assertion and short on empirical evidence."[75] Van de Ven agreed it was a "buzzing, blooming, confusing world" of organization and management theories resulting in "a tower of babbling and fragmented explanations" of differing paradigms, but was not perturbed by this, although these paradigms might be confusing and lacking empirical support, they were healthy signs of pursuit of knowledge.[76]

Subsequently, Miner identified 28 organization theories and found 8 "high" in estimated importance and scientific validity. The judges of Miner's theories were past presidents of the Academy of Management and past editors and editorial reviewers from the Academy's research and theory journals—knowledgeable academics. The application of these theories was in doubt: "Yet we have to a degree lost sight of the usefulness criterion, and the matter of practical application; perhaps some believe we have become too academic . . . [but] there is more to accomplish . . . a solid base has been created on which to build the future."[77] For Gerald F. Davis, it was a Cambrian explosion: "Organization theory has amassed an impressive armory of theoretical constructs and mechanisms over the past half-century . . . but at this stage in the field's development there is perhaps more value in careful empirical work on substantively important problems, even if its contribution to theory is minimal."[78] The venture continues as we learn and understand the past to advance teaching and scholarship and to incentivize studies that will increase our understanding and that of those we profess to serve.

U.S. Theories Abroad

Results of studies conducted in other nations signaled the singularity of organization theories and perspectives originating in the United States. As recalled by Geert Hofstede, the European Group for Organization Studies (EGOS) was formed (1974) to make research being conducted in different European countries more well-known and to thereby highlight "the influence of nationality

---

[75] Lex Donaldson, *American Anti-Management Theories of Organization: A Critique of Paradigm Proliferation* (Cambridge, England: Cambridge University Press, 1995), p. xi.

[76] Andrew H. Van de Ven, "The Buzzing, Blooming, Confusing World of Organization and Management Theory: A View from Lake Wobegon University," *Journal of Management Inquiry* 8 (June 1999), p. 119.

[77] John B. Miner, "The Rated Importance, Scientific Validity, and Practical Significance of Organizational Behavior Theories," *Academy of Management Learning & Education* 2(3) (September 2003), p. 262.

[78] Gerald F. Davis, "Do Theories of Organization Progress?" *Organizational Research Methods* 13(4) (October 2010), p. 707.

on organization theories".[79] With a similar intent, *Organization Studies* was found in 1980 as a European journal to provide an alternative way to look at organizations not reflected in dominant U.S. journals. Both of these events furthered the demise of the "culture-free hypothesis" as it became increasingly obvious that organizations are bound by national cultures. Hofstede has observed that not only are organizations culture bound, but so are organization theorists. He writes: "Give me a new theory and I will tell you the nationality of its author."[80] In Hofstede's opinion, organization theorists in the United States are driven by the market, the French by power, the Germans by rules, the Dutch by consensus, the Chinese by family, and he concludes there will be no universal theory of organizations because of cultural differences.[81] Hofstede adds that "[m]ore and more organizations are crossing national borders, and thus differences in nationality are increasingly a source of conflicts and contradictions in organizations."[82] As a consequence, negotiations between representatives from different countries are almost certain to be difficult unless an appreciation of cultural differences is front and center in any such situations.

In an interesting aside, Hofstede noted that whereas East Asia is fully developed economically, there are few "native theories" of organization, most having been formulated by individuals from Europe, the United States, and other non–East Asian countries.[83] For instance, Richard D. Whitley, an Englishman, has argued that the dominant forms of organizing in Japan, South Korea, and Taiwan reflect the values of a long-term orientation, desire for stability (uncertainty avoidance), group rewards (collectivism), personal authority relationships, and loyalty to an enterprise as a whole. Similar values shaped the powerful Japanese business alliances known as *keiretsu*, family-owned conglomerates (*chaebol*) in South Korea, and Chinese family businesses in Taiwan. Despite some variations, the basic form of organizing expatriate Chinese family businesses is similar in countries such as Taiwan, Hong Kong, and Thailand. Whitley concludes that "(a) there are a variety of forms of business organization which are competitive in world markets; (b) these vary in certain basic characteristics because of the institutional environment in which they become established, and (c) to a considerable extent, they are societally specific in that they would not function as effectively in different societal contexts."[84] All this suggests that a universal theory of organizations may be a false hope.

SUMMARY

As we moved toward the near present in understanding people and organizations, numerous developments shaped the evolution of management thought as human relations as a movement was overtaken by the emergence of a new generation of scholars devoted to the study of what became known as "organizational behavior." Moving beyond the "feel-good" reputation of human relations, organizational-behavior researchers addressed issues such as job design, work motivation, and effective leadership in an analytical fashion. Similarly, personnel management as a field began to build a firmer empirical base and over time evolved into HRM and, then, SHRM. At about the same time, organization theorists begin to debate the effect of technology on an organization's structure and explore how organizations adapt to ensure a proper "fit" between their management processes, structures, and strategies and changing environments. With the growing globalization of business following World War II, and the increasing need to manage with an appreciation of diverse cultures, there was also a growing focus on understanding differences in workplace dynamics across borders and how different national cultures might influence the applicability of management theories and practice. This chapter reviewed each of these developments.

---

[79] Geert Hofstede, "An American in Paris: The Influence of Nationality of Organization Theories," *Organization Studies* 17(3) (1996), p. 525.

[80] *Ibid.*, p. 531.

[81] *Ibid.*, pp. 534–535.

[82] *Ibid.*, p. 535.

[83] *Ibid.*

[84] Richard D. Whitley, "East Asian Enterprise Structures and the Comparative Analysis of Forms of Business Organization," *Organization Studies* 11(1) (1990), p. 69.

Science and Systems in an Information Age

Numbers have always held a fascination for humanity; people have ascribed mystical powers to some numbers, malignant qualities to others, and throughout history have used numbers to tally flocks of sheep as well as to reach for the stars. Numbers have no intrinsic value in themselves, but by lending a preciseness and orderliness to the world, they have become symbols of the continued quest for knowledge. An inborn inquisitiveness has led humans to explore, to attempt to explain the inexplicable, and to search for a force that binds the complexities observed in nature into some logical scheme. Humans have sought to bring order from chaos by searching for interrelationships among observed events and activities since time immemorial.

The preceding chapters have described numerous attempts to increase the technical efficiency and effectiveness. The need for reliable and valid information to gauge an organization's performance and monitor external events is also ancient. In earlier chapters, we saw how new technologies, such as the telegraph, enabled managers to systematically gather, record, and use information to make decisions. This chapter extends these deep roots to trace the emergence of operations research and management science, the new language of production/operations management, the rise of Japanese industry from the ashes of World War II, and the search for world-class manufacturing. The chapter concludes with a discussion of general systems theory, cybernetics, and the arrival of the "digital hand" of the Information Age.

The Quest for Science in Management

The scientific method denotes an objective approach to problem-solving through a statement of hypotheses, data collection and analysis, and the selection of a course of action based on the ensuing results. In breaking with the mystics who held that reality was unknowable, Aristotle laid the foundation for modern scientific inquiry.[1] After the fall of the Roman empire in the fifth century, scientific reason yielded to the Age of Faith, only to reemerge with the beginning of the Italian Renaissance in the late fourteenth century. It was during the Renaissance that the foundations for modern mathematics and science were established. René Descartes thought the world operated mechanistically and prescribed the use of mathematics to describe its movements.[2] Isaac Newton developed calculus and laws of motion and gravitation, furthering Descartes's conception of the world as a giant machine.[3] Mathematics was the building block for bringing the parts together into one grand formula. The rediscovery of Aristotle during this period of enlightenment and a renewed interest in mathematics and science led to vast technological changes that became known as the Industrial Revolution (see Chapter 4).

Charles Babbage, and to some extent Andrew Ure, applied a scientific approach to solving the challenges of the burgeoning factory system during the Industrial Revolution (see Chapter 4). Industrialization demanded order and predictability, and in the early twentieth century engineers such as Frederick W. Taylor, Carl G. Barth, Henry L. Gantt, the Gilbreths, and Harrington Emerson led the way in scientifically studying and systematizing work (see Chapters 7 and 8). The seeds of the modern industrial corporation—the forerunner of today's *Fortune* 500 company—were sown during this era.

Operations Research (OR)

World War I gave widespread recognition and acceptance to the use of a scientific approach to management as evidenced in Gantt's work for the Emergency Fleet Corporation and Wallace Clark's efforts for the U.S. Shipping Board (see Chapter 8). For more than 3 decades, the work of Gantt, Taylor, and other scientific-management proponents was carried forward and known as "industrial administration" or, more commonly, "production management." The goal during these years, however, was to improve the technical efficiency of a firm's industrial operations, rather than on the responsibilities of general management. Outside events would soon intervene, giving rise to a new focus.

World War II brought managers, government officials, and scientists together to bring order and rationality to the logistics of global hostilities. The British formed the first operations-research (OR) groups comprised of various specialists to bring their diverse knowledge together to develop radar systems, perfect ground-to-air and air-to-air gunnery, design antisubmarine measures, guide bombing runs, and provide civilian defense.[4] One of the best-known OR groups was under the direction of Patrick M. S. Blackett, an experimental physicist. Called "Blackett's circus," it was an interdisciplinary group that included three physiologists, two mathematical physicists, one astrophysicist, one army officer, one surveyor, one general physicist, and two mathematicians. It was in groups such as this that various specialists were brought together to solve the complex challenges of "modern" warfare.

---

[1] Aristotle, "Analytica Priora," ["Prior Analysis"], trans. Arthur J. J. Jenkinson in W. David Ross, ed., *The Works of Aristotle*, vol. 1 (Oxford: Clarendon Press, 1908). Written circa 350 BCE.

[2] René Descartes, *Discourse on the Method of Rightly Conducting the Reason and Seeking Truth in the Sciences*, trans. John Veitch (Chicago, IL: Open Court Publishing Company, 1899). Originally written in 1637.

[3] Isaac Newton, *Philosophiæ Naturalis Principia Mathematica* [*Mathematical Principles of Natural Philosophy*] (London: Joseph Streater, 1687).

[4] Joseph F. McClosky, "The Beginnings of Operations Research: 1934–1941," *Operations Research* 35(1) (January–February) (1987), pp. 143–152.

OR was conceived as the application of scientific knowledge and methods to the study of complex problems with the stated purpose of deriving a quantitative basis for decisions. Whereas the British formed the first OR groups, U.S. industrial organizations and private consulting firms, such as Arthur D. Little, Inc., as well as nonprofit institutions such as RAND Corporation soon followed suit.[5] The Operations Research Society of America (ORSA) was founded in 1952. It began publishing its flagship journal *Operations Research* the same year. Formed the next year, The Institute of Management Sciences (TIMS) sought "to identify, extend, and unify scientific knowledge that contributes to the understanding of the practice of management."[6] It began publishing the journal *Management Science* in 1954. ORSA and TIMS merged in 1995 to form the Institute for Operations Research and the Management Sciences (INFORMS).

The application of operations-research techniques came very naturally to production management, an area with structured problems (such as optimizing economic order quantities for inventories, service scheduling and dispatching, determining economic batch sizes, and quality control) where decision rules could be rationally devised. The Gilbreths spoke of the "one best way" as the objective of their scientific analysis (see Chapter 8). The "management scientists" merely put the quest more euphemistically: "The approach of optimality analysis is to take various alternatives into account and to ask which of these possible sets of decisions will come closest to meeting the businessman's objectives (i.e., which decisions will be best or optimal)."[7] The old school and the "new" management scientists both sought to apply the scientific method to rationally evaluate alternatives in an effort to make the best possible decisions. Operations research and management science were not so much the search for a science of management as a striving for the use of science *in* management. In this endeavor, the tools of mathematics and science were enlisted to solve the age-old challenge of optimally allocating society's scarce resources. This would, in turn, reshape the prevailing view of production management.

Production Management in Transition

The Gordon and Howell report on higher education in business had few kind words for production management: "Production management courses are often the repository for some of the most inappropriate and intellectually stultifying materials to be found in the business curriculum . . . many faculty members have little respect for such courses . . . and students complained more strongly to us about the pointlessness of the production requirement than of any other."[8] It was also critical of the typical business school's failure to require baseline math skills for a degree. In response, business schools began to incorporate statistics and mathematics in their curricula, and a new genre of production management textbooks emerged, heavily emphasizing operations-research techniques. The outcome for management education was a blend of the old and the new that became known as "production/operations management."

The new language of production/operations management was heavily oriented toward statistics and mathematics. As the scientific method was at its base, its body was comprised of specific techniques for quantifying variables and relationships; at its apex were models for optimally allocating scarce resources. Techniques such as probability theory, linear programming, queuing theory, decision trees, and simulation were an essential part of the new language. Probability theory was used in drawing random samples for quality control; linear programming facilitated the allocation of limited resources among competing uses to maximize benefits or minimize

[5] William Thomas, "Operations Research vis-à-vis Management at Arthur D. Little and the Massachusetts Institute of Technology in the 1950s," *Business History Review* 86(1) (Spring 2012), pp. 99–122.

[6] Merrill M. Flood, "The Objectives of TIMS," *Management Science* 2(2) (January 1956), p. 178.

[7] William J. Baumol, *Economic Theory and Operations Analysis* (Englewood Cliffs, NJ: Prentice Hall, 1961), p. 4.

[8] Robert A. Gordon and James E. Howell, *Higher Education for Business* (New York: Columbia University Press, 1959), p. 190.

losses; and queuing theory helped achieve an optimal balance between the cost of increasing service and the amount of time individuals, machines, or materials must wait for service. Decision trees could be drawn to calculate the benefits or costs likely to result from alternative courses of action. Competitive strategies could be developed utilizing game theory; simulation could be used to imitate different conditions so that the likely outcomes of different competitive strategies could be compared.

Along with applying these techniques, "decision theorists" sought to combine economic concepts such as utility and choice with probability theory to assess conditions of risk and uncertainty.[9] These applications also reshaped business-school curricula and created a new set of staff specialists with whom managers had to communicate. Postwar developments in computer technology furthered Gantt's early work with progress and performance bar charts (see Chapter 8). Beginning in 1956, the DuPont Company developed a computerized network method for planning and controlling, which became known as the Critical Path Method (CPM). At about the same time, the U.S. Navy, Lockheed Aircraft Corporation, and management consultants Booz, Allen & Hamilton created the Program Evaluation and Review Technique (PERT) for mapping the activities necessary for constructing the Polaris missile. PERT and CPM rely on diagrams depicting the interrelationships across time among those events and activities composing a project. These diagrams, called "networks," allow managers to total the required time for each activity along every sequence—or path—of activities necessary for project completion. The path having the longest time is the "critical path," indicating the earliest date that a project can be completed. Having identified the critical path, project managers can focus their attention on either reducing the time of activities in this path or at least watch closely for any delays. Although PERT and CPM are more complex than this brief description implies, they are really little more than Gantt's pioneering bar-charts enriched by increased computing power.

In brief, operations researchers, management scientists, and decision theorists reshaped the earlier notions of "industrial administration" or "production management." The techniques that they developed and applied enhanced the academic credibility of production/operations management in U.S. business schools. It would take a competitive challenge from abroad, however, to move production/operations management to a new stage of development.

"If Japan Can . . . Why Can't We?"

On June 24, 1980, a NBC television documentary titled *If Japan Can . . . Why Can't We?* was aired in the United States. It highlighted the rise of Japanese industry from the ashes of World War II to become a leader in the production of high-quality goods and is considered one of the most important events in the U.S. quality movement. Of note, the documentary credited U.S. engineer W. Edward Demings as the major force behind Japan's post–World War II success.

Quality and Quality Circles

After World War II, as part of U.S. efforts to revive the Japanese economy, a series of events occurred that would make Japan an industrial phoenix. The Japanese productivity "miracle" was based on ideas introduced by two U.S. civilian communication engineers given the task of helping Japanese industry rebuild. Charles W. Protzman, III, and Homer M. Sarasohn, assigned to the Civil Communications Section, Supreme Command for the Allied Powers, presented two seminars (in Tokyo in 1949 and Osaka in 1950) for Japanese executives on "the fundamentals of

---

[9] See, for example, David W. Miller and Martin K. Starr, *Executive Decisions and Operations Research* (Englewood Cliffs, NJ: Prentice Hall, 1960); *idem, The Structure of Human Decisions* (Englewood Cliffs, NJ: Prentice Hall, 1967).

industrial management."[10] Thereafter, the seminars were conducted by Nikkeiren, the federation of Japanese employers' associations, and continued until 1974. As Protzman was "on loan" from the Hawthorne Works of the Western Electric Company, his understanding of statistical quality control was based on the work of Walter A. Shewhart.[11]

Shewhart had begun working on quality-control problems at AT&T's Bell Telephone Laboratories (located in New Jersey) during the early 1920s. His goal was to replace the phrase "as alike as two peas in a pod" with "as alike as two telephones." He took samples of output and applied statistical analysis to identify variations in quality. Shewhart understood that there would always be some random variation in output over which workers had no control. Over numerous trials, however, there would be some limits to this random variation. It was what happened outside these limits that could be examined for corrective action. Shewhart is often referred to as the "Father of Statistical Quality Control." He described the basic principles of this new discipline in 1931 book *Economic Control of Quality of Manufactured Product*.[12] It would be one of Shewhart's followers, however, who would popularize statistical quality control in Japan during the post–World War II years.[13]

W. Edwards Deming was educated as a mathematical physicist. As an expert on statistical sampling, he was employed by the War Department during World War II to teach engineers how to use Shewhart's quality-control techniques in the production of war materiel. In 1947, he went to Japan to help prepare for an upcoming population census. Deming was pleased when Kenichi Koyanagi, managing director of the Union of Japanese Scientists and Engineers (JUSE), invited him (in 1950) to present a series of lectures on quality control. Koyanagi and his colleagues had continued their study of U.S. manufacturing methods after Sarasohn and Protzman's departure and had read Shewhart's 1931 book, as well as a set of lectures he had given at the U.S. Department of Agriculture. The lectures had been edited by Deming.[14]

Deming lectured and consulted in Japan for 3 decades.[15] Whereas U.S. audiences first became aware of Deming through the aforementioned NBC documentary, they did not find a smiling face. Deming was critical of U.S. management, perhaps because he had been ignored for so long, but more likely because U.S. firms were losing market share to other more quality oriented and productive foreign competitors. As he explained: "The wealth of a nation depends on its people, management, and government, more than its natural resources. The problem is where to find good management. It would be a mistake to export American management to a friendly country."[16]

Deming identified Seven Deadly Diseases of Management that were barriers to improved quality:

1. Lack of constancy of purpose to plan product and service that will have a market and keep the company in business, and provide jobs.

2. Emphasis on short-term profits: short-term thinking (just the opposite from constancy of purpose to stay in business), fed by fear of unfriendly takeover, and by push from bankers and owners for dividends.

---

[10] Kenneth Hopper and William Hopper, *The Puritan Gift: Reclaiming the American Dream Amidst Global Financial Chaos* (London: I. B. Taurus, 2009), pp. 290–327. See also Robert C. Wood, "A Lesson Learned and a Lesson Forgotten," *Forbes* (February 6, 1989), pp. 70–78, for Sarasohn's recollections of these events.

[11] Hopper and Hopper, *The Puritan Gift,* p. 442.

[12] Walter A. Shewhart, *Economic Control of Quality of Manufactured Product* (New York: D. Van Nostrand, 1931).

[13] Joe Stauffer, "SQC before Deming: The Works of Walter Shewhart," *Journal of Applied Management and Entrepreneurship* 8(4) (October 2003), pp. 86–94.

[14] Walter A. Shewhart with the editorial assistance of W. Edwards Deming, *Statistical Method from the Viewpoint of Quality Control* (Washington, DC: Graduate School, Department of Agriculture, 1939).

[15] For a discussion of Deming's work in Japan, see Peter B. Petersen, "The Contributions of W. Edwards to Japanese Management Theory and Practice," in Frank S. Hoy, ed., *Proceedings of the Annual Meeting of the Academy of Management* (1987), pp. 133–137.

[16] W. Edwards Deming, *Out of the Crisis* (Cambridge, MA: Center for Advanced Engineering Study, Massachusetts Institute of Technology, 1986), p. 6.

3. Evaluation of performance, merit rating, or annual review.

4. Mobility of management; job hopping.

5. Management by use only of visible figures, with little or no consideration of figures that are unknown or unknowable.

6. Excessive medical costs.

7. Excessive costs of liability, swelled by lawyers that work on contingency fees.[17]

Deming attributed 95 percent of all errors to the systems under which people worked, not the people themselves. He believed that quality control began with an organization's top managers, not with its lower level employees. The goal was the reduction of variations in quality through continuous improvement (*Kaizen*). Deming's slogan was "Plan-Do-Act," an iterative cycle that provides feedback for continual improvement. Deming repeatedly berated U.S. managers for their faults, igniting a quality-control revolution.[18]

Joseph M. Juran was another significant contributor to the early quality-control movement. Juran, who had also worked at the Western Electric Company's Hawthorne Works, and, like Deming, was taken with Shewhart's ideas on statistical quality control. After World War II, Juran resigned from Western Electric to become a quality-control consultant for Wallace Clark & Co. He subsequently formed his own consulting firm.[19] In 1954, the JUSE invited Juran to Japan to aid in its rebuilding efforts. Expanding on the work of Vilfredo Pareto, Juran popularized the notion that 80 percent of the defects in production are caused by 20 percent of the causes of all defects.[20] Juran, thus, advised managers to work on their most critical problems first, which he called the "vital few," before moving on to resolve the "trivial many."

Kaoru Ishikawa was a professor of engineering at the University of Tokyo. He gave voice to Shewhart, Deming, and Juran and is generally considered a key figure in developing "quality circles."[21] Quality circles are comprised of a group of employees who are brought together to discuss ways to improve the quality of a product or service. Ishikawa's work at the U.S. Kawasaki Plant in Lincoln, Nebraska, led to the adoption of quality circles at Hewlett-Packard Company and a host of additional firms.

Kaoru Ishikawa. Courtesy of Ichiro Kotsuka, Managing Director Union of Japanese Scientists and Engineers (JUSE).

Others would advance the quality-control mantle, including Armand V. Feigenbaum, who began his career at General Electric Co. and coined the phrase "total quality control," forerunner of GE's well-known "six sigma" quality program. Philip Crosby originated the "zero defects" concepts, believing that the benefits derived from implementing a quality philosophy far outweighed its costs, declaring "Quality is free." Those in Japan that continued Ishikawa's work included Genichi Taguchi, director of the Japan Industrial Technology Institute; Taiichi Ohno and Shigeo Shingo, at Toyota Motor Corporation; and Ichiro Ueno, son of Yōichi Ueno, who promoted scientific management in Japan (see Chapter 11).

---

[17] *Ibid.*, pp. 97–98.

[18] For more on Deming, see Peter B. Petersen, "Library of Congress Archives: Additional Information about W. Edwards Deming (1900–1993) Now Available," *Journal of Management History* 3(2) (1997), pp. 98–119.

[19] John Butman, *Juran: A Lifetime of Influence* (New York: John Wiley & Sons, 1997), pp. 75–76.

[20] See Vilfredo Pareto, *Cours d'économie politique* [*A Course on Political Economics*], 2 vols. (Lausanne: F. Rouge, 1896–1897).

[21] Greg Watson, "The Legacy of Ishikawa," *Quality Progress* 39(4) (April, 2004), pp. 54–57.

The Toyota Production System and Lean Manufacturing

Taiichi Ohno is known for developing the Toyota Production System, referred to as "lean manufacturing."[22] In particular, he is credited with the widespread acceptance of "just-in-time" inventory management. When asked how he got the idea for having suppliers deliver materials to a factory on the day they are needed (thus eliminating costly inventories), Ohno replied that it came to him from reading about Henry Ford's experiences at the Ford Motor Company.[23] Ford—but primarily Ernest Kanzler, his son-in-law—developed the idea of reducing inventory "float" by coordinating the arrival of raw materials.[24] This allowed Ford Motors to transform a myriad of parts into automobiles that could be on dealers' lots in 14 (rather 28) days, minimizing the cost of holding inventory. In a similar fashion, Toyota's assembly line, designed by Ohno, with the assistance of Shigeo Shingo, *pulled* parts in the necessary quantities "just-in-time," eliminating the need to maintain expensive stockpiles of materials.

Globalization and the International Organization for Standardization

Whereas the efforts of Deming, Juran, and others in the years following World War II highlighted the competitive advantage to be gained by global corporations bringing lower prices and quality products to an expanding share of the world's population, an interest in quality standards may be traced to the early twentieth century. The British Engineering Standards Committee was established in 1901 and the American Engineering Standards Committee in 1916.[25] Both groups sought to develop quality standards applicable across products, industries, and nations. The British Engineering Standards Committee is now known as the BSI Group, and the American Engineering Standards Committee has become the American National Standards Institute. On the international front, the International Federation of the National Standardizing Associations (ISA) was organized in 1926. In 1947, the ISA joined with the newly formed United Nations Standards Coordinating Committee to create the International Organization for Standardization (ISO), based in Geneva. The ISO is comprised of 162 member countries. The acronym (ISO) comes from the Greek meaning "equal." The ISO provides companies with standards to ensure that their products and services meet customer requirements. The latest standards, known as ISO 9000, emphasize the joint involvement of customers, employers, and employees in pursuit of continuous quality improvement.

Seeking World-Class Manufacturing

In 1980, Robert H. Hayes and William J. Abernathy charged that U.S. industry had forgotten how to compete, produce efficiently, keep prices down, and maintain product quality.[26] As global competition mounted, a renewed interest in production/operations management emerged. In contrast to the earlier focus of production management on improving the technical efficiency of a

---

[22] Taiichi Ohno, *Toyota Production System: Beyond Large-Scale Production* (New York: Productivity Press, 1988). Originally published in 1978.

[23] Norman Bodek, "Forward," *Today and Tomorrow* by Henry Ford (with the collaboration of Samuel Crowther) (Cambridge, MA: Productivity Press, 1988), p. vii. Originally published in 1926.

[24] Peter B. Petersen, "The Misplaced Origin of Just-in-Time Production Methods," *Management Decision* 40 (2002), pp. 82–88. See also *idem*, "The Light before the Dawn: The Origin of Quality Japanese Products During the 1920s," *Journal of Managerial Issues* 5(1) (Spring 1993), pp. 17–38.

[25] JoAnne Yates and Craig N. Murphy, "From Setting National Standards to Coordinating International Standards: The Foundation of the ISO," *Business and Economic History* (On-line) 4 (2006). See also *idem, The International Organization for Standardization (ISO): Global Governance through Voluntary Consensus* (London: Routledge Press, 2009).

[26] Robert H. Hayes and William J. Abernathy, "Managing Our Way to Economic Decline," *Harvard Business Review* 58(4) (July–August 1980), pp. 67–77.

firm's industrial operations, there was a call for viewing a company's product decisions as an aspect of its overall competitive strategy.[27] The challenge was whether the United States, in particular, could relearn the quality and efficiency lessons that it had been teaching the rest of the world since the scientific-management era.

To respond to this challenge, the desire to become "world-class" and the notion of "best practices" became popular.[28] "Best practices" involves identifying other companies whose performance is deemed superior and learning the reasons for their success. "World-class" is a term used to describe a company recognized as outstanding in its industry. A key part of becoming world-class involves "benchmarking," a process in which a company measures its performance against industry leaders in areas such as quality control and product design. Once a company is able to determine how others are able to achieve higher performance, it then uses this information to improve its own performance. Both "best practices" and striving to become "world-class" are attempts to learn from industry leaders.

As Hayes and Pisano have warned, however, "If managers pin their competitive hopes on the implementation of a few best-practice approaches, they implicitly abandon the central concept of a strategy in favor of a generic approach to competitive success."[29] If everyone is following best practices, how will companies differ? Companies seek to be different, or to offer the appearance of being different, so as to gain a competitive advantage in the marketplace. A "me-too" strategy simply based on imitating competitors is seldom a long-term recipe for success.

Systems and Information

Throughout history, people have observed order in nature. They saw an ecological balance in plant and animal life; noted that the planets and stars moved in predictable patterns and used them to chart their lives; and followed a rhythm in the coming and going of seasons to plant and harvest their crops. Primitive people built their lives around rituals that were a part of this natural order; such ceremonies gave them a sense of security.

As people designed organizations, they sought the same order they observed in nature. Early factory managers followed the dictates of systematic management to arrange their workplaces, assure the proper flow of materials, and facilitate the accomplishment of desired goals. Behavioralists spoke of social systems, studied workplaces as sociotechnical systems, and noted the need for equilibrium both within an organization and in relation to its surrounding environment. Each of these applications shares a number of common characteristics: (1) a goal or purpose; (2) presumed inputs, or what we have termed factors of production, which may include people, materials, money, or information; (3) transformation of these inputs into goods or services; and (4) feedback about whether the intended goal or purpose is met. This cycle of inputs, transformations, outputs, and feedback must be maintained if an organization is to exist over time. That is to say, an organization can only survive if it is capable of producing outputs that can be exchanged for the energy necessary to obtain new inputs and also to maintain itself in operating order. In a business setting, the value of the outputs an organization produces is measured by the amount that buyers are willing to pay for the goods and services it provides.

---

[27] Wickham Skinner, "Manufacturing – Missing Link in Corporate Strategy," *Harvard Business Review* 47(3) (May–June 1969), pp. 136–145.
[28] Robert H. Hayes and Steven C. Wheelwright, *"Restoring our Competitive Edge: Competing through Manufacturing* (New York: John Wiley & Sons, 1984), pp. 375–385. See also Richard J. Schonberger, *World Class Manufacturing: The Lessons of Simplicity Applied* (New York: Free Press, 1986).
[29] Robert H. Hayes and Gary P. Pisano, "Beyond World Class: The New Manufacturing Strategy," *Harvard Business Review* 72(1) (January–February, 1994), p. 77.

A business is considered profitable if this value exceeds the collective cost of procuring and transforming inputs into outputs. If excess profits exist, they can be held in reserve for hard times or used to finance growth.

General Systems Theory and Cybernetics

Although Chester I. Barnard (see Chapter 14) viewed organizations as open systems that included investors, suppliers, customers, and others, it was not until the 1960s that systems theory made an impact on management thought. K. Ludwig von Bertalanffy, a biologist, is credited with coining the phrase "general systems theory."[30] He noted the "openness" of all systems; that is, all organisms are both affected by and affect their environment. "Organism" has the same Greek and Latin roots as "organization," and both deal with the function, structure, and relationship of parts to a whole. It became appropriate, then, to think in terms of an organization as an open system; meaning a system that depends on other systems for its inputs (people, money, materials, and so forth) and, thus, cannot exist in isolation. An organization's managers cannot solve a production problem, for example, without considering whether supplier organizations (systems) will ship necessary materials on time or at a mutually acceptable price. As the work of Lawrence and Lorsch concluded, organization–environment interactions are crucial to understanding organization design (see Chapter 20).

Bertalanffy's efforts were an initial piece in a jigsaw puzzle from which others began to build. Norbert Wiener derived the word *cybernetics* from the Greek *kubernētēs*, meaning pilot or person at the helm, to label the study of organisms and machines as self-regulating systems.[31] Being self-regulating, the human body is, technically speaking, a cybernetic system. By contrast, artificially created systems, such as business firms, health-care facilities, and educational institutions, do not have automatic controls. Their performance must be continually monitored to detect and adjust for deviations from set standards. From a cybernetics perspective, an organization's performance can be monitored and, thus, controlled at three points: before, during, or after an activity is completed. Each of these points matches a different aspect of the input → transformation → output → feedback cycle that must be maintained if an organization is to exist over time. Wiener developed his theory of cybernetics while exploring interactions between humans and machines. He found that both rapidly adjusted to changing conditions based on feedback about whether an intended goal or purpose was met, suggesting that both could "learn" to adapt to their environment. This suggests a rather startling conclusion: "In tandem, humans and machines could form a dynamic and powerful system; left to themselves, machines could, in principle, develop intelligence and the ability to self-replicate. They might even replace humanity."[32]

On the heels of Wiener's work in cybernetics, the field of artificial intelligence (AI) emerged in the mid-1950s. AI combines the reasoning ability of the human mind with the processing

---

[30] K. Ludwig von Bertalanffy, "General Systems Theory: A New Approach to the Unity of Science," *Human Biology* 23(4) (December 1951), pp. 302–361.

[31] Norbert Wiener, *Cybernetics, Or Control and Communication in the Animal and the Machine* (Cambridge, MA: MIT Press, 1948), p. 23. Although Wiener claimed to have "invented" the word "cybernetics," it appears throughout ancient Greek writings dating back to Plato's *First Alcibiades*. On this point, see Pesi R. Masani, *Norbert Wiener, 1894–1964* (Basel, Switzerland: Birkhauser, 1989), p. 259. In claiming to have invented the term cybernetics, Wiener does note that "incidentally" he later learned that "the word had already been used by [André-Marie] Ampère . . . [and] a Polish scientist" (pp. 23–24). Ampère used the term *cybernétique* in his *Essai sur la philosophie des sciences* [*Essay on the Philosophy of Science* (Paris: Bachelier, 1834), p. 140] to refer to a new science of government. The unnamed Polish scientist appears to have been Bronisław F. Trentowski, who wrote of *cybernetyka* or the "art of governing a nation" in his book *Stosunek filozofii do cybernetyki czyli sztuki rządzenia narodem* [*The Relationship of Philosophy to Cybernetics, Or the Art of Ruling a Nation*] (Poznań, Poland: J. K. Żupańskiego, 1843), p. 9. See also Plato, *The Dialogues of Plato*, 3rd ed., vol. 2 trans. by Benjamin Jowett (Oxford: Clarendon Press, 1892), p. 508. Written circa 350 BCE. The passage in question reads: "SOC.[RATES]: Or again, in a ship, if a man having the power to do what he likes, has no intelligence or skill in navigation [*kubernētēs*], do you see what will happen to him and to his fellow-sailors?"

[32] Michael Saler, [Review of *Rise of the Machines*], *Wall Street Journal* (September 3–4, 2016), p. C6.

power of computers. Herbert A. Simon and Allen Newell were among the early pioneers in AI research.[33] By simulating human-information processing using "expert systems," Simon and Newell programmed a computer to play chess and prove mathematical theorems. As early as 1960, Simon predicted that "machines will be capable, within twenty years, of doing any work that a man can do."[34] Although AI could not account for unique parts of human existence such as ethics or aesthetics, it marked the beginning of computers designed to guide robots, drive automobiles, and make "virtual reality" a reality. Apple, Inc.'s Siri and Amazon.com Inc.'s Alexa digital assistants are AI applications, as are navigation apps that help plan the most efficient route to a destination or allow online retailers to recommend products and services based on past purchases. In 1975, Simon and Newell received the Turing Award from the Association for Computing Machinery for their contributions to artificial intelligence.

From the "Invisible Hand" to the "Digital Hand"

Suppose it is some 60 or so years ago and you are the Director of the Data Processing Department in your firm. When you arrive at work, you see numerous persons operating keypunch machines to make tiny holes in 80-column cards that carry a printed admonishment that they should not be folded, spindled, or mutilated; another employee is running a sorter to arrange these cards into various categories; another is operating a tabulator that reads these tiny holes and prints the results on long sheets of paper.

Assured that work is proceeding smoothly, you enter your office, check your flip-the-page calendar for your appointments, and finding some spare time, you check the financial pages of the *Wall Street Journal*. You see ads for computing machinery made by International Business Machines (IBM), Sperry Rand, Minneapolis-Honeywell, RCA, National Cash Register, and a few other firms, but IBM is definitely number one in the business. You begin thinking about taking a vacation and use your black, rotary dial phone to call your local travel agent, who can make plane, hotel, and rental-car arrangements and mail you some brochures describing how to find your destination, your accommodations, and other matters. Seeking some information about your destination, you go to your bookshelves and pull out the appropriate volume of your encyclopedia. Just in case you wish to verify the spelling or meaning of a word, you also have a dictionary handy.

Fast-forward to the present and the information world you know is quite different. You can accomplish all these tasks with a mobile device you carry in your pocket as you wait to order lunch or commute to work. Reading the *Wall Street Journal* you now see advertisements for Dell, Microsoft, Cisco, Intel, Apple, and other companies prominent in the computing industry. You use search engines such as Google to almost instantly locate information on arcane subjects such as the Boer War or what happened at the Battle of Waterloo. For your vacation, you arrange your own transportation, compare airfares, locate accommodations, and view the dining room, sleeping area, or other facilities in the hotel you have chosen; you are virtually there. What happened in those intervening 60 or so years?

It Is a Small, Smaller World

You have entered the Information Age, enabled by advancing computer technology. Of the 10 forces that Thomas L. Friedman has identified as "flattening the world," 8 are related directly in some manner to the Information Age: work-flow software, uploading, outsourcing, offshoring,

---

[33] Herbert A. Simon, *The Sciences of the Artificial* (Cambridge, MA: MIT Press, 1969); Allen Newell and Herbert A. Simon, *Human Problem Solving* (Englewood Cliffs, NJ: Prentice Hall, 1972).

[34] Herbert A. Simon, *The New Science of the Management Decision* (New York: Harper & Brothers, 1960), p. 38. On May 11, 1997, Garry Kasparov was the first world chess champion to be beaten by a computer, IBM's Deep Blue.

supply-chaining, insourcing, in-forming, and steroids.[35] James W. Cortada has characterized this flattening as an evolution from Adam Smith's "invisible hand" of the marketplace to Alfred D. Chandler's "visible hand" of management to the "digital hand" of the Information Age.[36] In Chapter 4, we discussed Charles Babbage's vision of a machine capable of performing any calculation. He encountered so many problems in constructing his Analytical Engine, however, he was never able to build a full-scale model.

Some 90 years later, British mathematician Alan Turing took a step toward fulfilling Babbage's vision. In 1938, as the armies of Adolf Hitler's Germany threatened Europe, the British Secret Intelligence Service (commonly known as MI6) became aware of a new German message-encoding machine called Enigma. If the Enigma code (called "Ultra" by the British) could be broken, MI6 could intercept and use the German messages to anticipate the movement of Hitler's armies. Cryptology (the devising and breaking of coded messages) was a complicated process, and Enigma had defied all traditional cryptanalysis. Building on the work of Marian Rejewski at the Polish Cipher Bureau, Turing, among others, was employed to fully break the Enigma code in 1932. Because almost all codes depend on the substitution of numbers for letters in various ways, and because a huge number of combinations are possible, only a machine that could process masses of numbers could hope to succeed. Turing led the successful effort to develop a general-purpose computer to handle the necessary calculations.[37]

As also noted in Chapter 4, Herman Hollerith created a punched-card tabulating machine to input data for the 1890 U.S. Census. In 1896 he formed the Tabulating Machine Company, which, after a period of time, became the International Business Machines Corporation (IBM).[38] During 1937–1944, with funding from IBM, Howard H. Aiken designed and built an electromechanical computing machine called Mark I. Lt. (later Rear Admiral). Grace Murray Hopper, who developed the computer programming language COBOL, was the lead programmer for Mark I. Computers are merely machines (hardware)—what makes them useful is "software," general-purpose symbols providing instructions. The Electronic Numerical Integrator and Computer (ENIAC) was programmed by a team that included Jean Jennings Bartik, Marlyn Wescoff Meltzer, Ruth Lichterman Teitelbaum, Betty Snyder Holberton, Frances Bilas Sopenc, and Kay McNulty Mauchly.[39] The ENIAC, built between 1943 and 1945, at the University of Pennsylvania, under the direction of John Mauchly and J. Presper Eckert, Jr., was the world's first electronic general-purpose computer. Mauchly and Eckert's underlying patents, however, were disputed in a lawsuit filed by Honeywell and Control Data Corporation. John V. Atanasoff, working with graduate student Clifford Berry, had built an automatic electronic digital computer at Iowa State University, beginning work in 1939. Mauchly had visited Iowa State as Atanasoff's guest for 4 days in 1943 and taken notes on what is now known as the Atanasoff–Berry Computer. Although neither Atanasoff nor Iowa State had applied for patent protection, the U.S. District Court for the District of Minnesota upheld Atanasoff's patent rights on the basis that he was the first person to both conceive and build "the calculating device that led to the invention of the computer."[40] As a result, royalties that had been going to computer manufacturer Sperry Rand (today's Unisys), which had acquired Mauchly and Eckert's patents, were discontinued in April, 1973. Worthy of mention, in the early 1980s, the

---

[35] Thomas L. Friedman, *The World Is Flat: A Brief History of the Twenty-First Century* (updated and expanded version) (New York: Farrar, Straus, and Giroux, 2007), pp. 51–199. Friedman uses the term "steroids" to reference increased computing power and capabilities rather than to describe class of organic compounds.

[36] James W. Cortada, *The Digital Hand: How Computers Changed the Work of American Manufacturing, Transportation, and Retail Industries*, vol. 1 (New York: Oxford University Press, 2004).

[37] Andrew Hodges, *Alan Turing: The Enigma* (New York: Simon & Schuster, 1983), especially pp. 166–170, 181–195.

[38] George E. Biles, Alfred A. Bolton, and Bernadette DiRe, "Herman Hollerith: Inventor, Manager, Entrepreneur – A Centennial Remembrance," *Journal of Management* 15(4) (December 1989), pp. 603–615.

[39] Walter Isaacson, "The Women of ENIAC," *Fortune* (October 6, 2014), pp. 160–165.

[40] Jane Smiley, *The Man Who Invented the Computer: The Biography of John Atanasoff, Digital Pioneer* (New York: Doubleday, 2010), p. 80.

computer programming language Ada, named after Lady Ada Lovelace, Babbage's close friend and collaborator (see Chapter 4), was developed by the U.S. Department of Defense.

During more than a century from Charles Babbage's vision to Atanasoff's reality, computers advanced rapidly in technological capability, allowing heretofore unrealized applications. The first computers were monster mainframes; it was thought that only a few computers would be necessary to handle the U.S. census, scientific calculations, and perhaps, someday, accounting, payroll, and inventory problems. "Electronic data processing" was the term used to refer to the automated methods used by computers to process data.

In 1960, IBM's revenues were twice the total of all other firms in the entire computer industry. Threats to break up the alleged IBM "monopoly" were made unnecessary, however, by advancing computer technology that moved from vacuum tubes, to transistors, to integrated circuits (the latter coinvented by Robert N. Noyce of Fairchild Semiconductor and Texas Instruments' Jack S. Kilby in 1958).[41] Integrated circuits triggered a host of changes in both hardware (equipment) and software (operating systems). "Microcomputers," which utilized circuit boards, became popular in the early 1970s. By 1977, some 72 percent of the microcomputer market was held by three firms: Apple, Commodore, and Tandy. Microsoft had been founded in 1975 by William H. Gates and Paul Allen. IBM decided to enter the microcomputer market in 1980, and personal computers, laptops, and mobile devices inexorably followed.

Enabling Global Trade through Information and Communication

Tom Standage reminded us (see Chapter 5) that the Victorians had an Internet of their own: the telegraph, which fostered romances, facilitated commercial transactions, reshaped distribution strategies, and swept away local trade barriers.[42] ARPANET (Advanced Research Projects Agency Network), the precursor of the Internet, was developed by the U.S. Department of Defense beginning in 1960. The Internet as we know it today was privatized starting in 1993. With the Internet's commercialization, a borderless economy emerged as goods and services could be bought and sold worldwide. True to Joseph A. Schumpeter's notion of creative destruction (see Chapter 18), the Internet abounded with innovations, including electronic mail, social media sites, messaging services, news and instant messaging services, and innumerable websites devoted to an endless list of subjects.

Technology is the handmaiden of management theory and practice. Information technology can provide an initial, but not necessarily unassailable, competitive advantage. At times it seems that virtually every facet of a manager's job is affected by computer technology. Based on an analysis of the development of communications in corporations prior to the widespread introduction of computers, Yates concluded that "technologies were adopted, not necessarily when they were invented, but when a shift or advance in managerial theory led managers to see an application for them. . . . The technology alone was not enough – the vision to use it in new ways was needed as well."[43] This conclusion appears to hold with respect to the Information Age, as computers have become more than giant electronic calculating machines, now fulfilling information needs at all levels of an organization and across continents, oceans, and time zones. Information can be distributed globally through network systems, stored in the "cloud" on virtual servers, input into decision support systems, and accessed remotely so that group members can work "together" from their own homes.

---

[41] Leslie Berlin, *The Man Behind the Microchip: Robert Noyce and the Invention of Silicon Valley* (New York: Oxford University Press, 2005), p. 3.

[42] Tom Standage, *The Victorian Internet: The Remarkable Story of the Telegraph and the Nineteenth Century's On-Line Pioneers* (New York: Walker and Company, 1998), p. 213.

[43] JoAnne Yates, *Control through Communications: The Rise of System in American Management* (Baltimore, MD: Johns Hopkins University Press, 1989), pp. 274–275.

Accurate information has always been essential for effective managerial decision-making. Over time, however, as transactions and interactions within organizations became more complex, information was needed for internal uses as well as for reporting to external constituents and regulatory agencies. As information-providing capabilities advanced, managers mastered as well as developed innovative workplace applications for new information technologies. Chandler commented on the importance of developing an information-rich "integrated learning base" that is rooted in the technical, functional, and managerial capabilities of an organization as a whole rather than individual managers.[44] These capabilities provide the basis for an organization's continued growth and competitiveness. *Technical capabilities* develop by learning from new and existing knowledge bases, which may be firm or industry specific. This involves gathering knowledge related to basic and applied research to improve existing products or to introduce new products. *Functional capabilities* refer to those activities in which an organization must successfully engage to acquire, transform, and market its products. These activities are essential for an organization's survival. *Managerial capabilities* are required to administer an organization's operational units, integrate its activities, and coordinate the flow of goods and services through the input → transformation → output → transformation cycle to retailers and final customers. Chandler's appreciation of the importance of developing an information-rich integrated learning base that is rooted in an organization's technical, functional, and managerial capabilities aligns with Edith T. Penrose's view that the productive services available or potentially available from its resources give each organization its unique character (see Chapter 19).

SUMMARY

The post–World War II era posed new opportunities in the global arena that would transform old ideas about markets and manufacturing. Japanese industry led the way in improving product quality and reliability with quality circles, just-in-time inventory management, and lean manufacturing. General systems theory and cybernetics underscored that organizations are open systems that interact with their surrounding environment. With the dawning of the Information Age, computer technology advanced rapidly from vacuum tube mainframes to lithium-powered miniature chips loaded with computing and information capabilities for mobile devices. This computational power enabled the testing of advanced mathematical models, reshaped production management, and created opportunities for innovative ventures in technology. The Internet has enabled unlimited communication around the world, opened markets, and created applications for multiple purposes. From the "invisible hand" of Adam Smith to Alfred D. Chandler's "visible hand of management" to the "digital hand" of the Information Age, our daily and work lives were changed. Perhaps only the Industrial Revolution could rival the social change experienced during this period.

---

[44] Alfred D. Chandler, Jr., *Inventing the Electronic Century: The Epic Story of the Consumer Electronics and the Computer Industries* (New York: Free Press, 2001), pp. 2–5.

Obligations and Opportunities

It was noted in Chapter 1 that managers face daily challenges and make decisions within a given set of cultural values and institutions. This chapter considers the increasing globalization of business and how competing in international markets with contrasting cultural values and institutions has influenced the evolution of management thought. It also discusses business ethics and society's expectations for business.

Managing in a Global Arena

As the Silk Road and spice trade attest, the exchange of goods between cultures in different parts of the world—what today is called the globalization of business—has a rich history going back to the dawn of the Stone Age. Coins, clay tablets, and the remains of once mighty trading forts tell the story of ancient empires engaged in exchanging gold, ivory, precious stones, and textiles. Commerce, whether by land or sea, bound early civilizations, and placed them in fierce economic competition with each other.[1]

The Globalization of Business

Trade among nations has, more often than not, been initiated and pursued as a political strategy. Little has changed with modern sanctions, embargos, and tariffs. Although many early adventurers were motivated by natural curiosity or the desire for a more varied diet or assortment of products, the economic interests of past kings, queens, and potentates provided the main driving force behind the great discoveries of unknown lands and peoples, with national treasuries financing the explorers who sailed uncharted waters to ply new trade routes, establish colonies, bring home exotic goods, and expand empires.

---

[1] Miriam Beard, *A History of the Business Man,* (New York: Macmillan, 1938).

As discussed in Chapter 2, as an economic philosophy, mercantilism held that governments should play a central role in financing and protecting trade to build strong national economies. Mercantilists used politics to subsidize local business, tariffs to keep out products from alien lands, colonies to ensure a steady supply of raw materials, and a strong navy to keep commercial sea lanes free from pirates. Trading companies—such as the East India Company, the Hudson's Bay Company, and the Dutch East India Company—benefitted from national monopolies to dominate trade in specific areas or items such as furs or spices. Canada, India, and the United States were British colonies; France, Belgium, Portugal, and Germany controlled colonies in Africa; Indonesia was a Dutch colony, then called Dutch East India; and French Indo-China (today's Vietnam, Laos, and Cambodia) was a colony ruled by France. In each case, these colonies provided the country that owned them with markets, raw materials, and labor serve as and are early examples of global business.

Mercantilism eventually fell of its own weight: Failing state-owned enterprises were kept alive, colonists were bound in economic servitude, and a strong military was required to protect a nation's economic privileges. As also discussed in Chapter 2, Adam Smith took issue with mercantilism. He believed that mercantilist tariff polices were destructive and that rather than protecting industry actually penalized efficiency and, consequently, misallocated a nation's resources. Smith felt that economic activity should be regulated solely by marketplace forces and competition. The "invisible hand" of the marketplace would ensure that resources flowed to their most efficient use and yield the greatest return. In this way, the self-interests of each person and nation, acting in a fully competitive market, would bring about the greatest prosperity for all.[2] David Ricardo, an early nineteenth-century British economist, suggested that what was needed was not a national economic policy, such as mercantilism, but rather a free-market that allowed each nation to find its "comparative advantage" over others in producing a particular good.[3] If one nation can produce a good at a relative advantage compared to another, and the other has a relative advantage in producing a second good, both countries can gain from trading with each other. Note that "comparative advantage" is different than "absolute advantage." If one of the nations in the foregoing example has an absolute advantage in producing both goods, the two nations can each still benefit by trading with each other "as long as they have different relative efficiencies."[4]

As colonialism and mercantilism faded, trade among nations continued to thrive. In its early economic development, the United States was a debtor nation, depending on capital from abroad. The J. & W. Seligman Company, a New York investment bank founded in 1864, had branches in London, Paris, and Frankfurt. Members of the Seligman family and other domestic bankers sold securities abroad to finance the growth of U.S. businesses. Wilkins observed that as late as 1914, the United States still had a balance of payment deficit, borrowing more from abroad than it invested worldwide.[5] The United States was a lively trader in the Pacific (some 80 U.S. firms had branches in China alone), South America, Africa, continental Europe, and Great Britain, but it still imported capital to finance the growth of its own industries.

Technology has always been an important factor in growing world markets. Early trade routes hugged the world's shorelines because of fragile ships and poor navigational aids. Stronger masts, larger sails, and advances in navigation techniques broadened trade horizons. Millennia passed before humans used hydrocarbons for energy: first, steam power for the Industrial

---

[2] Adam Smith, *An Inquiry Into the Nature and Causes of the Wealth of Nations*, vol. 2 (London: W. Strahan and T. Cadell in the Strand, 1776), p. 35.

[3] David Ricardo, *On the Principles of Political Economy, and Taxation* (London: John Murray, 1817), pp. 156–161.

[4] This seems to be an inescapable phrase in discussions of comparative advantage. We have been unable to discern its origin.

[5] Mira Wilkins, *The Emergence of Multinational Enterprise: American Business Abroad from the Colonial Era to 1914* (Cambridge, MA: Harvard University Press, 1970), pp. 201–207.

Revolution and travel, later to generate electricity for illumination and communication, and subsequently to drive internal combustion engines. Steam-powered ships, the telegraph, and transoceanic cables improved communication and reduced travel time. Faster ships, aircraft, and the wireless radio presaged the coming of jet travel and global communication by sky-based and orbiting satellites. The title of the book *The Lexus and the Olive Tree* is a metaphor for the globalization of business. The olive tree symbolizes cultural identity, old ways, ritual, and nationalism. The Lexus symbolizes the marvels of modern technology and global integration.[6] According to the book's author, Thomas L. Friedman, modern societies can either move toward free worldwide trade or engage in economic protectionism based on tribalism and nationalism. He sees globalization as the only alternative for economic viability.

What some scholars refer to as the "new" global competition is, in historical perspective, an extension of the past. The primary difference is improvements in communication and transportation that enable almost immediate international exchanges of products, services, and information. The United States' experience with multinational enterprise began in the 1850s, but did not grow rapidly until after World War II, when the book value of its direct investments abroad increased some 10-fold by 1970.[7] During the same period, other nations established manufacturing, distribution, and sales facilitates in the United States for products such as automobiles, tires, electronics, and pharmaceuticals. At present, the United States is the world's biggest importer as well as exporter of goods, with trillions of dollars in play annually.

Globalization has resulted in numerous multinational trade agreements. The North America Free Trade Agreement (commonly known as NAFTA), the European Union, and the Asia-Pacific Economic Cooperation agreement represent efforts to break down trade barriers among nations. Is this David Ricardo's law of comparative advantage coming to fruition? Will these alliances foster a new mercantilism, favoring a nation's commercial partners, but excluding free trade among all nations? Vernon warned of the tensions that can develop between nations as a result of multinational trade agreements, especially if such agreements restrict commerce through tariffs on imported goods, restrictive quotas, and other regulations.[8]

Individuals and Organizations: Relating to Evolving Expectations

Nicollò di Bernado dei Machiavelli wrote "there is nothing more difficult to carry out nor more doubtful of success, nor more dangerous to handle, than to initiate a new order of things. For the reformer has enemies in all those who profit by the older order, and only lukewarm defenders in all those who would profit by the new order."[9] Change can come from within, but it is far more likely to come from without. A firm's economic environment can bring new opportunities as well as unanticipated competition; technology can alter how people live and earn a living; political disruptions may lead to greater freedom or place limits on individuals and organizations; and evolving social mores can redefine appropriate behavior.

---

[6] Thomas L. Friedman, *The Lexus and the Olive Tree: Understanding Globalization* (New York: Farrar, Straus and Giroux, 1999).

[7] Mira Wilkins, *The Maturing of Multinational Enterprise: American Business Abroad from 1914–1970* (Cambridge, MA: Harvard University Press, 1974), Table XIII, p. 329.

[8] Raymond Vernon, *In the Hurricane's Eye: The Troubled Prospects of Multinational Enterprises* (Cambridge, MA: Harvard University Press, 1998). See also Frederick W. Smith, "How Trade Made America Great," *Wall Street Journal* (March 26–27, 2016), p. A9.

[9] Nicoló Machiavelli, *The Prince,* trans. Luigi Ricci (New York: New American Library, 1952), pp. 49–50. Written in 1513, but not published until 1532 because of its controversial nature.

Business Ethics

Ethics, or questions of human moral conduct, have occupied the thinking of theologians and philosophers since antiquity. Broadly viewed, ethics are the moral "oughts" that sustain a civilized society. Business practices have long been associated with moral guidelines beyond the confines of legal boundaries. Aristotle is credited with the search for "virtuous behavior" in one's moral character and justice in one's relations with others. His "commutative justice" addressed the voluntary exchange of goods and services, an important element of a free society; "distributive justice" is related to the distribution of wealth and income within a society and forms the basis for contemporary discussions of economic inequality.[10]

The notion of a "just price" has been debated since at least the ninth century.[11] Building on Aristotle's theory of justice, Saint Thomas Aquinas, writing in the thirteenth century, believed a just price is that which is determined voluntarily by a buyer and a seller.[12] In Chapter 2, we examined how the expansion of trade promoted the need for business ethics and how Dominican Friar Johannes Nider declared that goods should be "lawful, honorable, and useful"; prices should be just; sellers should beware (*caveat venditor*) and not engage in "trickery" or "intimidation" or sell to "simpletons," who would not be informed buyers; and those who buy "looking for nothing but a rise in prices [i.e., financial speculators], sin most gravely."[13]

As early as the beginning of the eighteenth century, moral-philosophy courses emphasizing "natural, rational ethics" were taught in U.S. institutions of higher learning.[14] Following in this tradition, Joseph Wharton, who donated $100,000 in 1881 to the University of Pennsylvania to establish the nation's first collegiate school of business, felt that an effort should be made "to inculcate and impress upon the students: The immorality and practical inexpediency of seeking to acquire wealth by winning it from another rather than earning it through some sort of service to one's fellowmen . . . . [and] the necessity of rigorously punishing by legal penalties and social exclusion, those persons who commit frauds, betray trusts, or steal public funds, directly or indirectly."[15] Wharton set his ethical standards high, hoping they would be attained in practice.

The Wharton School became a model for other collegiate programs. Instruction in business ethics began as early as 1904 at the University of California (today's University of California-Berkeley), Yale University, the University of Chicago, and Northwestern University. Economics departments in colleges of business coupled economics and sociology or social work with emphases on service and moral obligations. Other universities would follow with business-ethics courses and lectures. Abend provides a historical account of business-ethics courses and the people responsible for their development. He notes that our understanding of the ethical issues confronting business ethics has been lacking: "[E]arly twentieth century concerns and arguments were not all that different from early twenty-first century ones. . . . [Yet] each generation of business ethicists, politicians, and journalists seems to represent certain business ethics problems as novel problems . . . unique to their own age. But this is just mistaken. My historical research shows this novelty and uniqueness to be illusory."[16]

---

[10] Aristotle, *The Nicomachean Ethics* translated by Robert Williams (London: Longmans, Green, and Co., 1876), pp, 115–150. Originally published 350 BCE.

[11] Raymond de Roover, "The Concept of Just Price: Theory and Economic Policy," *Journal of Economic History* 18(4) (December 1958), especially pp. 420–423.

[12] Thomas Aquinas, "The *'Summa Theologiae'* of St. Thomas Aquinas" translated by the Fathers if the English Dominican Province (New York: Benziger Brothers, 1911), Part II, Second Number, pp. 317–320. Written between 1259 and 1272.

[13] Johannes Nider, *On the Contracts of Merchants*, trans. Charles H. Reeves, ed. Ronald B. Shuman (Norman, OK: University of Oklahoma Press, 1966), pp. 38–45. Written circa 1430 and originally published circa 1468.

[14] Perry Glanzer and Todd C. Ream, *Christianity and Moral Identity in Higher Education* (New York: Palgrave Macmillan, 2010), p. 39.

[15] Joseph Wharton quoted in Fairman Rogers, "The Wharton School of Finance and Economy," *The Penn Monthly* 12(1) (May 1881), p. 359.

[16] Gabriel Abend, "The Origins of Business Ethics in American Universities, 1902–1936," *Business Ethics Quarterly* 23(2) (April 2013), p. 172.

Robert Wood Johnson wrote the initial Johnson & Johnson Company Credo in 1943.[17] It currently reads:

> We believe our first responsibility is to the doctors, nurses and patients, to mothers and fathers and all others who use our products and services. In meeting their needs everything we do must be of high quality. We must constantly strive to reduce our costs in order to maintain reasonable prices. Customers' orders must be serviced promptly and accurately. Our suppliers and distributors must have an opportunity to make a fair profit.
>
> We are responsible to our employees, the men and women who work with us throughout the world. Everyone must be considered as an individual. We must respect their dignity and recognize their merit. They must have a sense of security in their jobs. Compensation must be fair and adequate, and working conditions clean, orderly and safe.
>
> We must be mindful of ways to help our employees fulfill their family responsibilities. Employees must feel free to make suggestions and complaints. There must be equal opportunity for employment, development and advancement for those qualified. We must provide competent management, and their actions must be just and ethical.
>
> We are responsible to the communities in which we live and work and to the world community as well. We must be good citizens-support good works and charities and bear our fair share of taxes. We must encourage civic improvements and better health and education.
>
> We must maintain in good order the property we are privileged to use, protecting the environment and natural resources.
>
> Our final responsibility is to our stockholders. Business must make a sound profit. We must experiment with new ideas. Research must be carried on, innovative programs developed and mistakes paid for. New equipment must be purchased, new facilities provided and new products launched. Reserves must be created to provide for adverse times. When we operate according to these principles, the stockholders should realize a fair return.[18]

The 1960s witnessed renewed interest in business ethics when The Reverend Raymond C. Baumhart, S.J. asked, "How ethical are businessmen?" More than half the approximately 1,700 readers of the *Harvard Business Review* he polled indicated they believe that business operators "would violate a code of ethics whenever they thought they could avoid detection."[19] *Business and Society Review*, the first journal entirely devoted to business ethics began publication in 1972.[20] Other business-ethics journals followed, including *Business and Professional Ethics* (1980), *Journal of Business Ethics* (1982), and *Business Ethics Quarterly* (1991).

When John Shad, chairman of the Securities and Exchange Commission from 1981 to 1987 donated $23 million in 1987 to the Harvard Graduate School of Business Administration for the teaching of business ethics, he called for knowledge accompanied by conscience: "It is not enough for these [business] schools to certify that their graduates have mastered the fundamentals of their profession. The schools must hone their ability to certify that their graduates have the character and integrity to use the knowledge gained for the benefit – rather than the abuse – of society."[21] Business schools do have an opportunity to influence the character and integrity of their graduates. Less evident in Shad's comment is the responsibility of parents, schools, religious groups, and communities to inculcate the moral "oughts" that sustain a civilized society.

---

[17] Robert Wood Johnson II, *Robert Johnson Talks It Over* (New Brunswick, NJ: Johnson and Johnson, 1949), p. 168.

[18] Available at http://www.jnj.com/sites/default/files/pdf/jnj_ourcredo_english_us_8.5x11_cmyk.pdf

[19] Raymond C. Baumhart, "How Ethical Are Businessmen?" *Harvard Business Review* 39(4) (July–August 1961), p. 19.

[20] Theodore Cross, "Why *Business and Society Review*?" *Business and Society Review* 1(1) (Spring 1972), p. 4.

[21] John S. R. Shad, "Business's Bottom Line: Ethics," *New York Times* (July 27, 1987), p. A19.

The Interstate Commerce Act (1887), the Sherman Antitrust Act (1890), the Clayton Antitrust Act (1914), the Federal Reserve Act (1913), and the Federal Trade Commission Act (1914) were early actions to control business practices (see Chapter 12). The Securities and Exchange Commission was established in 1934 to implement the Securities Act of 1933 and the Securities Exchange Act of 1934, which required full financial disclosure and independent audits of financial statements and prohibited "insider trading." The Sarbanes–Oxley Act (2002) created a board to oversee public auditing firms, mandated new financial disclosure requirements, imposed stronger criminal penalties for fraud, and prohibited public-accounting firms from serving as a consultant to the businesses they audit. Section 406 of the Sarbanes–Oxley Act requires publicly traded firms to prepare and make public a code of ethics. One study has found, however, the result of this requirement has been "cut and paste" documents in which the "content and language converge" in boilerplate language and provide little guidance tailored to ethical issues unique to firms or their industry.[22] Laws alone cannot overcome human frailties or prevent chicanery, and history's lesson is to be skeptical in legislating ethical conduct.

Acting Ethically and Globally

History is replete with examples of unethical behavior in business, politics, religion, education, sports, and all other human endeavors. As events in other nations have shown, unethical behavior knows no national boundaries. Ethical behavior, whether in business or life, more generally is not bounded by borders, ethnicity, religious beliefs, or other aspects of human experience. Is there an ethical imperative that spans all cultures?

There have been attempts to define "hypernorms," certain standards to be respected across cultures: the right to freedom of movement, freedom from torture, private property, physical security, a fair trial, freedom of speech and association, subsistence, a minimal education, political participation, and nondiscriminatory treatment on the basis of traits such as gender.[23] A study of normative guidelines endorsed by various international groups reveals some agreed-upon standards: adequate health and safety protections; the rights of all persons to life, liberty, personal security, and privacy; and environmental standards regarding pollution.[24]

The U.S. Foreign Corrupt Practices Act (FCPA, 1977; amended 1988) forbids publicly traded companies from making illicit payments to foreign government officials, to foreign political parties or their officials, and to intermediaries for acquiring or retaining business. FCPA has been controversial. It makes relatively small payments (called "grease") to expedite activities such as obtaining a work permit or visa legal, but forbids relatively large payments to political figures or their intermediaries to gain or retain business—this is considered bribery. The line between grease and bribery can be very thin. Such efforts to legislate ethical behavior make Aristotle's "virtuous conduct" a statute and a matter of advocacy not morality.

The search for hypernorms may be a worthy endeavor, but ethics (like management) is culturally bound by where a firm conducts business. Hypernorms are typically prepared by North Americans or Western Europeans versed in presumed individual rights. Western cultural tradition is indebted to John Locke who challenged the supposed divine right of kings to rule without the consent of the governed (see Chapter 2). As one observer has noted, however, "Some non-Western world views question the *primacy* of the 'inalienable dignity of the individual' as being a threat to the community or religious tradition. Sometimes, religion or a religious leader trumps

[22] Lori Holder-Webb and Jeffrey Cohen, "The Cut and Paste Society: Isomorphism in Codes of Ethics," *Journal of Business Ethics* 107(4) (June 2012), pp. 485–509.

[23] Thomas Donaldson, *The Ethics of International Business* (New York: Oxford University Press, 1989), p. 81.

[24] Christian J. Resick, Paul J. Hanges, Marcus W. Dickson, and Jacqueline K. Mitchelson, "A Cross-Cultural Examination of the Endorsement of Ethical Leadership," *Journal of Business Ethics* 63(3) (February 2006), pp. 345–359.

individual rights."[25] Constitutional guarantees to promote universal and inalienable rights are a part of a Western heritage that reflects an age-old struggle between autocracy, theocracy, and democracy.

Business and Society

The line between ethics and corporate social responsibility is likewise not always clear. Johnson & Johnson's Credo defines how its employees ought to behave, and recognizes the broader community in which they and the company play a role. Ethics refers to the moral conduct of individuals, whereas corporate social responsibility addresses society's expectations for business. Judgments relating to a person's moral conduct and acceptable corporate behavior rest on social values and legal requirements that evolve over time.

As noted in Chapter 6, businesspeople have been known throughout history as benefactors of literature, music, and art. Andrew Carnegie made a great deal of money and gave it all away because he believed that wealth imposed a duty:

> To set an example of modest, unostentatious living, shunning display or extravagance; to provide moderately for the legitimate wants of those dependent upon him; and, after doing so, to consider all surplus revenues which come to him simply as trust funds, which he is called upon to administer, and strictly bound as a matter of duty to administer in the manner which, in his judgment, is best calculated to produce the most beneficial results for the community – the man of wealth thus becoming the mere trustee and agent for his poorer brethren . . . .[26]

Carnegie's belief that wealth imposes a duty underscores that we all (both rich and poor) have a social responsibility to use our material resources wisely. In a review of the social role of business (and business operators such as Carnegie), Heald concluded:

> American businessmen fully shared the social concerns and preoccupations of their fellow citizens. Although they have often been depicted – indeed, caricatured – as single-minded pursuers of profit, the facts are quite otherwise. . . . Like others, they were frequently troubled by the conditions they saw; and, also like others, they numbered in their ranks men who contributed both of their ideas and their resources to redress social imbalance and disorganization.[27]

Wood's study of the forces behind the passage of the Meat Inspection Act (1906) and the Pure Food and Drug Act (1906) found that business operators were proactive, desiring laws to protect both themselves and consumers. The passage of these acts has often been attributed to Upton Sinclair's dyspepsia-inducing book on the Chicago (IL) stockyards, *The Jungle*.[28] The facts, however, do not support this claim. Manufacturers and producers such as Henry J. Heinz, Frederick Pabst, and Edward R. Squibb from the food processing, pharmaceutical, brewing, baking, and distilling industries joined together to support consumer protection laws.[29] They understood that these laws protected the honest seller from the adulterer and were in the interest of business, as

---

[25] Patricia H. Werhane, "Principles and Practices of Corporate Responsibilities," *Business Ethics Quarterly* 20(4) (October 2010), p. 699.

[26] Andrew Carnegie, *The Gospel of Wealth and Other Timely Essays* (New York: Century Co., 1901), p. 15.

[27] Morrell Heald, *The Social Responsibilities of Business: Company and Community 1900–1960* (Cleveland, OH: The Press of Case Western Reserve University, 1970), p. 1.

[28] Upton Sinclair, *The Jungle* (New York: Grosset & Dunlap Publishers, 1906). Originally serialized in 29 parts, February 25 to November 4, 1905, by the newspaper *Appeal to Reason*.

[29] Donna J. Wood, "The Strategic Use of Public Policy: Business Support for the 1906 Food and Drug Act," *Business History Review* 59(3) (Autumn 1985), pp. 403–432.

Keith Davis. Courtesy of Arthur G. Bedeian.

well as being sound public policy. Indeed, meatpackers favored the 1906 Meat Inspection Act. It helped market their products by giving them the federal government's mark of approval. An ensuant U.S. Department of Agriculture report on the Chicago stockyards debunked the harshest of Sinclair's claims, calling them "wilful and deliberate misrepresentations of fact" and "atrocious exaggeration."[30]

Howard R. Bowen, erstwhile president of the University of Iowa, spearheaded the modern concern for how business behaves toward society. In his Federal Council of the Churches of Christ in America sponsored book, *Social Responsibilities of the Businessman*, he defined social responsibility as "the obligations of businessmen to pursue those policies, to make those decisions, or to follow those lines of action which are desirable in terms of the objectives and values of our society."[31] Synonymous with this definition were the phrases "public responsibility," "social obligations," and "business morality." Bowen was the first writer to frame the social responsibilities of business operators as a moral imperative. He recognized, however, that businesses could not solve the problems of economic life alone: "Such an assumption would be unwise and dangerous not only for society . . . but also for businesses themselves. They cannot be saddled with responsibilities which they cannot hope to discharge effectively."[32] Drawing this distinction between what businesses could do and should do sparked a debate that continues today.

Keith Davis recalled that Bowen's book "crystallized" his thinking about social issues in management. "If you mess it up, you clean it up," a lesson from Davis's childhood, led him to the conclusion that because business influenced society, it had to accept the social obligations that followed.[33] In a widely cited article, Davis stated the pros and cons of social responsibility for business. Arguments in favor of social responsibility include: it serves the long-run interest of business; it improves the public image of business and increases its legitimacy in society; by being socially responsible corporations can avoid government regulation; and corporations have the resources and expertise to apply to social problems. Arguments against included: as a trustee for a corporation's stockholders, management should optimize corporate return; social involvement is costly and dilutes the primary economic purpose of corporations; and corporations should not be given social responsibilities for which they cannot be held accountable.[34] On balance, Davis favored social responsibility for business, but acknowledged Bowen's caveat that certain social challenges should be the province of others better equipped to meet them.

The belief that corporations have "stakeholders," or various constituencies whose interests should be considered in making decisions, became popular in the early 1960s. The term stakeholder was first coined in the 1950s.[35] In a 1963 internal memorandum circulated at the Stanford

---

[30] U.S. Congress, House of Representatives, *Hearings before the Committee on Agricultural on the So-called "Beveridge Amendment" to the Agricultural Appropriation Bill*, 59th Congress, 1st Session. (Washington, DC: Government Printing Office, 1906), pp. 350, 349.

[31] Howard R. Bowen, *Social Responsibilities of the Businessman* (New York: Harper & Brothers, 1953), p. 6.

[32] *Ibid.*, p. 7.

[33] Keith Davis, "A Journey through Management in Transition," in Arthur G. Bedeian, ed., *Management Laureates: A Collection of Autobiographical Essays,* vol. 1 (Greenwich, CT: JAI Press, 1992), p. 285. See also Keith Davis and Robert L. Blomstrom, *Business and Its Environment* (New York: McGraw-Hill, 1966).

[34] Keith Davis, "The Case for and against Business Assumptions of Social Responsibilities," *Academy of Management Journal* 16(2) (June 1973), pp. 312–322.

[35] As Freeman et al. note, the precise origin of the term "stakeholder" has been difficult to establish. See R. Edward Freeman, Jeffrey S. Harrison Andrew C. Wicks, Bidhan L. Parmar, and Simone de Colle, *Stakeholder Theory: The State of the Art* (Cambridge, England: Cambridge University Press, 2010), p. 31n.

Research Institute (now SRI International), it was defined as "those groups without whose support the organization would cease to exist."[36] Igor Ansoff, a corporate planner at Lockheed Aircraft, and staff at the Stanford Research Institute intended to convey the idea that a corporation's "objectives" could not be accomplished if stakeholder groups did not provide the necessary support. When Ansoff wrote of corporate strategy, however, he distinguished between "economic objectives" and "social or noneconomic objectives":

> The firm has both (a) "economic" objectives aimed at optimizing the efficiency of its total resource conversion process and (b) "social" or noneconomic objectives. . . . In most firms the economic objectives exert the primary influence on the firm's behavior and form the main body of explicit goals used by management for guidance and control of the firm . . . [whereas] the social objectives exert a modifying and constraining influence on management behavior. [37]

For Ansoff, the purpose of a firm was to maximize long-term return on its assets; secondary responsibilities could not be met unless a firm's economic objectives had been achieved. He acknowledged the earlier view of Peter F. Drucker that management must put economic considerations first and could justify a firm's existence only through the economic results it produced:

> [M]anagement has failed if it fails to produce economic results. It has failed if it has not supplied goods and services desired by the consumer at a price the consumer is willing to pay. It has failed if it does not improve or at least maintain the wealth producing capacity of the economic resources entrusted to it.[38]

Drucker recognized that there could be noneconomic consequences of managerial decisions, such as improved community well-being, but these were by-products made possible only by an emphasis on economic performance. The consensus of Drucker and Ansoff was that economic results took priority and that social or noneconomic objectives could be pursued only if a firm's primary objectives had been attained.

Although the stakeholder approach proved useful in understanding firms in a changing economic, social, and political environment, issues remained with respect to determining who would be the primary claimants and who would be secondary. Carroll helped clarify these issues by describing four categories of responsibilities: economic, legal, ethical, and discretionary (later labeled philanthropic). These were "not mutually exclusive, nor . . . intended to portray a continuum with economic concerns on one end and social concerns on the other. . . . They are neither cumulative nor additive . . . [but] are simply to remind us that motives or actions can be categorized as primarily one or another of these four kinds."[39] Economic responsibilities are primary, because a business firm is a fundamental producer and seller of products and services. Legal responsibilities are those regulations and rules created by political institutions to legitimize and govern business activities. Ethical responsibilities are expectations of how a firm should conduct its business beyond what the law required. Philanthropic responsibilities are voluntary. The intent of these categories is to show that corporate responsiveness was not an either or proposition; that is, profits were not mutually exclusive of other categories, but that each category can interact and overlap.[40]

---

[36] Cited in R. Edward Freeman, *Strategic Management: A Stakeholder Approach* (Boston, MA: Pitman, 1984), p. 31.

[37] H. Igor Ansoff, *Corporate Strategy: An Analytic Approach to Business Policy for Growth and Expansion* (New York: McGraw-Hill, 1965), pp. 37–38.

[38] Peter F. Drucker, *The Practice of Management* (New York: Harper & Row, 1954), p. 8.

[39] Archie B. Carroll, "A Three-Dimensional Conceptual Model of Corporate Performance," *Academy of Management Review* 4(4) (October 1979), pp. 499–500.

[40] Mark Schwartz and Archie B. Carroll, "Corporate Social Responsibility: A Three Domain Approach," *Business Ethics Quarterly* 13(4) (October 2003), pp. 503–530.

Social Entrepreneurship

Social entrepreneurship has been proposed as a way to match business capabilities with social-responsibility opportunities. Gregory Dees has suggested creating social value along with economic benefits by adopting an entrepreneurial approach to social problems. Entrepreneurship, of course, is not a new phenomenon. Social entrepreneurship, however, combines "the passion of a social mission with an image of business-like discipline, innovation, and determination." Beyond "innovative not-for-profit ventures, social entrepreneurship can include social purpose business ventures, such as for-profit community development banks, and hybrid organizations mixing not-for-profit and for-profit elements, such as homeless shelters that start businesses to train and employ their residents."[41] Porter and Kramer have suggested that social entrepreneurship can "enhance the competitiveness of a company while simultaneously advancing the economic and social conditions in the communities in which it operates."[42] This may involve rethinking all facets of a company's operations, including employee wellness and safety, product packaging, plant and distribution locations, supply-chain management, environmental impact, and energy and water usage. Social entrepreneurship proponents recognize that businesses cannot do everything, but believe that what businesses can do to enhance their competitiveness while also improving the economic and social conditions in their communities, they *should* do. This moves the discourse about corporate social responsibility to another level with the emphasis on "Doing Good" rather than simply "Looking Good."

Business and Its Environment

Expectations about the role of business in conserving the earth's natural resources have also changed over time. The Yellowstone Act, passed by the U.S. Congress in 1872, established the first national park in the world. By 1916, the year the National Park Service was created, there were 14 national parks in the United States, including Yosemite and Sequoia in California, Glacier in Montana, and Rocky Mountain in Colorado. There are now 61 national parks in the United States. Global concern for environmental matters escalated in the 1990s, and the terms ecology, "greening," sustainability, and climate change became common. Nongovernmental groups such as the Caux Roundtable (1994), the Ceres Principles (1999), and the United Nations Global Compact (1999) reflected this concern. The International Organization for Standardization (ISO) published the world's first standards on environmental management in 1992. It released its ISO 14000 Environmental Management System standards in 1996. ISO 14000 is a family of environmental standards that offers world-class specifications for products, services, systems, and reducing waste in energy and materials.[43] The same challenges associated with defining hypernorms for corporate social performance apply to setting standards for environmental performance, however. Nevertheless, it may be easier to define standards for air and water quality and product safety and performance than social responsibility, which is less quantifiable, and in 2010, the ISO released international standards (ISO 26000) to guide organizations in responsibly contributing to society's health and welfare.

---

[41] J. Gregory Dees, "The Meaning of 'Social Entrepreneurship'," Original Draft: October 31, 1998; reformatted and revised: May 30, 2001. Available at https://entrepreneurship.duke.edu/news-item/the-meaning-of-social-entrepreneurship/

[42] Michael E. Porter and Mark R. Kramer, "Creating Shared Value," *Harvard Business Review* 89(1) (January–February, 2011), p. 66. See also Michael A. Driver, "An Interview with Michael Porter: Social Entrepreneurship and the Transformation of Capitalism," *Academy of Management Learning & Education* 11(3) (September 2012), pp. 421–431.

[43] JoAnne Yates and Craig N. Murphy, "From Setting National Standards to Coordinating International Standards," *Business and Economic History On-Line* 4 (2006), pp. 1–25. See also Craig N. Murphy and JoAnne Yates, *The International Organization for Standardization (ISO): Global Governance through Voluntary Consensus* (London: Routledge, 2009).

SUMMARY

Chapter 22 examined the globalization of business and how competing in international markets with contrasting cultural values and institutions has influenced the evolution of management thought. It also discussed business ethics and society's expectations for business. Competing globally begets an obligation to behave in a legal, ethical, and socially responsible manner. Ethics, or questions of human moral conduct, have occupied the thinking of theologians and philosophers since antiquity. Broadly viewed, ethics are the moral "oughts" that sustain a civilized society. Business practices have long been associated with moral guidelines beyond the confines of legal boundaries. Corporate social responsibility addresses society's expectations for business. Judgments relating to a person's moral conduct and acceptable corporate behavior rest on social values and legal requirements that evolve over time.

Epilogue

Our goal throughout the preceding chapters has been to trace the evolution of management thought from its earliest informal days to the present. In doing so, we have focused on how our ideas about management as a body of knowledge and management as an activity have developed over time. We believe that to fully understand the management discipline in its broadest sense, one must also understand it historically. The historical record provides a bridge across time, uniting the past and present as they lead into the future.

Present management theory and practice are quite literally what the past—as received and interpreted by the present—have made them. The past repeatedly informs and reinforms the present such that the search for understanding is never finished. In this sense, the past exists in a reciprocal relationship with the present. Moreover, just as the past is seen through the eyes of the present, the present is judged in an unending dialogue with the past. Today is not like yesterday, nor will tomorrow be like today, yet today is a synergism of all our yesterdays.

A free commerce between the ages cements our kinship with times and places past and allows us to more fully appreciate our own time and place in the parade of history. It also allows us to repeatedly tap the past's greatest minds. With only the cost of one's intellectual effort, the insights of the past are available to repeatedly engage, delight, and pique one's curiosity at a moment's notice.

Our expedition into the past is now concluded. We hope that our readers have enjoyed the journey and will continue to benefit from having explored the management discipline's intellectual roots and having become acquainted with the work and lives of its many contributors from around the world. We likewise hope that they have come to recognize and appreciate "their place in history."

Name Index

Subject Index